Hermeneutic Philosophies of Social Science

Hermeneutic Philosophies of Social Science

Edited by
Babette Babich

DE GRUYTER

ISBN 978-3-11-052837-4
e-ISBN (PDF) 978-3-11-055156-3
Set-ISBN 978-3-11-055157-0

Library of Congress Cataloging-in-Publication Data
A CIP catalog record for this book has been applied for at the Library of Congress.

Bibliographic information published by the Deutsche Nationalbibliothek
The Deutsche Nationalbibliothek lists this publication in the Deutsche Nationalbibliografie; detailed bibliographic data are available on the Internet at http://dnb.dnb.de.

Printing and binding: CPI books GmbH, Leck
♾ Printed on acid-free paper
Printed in Germany

MIX
Papier aus verantwortungsvollen Quellen
FSC® C083411
FSC www.fsc.org

www.degruyter.com

Table of Contents

List of Abbreviations

René Descartes

CSM *The Philosophical Writings of Descartes*, ed. J. Cottingham, R. Stoothoff and D. Murdoch, 2 vols. Cambridge: Cambridge University Press, 1985.

Wilhelm Dilthey

DGS *Gesammelte Schriften*, 28 vols. Göttingen: Vandenhoeck & Ruprecht, 1914–2011.

SW *Selected Works*, ed. Rudolf A. Makkreel and Frithjof Rodi. Princeton: Princeton University Press, 1985ff.

Hans-Georg Gadamer

PCH *Le probleme de la conscience historique*. Louvain: Publications Universitaires, 1963.

WM *Wahrheit und Methode: Grundzüge einer philosophischen Hermeneutik*. Tübingen: Mohr, 1960.

Martin Heidegger

GA *Gesamtausgabe*. Frankfurt a.M.: Klostermann, 1975ff.

Edmund Husserl

BW *Briefwechsel*, ed. Karl Schuhmann and Elisabeth Schuhmann. In: *Husserliana Dokumente*, vol. 3. Dordrecht: Kluwer, 1994.

EU *Erfahrung und Urteil. Untersuchungen zur Genealogie der Logik*, ed. Ludwig Landgrebe. Prag: Academia, 1939 (reprint Hamburg: Claassen & Goverts, 1948; Hamburg: Felix Meiner, 1999).

HM *Husserliana Materialien*. Dordrecht: Kluwer/Springer, 2001ff.

Hua *Husserliana*. The Hague/Dordrecht: Nijhoff/Kluwer/Springer, 1950ff.

Immanuel Kant

CPR *Critique of Pure Reason*, tr. Norman Kemp Smith. London: Macmillan, 1929.

Friedrich Nietzsche

Quotations of Nietzsche's writings are from KSA (*Kritische Studienausgabe*). References for English translations are given in the authors' reference sections.

KSA Nietzsche, Friedrich, *Sämtliche Werke. Kritische Studienausgabe*, 15 vols., ed. Giorgio Colli and Mazzino Montinari. Munich/Berlin/New York: DTV/De Gruyter, 1980.

Abbreviations of Nietzsche's works:

BGE *Beyond Good and Evil*

BT *The Birth of Tragedy*

GM *On the Genealogy of Morals*

GS *The Gay Science*

WS *The Wanderer and His Shadow*

Z *Thus spoke Zarathustra*

Richard Rorty

CIS *Contingency, Irony, and Solidarity.* Cambridge: Cambridge University Press, 1989.

ORT *Objectivity, Relativism, and Truth, Philosophical Papers*, vol. 1. Cambridge: Cambridge University Press, 1991.

PMN *Philosophy and the Mirror of Nature.* Princeton: Princeton University Press, 1979.

PSH *Philosophy and Social Hope.* Harmondsworth: Penguin, 1999.

Babette Babich

Hermeneutic Philosophies of Social Science: Introduction

Interpretive philosophical reflection, hermeneutics, is inseparable from any philosophy of social science. Indeed, to the extent that the social sciences include the human subject, reflection on reflection is integral and such reflection constitutes, whether one names it as such, or not, part of the hermeneutic turn.

This collection of essays offers a range of hermeneutically minded philosophies of social science foregrounding understanding and including a specific attention to history as well as a methodological reflection on the notion of reflection but also subjective obstruction: 'prejudice' or 'pre-judgments' as Joseph J. Kockelmans speaks of these in his chapter below. This same approach informs what has been called a "humanist" by contrast with a naturalistic approach to the social sciences.[1] Currently, although fashions change constantly, some contemporary hermeneutic studies include so-called 'thing ontology' (there are other names), and hermeneutic philosophies of social science also embrace social studies of knowledge as well as social studies of natural science as these latter are themselves, as Bruno Latour has long argued, so many social practices.

Yet there is at the same time a tendency to resist the language of hermeneutics in connection with the philosophy of science. This may be further exacerbated today as part of the quantitative turn in today's university-level human and social sciences. In part, this is due to a certain hard-science anxiety on the part of the social scientists themselves who worry, rather as the title of Bent Flyvbjerg's book *Making Social Science Matter* seems to suggest,[2] that social inquiry is destined to fall short in those respects that make an inquiry seem to be significantly "scientific."[3]

Approaches to hermeneutic philosophies of social science that may be considered hermeneutic, quite in spite of this surprisingly durable constellation of anxiety and suspicion, can be found. Examples include James Bohman's *New Philosophy of Social Science* (1991) and Harvie Ferguson's *Phenomenological So-*

---

1 Note that Roger Trigg (1985) reflects on this in his survey.

2 Bent Flyvbjerg's book *Making Social Science Matter: Why Social Inquiry Fails and How It Can Succeed Again* (Flyvbjerg 2001).

3 This concern is also evident in Bruno Latour's recent *An Inquiry into Modes of Existence: An Anthropology of the Moderns* (Latour 2013) and Steve Fuller's *Philosophy of Science and Its Discontents* (Fuller 1989).

https://doi.org/10.1515/9783110551563-001

ciology (2006), as well as (analytically styled, despite its title), Yvonne Sherrat's *Continental Philosophy of Social Science* (2006) and, in spite of an explicit antipathy to hermeneutics in favor of the generic titling of her book, Karin Knorr-Cetina's *Epistemic Cultures* (1999).[4] Thus, in addition to general approaches to the philosophy of the social sciences as such, one must also consider the range of "Social Studies" of science, natural and social, including studies of technique and technology, ranging from John Ziman to Bruno Latour and Stephen Woolgar in the early days of their collaboration, together with Barry Barnes and Harry Collins and Trevor Pinch and arguably including even Andrew Pickering along with the analytically minded but *sui generis* reflections of Steve Fuller.[5] Other contributions drawing on history have grown into a separate discipline often analytically articulated as part of what is generically known as "history of philosophy." In this tradition, authors comventionally feel constrained to exclude hermeneutics as well as feminist approaches which (when these are not ghettoized in the philosophy of science) can also be lumped in with hermeneutic approaches to social science in the work of Lorraine Code and Hilary Rose[6] as well as Andrea Nye's work on logic, although Nye's loyalties are explicitly analytic and thus "historicist," alongside other work in feminist epistemology and philosophy of science, both natural and social, although, once again, the great majority of these studies remain 'analytically' rather than 'continentally' minded.

Hans-Georg Gadamer (1900 – 2002) reflected on hermeneutic philosophies of social science in a series of chapters included in his *Reason in the Age of Science*.[7] Gadamer's concern emerges in two successive chapters, "Hermeneutics as Practical Philosophy" and "Hermeneutics as a Theoretical and Practical

---

4 See here Bohman 1991 but also Ferguson 2006 as well as Baumann 2010. Thus although analytic in approach Yvonne Sherrat's *Continental Philosophy of Social Science* (Sherrat 2006) duly encompasses all "other" approaches to philosophy of science in a specifically "history of philosophy" styled frame and see too, if more in the tradition of history of science studies, Knorr-Cetina 1999. But see, for a discussion including Dilthey, Weber, and Schütz, Harrington 2001.

5 John Ziman was author of many studies in this direction, see in particular his book, *The Force of Knowledge: The Scientific Dimension of Society* (Ziman 1976) as well as his chapter contribution "No Man is an Island" along with Rom Harré's "Science as the Work of a Community" and Tony O'Connor's "Human Agency and the Social Sciences: From Contextual Phenomenology to Genealogy" all included in the section "Hermeneutics and the Philosophy of Science" in Babich (ed.) 2002, pp. 187 – 194, 203 – 218, 219 – 229.

6 See Code 1991. Code, like Gadamer although her formation is more traditionally analytic, focuses on language and centers on autonomy. See too, if likewise more focused, like Code, on the natural as opposed to the social sciences and more analytically minded than continental, Rose 1994. See too Apel 1979.

7 Gadamer 1983.

Task."[8] With his accustomed methodological exigence, Gadamer raises the question not of the social sciences as such, nor of hermeneutics in particular but philosophy itself. Thus Gadamer notes the enduring concern of philosophy to keep pace with the sciences, not only as a science among the sciences but also, this would be a double effect, as charged to provide science as such with theory—"*Wissenschaftstheorie*," for Gadamer, refers to the claims of philosophy with respect to the dominion of the sciences in all their diversity, natural and social—but also corresponding to "the claim of philosophy to be a giving of accounts [*Rechenschafts ablegen*]."[9]

The task of philosophy in our technoscientific era is to think where, as Heidegger said, "science does not think" and not less to communicate, needful where, as Gadamer says, science "does not really speak a language in the proper sense."[10]

Here, we consider Gadamer's observation, inspired by Nietzsche's "demand that one doubt more profoundly and fundamentally than Descartes"),[11] and further amplified by the "critique of ideology" that

> called scientific neutrality into doubt. It questioned not merely the validity of the phenomena of consciousness and of self-consciousness (which was the case with psychoanalysis) but also the purely theoretical validity of scientific objectivity with which the sciences laid claim.[12]

Beginning with Heidegger's reflections on the Greek legacy of rationality inspires "the new notion of interpretation,"[13] whereby

> The very idea of a definitive interpretation seems to be intrinsically contradictory. Interpretation is always on the way. If, then, the word interpretation points to the finitude of human being and the finitude of human knowing then the experience of interpretation implies something that was no implied by the earlier self-understanding when hermeneutics was coordinated with special fields and applied as a technique for overcoming difficulties in troublesome texts. Then hermeneutics could be understood as a teaching about a technical skill—but no longer.[14]

---

8 Gadamer 1983, pp. 88–112 and pp. 113–138. See, further, below, the chapters authored by Kockelmans, Madison, Geniusas, and Franeta.
9 Gadamer 1983, p. 2.
10 Gadamer 1983, p. 3.
11 Gadamer 1983, p. 100.
12 Gadamer 1983, p. 100
13 Gadamer 1983, p. 102.
14 Gadamer 1983, p. 105.

The challenge for Gadamer is to decide between "theory of science" and "philosophy" of science.[15] Thereby we can begin with his invitation to consider

> the traditions within which we stand—and every tradition that we creatively or appropriatively pass on—offer less an objective field for the scientific mastery of a subject matter or for the extension of our domination by knowledge of the unknown than a mediation of ourselves with our real possibilities engulfing us—with what can be and what is capable of "happening" to and becoming of us.[16]

Gadamer argues that "science is no less science where it is aware of the humaniora as its integrative function." By attending to its hermeneutic dimensionality we enhance rather than diminish science.

Hermeneutic philosophies of the social science as these are represented in the present collection of essays have drawn inspiration from Gadamer's work as well as Paul Ricoeur, Michel de Certeau, and Pierre Bourdieu, in addition to Michel Foucault and Jean Baudrillard. Other contributions foreground Wilhelm Dilthey in addition to Edmund Husserl and Maurice Merleau-Ponty as well as Heidegger's expressly hermeneutic phenomenology in addition to Max Scheler and Alfred Schütz among others.[17]

The term hermeneutics is not without its own attendant baggage, as a methodological approach that has been alternately foregrounded and eclipsed and is currently enjoying renewed attention. Still the word can often be a problem and some reflections are hermeneutic even where the term is not explicitly mentioned or even deliberately kept at a distance. Hence writing on Durkheim and tracing a similar trajectory of influence, Warren Schmaus reflects on interpretation as such, foregrounding method while avoiding the mention of the word "hermeneutics"—thus his book is subtitled "Creating an Intellectual Niche," pointing to the lack of space for the range of approaches that might foreground interpretation as such. Schmaus is hardly the only scholar who favors this tactic: arguably both Clifford Geertz and Paul Rabinow do so as do many others. In turn, this sensitivity highlights the still riven chasm between 'analytic' and 'continental' approaches to philosophy of science,[18] a separation only deepened by the hierarchical distinction between the natural and the social sciences, Thus, although a number of approaches toward a range of hermeneutic philosophies

---

15 It is significant that when Gadamer wrote this, the conventional German rendering of 'philosophy of science' was *Wissenschaftstheorie*. Today the terminology has shifted to a more or less direct translation of philosophy of science: *Wissenschaftsphilosophie*.

16 Gadamer 1983, p. 167.

17 See, for example, Schmaus 1994, more generally, again, Ferguson 2006.

18 See Babich 2010, 2012, and 2015a.

of the social sciences exist,[19] the authors, even when they are continental themselves, can be inclined to downplay the specific role of hermeneutics in the approaches they argue.

Today, most philosophers of science are trained in analytic philosophy, not "continental philosophy"—largely because universities are almost uniformly analytic. Thus even schools that had been traditionally "continental" have since hired analytically trained scholars even for continental appointments (the academic political element being the missing shade of blue in Thomas Kuhn's *Structure of Scientific Revolutions*). Thus the painful wake of the so-called science wars foregrounds "genealogy" by which is meant more Foucault than Nietzsche. As a kind of micro-illustration of the same point, although Nietzsche himself wrote sustained hermeneutic reflections on history, analytic studies of Nietzsche's philosophy of history, including Emden and Jensen as well as, on the political side, Drochon, etc., rather uniformly tend to elide, often in good conscience and often, in good analytic fashion, describing their own approaches as 'continental,' exclude hermeneutics along with critical theory. Here it should also be noted that formations are mixed in the case of the contributions here included, not only advancing hermeneutic philosophies of social science, but drawing on other approaches including pragmatism, and "process" philosophy and other traditions.

The strength of this book collection thus reflects the richness of the hermeneutic tradition just as it draws on every area of philosophical reflection, illustrating the past diversity of hermeneutic approaches as well as the future possibilities for hermeneutic and phenomenological philosophies of social science. The interpretation of texts and practices, including hermeneutic phenomenology's special attention to the life-world is seen in the contributions to follow as articulating questions of the sociology of knowledge as well as specifically applied ethics and the law, cultural theory, as well as reflections on education and exploration of themes drawn from history of philosophy, from Plato to Descartes.

---

19 See, on the continental side, the contributions of Kockelmans and Heelan in particular, but see also, albeit more analytically minded (this has regrettably not led to a reception among his analytic peers), Dmitri Ginev's many studies, perhaps especially his contribution "Micro- and Macro-Hermeneutics of Science" to a volume Ginev edited with the late Robert S. Cohen (in honor of Azarya Polikarov), *Issues and Images in the Philosophy of Science* (Ginev and Cohen 1997), pp. 87–94 in addition to Ginev's own "Rhetoric and Double Hermeneutics in the Human Sciences" (Ginev 1998).

I Kinds of Hermeneutic Philosophies of the Social Science

The very notion of a hermeneutic philosophy of social science highlights reflexive plurality. Typical hermeneutic approaches to the social sciences may, as already noted, be traced in the writings of Dilthey,[20] Schütz,[21] Scheler[22] but not less Weber[23] as well as Gadamer,[24] Ricoeur as well as, from the perspective of Critical Theory, Theodor Adorno. To this list can be added, in differing interpretive fashions, Bourdieu, Alasdair MacIntyre, Niklas Luhmann, Jacques Ellul, Baudrillard, as well as de Certeau (who himself reads between Foucault and Baudrillard) and Paul Virilio, etc. We have already seen that to this must be added the tendency of theorists like Geertz and Charles Taylor to adopt some of tactics and foci of hermeneutics while excluding engagement with the tradition (all those other names of all those many philosophers and fellow travelers) and routinely excluding the term hermeneutics from their discussions.[25] Such terminological suppression is part of the politics and thus the professional tactics of institutional or university philosophy of science, be it of a social or natural kind.

Already one needs a definition of a specifically hermeneutic philosophy of social science. At the same time there are debates about whether one ought to

---

20 See here, very directly, Wilhelm Dilthey's own *Introduction to the Human Sciences: An Attempt to Lay a Foundation for the Study of Society and History* (Dilthey 1988). In addition to Bulloff 1980 as well as Bakker 1999, including a discussion of the tensions between Heidegger's and Dilthey's hermeneutic approaches. And see too in the present volume, Nelson and Scharff below. Useful here too is Bambach 1995. And see, if more recondite than a first introduction can reasonably expect to be, Thouard 2005.

21 See, in general, the contributions to Michael Staudigl and George Berguno's collection, *Schutzian Phenomenology and Hermeneutic Traditions* (Staudigl and Berguno 2014), particularly, in that same volume, Martin Endress' "Interpretive Sociologies and Traditions of Hermeneutics" (Endress 2014).

22 Scheler 1980.

23 See for a useful discussion focused in particular on Weber's appropriation of Aristotle, McCarthy 2009, pp. 100 ff.

24 In addition to Joseph Kockelmans's useful discussion below, together with Hans-Georg Gadamer's own contribution to an issue of the New School journal dedicated to his work, "The Problem of Historical Consciousness" (Gadamer 1975), see, very classically, and note that both of the examples are counterpoised with other names, Georgia Warnke, "Hermeneneutics and the Social Sciences: A Gadamerian Critique of Rorty" (Warnke 1985) as well as, more recently, Edward W. Gimbel, "Interpretation and Objectivity: A Gadamerian Reevaluation of Max Weber's Social Science" (Gimbel 2016). But see too, Rorty 2003.

25 There are exceptions as I note some of them here and throughout this introduction, see for example Fred Dallmayr's "Hermeneutics and Cross-Cultual Encounters: Integral Pluralism in Action" in Dallmayr (2010), pp. 103–122. And see too Mohr/Rawlings 2013, Gibbons 2006, and Heller 1989.

speak of a hermeneutic or else of a phenomenological approach (thus the utility of combination approaches such as the Heideggerian hermeneutico-phenomenological approach) to the social sciences. To these debates, not that adding things to the mix is especially helpful apart from indicating the breadth of the problem, one may add the important dispute concerning Emile Durkheim (there is a hermeneutic dispute about this given the differing attributions of positivism between Francophone and Anglophone traditions along the periphery of which one place the German and the Dutch and Flemish traditions).[26] In addition to the disparate foci between Francophone and Anglophone taxonomies of the hermeneutics of social science, there is also a distinctive German tradition. One may note, for example the range of contributions to the book collection on specifically *hermeneutic* sociology of knowledge[27] in addition to methodological explorations.[28] And in the literature of the 1980s, in addition to Simon Glynn's 1986 *European Philosophy and the Social Sciences*[29] we may note Dieter Misgeld's 1989 and overtly preliminary discussion of the articulation between phenomenology and hermeneutics in sociology. [30] In addition, read from a more general as well as more mainstream perspective in the philosophy of science, writing in 1979, on the cusp of the1980s, Dagfinn Føllesdal makes the (now standard analytic) case that the hermeneutics of science may be regarded as a special case of philosophical (analytic) approaches to scientific methodology.[31] In just this way, to be sure, analytic philosophy has typically tended to discredit the value of hermeneutic philosophical approaches claiming that it was something they were already doing. Such assertions have however also been combined with claims of

---

26 Thus Jeffrey C. Alexander can claim at the start of his own discussion of this dispute in his book *Durkheimian Sociology: Cultural Studies* (Alexander 1990) that Steven Lukes may well take responsibility for excluding Durkheim from the hermeneutic tradition on the grounds that "Durkheim took a positivist rather than a hermeneutic position." Alexander 1990, p. 16. Cf., here, Lukes 1972. Of course this is a complex point and see further Bloor 1982 as well as Johan Heilbron 2004. See Alexander's more recent article, co-authored with Philip Smith, "The Strong Program in Cultural Theory: Elements of a Structural Hermeneutics" (Alexander and Smith 2001). The thematic remains relevant and Stjepan Mestrovic reads Durkheim as a hermeneuticist to assist a finer point with respect to sociological method contra his topical assessment of *Anthony Giddens: The Last Modernist* (Mestrovic 2005).

27 Hitzler, Reichertz and Schröer 1999.

28 Moses and Knutsen 2012.

29 Glynn 1986.

30 Cf. Misgeld 1989.

31 Føllesdal 1979.

incomprehensibility (vague, badly written, what is the argument?) along with declarations of a lack of interest (dated, tiresome, and so on).[32]

Not at lot would seem to have changed in contemporary Anglophone philosophy, which may still be named, for better or for worse, "analytic"—although the designation is increasingly refused to the extent that analytic philosophy having long refused to recognize the value of continental philosophy regards its own approach to traditionally continental themes and thinkers as the only valid or viable approach. We are beyond the analytic-continental divide, so we are told (this claim arguably dates back to the beginning of the division). And the assertion is as good as true—not because the divide has been abolished or differences overcome or bridges built and borders dissolved but simply because analytic philosophy (hence the near ubiquity of its terminological conventions, like "naturalism"), is by and large the philosophy taught at university. Thus most the overwhelming majority of professional philosophers today enjoy an analytic background, This is because for the last two or three decades, university appointments in the US, the UK, France, and Germany and Italy and so on have gone to analytically informed or formed academics who nonetheless vociferously resist the designation as analytic and sometimes, the most notable case being Brian Leiter, regard themselves as 'continental.'[33]

Quite apart from such terminological tensions, the hermeneutic approach remains unsettling as the social sciences continue to be embroiled in a certain crisis of method arguably attributable to the dominant model of the natural sciences. This is witnessed in recent years by a turn toward the quantitative (and thus the quantifiable) compounded by the new, so-called "datalogical" or digital turn, which although it promises new insights, continues the modeling of the social sciences on the paradigm of the hard sciences. Paradoxically perhaps, current discussions of "big data," with its strange properties of emergence and relation, can only require (which is not to say that today's theorists embrace) a hermeneutic turn.[34]

---

32 Thus some three decades ago now, Mark Okrent offered such a strategization in his essay on hermeneutics and social science. Okrent 1984: 23–49.

33 I discuss some of these problems in a dialogue with the philosopher and gaming designer and theorist, Chris Bateman, see Babich and Bateman 2016. The dialogue is one of series of dialogues, published at the end of 2016, continuation ongoing through 2017.

34 This has not yet been completely developed. Though not expressly hermeneutic, see, Lynch 2016 as well as the contributions to Pietsch et al., 2017 and Stingl 2015. I discuss this and related elements in Babich 2018.

Where the natural sciences appear to have a clear hierarchy—physics at the top, followed (with some contentiousness) by chemistry,[35] biology and so on with some debate as to where to find or to set sciences like cosmology, clearly with astronomy, at least on some accounts at the same level as physics itself, or oceanography and the earth sciences, as well as cross-over sciences such as geography and, complicated by today's political debates, meteorology and climate science, in this volume there will be some discussion of the latter sciences in connection with coastal science (and engineering) politics—there is, by contrast, no clearly privileged top "social science," although as the late Gary Madison points out, many have sought to give this title to economics, precisely owing to its precision.[36] Nevertheless, among what the Germans call the sciences of spirit or intellect or mind, the *Geisteswissenschaften*, may be counted economics, history, political science, sociology, anthropology, psychology, sociolinguistics but not less educational theory and reflection[37] as primary social sciences, to which sciences some cultural traditions include theology and philosophy as well as among the other historical and human and social sciences.

VI Plan of the Text

VI.1

The first section, entitled *Science and Method: Towards Hermeneutic Phenomenology of Social Science*, takes its inspiration and point of departure from an explicit reflection on this very topic in a classic study, key to this collection as whole, in the essay by the Dutch philosopher of science Joseph J. Kockelmans (1923–2008): "Toward an Interpretative or Hermeneutic Social Science." In his essay, Kockelmans raises the question of the role and use of hermeneutic philosophy in the philosophy of the social sciences. Taking as point of departure Heidegger's hermeneutic phenomenology, Kockelmans reads Gadamer's reflections on history as well as his *Truth and Method*. In each case, for Kockelmans, what is methodologically essential is to articulate what can be elicited for the purposes of a philosophy of the social sciences, including an overview of objections that

35 See for example the contributions to Baird, Scerri and McIntyre 2006 and my own review of this disciplinary claim with additional literature in Babich 2010.

36 See Madison 1990.

37 See Babich 2012. Bruno Latour's own contributions to this review are discussed among others in Babich 2015a and briefly in my own essay in this volume. Cf. Felder 2013 and Pierozak 2016 in addition to Feussi 2016.

may be offered. Thus Kockelmans explores the sense in which Heidegger's and especially Gadamer's ideas about philosophy can be valuable for a philosophy of the social sciences.

This second chapter was composed in direct correspondence with Kockelmans by his friend and intellectual co-traveler, the Belgian-Irish physicist and philosopher of science, Patrick Aidan Heelan (1926–2015). Heelan's own expertise was in measurement and waves, in developed in his work with Erwin Schrödinger which lead to the quantum philosophy, as Heelan would speak of it, of Werner Heisenberg.[38] In "Quantum Mechanics and the Social Sciences," Heelan develops the argument that quantum mechanics may be interpreted, in the spirit of Niels Bohr and Werner Heisenberg, as being about physical objects in so far as these objects themselves are revealed by and within the local, social, and historical process of *measurement*. Heelan shows that a reading of the hermeneutical aspect of quantum mechanical measurement reveals close analogues with hermeneutical social/historical sciences. In conclusion, Heelan argues that the hermeneutical analysis of science requires the move from the epistemological attitude to an ontological one.

The next chapter follows, as it were, this very move to social theory, not qua traditionally received and not only in terms of conventional social studies of science but critically reflected. Thus the intersection between hermeneutics and critical theory is explicitly thematized in the chapter contributed by Hans-Herbert Koegler, a German philosopher who has taught for many years in Florida: "A Critical Hermeneutics of Agency: Cultural Studies as Critical Social Theory." Observing that research practices commonly labeled as "cultural studies" are the productive continuation of the epistemic interests pursued by the early Frankfurt School, Koegler argues that cultural studies represent the reflexive and creative diversity emblematic of everyday practices, whereby, following Adorno, it is common to underscore an element of subversion of resistance even in standardized "entertainment-products." Koegler asks how social practices of power influence, by means of producing meaning, the self-understanding of subjects, and how those subjects themselves are in turn capable of influencing and changing their respective cultural and social practices. Koegler's further question, given all the contradictions of individual self-understanding, asks how power might be "anchored" in subjective interiority?

In the next chapter, Eric S. Nelson, "Overcoming Naturalism from Within: Dilthey, Nature, and the Human Sciences" focuses on Dilthey's understanding

---

38 For a retrospective and overview of this, see Heelan's posthumously published book, *The Observable*, Heelan 2016.

of nature and spirit in the 1890s, in terms of the debate between naturalism and anti-naturalism. For Nelson, Dilthey outlines the limits of natural scientific methods in the face of the felt reflexivity of the subject, the singular nexus of individual life, together with the inability of humans to know and comprehend life as a comprehensive universally valid systematic whole. Thus Dilthey *immanently* demonstrates naturalism's possibilities and limits in relation to the psychological, historical, and ethical life of individuals without appealing to essentialist, religious, or metaphysical conceptions of a substantial self. Because lived-experiences are complex relational wholes involving purposiveness, they cannot be coherently and adequately reduced to or reconstructed as discrete "natural" elements abstracted from the complex nexus of life.

In the final contribution to this first section, Steve Fuller, the US born philosopher of science and sociologist, based at Warwick, offers an intentionally explosive reflection: "Hermeneutics from the Inside-Out and the Outside-In—And How Postmodernism Blew It All Wide Open." Fuller's language of an 'inside-out' vs. 'outside-in' approach to hermeneutics, distinguishes the human sciences from the natural sciences. As Fuller reminds us, the social sciences have been the historic testing ground for both approaches. But today, on Fuller's view, the postmodern condition has exploded this traditional dialectic, challenging the shared assumption that the 'human' is a member of *Homo sapiens*, a classificatory assumption from the second half of the 18th century to the second half of the 20th century. Fuller concludes his chapter by raising the question of the viability of hermeneutics in a world where the 'human' is thus ontologically indeterminate.

VI.2

The next section, *Reflexive and Relational Hermeneutics*, begins with a contribution by the philosopher and historian, Steven Shapin. In his chapter, "The Sciences of Subjectivity," Shapin talks about one of the subjective sciences via what can seem to be the most subjective of all the senses: gustation, that is, taste and tasting. Shapin sets up his reading by referring to what he calls a "long-standing fascination with deflating certain stories about objectivity." Foremost in this deflationary enterprise is subjectivity as such which presents difficulties for objective demonstration by contrast with standard sorts of knowledge. To focus on subjectivity, Shapin traces potentially constructive links between contemporary science studies and resources in 18th-century philosophical aesthetics. In particular, looking at wine, Shapin's focus concerns available engagements with the mode of subjectivity known as taste, and, especially, gustation and olfaction, to suggest ways in which we might study the achievement of intersubjectivity in these domains.

In his contribution, Dimitri Ginev calls upon the notion of double hermeneutic to address both reflexivity and the elusive notion of the ontological difference. Ginev's chapter, "Studies of Empirical Ontology and Ontological Difference," criticizes the tendency to radical empiricization of empirical ontology while supporting the anti-foundational ontological turn in science and technology studies. On the cognitivist argument, the empirical immediacy is inevitably shaped and mediated by non-empirical assumptions. However, according to the hermeneutic argument, any empirically immediate state of affairs is the upshot of actualizing possibilities projected by interrelated practices upon horizons of practical existence. Thus, the actually given qua empirical immediacy is ineluctably "produced" within the potentiality for practical being. Following this, Ginev suggests a non-empirical extension of empirical ontology, specifically illustrated by way of the integration of radical reflexivity in ethnographic descriptions of multiple realities before reflecting on the introduction of double hermeneutics in the studies of empirical ontology.

The third chapter in this section, Babette Babich, "Hermeneutics and Its Discontents in Philosophy of Science: On Bruno Latour, the "Science Wars", Mockery, and Immortal Models " reviews the fortunes of Alan Sokal's 1996 hoax, including the politics of mockery. A hermeneutic reflection on the history and philosophy of science highlights the relevance of the hegemony of analytic style in philosophy, discussed in terms of both the Forman thesis in the History of Science as well as the fate of Latour's lab-ethnography cum field ethnography, along with socio-linguistics and the political force of rhetoric as a means of excluding other voices, especially within professional philosophy and philosophy of science in particular. The paper concludes with a discussion of the politics of scientific publishing in the context of shoreline modelling, "immortal" or zombie models as these persist in the face of (or better said: absence of) empirical feedback.

In the first of the last two dialogically-related concluding contributions in this section, the late Canadian philosopher, Gary Madison (1940–2016) writes "On the Importance of Getting Things Straight" to emphasize the order of knowing, including clarification, requests for further information, etc. Thus Madison argues that it is curious that phenomenological (or philosophical) hermeneutics, a systematic theory of human understanding in all its various forms, continues to be so widely misunderstood as it has been. Nevertheless, as phenomenology has shown, human understanding invariably tends to misunderstand itself. Madison finds it striking that the two chief ways in which hermeneutics is commonly misunderstood are themselves diametrically opposed to one another. With this advance response, the reader is better prepared to approach the final chapter of this section, the Lithuanian philosopher, Saulius Geniusas' reflections on "Hans-Georg Gadamer's Concept of the Horizon and Its Ethico-Political Critique." Geniusas focuses on the relevance of Gadamer's hermeneutics in the context of today's socio-political concerns. In question are ethically and politically motivated critiques of Gadamer's hermeneutics, especially those of Richard Kearney, who suggests that Gadamer fails to offer a satisfactory account of the relation between ipseity and alterity. Geniusas argues, per contra, that Gadamer's hermeneutics does not overlook the otherness of the Other. Here, Geniusas concludes that the fusion of the horizons abolishes neither the self, nor the Other, but raises both to a higher universality. The oneness of the horizon(s) thereby proves to be the dialogue that we ourselves are.

VI.3

The third section of this book focuses on *Practice and Application: Hermeneutics, Social Theory, Pragmatics.* The first contribution is offered by the hermeneutic legal scholar, Duška Franeta, offering a reading of "Gadamer's Hermeneutics as Practical Philosophy" in an explicitly applied context. Franeta explores the connection of philosophical hermeneutics in Aristotle's practical philosophy, noting that the fundamental notions of prejudice, hermeneutical circle, tradition, situation, effective-historical consciousness, fusion of horizons and application underwrites Gadamer's central thesis that our understanding is never mere subject-oriented behavior but always also historically limited. Thus Gadamer intends to show that we can never fully escape from all of our prejudices but not that we cannot encounter them critically. Indeed, the fact that we cannot erase our own horizon when approaching someone else may invite us to seek instead to find a common ground with them inasmuch as the process of understanding always has a dialogical character. Franeta concludes by outlining the revival of self-understanding of humanities, universal competence of scientific experts and domain and objectives of contemporary education.

In the following contribution, the German theorist of the sociology of knowledge, Bernt Schnettler (Bayreuth), along with his co-authors, Hubert Knoblauch (TU Berlin) & Jürgen Raab (Koblenz-Landau), offers a review of what has been, in a German context, known as "The 'New' Sociology of Knowledge." This novel approach was developed in a characteristic context as philosophical reflection on the conditions of human thinking and reasoning, subsequently evolving into a specific sociological perspective on the social conditions of knowledge production and dissemination. The social character of thinking has long been observed from Bacon to Marx, and numerous theorists, as Schnettler/Knoblauch/Raab point out, have emphasized the distorting effects social influences have upon individual thinking. Ultimately, the authors argue, thinking and knowledge production depend fundamentally on their social genesis.

In his contribution to this collection, the French sociolinguist, Didier de Robillard looks at de Certeau in connection with both history and sociolinguistics in his chapter, "Taking Plurality Seriously with Michel de Certeau: From History to 'Reception Sociolinguistics'," specially translated for this volume by Tracy Burr Strong, who was himself de Certeau's colleague in San Diego for several years. As one of the most important theorists of practical or engaged hermeneutics in everyday social engagement, de Robillard shows that the French sociological and praxical philosopher, Michel de Certeau. But de Certeau was also concerned with sociology and with language in addition to history. De Robillard details the conjunction of hermeneutics and sociolinguisitics via a reading not only of de Certeau but also the French research tradition of sociolinguisitics as a hermeneutic practice of Certeaulian everyday life.

The penultimate chapter of the second section is offered by the pragmatic philosopher and student of (and collaborator with) Richard Rorty, Barry Allen, "Pragmatism and Hermeneutics." Here, Allen offers a kind of hermeneutics of pragmatism itself, bringing his own signature style together with the resources of hermeneutics to explicate the intersection of "Practice" as a kind of applied pragmatism. Still, if perhaps surprisingly, the word *pragmatism* scarcely appears in Rorty's *Philosophy and the Mirror of Nature.* Rorty's terminology, on Allen's report, is *epistemological behaviorism* which was a term quickly replaced by anti-representationalism, and which, together with thoughts on literature and politics, formed Rorty's version of pragmatism. Yet Allen points out that *Philosophy and the Mirror of Nature* was written for "professional consumption." Thus Allen underscores that Rorty would have had no need to *reach out* to analytic epistemologists, inasmuch as he himself was already one of them. For Allen, the writing of *Philosophy and the Mirror of Nature* would take Rorty beyond that tradition, indeed and as the title of one of Rorty's chapters suggests, "From Epistemology to Hermeneutics."

Paul Fairfield's contribution rounds out this section and in his comprehensive set of reflections, "Make It Scientific: Theories of Education from Dewey to Gadamer," Fairfield notes that faculties of education have always been keen to associate their discipline with the social sciences. Thus university schools of education assert a claim to scientificity in ways largely reminiscent of the early days of sociology, psychology, political science, and other established disciplines of the social sciences. Research produced by "educationalists" is expected to conform to all the protocols of empirical and quantitative methodology, raising the hope in many minds that the essential business of education might finally transcend the contested realm of art and philosophy and be placed on the secure path of a science. As educational discourse assumed an increasingly empirical and psychological guise through the course of the 20th century, the imperative to legitimate teaching methods as "scientific" is ubiquitous both on the side of conservatives and progressives as faculties of education seek to establish their credentials within academe.

VI.4

The final section of this collection, *Truth and Life: Philosophy and History, Psychology and Method*, is broader in its scope and consequently in detail. To this extent, this collection endeavors to go some way to inciting continued reflection on just this broad range of possibilities. In his lead contribution, the English philosopher by origin, though a securely native Floridian by now, perhaps owing to his brilliant dedication as a swimmer and part-time (if non-Nietzschean) Dionysian, Simon Glynn's "The Hermeneutical Human and Social Sciences" offers a review of the hermeneutic social and human sciences themselves including a subject focused reflection and illustration. Glynn reflects on the original function of hermeneutic interpretation for textual exegesis of scripture as well as classical philological and legal texts. Glynn takes the broadening application of literary approaches to cultural artifacts including theatrical performances. In this context, Glynn argues that hermeneutic interpretation offers a valuable tool for understanding of human behavior including social, cultural, historical, political and economic etc., action, interactions and relations and not less related institutions.

In his contribution, the German philosopher, Harald Seubert, who is currently professor in Basel, offers us a philosophy, systematically articulated, of life. In "Life, Metaphysics, History: Reflections on the Contemporary Relevance of Dilthey's Philosophy of Life," Seubert reviews Dilthey's later life dream interpretation of nothing less quintessentially academic than Raphael's *School of Athens*. Beginning with Dilthey's dream division of the philosophical schools into the irreconcilable camps of positivism, freedom idealism and objective idealism, each internally coherent and incommunicative and thus other-excluding, Seubert argues that Dilthey's signal insight into the irreversible deficiencies of freedom begins in historical awareness. After Fichte and Hegel, and via Husserl and Heidegger, Yorck and Ranke, Seubert draws on both Stephan Otto and Manfred Riedel to illuminate Dilthey's philosophy of life as a first (or foundational) hermeneutic science.

The concluding three chapters exemplify the breadth of this collection, focusing on the history of philosophy, considered through the lens of Alfred North Whitehead's enduring aperçu, elevating and relegating us at once to mere footnotes to Plato in addition to a discussion of Heidegger and Dilthey on history to conclude with an elegantly hermeneutic reading of Descartes. In the antepenultimate chapter, "Four Fundamental Aspects of the Reversal of Platonism," Lawlor argues that any attempt to reverse Platonism is itself derivative from Plato's dialogues and the interiority of thought (*Theatetus*), its multiplicity (*Parmenides*) and spontaneity (*Republic*, Book VII) as well as the imagination of the political as the life of the mind: the soul (Book II). Lawlor argues that the reversal of Platonism means conceiving forms or essences as events and, on Derrida's suggestion, aims to reduce violence to a minimum. Where Platonism wills the end, hence on Derrida's terms, directed to the violence of the worst, Lawlor argues for a "hyperbolic *Gelassenheit*" as the only genuine reversal of Platonism.

The next contribution by Robert C. Scharff is addressed to the philosophy of history: "Heidegger: Hermeneutics as 'Preparation' for Thinking." For Sharff, Dilthey's understanding of historical life "in its own terms" inspired Heidegger's early conception of phenomenology as a philosophy requiring "hermeneutical" preparation. In this context, Scharff maintains that it is likewise through Dilthey that Heidegger would contend that in Nietzsche's second *Untimely Mediation*, Nietzsche "understood more about [being historical] than he made known."

The final chapter of this book contributed by the American philosopher, David Blair Allison (1944–2016) leaves us with a hermeneutic reading as an art, *in lento*, focused on René Descartes, the philosopher of the clear and the distinct, the philosopher whose turn to subjective certainty inaugurates modernity and might to this same extent seem to require the resources of hermeneutics least of all. But Allison's review of "Hermeneutic Reflections on Descartes' Introduction to His *Meditations on First Philosophy*" includes a reading of Descartes' own account of his project. Allison's beautifully written exploration adumbrates the key method of any hermeneutic approach to a philosophical text in a philosophically interpretive parallel to Ranke's ideal of history as it itself actually was [*eigentlich gewesen*], what Descartes himself "actually" says. Inevitably such a reading offers profound and provocative insights into Descartes' epistemological project beyond traditional accounts.

References

Alexander, Jeffrey C. (1990) *Durkheimian Sociology: Cultural Studies.* Cambridge: Cambridge University Press.

Alexander, Jeffrey C. and Smith, Philip (2001) "The Strong Program in Cultural Theory: Elements of a Structural Hermeneutics." In: Jonathan H. Turner (ed.), *Handbook of Sociological Theory*. Frankfurt a.M.: Springer, pp. 135–150.

Apel, Karl-Otto (1979) "The Common Presuppositions of Hermeneutics and Ethics: Types of Rationality beyond Science and Technology." *Research in Phenomenology* 9(1): 35–53.

Babich, Babette (2002) "Sokal's Hermeneutic Hoax: Physics and the New Inquisition." In: *Hermeneutic Philosophy of Science, Van Gogh's Eyes, and God*. Dordrecht: Kluwer, pp. 67–78.

Babich, Babette (2003) "On the Analytic-Continental Divide in Philosophy: Nietzsche's Lying Truth, Heidegger's Speaking Language, and Philosophy." In: Carlos Prado (ed.), *A House Divided: Comparing Analytic and Continental Philosophy*. Amherst, NY: Humanity Books, pp. 63–103.

Babich, Babette (2010) "Towards a Critical Philosophy of Science: Continental Beginnings and Bugbears, Whigs and Waterbears." *International Journal of the Philosophy of Science* 24 (4): 343–391.

Babich, Babette (2012) *La fin de la pensée? Philosophie analytique contre philosophie continentale*. Paris: L'Harmattan.

Babich, Babette (2013) "*O, Superman!* or Being Towards Transhumanism: Martin Heidegger, Günther Anders, and Media Aesthetics." *Divinatio* (January 2013): 83–99.

Babich, Babette (2015a) "Calling Science Pseudoscience: Fleck's Archaeologies of Fact and Latour's 'Biography of an Investigation' in AIDS Denialism and Homeopathy." *International Studies in the Philosophy of Science* 29(1): 1–39.

Babich, Babette (2015b) "Sakrale Huren und das Fetisch-Fragment. Batailles Kriegstagebücher Sur Nietzsche." In: Artur R. Boelderl (ed.), *Bataille*. Vienna: Turia & Kant, pp. 275–298.

Babich, Babette and Chris Bateman (2016) "The Last of the Continental Philosophers." Online. 29 November 2016. http://onlyagame.typepad.com/only_a_game/2016/11/babich-and-bateman-1.html.

Babich, Babette (2018) "Hermeneutic Perspectives on the Politics of Technology: GPS Hacking Hackers, Virilio's Teratology of Pain, and Airport Security" In Nolen Gertz and Peter-Paul Verbeek, eds., *Security and the Political Turn in Philosophies of Technology*. Forthcoming.

Babich, Babette (ed.) (2002) *Hermeneutic Philosophy of Science, Van Gogh's Eyes, and God*. Dordrecht: Kluwer.

Baird, Davis, Scerri, Eric and McIntyre, Lee (eds.) (2006) *Philosophy of Chemistry: Synthesis of a New Discipline*. Dordrecht: Springer.

Bakker, J.I. (1999) "Wilhelm Dilthey: Classical Sociological Theorists," *Journal of Alternative Perspectives* 22: 43–82.

Bambach, Charles (1995) *Heidegger, Dilthey, and the Crisis of Historicism*. Ithaca: Cornell University Press.

Bataille, George (1985) "The Notion of Expenditure." In: George Bataille, *Visions of Excess*, tr. Allan Stoeckl. Minneapolis: University of Minnesota Press, pp. 116–129.

Bataille, George (1991) *The Accursed Share*, tr. Robert Hurley. Cambridge: MIT Press.

Baumann, Zygmunt (2010) *Hermeneutics and Social Science: Approaches to Understanding*. London: Routledge.

Birault, Henri (1966) "De la beatitude chez Nietzsche." *Nietzsche: Cahiers de Royaumont* 6: 13–28

Birault, Henri (1977) "Beatitude in Nietzsche." In: David B. Allison (ed.), *The New Nietzsche.* New York: Dell, pp. 219–231.

Bloor, David (1982) "Durkheim and Mauss Revisited: Classification and the Sociology of Knowledge." *Studies in History and Philosophy of Science Part A*, Volume 13, Number 4 (December): 267–297

Bohman, James (1991) *New Philosophy of Social Science.* Cambridge: MIT Press.

Braver, Lee (2015) "Hermeneutics and Language Philosophy." In: Jeff Malpas and Hans Helmuth Gander (eds.), *The Routledge Companion to Hermeneutics.* London: Routledge, pp. 634–643.

Brown, Mark B. (2009) "Bruno Latour and the Symmetries of Science and Politics." In: Mark B. Brown, *Science in Democracy: Expertise, Institutions, and Representation.* Cambridge: MIT Press.

Buloff, Ilse (1980) *Wilhelm Dilthey: A Hermeneutic Approach to the Study of History and Culture.* The Hague: Nijhoff.

Code, Lorraine (1991) *What Can She Know? Feminist Theory and the Construction of Knowledge.* Ithaca: Cornell University Press.

Dahlstrom, Daniel O. (1994) *Das Logische Vorurteil: Untersuchungen zur Wahrheitstheorie des frühen Heidegger.* Vienna: Passagen.

Dallmayr, Fred R. (1989) "Life-World: Variations on a Theme." In: Stephen K. White (ed.), *Life-World and Politics: Between Modernity and Postmodernity: Essays in Honor of Fred Dallmayr.* Notre Dame: University of Notre Dame Press, pp. 25–65.

Dallmayr, Fred R. (2010) *Integral Pluralism: Beyond Culture Wars* (Lexington: University of of Kentucky Press.

Dilthey, Wilhelm (1988) *Introduction to the Human Sciences: An Attempt to Lay a Foundation for the Study of Society and History*, tr. Ramon Betanzos. Detroit: Wayne State University Press.

Dilthey, Wilhelm (2002) *The Formation of the Historical World in the Human Sciences.* Collected Works, Volume III. Princeton: Princeton University Press.

Dolling, Lisa (2002) "Dialogue as Praxis: Philosophical Hermeneutics, Historical Epistemology, and Truth." In: Carol C. Gould (ed.), *Constructivism and Practice: Toward a Historical Epistemology.* Lanham, MD: Rowman & Littlefield, pp. 33–46.

Ellul, Jacques (1967) *The Technological Society*, tr. John Wilkinson. New York: Vintage.

Endress, Martin (2014) "Interpretive Sociologies and Traditions of Hermeneutics." In: Michael Staudigl and George Berguno (eds.), *Schutzian Phenomenology and Hermeneutic Traditions.* Frankfurt a.M.: Springer, pp. 33–54.

Felder, Ekkehard (ed.) (2013*) Faktizitätsherstellung in Diskursen: Die Macht des Deklarativen.* Berlin/Boston: De Gruyter.

Ferguson, Harvie (2006) *Phenomenological Sociology: Experience & Insight in Modern Society.* London: Sage.

Feussi, Valentin (2016) "'Croyance originaire' et élaboration de sens. Quelles conséquences pour la sociolinguistique?" *Glottopol* 28: 226–241. Online: http://www.univ-rouen.fr/dyalang/glottopol.

Flyvbjerg, Bent (2001) Making Social Science Matter: Why Social Inquiry Fails and How It Can Succeed Again. Cambridge: Cambridge University Press.

Føllesdal, Dagfinn (1979) "Hermeneutics and the Hypothetico-Deductive Method." *Dialectica* 33(3–4): 319–336.

Fuller, Steve (1988) *Social Epistemology.* Bloomington: Indiana University Press.
Fuller, Steve (1989) *Philosophy of Science and Its Discontents.* Boulder: Westview Press.
Gadamer, Hans-Georg (1975) "The Problem of Historical Consciousness." *Graduate Faculty Philosophy Journal* 5(1): 8–52.
Gadamer, Hans-Georg (1977) *Philosophical Hermeneutics.* Berkeley: University of California Press.
Gadamer, Hans-Georg (1983) *Reason in the Age of Science*, tr. Frederick G. Lawrence. Cambridge: MIT Press.
Geertz, Clifford (1971) *The Interpretation of Cultures. Selected Essays.* New York: Basic Books.
Geertz, Clifford (1983) *Knowledge: Further Essays in Interpretive Anthropology.* New York: Basic Books.
Gibbons, Michael T. (2006) "Hermeneutics, Political Inquiry, and Practical Reason: An Evolving Challenge to Political Science." *American Political Science Review* 100(4): 563–571.
Gimbel, Edward W. (2016) "Interpretation and Objectivity: A Gadamerian Reevaluation of Max Weber's Social Science." *Political Research Quarterly* 69(1): 72–82.
Ginev, Dimitri (1997) *A Passage to the Hermeneutic Philosophy of Science.* Amsterdam: Rodopi.
Ginev, Dmitri (1998) "Rhetoric and Double Hermeneutics in the Human Sciences." *Human Studies* 21: 259–271.
Ginev, Dmitri and Cohen, Robert S. (1997) *Issues and Images in the Philosophy of Science.* Dordrecht: Kluwer.
Glynn, Simon (1986) *European Philosophy and the Social Sciences.* Aldershot: Gower.
Habermas, Jürgen (1988) *On the Logic of the Social Sciences*, tr. Shierry Weber Nicholsen and Jerry A. Stark. Cambridge: MIT Press.
Harrington, Austin (2001) *Hermeneutic Dialogue and Social Science: A Critique of Gadamer and Habermas.* Abingdon, Oxon: Routldge.
Heelan, Patrick A. (1998) "Scope of Hermeneutics in the Philosophy of Natural Science." *Studies in the History and Philosophy of Science* 29: 273–298.
Heelan, Patrick A. (2016) *The Observable: Heisenberg's Philosophy of Quantum Mechanics*, ed. Babette Babich. Oxford: Peter Lang.
Heilbron, Johan (2004) "The Rise of Social Science Disciplines in France" [La sociologie durkheimienne: tradition et actualité] *Revue européenne des sciences sociales*, T. 42, No. 129: 145–157.
Heller, Agnes (1989) "From Hermeneutics in Social Science toward a Hermeneutics of Social Science." *Theory and Society* 18(3): 291–322.
Hitzler, Ronald, Reichertz, Jo and Schröer, Norbert (eds.) (1999) *Hermeneutische Wissenssoziologie. Standpunkte zur Theorie der Interpretation.* Constance: Universitätsverlag Konstanz.
Knorr-Cetina, Karin (1999) *Epistemic Cultures: How the Sciences Make Knowledge.* Cambridge: Harvard University Press.
Kockelmans, Joseph J. (1976) "Hermeneutic Phenomenology and the Science of History." *Phënomenologische Forschungen* 2: 130–179.
Kockelmans, Joseph J. (1978) "Reflections on Social Theory." *Human Studies: A Journal for Philosophy and the Social Sciences* 1: 1–15.

Kockelmans, Joseph J. (1979) “Deskriptive und interpretierende Phanomenologie in Schütz’s Konzeption der Sozialwissenschaft.” In: Walter Sprondel and Richard Grathoff (eds.), *Alfred Schütz und die Idee des Alltags in den Sozialwissenschaften*. Stuttgart: Enke, pp. 26 – 42.

Latour, Bruno (1987) *Science in Action: How to Follow Scientists and Engineers through Society*. Cambridge: Harvard University Press.

Latour, Bruno (1999) *Pandora’s Hope: Essays on the Reality of Science Studies*. Cambridge, MA: Harvard University Press.

Latour, Bruno (2013) *An Inquiry into Modes of Existence: An Anthropology of the Moderns*, tr. Catherine Porter. Cambridge: Harvard University Press.

Latour, Bruno and Woolgar, Steve (1979) *Laboratory Life: The Construction of Scientific Facts*. London: Sage.

Lukes, Steven (1972) *Emile Durkheim: His Life and Work*. New York: Harper and Row.

Lynch, Michael (2016) *The Internet of Us: Knowing More and Understanding Less in the Age of Big Data*. New York: W.W. Norton

Madison, Gary (1990) “Getting Beyond Objectivism: The Philosophical Hermeneutics of Gadamer and Ricoeur.” In: Dan Lavoie (ed.), *Economics and Hermeneutics*. London: Routledge, pp. 32 – 57.

McCarthy, George E. (2009) “Understanding Historical Hermeneutics and Practical Science in Weber.” In: George E. McCarthy, *Dreams in Exile: Rediscovering Science and Ethics in Nineteenth-Century Social Theory*. Albany: State University of New York Press.

Mestrovic, Stjepan (2005) *Anthony Giddens: The Last Modernist*. London: Routledge.

Misgeld, Dieter (1989) “Common Sense and Common Convictions: Sociology as a Science, Phenomenological Sociology and the Hermeneutical Point of View.” *Human Sciences* 6 (1): 109 – 139.

Mohr, John W. and Rawlings, Craig (2013) “Four Ways to Measure Culture: Social Science, Hermeneutics, and the Cultural Turn.” In: Jeffrey C. Alexander, Ronald Jacobs and Philip Smith (eds.), *The Oxford Handbook of Cultural Sociology*. Oxford: Oxford University Press, pp. 70 – 113.

Moses, Jonathon and Knutsen, Torbjørn (2012) *Ways of Knowing: Competing Methodologies in Social and Political Research*. London: Palgrave Macmillan.

Okrent, Mark (1984) “Hermeneutics, Transcendental Philosophy and Social Science.” *Inquiry* 27: 23 – 49.

Pierozak, Isabelle (2016) “Pourquoi une sociolinguistique (de la /) en réception? Citation et conception de la recherche / professionalité du chercheur.” *Glottopol* 28: 206 – 225. Online: http://www.univ-rouen.fr/dyalang/glottopol.0

Pietsch, Wolfgang, Jörg Wernecke, Max Ott, eds. (2017) *Berechenbarkeit der Welt?: Philosophie und Wissenschaft im Zeitalter von Big Data*. Frankfurt: Springer.

Rorty, Richard (2003) “Analytic and Conversational Philosophy.” In: Carlos Prado (ed.), *A House Divided: Comparing Analytic and Continental Philosophy*. Amherst, NY: Humanity Books, pp. 17 – 32.

Rose, Hilary (1994) *Love, Power and Knowledge: Towards a Feminist Transformation of the Sciences*. Bloomington: Indiana University Press.

Scheler, Max (1980) *Problems of a Sociology of Knowledge*, tr. Manfred Frings. London: Routledge.

Schmaus, Warren (1994) *Durkheim's Philosophy of Science and the Sociology of Knowledge: Creating an Intellectual Niche.* Chicago: University of Chicago Press.
Schütz, Alfred (1967) *The Phenomenology of the Social World.* Evanston: Northwestern.
Sedgwick, Peter R. (2007) *Nietzsche's Economy: Modernity, Normativity and Futurity.* London: Palgrave McMillan.
Sherrat, Yvonne (2006) *Continental Philosophy of Social Science: Hermeneutics, Genealogy, and Critical Theory from Ancient Greece to the Twenty-First Century.* Cambridge: Cambridge University Press.
Simon, Joseph (1989) *Philosophie des Zeichens.* Berlin/New York: De Gruyter.
Staudigl, Michael and Berguno, George (eds.) (2014) *Schutzian Phenomenology and Hermeneutic Traditions.* Frankfurt a.M.: Springer.
Stingl, Alexander (2015) *The Digital Coloniality of Power: Epistemic Disobedience in the Social Sciences and the Legitimacy of the Digital Age.* Lanham: Lexington.
Thouard, Denis (2005) "Wie Flacius zum ersten Hermeneutiker der Moderne wurde. Dilthey, Twesten und Schleiermacher und die Historiographie der Hermeneutik." In: Jörg Schönert and Friedrich Vollhardt (eds.), *Die Geschichte der Hermeneutik und die Methodik der textinterpretierenden Disziplinen.* Berlin/New York: De Gruyter, pp. 265–280.
Trigg, Roger (1985) *Understanding Social Science.* Oxford: Basil Blackwell.
Warnke, Georgia (1985) "Hermeneneutics and the Social Sciences: A Gadamerian Critique of Rorty." *Inquiry: An Interdisciplinary Journal of Philosophy* 28(1–4): 339–357.
Weber, Max (1949) *The Methodology of the Social Sciences.* New York: Free Press.
Weber, Max (1988 [1922]) *Gesammelte Aufsätze zur Wissenschaftslehre*, ed. Johannes Winckelmann. Tübingen: Mohr/Siebeck.
Ziman, John (1976) *The Force of Knowledge: The Scientific Dimension of Society.* Cambridge: Cambridge University Press.

I Science and Method: Towards Hermeneutic Phenomenology of Social Science

Joseph J. Kockelmans

Toward an Interpretative or Hermeneutic Social Science

Abstract: In this essay I wish to reflect on the question of whether or not hermeneutic philosophy in principle can make a positive contribution to the philosophy of the social sciences. My reflections are inspired by Heidegger's conception of hermeneutic phenomenology as developed in *Being and Time*. On the basis of this conception, which I presuppose here, I shall try to develop a number of theses which were derived from two of Gadamer's major publications: *Le probléme de la conscience historique* and *Wahrheit und Methode*. In view of the fact that the three works referred to are concerned with the foundations of philosophy itself, and not with the philosophy of the social sciences, I wish to explain first in what sense Heidegger's and Gadamer's ideas about philosophy can be made profitable for a philosophy of the social sciences and how some objections that have been raised against this position and which are immediately relevant to the main topic of this essay can perhaps be met successfully. Since in the pages to follow I shall be concerned explicitly with Gadamer's publications only, I shall try to explain my view in this regard predominantly in reference to his book *Wahrheit und Methode*.

I Hermeneutic Philosophy and Its Critics

Gadamer's concern (the suggestion implicit in the title of his magnum opus notwithstanding) has never been to develop a method for the human sciences in the sense of either Schleiermacher or Dilthey. No doubt his main concern was with understanding and interpretation; but instead of trying to help the humanities find new methods which would place them on a par with the natural sciences, Gadamer is concerned with discovering what actually happens in any form of understanding, almost independent of our deliberate activities, on a level where "understanding is not so much a method ... as a standing within the happening of tradition" [*Überlieferungsgeschehen*].[1] Taking hermeneutics to be a "theory of the actual experience that understanding is,"[2] Gadamer attempts to describe the conditions that make all understanding possible. Such an endeavor

1 Gadamer, *Wahrheit und Methode* [Hereafter cited as WM], pp. 293, xiv. Cf. Kisiel 1969.
2 Gadamer, WM, p. xxii.

https://doi.org/10.1515/9783110551563-002

obviously cannot replace methodological investigations, but it tries to explore dimensions which are presupposed in reflections on hermeneutic methodology. One could formulate this also as follows.

By showing "how much happening is operative in any form of understanding,"[3] philosophic hermeneutics wishes to clarify the conditions under which all understanding actually occurs. Gadamer takes from Heidegger the basic thesis that all human understanding is basically hermeneutic and that this is so because of the fact that man himself and, thus, all of his activities, are essentially determined by finite temporality and historicity. All genuine human experiences in science, art, social praxis, morality, religion, philosophy are characterized by the operative presence of two components: there is always an element coming from the tradition of the society to which each man belongs, and there is a creative element in which that which is handed down is overcome or transcended. That is why Gadamer is preoccupied with the endeavor of exploring the movement of understanding in its concrete appropriation of the possibilities which flow from the transmitted heritage of the past.

Understanding itself is not to be considered so much an action of a given subjectivity, but rather as an entering into the occurrence of the happening of the tradition in which past and present are constantly being mediated. This is what must gain acceptance in hermeneutic theory, which until now has been too much dominated by the idea of procedure and method.[4]

Gadamer adopts here the attitude that the radical finitude, "temporality," and historicity of man's ek-sistence is to be accepted as a basis which one cannot transcend by an appeal to an absolute spirit or a transcendental ego (Hegel, Husserl). Once the radical facticity of man is realized it makes no sense to try to overcome it; what is of prime importance then is the task of grasping the full significance of what it means to belong to a tradition and of the realization that a man belongs more to his tradition than he ever belongs to himself. "Long before we understand ourselves in retrospect, we understand ourselves as a matter of course in the family, society, and nation in which we live .... Thus the individual's pre-judgments much more than his judgments are the historical reality of his Being."[5] Before our prejudgments can ever become an epistemological problem, they are already an ontological fact, the facticity of our standing in a tradition which has already been handed down to us and on the basis of which we understand whatever we are able to understand. The basic epistemological problem for

3 Gadamer, WM, p. 279.
4 Gadamer, WM, pp. 275, xiv, xxvii.
5 Gadamer, WM, p. 261.

our finite understanding is therefore not a matter of discarding our pre-judgments in order to begin absolutely, but to distinguish between legitimate pre-judgments and pre-judgments which obstruct understanding. The tradition is not to be rejected, but to be taken up in such a manner that by giving us access to our past it continually opens up new possibilities for the future. It is in this context that the hermeneutic circle, as understood by Heidegger, receives its positive meaning. The circle appears in the circular relation between a living tradition and its interpretation, which itself is and remains a constitutive part of that tradition. That is why the interpretation will always remain partial, finite, governed by the historical situation in which it takes place. One interprets a tradition from within that tradition. The tradition first provides the basis for our interpretation; it is our innovative and creative interpretation that keeps our tradition alive. The movement of interpretation is evoked by the more primordial movement of the transmission; the two movements together constitute the circular movement of the historical happening. As such the circle reflects the intrinsically circular structure of our temporal eksistence whose future projects are necessarily determined and guided by past presuppositions.

Although Gadamer himself is not concerned with methodological issues, the importance of these reflections for the social sciences is nevertheless evident. For if it is true that all understanding of inherently human phenomena is hermeneutic in character, then our scientific knowledge of social phenomena must contain a hermeneutic dimension. For although it is true that social phenomena take place in the present, they are nonetheless historical also, in the sense that together with other phenomena they constitute what Gadamer calls "the happening of the tradition." I shall return to this basic thesis as well as to its implications for the methods to be employed in the social sciences, in the pages to follow. First, however, I wish to consider a few objections which have been raised against Gadamer's position, in that they are immediately relevant to the application of his view to the methodology of the social sciences.[6]

Almost all of the objections to Gadamer's view are directly or indirectly aimed at his basic thesis, namely that interpretation can never lead to science, if by science is understood a discipline which tries to achieve objectivity and permanent knowledge. Truth cannot reside in the genuine re-cognition of an author's or an agent's meaning, for such an unrealizable ideal naively disregards the fact that every putative re-cognition of a text or a pattern of behavior is really a new and different cognition of which the interpreter's own historicity is a constitutive part. Since no method can help us transcend the historicity of the inter-

6 Gadamer, WM, pp. xvii, 280, 289–290; see Hirsch 1967, pp. 245–246, 252–255, 258–264.

preter's own understanding, truth cannot be achieved by means of methods. Thus, contrary to what the title of Gadamer's main work, *Wahrheit und Methode*, seems to suggest, method is *not* the way to truth. According to the critics this view necessarily leads to relativism in all domains where interpretative methods are to be applied. It seems to me that Gadamer's view according to which interpretative methods cannot achieve objectivity and permanent knowledge is correct and that the arguments he gives for this thesis are convincing. It is undeniably true that the historicity of the interpreter's own understanding is a constitutive part of his knowledge of any phenomenon he approaches with the help of interpretative methods. However, it is my opinion that the critics are mistaken when they claim that defending this view leads to relativism in all domains or disciplines in which interpretative methods are employed. For it seems to me that a careful distinction between "objectivity" and "intersubjective validity" takes most of the wind out of the critics' sails. In view of the fact that interpretative disciplines do not apply any processes of objectivation, it is obvious that no objectivity can be achieved in these disciplines. Furthermore, since these disciplines do not take the subject matter to be understood out of the historical context to which it belongs and, thus, do not try to achieve a demundanization [*Entweltlichung*] as found in the objectifying empirical sciences of nature for instance, their investigations cannot bring about insights which are true for all people at all times. On the other hand, however, in view of the fact that the interpretation recommended by hermeneutic theory is bound by the canons of hermeneutics, it is, in principle at least, always possible to come to an interpretation which is intersubjectively valid for all people who share the same world at a given time of history. Finally, as for the irony found in the title of Gadamer's book, *Truth and Method*, one must realize that the word "truth" here stands for the Heideggerian conception of truth, i.e., the process of unconcealment, and not for the classical conception of truth, i.e., the correspondence between what is and what is understood or claimed. The title of Gadamer's book, thus, tries to express that truth as unconcealment always and necessarily precedes the application of all interpretative methods on account of the hermeneutic situation in which all genuine understanding must take place.

It is often said that Heidegger's and Gadamer's conception of hermeneutics continuously falls into contradiction in that these authors do not make a careful distinction between the meaning of a phenomenon or a text, and the significance of that meaning for people who find themselves in a particular situation. Anyone who does not make this distinction has to admit, at the same time, that a historical phenomenon has a self-identical and repeatable meaning, and that the meaning of that phenomenon changes over time. Thus, the critics argue, Heidegger and Gadamer should have tried to resolve the paradox arising here by observing that the word “meaning” has been given two different senses in this case: there is a difference between the meaning of a phenomenon in itself which does not change over time and the meaning of the same phenomenon which changes for us. In making this distinction the critics must obviously assume that the unchanging meaning of a phenomenon or a text is that which the agents involved in the phenomenon or the author of the text meant by their behavior or their use of particular linguistic elements. Heidegger and Gadamer have tried to explain why in the realm of meaning no distinction can possibly be made between an in-itself and a for-us, i.e., between the meaning of a phenomenon in itself and the meaning which this phenomenon has for us. For the meaning of something is inherently related to someone and this human being (or this group of human beings, as the case may be) is in his understanding of the phenomenon's meaning essentially determined by the hermeneutic situation in which he finds himself. The only legitimate distinction which can be made in this context as far as social phenomena are concerned, is the distinction between the meaning a phenomenon has for a society and the meaning the same phenomenon may have for a particular individual who finds himself in this or that particular situation. If a society engages itself in a public ceremony it does so because its tradition has attached a certain meaning to this ceremony. However, this by no means entails that this particular ceremony will have the same meaning for everyone who actually takes part in it. One should note that in this case no distinction is made between the meaning of a phenomenon taken in itself, and the meaning of the same phenomenon for us. Whereas the distinction suggested by the critics cannot possibly be made, the latter distinction is of importance in the realm of the social sciences, because it helps us in determining the precise subject matter of these disciplines, as we shall see later. Some critics have argued that if, indeed, the distinction between the meaning of a phenomenon taken in itself and the meaning of the same phenomenon for us cannot be made legitimately, then Gadamer contradicts himself where he speaks of the *Horizontverschmelzung* which must take place in all interpretation.

According to Gadamer, the real meaning of a phenomenon as it addresses itself to an interpreter is always codetermined by the hermeneutic situation of the interpreter.[7] In the case of a historical phenomenon that took place in the past, the meaning of that same phenomenon was co-determined by the perspective of the agents involved in it. What the interpreter understands is neither wholly determined by his own perspective, nor is it wholly the result of the original perspective. That which the interpreter understands is rather the product of a fu-

7 Gadamer, WM, p. 280.

sion between these two perspectives or horizons. "In the process of understanding there always occurs a true fusion of perspectives in which the projection of the historical perspective really brings about the sublation of the same."[8] However, the critics say, if this is the case, then the question must be asked how an interpreter can fuse two perspectives (his own and that of the agents actually involved in the phenomenon), unless he has somehow appropriated the original perspective. But this (according to Gadamer's own testimony) the interpreter can never do, because in principle he cannot overcome the "distorting" perspective of his own historical situation, no matter how hard he tries: "one understands differently when one understands at all."[9]

It seems to me that in this particular case the critics' interpretation of Gadamer's view is unfair. Gadamer makes it perfectly clear that the perspectives [*Horizonte*] introduced here should not be taken in the sense the critics understand them. It is precisely in order to avoid anyone's conceiving of the situation in terms of a meaning-in-itself which appears to the original agents from the perspective of their epoch and the same meaning-in-itself which appears to the interpreter from the perspective of his own conception of the world, that Gadamer speaks of afusion of horizons and not of a replacement of the one by the other. Furthermore, one must realize here that the perspectives or horizons referred to, in both cases are an integral part of the meaning of the phenomenon in each separate case, so that taken by themselves they are purely ideal constructs. As Gadamer states it: in interpretative understanding we always find a fusion of horizons which only putatively are assumed to exist by themselves [*die Verschmelzung solcher vermeintlich für sich seiender Horizonte*].[10]

It is sometimes said that Gadamer's conception of hermeneutics is inherently relativistic in that he claims that prejudices [*Vorurteile*] are not to be avoided but welcomed in every attempt at interpretation.[11] Although I do not believe that the concept of *Vorurteil* in Gadamer's opinion has as negative a meaning as his critics claim it has, nonetheless I agree with these critics that misunderstanding can be avoided by using a more careful terminology. That is why in the pages to come I shall use Heidegger's term *pre-judgment* instead of Gadamer's *prejudice* in order to stress the point that in many instances our anticipated knowledge and pre-understanding of phenomena by no means has the character of a mere prejudice. These reflections may suffice to set the stage for our investigation concerning the possible application of these ideas to the methodology of the social sciences.

---

8 Gadamer, WM, p. 290.

9 Gadamer, WM, p. 280; cf. Hirsch 1967, pp. 252–254.

10 Gadamer, WM, p. 289.

11 Hirsch 1967, pp. 245–246, 258–264.

II Interpretative Social Science

First I wish to explain briefly what is to be understood by "interpretative social science" or also "hermeneutic social science," and how hermeneutic social science is to be related to empirical and descriptive social science. It will not be possible here to deal with all the problems involved, but I hope to be able to briefly indicate how most of these problems can be solved in principle. Instead of focusing predominantly on philosophical issues to which the problems referred to are related, I wish to deal mainly with methodological issues. Yet a few introductory remarks of a more philosophical nature appear to be necessary.

The subject matter of interpretative social science consists in the totality of all social phenomena which function in a meaningful way in our society, i.e., our social world (or the world of a given society, as the case may be). Interpretative social science is not interested in the factual occurrence of these phenomena, nor in the way these phenomena can be "explained" by relating them to one another. This would be the task of empirical social science. Interpretative social science is not interested either in discovering invariable structures which are found in social phenomena of a certain kind. For this would be the task of descriptive or phenomenological social science. Interpretative social science focuses its attention on an attempt to understand the social meaning of these phenomena, i.e., the meaning which these phenomena have in our or, as the case may be, in a given society.[12] It will be clear that interpretative social science is not interested in discovering the meaning which a private individual or a group of individuals who happen to be concerned with, or involved in, these phenomena may attach to them, nor in the meaning which social agents "deep in their hearts" may attach to certain social actions they perform. Interpretative social science is concerned only with discovering the social meaning which a society attaches to certain phenomena and certain patterns of social behavior. Although this meaning is never "objective" in the sense in which this term is used in the natural sciences (for this meaning is by no means the result of a process of objectivation), nonetheless this meaning is in no sense of the term "subjective" either. This meaning is intersubjectively shared by the members of a society and thus intersubjectively accessible, so that a community of scholars in principle can achieve an intersubjectively acceptable understanding of the

12 The term "interpretative social science" or "interpretative sociology" was suggested by Alfred Schutz. The expressions "empirical social science," "descriptive social science," and "interpretative social science" do not refer to three different sciences or disciplines, but rather to three different basic possibilities in each social science. For the distinction between the empirical, descriptive, and interpretative components of every human discipline, cf. Kockelmans 1973.

meaning of these institutions, phenomena, patterns of behavior, etc. Let us clarify this basic point with a few examples taken from our everyday world. Let us suppose the mayor of a town dies and his funeral has been arranged. Interpretative social science is interested in the meaning we attach to the funeral ceremony as it takes place there. Perhaps one may be interested in trying to understand the meaning which family members, friends, the members of a church, political friends and enemies, the organizers of funeral homes and cemeteries, etc., attach to this ceremony as such, or to the ceremony precisely insofar as it involves a politician. In other words, interpretative social science explicitly admits that such a complex social phenomenon can be the subject matter of various interpretative approaches. But interpretative social science is in no case interested in the thoughts, feelings, emotions, fears, anxieties, hopes, etc., which isolated individuals may experience during, or in connection with, this ceremony, except insofar as all of this is an inherent part of the public ceremony and is expressed in a manner which is open to systematic inspection. To give another example, in the American society professional sports and games play an important social role. Interpretative social science is interested in understanding the meaning of this social phenomenon. It may approach this meaning from an economic or a social point of view; it may approach this meaning from the viewpoint of those who own the team, the club, or the stadium; it may approach the problems involved from the viewpoint of those actively involved in the sport: the players, the spectators, or those who indirectly earn a living from these events, etc. But in all these cases interpretative social science is not immediately interested in the thoughts, feelings, and emotions of the actual human beings under consideration, except insofar as all of this is constitutive for the phenomena as such. The following, too, could clarify the issue at hand. Over the past decades the American society has been in the process of adopting a different attitude in regard to sex. This manifests itself in almost all public forms of life, ranging from nightclubs, entertainment places and events, movies, novels, poetry, periodicals, and the concrete ways in which individuals become involved in sexual relationships. This enormously complex phenomenon is difficult to understand. Interpretative social science wishes to understand the meaning of this change in attitude. It can approach the problems involved from many perspectives and focus on the phenomenon as a whole, or on certain aspects of it. But it certainly is not concerned with the private thoughts, feelings, emotions, hopes, or fears which individuals experience when they engage in sexual relationships. Obviously it is interested in trying to understand the motives, justification, and rationale, which various groups of people have for their actual behavior and attitudes (married people, teenagers, nudists, prostitutes, "liberated" men and women, homosexuals, movie-producers, owners of bars and public places, etc.), but all of this is relevant only to the degree that it is constitutive for the meaning of the phenomena under consideration. In trying to understand the social meaning of social phenomena, institutions, and actions, interpretative social science employs hermeneutic methods. Before we can turn to a more detailed description of these methods, it should be noted that the expression "interpretative understanding" [*Verstehen*] has nothing at all in common with empathy, subjective feeling, private conception, personal conviction, etc. The term is taken here in the sense in which the members of a nation that has been in a war and finally has reached peace, can say that they understand what war and peace mean; or also in the sense in which adults who have children of their own can say that they understand what it means to be married and to take care of a family. Although this type of understanding has relatively little in common with the understanding of a mathematician who says that he understands the proof for a certain theorem of geometry, nonetheless it should be pointed out that this type of understanding is by no means necessarily subjective in any sense of the term. Furthermore, it should be noted that in employing this type of understanding interpretative social science binds itself to hermeneutic rules whose goal it is to achieve intersubjective validity in regard to the results obtained via this type of understanding. Thus, contrary to Dilthey's view, such a systematic attempt which binds itself to rules, does not lead to, or in any way involve, relativism.

It is true that the understanding of the meaning of social phenomena, institutions, and actions which can be achieved in this way, will not always have validity for all peoples of all times; nonetheless it certainly, in principle, can have intersubjective validity for all those who are members of a given society at a given moment in time. This fact has been one of the reasons why Weber tried to combine the method of *Verstehen* with empirical methods, in order through this combination to reach a higher degree of objectivity. It is obviously true that if one employs empirical methods in the study of social phenomena, methods which imply abstraction, formalization, and idealization, one can in many cases discover insights which transcend the limitations of place and time. This is due to the fact that the processes mentioned precisely place the phenomena under consideration outside the historical process in which they developed and in which they have the meaning the members of a community actually attach to them. But it is equally true that if one precisely is interested in the understanding of the meaning of these phenomena as they actually occur, the results have validity only for the society under consideration taken in a given epoch. However, this does not mean that this latter type of knowledge is inferior or in any sense of the term subjective or unscientific. This does mean that interpretative social science is to some degree a historical science. For it is clear that the meaning of social phenomena cannot be understood genuinely if it is not studied as the meaning of a historic event, process, or institution whose origin goes back far into the life of a community or individual.

Yet there is a difference between history and interpretative social science. In the past it has been said that sociology and social science in general are the sciences of the present, whereas history is the science of the past. Whatever one thinks about this characterization of the distinction between social science and history, it becomes clear here that social science certainly is continuous with history. Interpretative social science tries to understand the historical situation in which social phenomena arise and to show how they are incorporated in the context of a living tradition in which each individual of a society forms his identity. Thus it must study traditions with the intention of displaying alternatives and instigating changes; in other words interpretative social science is interested in the past because it is concerned with the future.[13] Interpretative social science is therefore equally continuous with social philosophy. This brings us to a last point that must be clarified before we can turn to the canons which interpretative social science has to employ in order to achieve intersubjective validity. One will recall that both Dilthey and Weber have claimed that social science should be value-free, i.e., social science must be "scientifically objective" and avoid all reference to practical affairs.

Social phenomena must be studied in as value-neutral a way as possible. No claims to normative bonds can be made and the interpretation must progressively objectify the meaning of the social phenomena under consideration, through abstracting from a decision about the credibility of assertions and about the acceptability of norms and values. The interpreter is not permitted to take any responsibility with respect to the truth claims of the conceptions held about these phenomena, or to formulate prescriptions concerning what should be done about them.

It is to be observed here first that the discussion concerning the distinction to be made between fact and value gained importance the moment empirical methods were applied to human phenomena. For originally it was believed that in order to achieve objectivity and intersubjective validity empirical science had to abstract from all value aspects of the phenomena to be considered in that they were said to be inherently subjective and thus beyond the possible concern of science. However, it is now quite generally assumed that this view is in error and that phenomena which have value can be brought within the compass of empirical research without any such explicit abstraction. Secondly one should

13 See Radnitzky 1968, pp. 147–153, and the literature quoted there.

realize that although some individuals may indeed have a highly subjective conception of the value of these phenomena, the values themselves are by no means subjective.

Furthermore, it should be noted that the terms "fact" and "value" are very vague and confusing, unless they are taken in the sense given to these expressions in the various value-theories which have been developed between Lotze and Nicolai Hartmann, and that in Weber's case the distinction is to be understood from the viewpoint of Rickert's Neo-Kantianism. However, if these terms are taken in that philosophical perspective, the question must be asked as to whether or not philosophy of value is an acceptable form of philosophy. Elsewhere I have tried to explain why I am convinced that any value-theory rests upon a basic misunderstanding which in the final analysis has its roots in a scientistic interpretation of the meaning and function of empirical science. Let me briefly summarize the conclusions reached in that essay,[14] in objecting to any form of value philosophy it was not my intention to state that there are no values, nor that philosophy should not be concerned with them. Philosophy must certainly be concerned with the values things and events have for us, but in so doing it should not separate from one another ontology (dealing with what is) and axiology (dealing with what ought to be). For one must realize that the distinction between facts and values rests upon an abstraction and that in the "real" world there are no bare facts nor mere values. On the level of our pre-philosophical and pre-scientific experience we never experience things without values, nor do we ever experience values which are not the values of things or events. Anyone who begins his reflection on values by isolating that which ought to be from that which is, will find himself confronted with pseudo-problems. From an epistemological point of view the problem is: how do we know values?; and from the ontological perspective the question is: how can values be? It can be shown that (once this distinction between fact and value has been made) anyone who is able to find an adequate solution for the epistemological problem will find himself confronted with a mystery as far as the ontological problem is concerned. For if we are able to know values, then these values must be human, temporal, and historical; however from an ontological point of view merely relative values are incapable of solving the problems they were supposed to solve. On the other hand, if values are to fulfill the function for which they have been suggested in the various axiologies, they must be absolutes of some kind, but in that case they obviously cannot be known by man. However, on the level of our immediate experience upon which philosophy must reflect, it

14 Kockelmans 1970, especially pp. 246–249.

is undeniable that there are values, that we do know them, and that we know them as the values which things and events have for us.

As soon as the distinction between separated facts and separated values has been replaced by the conception of meaning [*Sinn*] as found in hermeneutic phenomenology, it is clear at once that interpretative social science cannot possibly be value-neutral or value-free, if by this is meant that this type of social science should try to establish facts without having an opinion about their value or meaning. However, there is a great difference between an attempt to understand the meaning of social phenomena by means of interpretation, and to formulate a set of ethical standards or norms with which the social meaning of these phenomena can be evaluated. Whereas the former is, indeed, the main concern of interpretative social science, the latter is the task of social philosophy and ethics. Let us turn now to some methodological reflections which follow from these basic insights.

III The Canons of Hermeneutics and Interpretative Social Science

Interpretative social science is the social discipline which tries to understand the meaning of social phenomena by interpreting these phenomena according to the canons of hermeneutics which, in principle at least, guarantee the intersubjective validity of the interpretation. It should be noted here that these canons have nothing in common with the rules developed in formal logic for considering valid syllogisms or for checking the validity of arguments. For the rules of logic, if properly applied to the proper subject matter, automatically lead to the desired result. The canons of hermeneutics, on the other hand, cannot be applied (as it were from the outside) to a subject matter we understand already, at least to some degree. In the case of hermeneutic interpretation it is assumed that before the interpretation can be developed, the interpreter knows the phenomena he wishes to understand and has at least some knowledge of the context of meaning in which these phenomena appear and to which they belong. It is assumed, also, that to some degree he knows the world in which these phenomena occur. The task of hermeneutic interpretation is to critically examine this fore-knowledge of the world and of the phenomena we encounter there, with the intention of coming to a deeper comprehension of these phenomena and, thus, to a type of understanding [*Verstehen*] which leads to an intersubjectively acceptable result. In other words, the canons have no other function than to help us make explicit systematically what implicitly was already there before us. It is in that sense that one could say that that to which we wish to "apply" the canons of hermeneutics determines, from the very start and in its entirety, the effective and concrete content of the understanding itself.

Furthermore, it should be noted once more that hermeneutic interpretation is inherently oriented toward historical understanding and that historical understanding cannot be modeled after the objectivist knowledge found in the empirical sciences, because this understanding itself is a process which has all the characteristics of a historic event. Even as historians, that is, as representatives of a modern, methodical science, we are and remain members of a community in which (through an uninterrupted chain) the past addresses itself to us. In other words, the historicity of the historian's interpretation is one of the necessary preconditions of his hermeneutic understanding. Only a person who himself stands in history can hope to understand history. Historical thinking cannot but reflect upon its own historicity. There is no neutral standpoint outside of history upon which the historian could found himself.[15]

But let us now turn to a brief reflection on the various canons and explain their meaning in the light of the preceding considerations.[16] The first canon states that the meaning of a phenomenon cannot be projected into that phenomenon, but must be derived from this phenomenon itself. The canon of the autonomy of the object thus states that one must understand a phenomenon from within itself; the phenomenon itself is the primary and final source of as well as the criterion for the legitimacy of the interpretation. The canon obviously does not demand that the social phenomenon be taken in isolation; for the phenomenon is what it is precisely in the context to which it harmoniously belongs; nor does it require a passive adherence to the meaning which is already articulated and expressed in our advance knowledge of it. The canon merely tries to prevent insights and conceptions extraneous to the phenomenon itself being forced upon it, or the phenomenon's being further articulated by concepts which themselves do not flow from a careful analysis of the phenomenon itself. In the social sciences we are often inclined to clarify social phenomenon with ideas which really have their origin in certain philosophical prejudices, rather than in the phenomena themselves. Someone interested in the question of why college students become alienated from the church communities to which they originally belonged may be inclined to take the concept of alienation as found in either Hegel or Marx, or in the sense given to it in psychoanalysis, without carefully trying to understand this very typical form of alienation from the

15 Gadamer, *Le probleme de la conscience historique* [Hereafter cited as PCH], pp. 65–67.

16 For what follows cf. Betti 1967, pp. 211ff.; Radnitzky 1968, pp. 19–40; Seebohm 1972, pp. 7–43.

phenomenon itself, taken in the concrete context in which we encounter it today in our world. Obviously this does not mean that these determinations of the phenomenon of alienation as given by philosophers and scientists may not be used as hints pointing to what one should look for, because we may assume that these authors themselves derived their views from analogous phenomena they experienced or observed. Yet, in a hermeneutic interpretation, the source and criterion of the articulated meaning "is and remains the phenomenon itself." The second canon states that one must search for an interpretation which makes the phenomenon maximally reasonable, or perhaps better: human. In order to understand the meaning of this canon one must realize that many social phenomena are so complex and so richly structured, so deeply rooted in the past of a society, that their genuine meaning often cannot be made explicit on the basis of the phenomena as they actually manifest themselves at a certain moment in time. In many instances the original, and often the genuine, meaning of patterns of social behavior, types of action, the adherence to social institutions, and the institutions themselves, may have been covered up by secondary and tertiary layers of meaning so that those actually involved in these actions or confronted with these institutions no longer explicitly realize the original meaning. Anyone who has made a serious study of institutions as well as of social customs will have encountered this fact on many occasions, In that case the interpreter must complement the phenomena as they immediately manifest themselves with suitable assumptions so as to make these phenomena maximally reasonable and human. So it is that the interpreter tries to understand the relevant phenomena "better" and "more deeply" than those who are actually involved in or confronted with them. The second canon obviously must be counterbalanced by the first, and the assumptions mentioned should be chosen in such a way that they are inherently connected with the given phenomena. The question as to whether or not a given assumption is, indeed, inherently connected with a phenomenon can often be solved only through careful historical research.

In all of this it is presupposed that the interpreter bring himself into a harmonious relationship with the phenomena to be interpreted. Thus a third canon states that the interpreter must try to achieve the greatest possible familiarity with the phenomenon whose meaning he wishes to understand interpretatively. In the older school of hermeneutics (Schleiermacher, Dilthey), it was often said that the interpreter should empathize with the social agents involved in these phenomena. Imaginative re-enactment as well as the placing of oneself in the situation of the agents may, psychologically, have a heuristic value in the first explorative stages of the process, but this is most certainly not what the third canon attempts to accomplish. If one wishes at all to speak of imagining oneself in the place of some other person, he must realize that it is not with the other's thoughts that he should be concerned, but with what these thoughts are about, i.e., the social meaning of the phenomena under consideration. Since hermeneutics is really concerned with the mediation of traditions, the interpreter has to familiarize himself with the phenomena in their historical origin, with the various components of meaning which have been gradually attached to the original meaning in a long historical process, and with the various traditions themselves which influenced the origin and the further development of the phenomena.

The most important canon, however, is to be found in the hermeneutic circle. Before discussing this all-important canon in detail, I wish first to give a brief description of the meaning of this canon for interpretative social science and to relate it to a last canon according to which one must show the meaning of social phenomena for one's own situation. The hermeneutic circle is essentially a very general mode of the development of all human knowledge, namely, the development through dialectic procedures. It is assumed that there cannot be any genuine development of knowledge without some fore-knowledge. The anticipation of the global meaning of an action, of a form of life, of a social institution, etc., becomes articulated through a dialectic process in which the meaning of the "parts" or components is determined by the fore-knowledge of the "whole," whereas our knowledge of the "whole" is continuously corrected and deepened by the increase in our knowledge of the components. The hermeneutic circle involves four different aspects. For, the part-whole-relationship holds first for the phenomenon taken as a whole and all of its constituent parts or elements. Furthermore, this relationship also holds between this particular phenomenon and all other related phenomena from which, in the final analysis, it derives (part of) its meaning. Then, this relationship holds between the social agents as involved in this phenomenon and the world in which they live. Finally, this relationship holds between our Western civilization taken as a whole and the particular phenomenon taken as appearing in the agents' world as a constitutive part of this civilization. It is because of all of these circular and spiral relationships that a definitive and all-encompassing interpretation can never be achieved. The dialectic process is quasi-infinite, both on the side of our knowledge of the relevant wholes and on the side of their parts. However, in most instances an interpretation can be reached which genuinely can be said to be adequate in regard to the phenomena under consideration.

The final canon to be mentioned here is that which states that in all of these steps the interpreter must try to show the meaning of a phenomenon for his own situation. No one is really interested in understanding something that is totally irrelevant for himself and the society in which he lives. Thus, after trying to understand a phenomenon in its historical origin and further development he must try to come to a view which states the meaning of all of this for his own situation.

This cannot be done except on the basis of certain prejudgments which in many cases may appear to be mere prejudices and often are inherent in the situation itself in which the interpreter finds himself. One of the main tasks of hermeneutic interpretation is to carefully stipulate these pre-judgments and to examine them critically for their inner human meaning. After this brief summary of the most important canons to be used in hermeneutic interpretation, I wish now to return to a more detailed discussion of the last two canons listed, in that not only are they essential to any acceptable interpretation, but also lead to a number of significant problems.

IV The Hermeneutic Circle in Interpretative Social Science

In our attempt to determine more concretely the structure of the interpretative understanding which is constitutive for all hermeneutics, we must stress once more that this type of understanding essentially implies an affinity with the tradition of the phenomena to be understood. Hermeneutic interpretation tries to bring about a mediation of traditions in that it tries to understand all social phenomena as inherently historical. With this reminder let us turn now to a careful examination of the basic rule of hermeneutics: the circular relationship between the whole and its parts. The anticipated understanding of the whole is to be complemented and deepened by means of a better understanding of the parts; and yet, it is only within the light of the whole that the parts can play their clarifying roles. This can easily be explained by considering the example of working with a foreign language. When one begins to translate a text written in a foreign language, he starts by structuring the text provisionally on the basis of a global understanding of its content or subject matter (as suggested by its title, subheadings, the overall context to which the text belongs, similar or analogous texts, etc.). This is true not only for the text taken as a whole, but also for its major parts, and ultimately even for the paragraphs and sentences of which it consists. During the process of translation this global idea guides our translation, but it will be rectified, corrected, or even rejected on the basis of a more careful study of its parts. What every translator aims at is the complete coherence of this global meaning with the "final" meaning; for this is the most important criterion for his own correct understanding of the text.

What is said here about translating a text holds analogously for our understanding of any inherently historical phenomena, and thus for all social phenomena. To give an example: it seems to me that a sociologist can learn a great deal about a society by studying the ways in which the society as a whole and particularly its families take care for their deceased members, and the function which the dead continue to play in the society and its families. It is obvious that such a study will lead to completely different results if it is made of an Indian tribe living on a reservation than if it is made of people living in New York City. Let us suppose that someone living in New York undertakes such a study. He will approach this highly complex phenomena with a certain fore-knowledge based on his own experience, his contacts with other people, and all he has read about the subject. With this fore-knowledge he will then make a careful study of all the elements which seem to be relevant to this complex phenomenon, beginning with the attitude, actions, and behavioral patterns of the family members, friends, neighbors, church members; the ritual in the funeral home, the church ceremony, the burial or cremation; and finally, the various ways in which people try to keep the memory of the dead alive, or perhaps the manner in which they try to forget. It is obvious that the fore-knowledge of the whole which guided the researcher in selecting the relevant phenomena (parts) will gradually change when more and more accurate information has been obtained about the specific phenomena. It is obvious to me, also, that the genuine meaning of the phenomena taken as a whole will remain misunderstood as long as the researcher limits his interest exclusively to the present. Many aspects of the totality of the phenomena have a deep historical root and only when this has been taken into consideration will it become understandable why people try to take care of their dead as they actually do.

Schleiermacher and Dilthey, speaking about the hermeneutic circle, make a distinction between a subjective and an objective interpretation. "The art" [of interpretation] can develop its rules only from a positive formula, namely: the historical and divinatory, objective and subjective, reconstructing of a given "utterance" or phenomena.[17] The goal of the subjective interpretation is to discover the mental experiences of the author of a text or the agents involved in social phenomena and to reconstruct their thoughts, intentions, feelings, etc. On the other hand, the aim of the objective interpretation is to come to an understanding of the meaning of the text or the historical phenomenon as it presents itself to the interpreter. In making this distinction both Schleiermacher and Dilthey were guided by the historicist prejudice that even in history no genuine scientific insight can be achieved if the final result does not possess a kind of objectivity which is somehow comparable to that found in the natural sciences. In order to achieve this Schleiermacher and Dilthey tried to separate two realms, one in which genuine objectivity can be achieved, and one in which this objectivity cannot be achieved, but which nonetheless is of great heuristic value in regard to

17 Schleiermacher 1959, p. 87.

the first. In the preceding pages we have seen that this distinction was a very unfortunate one; it led to a great number of quasi-problems and was an easy target for criticism, particularly from the neo-positivist point of view. The goal of hermeneutic interpretation is not to be found in the interpreter's reliving of the experiences of those involved in the phenomena to be understood. The interpreter does not wish to place himself in the position of someone else (the agent) and to penetrate his mental activities; he wishes merely to understand the meaning of the phenomenon in question as it has been handed down to us by our tradition. Thus the goal of interpretation is to unveil the miracle of the mediation of traditions, and not the mysterious communication between souls. Interpretative understanding is a typical kind of participation in something that in principle can be seen by everybody. What is typical for this kind of participation is that it is critical and binds itself to methodical rules and principles.

As for the objective aspect of the hermeneutic circle as explained by Schleiermacher and Dilthey, it should be noted that the type of objectivity: they wished to achieve is impossible and even if it were possible, would be undesirable. One has to realize that what determines our anticipation and foreknowledge and what guides us in our understanding of a phenomenon, is precisely that which we have in common with that tradition insofar as this manifests itself in the phenomenon under consideration. Thus it is impossible to tear oneself completely away from that tradition, to adopt a "neutral" and "objective" attitude, and, in this way, to achieve an "authentic" understanding. The intention of the interpreter is rather to mediate between the phenomenon and the tradition which is pre-understood in that phenomenon.[18] I shall return to this problematic shortly. In order to understand the genuine meaning of the hermeneutic circle, let us turn to a text by Heidegger. Speaking about the implications of the circle for the analytic of man's Being he writes:

> But if we see this circle as a vicious one and look out for ways of avoiding it, even if we just "sense" it as an inevitable imperfection, then the act of understanding has been misunderstood from the ground up ... What is decisive is not to get out of the circle but to come into it in the right way. This circle of understanding is not an orbit in which any random kind of knowledge may move; it is the expression of the existential fore-structure of Dasein itself. It is not to be reduced to the level of a vicious circle, or even of a circle which is merely tolerated. In the circle is hidden a positive possibility of the most primordial kind of knowing. To be sure, we genuinely take hold of this possibility only when, in our interpretation, we have understood that our first, last, and constant task is never to allow our fore-having, fore-sight, and fore-conception to be presented to us by fancies and popular conceptions,

18 Gadamer, PCH, pp. 67–69; cf. Radnitzky 1968, p. 27.

> but rather to make the scientific theme secure by working out these fore-structures in terms of the "things themselves."[19]

It is clear that here in this text the positive, ontological meaning of the circle is stressed for the first time. This dimension was still lacking in Schleiermacher as well as in Dilthey. Anyone who wishes to understand something should adhere to "the things themselves" and try to overcome his prejudices, regardless of whether they have their origin in his personal life or in the tradition to which he belongs. For what is to be discovered by means of the interpretation, is what has been the case, not what should have been the case, or what I and other people would have liked to have been the case.

Let us take a historical document as an example to illustrate what is meant here. As soon as the interpreter has found some elements he thinks he understands, he projects a provisional conception concerning the meaning of the whole text. But this first understanding of some of its parts has been motivated not only by the statements found in the text, but also by the general context in which, in his view, such statements should fit. To understand "the thing itself" that in this way begins to emerge before him, means to project a provisional conception of the whole which is to be corrected as his reading of the document proceeds. Eventually he will have to adopt another point of view in regard to the document and its overall meaning; but this new perspective, too, is perhaps still to be broadened, changed, specified. In all of this "the thing itself," as it emerges for him in the process of "deciphering," keeps guiding him. It is this perpetual oscillation of our interpretative conceptions which Heidegger tried to describe in the text just quoted: namely our comprehension of something in terms of a process in which an anticipated understanding is to be examined critically on the basis of ever new projects, as long as the situation requires it, i.e., until finally "the thing itself" begins to manifest itself.

Anyone who tries to do this continuously runs the risk of getting entangled in his own prejudices and of finding that the conceptions he has projected in anticipation appear not to conform with "the thing itself" as it emerges there before him. That is why it is the interpreter's continuous task to elaborate ever new projects and to examine critically the pre-judgments which they imply, until he reaches the point where his anticipated understanding appears to be "authentic" in that it is proportionate to the thing to be brought to light. The only form of objectivity which is found in such a process consists in the fact that my anticipation is gradually confirmed when (in studying the various elements and as-

---

19 Heidegger 1962, pp. 194–195.

pects involved) I try to test this anticipation time and again on the thing which emerges before me in so doing. Thus each interpretation of a phenomenon must be begun with a reflection by the interpreter on his own preconceived ideas which necessarily result from the hermeneutic situation in which he finds himself. He must try to justify them, i.e., to clarify their origin and meaning.

From this it follows that the hermeneutic task as Heidegger conceives of it, does not consist merely in recommending a method for studying historical documents. We have seen that he tried to radicalize that type of understanding which everyone attempts to accomplish when he genuinely tries to comprehend something. What we encounter in our attempt to understand a text or document, is already found in all forms of our understanding, provided the subject matter of our understanding is something intrinsically human, and for that reason essentially historical. That is why Heidegger's ideas are particularly relevant for reflections on the methods of interpretative social science.

For in all the cases in which man tries to understand something inherently human, he has to follow the same procedure. He begins by assuming that such and such is the meaning of the phenomenon under consideration. In this pre-conception of the meaning of the phenomenon many factors play a part: his personal outlook on the world, his moral standards, his religious convictions, the tradition to which he belongs and in which he lives, his knowledge of the field connected with the phenomenon, his interest, etc. Obviously, his main guide in forming his pre-conception is that which here and now already shows itself, however partial this may be. Hermeneutics does not demand that one give up the subjective co-determinants of our pre- conceptions. It does not require either that one try to come to an objective neutrality in regard to the phenomena, for such neutrality is excluded in principle. The hermeneutic attitude asks merely that one be willing to qualify prejudices as prejudices, and to take mere opinions as opinions, and to give them up the moment the phenomenon, i.e., the thing itself, appears to be incompatible with them. It is only when one adopts this "critical" attitude that he gives a phenomenon, an institution, a document, a thing, the possibility of manifesting itself in its being-different, i.e., to show its truth against the preconceived ideas which originally we tried to substitute for it.[20] Another element of the circle that has become manifest through Heidegger's investigations is the fact that the hermeneutic circle does not have a merely formal character. Schleiermacher and Dilthey speak only about a formal relationship between a whole and its parts; they speak of a dialectic between the "guessing" concerning the meaning of the whole and its later

20 Gadamer, PCH, pp. 70–76.

explanation "by means of the parts." In this romantic conception of the circle, the circular movement is nothing but a deficient, although necessary, form of investigation.

Schleiermacher suggests that once we have gone through the circle we finally reach certainty. At that moment, our circular form of understanding is no longer necessary; our original pre-conception has been verified (or falsified) and, thus, is no longer needed as such. Heidegger on the contrary defends the thesis that our comprehension of human phenomena never ceases to be determined by the anticipatory impetus of our pre-conception. But there is more. We have just said that all comprehension must be characterized as a totality of circular relationships between a whole and its parts. Now we have to add to this that these circular relationships themselves must be characterized by our anticipation of a perfect coherence. This means that in the final analysis only an interpretation which is intrinsically coherent in itself as well as with all of its parts can be admitted. This requirement could still be understood in a purely formal way. However, if one reflects on the meaning of this requirement it becomes clear that the coherence we assume to be present in a series of phenomena transcends this series in that this coherence is also assumed to be referring to what happens to be the truth, thus to the things themselves re-presented by them. In other words when I claim that a text must be coherent in order to be understandable, I make this claim because I am convinced that this coherence is a necessary condition for the text's describing the truth, and thus for my finding the truth via a historic-critical analysis of the text. What I am ultimately interested in are the things themselves, not the way in which they have been handed down to me. In other words, finally, the anticipation of perfect coherence presupposes not only that the text is an adequate expression of an idea, but also that this idea corresponds with what is the case. If we apply this requirement to our attempt to understand the social phenomena with which interpretative social science is primarily concerned, it will obviously have to be mitigated in that in this realm a perfect coherence can very seldom be achieved due to the fact that human beings are not always consistent in their social activities. And yet even here hermeneutic interpretation tends toward "the things themselves" and thus cannot rest until all inconsistencies are explained, if not in harmony with the laws of a rigorous logic, then at least in the light of a typically human logic.

These reflections also explain in what sense the interpreter is related to the tradition through affinity in his hermeneutic interpretation of historical phenomena. Hermeneutics takes its point of departure in the conviction that to comprehend means to be in direct relation with "the things themselves" while at the same time being related to the tradition from which these "things" address themselves to us. Interpretation is necessary here precisely because there is a tension between what is familiar to us in the present and that which has become strange to us in the relevant tradition. But this tension is not merely psychological in character (Schleiermacher); it constitutes precisely the meaning and structure of man's historicity. Thus what hermeneutic interpretation takes as its subject matter of investigation is not the psychic states of actors, agents, and interpreters, but "the things themselves" as they have been handed down by a tradition which is no longer genuinely mine.[21]

What been said previously about the hermeneutic situation sheds light on another important element of all hermeneutic interpretation, namely the genuine meaning and function of temporal distance in any attempt to understand historical phenomena. Temporal distance has nothing in common with a distance one can travel through. This was one of the basic, but naive, prejudices of historicism. It was assumed there that it is possible to reach historic objectivity by going back and placing oneself within the perspective of an earlier epoch and rethinking the facts in terms of conceptions characteristic of that time. In truth, however, one must try to conceive of temporal distance as an essential element and as the positive and productive possibility of hermeneutic interpretation and comprehension. Thus, temporal distance is not a distance to be traveled through, but a living continuity of elements which as links in a chain constitute the tradition which, taken as a whole, functions as the light in which everything with which we are confronted (i.e., which is now being handed down to us) can appear as that which it really is. The reason it is difficult to genuinely appreciate contemporary works of art or contemporary changes in our social structure is to be found in the lack of temporal distance which purifies and separates the universally valuable from the non-universally valuable.

Obviously one can make the remark that if one approaches social phenomena in this way, many prejudices necessarily must be at work in any attempt to interpret their meaning. However, one must realize again that hermeneutics does not deny that there are prejudices. It itself, by means of its critical methods and careful application of the canons of hermeneutics, precisely tries to separate true from false pre-judgments, i.e., pre-judgments which clarify from pre-judgments which obscure. Prejudices are dangerous merely as long as one does not recognize them as such. But in order for us to be able to recognize them, they must have been at work. It is true that unobserved prejudices have determined the opinion of people concerning a great number of things. In critically looking back upon the course of history, it is often possible to unmask false prejudices.

---

21 Gadamer, PCH, pp. 76–80.

But this again is possible only after one has been provoked by them and this, in turn, is possible only by returning to a tradition by means of a renewed contact with it and by critically examining the motives of its beliefs.[22]

This brings us to a final aspect of the hermeneutic approach to social phenomena. Let us suppose that in trying to explain the meaning of a social phenomenon one becomes aware of having used a pre-judgment which appears to be a mere prejudice. Let us assume also that he substitutes another prejudgment in the place of the former. In that case the second pre-judgment obviously cannot be conceived of as being the "definitive" truth, for that would again mean a return to the naive thesis of objectivist historicism. Such a conception forgets that the prejudice which was denounced and the pre-judgment which was substituted for it both belong to an uninterrupted chain of events of which both are members. In other words, one must realize here that the original prejudice continues to play an important part, even though this part is different from before. Everyone knows how difficult it is to give up a prejudice and to substitute a new conviction in its place. The reason for this is that the new conviction can never be presented as the eternal truth. And what is more, the new conviction can never be specified adequately except in connection with the original prejudice whose part it now plays. It is by dialectic opposition that convictions become evaluated. Thus, we are led here to a new element, namely the dialectic between old and new. The original, implicit prejudice which was not yet understood as a prejudice, functioned within the overall conception concerning a set of phenomena.

My new conviction is not in harmony with the original overall conception. Adopting a new conviction means to give up part of my original overall understanding of those phenomena. Thus a dialectic process begins to take place between what is mine but appears to be inauthentic, and what is authentic but is not yet mine. Our interrogation which is the universal mediator of this dialectic will never reach a point where it becomes impossible to replace an implicit prejudice by a new conception which is still alien to me but which I shall have to make mine if I am really willing to comprehend the relevant set of phenomena.

In other words, what naive, objectivist historicism has never understood is that the process of interpretation is itself inherently a finite process that in itself is as historical as the historical phenomena which it tries to explain. For historicism, there is a kind of historicity that is found in all objects of historical investigation, but this historicity is ultimately an illusion that can be overcome. At the end there will be a veritable object which is no longer historical. Thus for naive

22 Gadamer, PCH, pp. 81–83.

historicism the historical object is a kind of mixture of an in-itself and a for-us, a mixture of an ahistorical veritable object and our historic illusion. However, a more careful examination of historical phenomena which includes a careful examination of all the pre-judgments inherent in the methodical procedures we employ while studying these phenomena systematically shows that such a conception of the "historic object" is unacceptable and that it finally leads either to complete subjectivism (the "in-itself" is a pole which never can be reached), or to radical objectivism (the for-us seems to be mere appearance). According to the hermeneutic conception of the "historic object" the historic reality itself and our historic understanding of that reality can never be separated. What we call the "historic object" is the affinity, the dialectical relationship, which necessarily exists between these two poles, poles which in reality do not exist in separation.[23]

V Interpretative, Descriptive, and Empirical Social Science

Before concluding these reflections on interpretative social science we must try to answer the question of how interpretative social science is to be related to the two other social disciplines distinguished here, namely empirical and descriptive social science. It seems to me that Max Weber, although not subscribing to the basic thesis defended in this study, has indicated the way in which perhaps this question can be answered satisfactorily. Weber distinguishes four different phases in any attempt by social science to acquire knowledge of social reality with respect to its cultural significance and "causal" relationships.[24] First, the investigator must try to establish the hypothetical laws and factors capable of explaining the relevant phenomena. Second, he must try to render intelligible their meaning. Third, he must trace as far into the past as possible "the individual features of these historically evolved configurations which are contemporaneously significant," and explain them historically "by antecedent and equally individual configurations."[25]

Finally, we must add to all of this that in Weber's view his conception of ideal types must mediate between empirical explanation and interpretative understanding.[26] It seems to me that these remarks can be applied to the ideas developed in this essay. If we look at the problematic not from a pedagogical, but merely from a methodological point of view, it seems apparent that any social

23 Gadamer, PCH, pp. 83–87.
24 Weber 1963, especially p. 381.
25 Weber 1963, p. 382.
26 Weber 1963, pp. 391ff., 401–402, 408, 417.

scientist confronted with social reality will first ask what the facts are and why they are the way they appear to be. In order to answer these questions he will have to examine the question of what these facts mean and how they came to have this meaning. To give an example used earlier in this essay, suppose someone wishes to study the alienation of university students from the church communities to which they originally belonged. It is obvious that there is very little to ask and wonder about as long as one does not know precisely what the facts are. However, once the facts have been established the question of why they are the way they appear to be must be asked. In order to specify the variables which should be selected in empirical explanation, in order to come to a better understanding of the facts and to make predictions possible, it will be necessary to study the question of what alienation means in this concrete case and how this type of alienation originates. To answer this question interpretative social science, in addition to theology, is indispensable. Finally, in order to be able to establish a common ground where empirical research and interpretative social science can meet, descriptive methods must be used to clarify the essential structures of all the partial phenomena which as its components constitute the complex phenomenon. Thus by means of a careful description and "definition" of "ideal types" it will then be possible to separate the variables which perhaps can shed light on the question of why the facts are as they appear to be. Once an explanation of the facts has been achieved, predictions can be made as to what may be expected in the future, either assuming that substantially the circumstances will remain the way they are, or under the assumption that some of the antecedent conditions may be changed appropriately.

Over a period of time it may be possible to test some of these predictions and to find a confirmation of the theory thus established. However, it seems to me that the results of the descriptive and empirical approaches should finally be reinserted in the totality of meaning which the interpretative approach has structured, articulated, and clarified. For it is in the concrete world which has now been understood more deeply that future events will take place and have the meaning which the interpretative approach tried to make explicit.

Acknowledgments

This article was originally published in the *New School Graduate Faculty Philosophy Journal* 5(1) (1975): 73–96. Permission to reprint was granted by the late author himself as well as, very graciously, the journal's current editors.

References

Betti, Emilio (1967) *Allgemeine Auslegungslehre als Methodik der Geisteswissenschaften.* Tübingen: Mohr.
Heidegger, Martin (1962) *Being and Time*, tr. John Macquarrie and Edward Robinson. New York: Harper & Row.
Hirsch, Eric D. (1967) *Validity in Interpretation.* New Haven: Yale University Press.
Kisiel, Theodore (1969) "The Happening of Tradition: The Hermeneutic of Gadamer and Heidegger." *Man and World* 2: 358–385.
Kockelmans, Joseph J. (1970) "Metaphysics and Values." In: Robert E. Wood (ed.) *The Future of Metaphysics.* Chicago: Quadrangle Books, pp. 229–250.
Kockelmans, Joseph J. (1973) "Theoretical Problems in Phenomenological Psychology." In: Maurice Natanson (ed.), *Phenomenology and the Social Sciences*, 2 vols. Evanston: Northwestern University Press, vol. 1, pp. 225–280.
Radnitzky, Gerard (1968) *Continental Schools of Metascience.* Goteborg: Akademiforlaget.
Schleiermacher, Friedrich (1959) *Hermeneutik*, ed. H. Kimmerle. Heidelberg: Winter.
Seebohm, Thomas M. (1972) *Zur Kritik der hermeneutischen Vernunft.* Bonn: Bouvier.
Weber, Max (1963) "'Objectivity' in Social Science and Social Policy." In: Maurice Natanson (ed.), *Philosophy of the Social Sciences.* New York: Random House, pp. 355–418.

Patrick Aidan Heelan

Quantum Mechanics and the Social Sciences

Abstract: Quantum mechanics is interpreted, in the spirit of Niels Bohr and Werner Heisenberg, as about physical objects in so far as these are revealed by and within the local, social, and historical process of measurement. An analysis of the hermeneutical aspect of quantum mechanical measurement reveals close analogues with the hermeneutical social/historical sciences. The hermeneutical analysis of science requires the move from the epistemological attitude to an ontological one.

Elsewhere I have written widely on hermeneutics and the physical sciences[1] and I want now to show by a hermeneutic analysis that quantum mechanics can be interpreted as a bridge between the physical and social sciences.

According to Niels Bohr and Werner Heisenberg, the quantum theory of physics differs from classical physics in this respect above all that while classical physics characterizes a physical object by what is real and objective, the quantum theory characterizes a physical object only by what can actually be simultaneously measured. Since, however, measurement can perturb the object measured and (allegedly) does so significantly at the level of quantum physics, what is actually measured in quantum physics is significantly the outcome of a human interaction with the physical reality, and this interaction leaves the system irreversibly changed with respect to some of its parameters. That was the view of Niels Bohr and Werner Heisenberg and it constitutes the original core of what is called "complementarity." It is the view I am provisionally adopting for the purpose of this paper. I also think it is more right than wrong and that the rightness it contains has been undervalued.

Let me expand on what this view entails. It entails that the secular structure of a "quantum phenomenon" is not an objective reality, but is revealed only and strictly within the context of measurement, while recognizing that measurement has to be taken as a socio-historical process of empirical inquiry based on standardized technologies and skills and performed by (spatially and temporally) local scientific inquirers. When compared with the old physics, the new picture of scientific inquiry introduces elements of a socio-historical nature as essential

1 See the list of references.

https://doi.org/10.1515/9783110551563-003

to the analysis of the process of scientific inquiry, such as where, when, by what expert group, in what sequence, for what purpose, etc. In the Bohr/Heisenberg view, the relevance of two non-classical freedoms, namely, social factors and history, is implicit in their understanding of quantum theoretic inquiry. In this view, the quantum theory incorporates within it essentially the socio-historical processes of measurement and relates to the socio-historical path of the system's disclosure within the world. Such knowledge is essentially hermeneutical.

Conversely, wherever these non-classical elements (where, when, by whom, in what sequence, for what purpose, etc.) are intrinsic to and inescapable factors of a scientific process, Bohrians and Heisenbergians would direct you to the quantum theory as a trusty model of such a process. Measurement always involves a local community of expert scientific operators and witnesses—henceforth, the "local research community," or simply, the "local community"—and a laboratory niche in the local community's perceptual world; this is the local niche within which the phenomenon is disclosed through a measurement. A sequence of measurements defines a socio-historical path of disclosure. Using a Merleau-Ponty metaphor,[2] any phenomenon takes "flesh" in the world only along definite socio-historical paths each defined by a particular sequence of decisions taken by local communities. A different sequence of decisions will define a different socio-historical path. To vary the metaphor, if the phenomenon is "dressed" for disclosure in a certain way by each measurement, then different socio-historical paths are characterized by different irreversible sequences of "dresses" resulting from the human decisions that are locally made.[3] Firstly, the quantum theory gives an account of the essential or secular unity of a phenomenon vis-a-vis local communities since all presentable data are united formally by a single theory.

Secondly, under the interpretation given above, it is reasonable to take the "superposition" of two theoretical states to represent the disclosure possibilities of the system relevant to two different possible local communities. The "reduction of the wave packet" would then represent both the decision of a particular local community to equip itself to act, and the post-measurement disclosure of the phenomenon to that community. These are real changes in the world.[4]

---

2 See Merleau-Ponty 1962.

3 There is, of course, no such thing as an "undressed" phenomenon. (The metaphors of "flesh" and "dress" are introduced to substitute for Aristotle's "quality" while relativizing it to human communities and history; cf. Heelan 1989.)

4 Choosing to represent a state as a superposition state relative to a data operator Q is, I take it, the first step toward a decision to measure the quality represented by the operator Q.

Thirdly, the disclosure of a phenomenon is characterized by path dependent data. For example, in quantum physics, a change in the order of some pairwise decisions or measurements, such as momentum and position, or up-down and left-right spin (each measurement associated with a different possible local research community), would (according to the quantum theory) yield different sets of data irreversibly. The elements of each pair, though mutually exclusive in their local historical realizations, belong nevertheless to the definition of the same phenomenon insofar as this is full of real historical potentiality. We could speak of the same phenomenon as "fleshed out" by and for a particular local research community by the sequence of decisions made by past inquiries, i.e., by past research communities; it is this inquiry sequence that determines the historical path of its worldly disclosure. The phenomenon remains, however, throughout its evolution the *identical* secular phenomenon.

This hermeneutical account of data constitution confronts the ontology (rather than the epistemology) of social-historical time as constitutive of human understanding and experience, and the sequential order of local human decision-making as branch-points of real-world novelty. In the model here proposed, data production is path-dependent. Different local and historical communities can prepare and recognize the same phenomenon, but they will find it "dressed" or "fleshed out" differently—exhibiting the phenomenon's social and historical, in the sense of hermeneutical, dimensions.

The ontological interpretation implies a role in the scientific account for two non-classical freedoms, i.e., for social factors and for history. Social factors enter at decision points where local communities decide what representational superpositions are to be broken by measurement. History enters through the path-dependence of the data that trace the life history of the real phenomenon. Although both of these freedoms are real and can lead to real novelty, they are constrained by the essential secular unity of the socio-historical phenomenon which is what the quantum theory defines.[5]

---

5 The discussion at this point naturally leads to the topic of how secular changes in the ways the phenomenon is "dressed" over longer historical periods can be reflected in models of the quantum type. I can only offer some provisional comments here. For communities separated in time, some secular changes are perceived as evolutionary, some as revolutionary. The quantum model has the potentiality of incorporating revolutionary changes in science as evolutionary—that is, as preserving continuity with the past—by adding new data operators to the infinite-dimensional Hilbert space of wave-functions, leaving the rest of the structure intact. An example of this is the enlargement of the traditional set of operators to include the spin operators.

Many of the sciences but especially the social sciences rely on methods of statistical analysis originally developed for the physical sciences; in these methods it is assumed that data are in principle *objective*, i.e.,

1. that what a datum is (how it should be described) does not depend on the local interests people may have in measuring and recording it; in other words, that the descriptive categories for data and phenomena are not derived from the local character of the scientific community but are rather in Newton's terms "universal" qualities (see Newton's "Rules of Reasoning in Philosophy") and,
2. that whether or not a datum is recorded (i.e., a data judgment is made) does not change the course of things in the world; in other words, the decision of the local community to equip itself and to act leaves the world unchanged.

In this classical view, scientific inquiry is a view from outside the world, disengaged from the course of events in the world.

Of the two components of objectivity stated above, the former, is concerned with the categories of objective knowledge, let me call it an *epistemological principle*; the latter, is concerned with the being of the world, let me call it an *ontological principle.* It is well known that quantum physics has undermined the latter of these principles, since a measurement leaves the measured phenomenon irreversibly changed; on the terms of the interpretation given above, quantum physics also undermines the former. With respect to both these principles, it is not clear what should replace them.

These objectivity principles have been challenged in recent years by many scholars, including philosophers, sociologists, anthropologists, and historians of science. I find all of these discussions turn on the relation between the domains of the mental (or more generally, the representational) presumed known and the physical presumed derivable from the representation by a set of principles. It should be clear to a critical reader that epistemological problems are not resolvable in this way but require a prior ontological analysis.

What is the meaning of ontology? And what is the ontology of an act of research? Research is the search for an understanding of what we experience. Understanding and ontology are linked. Inquiring, searching, understanding are, as Aristotle said in the *Metaphysics*, of the defining essence of being human. The domain of this activity is traditionally called Being. Acts of understanding relate people to the world by recalling where they are, where they have been, and where they might want to go. Each act of human understanding foresees possibilities and envisages choices against the background of the World; World in this hermeneutical sense is Being. Heidegger puts it well when he says that to be human is to-be-There-in-the-World, to be *Da-sein.*[6] By Being and World, I do not mean the set of all ready-made things and events (i.e., beings); I mean rather the background essential to human life that makes all things and events possible and understandable. Being is all there is and *can be* and human life is ultimately concerned with nothing but this.

Heidegger made a distinction, the rudiments of which are also found in Aristotle, between "*ontic*" beings and "*ontological*" Being; this he called "the ontological difference".[7] Ontic beings are given as ready-made things and events distributed in objective space and time and belonging from the theoretical viewpoint to the inventory of a local Euclidean world—this is *reality* as it is usually taken in modern philosophy—while ontological Being is the common essential and hermeneutical background of human life which makes ontic beings understandable and which, when interpreted by human life, confers affirmable reality on local worlds. Aristotle and Heidegger are representative of a tradition that addressed the activity of human understanding and research first and foremost as *ontological*, and only secondarily as the ontic.[8]

The activity of understanding then is to be defined as the ontological activity of local communities constituting local beings as known within the hermeneutical and ontological horizon of Being. Note that since understanding (the activity of) understanding does not presuppose prior epistemological principles (in the classically modern sense), it avoids the basic *petitio principii* of an epistemological starting point. One of the functions of such *constitution* is to construct and use representations; what these are and how they are used is then to be studied in this connection.

For Aristotle and, more generally, prior to Descartes and Locke, epistemological questions were formal, regional, and local in character, subsidiary to the ontology of knowledge. After Descartes and Locke, however, the general cultural consensus characteristic of modern times was formed; it had two parts, that science provides the single, true, and privileged account of Nature and that the scientific account ought to replace all other accounts of Nature. Modern philosophy turned to epistemology largely because of the dissonance between Nature as (ontically) pictured by the new science and Nature as assumed for the purposes of human life. The newly emerging scientific picture of Nature was bereft of those

6 See 1962, p. 27, and in general, sect. 32; see also Heelan 1983a and 1983b and 1989.

7 See Heidegger 1966.

8 Pragmatism has tried to escape the rigidity of modern philosophy's ontic framework by introducing human life and culture into the specification of the world (Dewey 1960), but such specifications fail to raise the ontological dimension, and Pragmatism consequently fails to be able to justify itself on other than instrumentalistic grounds.

sensible qualities and feelings, moral purposes, and social organization that constituted the hermeneutical arena—the World—of human life; it had of itself no "meaning," i.e., no human, social "meaning" (whatever other meaning it had in modern philosophy was in the cold eye of an impersonal God). In this cultural transformation, it was inevitable that a new branch of philosophy would grow up, a general epistemology, which was both the science of scientific knowledge and claimed to be the foundation of all philosophy.

When epistemology moved to center-stage, problems were created that could at first be postponed: the problem, for instance, about how knowledge can build bridges between representations, such as scientific theories, diagrams, or data reports, and reality without presupposing a prior grasp of reality. The changes that have taken place in science since the 17th century have brought new and very different models of scientific knowing and with them confusion to those who believed that science provided unchangeable and privileged paradigms of objective knowledge. Certainly, it was the advent of quantum mechanics that dealt the severest blow to the view that scientific knowledge is objective. It is to solve these problems that I turn to an ontology of the activity of scientific research.

Between an epistemology and an ontology of scientific research, there are significant differences in starting point and method. In the *first* place, the ontological starting point drops the Cartesian supposition that whatever functions as a representation can itself be known and judged by internal criteria (e.g., clarity and distinctness) and one returns instead to the Aristotelian position that representations (or *species*, as they were called) are not generally known in themselves but only in what they make known. The ontological starting point works from the principle that whatever scientific representations do, they do it only as a function of what human understanding is.

In the *second* place, the ontological starting point supposes that *real* or *evident* knowledge activity has somehow antecedently been identified and described—but not by an epistemological inquiry in the classically modern sense (i.e., concerned with the justification of mental or other representational contents), but in some other way, for example, by phenomenological inquiry. Phenomenology is explicitly concerned with the ways Being is given critically and evidentially to human understanding; it is not about representations and their validity, but about "*die Sache selbst*", i.e., about what is presented to the knower with evidence in the act of knowing.[9] Turning to phenomenology, however, is not without its problems for someone doing the philosophy of science.

---

9 See Husserl 1970, Heidegger 1962, and Merleau-Ponty 1962.

In the *third* place, we take the paradigmatic fulfillment of scientific knowing to be the recognition of occurrences in the world of what science speaks, i.e., of scientific data. *Data constitution is the starting point and the central philosophical question of an ontological inquiry into science.* Data production and analysis is a part of the experimental, i.e., laboratory, side of science. Compared to the interest philosophers have shown in theories, interest in experimental work has been small until recently.[10] Recent work, however, has failed adequately to clarify the notion of *data* and to address the central philosophical problems of the phenomenology and ontology of *data constitution.*[11]

Data

I shall first present a preliminary clarification of the notion of *data*, and then return to the proposal discussed at the beginning of this paper. We start with a hermeneutic phenomenology of data observation.

Every datum is in relation to a phenomenon and in relation to a local suitably prepared community of data producing observers or expert witnesses.[12] By *community*, I mean, a group that shares outlooks and tasks and monitors the activity of its members so as to pass judgment on its quality as an expression of community goals. By a *local* community, I mean, one that exists in a certain place and time, not an ideal, universal, or global community. By *suitably prepared*, I mean, sharing an expertise and equipped with the appropriate instruments to constitute a community. By *data producing*, I mean, preparing, recognizing, and reporting data in question. In sum, I am speaking of the activity of research, particularly of laboratory science. I shall use the terms "observer" or "local observer" for such a local suitably prepared community of data producing observers or local community of expert witnesses.

In order to have a philosophical perspective, the local observer must be raised above the everyday attitude (i.e., ontic, instrumental, technical, or

---

10 The recent interest in experimentation grew out of the seminal studies of L. Fleck (1979), G. Holton (1973, 1978), T.S. Kuhn (1962, 1977), C. Bernard (1957), and others. Among the more significant books on this topic recently published with a hermeneutical interest, are B. Babich (1993), R. Crease (1993), I. Hacking (1983), P. Heelan (1983b), D. Ihde (1979), J. Kockelmans (1993), J. Rouse (1987). See also, in the history of science, R.P. Galison (1987), S. Shapin and S. Schaffer (1985); and in the social sciences, B. Latour (1987), A. Pickering (1984), B. Latour and S. Woolgar (1979).

11 See Heelan 1989.

12 See Heelan 1989.

other) to become critically self-aware as *Dasein*, i.e., as understanding Being; they now are ready to become philosophers of science, i.e., to begin the work of interpreting science against the background provided by the textual and other resources of the philosophical community.

Considered phenomenologically, every datum is *for* an observer and *about* a phenomenon. The datum is some (real) *appearance* of a phenomenon to an observer; the datum judgment then is always about some secular phenomenon revealed through a datum, e.g., "The energy of this (just arrived) electron is 5 Mev." A (real) appearance of a phenomenon is often called a "profile" of the phenomenon, *having energy of 5 Mev* is a profile of the (just arrived) electron.

The phenomenon is the existential unit and essential secular invariant to which a multiplicity of data can be ascribed by the observer. The "about-ness" or "of-ness" of a datum implies that every datum is *intentional*, i.e., that every datum is an appearance *of* something else that is individually present.[13] The intentionality of a datum is threefold.

1. In the first place, a datum is not known for its own sake, but for the sake of something with a secular structure that it reveals as present in the ambience of the observer; we call this **the** *phenomenon.*
2. In the second place, the datum judgment is synthetic (joins predicate [P] to a subject [S], e.g., S is P), since it is of the nature of a phenomenon (S) that, while remaining essentially the same, it is capable of showing itself to an observer under many different appearances (P's); the phenomenon then is the subject (*subjectum*, see below) to which is attributed a possible multiplicity of connected data.
3. In the third place, since the phenomenon in fact endures between appearings to observers, the phenomenon is more than any data accumulated about it and more than the law of data synthesis. Aristotle, though far removed from the sophistication of modern science, saw this point clearly and called what is so posited "substance" as "*subjectum*". This position re-asserts something that modern philosophy denied, namely, that human understanding has an *intuition of existence or being* that goes beyond the primary sensibles of spatial and temporal extention or the categories. It is this insight we are trying to recover when we say that the datum judgment affirms, in addition to the synthesis (e.g., S is P), the presence of a phenomenon as a being beyond both the data and the synthesis; more precisely, the

13 With respect to observers, data perform a role analogous to what *sensations* would perform in classical theories of perception, *if these were ontological theories rather than epistemological theories*; they mediate the real presence of an object to an observer, but with the difference that instruments play the part of sense organs.

synthesis is not just one of correlations among data, but of attribution to a common *subjectum*.

In relation to the research activity of any local observer, the *epistemological datum* is the content of what is *objectively represented* when a datum judgment is formulated as a report through the medium of some language and some theory. Data reports are offered in the form of numerical indices or values estimated by instrumental measurement and attributed to the qualities possessed by the phenomenon according to the theory in use.[14] Data reports are both *concrete*, denoting what has appeared to observers in space and time, and *abstract*, connoting the essential qualities of a kind that can occur again and again in observation or be prepared in standard ways under standard circumstances for observation. The language of data reports is, on the one hand, sensibly realistic and environmentally worldly, and on the other, loaded with numbers and theoretical vocabulary. This creates a paradox but it is not here my intention to resolve this.[15]

Data reports are the product of constitution and, once made, all reference to the process of constitution and representation is dropped; in contrast, the *ontological datum*, taken in the context of the *observer-being-in-or-coming-into-the-presence-of-a-datum*, retains this reference.

In the formation of an epistemological datum, a purge of locally irrelevant but ontologically significant factors may have, indeed usually has already, occurred. Measurement in quantum mechanics is accompanied by such a loss of information (an increase in entropy). *It is this feature that suggests a comparison with the quantum mechanical model of a transition from superposition states (before measurement) to a pure state (following the datum judgment).* The constitution of the datum in the kind of theory we are considering is then the ontic realization of one possibility, executed at the expense of some excess of ontological possibilities that are lost irreversibly in the process; this irreversible change in the real course of historical events brings about the above mentioned increase in entropy. What this original excess of ontological possibilities is will need a more thorough discussion.

---

14 Ackermann 1985 presents this view but without the hermeneutical refinement.

15 The topic was addressed in Heelan 1989.

Conclusions

Finally, some conclusions: theories of a quantum type are suggested wherever the phenomena under study have an essential socio-historical dimension on account of which data appear only as related to a specific path, i.e., 1. to specific local communities of expert witnesses, such as different laboratories, historians, even nationalities, and 2. to the sequencing of the phases of the inquiry (the order in which decisions are made and executed). Examples of the former are presently used to cast doubt on the existence of a single phenomenon; while examples of the latter are now turning up in the sequencing of questions in questionaires, of pedagogical materials in teaching, of stages of economic development, etc.

References

Ackermann, Robert John (1985) *Data, Instruments, and Theory.* Princeton: Princeton University Press.

Babich, Babette (1993) "Continental Philosophy of Science: Mach, Duhem, and Bachelard." In: Richard Kearney (ed.), *Routledge History of Philosophy.* Vol. 8. London: Routledge, pp. 175–221.

Bernard, Claude (1957) *Introduction to the Study of Experimental Medicine*, tr. Henry C. Greene, foreword by I.B. Cohen. New York: Dover.

Crease, Robert (1993) *The Play of Nature: Experimentation as Performance.* Bloomington/Indianapolis: Indiana University Press.

Dewey, John (1960) *The Quest for Certainty.* New York: Putnam.

Eger, Martin (1993) "Hermeneutics as an Approach to Science: Parts I and II." *Science and Education* 2: 1–29, 303–328.

Fleck, Ludwik (1979) *Genesis and Development of a Scientific Fact*, ed. Thaddeus Trenn and Robert Merton, tr. Fred Bradley and Thaddeus Trenn, foreword by T.S. Kuhn. Chicago: University of Chicago Press.

Galison, Peter (1987) *How Experiments End.* Chicago: University of Chicago Press.

Hacking, Ian (1983) *Representing and Intervening.* Cambridge: Cambridge University Press.

Heelan, Patrick A. (1975) "Hermeneutics of Experimental Science in the Context of the Life-World." In: Don Ihde and Richard M. Zaner (eds.), *Interdisciplinary Phenomenology.* The Hague: Nijhoff, pp. 7–50.

Heelan, Patrick A. (1983a) *Space-Perception and the Philosophy of Science.* Berkeley/Los Angeles: University of California Press.

Heelan, Patrick A. (1983b) "Natural Science as a Hermeneutic of Instrumentation." *Philosophy of Science* 50: 181–204.

Heelan, Patrick A. (1987) "Husserl's Later Philosophy of Science." *Philosophy of Science* 54: 368–390.

Heelan, Patrick A. (1989) "After Experiment: Research and Reality." *American Philosophical Quarterly* 26: 297–308.

Heelan, Patrick A. (1991) "Hermeneutical Phenomenology and the History of Science." In: Daniel Dahlstrom (ed.), *Nature and Scientific Method: William A. Wallace Festschrift*. Washington, D.C.: Catholic University of America Press, pp. 23–36.
Heelan, Patrick A. (1992) "Experiment as Fulfillment of Theory." In: D.P. Chattopadhyaya, Lester Embree and Jitendranath Mohanty (eds.), *Phenomenology and Indian Philosophy*. New Delhi: Council for Philosophical Research, pp. 169–184.
Heelan, Patrick A. (1993) "Galileo, Luther, and the Hermeneutics of Natural Science." In: Timothy Stapleton (ed.), *Festschrift for Joseph Kockelmans*. Dordrecht: Kluwer, pp. 363–374
Heidegger, Martin (1962) *Being and Time*, tr. John Macquarrie and Edward Robinson. New York: Harper and Row.
Heidegger, Martin (1966) *The Essence of Reasons*. Evanston, IL: Northwestern University Press.
Holton, Gerald (1978) *Scientific Imagination: Case Studies*. Cambridge: Cambridge University Press.
Hughes, R.I.G. (1989) *The Structure and Interpretation of Quantum Mechanics*. Cambridge, MA: Harvard University Press.
Husserl, Edmund (1970) *The Crisis of European Sciences and Transcendental Phenomenology: An Introduction to Phenomenological Philosophy*, tr. David Carr. Evanston: Northwestern University Press.
Ihde, Don (1979) *Technics and Praxis*. Dordrecht: Reidel.
Kockelmans, Joseph J. (1993) *Ideas for a Hermeneutic Phenomenology of the Natural Sciences*. Dordrecht: Kluwer.
Kuhn, Thomas S. (1962) *The Structure of Scientific Revolutions*. 2nd ed. Chicago: University of Chicago Press.
Kuhn, Thomas S. (1977) *The Essential Tension: Selected Studies in Scientific Tradition and Change*. Chicago: University of Chicago Press.
Latour, Bruno (1987) *Science in Action*. Cambridge, MA: Harvard University Press.
Latour, Bruno and Woolgar, Steve (1979) *Laboratory Life: The Social Construction of Scientific Facts*. Beverly Hills: Sage.
Merleau-Ponty, Maurice (1962) *Phenomenology of Perception*, tr. Colin Smith. London: Routledge and Kegan Paul.
Newton, Isaac (1962) *Mathematical Principles of Natural Philosophy and His System of the World*, tr. Andrew Motte, ed. Florian Cajori. Berkeley/Los Angeles: University Press.
Pickering, Andrew (1984) *Constructing Quarks: A Sociological History of Particle Physics*. Chicago: Chicago University Press.
Rouse, Joseph (1987) *Knowledge and Power: Toward a Political Philosophy of Science*. Ithaca: Cornell University Press.
Shapin, Steven and Schaffer, Simon (1985) *Leviathan and the Air-Pump: Hobbes, Boyle, and the Experimental Life*. Princeton: Princeton University Press.

Hans-Herbert Kögler

A Critical Hermeneutics of Agency: Cultural Studies as Critical Social Theory

Abstract: This chapter reconstructs the project of cultural studies as the productive continuation of the epistemic interests pursued by the early Frankfurt School. Both critical theory and cultural studies are interested in culture as a medium in which power and subjectivity intersect. For the two social-scientific paradigms, the central question is the relation between power and agency, i.e., how social practices of power influence the hermeneutic self-understanding of subjects, and how those subjects in turn are capable of influencing their respective cultural and social practices. The reconstruction of the methodological paths of both perspectives leads to a critical-hermeneutic position able to provide a methodological framework for empirical social research with normative intent.

My contribution to the research logic of cultural criticism attempts to clarify the extent to which the early Frankfurt School and the currently flourishing cultural studies differently conceive an agent's cultural self-understanding as determined by social power. To be sure, both paradigms assume that objective social processes and practices have a structuring impact on subjective self-understanding, without, however, reducing the self-consciousness of the subjects to an epi-phenomenon of power or economy. Yet the conceptualization of the realm of mediation, which is supposed to both allow for an analysis of effects of power on consciousness (say as 'ideologically distorted consciousness') and still retain the relative autonomy of selves, is utterly different in both. Critical theory explains ideological schemes through recourse to depth psychology, and then grounds the force of criticism in the theorist's capacity to make conscious such implicit and hidden schemes for the agents. In contrast, cultural studies, or so I will argue, conceive of mediation in terms of the *symbolic dimension of language*, on the basis of which subjects make sense and interpret themselves. The power for critical reflexivity as well as the capacity for creative social action emerges as a potential built into the interpretive cultural practices as such.

My thesis is that the symbolic paradigm of cultural studies constitutes a substantial progress in comparison to the grounding of cultural criticism in a depth psychology of consciousness, yet I argue that a complete and satisfying theory of symbolic mediation still requires social-psychological elements. The quasi-ar-

https://doi.org/10.1515/9783110551563-004

chaeological reconstruction of the epistemic frameworks of critical theory and cultural studies will reveal that, for one, the move from a depth psychology of understanding to a symbolic theory of cultural meaning can free us from the aporias of the early Frankfurt School. We are going to show that an adequate conceptualization of symbolic mediation—that is, one that can both detect power effects in self-understanding and yet ascertain the potential for creativity and reflexivity—asks for a critical hermeneutics of agency that can fuse symbolic forms and psychic aspects of meaning.

The analysis will proceed along the following path: to begin, I will introduce Horkheimer's early project of a critical social theory, according to which depth-psychological mechanisms explain the (power-determined) integration of selves into (a highly stratified and unjust) society. The need for social recognition and integration illuminates how ideological distortions of experience can gain hold of subjective consciousness, while the existence of the psychic mediation entails the possibility that agents become reflexive and critical with regard to internalized ideological schemes. However, by the time of the *Dialectic of Enlightenment*, the earlier hope for resistance and critique has disappeared. Now convinced that in late capitalism individuals have become unable to build up the psychic autonomy necessary for reflexive thought, the ground for resistance and critique is lost. Yet with that result, the original project of a critical theory of society aiming at a reflexive understanding of power by the agents themselves becomes aporetic; the 'end of the subject' thesis thus drives critical theory into deep and devastating contradictions (I). In order to point to a way out of this pessimistic impasse, I claim that the aporias resulting from the conceptual elimination of the psychic dimension can be overcome if we turn to a *hermeneutically inspired theory of symbolic mediation.* Such a conception, as we will see, can *both* integrate the argument concerning a power-shaped schematism of experience *and* do justice to the specific utopian and ethical intuitions of openness to otherness and subjective critical reflexivity which early critical theory introduced into the discussion (II). In a final step, I will show that the project of cultural studies, as conceived and practiced by Stuart Hall and many others, can be understood as the institutional realization of precisely that perspective. The core problem of cultural studies consists in a non-reductive mediation of agency and power, while its methodological imperatives are based on the most advanced tools concerning symbolic forms and social practices. In order to ground this perspective methodologically, I present the sketch of a hermeneutic theory of linguistically mediated agency which allows for the methodological reconciliation of a power-shaped meaning with reflexive and creative modes of interpretation. The basic idea behind this perspective consists in the claim that the socio-psychic need for social recognition leads to the power-influenced pre-schematization of a potentially infinite and open symbolic meaning; yet, due to the inherent openness and indeterminacy of symbolic world-disclosure, schemes of understanding can always be challenged and overcome by reflexive and creative practices (III).

I Horkheimer's Early Program and the Dilemma of Critical Theory

According to Horkheimer's opening address at the Institute for Social Research, critical social theory should attempt to bring social philosophy and social research in fruitful contact with one another.[1] The aim is to reconstruct the constitution of subjective experience in the general societal context without abandoning the self to social forces. Philosophical questions—such as the relation between individual and society, the significance of culture, the formation of social solidarity, and the structure of social life in general—are to be renewed in an empirical research context. While Kantian and Mannheimian social philosophies are divorced from social reality, empirical research is fragmented into too many positivistic endeavors. A renewal of social philosophy has to reunite philosophical questions and social research in a way "that philosophy—as a theoretical understanding oriented to the general, the 'essential'—is capable of giving particular studies animating impulses, and at the same time remains open enough to let itself be influenced and changed by the concrete studies."[2]

Horkheimer's claim for such an integration is motivated by the concern for a non-reductive yet socially-situated theory of experience. In order to define the methodological premises of that project, which needs to be laid out pragmatically rather than in a priori fashion, we need to distinguish three levels: (1) the economic dimension of society, (2) the psychic dimension of individual experience, and (3) the dimension of culture. According to Horkheimer, the essential question for critical social theory consists in the analysis and determination of the relations between those dimensions. At stake is "the question of the connection between the economic life of society, the psychical development of individuals, and the changes in the realm of culture in the narrower sense (to which belong not only the so-called intellectual elements, such as science, art, and religion,

1 See Horkheimer 1995a, pp. 1ff.
2 Horkheimer 1995a, p. 9.

but also law, customs, fashion, public opinion, sports, leisure activities, lifestyle, etc.)."[3]

However sketchy this might appear, we can detect three essential claims. First, in contrast to orthodox Marxist positions, economy, while an important factor, is not granted a fully determining force. Horkheimer equally rejects a 'bad Spinozism' that explains the social in terms of its spiritual expressions and a 'misunderstood Marxism' that would deduce the psychic and cultural dimensions directly from economic life. Second, culture is not to be identified with 'high culture.' Horkheimer accepts the late Dilthey's fusion of Hegel's absolute with the objective spirit, thus acknowledging the equal importance of all cultural practices. Finally, and this will turn out to be crucial for our discussion, a distinction between individual psyche and culture is introduced. The emphasis on a psychic dimension that mediates culture and economy indeed defines the major (yet controversial) contribution of the Frankfurt School to social criticism.

It is important to properly understand the role of the psychic dimension in Horkheimer's early project. The psychic level gets introduced as the *mediation* between the economic 'base' and the cultural 'superstructure.' According to Horkheimer, culture cannot be connected directly with economy because "such dogmatic convictions ... presuppose a complete correspondence between ideal and material processes, and neglect or even ignore the complicating role of the *psychic links* connecting them."[4] Yet culture is nonetheless not to be idealized as a purely autonomous realm of subjective self-expression. True, the reference of thought is the concrete individual: "Thought, and thus concepts and ideas, are modes of functioning of human beings, and not independent forces,"[5] which forces us to take into account the psychological perspective. However, since the self is itself socially situated, "economic (rather) than psychological categories are historically fundamental."[6] The rejection of an abstract isomorphism between economic life and cultural forms leads to the concrete, thinking and speaking individual, and thus to psychology. Yet because the individual is situated in the context of economic social forces and its historical expressions, economic categories still take precedence over the psychological level.

At first, it might seem that Horkheimer is entangled in a problematic circle here. On the one hand, economic reductionism is rejected by referring to the irreducibly subjective acts of understanding which originate in the individual. Thus the necessity of the psychological perspective. Yet on the other hand an ab-

3 Horkheimer 1995a, p. 11.
4 Horkheimer 1995a, p. 12.
5 Horkheimer 1995b, p. 116.
6 Horkheimer 1995b, p. 118.

stract universalistic psychology is equally rejected, because the individual is unavoidably situated in a concrete economic-historical constellation, and thus subject to economic forces. The way out of this circle is provided by the *dialectical function* that depth psychology plays for Horkheimer. Psychological explanations of cultural beliefs and practices are necessary because only they can account for how agents accept otherwise intolerable and overtly absurd social conditions. The individual act of thought has to be seen as mediated by a psychic apparatus in order to 'make sense' of the smooth adjustment of individuals: "That human beings sustain economic relationships which their powers and needs have made obsolete, instead of replacing them with a higher and more rational form of organization, is only possible because the action of numerically significant social strata is determined not by knowledge but by a drive structure that leads to false consciousness."[7]

The reference to a "drive structure" should not be construed as a unsophisticated biological essentialism, but rather as the indication of co-determining emotive and affective factors in experience. Horkheimer's model of how socially situated experience takes shape involves the following steps. To begin with, we have to see that accounting for ideological distortions of reality and experience requires the explanatory help of a depth-psychological perspective. Obvious contradictions, counter-evidence and false generalizations remain unexperienced and undiscovered by the situated selves—thus forcing us to assume that a particular mode of experiencing reality *systematically overlooking those distortions* is involved.[8] In order to account for this phenomenon, we have, in a second step, to introduce the idea of an *implicit pre-structuration of thought and perception.* Obviously, reality must be *constructed* in a certain manner of disclosure so as to adjust agents to otherwise problematic social conditions. Naming Kant's concept of schematism, Horkheimer claims that capitalist society pre-constructs experience differently for differently situated social individuals: "On the basis of their psychical apparatus, human beings tend to account of the world in such a way that their action can accord with their knowledge ... Psychology must explain that particular preformation, however, which has as its consequence the harmony of worldviews with the action demanded by economy."[9] And he adds: "it is even possible that something of the 'schematism' referred to by Kant might be discerned in the process." The deeper source of acceptance of

7 Horkheimer 1995b, p. 120.

8 These early assumptions have later been supported by analyses with regard to American antisemitism. See Adorno 1982 [1950], esp. pp. 297 ff.

9 Horkheimer 1995b, p. 122, 123.

such partial interpretive schemes is, finally, taken to be located in a *basic need for social recognition and acceptance*. The concept of need is not, again, to be reduced to mere bio-sexual functions, but includes instead truly social wants like security in the group and social recognition.[10] Basic survival or self-preservation, then, becomes the question of one's social integration in the collective which requires the adjustment to the symbolic as well as practical structures that define one's concrete environment.

I want to emphasize the dialectical tension with which that model attempts to capture how social power gets internalized and reproduced on the subjective-experiential level. The depth-psychological analysis gives us a tool for understanding how subjects can adapt to objectively challenging and problematic situations. However, the mediating dimension of the psyche equally entails the possibility of a reversal and displacement of the objective socio-economic structure. Horkheimer's theory, which looks at times like an anticipation of Bourdieu's conception of social habitus, precisely foregrounds the psychic in order to avoid and reject a complete isomorphism between *subjective agency and social fields*.[11] Such an isomorphism would deliver the individual entirely to social formations; in contrast to this, the existence of a *psychic mediation* entails the seeds for a political subversion, the potential for the expanded establishment of subjective and rational autonomy: "The disclosure of psychical mediations between economic and cultural development ... may lead not merely to a critique of the conception of the functional relations between the two, but instead to a strengthening of the suspicion that the sequence may be changed or reversed in the future."[12]

Indeed, the very distinction between "traditional" and "critical" theory is modelled on the promise that the (ideologically necessary) construction of culture through psychic adjustments also entails the hope for a critical reversal, for a resistance and 'dis-entanglement' from existing economic and social conditions.[13] The possibility, as we have seen, for such a critique and resistance is

10 Horkheimer 1995b, pp. 120 ff.

11 Indeed, Horkheimer even refers to the concept of 'l'habitude' in (contemporary) French sociology. However, Horkheimer discussion remains extremely sketchy at this point, and will need to be specified. In particular, there is no clear distinction between (a) the need to identify with one's social situation so as to accept one's objective social chances by being socialized into a specifically constrained social identity (as woman, as Jew, as worker) as defined by the whole society; and (b) the need to be accepted and recognized as a member within one's concrete social environment, and thus to have to adjust to the specific norms, values, practices, rules of conduct that are essential for one's social group.

12 Horkheimer 1995b, p. 120.

13 See Horkheimer 1987b.

grounded socio-ontologically in the *psychic mediation of experience*, yet precisely this psychological grounding is later abandoned due to the experience of fascism and mass culture changed by the Frankfurt School theorists. Instead of a social-philosophical synthesis undertaken in revolutionary spirit, the *Dialectic of Enlightenment* (1944/47) now projects a skeptically-distanced, somewhat withdrawn theory of a quasi-total reification. Instead of the empirical analysis of relations between economic power, psychic attitudes, and symbolic forms, we now encounter an analysis of the master concept of "instrumental reason." A pre-classifying thought itself is now supposed to exercise the functions of social power and the organization of subjective experience, while we still also find the idea of a correlation between socially schematized experience and the need for social recognition acknowledged at the very core of social existence: "The dutiful child of modern civilization is possessed by a fear of departing from the facts which, in the very act of perception, the dominant conventions of science, commerce, and politics—cliché-like—have already molded; his anxiety in none other than the fear of social deviation."[14]

Yet the very suggestion of the identity of cognitive and social conformism now indicates that the social-psychological perspective has given way to the historical-philosophical meta-narrative of "identifying thought." Confronted with the explanation of the pervasive standardization of culture (as well as with the lack to any substantive resistance to fascism), Horkheimer and Adorno propose the hypothesis of the 'end of psychic mediation of experience.'[15] We are witnessing here a clear theoretical break from the earlier conception. Drawing on Freud's triad of ego, super-ego, and id, the amazing lack of resistance is explained with the elimination of the level of the super-ego. Accordingly, internalization has come to an end in late capitalism,[16] as the macro-structural constellations of late-capitalism have effectively undermined the micro-structural conditions necessary for the (familial) development of ego-strength. For Horkheimer and Adorno, the family once provided a socializing threshold, a life-worldly buffer-zone against an all-too-pervasive influence of social power on self-constitution. Through identification with a strong father and a loving mother, the constitution of internalized authority, which could oppose external authority and influence, had been possible: "There was a force in the life of the child which allowed her to develop, inasmuch as she adjusted to the external world, her unique individuality as well."[17] The internalized institution of self-

14 Horkheimer and Adorno 1996, p. xiv.
15 Horkheimer 1987c, pp. 377 ff.
16 See Benjamin 1977, pp. 42 ff.
17 Horkheimer 1987c, p. 386.

control via the super-ego provided ego-strength, because it allowed the self to control its desires and thus to conduct herself autonomously, to practice self-control. According to Horkheimer and Adorno, the destruction of (male) economic independence in late-capitalism, in the course of which the familial autonomy of the father gets dissolved, leads equally to the deconstruction of the micro-constellation necessary for successful socialization: self-governed ego-identity—and thus resistance against power—have now become impossible.

For our discussion, it is important to see how this reinterpretation of the schematism of experience leads to the dialectical dilemma, or even self-dissolution, of critical theory. Yet in contrast to a widespread assumption, holding that critical theory's aporias stem from its radical break with the early model, the problem rather derives from an underlying continuity. Indeed, the contradiction results from the assumption that *resistance needs to be grounded in the psychic autonomy of subjects.* Since the *Dialectic of Enlightenment* holds that the exclusive source of resistance, the autonomous individual, has been eradicated by late capitalism, any foothold of critical theory in the agents' lifeworld appears to have been evaporated. Thus by clinging to the idea of a "psychic center" as basis for resistance, Horkheimer and Adorno lead their early project into a deadly impasse.[18]

There are two versions of this end-of-mediation theory. In the stronger account, the 'end of internalization' suggests the end of psychic mediation as such. Fascist propaganda as well as "*Kulturindustrie*" are now taken to have a direct and unmediated access to the desires, emotions, and dispositions so as to employ the individual for their strategic and functional purposes. In the less radical version, the development of an internalized super-ego is still assumed, but a weakened ego is now taken to be fully determined by an overpowering and strong super-ego; ideals of leadership and star-cult are seen as hooking onto the internalized authority-schemes of a weak ego, which the child—because of the lack of strong parental identification—internalized at an early age.[19] To be sure, while only the first version presents a full break with the

---

18 I am aware that at several points in the *Dialectic of Enlightenment*, usually at the end of the chapters, the hopeful resources of human reason are invoked. However, the unmediated and abrupt nature of those pleas, which are as desperate as they are unreconciled with the rest of the text, rather support the impression of a utterly pessimistic work. See also Horkheimer (1996 [1947]).

19 See Benjamin 1977 and 1978; Cook 1996, esp. p. 13–22 and 53–56. Since our analysis will unearth the importance of implicit schemes of understanding, the second thesis would make more sense. Also, it is compatible with the earlier version that presumes the psychic mediation between economy and culture. According to that move, we can preserve the theoretical continuearly conceptual framework of psychic mediation, both theories lead to the factual elimination of a socially-constructed ego-strength, and thus to the denial of any socially-situated potential for critique and resistance. Thus, the two versions lead to the following two aporetic implications:

Assuming that the analysis of the breakdown of the family-based constitution of ego-strength is true—which has been challenged empirically[20]—resistance and critical reflexivity have now lost any identifiable location in sociopolitical reality. Due to the fact that the psychic dimension was introduced as the essential source of resistance, the negative assessment with regard to autonomous subjectivity must effect the project of a critical theory as a whole. Critical theorists cannot address themselves any longer to really existing subjects who can understand and take up the subversive messages delivered by critical theory.

However, even if the internalization of paternal authority (and the conjoined constitution of self-control) would still be possible, there would arise a contradiction between the related ideal of ego-strength (which is based on the construction of internalized power) and the use of that model for resistance. After all, the 'dialectic of enlightenment' consists precisely in the repression of one's own inner nature through the processes of the domination of outer nature, which were initially supposed to set the human being free. Accordingly, 'inner repression' gets employed as the necessary condition for resisting power, even though it is itself a form of domination. Critical theory has indeed arrived at its own, devastating dialectic, since the source of resistance is dependent on the power against which one attempts to resist.

That double dilemma of critical theory, which consists in seeing the psyche as both eliminated (which leaves the theory without addressees) and as a normative ideal (which contradicts its own analysis of subjugated subjectivity) forces us to take up the basic question of social criticism again: how can we reconstruct the internalization of power in subjective experience without eliminating conceptually the possibility of critical reflexivity and transformative resistance?[21]

ity with Horkheimer's earlier social ontology, while the capacity to reflexively thematize and challenge existing social structures is now empirically questioned. The super-ego and the individual ego thus merge into one interpretive schematism, and thus lack any reflexive break or distanciation between the two levels.

20 Benjamin 1978.

21 Faced with such aporias, it occurred to the critical theorists themselves that an alternative framework for theorizing resistance is needed. Marcuse attempts to place hope in an emphatically interpreted libido, while Adorno and Horkheimer replace their vision of 'innerworldly transcendence' with either aesthetic or negative-theological reflections (Marcuse 1964; Adorno (1990). However, in these perspectives the utopian dimension of social criticism remains largely

II. Language and Symbolic Mediation in Early Critical Theory

I suggest that in order to point a way out of this impasse, it is helpful to turn to the productively ambiguous function that pertains to the linguistic mediation of reality. The basic idea here is that language, as the master-medium of cultural experience, entails traces and trajectories of power without ever becoming merely its instrument or expression. Openness toward new experience, reflexivity with regard to our experience, and the dialogic dimension of intersubjectivity are all inherent in our linguistic practices; I will argue that these aspects, in conjunction with a theory of symbolic power, can serve as a guiding thread for a normatively oriented social critique.

At first, it seems clear why such an alternative might never have seriously been considered by Horkheimer and Adorno: experience and culture appear to them as fully determined by "identifying thought." In light of an almost desperate reversal of Hegel's claim concerning the absolute mediation of the particular by the universal, no escape from totalizing thought seems possible. Thought as well as language are taken to be fully dominated by a will to total subsumption, according to which the individual exists only as the case of the universal law: "*Die Sprache stempelt ab*."[22] The refusal or even incapacity to see more than a late-capitalist will to power *in our linguistic practices* is even more startling since, as Habermas has shown, the identification of symbolic thought with power creates a unique impasse for early critical theory, since it takes itself to be the *reflexive* analysis of power in light of its practical overcoming. If, however, thought as such becomes identical with power, and if thus no distinction is possible between reified meaning and critical modes of discursive understanding, then the project of a reflexive transformation loses any normative ground. The (abstract) utopian referral to a pre-symbolic mimesis, or to a trans-symbolic aesthetic or theological dimension (all of which resist conceptual explication) re-

---

unmediated with social reality, which itself is understood in terms of a totalizing framework of an all-pervasive power-system.

22 "Die Sprache läßt das Neue als Altes erscheinen, sie beweist, das alles im Rahmen des je Bestehenden sich begibt. Die Sprache stempelt ab ... Sobald man spricht, wird ein Besonderes als ein Allgemeines bezeichnet," Horkheimer 1987d, p. 70, 71. With regard to Hegel, it is explicitly stated that "even Hegel's Logic is subservient to the philosophy of identification," p. 72. For a subtle defense of Hegel's conception of normative critique, in particular in comparison to Adorno's criticism, see Buchwalter 1987.

main mere gestures—and are thus insufficient to guide critical reflection of social controversies.[23]

Why, then, have Horkheimer and Adorno never really pondered the alternative of a symbolically grounded theory of resistance? That question is, I need to emphasize, not arbitrarily posed. Indeed, Horkheimer and Adorno have, while working on the *Dialectic of Enlightenment,* intensively reflected upon the possibility of a new philosophy of language. The goal in mind was to develop a theory of experience that can both capture and transcend the effects of totalizing power. According to that perspective, we have to acknowledge the force of schematism that denigrates and instrumentalizes language as an expression of identifying thought, but nevertheless consider that language constitutes a mode of transcending power, a mode, remarkably, that is even independent from the psychic constitution of the speaking individual. As Horkheimer put it: "Independent from the psychological intention of the speaker, language points toward a universality that we have usually attributed to reason. The interpretation of that universality leads to the idea of the just society."[24]

According to Horkheimer—yet emphatically supported by Adorno—'language' is by no means identical with identifying thought. Linguistic practices are rather characterized by an in-built tension which shows itself by indicating, through the filters of encrusted and crystallized meanings, alternative forms of existence. On the one hand, to speak means to give expression to existing power relations, and thus to reproduce that power by conforming to the available schemes and expectations regarding correct and comprehensible self-expression: "There is a tendency that all sentences, whatever they might say, just express the very same meaning. That tendency comes right along with, and is actually the same, as schematization."[25] Yet in another dimension language also points, and here it is equally independent from the individual intentions, to a trans-empirical and more utopian form of meaning: "To address someone in speech really implies that we recognize him as a possible member of a future association of free human beings. Speech presupposes a common relationship to truth, and thus entails the deepest assertion of the alien existence to whom one speaks, indeed of all existences as possibilities."[26] Language thus is to be understood *dialectically,* inasmuch as it is always embedded in forms of

23 The utopian or normative dimension, which aims at reconciliation in spite of a reified and alienated experience, thus becomes ineffable. (See Habermas 1983).

24 Max Horkheimer, "Letter to Th. W. Adorno, Sept. 14th 1941," in: "Horkheimer 1987 f, vol. 17 p. 171.

25 "Horkheimer 1987 f, vol. 17", p. 172.

26 "Horkheimer 1987 f, vol. 17", p. 172

power, and yet, as relating to 'truth,' indicates a transcending move beyond such power-saturated crystallizations: "The contradiction would always be the one between the service (of language) to the existing praxis and its necessary intention toward a just universality."[27]

Now, especially given Adorno's participation, it seems clear that we are not asked to think of 'truth' in an ahistorical or transcendentalist manner, say in the recognition of universal validity claims, or of general rational features of speech or language as such.[28] Rather, a true community of speakers would have to entail the quasi-mimetic openness toward concrete otherness as well as the critical reflexivity of situated subjects. As we shall presently see, both aspects, in combination with the power-structuration of meaning, define the linguistic conception of cultural studies. The undeniable fact, however, that Horkheimer and Adorno never developed their project of a 'dialectics of linguistic world disclosure' (they never wrote the planned successor to *Dialectic of Enlightenment*), indicates ultimately a clinging to the paradigm of psychic autonomy: speech acts are, after all, expressions of the individual subject, who, since the end of internalization, lacks the resources to achieve true autonomy. The reduction of speech to deprived subjectivity appears to us as a methodological blindness with regard to the creative and reflexive potentials inherent in everyday linguistic practices, which would have allowed to break free from the pessimism of the *Dialectic of Enlightenment.*

Central to the theory of experience, as developed in *Dialectic of Enlightenment*, is the necessary *pre-schematization of any subject-object relation.* The pessimistic radicalization of such "projections" consists in the anti-mimetic closure of any subjective experience with regard to new or challenging encounters: the ossification or 'crystallization' of *experiential schemes* can then be understood as the loss of any reflexivity of one's own participation in this process, which amounts to the unconscious fixation of the subject to its own yet unacknowledged interpretation. Horkheimer and Adorno assume that every perception is pre-constructed, since the basic will to survival will necessarily project its needs onto the environment so as to discern the relevant features for self-preservation: "In a certain sense all perception is projection ... In human beings projection has been automatized, like other attack or defense behaviors which have

---

27 "Horkheimer 1987 f, vol. 17", p. 171.

28 At this point, we can clarify a major point of difference between a hermeneutic foundation of cultural criticism and the theory of communication by Habermas, who reconstructs the "linguistically intended universality" in a Neo-Kantian manner in terms of universal validity claims, while cultural studies and its conception of meaning emphasize the intersection of schematizing power and subjective self-understandings; in such a power-embedded hermeneutics, the situated and intertwined relations between universal and particular are the focus of attention.

become reflexes."[29] In order to criticize distortions and pathologies which exist in form of rigid schematizations of reality, we can thus not simply invoke an 'undistorted' or objective point of view; rather, what is required is the *reflexive consciousness of the conceptual contributions to world disclosure* so as to make a more adequate understanding of reality possible: "In order to reflect the thing as it is, the subject must return to it more than he receives from it."[30] Since the object is formed only as the subject is distinguished from it, the denial of the constructive dimension of world disclosure constitutes a pathological distortion; in contrast, its acknowledgment allows for a self-reflexive relation to the world.

While *reflexive consciousness* can differentiate itself from the object, and is thus capable to see its own disclosing perspective as what it is, *pathic consciousness* remains imprisoned within its 'self'-constructed schemata, which are accordingly experienced as 'reality-in-itself.' The subject has thus become incapable toward a reflexive openness vis-a-vis experience: "True madness lies primarily in immutability, in the inability of thought to participate in the negativity in which thought—in contradistinction to fixed judgment—comes to its own."[31] This attractive model, including a critically-reflexive and a pathically-fixated consciousness, becomes aporetic only because it is not placed in the context of a theory of symbolic mediation. Because the capacity to reflexivity as such is seen as anchored in psychic autonomy, which in turn is taken to be eradicated by late capitalism, transcendence can only be posited in (aesthetic or theological) spheres beyond the mundane capabilities of situated and potentially reflexive selves. If we, however, relocate the critique of ideology within a theory of symbolic mediation, according to which the critical reflexivity and creative potential inheres in linguistic world disclosure, and not in the subject, the potential for a reflexive awareness of the 'subjective contribution' is ontologically entailed within all social and cultural practices.[32] Instead of identifying "linguistic world disclosure" *in toto* with the identifying logic of subsumption, we can now understand that the very experience of something as something, and thus as something concrete and different, is a process *made possible* by linguistic means. "Mimesis" must then not be pre-symbolic, or even be distorted by symbolic mediation, but a 'hermeneutic mimesis' rather exemplifies a superbly articulated and expressed experience of the phenomenon, in the stylistically ade-

29 Horkheimer and Adorno 1996, p. 187, 188.

30 Horkheimer and Adorno 1996, p. 188.

31 Horkheimer and Adorno 1996, p. 194.

32 This move thus allows for the reconstruction of a non-totalizing experience of the other which does not have to resort to a pre-symbolic myth of mimesis.

quate use of formulations, in the openness and adequacy of choosing the right word. The idea of the hermeneutic circle, which lies at the heart of any symbolic understanding of the world, entails that language 'reads' and discloses the particular being which shows itself in the to-and-fro movement between its subject-matter and the projected interpretive frame. It thus encompasses a permanent relationship as well as the differentiation between the subjective and the objective side of meaning.[33]

We would thus be able to reconstruct the empirical loss of reflexivity in situated agents without having to abandon the potential for critical reflexivity ontologically. According to Horkheimer and Adorno, the essential aspect of modern power is the *coupling of interpretive schemes with power mechanisms*, which in late capitalism is taken to destroy the psychic links that 'fraction' the connection between symbolic meaning and social power: "In the world of mass series production, stereotypes replace individual categories. Judgments are no longer based on a genuine synthesis but on *blind subsumption* ... The perceiver is no longer present in the process of perception."[34] Yet even for Kant the schematism (with which he attempts to mediate forms of intuition and categories with sense perception) is no conscious achievement. Horkheimer himself points out that by discerning the 'schematism of experience' we are dealing with a "hidden art in the depth of the human soul."[35] Accordingly, *any* mode of conscious experience —reflexive or pathic—is dependent on some implicit background schematism. It is thus misleading to oppose harshly the real or conscious process of synthesis with "blind subsumption." Rather, the reflexivity of situated agents is generally *mediated by a cultural preunderstanding*, with regard to which agents conduct in a more or less reflexive attitude. The hermeneutic model of a preunderstanding necessary for explicit conscious acts can provide the context for a less rigid mediation of power-saturated schemes and reflexive agency.[36]

---

33 See Gadamer 1990; especially the third (and often neglected) part, in which the structural openness of linguistic concept formation with regard to experience is emphasized. See also Kögler 1999.

34 Horkheimer and Adorno 1996, p. 201, 202, my emphasis.

35 Horkheimer and Adorno 1996, p. 188; the same passage is quoted in Horkheimer 1995b, p. 122, where it reads "Kant spoke of a hidden art in the depths of the human soul 'whose real modes of activity nature is hardly likely ever to allow us to discover, and to have open to our gaze.'" See Kant, CPR B 180 f.

36 I have developed such an account of a power-saturated yet non-reductive preunderstanding in *The Power of Dialogue: Critical Hermeneutics after Gadamer and Foucault* (Kögler 1996), Part One: "The Preunderstanding of the Interpreter." As shown by numerous cultural studies, conscious acts are embedded in power-shaped frames of meaning, without, however, disempowering the agents fully or disarming them of any possible reflexive attitude. In other words, the turn

III. Towards a Critical-Hermeneutic Grounding of Cultural Studies

The dialectic of conscious speech and implicit social power mediated by a cultural preunderstanding leads directly into cultural studies and its basic questions, which we may now pose and answer without entering into an aporetic situation: How do symbolic schemes structure the conscious experience of subjects? To what extent are the relevant forms of meaning shaped by power relations, and what is their function in the economy of reproducing symbolic and material domination? Finally, to what extent are subjects aware of the existence of power-influenced schemes of meaning, and to what extent are they capable of critical examination and practical transformation with regard to them?[37]

In order to set the stage for our critical-hermeneutic grounding of cultural studies, we propose to define the paradigm of cultural studies in the four following ways:

1. The methodological orientation of cultural studies has to be focused on *the symbolic construction of reality.* This is what prompts for instance Stuart Hall to integrate aspects of structuralism and semiotics into cultural studies, and this is what paved the way for the central place that Foucauldian discourse analysis today occupies in cultural criticism.[38] The symbolic perspective provides a common frame, since power relations 'articulate' themselves always through interpretive schemes; at the same time, this vision provides a truly inter-disciplinary orientation inasmuch as the theme of power-shaped meaning can be dealt with according to the methods and concepts of the respective particular disciplines.[39]

---

to a theory of symbolic mediation allows us to detect and analyze the pervasive features of power by preserving a level on which to locate the potential for critical reflexivity and political transformation

37 Due to the fact that cultural studies represent a highly heterogeneous and complex field of research, ranging from the effects of globalization to audience reception of mass media, from social power struggles to 'race, class and gender' studies, the following analysis of methodological premises of cultural criticism must abstract from many particular issues. The emphasis I place on the *symbolic* mediation is by no means intended to downplay the importance of bodily practices, as defined, say, by Foucault or Bourdieu; however, the possibility of reflexive criticism and informed resistance, as much as the full cultural meaning of social practices, are based upon the linguistic dimension of our experience.

38 See Hall 1981; 1996a.

39 In this context, the dialogic conceptions of language and communication by Bahktin and Voloshinov, the conception of cultural practices by de Certeau, and the Marxist philosophy of

2. In order to prevent any academic ossification into a sterile semiotic discourse cut-off from social praxis, research has to be tied immediately to the ongoing political life. Especially Larry Grossberg supports such a pragmatist self-understanding of cultural studies.[40] The 'research logic' of cultural studies should never become autonomous or automatic; it always needs to be linked to political issues such as Aids, xenophobia, sexual and gender identities, globalization, etc. The symbolic perspective thus 'networks' the specific disciplinary orientations (art-historical, sociological, communicational, anthropological) with concrete problems.[41]
3. The envisioned connection of symbolic theory to political praxis is undertaken in a spirit indebted to the situated self-understanding of the subjects. According to the Gramscian version of Marxism, we have to reject any elitist conception of culture. Culture is, in the words of Raymond Williams, 'ordinary'—and as such needs to be defended against any denigration from above. At the same time, however, we should also avoid a naïve leftist populism that celebrates any existing cultural practices and identities as *de facto* legitimate and self-chosen. Precisely the adoption of the concept of ideology commits us to a position equally beyond an 'elitism of high culture' or a 'populism of low culture.' At stake is rather the reconstruction of reflexive and creative potentials in the discursively and socially limited contexts of experience.[42]
4. Such a symbolically mediated, politically motivated, and culturally situated model finds its final fulfillment in the analysis of the *cultural construction of subjective identity.* Implied already in the discourse analysis of media experience, and yet even more pronounced in studies concerning race, class, and

---

language by Gramsci, have been used to infuse into Foucault (and recently into Bourdieu as well) more open and flexible conceptions of meaning and agency in various disciplines.

40 See Grossberg 1997.

41 Especially the 'politics of representation,' in which the symbolic self-understanding with regard to basic interpretive concepts is at stake, has thus become highly relevant for cultural studies. Indeed, 'meaning' and 'sense' are now seen as controversial and contested political goods, the 'definition' or even 'conquest' of which presents one of the most important aims of any critical intervention into politics. Stuart Hall himself has intervened in such a way into the politics of Great Britain in the 80s with his book *The Hard Road to Renewal: Thatcherism and the Crisis of the Left* (Hall 1988).

42 These dialectic formulations are intended to indicate a position *beyond* the elitist criticism of Adorno *and* any unreflected populism. While the Frankfurt School frequently overlooked the traces of subversion in the reception of mass culture, in cultural studies we find tendencies toward an uncritical acceptance of consumerist hedonism. The following discussion tries to overcome those bad alternatives.

> gender, this perspective questions the symbolic (and social) constructions implicit in subjective experiences. We come here full circle with regard to the methodological program of cultural studies, since the general thesis of the symbolic mediation of reality is now concretely applied to the lived experience of situated selves. The problem consists in showing how we can, within the framework of our methodological perspective, reconstruct the impact of social power on self-understanding without, however, eliminating conceptually the capability of subjects for critical reflexivity and resistance.[43]

We can now pursue the methodological grounding of cultural studies by integrating Horkheimer's concept of social recognition into a hermeneutic theory of symbolic self-construction. According to such a perspective, the developing self slowly takes on social schemes of identification since it has to assure itself of the recognition and solidarity of its social environment. The will to recognition, consisting in a deep-seated longing to be accepted and supported, can be satisfied only by more or less conscious acts of adjustment to the symbolically structured world. The encounter of the self with the other, in the course of which one's identity takes shape, crystallizes in the adaptation of typical self-images; those schemes are projections of the other onto my being, and they become, inasmuch I adopt the other's stance toward myself, my own modes of self-understanding. This process already begins in the pre-symbolic phase of the mother or parent relation, and continues in the later, symbolically mediated phases of life. However, since neither the attachment of one's deepest fantasies to discursive structures nor the symbolic self itself are fixated, as Hall has shown,[44] any self-identification in the context of socially established schemes of interpretation essentially remains an open and criticizable project.

While we thus require the concept of *recognition* as an explanatory mechanism for the power-induced adjustment to discursive schemes, we equally need to emphasize the idea of reflexive self-realization. The task is now to do so without succumbing to a Kantian model of self-ruling, since it led, as we saw, early critical theory into one of its aporias by introducing an authoritarian model of subjectivity as grounds for resisting power and authority. The normative intuition

---

43 Precisely this problematic has recently become a new central focus of discussion in cultural studies. Stuart Hall himself reflects on this issue in the context of the neo-existentialist writings of late Foucault, and considers, following Lacan and Butler, the reintegration of psycho-analytic models into discourse analysis. My contribution relates directly to that discussion. See Hall 1996b.

44 See Hall 1996a, 1996b.

of a self-governed existence is indeed crucial for any life opposed to power; nonetheless, such an intuition cannot be explicated by reference to the heterogeneity of pre-symbolic drives, nor is it to be derived from interpretive openness of meaning alone. With regard to pre-discursive desires, Judith Butler has rightly emphasized that the cleavage between desire and discourse is not sufficient to ground a socially progressive resistance. This is because such a 'resistance from below' seems to be capable only of destabilizing and shaking-up established meanings, while its rootedness in pre-symbolic drives do not allow for a discursive reformulation of our cultural self-understanding.[45] Similarly, the Derridean play of differences entails no valid model for reflexive self-determination, since in this model, interpretation traverses the symbolically disclosed realm of meaning without any limits and constraint; yet such a never-ending, never consummated process of understanding might even work in support of existing social and institutional divisions, since their impact on schemes and content of subjective self-understanding gets denied in its course.[46] If we can ground critical reflexivity neither in the desire/discourse gap nor derive it from interpretive indeterminacy, the question remains: How are we going to reconstruct the conditions of possibility of critical self-reflexivity without losing sight of the empirical structuration of meaning through power?

We can conceive of a solution to this issue if we replace, as consistently argued in this chapter, the thesis of a psychic mediation of experience with a theory emphasizing the symbolic nature of understanding. In contrast to the early Frankfurt School, this approach rejects any conceptual relation between the capability to creative interpretation or reflexive self-determination and the independent development of a certain psychic structure; instead, creativity and reflexivity are seen as structural aspects of symbolic world disclosure itself. Such reflexivity is exemplified through the manifold interpretive practices in everyday life, without, however, already presenting us with a fully developed reflexive understanding. In a critical hermeneutics of language, the symbolic (that is, non-causal) relation of speech acts to their meaning is rather seen as a resource which can be unfolded in terms of a both socially situated and yet theoretically informed self-reflection. Linguistic world disclosure encompasses

45 "What do we make of a resistance that can only undermine, but which appears to have no power to rearticulate the terms, the symbolic terms—to use Lacanian parlance—by which the subjects are constituted, by which subjection is installed in the very formation of the subject?" Butler 1997, p. 88.

46 For a similar criticism of a merely interpretive or symbolic multiculturalism that ignores the social and economic factors operative within and behind cultural forms of meaning, see Matustik 1998.

the possibility of a reflexive self-relation, and thus can be developed into a conscious explication of the underlying symbolic forms of meaning. This is because language not only discloses entities within the world, but equally allows to represent such a representation itself. The reflexive structure of symbolic relations vis-à-vis the world is independent from the intra-psychic control of drives.

This move allows for the reconstruction of the normative-practical orientation of critical theory since agents, as the addressees of the reflexive messages, are now *eo ipso* equipped with the tools necessary for such criticism. The problem of the 'loss of situated agents' capable of being addressed by cultural criticism, which emerged from the thesis of the end of the autonomous individual, thus dissolves. Similarly, we can now do away with the aporetic justification of the source of resistance against authoritarianism in a psychic structure which is itself authoritarian. If reflexivity is an in-built feature of symbolic understanding, then there is no need for an additional theory of psychic self-domestication, that is, for a conception of authoritarian self-discipline in one's psychic economy.[47] Moreover, reflexive self-determination now need not be conceived in opposition to sensuous experience: the subject qua speaker can draw on the reflexive resources of language without having had formerly to subject one's desires and wishes to repressive control. Indeed, the conceptual separation between reflexive acts, enabled by symbolic means, and psychic autonomy, grounded in the repression of drives, might open up a perspective of a reflexive yet non-repressive relation between understanding and sensuality.[48] Finally, insofar as symbolic understanding takes place in the context of a dialogic interaction between self and other, this model further captures the normative intuition of *openness and recognition with regard to the radical other.* As indicated above, hermeneutic experience thrives through the open dialectic between the general and the particular; accordingly, the other or the 'non-identical' (Adorno) is never to be subjected to the subsumption under a pre-established general concept, but always taken to present a challenge to one's taken-for-granted beliefs

47 The fact that reflexivity is entailed in our linguistic practices as a normative orientation can be seen by our attitude to ask agents for reasons for strange or unusual actions or for acts that run counter to established norms or habits of behavior. We thus assume the potential of a reflexive self-relation to be built into our shared practices by holding people accountable to give reasons for their actions. Reflexivity can be considered a meta-value of our communicative practices since we would consider a person that refuses to give any reason for their action 'irrational' in a more basic way than a person that would give an unconvincing or insufficient one.

48 The harmonious relation between understanding and the senses is also normatively relevant since repressed characters might be more inclined to (racist, sexist, nationalist) project others as beings that can realize what they themselves are forbidden to do, and that are 'therefore' to be hated (without consciousness of that deep-psychic structure, of course).

and prejudgments. Such a methodology therefore entails the normative respect for the culturally, sexually, and socially other.[49]

Crucial in the context of a critical hermeneutics of agency is, however, that the symbolic emergence of the reflexive self takes place against the background of power-influenced structures of meaning. We are thus dealing with the twofold thesis that the need for social recognition explains the internalization of power-saturated schemes, yet that linguistic meaning entails the potential for transgression and the critique of power. In contrast to the *Dialectic of Enlightenment*, I argue that linguistic world disclosure, by its very nature of being a symbolic (that is, non-causal) relation to the world, contains the seeds for a creative and reflexive thematization. This potential, however, is 'domesticated' by numerous and pervasive social practices of normalization, standardization, and stereotypification of the experiencing self.[50] The basic idea of fusing a theory of symbolic mediation with a social psychology of recognition states that the potential infinity of experience and expression is constrained by the need for social recognition (and yet is never fully controlled by it). Subjects thus adjust themselves, by means of the habitualized pre-schematizations of their symbolic competence, to the thought, perception and action-schemata of their group. This process provides agents with recognition and self-esteem as group members, which they require for their social-symbolic survival; at the same time, the acceptance as a member of 'general society' [*Gesamtgesellschaft*] is granted solely on the subject's conforming attitude toward the expected, usually gender, class and ethno-specific schemes.[51]

49 See Kögler, "Ethical and Methodological Recognition of the Other," in: Kögler 1996a, p. 141–157. The basic point is that the normative recognition of the other as a dialogic self is derived from within the interpretive encounter itself, and thus can be justified by means of an explication of the normative dimension that is already implicitly present in our interpretive practices.
50 Foucault, 1976; 1978. I have argued elsewhere that Foucault's thesis concerning the power-based construction of selfhood makes sense only in the context of a hermeneutic theory of experience that can treat the internalization of power in a non-behavioristic manner. See Kögler 1996b. Here I shall further develop the concept of internalization.
51 We thus employ Horkheimer's early conception of a *need for social recognition* in order to explain how subjective acceptance and internalization of power-saturated schemes becomes possible. We thus preserve the social-psychological dimension, which gets productively combined with discourse analysis, insofar as it illuminates the constitution of socially constructed subjective experience. Similarly, we replace the idea of subjective autonomy as the source of resistance with a theory of linguistic meaning that entails the potential for reflexive criticism and creative meaning. *Subjectivity, then, is rather the goal than the unavoidable starting point.* This argument applies also to poststructuralist discussions of subjectivity, insofar as we should not see those analyses as destroying the possibility of autonomy, but rather as showing how non-autonomous forms of subjectivity are socially created, and how we can, without relying al-

The dialectic of symbolic power thus ties the self, through its recognition needs, to socially normed patterns of self-understanding which form the horizons of self-evaluation and self-esteem. Studies ranging from feminine body culture, the self-experience of ethnic minorities, or the cultural hegemony of social classes have shown the extent to which subjects experience themselves through such prescribed standards and schemata.[52] Tied to such schemes by fear of social exclusion or even 'social death,' the subjects adopt those modes as their own.[53]Especially members of non-integrated groups are forced to a permanent reflection on the symbolic violence inherent in language, if labeled as "foreigner," "negro," "prostitute," etc. They are, we may say, dialectically integrated by being both part of the general symbolic order—which amounts to the sense of shame and self-denigration, and through their ties to particular social lifeworlds, which makes them outcasts. While such a situation may put these agents in a more 'natural' position to question and reject the existing modes of evaluation, it may also lead to over-adjustment or self-denial, and even to self-destructive practices. The alienated attitude, however, has a unique potential to reveal the (constructivist) truth about all of our symbolically constituted identities, which express themselves in seemingly 'natural' expressions like "woman," "worker," "intellectual" in respective schemes of identity.

The concept of a 'schematism of experience,' which constitutes the deep-psychological or deep-symbolical relays between the need for social recognition and social power relations, can be explicated through the hermeneutic model of understanding. The idea that subjective speakers necessarily rely on a meaning-constitutive background is of crucial importance here.[54] As speech act theory as

ready on the autonomous self, nonetheless develop and create new forms of self-understanding and self-realization. This move of theorizing is crucial, because it could show how oppressed selves can in fact overcome and re-create themselves from their oppressed position (see Fanon on colonized selves), without having to be 'autonomous' already.

52 See Diamond and Quincy 1988; Fanon 1967; Bourdieu 1991. For black youth, it may be the sports career, as suggested in the documentary movie *Hoop Dreams*. Bourdieu's analysis of habitus provides overwhelming evidence how agents define themselves in terms of their social position.

53 I have analyzed the relationship between female identity and the need for social recognition with regard to practices such as female excision and abortion in Kögler 2014.

54 Both Heidegger with regard to a 'circumspective understanding' of Being-in-the-World, and Wittgenstein in his crucial reflections "On Certainty,' have shown that our explicit understanding of something as something is based upon an implicit preunderstanding. That preunderstanding defines the meaning of explicit expressions while not being thematically present as such. The language-hermeneutic reflections of Gadamer and Searle have extended those insights directly to the realm of linguistic meaning. Methodical control in the human sciences is never complete, as Gadamer argues, since the interpreters comprehension is subject to a historical horizon

well as semiotics have shown, speaker and hearer can communicate about something only insofar as they employ shared symbolic means, as they follow shared conventions that regulate the common use of signs.[55] In order to be grasped by B as y, the communicative intention of A to communicate y to B has to rely on shared assumptions followed by both communicators. Whether something can count as a question, a statement, an order or an emotional expression depends on the communicative or 'illocutionary' force, the sense of which is learned by being socialized into language games. Now, for our context it is crucial that the shared understanding between speakers is not fully determined by the 'rules' of the game. Indeed, the mutual understanding of communicators is only given if the 'hermeneutic background' sufficiently overlaps in order to establish shared conceptual and practical understanding. The 'background' is not fully explicable in terms of rules; it is acquired through socialization, and as such tied to the particular cultural and social context.[56] In other words, social differences and distinctions that prevail in the respective contexts leave their impression on preunderstanding. Subjective intentions in communication are thus not only shaped by explicit communicative needs, but also by a 'horizon of intelligibility' which defines a socially situated scope of understanding; insofar as the social context is pervaded by power relations, they will appear indirectly on the level of meaning.[57]

This process leads, on the one hand, to the internalization of the power structures, because the objective opportunities for self-realization are unevenly distributed among different social groups. The pre-schematization of experience adjusts the reflexive and creative potential to the socially accepted schemes, and

---

the scope of which lies beyond individual consciousness. In everyday communication, as Searle argues, any clearly defined sentence is intersubjectively understood only because the communicators possess a shared practical horizon of understanding the situation.

55 Searle 1969; Habermas 1987. This position is contested by Davidson 19 where Davidson argues that contextually invented 'passing theories' can account for intersubjective understanding. However, the communication breakdown between speakers who speak the same language yet coming from radically different social or cultural milieus suggests something like a hermeneutic background as a source of shared meaning.

56 Searle 1983, pp. 141ff.

57 Pierre Bourdieu's sociolinguistics of the symbolic habitus, which is grounded in the social habitus and thus points back to the social status based on recognition, can serve such a critical reconstruction as a guiding thread. However, as I have shown in the target essay of a discussion of Bourdieu, we have to integrate Bourdieu's conception in a more refined hermeneutics including reflexivity and innovative self-interpretation. See Bourdieu 1991, and for critical readings of Bourdieu, the special issue "New Directions in the Sociology of Knowledge," *Social Epistemology*, Spring 1997.

thus helps to reproduce, symbolically as well as practically, existing structures of domination.[58] Yet on the other hand, the fact that those experiences are *symbolically mediated* implies that subjects—as speakers—are never totally determined by objective power structures. The medium of language entails the possibility of infinitely many expressions and interpretations, which thus can only be constrained empirically, and never absolutely.

The task of cultural studies is thus to make explicit the hidden contexts that implicitly shape our conscious understanding, and thereby to push reflexivity and self-understanding onto a higher plane. Despite the fact that the hermeneutic background is permeated by power, it nonetheless remains 'hermeneutic;' as such, it is in principle accessible to the agents themselves, and remains always a negotiable part of the agents' own self-understanding. Interpretive schemes are not as fixed and static as the classical structuralist or discourse-analytical models assume; especially in struggles concerning the cultural, political, social and 'gendered' identity of groups, the meanings of basic terms are up for grasp and targets of ongoing re-negotiation.[59] With regard to the power-induced socialization into symbolic forms, we are thus fortunately dealing with an *ambiguous process*. True, the symbolic schemes often demarcate relatively rigid boundaries for individual self-expression; and yet the situated self-understanding is still never fully delineated by the socio-symbolic logic of identification. This is not, as Hall and others have argued, because of the desire/discourse gap or the indeterminacy of the signifier. If we want to relate symbolic identification to reflexive agency, we should rather emphasize that the *self-reference of the first person* can never be fully inscribed into a definite description: this act—as an act of *self-identification*—is dependent on the spontaneous agency of the subject itself,

---

58 The 'domestication' or 'reduction' of our reflexive and creative powers, which we as speaking beings always possess as potentials, is brought about by a will to social recognition; the need to be integrated makes us constrain, usually unconsciously, *the open horizon of interpretive possibilities in order be allow us to participate in the acceptable and socially established rules of meaning.* Foucault defends a similar conception of discourse, albeit more inspired by Bergsonian and surrealist themes, in "The Discourse on Language," in: Foucault 1972.

59 Such 're-negotiations' are well described by Fiske 1996. To be sure, we have to ask further what aspects of the social background can be immediately expressed in the language and 'world view' of the situated selves, and what features require an objectifying theoretical framework. In any event, the interpretive schemes that agents themselves have access to and that they can understand as their meaning have to be kept in mind by every objective analysis. It has to be shown how these schemes derive from or are related to objective functional mechanisms or structures. To show this, I think, might also help situated agents to understand the meaning and the relevance of abstract theoretical languages.

and can thus never by ossified by a general classification or typification.[60] Similarly, every interpretive self-image, just as much as it is defined by linguistic meaning, remains embedded in complex practical contexts and thus dependent on a host of implicit background assumptions. Since that background understanding is complex and diversified, and thus cannot be circumscribed in a definite set of rules, the very 'identity' of the 'identified' self must equally remain open. Self-reference and background dependency thus imply that self-understanding withstands a rigid fixation in definite interpretations.

Finally, with our proposed hermeneutic conception of symbolic mediation we can also avoid the complementary mistake consisting in an excessive over-estimation of the reflexive and creative powers of situated selves. While we need to emphasize the transcending potential inherent in interpretive practices, we need not overlook the actual power-shaped and constraining contexts of meaning constitution. From its inception, being socialized into practices of speech and communication is associated with practices of evaluation, normalization, and adjustment, which agents obey for the sake of social recognition. The deep-seated need for social acceptance moves subjects to internalize the expected patterns of behavior and expression, which crystallize into the agent's second nature. Our model thus rejects that agents stand as free and reflexive subjects 'before' a host of social possibilities. Rather, the *situated* subject is always already embedded in its social positions which in turn shape the outlook of its interpretive endeavors. It is because of such a situatedness of experience that a more radical reflexive break—by means of semiotic and discourse-theoretic tools—with the agent's self-understanding is necessary.

Accordingly, the reflexivity and creativity that is entailed in our linguistic practices can provide the situated springboard for a critical interpretation. Cultural Studies should be understood as the theoretically-informed continuation of our everyday potential for reflexivity, by means of a reflexive reconstruction of power-laden interpretive schemes, and as such as the legitimate heir to the Frankfurt School. The task is to enhance our understanding of the implicit mechanisms of power, and thereby to lead to a less constrained unfolding of our creative capabilities.

60 Here, the relation between an internalized social 'me' and a transcending, reflexive and creative 'I' as suggested by George Herbert Mead helps for theorizing internalized power and reflexive criticism. See Mead 1934. See also Kögler 2012.

References

Adorno, Theodor W. (1991) "On the Fetish Character in Music and the Regression of Listening," in Adorno, *The Culture Industry*. London and New York: Routledge, pp. 29–60.

Adorno, Theodor W. (1941) "Review of Wilder Hobson 'American Jazz Music' and Winthrop Sargent 'Jazz Hot and Hybrid'." *Zeitschrift für Sozialforschung* 9(1): 169.

Adorno, Theodor W. (1971) "Perenial Fashion—Jazz." In: Theodor W. Adorno, *Prisms*. Cambridge: MIT Press, pp. 119–132.

Adorno, Theodor W. (1990) *Negative Dialectics*. London: Routledge.

Adorno, Theodor W. et al. (1982 [1950]) *The Authoritarian Personality*. New York/London: Harper and Brothers.

Ang, Ien (1985) *Watching Dallas*. London/New York: Routledge.

Benjamin, Jessica (1977) "The End of Internalization: Adorno's Social Psychology." *Telos* 32: 4211–64.

Benjamin, Jessica (1978) "Authority and the Family Revisited, or: A World without Fathers." *New German Critique* 5: 35–57.

Bourdieu, Pierre (1991) *Language and Symbolic Power*. Cambridge, MA: Harvard University Press.

Buchwalter, Andrew (1987) "Hegel, Adorno, and the Concept of Transcendent Critique." *Philosophy and Social Criticism* 12: 297–328. Butler, Judith (1997) *The Psychic Life of Power*. Stanford: Stanford University Press.

Cook, Deborah (1996) *The Culture Industry Revisited: Th. W. Adorno on Mass Culture*. London: Routledge

Donald Davidson (1986) in Ernest Lepore (ed.), *Truth and Interpretation: Perspectives on the Philosophy of Donald Davidson*. London: Blackwell p. 433–446. Diamond, Irene and Quincy, Lee (eds.) (1988) *Feminism and Foucault*. Boston: Northeastern University Press.

Fanon, Frantz (1967) *Black Skin, White Masks*. New York: Grove.

Fiske, John (1987) *Television Culture*. London/New York: Routledge.

Fiske, John (1996) *Media Matters: Race and Gender in U.S. Politics*. Minneapolis: University of Minnesota Press.

Foucault, Michel (1972) *Archaeology of Knowledge*. New York: Pantheon.

Foucault, Michel (1976), *Discipline and Punish*, New York: Random House.

Foucault, Michel (1978), *The History of Sexuality, Vol. 1*, New York: Random House.

Gadamer, Hans-Georg (1990) *Truth and Method*. Continuum: New York.

Grossberg, Larry, Nelson, Cary and Treichler, Paula (eds.) (1992) *Cultural Studies*. London/New York: Routledge.

Grossberg, Lawrence (1997) *Bringing It All Back Home: Essays on Cultural Studies*. Durham/London: Duke University Press.

Habermas, Jürgen (1983) *Theory of Communicative Action*. Vol. 1. Beacon Press: Boston.

Hall, Stuart (1981) "Cultural Studies: Two Paradigms." In: Tony Bennet et al. (eds.), *Culture, Ideology, and Social Process*. London: BT Batsford Ltd.

Hall, Stuart (1988) *The Hard Road to Renewal: Thatcherism and the Crisis of the Left*. London/New York: Verso Books Hall, Stuart (1996a) "Signification, Representation, Ideology: Althusser and the Post-Structuralist Debates." In: J. Curran, D. Morley and V. Walkerdeen (eds.), *Cultural Studies and Communications*. London/New York/Auckland: Bloomsbury Academics, p. 11–34.

Hall, Stuart (1996b) “Introduction: Who Needs Identity?” In: Stuart Hall and Paul du Gay (eds.), *Questions of Cultural Identity.* London/Thousand Oaks/New Delhi: Sage, pp. 1–17.
Hall, Stuart and Du Gay, Paul (1996) *Questions of Cultural Identity.* London: Sage.
Horkheimer, Max (1987a) *Gesammelte Schriften.* Frankfurt a.M.: Frankfurt: Suhrkamp
Horkheimer, Max (1987b) “Traditionelle und Kritische Theorie In: Horkheimer 1987a, Vol. 4. P. 21–225. Horkheimer, Max (1987c) “Autorität und Familie in der Gegenwart.” In: Horkheimer 1987a, Vol. 5. Horkheimer, Max (1987d) “Kopula und Subsumtion.” In: Horkheimer 1987a, Vol. 12. P. 69–74.Horkheimer, Max (1987e) “Ursprung und Ende des Individuums.” Discussion with Th. W. Adorno. In: Horkheimer 1987a, Vol. 12. p. 436–466.
Horkheimer, Max (1987f), “Briefwechsel 1941 – 1948,” in Horkheimer 1987a, Vol. 17.
Horkheimer, Max (1995a) “The Present Situation of Social Philosophy and the Tasks of an Institute for Social Research.” In: Max Horkheimer, *Between Philosophy and Social Science. Selected Early Writings.* Cambridge: MIT Press.
Horkheimer, Max (1995b) “History and Psychology.” In: Max Horkheimer, *Between Philosophy and Social Science. Selected Early Writings.* Cambridge: MIT Press.
Horkheimer, Max (1996 [1947]) *Eclipse of Reason.* Continuum: New York.
Horkheimer, Max and Adorno, Theodor W. (1996) *Dialectic of Enlightenment.* New York: Continuum.
Kögler, Hans-Herbert (1996a) *The Power of Dialogue: Critical Hermeneutics after Gadamer and Foucault.* Cambridge, MA: MIT Press.
Kögler, Hans-Herbert (1996b) “The Self-Empowered Subject: Habermas, Foucault, and Hermeneutic Reflexivity.” *Philosophy and Social Criticism* 22(4): 13–44.
Kögler, Hans-Herbert (2012) “Agency and the Other: On the Intersubjective Roots of Self-Identity.” Special issue on ‘Human Agency and Development,’ in *New Ideas in Psychology (NIP)*, B. Sokol, J. Sugarman, (eds.), p. 47–64.
Kögler, Hans-Herbert (2014) “Empathy, Dialogue, Critique: How should we *understand* (inter-) cultural violence?” in *The Agon of Interpretations. Towards a Critical Intercultural Hermeneutics*, Ming Xie (ed.), Toronto: University of Toronto Press, pp. 275–301.
Marcuse, Herbert (1964) *One-Dimensional Man.* Boston: Beacon Press.
Matustik, Martin B. (1998) “Ludic, Corporate, and Imperial Multiculturalism.” In: Cynthia Willett (ed.), *Theorizing Multiculturalism.* London: Blackwell, p. 100–117.
Mead, George Herbert (1934) *Mind, Self, and Society.* Chicago: University of Chicago Press.
Searle, John (1969) *Speech Acts.* Cambridge: Cambridge University Press.
Searle, John (1983) “The Background.” In: John Searle, *Intentionality.* Cambridge: Cambridge University Press, p. 141–159.
Searle, John 1985) “Literal Meaning.” In: John Searle, *Expression and Meaning.* Cambridge: Cambridge University Press, p. 117–136.

Eric S. Nelson

Overcoming Naturalism from Within: Dilthey, Nature, and the Human Sciences

Abstract: Dilthey's middle works offer alternative strategies for interpreting the debate between naturalism and anti-naturalism. These works traced the limits of natural scientific methods in the face of the felt reflexivity of the subject, the singular nexus of the individual's life, and the epistemic inability to comprehend life as a universally valid whole. Dilthey naturalistically critiques claims appealing to an uninterpreted immediate givenness and the direct self-access and self-evidence of uninterpreted "inner experience," while minimalistically confronting naturalism with the reflexively felt, interpretively processed, and reflectively conceptualized and mediated character of the given. Lived-experiences are complex relational wholes, involving purposiveness, which cannot be reduced to discrete "natural" elements abstracted from the life-nexus. Naturalism is the primary orientation of modern science; yet the contents of life and the objects themselves call us to methodological differentiation and the articulation of reality in more complex and multifaceted ways.

I Introduction

Wilhelm Dilthey's epistemic project is to a certain extent "naturalizing," as his Neo-Kantian, phenomenological, and later hermeneutical critics have noted. At the same time, it is "anti-naturalistic" according to the positivistic and scientistic reception of his works. It is ironic that a holistic thinker of the self-generative interconnected "life-nexus" [*Lebenszusamenhang*] has been identified in this reception with a dualistically (mis-)construed reification of the distinction between nature [*Natur*] and spirit [*Geist*], and explanation [*Erklärung*] and understanding [*Verstehen*].

In this essay, I suggest a more complex and nuanced approach to Dilthey's thinking of nature and spirit that reveals his current relevance to ongoing debates between proponents of naturalism and anti-naturalism by reconsidering the mediated nexus of nature and history articulated in Dilthey's works, particularly the writings of the 1890s that are closer to a naturalistic and positivistic perspective without embracing it. I argue that Dilthey's project is more coherent than his naturalistic and anti-naturalistic critics have proposed. Such a reconsideration of Dilthey's project offers a significant alternative strategy for responding

https://doi.org/10.1515/9783110551563-005

to the opposition between naturalism and anti-naturalism that continues to inform contemporary philosophy.

Beginning with the naturalistic perspective presupposed by and established in the modern natural sciences, the "fact of science" that is the point of departure for Neo-Kantianism and positivism, Dilthey immanently unfolds its scope, possibilities, and limits in relation to the psychological, historical, and ethical life-contexts of concrete embodied individuals. He does so without relying on essentialist religious or metaphysical conceptions of being, ideal validity, or an unchanging self. Dilthey not only accepted the validity of the modern natural sciences, he sought to clarify and justify them by historically and anthropologically contextualizing them. Nature and history do not necessarily indicate the elimination of knowledge and truth in relativism and skepticism, as Husserl feared in his polemical "Philosophy as Rigorous Science"; they are its contexts and conditions as Husserl later emphasized in a line of thinking that culminated in *The Crisis of European Sciences and Transcendental Phenomenology.*[1] Without these life-processes, and the emergence of the cognitive from the non-cognitive, and rationality from the life-nexus, there would be no science as a socially constituted practice of knowing or as the human enactment of truth.

II The Promise and Crisis of Naturalism

Dilthey's attention to natural science and writings about the historical formation of the modern natural sciences and the naturalistic life-comportment are underemphasized.[2] In these writings, such as his account interpreting the constitutive role of Stoicism in the formation of early modern natural philosophy, Dilthey helped pioneer the history of science as a philosophical enterprise.[3] Dilthey's this-worldly and historical justification of the sciences, and corresponding transformation of the modern project of epistemology, critically traced the extent and limits of scientific knowledge in the life-nexus and context.

1 Husserl 1981; Husserl 1970.

2 In addition to works on the emergence of modern science, Dilthey discussed contemporary natural scientific developments in review essays published in DGS volumes 15–17. References to Wilhelm Dilthey's works are to: *Gesammelte Schriften*, 28 vols. Göttingen: Vandenhoeck & Ruprecht, 1914–2011 (cited as DGS); English translations are from Wilhelm Dilthey, *Selected Works*, ed. R.A. Makkreel and F. Rodi. Princeton: Princeton University Press, 1985– (cited as SW).

3 See the essays in DGS 2; on Dilthey's account of the transition to modern science and modernity, see Frohman 1995.

Dilthey's rethinking of the epistemology of the sciences required their social-historical contextualization; the sciences are rethought in relation to their psychological, anthropological, and natural conditions that are embedded and enacted in historically mediated forms of life yet irreducible to pure historicity. In the context of the natural-historical finitude of human life, Dilthey contested reified visions of human reason with the felt self-relational reflexivity [*Innewerden*] of the self, the singular individuation of natural and historical life in an individual life, and the inability of humans to fathom and comprehend the whole of life as an integrated universally valid metaphysical system.

Dilthey's critique of historical reason revealed the conditional on-going process character of knowledge and the one-sidedness of the claims of the naturalistic worldview. The idea of truth in the naturalistic worldview that orients natural scientific inquiry has no theoretical limits in the continuing practice of the natural sciences. The natural standpoint enters into crisis and aporia when it is illegitimately extended beyond its experiential life-contexts and reified as a metaphysical world-system independent of its life-nexus.[4]

Dilthey's double strategy naturalistically contextualized epistemic claims involving an appeal to what transcends experience and the categories of life enacted through experience, while hermeneutically resituating claims about nature and naturalness. He rejected the naïve empiricism and intuitionism that entail appeals to a non-interpreted immediate givenness. For Dilthey, there is no access to experience independent of the mediation of expression and understanding; the direct self-access and transparent self-evidence of an uninterpreted intuitionist "inner experience" or an unmediated empiricist "sensuous experience" prove to be illusory. In contrast to vulgar life-philosophy and growing irrationalist appeals to a pure stream of life without the mediation of words and concepts, which Dilthey would challenge with a scientific conception of life-philosophy for the sake of life that cannot live without knowledge, Dilthey noted how concepts and intuitions are inappropriately separated from their life-contexts. Through the overextension and abuse of both reason and intuition, lived-experiences are fixated and dynamic life-perspectives become reified metaphysical world-pictures.

Dilthey's critical defense of naturalism is a limited and conditional one insofar as he resituated naturalistic claims vis-à-vis the subject in the experience. Dilthey's epistemic subject is a situated, experiential, and embodied one within the life-nexus. Insofar as it involves more than being an impersonal product of natural and social forces, this experiential subject requires a "weak transcenden-

4 On Dilthey's hermeneutical empiricism, see Nelson 2007.

tal" argument. Dilthey liberalizes the naturalistic thesis through this completely conditional yet still significant and meaning-creating self. Due to Dilthey's moderate nominalism and experientialism, Dilthey minimalistically reinterpreted Kantian a priori transcendental categories as conditionally enacted and contextually embodied life-categories [*Lebenskategorien*]. Dilthey confronted naturalism, as the exteriority of worldly causal relations, with the reflexively felt and interpretively mediated character of the phenomenally given and the factical in the lived-experiences of an individual life that is experienced as my own.

The experiential hermeneutical perspective of an individual life cannot disregard or escape the natural causal relations with which it is entangled. This contingent self, as the individuation of meaning in the midst of its natural and social conditions, cannot be coherently and adequately reduced to, or reconstructed as, a discrete set of "natural" elements abstracted from the complex life-nexus. In the co-givenness of self and world, spirit and nature, to be a self is to have a world "there-for-me." The world, as a relational nexus of significance, presupposes its being-there for someone. The individual is ineffable from the perspective of the natural standpoint. It is the individual person as a living ethical reality that is the other defining feature of modernity and the primary focus of the human sciences in Dilthey's historical analysis.

Despite the role of the ethical individual in the human sciences, naturalism is the primary methodological orientation for all modern science. Yet it is exposed to a dialectic that results in dogmatic metaphysical theses and explosive aporias that force its liberalization. The naturalistic standpoint is caught in perplexity and crisis in being extended to ethical life and challenged with issues of value, purpose, and meaning that it cannot appropriately address. It is the contexts and contents of life—as mediating nature and spirit—that motivate the methodological differentiation of the sciences and the articulation of reality in more complex and multifaceted ways.

III Dilthey and Naturalistic Positivism

Dilthey's name is invoked in Anglo-American contexts in conjunction with the idea—articulated by C.P. Snow—that the natural sciences and humanities constitute two distinct cultures. Dilthey is understood as a radical dualist in this discussion and this remains the predominant way of construing his distinction between interpretive understanding in the human sciences and causal explanation in the natural sciences. Moreover, Dilthey has been interpreted as proposing the supremacy of one culture over the other within philosophical discourses.

One reading of Dilthey identifies his project's basic tendency as in some sense "naturalizing" and "positivistic." Although this judgment might appear peculiar, Dilthey himself affirmed the family affinity between these two movements—along with materialism—as developmental variations of a common "natural standpoint" or "natural worldview." Dilthey not only noted their affinity with and resonance with one another but with his own critical empirical project that also begins with the fact of the modern natural sciences. Broadly construed, the naturalistic standpoint encompasses a guiding commitment to a non-supernatural and scientific conception of the world. Naturalism is transformed into natural scientific positivism, according to Dilthey, when the critical standpoint of the phenomenal character of the physical world is recognized.[5] The positivist turn in the modern natural sciences entails that naturalism and materialism as doctrinal metaphysical systems or theses about reality are abandoned.

Dilthey's later hermeneutical critics maintain the continuity between Dilthey and scientism.[6] Heidegger claimed that Dilthey's differentiation of two varieties of sciences, natural and human, remains a positivistic distinction. It is derivative of the more original question of being [*Sein*] as such and as a unified whole in contrast with the ontic investigation of beings as entities [*Seiende*]. Gadamer maintained that Dilthey was trapped between the scientistic methodologically reductive conception of the world and the romantic experience of an affectively moved and felt vital individuality.[7] Because of his affinity with positivism, Gadamer has stressed how Dilthey remained a student of Comte and Mill as well as of Goethe and Schleiermacher. This characterization of Dilthey makes little sense if "naturalistic positivism" is defined in the limited sense of, in Croce's words, "the enemy of everything spiritual and historical."[8] An expanded and historically fairer exposition of positivism, one that allows us to productively and critically clarify Heidegger and Gadamer's portrayal of Dilthey, is that it is naturalistic and positivistic in the sense that it encompasses: (1) the critique of metaphysical conceptions of reality for the sake of encountering and investigating reality in its empirical givenness and phenomenality and (2) the epistemic priority of the methods, models, and results of the modern natural sciences. Dilthey endorsed the former thesis while modifying the latter one with a broader conception of science that encompassed the natural and social-historical world.

---

5 DGS 5, p. 403.

6 On Dilthey and positivism, see Sommerfeld 1926; on Heidegger's analysis of Dilthey's positivism as the culmination of metaphysics, see Gander 1988.

7 Gadamer 2004, p. 214.

8 Croce 1941, p. 129.

In another variation of this criticism, developed in Georg Simmel and adopted by Walter Benjamin and Theodor Adorno, Dilthey could not overcome the last residues of naturalistic biology and universalistic anthropology by adequately historicizing and socializing human existence.[9] This restraint is intentional. Dilthey opposed the historical school's one-sidedness as much as reductive naturalism. Dilthey's anthropological dimensions were critiqued by historicizing thinkers on the right and the left. In an early response to Dilthey's criticism of the notion of a folk soul [*Volkseele*], or collective agent, Simmel contended that there are no real individuals for the same reasons that Dilthey used to conclude that there are no real collective entities. The collective and the individual are equally constituted products of natural conditions and social forces.[10] Simmel proposed that this position, Dilthey's hermeneutical o individualism is left unnamed, was a positivism that inconsequentially stopped short in the face of the myth of the person.[11]

IV Dilthey and Anti-Naturalism

A second way of reading Dilthey has made his thought the target for proponents of the thorough naturalization of the human sciences and everyday life. Dilthey appears as a major antagonist of scientific naturalism from Otto Neurath's polemical assessment to Mantzavinos's *Naturalistic Hermeneutics*. According to this argument, Dilthey cannot successfully prove that the human and natural sciences are discrete autonomous unities and that this thesis dangerously undermines the unity, coherence, and integrity of the sciences.[12] Dilthey is read as placing inherent limits on the progress of positive scientific knowledge and rejecting a naturalistic conception of the world for one inhabited by biographical persons, felt and conceptual motivations, social groups, cultural patterns, political institutions, and other mythical folk-concepts. Dilthey's differentiation of the human sciences consequently places them outside the realm of legitimate scientific inquiry. The expanded notion of rationality and science promoted by Dilthey inevitably leads to irrationality and anti-science for these critics. This positivist criticism is echoed in Marxist materialism; Lenin and Lukács depicted Dilthey

9 On Benjamin's reading of Dilthey's as an anthropologically based and naturalistic opponent of radical historicity, see Hanssen 2000, p. 53.

10 Compare Udehn 2001, pp. 68–74.

11 Udehn 2001, pp. 68–74.

12 Neurath 2006, p. 285; Mantzavinos 2005.

and Weber's justification of interpretive understanding [*verstehen*] in the human sciences as a higher obscurantism and non-clerical form of idealism.[13]

There are earlier suspicions concerning the meaning and implications of interpretive understanding, which is the elementary stumbling block for Dilthey's science oriented commentators. Theobald Ziegler warned in the late 19th century of a "dictatorial *Ignorabimus*" ("we will not know") that he proposed stemmed from Dilthey's interpretation of Augustine. Dilthey emphasized Augustine's articulation of an irrational subjective interiority and ineffable individuality that can only be comprehended through an intuitive felt understanding. Such a feeling-to-feeling transmission between persons cannot be reproduced and thus endangers the objectivity and rationality of science.

A disagreement concerning Dilthey's import for the sciences is evident in the von Mises brothers. The Austrian school economist Ludwig von Mises accepted Dilthey's methodological individualism, criticized by Simmel, and the incalculable character of life in the 1920s in his confrontation with Neurath's conception of socialist calculation. The logical positivist Richard von Mises maintained, however, that *ignoramus et ignorabimus*—the "we do not know and will not know" that Emil Du Bois-Reymond introduced in a 1872—is a consequence of Dilthey's differentiation of explanation [*erklären*] and understanding [*verstehen*].[14]

Walter Pollack and Georg Misch argued against the claim that understanding the finitude and conditionality of cognitively established theoretical knowledge as entailing an obscurantist prohibition on further research and inquiry.[15] Dilthey rejected in his discussions of Du Bois-Reymond's thesis the idea that there are intrinsic limits to scientific inquiry even as he argued that the sciences are internally differentiated and varied by their objects of inquiry.[16] The scope and unity of science are not to be dogmatically limited from outside; the sciences are differentiated through the multiplicity that constitutes the empirical world. Dilthey would consequently agree with Haeckel's critical reply—*Impavidi progrediamur* ("advance fearlessly")—to Du Bois-Reymond's *ignorabimus* and Virchow's *restringamur,* while disputing positivistic claims about the import of the sciences within everyday life.

In a *Literaturbrief* from 1876, Dilthey describes how Du Bois-Reymond's thesis is as unscientific as the dogmatic scientific materialism that it opposes.[17] The

13 On Dilthey's relationship with Marxism, see Rockmore 1992, p. 212.

14 Mises 1968, p. 209.

15 Pollack 1907, p. 119; Misch 1947, p. 49.

16 Pollack 1907, p. 119.

17 DGS 17.

current configuration of the scope and limits of the sciences can and will be redrawn. Crises and alternative hypotheses and theories reconfigure the scope and limits of scientific knowledge. However, inclining toward Hume's argumentation concerning what theory and scientific theory can achieve, and prefiguring Carnap's distinction between science and ethics, Dilthey concluded that there are no internal limits to science in its own domain yet, even if every question could be scientifically resolved into natural laws, the riddles and tasks of practical life would still remain unanswered.[18]

Jürgen Moltmann argued that Dilthey did not advocate obscurantism in response to science and reason. Dilthey identified a scientistic obscurantism in the disregard of historical life, and delusion that truth is gained independently of its intersubjective conditions.[19] Their ahistorical lack of vision resembles the priestly princes of metaphysics who refuse to acknowledge the constitutive role of the affective, the subjective, and the individual that are the conditions of both life and knowledge. No desires and sentiments run through the veins of their knowing subjects and such subjects are constitutively incapable of living and knowing. The thesis that reason is grounded in sentiment and historical life is another argument with precedents in Hume's philosophy of common life.

Misch maintained that Dilthey adopted the same phenomenalist epistemic basis as the positivist advocates of the natural sciences, whilst reinterpreting its significance. There can be in Dilthey no "we will not know" that limits processes of intellectual development.[20] There is only a reasonable recognition that we cannot know in an absolute "royal" way. This pluralist claim cuts against both reductionistic naturalism and anti-naturalism. Insofar as anti-naturalism assumes a royal route to truth through intuition, dialectic, or abstract reason, it commits the same error as its opponents.[21]

There is a suggestive alternative conception of nature and spirit in Dilthey. Ermarth describes him as an idealist inculcated "with a considerable dose of naturalism." But more adequately, as Dilthey did not idealistically deny natural and social exteriority, others stress Dilthey's intermediate and mediating role in these disputes.[22] Dilthey articulated an expansive and liberal in contrast with a cramped and illiberal naturalism; one encompassing value, validity, and the ideal as

18 On Carnap's relationship to Dilthey and Heidegger, see Nelson 2012 and Nelson 2013a.

19 Moltmann 1971, p. 60.

20 Misch 1947, p. 49.

21 Harrington contends that Dilthey cannot be assimilated to either naturalism or the anti-naturalism of Husserl and Neo-Kantianism in Harrington 2001. Compare the arguments for a common anti-naturalism in Jalbert 1988.

22 Keller 1895: 126.

the content of consciousness in accordance with a scientific- and person-oriented principle of phenomenality [*Satz der Phänomenalität*] in which nature and the world are not neutral and impersonal but "there-for-me."[23]

V Nature and Spirit

In a late short retrospective piece, his "Draft for a Preface" (1911) for a collection of his epistemological and psychological writings, Dilthey noted that the dominant positivist model of the natural sciences had "truncated the spiritual-cultural world" by transforming it into a mere folk-illusion.[24] This illusion—from the perspective of mere natural material relations—is, however, not a groundless illusory projection but functionally real in how individuals live. The most reductive naturalist and materialist presuppose the practices of the human world and the enactment, expression, and understanding of human life. All sciences presuppose this life-nexus. But it is this practical life-context, which has been bracketed by the natural sciences, that allows human scientists to recognize the individual self in its sociality and its productive creative relations with the whole of its life.

Dilthey revealed the aporias of constitutive idealism and its problematic intellectualist and representationalist assumptions about mind and reality, arguing that life is given through its phenomenality. Yet life is not merely a phenomenal appearance constituted by an empirical much less an ideal consciousness. It is significant for someone. Whereas only nature comes from nature, life in its relational tensions and living actuality is "there-for-me." Life is given as a complexly mediated productive nexus that can form awareness, meaning, and value for itself. This relationally emergent life is in need of words and the cultivation of its relational capacities for expression. As such, life is not immediately or intuitively given to itself. It is reflexively aware, which is "the most simple form in which psychic life can appear."[25] The simple and elemental is already reflexively relational and mediated. That is to say, it must be understood and interpreted through its expressions, objectifications, and practices. There is no knowledge of a world independent of perception and lived-experience, which provide the context and actuality for idealism's consciousness and naturalism's material nature.

---

23 DGS 5, p. 90; SW I, pp. 245–246.
24 SW II, p. 2.
25 DGS 19, p. 66; SW I, p. 254.

The naturalizing approach to reality based on a materialistic understanding of the natural sciences continues to be the prevailing tendency of our time despite the anti-naturalistic calls to re-enchant the world and the theological turn in some forms of recent philosophy. The anti-naturalistic distrust of the sciences is scrutinized by Dilthey in the same preface. Dilthey maintained that it is not modern science and its successes that are the problem but the triumph of a narrow conception of scientific method over science.

Despite the limitations and dogmatic overextension of positivism, and thus of the naturalistic worldview as a metaphysical doctrine about the totality of the world, Dilthey articulated the empirical dynamic of knowledge while rejecting positivism's speculative opponents, "who tore thought away from sense-perception."[26] According to Dilthey, both positivism and Kantian inspired critical empiricism are correct to stress both experience and its limits, since the natural and historical empirical conditions and contexts of life cannot be transcended even as further articulation and evaluation pushes individuals beyond the factuality of real conditions.

In contrast to the one-sided reduction of life to biological and physiological instincts, drives, and the senses that are its natural basis or to the activity of a non-sensuous spirit or constitutive consciousness, Dilthey proposed a suggestive alternative strategy: to "understand life on its own terms," immanently interpreting it from out of itself—without eliminating its fullness for the sake of one of its elements—and bring it through its felt reflexivity, methodological interpretation and inquiry, and self-reflection [*Selbstbesinnung*] to reflective cognition and validity about itself.[27] To this extent, science [*Wissenschaft*] is not excluded or demeaned, as Dilthey's scientistic critics maintain. It has a central role—along with art and ethics—in the formation [*Bildung*] and self-reflectiveness [*Besinnung*] of modern individuals in relation to the contingency of natural forces and social conditions.

Dilthey remarked earlier in *Life and Cognition* (1892–1893) that "thought, which sets out to ultimately comprehend the universe, is bound to the transient existence of organic life. Thought is fragile; it appears only at isolated points in organic life and as such only at intervals as a temporary function. Everywhere it appears as a part of life and in its service."[28] Dilthey is pursuing here a naturalistic strategy insofar as he analyzes how things emerge from contingent natural conditions and circumstances and the common bodily sensuous schema of ani-

---

26 SW II, p. 2.
27 SW II, p. 2.
28 SW II, p. 345.

mal and human life. Thought strives to universalize itself, and the person to individuate herself in the context of these life-conditions. This universalizing from out of the facticity and finitude of one's situation and milieu is possible because of the pre-conceptual felt self-reflexivity and the intensified self-reflectiveness in which life turns back on itself and through which life becomes aware of itself, articulating itself as *a* life.[29]

The individuation and cultivation of a self occurs through an immanent intercrossing movement, encompassing the natural-biological as well as the social-historical, toward the possibility of the ideal and potentially even the religious. It is here that the ethical, the individual other worthy of respect, becomes visible within the context of the world and society. Dilthey described this process of the becoming of knowledge as "a real natural epistemology." It requires an expansive conception of naturalness, without doctrinal naturalism's confinement of the phenomena, in contrast with its reductive and eliminative forms.

VI Becoming a Self

Dilthey did not conclude his argumentation with the assertion of naturalness in this expanded sense. Dilthey critically traced the boundaries of natural scientific methods in the face of the felt reflexivity of the subject, the singular nexus of the individual's life [*Individuation*], and the inability of humans to know and comprehend life as a comprehensive universally valid systematic whole. Beginning with naturalism as a general point of departure in his writings of the 1890s, Dilthey immanently demonstrated its possibilities and limits in the context of the psychological, historical, and ethical life of individuals while declining to appeal to essentialist, religious, or metaphysical conceptions of a substantialized self.

Dilthey's project extends beyond the theory of knowledge as it is shaped by the concern for recognizing and valuing an ethical individual self within the context of the natural and social-historical determinants that appear to undermine the identity of such a self. Dilthey does not consequently posit a self as an atom of analysis outside the social, as Simmel charged, since Dilthey articulated the individuation of a thoroughly relational self. Simmel dismantled this individuality, which for Dilthey is not merely a theoretical thesis but a practical vocation, as an undigested naturalistic remnant resisting full social mediation. There is nei-

29 See Nelson 2011a.

ther an unmediated individual nor an ahistorical biological organism in Dilthey. He revealed how the self is expressed and cultivated only within and through the immanent structures and conditions of social-historical life. The individual self establishes itself and other selves as a universal value in and through this nexus, as an intersectional point of intercrossing forces that extend beyond it in processes of individuation.

Dilthey's practical ethical orientation constituted the genuine turning point from the natural to the human world. This transition from nature to spirit furthermore has its own epistemic conditions. While Dilthey naturalistically critiques claims appealing to a non-interpreted immediate givenness and the direct self-access and self-evidence of an unmediated "inner experience" or an unmediated sensuous perception, which lead to problematic transcendent claims about reality as a systematic totality, Dilthey critically—if minimalistically due to his reinterpretation of transcendental categories as embodied life-categories—confronts naturalism with the reflexively and interpretively processed and mediated character of the given and the factical. Since facticity and givenness must be there-for-me (there for a self) as lived-experiences are complex relational wholes involving purposiveness, Dilthey concludes that they cannot be coherently and adequately reduced to discrete "natural" elements abstracted from the complex life-nexus.

Naturalism is the most fundamental worldview and the primary orientation of modern science in Dilthey's *Weltanschauungslehre*; but the contents of life and objects themselves necessitate methodological pluralism and articulating reality in more multifaceted and nuanced ways.

VII Psychology's Mediating Role

Dilthey reinterprets epistemology as having a social, psychological, and biological dimension that cannot be eliminated without distorting the activities, processes, and tasks of cognitive knowledge [*Erkenntnis*] in the context of articulating and justifying ordinary and human scientific communicative understanding. Dilthey challenges metaphysical and scientistic formalisms that interpret knowledge to consist of worldless validity and value claims. The sense of actuality is not a product of intellectual positing; it is shaped by the interaction of cognition with feeling, instincts, and volitions that develop as a complex whole in a person through experiences of resistance, limitation, and restraint.

"The Origin of Our Belief in the Reality of the External World and Its Justification" (1890) illustrates how reality is neither a representationally constructed phenomenal object nor an immediately given in intuition or inner experience.

Reality as "there for me" is exhibited as immediate in empirical consciousness through felt reflexive awareness [*Innewerden*]. This apparent immediacy is mediated through biological drives, environmental adaptations, and practical interests formed through the play and work of impulse and resistance. Our sense of reality presupposes the elemental interaction and mediation of self and world prior to their differentiation; reality is irreducible to a worldless subject or an unperceived and non-given object, to pure consciousness or materiality, or their metaphysically reified manifestation as idealism and materialism.

Dilthey's philosophical and psychological writings from the 1890s represent a highly productive and controversial period in his intellectual development. Dilthey's endeavors to give both naturalistic and humanistic strategies their due regard and reconceive epistemology through the methods and data of the sciences, particularly history and psychology, led to the negative reaction of both positivists and idealists. No aspect of his thought was more provocative than his advocacy of a descriptive and analytic psychology as a "human science" [*Geisteswissenschaft*], which was opposed by those who considered psychology an exclusively naturalistic experimental science, including pioneering experimental psychologists such as Ebbinghaus and Wundt who pursued reductionist programs that uprooted individuals from their environing world and social existence. Dilthey's critics included Neo-Kantian philosophers. Windelband and Rickert protected the distinctiveness of the "cultural sciences," as sciences of individual persons and ideal values, from naturalism by abandoning psychology to the universalizing hypothetical-causal natural scientific explanations.

These debates continue to haunt later reflections on the possibility of a humanistic or interpretive psychology. Dilthey's contributions to these disputes over the actuality of the self and its experiences of the world are worth reconsidering for their historical significance, and—given the increasing albeit still too limited appreciation for the social, historical, cultural, and aesthetic dimensions of psychological inquiry—because we are perhaps in a better position today to recognize the continuing relevance of Dilthey's contextualizing epistemology and individual-oriented interpretive psychology.[30]

"The Ideas for a Descriptive and Analytic Psychology" (1894), Dilthey's most controversial work, raised the ire of positivistic psychology (Ebbinghaus and Wundt) and philosophers committed to a transcendental realm of validity and value claims (Rickert and early Husserl). Dilthey articulates—through a complex and nuanced reading of the psychological literature of his times—the possibility of a descriptive and analytic (interpretive) psychology. He did not maintain an

30 On the impure plural character of Dilthey's psychology, see Nelson 2010.

opposition of methods—understanding and explanation—and a duality of sciences—natural and human. Dilthey does not advocate abandoning or bracketing the causal nexus of reality; he reminds his readers that mechanical and efficient causal explanation in the natural sciences construct an abstract causal nexus linked by hypotheses and separated from the dense bonds and thick relations of life's effective nexus [*Wirkungszusammenhang*].

In kinship with Max Weber's later conception of interpretive understanding, relations of meaning and causal relations are mutually entangled. Neither one dissolves the efficient causal and conditional nature of scientifically explainable reality. Nowhere is the connectedness of meaning and causality more significant than in the human sciences themselves. Dilthey consequently did not reduce human scientific inquiry to pure interpretive understanding. Dilthey utilized both efficient causal explanation and interpretive understanding in his psychology as well as other human scientific strategies such as functional and structural explanation of social and cultural systems.

Dilthey did not deny causality; he critiqued the misuses and abuses of causality in reductive empirical experimental psychology and scientism for the sake of genuine scientific inquiry. Misch identified Hume as an important source for Dilthey's historical project. As with Hume's moderate and life-nexus oriented skepticism, which can be employed against dogmatic metaphysics and radical skepticism, Dilthey interrogated the possibility of fathoming causal connections to achieve certainty or metaphysical truth, whether this is materialist or idealist, while articulating the social reproduction and transformation of meaning and knowledge within the contexts of the daily communicative practices of everyday life. Counter to justifying the sciences through an appeal to a transcendent reality or transcendental conditions, Dilthey followed a Humean strategy of defending the sciences by skeptically abandoning exaggerated knowledge claims and through the sciences' anthropological-historical contextualization.[31]

Given the mediation involved in concrete individual life, psychology cannot be appropriately understood as a subjective self-intuition and introspection. This approach denies the facticity of life and mind, as mediated phenomena demanding interpretation, and undermines psychology's scientific—intersubjective and universalizing—task. Nor is psychology adequate to its task of illuminating individual human life if it is the collecting of discrete data—abstracted from and dissolving the life-nexus of individual and social life—externally reconstructed and organized through causal hypotheses.

31 This reading runs contrary to the account in Beiser 2012, p. 433.

Objectifying third-person methods are useful in science but should be contextualized in a human-oriented psychology that recognizes the conditional, negotiated, and fragile unity and identity of the individual person and the person's interpretive, mediated, and self-reflexive life. Because of the multifaceted mediation of the "acquired psychic nexus," which as structured contrasts with an atomistic bundle of elements and as acquired differs from the vision of an innate intrinsic self, psychology cannot be merely descriptive but must also be analytic, comparative, and structural. Structural psychology reveals the temporal enactment of the categories of life in lived-experience and provides additional support for his reinterpretation of epistemology and the human sciences in contrast with movements that disregard empirical psychology.

Dilthey did not abandon this psychological program even as it became more deeply hermeneutical in his later works. "Contributions to the Study of Individuality" (1895–96) further articulates the comparative-morphological strategy of elucidating individuality in its relational contexts. Through the hermeneutical oscillation between singular and whole, both are further elucidated. Dilthey rejected Windelband's Neo-Kantian model of the ideographic character of the cultural sciences developed. Dilthey illustrated how (1) natural sciences such as astronomy encompass an ideographic dimension and (2) the human sciences presuppose and propose generalizing and systematizing claims that allow the effective life-nexus to be interpreted through the typical and the singular. It is in such natural-historical contexts that the actual and not merely ideal individual can be recognized and respected.

The world overflows the individual for Dilthey: "The infinite richness of life unfolds itself in individual existence because of its relations to its milieu, other humans and things. But every particular individual is also a crossing point of contexts which move through and beyond its particular life ..."[32] The conditional and situated yet meaningful and purposive individual person is the basic point of departure and task for the human sciences and of Dilthey's hermeneutical justification of methodological individualism against the radical collectivist tendencies dominant in German cultural criticism and social theory.

Dilthey's methodological individualism differs from other varieties because it grasps the individual as a contextual historical reality rather than as a Hobbesian fiction and allows for the use of social concepts. Social realities such as the state, society, and community are given in experience and need to be interpreted in order to understand social life. Their experiential givenness does not justify positing them as independent much less metaphysical realities. Dilthey's cri-

32 DGS 7, p. 135.

tique of reified notions of the spirit of the people [*Volksgeist*] and community [*Gemeinschaft*] for the sake of the relational yet distinctive individual, which was reformulated by Plessner in response to its fascistic forms, proved to be prescient.[33]

VIII Naturally Interpreting Persons

Dilthey's philosophy of the human sciences appears anti-naturalistic from the perspective of an impoverishing and reified monistic naturalism. Dilthey's quasi-naturalism is such that the appropriate recognition of each object and class of objects calls for recognition. It is methodologically pluralistic and opposed to the minimalistic naturalism of philosophers like Quine. From Quine's eliminative viewpoint, Dilthey would appear even more dogmatically empirical in his defense of the unrestricted and unprejudiced empirical inquiry [*unbefangene Empirie*] against empiricism and more laxly lenient and baroque than Carnap's—from Quine's perspective—overly tolerant logical positivism.

Dilthey's critique of metaphysics places transcendent objects into suspicion as being beyond the limits of cognitive knowledge. This critique does not extend to phenomenal objects given in experience, all of which (natural and human) are mediated. The mediation of each object does not entail a reduction to isolated elements that suppresses their sense and significance. It requires that they be described and analyzed as wholes. Although sciences are expressions of life, which cannot escape life's conditions, the human sciences are constituted in intersubjective relations by ethical and social-political interests in a way that distinguishes them from the natural sciences that rest more securely in the objectified world.

Dilthey's vision encompasses naturalism without being limited by it. His strategies prefigure philosophical anthropology in Misch, Plessner, and Scheler. This contextualized, nuanced, and tolerant form of historically contextualized and liberated—as a human attitude and product—naturalism proceeds from the natural-biological and anthropological conditions of human life through their social-historical configurations to their unique intersection in the life, self-reflection, and individuation of a conditional yet meaningful and purposive nexus of *an* individual biographical life.

Heidegger construed Dilthey's project as a flawed anti-naturalist personalism and consequently a failed phenomenology that gave the naturalistic and sci-

33 Plessner 1999.

entific perspective too much purchase.[34] Dilthey's works are an ambiguous source for the new phenomenology, as Husserl noted in his defensive justification in "Philosophy as Rigorous Science" of the primacy of an absolute science opposing all natural, anthropological-psychological, and social-historical conditions and contexts.[35] Given their common sources in the descriptive and analytic empiricist philosophy of Trendelenburg, Dilthey appreciated the description of the emergence of higher forms of understanding, meaning, and validity described in Husserl's *Logical Investigations* and its tendency toward the a realist worldly referentiality. Husserl, Scheler, Heidegger learned from Dilthey's psychology and depiction of an immanent self-interpreting affective, worldly, and historical life.[36]

Dilthey's project is incommensurable with the Neo-Kantian and phenomenological transcendental-ontological turn in philosophy. Dilthey did he bracket the natural and the objective for the sake of a pure phenomenological starting point that is independent of the social-historical life-nexus. He would not attempt to replace metaphysics—placed in doubt by cultural-historical and epistemic-reflective critique and revealed to be more affective and individual than cognitive and universal—with a new transcendental-ontological philosophy. Philosophy should become a more modest project of critical reflectiveness that cannot abandon its close relations with either the natural and human sciences or with the questions of practical life. The multiplicity of ways of life and worldviews is in this context irrevocable.[37] Human life's intercontextuality and the value of individual personality are articulated through interdisciplinary human scientific research. As von Aster noted, metaphysics is abandoned in Dilthey for philosophical anthropology and universal history.[38]

Aster and Misch maintained that a philosophical reflection that informs and is informed by the human sciences and modestly remains within the immanence of nature and life is incompatible with the rehabilitation of the metaphysical, theological, and transcendence in the phenomenology of the 1920s.[39] Misch describes how Dilthey's anti-metaphysical critical philosophy directs us back toward empirical life and its problems, while the new "life-philosophical" ontology departs from that life to return to the metaphysical.[40] Dilthey's advocacy of the

---

34 Heidegger 1985, GA 20, p. 161. See Nelson 2013b.
35 Husserl 1981.
36 See Heidegger, GA 20, p. 161; Aster 1935, p. 149, 155.
37 On Heidegger's criticism of Dilthey's "ontic pluralism," see Nelson 2011b.
38 Aster 1935, pp. 51–52, 103.
39 Aster 1935, pp. 103–104.
40 Misch 1967, pp. 281–282.

Enlightenment's anti-metaphysical legacy and critical-positivist prioritization of experience and the experiential sciences are sources of resistance to the powers of authoritarianism and re-enchantment.[41]

IX Feeling and the Transformation of Nature in Dilthey's Aesthetics

Dilthey's aesthetics provides another example of his resistance to enchantment and critical appreciation of naturalism and modernity. Dilthey's aesthetics has been portrayed as a continuation of Romanticism that—due to the emphasis on feeling, imagination, and the free responsiveness of the subject—is incompatible with 19th century realism and naturalism. But in his aesthetic writings, particularly "The Three Epochs of Modern Aesthetics and Its Present Task" (1892), Dilthey emerged as a more sympathetic aesthetic theorist who criticized the limitations while articulating the significance and possibilities of literary realism and naturalism—e.g., modern artistic articulations of the naturalistic feeling of life—against their Neo-Romantic detractors and the emergence of symbolist spiritualism with its visionary enthusiasm.

Realism's power lies in how it critically reveals the discrepancy between outer appearance and internal reality, even as its weakness is its inability to reflectively generalize and interpretively focus on what is essential to evoking and heightening the "feeling of life." Rather than defending Romantic aesthetics and rejecting naturalism and, naturalism is understood as achieving its truth when it not only copies and reproduces but elucidates, intensifies, and transforms the life it portrays. Dilthey reinterprets realism through the tension of reality and feeling, resistance and will, and the objectivities of social life and lived-experience of the individual.

The naturalism of social novels expresses the emergence of a new style and sensibility appropriate for the modern technological conditions of life that has not yet achieved a "new inner form" for the work of art in relation to the subjectivity of the artist and audience. Dilthey reinterpreted both romanticism and realism as revealing two sides of the tensions of reality and feeling, resistance and will, and the objectivities of social life in the relational context of individual lived-experience.

Life-philosophically and hermeneutically interpreted, the aesthetic realism and naturalism prove to be one-sided and incomplete in contrast to the expan-

41 Misch 1967, pp. 281–282.

sive and liberal unfolding of naturalism in Goethe. Dilthey emphasized the naturalistic dimensions of Goethe and Schleiermacher, relying on them to formulate his objections to narrow naturalism. Nonetheless, despite his criticisms, literary naturalism and realism are more aesthetically promising for the "present task of aesthetics" than the abandonment of the tension between reality and feeling in a romantic literature that one-sidedly embraces organic vitality, intuitive vision, and irrational feeling. Dilthey' s critique of radical subjectivism in aesthetics illustrates his wider hermeneutical empiricist strategy of critiquing idealism by re-situating spirit within social-historical, psychological, and natural life-conditions. Dilthey is accordingly an ambiguous heir to Romanticism and a critic of its pathologies.

Acknowledgments

An earlier version of this chapter appeared as Eric S. Nelson, "Between Nature and Spirit: Naturalism and Anti-Naturalism in Dilthey," in: Giuseppe D'Anna, Helmut Johach and Eric S. Nelson (eds.), *Anthropologie und Geschichte. Studien zu Wilhelm Dilthey aus Anlass seines 100.Todestages.* Würzburg: Königshausen & Neumann, 2013.

References

Aster, E. von (1935) *Die Philosophie der Gegenwart.* Leiden: A.W. Sijthoff.
Beiser, F.C. (2012) *The German Historicist Tradition.* Oxford/New York: Oxford University Press.
Croce, B. (1941) *History as the Story of Liberty.* London: Allen and Unwin.
Frohman, L. (1995) "Neo-Stoicism and the Transition to Modernity in Wilhelm Dilthey's Philosophy of History." *Journal of the History of Ideas* 56(2): 263–287.
Gadamer, H.-G. (2004) *Truth and Method.* London: Continuum.
Gander, H.-H. (1988) *Positivismus als Metaphysik: Voraussetzungen und Grundstrukturen von Diltheys Grundlegung der Geisteswissenschaften.* Freiburg: Alber.
Hanssen, B. (2000) *Walter Benjamin's Other History: Of Stones, Animals, Human Beings, and Angels.* Berkeley: University of California Press.
Harrington, A. (2001) "Dilthey, Empathy and Verstehen: A Contemporary Reappraisal." *European Journal of Social Theory* 4(3): 311–329.
Heidegger, M. (1985) *History of the Concept of Time: Prolegomena.* Bloomington: Indiana University Press.
Husserl, E. (1970) *The Crisis of European Sciences and Transcendental Phenomenology: An Introduction to Phenomenology*, tr. David Carr. Evanston: Northwestern University Press.

Husserl, E. (1981) "Philosophy as Rigorous Science." In: *Husserl: Shorter Works*, ed. Peter McCormick and Frederick A. Elliston. Notre Dame: University of Notre Dame Press, pp. 166 – 197.

Jalbert, J.E. (1988) "Husserl's Position between Dilthey and the Windelband-Rickert School of Neo-Kantianism." *Journal of the History of Philosophy* 26(2): 279 – 296.

Keller, L., ed. (1895) *Monatshefte der Comenius-Gesellschaft* 4 – 5.

Mantzavinos, C. (2005) *Naturalistic Hermeneutics*. New York: Cambridge University Press.

Misch, G. (1947) *Vom Lebens und Gedankenkreis Wilhelm Diltheys*. Frankfurt a. Main: G. Schulte-Bulmke.

Misch, G. (1967) *Lebensphilosophie und Phänomenologie: Eine Auseinandersetzung der Diltheyschen Richtung mit Heidegger und Husserl*. Stuttgart: Teubner.

Mises, R. von (1968) *Positivism: A Study in Human Understanding*. New York: Dover.

Moltmann, J. (1971) *Hope and Planning*. New York: Harper & Row.

Nelson, E.S. (2007) "Empiricism, Facticity, and the Immanence of Life in Dilthey." *Pli: Warwick Journal of Philosophy* 18: 108 – 128.

Nelson, E.S. (2010) "Impure Phenomenology: Dilthey, Epistemology, and Interpretive Psychology." *Studia Phaenomenologica* 10: 19 – 44.

Nelson, E.S. (2011a) "Self-Reflection, Interpretation, and Historical Life in Dilthey." In: H.-U. Lessing, R.A. Makkreel and R. Pozzo (eds.), *Recent Contributions to Dilthey's Philosophy of the Human Sciences*. Stuttgart: Frommann-Holzboog, pp. 105 – 134.

Nelson, E.S. (2011b) "The World Picture and Its Conflict in Dilthey and Heidegger." *Humana.Mente: Journal of Philosophical Studies* 18: 19 – 38.

Nelson, E.S. (2012) "Dilthey and Carnap: Empiricism, Life-Philosophy, and Overcoming Metaphysics." *Pli: Warwick Journal of Philosophy* 23: 20 – 49.

Nelson, E.S. (2013a) "Heidegger and Carnap: Disagreeing about Nothing?" In: F. Raffoul and E.S. Nelson (eds.), *Bloomsbury Companion to Heidegger*. London: Bloomsbury, pp. 151 – 156.

Nelson, E.S. (2013b) "Dilthey, Heidegger und die Hermeneutik des faktischen Lebens." In: Gunter Scholtz (ed.), *Diltheys Werk und seine Wirkung*. Göttingen: Vandenhoeck & Ruprecht, pp. 97 – 109.

Neurath, O. (2006) "Soziologie im Physikalismus" (1931). In: M. Stöltzner (ed.), *Wiener Kreis. Texte zur wissenschaftlichen Weltauffassung*. Hamburg: Meiner, pp. 269 – 314.

Plessner, H. (1999) *The Limits of Community: A Critique of Social Radicalism*. New York: Prometheus.

Pollack, W. (1907) *Über die philosophischen Grundlagen der Wissenschaftlichen Forschung, als Beitrag zu einer Methodenpolitik*. Berlin: F. Dümmler.

Rockmore, T. (1992) *Irrationalism: Lukács and the Marxist View of Reason*. Philadelphia: Temple University Press.

Sommerfeld, H. (1926) *Wilhelm Dilthey und der Positivismus: Ein Untersuchung zur "Einleitung in die Geisteswissenschaften."* Berlin: J. Herper.

Udehn, L. (2001) *Methodological Individualism: Background, History and Meaning*. London: Routledge.

Steve Fuller

Hermeneutics from the Inside-Out and the Outside-In—And How Postmodernism Blew It All Wide Open

Abstract: This paper distinguishes the human sciences from the natural sciences in terms of a difference between an 'inside-out' and an 'outside-in' approach to hermeneutics, the former rendering us empirical geniuses and transcendental dopes and the latter transcendental geniuses and empirical dopes. The social sciences have been the historic testing ground for these two approaches. However, the postmodern condition has blown open this dialectic by challenging the shared assumption that the 'human' is a member of *Homo sapiens*, which had been in place from the second half of the 18th century to the second half of the 20th century. The paper ends by questioning whether hermeneutics is possible in a world where the 'human' is so ontologically indeterminate.

The starting point for this reflection on 'hermeneutics' in its broadest sense—that is, as the theory of meaning-making—is a curious yet largely taken-for-granted feature of the methodology of the human sciences, understood as *Geisteswissenschaften*. It amounts to a schizoid epistemic stance, which effectively renders us *empirical geniuses and transcendental dopes*. On the one hand, just because each of us happens to inhabit a unique configuration of space-time with which we are in direct sensory contact, we are presumed to be epistemic masters of that region. On the other hand, just because we do not happen to inhabit what lies outside that region, we are doomed to perpetual ignorance, unless we undergo a fundamental change in world-view to adopt a stance of a being who inhabits that region. It amounts to the sort of Gestalt switch which Kuhn (1970) notoriously claimed that both revolutionary scientists and historians have had to undergo —on the one hand, to project themselves into the next paradigm; on the other, to recover a past paradigm. In what follows, I take issue with this general 'inside-out' sensibility, whereby our knowledge is positively correlated with our sensory reach. In the process, I shall also present an 'outside-in' anti-hermeneutical sensibility, which I associate with a more 'natural-scientific' approach to human beings. In the end, however, I discuss how Postmodernism has disturbed this dialectic by challenging the ontological stability of the 'human.'

According to what I have presented as the default hermeneutical position, ontology amounts to an epistemological projection of the range of possible expe-

https://doi.org/10.1515/9783110551563-006

rience, or 'reification,' as Marxists following Lukacs say. Thus, the most that one can say (positively) about the language of 'transcendence' is that it refers not to something beyond human experience but to some deeper version of that experience, some ultimate sense of species being that one shares with other experiencers, perhaps due to common genetic make-up, morphology or simply lifeworld. George Santayana (1923) believed that this lay behind the philosophical valorization of 'common sense,' which he generalized across species with the idea of 'animal faith.' But others, influenced by Schopenhauer's account of the will, have called it the 'unconscious,' more specifically the 'libido' by Freud and the 'collective unconscious' by Jung. In any case, some such version of 'depth experience' is presumed to be necessary for getting into the mind of others who otherwise express radically different existential horizons.

I have exaggerated—slightly—for the sake of clarity. Nevertheless, an obvious expression of this general sensibility is the idea that understanding another culture requires total immersion in a 'different world,' a turn of phrase that even Kuhn uses for scientists. It has been the default attitude of such human sciences as history and anthropology which treat the 'human' as a specifically situated and embodied mode of being. It also helps to explain why the great theorist of the *Geisteswissenschaften*, Wilhelm Dilthey, fought his fiercest battles with proponents of experimental psychology, especially Wilhelm Wundt, whereas he was content to reinterpret theology—the original hermeneutical discipline—in largely symbolic terms, whereby, say, Martin Luther (to recall Dilthey's own extended study) organizes his personal experience into a 'perspective' [*Anschauung*] which then acquires world-historic significance as a *Weltanschauung*, not by virtue of some superhuman cognitive feats but rather by literally 'contaminating' other human minds. For Dilthey, then, the true field of contestation for the human sciences is the empirical—not the transcendental. And the question on the table for Dilthey and his opponents was whether 'the empirical' is best understood hermeneutically or experimentally.

Now suppose the natural sciences had refused to take a resolutely experimentalist stance to human experience, but instead treated the human in Dilthey's schizophrenic manner, emptying the category of transcendence into some interpretively deeper conception of human experience, while relegating transcendental discourse to a glorified syndrome. In that case, fields such as physical cosmology and evolutionary biology would be classed as science fictional diversions rather than as among the most esteemed and influential theoretical pursuits in contemporary science. After all, both fields require feats of the imagination that set aside much of the experiential basis on which hermeneutics builds. Progress in these fields is conducted via thought experiments and computer simulations, not feats of sympathetic understanding. Moreover, the natural scientists are not alone in taking this sort of 'anti-hermeneutical turn.' Much of popular thought assumes that it makes sense to propose and test hypotheses about regions of space-time so liminal that they would be impossible to occupy in our current mode of being. Thus, there remains considerable appetite for both psychical research (popularly known as 'extrasensory perception' or 'parapsychology') and the search for extra-terrestrial intelligence, despite numerous frauds and methodological difficulties more generally, all of which have also been in public view.

It is worth noting that the dubious status of these liminal inquiries could change were we, say, to travel faster than the speed of light, giving us the H.G. Wells' style *Time Machine* capacity to bounce back and forth in time—and thereby empirically settle otherwise transcendental issues about the beginning and the end of the world. Another possibility is that space-time itself may have the character of a 'tesseract,' namely, a four-dimensional analogue of a cube's projection of a surface. In that case, paranormal phenomena may simply reflect our imperfect grasp of the fourth dimension, which appears from our normal three-dimensional standpoint as 'distant' in some elusive sense. A vivid model of this sensibility appears in the 2014 film *Interstellar*, whose library-like image of 4-D hyperspace was inspired by several Jorge Luis Borges stories referencing tesseracts as the structure of the worlds contained in books.

In both the Wells and Borges fictions, the transcendental is placed within empirical reach. More interestingly, scientists actively pursue these prospects, even though they generally concede that they would require humans to enjoy a greater degree of what transhumanists call 'morphological freedom' than they currently do: We need to become, in some sense, 'shape-shifters' (Fuller 2016). To be sure, there is an interesting difference between the kind of morphological freedom that Wells and Borges would require: For Wells' time machine to work, our bodies would probably need to undergo radical transformation; whereas Borgesian tesseracts may require more simply a reorientation of ourselves to the world, whereby we operate with an extended sense of personal identity across multiple dimensions. In any case, the counter-intuitiveness of either prospect does not deter natural scientists from engaging in the relevant self-transcending feats of the imagination, often with advanced mathematics attached yet popular audiences still in toe (e.g. Krauss 2005).

At the same time, in an ironic turn, the natural scientific style of studying humans—characteristic of, say, experimental psychology and evolutionary biology—has concluded that humans are subject to various motivated and unmotivated forms of finitude ('biases') that undermine the reliability of first-person testimony with regard to just about anything, including the 'self' in which one's own being is situated.[1] All told then, the epistemology of the *Naturwissenschaften* is the evil twin of the *Geisteswissenschaften*'s: Natural scientists believe that we are *empirical dopes and transcendental geniuses:* As we confidently hypothesize about the beginning and the end of time, as well as various strange and unobservable entities near and far, we fail to recognize and track the causes of our own much more locally inscribed behavior. We are windows to the world but opaque to ourselves. This position is not quite as strange as it sounds. It is arguably the one that resulted in Europe's 17th century 'Scientific Revolution.' Although we cannot pursue this here, one would need to examine the role of what Alistair Crombie called the 'metaphysics of light' in converting the Christian doctrine of Original Sin into a positive heuristic for research in the late medieval and early modern periods. In this context, the experimental method—especially as introduced by Francis Bacon—can be seen as converting the human being into a living prism through which God's light might shine, resulting in a spectrum of actions corresponding to a range of conditions much wider than what one encounters in everyday life (Harrison 2007).

In any case, the 'social sciences,' understood as a body of knowledge that is distinct from both the humanities and the natural sciences, have been the site of contestation for the radically opposed epistemological horizons of the *Natur-* and *Geisteswissenschaften.* The discipline of sociology has provided the most explicit battleground, enshrined in terms of a 'qualitative' versus 'quantitative' methodological approaches to social inquiry, both sides of which are played out in the writings of such founding figures as Marx, Pareto, Durkheim and Weber. Instead of the proverbial 'God's eye-view,' 'Mind of God' or 'View from Nowhere' which has animated physics in the modern era, the figure of the 'Leviathan,' the unconditional authorizer of the social order regardless of particular social arrangements, the necessity whose recognition enables our liberty, has operated as the *de facto* starting point of the field. Although Hobbes first presented this figure as a materialistic deity, over the past 350 years the Leviathan has acquired more abstract guises—structures, laws, systems, etc. All of these have been subject some sort of mathematical treatment, often following—if not outright imitating—cognate developments in the natural sciences. Yet, at the outset there was a hermeneutical dimension.

On Hobbes' original telling, the Leviathan only comes into being because a group of individuals spontaneously realize their own finitude. On this basis they agree to pool their common self-understanding in order to invest absolute power

1 The classic textbook for this research, called 'attribution theory' in social psychology, is Nisbett and Ross (1980), which was influential on Fuller (1993) and Fuller and Collier (2004).

in some third party who can ensure a sphere of operable freedom in a way that they could not do simply left to their own individual devices. To be sure, starting with Gauthier (1969), Hobbes' tale of the social contract's emergence from the state of nature has been colonized by rational choice theory. Yet Hobbes himself does not resort to mathematics, let alone economics. Instead he avails himself of considerable moral psychological speculation, which he imagines is also available to individuals in the state of nature. These supposedly 'pre-social' individuals think of themselves very much as Adam and Eve did after their expulsion from Eden. They are not only sentient but also self-sentient—each possesses a conscience, which enables him or her to observe whatever he or she does. The hackneyed label 'self-interest' only masks the transcendental dimension of the condition. It fails to capture the extent to which humanity's 'diffident' frame of mind in the state of nature actually motivates their collectively taking a 'leap of faith' to invest absolute power in the Leviathan. They take more comfort in being equally powerless before one agent than existing in uncertain power relations with many agents. When Voltaire said in the century after Hobbes that humanity would have had to invent God if he did not already exist, this is arguably what he had in mind.

By the dawn of disciplinary social science in 1900, the artificial personhood of Hobbes' Leviathan had largely yielded to a more 'naturalized' conception, which allowed Emile Durkheim to speak of society as a *sui generis* entity that is not reducible to the psychological dispositions of a collection of agents. To be sure, the founders of German sociology, Ferdinand Tönnies and Max Weber, were notable in resisting such naturalization, as they continued to see society in Neo-Hobbesian terms as a complex of normatively binding transactional arrangements. Nevertheless, the first half of the 20th century spawned a tendency which C. Wright Mills (1959) notoriously dubbed 'grand theory,' with specific reference to the leading US sociologist of the time, Talcott Parsons. What bothered Mills was that Parsons operated with a fixed conception of 'society'—in his case, as a 'system' divided into 'functions' which are maintained by a range of 'structures,' depending on the particular character of the 'society' in question. The sociologist could then tell whether a society was 'functional' or 'dysfunctional,' depending on its capacity for self-maintenance in the face of changing environmental conditions. In this way, sociology could address 'social problems' of the sort to which a welfare state could administer. Parsons' conception, though clearly traceable to Durkheim, had been fortified by his exposure to the work of the Italian political economist Vilfredo Pareto from colleagues at Harvard. Pareto explicitly understood societies as 'organisms' in the physiological sense that dominated the early 20th century medical imagination. It implied a hierarchical social epistemology, whereby the sociologist effectively plays physician to society's patient: The former possesses a higher-order level of knowledge of the latter's activities, resulting in asymmetrical relations of communication and control (Fuller 2014).

Conspicuously absent from such grand-theoretic sociology was any consideration of 'people' in their expressive individuality, the default site of hermeneutics. In a homely attempt to reinvent Dilthey, Mills (1959) advocated that biography should be included among prescribed sociological methods. However, the general shift in focus from macro- to micro-level social behavior in the 1960s was insufficient to cause sociology to take a hermeneutical turn. Consider Erving Goffman, who has been the most influential sociologist of interpersonal behavior of the past half-century. He continued to share Parsons' 'behind the scenes' character of the social analyst, which led many to dub him 'cynical.' What Parsons had called 'functions' Goffman called 'roles,' simply because Goffman was interested in how those who made the social system work related to each other rather than how each of them related to the system as a whole. Parsons 'modeled' society while Goffman 'scripted' it, but neither had much interest in talking to people unless they were talking to each other. In other words, the *sui generis* object already needs to be in view before the sociologist (who is presumed to be 'other' to the proceedings) has something to study. Thus, perhaps the most learned of contemporary US sociological theorists, Randall Collins (2004), had no trouble joining the dots from Durkheim to Goffman, notwithstanding the 'macro vs. micro' difference in their style of sociological inquiry.

Even more instructive is the case of 'grounded theory,' the methodology developed by Anselm Strauss and Barry Glaser in the 1960s in explicit opposition to Parsons. In effect tackling the medical unconscious of Parsons' sociological gaze, Glaser and Strauss (1967) adopted the standpoint of someone on the floor of a psychiatric hospital with no special knowledge of either the psychiatrists' esoteric theories of mental illness or the psychiatric patients' personal experiences. This posture anticipated the early ethnographies of what is now called 'science and technology studies' (e.g. Latour and Woolgar 1979). In its original '60s setting, grounded theory enabled the otherwise voiceless to enunciate their concerns in their own terms. This generally emancipatory move became the signature principle of grounded theory, namely, that the analyst does not introduce categories into the analysis that are not available to the agents under investigation. One may quibble about whether this entails that the analyst is forbidden from trying to persuade the agents of analyst-based categories (e.g., any such prohibition would make grounded theory an enemy of Marxist-style 'consciousness raising'). However, the method's import was clear: The self-understanding of agents is presumptively privileged and the first job of the analyst is to perspicuously account for that.

In a psychiatric context, Glaser and Strauss had made quite a provocative move against the Parsonian orthodoxy, which presumptively cast patients as 'deviants' from some norm of mental health and hence a 'problem' requiring a solution, as provided by the structures of the healthcare system. However, Glaser and Strauss would be given their own comeuppance, as mental—specifically cognitive—deficiencies were shown to be found across the entire human population, not least in the minds of experts who are trained to know better, which presumably include the minds of scrupulous sociologists like Glaser and Strauss. This observation has even struck fear in the hearts of elite economists, who awarded one of the experimental psychologists behind it, Daniel Kahneman, the 2002 Nobel Prize in Economics, notwithstanding the field's self-appointed role as the guarantor of 'rationality' as an explanation of human behavior. Such generally recognized pervasiveness of 'irrationality' creates a problem for the epistemic positioning of grounded theory, since it derives much of its rhetorical force from championing minority rights in the face of a hegemonic rational order that willfully and knowledgeably represses them. But if this 'rational order' is nowhere to be found among in the minds of either the analysts or the agents, then in what sense can such an order even be said to have been 'maintained'? Could it be that 'rational order' is simply the collective hallucination that serves to render agents and analysts natural adversaries in social scientific inquiry without resolving their differences in perspective—a kind of failed Leviathan?

In the empirical rationality literature, one standard response has been to argue that in fact there is a more 'contextual' sense of suboptimal rational performance through which the agent remains sufficiently intact following the outcomes of her decisions to continue making more decisions with a comparable range of options in the future. Such an approach may be associated with time-pressured administrators, gamblers who budget their bets so that they can always return to the casino, or the reproduction patterns of entire populations in a resource-stretched ecology. Herbert Simon originally called this strategy 'satisficing,' but Gerd Gigerenzer, who studies statistical inference as an evolutionary adaptation, nowadays uses the label, 'fast and frugal heuristics' (Gigerenzer and Todd 1999). However, despite the relatively flattering gloss which this interpretation places on what would otherwise seem to be systematic violation of the canons of rationality, it is unlikely that it would correspond to the *self-understanding* of normal social agents—i.e. ones not in the ideal-typical situations just mentioned. Indeed, as with many other attempts to reframe the classically irrational as the evolutionarily adaptive, the agents might wish to disown their behavior as described in those terms because they actually uphold the standards of rationality which they failed to meet in practice. As a result, they might feel guilty, regretful, chastened, etc., when presented with Gigerenzer's cheery diagnosis. In short, however compelling the satisficing image of suboptimal rationality may be as an explanation of agents' behaviors, it belongs squarely to the analyst's—not the agent's—interpretive categories.

But does this mean that agent categories are completely without epistemic validity? One especially clever—perhaps even sophistic—answer comes by way of the social phenomenologist Alfred Schutz (1946), who in elaborating on William James' conception of 'multiple realities' wrote of 'spheres of relevance,' each with its own epistemic range. What Schutz added to James was a more vivid sense of the limits of such spheres, which correspond to the spatio-temporal range in which the agent can act meaningfully. In principle this general approach could be interpreted in a rather Borgesian way—if, say, the agent's encounter with specific books were seen as extending one's potential for action into the realities referenced by the books. However, in fact Schutz and his followers—notably Berger and Luckmann (1966) and the classic ethnographers in science and technology studies—returned to an understanding of the agent whose various 'spheres of relevance' coexist in a 'lifeworld,' which is largely defined by the sensory experience normally available to the agent's body. Thus, the great 'defamiliarizing' move that marked Latour and Woolgar (1979) was to treat scientific texts as referring not to timeless propositions or objective truths but simply to other such texts and such non-texts as lab equipment—all within the scientists' existential horizon.

In hermeneutical terms, Schutz marked a temporary victory for the inside-out over the outside-in perspective. The 'multiple realities' turn out to be multiple ways of coding the same general field of reality, namely, the agents' lifeworld, which makes 'epistemic validity' relative to specific coding standards. Thus, the same laboratory can be coded in scientific discourse or in lay discourse, and the key difference between scientists and lay people is the extent to which they can switch between them (high vs. low). A Janus-faced conclusion follows. On the one hand, the agent is now potentially 'rational' in a many-splendored way, by virtue of his or her Gestalt-switching capacities. On the other hand, as stressed not only by Schutz himself but also his ideological fellow traveler Walter Lippmann and Schutz's latter-day follower Harry Collins, there is a limit to any given agent's Gestalt-switching capacities, beyond which one rationally defers to those who can switch more effectively (aka 'experts' which is a contraction of 'experienced ones').

Much of the 'postmodern turn' in the human sciences has been about resisting Schutz's crypto-hermeneutics. The main postmodern strategy has been to change the question by philosophically relocating the topic of social agency from epistemology to ontology. Bruno Latour's intellectual journey over the past forty years represents one notable way of doing it. It amounts to a shift in the semantics—and more broadly, the semiotics—of what social agents say and do. Put more precisely: The arrow of reference is reversed. Instead of agents' words and deeds being interpreted as corresponding (or not) to some relation in which they stand to a larger reality, they are read as establishing the agents' own sense of identity, the maintenance of which others participate in through acts of mutual recognition. In that case, the only sense in which you can be 'wrong' is that your existence is invalidated by your presumptive ontological co-dependents. You thus become a literal 'non-entity.' In this respect, non-entities are not ignored but negated, yet negation may involve modes of liminality that stop short of death. Giorgio Agamben (2005) brought this point into vivid relief by distinguishing *bios* and *zoe:* that is, life understood as the embodiment of spirit or will and life understood as the mere animation of matter. The transition of the human from *bios* to *zoe* is evident in contexts, such as internment in concentration camps, where prisoners are divested of their rights and relegated to a state of animality, where by dint of torture they are rendered 'informants,' that is, wetware-based information providers, full stop.

In conclusion, more needs to be said about how the postmodern turn upset the implicit dialectic between the inside-out and the outside-in epistemologies of the *Geistes-* and *Naturwissenschaften*, rendering problematic the prospects for either hermeneutics or anti-hermeneutics. What both sides of the dialectic share is a clear sense of the material boundary between the human and the non-human. It is tied to whether an entity is born of parents who are members of the biological species, *Homo sapiens*. Michel Foucault's (1970) most lasting substantive contribution to historical scholarship may be his identification of Carolus Linnaeus's coinage of *Homo sapiens* in the mid-18th century as the moment when the 'human' acquired this default material identity, thereby enabling a specific set of sciences devoted to the human, the 'social sciences.'

In the wake of Linnaeus, the relevant sense of 'non-human' shifted from the superhuman (i. e. God) or even the subhuman (i. e. animals as such) to quite specifically the apes, which Linnaeus had observed do not look so very different from humans. However, so he thought, our essential difference from them comes from possession of a soul, the source of our 'sapient' powers. At that point, much thought started to be given to what makes us different from apes —and even whether apes might be trained up to become acceptable in human company (Corbey 2005). Also, it became scientifically respectable to set up a gradient of 'degrees of humanity' ranging roughly from apelike to non-apelike features of various human cultures. Thus, today's ethnic minority activists in the academy point to Kant's 1798 work entitled *Anthropology*, which Foucault notes as the first book to use the term, as the fountainhead of modern scientific racism. Somewhat less controversially, in the early 20th century, a field of 'philosophical anthropology' emerged, which treated the simian specificity of our bodies as a Rosetta stone for discerning the full extent of human capacities, biasing it towards a focus on technology as extending our biologically senses in various ways.

This 'primatocentric' way of posing the problem of the human continues to inform popular evolutionary thinking—albeit minus Linnaeus' original religious overtones. Thus, today we are said to be not merely differentiated from apes but 'descended' from them. However, this turn of thought was not readily available to Biblical and classical pagan authors. They had limited—if any—contact with apes. The nearest ape ecology, consisting of macaques (the so-called Barbary apes), inhabited the Atlas Mountains of North Africa. Instead, in the pre-Linnaean world, the 'human' tended to be seen as a rather generically defined animal (e.g. Socrates' 'featherless biped') with certain distinctive powers of mind, whose expression enables a level of freedom not enjoyed by other animals. Aristotle and many after him associated those powers with the capacity for language; hence, rhetoric's centrality to Aristotle's definition of the human as *zoon politikon*. Moreover, it is telling that of the many animal-based fables attributed to Aesop, in which the characters typically speak to each other, only one involves an ape.

But note my qualified phrasing, 'tended to be seen,' in characterizing the pre-Linnaean world. I also want to take into account the Abrahamic tendency —perhaps most pronounced in Islam—of regarding the human as a specially designed receptacle for the expression of God's being. In other words, it is not at all clear in the Abrahamic tradition that humans either were created as animals or are required to be animals, especially if one takes literally the original creation account of humans in Genesis from mud and clay and subsequent Biblical references to the 'golem' as a clumsy human attempt at God's handiwork based on the same principles. This looks more like the genealogy of artificial intelligence, a point that Norbert Wiener (1964) updated for contemporary audiences. It also sheds a different light on a bone of contention between Darwin and the scientific creationists of his own day—namely, whether humans descended *from* or *into* apes, especially if one interprets (as Biblical literalists did) humanity's simian likeness as a stigma of our fallen state.

In any case, pre-Linnaeus, the 'human' was located primarily in a normative aspiration, which then served as a standard for crafting and judging particular individuals. On this view, individuals are born potentially—but only potentially —human. This is the metaphysical backdrop for most discussions of education in the Western tradition, in which 'liberal arts' is the name of the skills and knowledge one needs to activate that potential. After Linnaeus, the locus for crafting the human became quite specifically an ape bearing a unique sort of soul, one capable of recognizing itself as a human in the making. By the second half of the 18th century, education itself came to be identified with this sense of self-recognition [*Bildung*], which Hegel then turned into a project for the collective realization of all humanity. Hermeneutics arises from this tradition, in which one can speak clearly of 'lifeworld' as the environment in which the crafting of humanity takes place. But suppose 'human' need not be an upright ape of a certain sort at all. For example, 'human' may be subject to multiple embodiments (e. g. uploaded and downloaded between carbon and silicon) or (*à la* Agamben) one may pass in and out of the state of being 'human.' Is hermeneutics possible in a world where the human is not so much promethean as simply protean?

References

Agamben, G. (2005) *The State of Exception*. Chicago: University of Chicago Press.
Berger, P. and Luckmann, T. (1966) *The Social Construction of Reality*. Garden City NY: Doubleday.
Collins, R. (2004) *Interaction Ritual Chains*. Princeton: Princeton University Press.
Corbey, R. (2005) *The Metaphysics of Apes*. Cambridge UK: Cambridge University Press.
Foucault, M. (1970) *The Order of Things*. (Orig. 1966). New York: Random House.
Fuller, S. (1988) *Social Epistemology*. Bloomington IN: Indiana University Press.
Fuller, S. (1993) *Philosophy of Science and Its Discontents*. 2nd ed. (Orig. 1989). New York: Guilford Press.
Fuller, S. (2014) "'The Higher Whitewash.' Review of J. Isaac, *Working Knowledge: Making the Human Sciences from Parsons to Kuhn*." *Philosophy of the Social Sciences* 44(1): 86–101.
Fuller, S. (2015) *Knowledge: The Philosophical Quest in History*. London: Routledge.
Fuller, S. (2016) "Morphological Freedom and the Question of Responsibility and Representation in Transhumanism." *Confero* 4(2): 33–45.
Fuller, S. and Collier, J. (2004) *Philosophy, Rhetoric and the End of Knowledge*. 2nd ed. (Orig. 1993, by Fuller). Mahwah NJ: Lawrence Erlbaum Associates.
Gauthier, D. (1969) *The Logic of Leviathan*. Oxford: Oxford University Press.
Gigerenzer, G. and Todd, P. (1999) *Simple Heuristics that Make Us Smart*. Oxford: Oxford University Press.
Glaser, B. and Strauss, A. (1967) *The Discovery of Grounded Theory: Strategies for Qualitative Research Practice*. Chicago: Aldine.
Harrison, P. (2007) *The Fall of Man and the Origins of Modern Science*. Cambridge: Cambridge University Press.
Krauss, L. (2005) *Hiding in the Mirror: The Mysterious Allure of Extra Dimensions, from Plato to String Theory and Beyond*. New York: Viking.
Kuhn, T. (1970) *The Structure of Scientific Revolutions*. 2nd ed. (Orig. 1962). Chicago: University of Chicago Press.

Latour, B. and Woolgar, S. (1979) *Laboratory Life: The Social Construction of Scientific Facts.* London: Sage.
Mills, C.W. (1959) *The Sociological Imagination.* Oxford: Oxford University Press.
Nisbett, R. and Ross, L. (1980) *Human Inference: Strategies and Shortcomings of Human Judgement.* Englewood Cliffs, NJ: Prentice-Hall.
Santayana, G. (1923) *Scepticism and Animal Faith.* New York: Charles Scribner's and Sons.
Schütz, A. (1946) "The Well-Informed Citizen: An Essay on the Social Distribution of Knowledge." *Social Research* 13: 463–478.
Wiener, N. (1964) *God and Golem, Inc.* Cambridge, MA: MIT Press.

II Reflexive and Relational Hermeneutics

Steven Shapin

The Sciences of Subjectivity

Abstract: In historical and ethnographic studies of the making of scientific knowledge, there has been a long-standing fascination with deflating certain stories about objectivity. Among the resources used to achieve that deflation have been the notions of subjectivity, which has been treated more as a trouble for objectivity than as a knowledge-making mode open to systematic study. I describe notions of subjectivity implicated in that inattention; I trace potentially constructive links between contemporary science studies and resources in 18th-century philosophical aesthetics; I draw notice to available engagements with the mode of subjectivity known as taste, and, especially, gustation and olfaction; and I suggest ways in which we might study the achievement of intersubjectivity in these domains.

In the science studies world, for quite a long time we've been fascinated by objectivity. We've long since stopped taking it for granted; we've displayed its historicity, its contingency, its shifting meanings.[1] We've described the practices of securing its appearance, and we've described those practices not as the application of off-the-shelf Method but as hard political and cultural work. We've pricked the objectivity balloon. Objectivity, we say, is an ideal for science—and some have asked whether it is actually a coherent and stable ideal—but it's not a reality about science, not in a form easily recognizable from its ideals. And science has been traditionally seen as the major, if not the only, domain where objectivity lives.

Objectivity is not something we can straightforwardly be against—how else do we commend our own stories but through some warrant bearing a family resemblance to objectivity?—but it is something whose specifications we have tended to deflate. Overwhelmingly, what we've done is to bring the ideal of objectivity into alignment with reality—ironically, to make it more objective—by adding to it doses of subjectivity. We historicize objectivity by drawing attention to what has counted as objectivity at various times and in various places. We take supposedly objective claims, beliefs, practices, people, institutions, stipulations,

1 See, among many examples, Markley 1983, Bloor 1984, Shapin 1994 and 1999, Shapin and Schaffer 1985, Pickering 1991, Dear 1992, Daston 1992, Miller 1992, Gieryn 1994, Porter 1995, Poovey 1998, especially chs. 1–3, Solomon 1998, Ashworth 2004, and Jasanoff 2011.

https://doi.org/10.1515/9783110551563-007

and intentions and we show their impurity, the presence in them of disparate subjective things. That which seems to be transparently about objects in the world contains ineradicable elements belonging to subjects, their background knowledge, their categories, customs, conventions, and purposes. Our scientific knowledge is about the world and it is also irremediably about us, as knowers. And the condition of our knowledge being intelligibly about the world is that it contains a bit of us. I take that to be lesson number one of the sociology of scientific knowledge.[2]

Giving accounts of whatever has counted as objectivity, we have—often without noticing it—made subjectivity into a matter of potential interest. Subjectivity has indeed been a scholarly focus, but typically in philosophical, historical, and ethnographic treatments of subjects and changes in the attributed make-up of those subjects: What is, and what is thought about, the entity that experiences, feels, acts, acts with, and is acted upon? That literature is important and extensive.[3] But scholars have not written so much or so incisively when subjectivity and objectivity are considered with respect to knowledge-making. Here, the categories of the objective and the subjective are arrayed in opposition, both in description and in evaluation. Subjectivity is then called upon to deflate objectivity. The two notions go together, but as doppelgänger, the good child and its evil twin, where the one is the positive image, the other the negative: a disruptive and disordering influence on knowledge; a trickster figure making a mess out of everything.

Subjectivity is seen as a philosophical trouble; it's what pollutes objective knowledge. You can find subjectivity as an item in philosophy encyclopedias, but more usually it's encompassed within the entry on objectivity—the grit in the knowledge-machine. There are works in science studies and the philosophy of science—two notable old-time examples are Israel Scheffler's (1967) *Science and Subjectivity* and Ian Mitroff's (1974) *The Subjective Side of Science*—in which subjectivity features in the title and then becomes practically invisible in the text, which shows little to no focused concern with what subjectivity is or how it might work in knowledge-making. A doppelgänger conception of objectivity and subjectivity is classical. Aristotle and the Stoics circulated the image of the two standing epistemically in the same relation as the wax to the seal; that image worked for Descartes and Locke in the 17th century; and more recently it served for Lorraine Daston and Peter Galison in their historical survey of objec-

---

2 For example, Barnes et al. 1996, Bloor 1996.

3 For example, Foucault 1988 [1984], Taylor 1989, Ellis and Flaherty 1992, Haraway 1991 [1985], Cussins 1996, Hall 2004, and Biehl et al. 2007.

tivity. "Objectivity" they write, "is related to subjectivity as wax to seal": the two are "as inseparable as concave and convex; one defines the other."[4]

Objectivity is a candidate for membership in J.L. Austin's class of "trouser words," taking their meaning from the words to which they are customarily opposed, where the negative (in now-strange language) "wears the trousers."[5] You might think, if we believed this or something like this, that subjectivity would be as much a topic of focused theoretical and empirical inquiry as its twin. We'd be greatly interested in what it is; we'd want to distinguish its specific forms and modes; we'd be interested in how it figures in concrete knowledge-making practices; and we'd be engaging with it in a naturalistic sort of way. But in science studies we've done almost none of those things. And that's odd since, if we no longer believe in the objectivity of legend, that puts quite a load on the subjective items we use for deflationary purposes: oddly, it seems here that objectivity doesn't exist, but subjectivity does. There are probably two reasons for this general neglect. One is the strength of the identification of scientific knowledge with ideas of objectivity and the intellectual capital that accrues from deflating what we take as legend; the other is what might be called the dustbin conception of subjectivity, the bin that holds the heterogeneous bits and pieces of whatever it is that makes trouble for objectivity-stories. We take objectivity as an ideal to be historicized and subjectivity as what we're sadly stuck with if we don't watch out.

The idea that there is nothing coherently and stably to be said about the subjective element in knowledge-making, that it is inchoate, arbitrary, unstable, and endlessly varying, fits subjectivity for its supposedly contaminating task and also excuses us from making its workings an explicitly framed topic of inquiry. What could we possibly find out? That sentiment too is classical. Subjectivities, like the practices of making the knowledges called objective, have their modes, and the naturalistic impulse rightly considers them in their specificities. That is, from the grab-bag of capacities and cultural practices widely regarded as subjective and as yielding subjective claims and knowledge, we can select and describe concrete forms, just as it has proven useful to select and describe the specific modes of knowledge-making known as solid-state physics or botanical taxonomy rather an entity like 'science as a whole.' So let's consider one mode of subjectivity among very many, the one called taste. Here the famous Latin tag is *De gustibus non est disputandum.* No one seems to know where the phrase originat-

4 Daston and Galison 1992, p. 82; Daston and Galison 2007, p. 197, 209; cf. Stengers 2000 [1993], ch. 2.
5 Austin 1962, p. 70.

ed, though some think it must be scholastic. Common English renderings are 'There's no disputing about taste,' 'There's no arguing about taste,' and 'There's no accounting for taste.' To each his own. You like Wagner and I like Verdi, and there is nothing we can say to each other that would alter our aesthetic responses or our expressed opinions, nor is there anything I can say or point out to you that would effectively communicate why Rigoletto is a great opera and *Götterdämmerung* is pompous drivel. It is widely thought that neither the facts of the matter nor rational persuasion can conceivably have any place in such things. In its normative sense, *De gustibus* counts as advice—don't argue when differing tastes present themselves in social situations, or at least don't expect that such arguments can lead to any worthwhile outcome. People who argue about taste—beyond a certain point or too energetically—can be a pain. It's rude, it's pointless, and it's likely to be disruptive.

In science studies, a telling instance of that view appeared in an important 1973 essay by Thomas Kuhn, in which he was concerned to defend himself from charges of subjectivism. Suppose, Kuhn said, he and a friend go to a movie, a western, and afterwards here marks to his friend 'How I liked that terrible potboiler!' That the movie was a potboiler is, Kuhn writes, a matter of *judgment:* he and his friend can argue all night, invoking all sorts of standards and criteria, about whether or not it was a potboiler. Judgment is, Kuhn says, 'discussable,' if you like, it can be rational. Maybe, Kuhn implied, he and his friend can, by trading arguments and evidence, come to share the view that the movie was indeed a potboiler. But, by contrast, that he liked the film is what Kuhn called a matter of *taste*; the experience of liking is incorrigibly subjective; it is private; and for that reason there's nothing to be said about it that has any consequence:

> short of saying that I lied, he cannot disagree with my report that I liked the film or that what I said about my reaction was wrong. What is discussable in my remark is not my characterization of my internal state, my exemplification of taste, but rather my judgment that the film was a potboiler.[6]

Where taste is concerned, there's just nothing to be discussed. Kuhn defended his work in the philosophy and history of science by saying that, of course, scientific theory choice is a matter of judgment—like finding evidence and criteria by which you can say a movie is or is not a potboiler; but it's not a matter of taste, about which, he claims, you cannot discuss, cannot find criteria, cannot

---

6 Kuhn 1977 [1973], p. 336–337.

advance evidence, cannot go on in a rational way, cannot reach any sort of agreement, cannot account for differing outcomes.[7]

Kuhn here implicitly assimilated positions in the philosophy of science to a body of thought rarely considered in connection with science. The taste/judgment distinction has traditionally had its being in aesthetics, especially in the 18th-century efflorescence of concern with the beautiful and the good, and, though Kuhn didn't say so, thinking of scientific and aesthetic judgments in the same frame is quite a productive thing to do.[8] If it's not exactly Keats's 'truth is beauty, beauty truth,' at least it's that, properly understood, concrete procedures for rendering truth and beauty judgments resemble each other quite a lot—or at least that's my claim. I briefly say how they do, and, along the way, I suggest how we might get interested in some historical and contemporary practices of subjectivity as forms of science. I say practices of subjectivity, since the notion becomes accessible in its specifics. Taste is one among many practices of subjectivity and the specific modes of taste involved in the organoleptic properties of aliment—notably taste and odor—have been widely accounted among the most private, arbitrary, and least discussable of all subjective modes. Taste is a mode of subjectivity; its sub-modes include the taste and smell of foods as well as the assessment of artistic beauty; but all forms of taste have been recognized as problems for philosophical treatments of knowledge and order.[9] How did 18th-century aesthetic philosophers think about taste judgments? There were writers in a direct genealogical line with Kuhn's distinction. Thomas Reid, for instance, surveyed existing philosophical opinion about

---

7 Kuhn 1977 [1973], p. 337.

8 Given Kuhn's friendship with the philosopher Stanley Cavell, it is interesting here to compare his treatment with Cavell's (1969 [1965]) account of the distinction between taste and judgment in aesthetics. In acknowledgments to *Must We Mean What We Say?*, Cavell (1969 [1965], p. xiv) specifically thanked Kuhn for conversations in 1956–1958 when both were teaching philosophy at Berkeley, which Kuhn had already noted in his 1962 *Structure* (Kuhn 1962, p. xiii).

9 18th-century philosophers concurred in using the word for palate responses to designate also 'higher' aesthetic judgment, even while some considered the link to be merely metaphorical rather than properly substantive: "How could it have happened," Kant (2006 [1798], pp. 139–140) asked, "that modern languages ... have designated the aesthetic faculty of judging with an expression (*gustus, sapor*) that merely refers to a certain sense organ (the inside of the mouth) and to its discrimination as well as choice of enjoyable things? ... [T]he feeling of an organ through a particular sense has been able to furnish the name for an ideal feeling; the feeling, namely, of a sensible, universally valid choice in general." Kant treated judgments that something is *pleasant* or *agreeable*—as in "this is a good roast chicken"—as wholly subjective, unlike judgments that a work of art is beautiful or sublime. These latter contain a presumption that other people *should* agree with one's judgment, even if they happen not to (Kant, 1914 [1790], especially pp. 48–63; see also Korsmeyer 1999, Dickie 1996).

the relationship between the categories of judgment and taste. Philosophers had situated the domain of judgment in means-ends deliberations, but reckoned judgment impotent in deciding between ends or in fixing upon what was good. Here, they thought, "we must be guided, not by judgment, but by some natural or acquired taste, which makes us relish one thing and dislike another,"[10] a taste we could not discuss. Reid's examples were a food choice and amoral choice, and he was concerned with the question of whether both could be viewed within the same frame:

> [I]f one man prefers cheese to lobsters, another lobsters to cheese, it is vain, say they, to apply judgment to determine which is right. In like manner, if one man prefers pleasure to virtue, another virtue to pleasure, this is a matter of taste, judgment has nothing to do in it. This seems to be the opinion of some philosophers[11]

Reid dissented, thinking that "we may form a judgment, both in the question about cheese and lobsters, and in the more important question about pleasure and virtue." Reid granted that individuals' preference between cheese and lobsters required no judgment, depending only on "the constitution of the palate." But if the question is who has the best taste, judgment can and should return an answer: each to his own—"the two tastes are equally good, and ... both of the parties do equally well, in preferring what suits their palate and their stomach." Palate relativism didn't disturb Reid, because he evidently cared far more about preserving the discussability of what was called judgment than establishing the accessibility of taste: "the two persons who differ in their tastes will, notwithstanding that difference, agree perfectly in their judgment, that both tastes are upon a footing of equality, and that neither has a just claim to preference."[12] There was a taste/judgment distinction, but judgment could function in the domain of taste, and the each-to-his-own outcome which some philosophers deplored was itself owing to judgment: "[I]t appears, that, in this instance, the office of taste is very different from that of judgment; and that men, who differ most in taste, may agree perfectly in their judgment, even with respect to the tastes wherein they differ." Judgment about taste was tolerant; judgment between a life of virtue and a life of pleasure neither was nor should be so casual. Anyone who could not see the obligation of virtue was not a 'moral agent,' giving

10 Reid 1788, p. 71.
11 Reid 1788, p. 71.
12 Reid 1788, p. 71.

evidence that his faculties were deranged. A taste for lobsters and the worth of a life given over to lobster eating were not on a level.[13]

A different genealogy stems from David Hume's (1758 [1757]) great *Essay Concerning the Standard of Taste*, and here its development would lead to an understanding of taste different from the one Kuhn commended. Hume's question was whether there could be such a thing as a standard in matters of taste, and the first response he canvassed was no. He invoked *De gustibus* and he talked about taste in the same sort of way that Kuhn later did:

> To seek the real beauty, or real deformity is as fruitless an enquiry, as to pretend to ascertain the real sweet or real bitter. According to the disposition of the organs, the same object may be both sweet and bitter; and the proverb has justly determined it to be fruitless to dispute concerning taste.[14]

But the richness of Hume's essay comes from not leaving the matter there. He also considered the coherence and legitimacy of the view that tastes are neither arbitrary nor incapable of being shared. Indeed, it was a common sentiment among 18th-century Scottish philosophers that the arbitrariness implied by *De gustibus* was refuted by the everyday practices of those who articulated it. Alexander Gerard, for example, perceptively noted that:

> The proverb, though frequently expressed, is never steadily or consistently adopted. Its authority is sometimes urged by persons whose sentiments are called into question; but it is disregarded by the same persons, whenever they are disposed to call in question the sentiments of others.[15]

You take refuge in *De gustibus* when you can find no principle or evidence to justify your taste, but when you find fault with another's taste, you believe and act as if there is a standard of taste, a right and a wrong in the matter.[16]

When I say that a Vermeer is beautiful, I mean it to be understood that there is something about the painting that is the occasion of my saying so and ought to cause you to respond as I respond. It's hard to imagine the point of my saying the Vermeer was beautiful if what I meant was nothing to do with observable aspects of the painting, aspects to which I can draw your attention and which I might be able to associate with more or less robust features of beautiful paintings. My sense of its beauty has, of course, got to do with me, but it also has got to do

---

13 Reid 1788, pp. 71–72.
14 Hume 1758, p. 136.
15 Gerard 1780, p. 208.
16 Gerard 1780, p. 208.

with the painting. And, in thinking that, I do not have to believe in any such notion as universal aesthetic standards. As we reckon that taste responses have got to do with objects, not just subjects, we then quite forget, Hume reminds us, "the natural equality of tastes," and, he might have said, we argue, dispute, and discuss quite a lot. It's "natural" for us, Hume said, to call on evidence and reasoned argument in order to arrive either at agreement or adjudication.[17] You and I can discuss things about the painting that flow from what I notice and you may not (or the other way round). We do not then act as if we regard our judgments as arbitrary or essentially private; insofar as we think that there are aspects of the object that elicit our aesthetic responses, we are talking about the objects, the same objects available to you as well as me—and we can and do refer to, even point at, aspects of those objects as we talk about our responses. That position too was staked out, turned over, and debated in 18th-century aesthetics.

Kant's *Critique of Judgement* named and discussed what he called the "antinomy of taste."[18] There are, he observed, two principles of judgment, each of which is valid but each of which seems to rule out the other. On the one hand, taste is an internal, private, felt response—subjective in the sense that there is no way that I can feel just what you feel—and, on the other hand, taste is something we might be able to give reasons for, reasons which we might communicate—objective in the sense that such reasons exist and that we can attach them to the object in question. Kant formalized the antinomy of taste, but he was not the only 18th-century philosopher centrally to confront these conflicting notions.[19] While no major aesthetic thinker omitted to mention the individuality and unaccountability usually conveyed by *De gustibus*, many reckoned that taste was in fact, as they said, 'improvable'—that there were social and cultural practices through which people could, if they wished, find more or less robust standards of taste and convey their assessments from one to another. Hume, for example, thought that there were people whose taste was accounted experienced, delicate, and correct; that others looked for, and to, these people to constitute a standard of taste; and that there were certain marks by which such people might be identified, among them experience and integrity. Taste was personal and subjective; people looked for ways to instruct taste and to repair the privacy of the subjective; they often found resources for that repair in the judgment of certain sorts of people; and, closing the circle, personal taste could be

---

17 Hume 1758, p. 136.
18 Kant 1914 [1790], pp. 229–241.
19 Costelloe 2003 and 2004, Stern 1991.

instructed through social knowledge and modified through social interaction. Hume's account struck many contemporaries as an imperfect notion of a standard of taste, but he never promised an aesthetic rose garden.[20] Other 18th-century aesthetic writers also viewed taste as a conversation between private responses and more or less robust social standards, a conversation that might, so to speak, go somewhere. The Scottish rhetorician Hugh Blair strongly argued that there was a cultural capacity to adapt, modify, and (as he said) 'improve' taste—to constitute taste as collectively held—placing his biggest bet on a consensus theory of taste formation: "That which men concur the most in admiring, must be held to be beautiful. His taste must be esteemed just and true, which coincides with the general sentiments of men. In this standard we must rest."[21]

For all the points held in common, 18th-century aesthetics does not offer a stable understanding of taste, no more than the philosophy of science offers a stable picture of scientific judgment. Edmund Burke, for example, disagreed with Hume's suggestion that a food might be bitter to some and sweet to others; we all have the same sense organs, he said, so what's bitter to me is, of course, bitter to you. What may vary is what we say about how the food strikes you.[22] (This is a recurrent move in the philosophy of taste: you can either make a distinction between the tasting act and reporting on the tasting act, or you can wonder about the intelligibility or legitimacy of any such distinction. It is, however, hard to understand the grounds on which that distinction is so confidently insisted upon.) Nor did the aesthetic philosophers of the 18th century resolve the antinomy of taste. The value for us in considering their work is that they recognized, confronted, and discussed the antinomy. They did not conduct ethnographic research on taste-formation, nor did they produce detailed historical studies of how tastes were made and how the aesthetic private became pub-

---

20 Hume 1758, pp. 136–140. Modern aesthetic philosophers and critics have become adept in identifying, and undermining, Hume's standard of taste because of its 'circularity': masters of taste are said to be recognized by their possession of good taste, and good taste is what masters have (for example, Noxon 1961, Smith 1988, p. 36–64), but the attributed experience, integrity, and overall good sense of supposed masters of taste are in principle independent of their judgments of aesthetic objects. Other commentators are unworried by any apparent circularity, since Hume was concerned to describe a social practice, and learning any social practice is learning who counts as a competent practitioner (Costelloe 2004, pp. 99–100, Jones 1993, p. 274).

21 Blair 1829 [1783], p. 24.

22 "We do and we must suppose, that as the conformation of their organs are nearly or altogether the same in all men, so the manner of perceiving external objects is in all men the same, or with little difference. We are satisfied that what appears to be light to one eye, appears light to another; that what seems sweet to one palate, is sweet to another; that what is dark and bitter to this man, is likewise dark and bitter to that ..." (Burke 1834 [1757], p. 25).

lic, to the extent it did. They acknowledged that the sharing of taste—rendering it social rather than individual—in this domain was a massive problem, but they reckoned that taste communities could be, and were, brought into being. In modern philosophical terminology, they were looking for the concrete means by which *intersubjectivity* might be secured, with difficulty and under specific conditions.[23]Their experiences and their precedents are instructive.

Traditions of aesthetics offer resources for thinking about scientific judgments, picking up, so to speak, the other end of the epistemic stick. In the study of science, we start from the notion of unproblematic and universal objectivity and then we add dollops of subjectivity, while in the study of taste, we start from the disposition to find judgments merely subjective, wholly arbitrary, and incorrigible, and then put ourselves in a position to appreciate that they have a referential character and that they may be discussable. That is to say, in judgments of taste and in judgments of truth, we approach intersubjectivity from different directions, but that is where, in both cases, we tend to wind up.

In fact, to the proverbial 'There's no arguing about taste,' I'd counter we argue about little else and, indeed, that absent such arguments and discussions, we would not be able to recognize the fabric of our quotidian social life. We do not much argue (or discuss) whether 2 + 2 = 4 (except in philosophy classrooms) or about the facts of the matter (except in law courts), but the texture of our conversations centers precisely on whether *An Affair to Remember* is a good movie, whether *Catch 22* is a great novel, whether Texas BBQ is better than Carolina BBQ, whether the poetry of Bob Dylan is as good as that of Dylan Thomas. So far as the practices of everyday life are concerned, including the everyday life of science-making, we should get better at understanding judgment and how it happens. As Richard Rorty once said,[24] if the objectivity of legend is not on the table, nevertheless we might be interested in something that he thought served the purposes for which objectivity is commonly invoked—which is the achievement, wherever it happens, of 'unforced agreement,' of coming to free and practical interactional assent about what is, from another point of view, private to the experiencing and knowing subject: "Objectivity is intersubjectivity."

So what do we know about how taste judgments are formed and how they may come to be shared? The answer is: not a lot. There's usually some misunderstanding when I say that: there is a huge sociological literature about this, I am told. But there isn't. The sociological treatment of taste has focused overwhelm-

23 For intersubjectivity, see Schutz 1964 [1951] and Crossley 1996; for rhetoric and the creation of shared judgment, see Booth 1974, pp. xii–xiii, 98–99.

24 Rorty 1987, pp. 41–42.

ingly on the social uses of taste, on taste as a social marker, as a mode of distinction, on explanations of changing tastes, on fashion as a social phenomenon.[25] These are all worthy topics, but they are not the same thing as a focused engagement with making and communicating taste. Antoine Hennion has described (and deplored) sociologists' interest in what taste does to the neglect of what taste is and how it is formed in the interactions between people and objects, people and people. Describing the tasting of wine, he advocates a "sociology of attention" as an appreciation of tasters' efforts momentarily to make themselves objects rather than subjects, to arrange "a stronger presence of the tasted object," to attend to and respond to what the tasted object reveals, what it is saying.[26] What would be good to have are ethnographies—contemporary and historical—of how taste judgments come to be formed, discussed, and sometimes shared. Such ethnographies would look a lot like those produced by laboratory studies of science, concerned with how fact and theory judgments come to be formed, discussed, and sometimes shared.

One reason, I suspect, that we have so few examples of this sort of thing is the sway of the *De gustibus* sensibility. It is considered either that there is no possibility of discussing taste or there is no point in any such discussion. But there is both the possibility and the point, and there exist, in fact, a handful of exercises showing varying degrees of interest in how, on a concrete level and in a quotidian frame, taste happens.[27] A noteworthy example is a study of how one becomes an opera buff by the sociologist Claudio Benzecry.[28] How do you learn to respond to opera the way that opera lovers do, to be an opera lover? You hang out with opera lovers, observe the moments and circumstances that elicit approving and disapproving responses, note the words, phrases, and gestures attached to descriptions and evaluations of opera passages and performances. As you listen to the opera, so you listen to the associations and distinctions made between different performances. And you get better at becoming an opera lover as you see more operas and get reactions to your descriptions and evaluations. Becoming an opera lover is knowing about opera and knowing about opera lovers and knowing about how opera lovers know about opera and how

25 See the classic studies by Veblen (1899, especially ch. 6) and Simmel (1957 [1904]). The most influential modern work is, of course, Bourdieu 1984, but see also Dimaggio 1987, Lamont 1992, Davis 1992, Peterson and Kern 1996, and Johnston and Baumann 2007.

26 Hennion 2007. See also Hennion 2001 and 2005, Hennion and Teil 2004, and Teil and Hennion 2004.

27 See, for example, McCormick 2009, DeNora 1995, Guilbaut 1983, Shrum 1996, Lieberson 2000, Lamont 2009, and, of course, the excellent Becker 1982, especially ch. 5.

28 Benzecry 2009 and 2011.

they know about other opera lovers; it's about the external world and about co-ordinating or distinguishing one's private aesthetic responses with the private aesthetic responses of others. Benzecry[29] acknowledges inspiration by early work of Howard Becker (1953) about how you learn to be a marijuana user, indeed how you learn to experience what a marijuana user experiences and how to value and talk about those experiences. You need both cannabis and community, both objects in the world and fellow experiencing subjects. Everyone gets stoned alone, together.

Academics haven't been greatly interested in naturalistic understandings of the practices of taste and judgment, but there are many other sorts of people to take up the slack. And there are two kinds of communities that have more or less systematically reflected on how tastes may be formed, described, and shared. The community of connoisseurs and those allied to connoisseurship make up one sort. The usage of the word 'connoisseur,' by the way, evidently came into English in the context of the 18th-century culture of refinement and politeness: the man of knowledge as a man of taste. In the French from which it was borrowed, it simply meant knowing in the sense of being acquainted with, on the *kennen* side of the German *kennen–wissen* distinction, but in English it was attached to the special sort of knowing, which was discernment in matters of taste.

Connoisseurship and scientific judgment aren't usually considered together, but they should be, and indeed they were by the physical chemist and philosopher Michael Polanyi. Judgment for Polanyi wasn't rigidly rule-governed, but neither was it arbitrary nor private. And this is what he signaled by repeatedly assimilating scientific judgment to practices like knowing the characteristics and qualities of wine. "Connoisseurship, like skill," Polanyi wrote, "can be communicated only by example, not by precept. To become an expert wine-taster, to acquire a knowledge of innumerable different blends of tea or to be trained as a medical diagnostician, you must go through a long course of experience under the guidance of a master."[30] "Scientific beliefs are necessarily indeterminate. They are like rules of art. They are guides in the art of making scientific discoveries and guides of connoisseurship in assessing the value of a scientific claim."[31] Thomas Kuhn, who incorporated elements of Polanyi's views into his *Structure of Scientific Revolutions* (1962), avoided using the notion of connoisseurship, but other than that, his view of scientific judgment was markedly similar. The knowledge of the connoisseur proceeds from example to example, as

29 Benzecry 2011, p. 66.
30 Polanyi 1958, p. 56.
31 Polanyi 1950, p. 196.

Polanyi said, but it isn't true that is can be communicated only by example. Wine connoisseurs, for example, talk a lot about the flavor and odor characteristics of wines.[32] Much of their talk is referential, that is, it points to characteristic sin the wine that connoisseurs come to know about, and taste communities can and do coalesce around more or less stable ways of designating these characteristics. You can learn to apply the descriptor 'black curranty' to a wine made from cabernet sauvignon and 'flinty' to a Chablis. You can believe that you are then doing something different from what you might be doing if you said that the wine reminded you of a spring morning, and you can believe that the black curranty odor arises from a substance that is indeed present in both the wine and the fruit. More to the point, you can come to be a member of a community using the same predicates to refer to their experiences and to the aesthetic properties of the wine. That sort of community can refer judgment of goodness to an assemblage of such properties.[33] There is a copyrighted device called a Wine Aroma Wheel—devised by a professor in the UC Davis viticulture and oenology department.[34] It allows users—and there are evidently many thousands around the world—reliably to assign stable descriptors to wine odors and tastes, proceeding from such basic categories as 'fruity,' 'floral,' and 'nutty' to more finely gauged descriptors such as 'peach,' 'apricot,' and 'apple.' The users are instructed to provide themselves with index samples of descriptors, for the 'asparagus' odor, several drops of the brine from tinned asparagus in a neutral white wine. The point is not taste objectivity; it is taste intersubjectivity. The Aroma Wheel is a homespun intersubjectivity engine. Taste communities coalesce around practices like that—practices that refer to mutually accessible external properties as the causes of internal states. These taste communities are neither universal nor easy to join, but then neither are the thought communities of particle physics and genomics.

The Wine Wheel is small beer, but many forms of modern commercial and academic taste expertise are immensely influential. Among the less visible bits of modern corporate and academic science are what I want to call the sciences of subjectivity, embedded within what I'd also like to call the aesthetic-industrial complex. A brief but instructive example: during the Second World War, the US Army Quartermaster Corps became aware that rations for the troops designed for their nutritional value were not performing their role because the men didn't

---

32 Shapin 2012 and Shapin 2016.

33 Donner 1991. Shapin 2012.

34 Available at http://winearomawheel.com/ (accessed December 10, 2011); see also Brenner 2007, pp. 17–23.

like how they tasted and looked.[35] Aesthetic responses were made into a focused topic of inquiry: that is to say, there was a practical demand for objective information about subjective states. Here the Army added impetus to industrial and academic concerns with taste that were emerging in the 1940s and1950s as the technologies of sensory evaluation, notably in connection with the wine and food scientists of UC Davis.[36] The industrial consulting company Arthur D. Little, Inc., in Cambridge, MA, together with commercial food and beverage companies (including Coca Cola and Pillsbury), developed the so-called Flavor Profile Method for eliciting and objectifying taste responses and the chillingly named Hedonic Index to quantify liking.[37] These methods and their successors, often used in connection with focus group techniques pioneered by Robert Merton, now form a vast complex of technical resources that help shape not just our alimentary environment but also practically everything that is commercially formulated, designed, and marketed—from pretzels to presidents, cabernets to Cadillacs, apples to Apples. The sciences of subjectivity are world-making. With some honorable exceptions, modern philosophers have either relegated taste to the domain of the inaccessible and the inchoate or carried on the fight to identify universal standards; sociologists have engaged with the functions rather than the formation of taste; and a few historians have written about olfactory reactions as indexes of the civilizing process. Meanwhile, the modern sciences of subjectivity go on their way, largely unattended to by people like us. Their practitioners are unaware of the inaccessibility and arbitrariness of taste responses, because they have found ways of accessing them, operationalizing their meaning, manipulating them, and even turning them into profit. If there is no accounting for tastes, that's news to the accountants.

Acknowledgments

This paper is adapted from a Presidential Plenary talk for the Society for Social Studies of Science in Cleveland, OH, on November 4, 2011. It is intended as a provocation and constructive prod, not as a research paper. Improvements to the original were suggested by Rebecca Lemov, Sophia Roosth, and Michael

35 See Peyram et al. 1954 and Meiselman and Schutz 2003.

36 See Peyram and Swartz 1950, Peyram et al. 1960, Amerine and Roessler 1976, and Stone and Sidel 2004, p. 7.

37 See Cairncross and Sjöström 1950, Sjöström et al. 1957, Peyram and Pilgrim 1957, Caul 1957, and Amerine et al. 1965, pp. 366–391.

Lynch. This essay was originally published in *Social Studies of Science* 42(2) (2012): 170 – 184.

References

Amerine, M.A., Pangborn, R.M. and Roessler, E.B. (1965) *Principles of Sensory Evaluation of Food*. New York: Academic Press.

Amerine, M.A. and Roessler, E.B. (1976) *Wines: Their Sensory Evaluation*. San Francisco: Freeman.

Ashworth, W.J. (2004) "Practical objectivity: The excise, state, and production in eighteenth century England." *Social Epistemology* 18: 181 – 197.

Austin, J.L. (1962) *Sense and Sensibilia*. Oxford: Oxford University Press.

Barnes, B., Bloor, D. and Henry, J. (1996) *Scientific Knowledge: A Sociological Analysis*. Chicago: University of Chicago Press.

Becker, H.S. (1953) "Becoming a marihuana user." *American Journal of Sociology* 59: 235 – 242.

Becker, H.S. (1982) *Art Worlds*. Berkeley: University of California Press.

Benzecry, C.E. (2009) "Becoming a fan: On the seductions of opera." *Qualitative Sociology* 32: 131 – 151.

Benzecry, C.E. (2011) *The Opera Fanatic: Ethnography of an Obsession*. Chicago: University of Chicago Press.

Biehl, J., Good, B. and Kleinman, A. (eds.) (2007) *Subjectivity: Ethnographic Investigations*. Berkeley: University of California Press.

Blair, H. (1829 [1783]) "On taste." In: H. Blair, *Lectures on Rhetoric and Belles Lettres*, ed. Abraham Mills. New York: Carvill, pp. 16 – 26.

Bloor, D. (1984) "A sociological theory of objectivity." In: S.C. Brown (ed.), *Objectivity and Cultural Divergence*. Cambridge: Cambridge University Press, pp. 229 – 245.

Bloor, D. (1996) "Idealism and the sociology of knowledge." *Social Studies of Science* 26: 839 – 856.

Booth, W.C. (1974) *Modern Dogma and the Rhetoric of Assent*. Chicago: University of Chicago Press.

Bourdieu, P. (1984) *Distinction: A Social Critique of the Judgment of Taste*, tr. R. Nice. London: Routledge & Kegan Paul.

Brenner, D. (2007) *Women of the Vine: Inside the World of Women Who Make, Taste, and Enjoy Wine*. Hoboken, NJ: John Wiley.

Burke, E. (1834 [1757]) "A philosophical enquiry into the origins of our ideas of the sublime and beautiful." In: E. Burke, *The Works of the Rt. Hon. Edmund Burke*. Vol. I. London: Samuel Holdsworth, pp. 22 – 74.

Cairncross, S.E. and Sjöström, L.B. (1950) "Flavor profiles: A new approach to flavor problems." *Food Technology* 4: 308 – 311.

Caul, J.F. (1957) "The profile method of flavor analysis." *Advances in Food Research* 7(1): 1 – 40.

Cavell, S. (1969 [1965]) "Aesthetic problems of modern philosophy." In: S. Cavell, *Must We Mean What We Say? A Book of Essays*. New York: Scribner, pp. 73 – 96.

Costelloe, T.M. (2003) "Hume, Kant, and the 'antinomy of taste'." *Journal of the History of Philosophy* 41: 165–185.
Costelloe, T.M. (2004) "Hume's aesthetics: The literature and directions for research." *Hume Studies* 30: 87–126.
Crossley, N. (1996) *Intersubjectivity: The Fabric of Social Becoming.* London: Sage.
Cussins, C. (1996) "Ontological choreography: Agency through objectification in infertility clinics." *Social Studies of Science* 26: 575–610.
Daston, L.J. (1992) "Objectivity and the escape from perspective." *Social Studies of Science* 22: 597–618.
Daston, L. and Galison, P. (1992) "The image of objectivity." *Representations* 40: 81–128.
Daston, L. and Galison, P. (2007) *Objectivity.* New York: Zone Books.
Davis, F. (1992) *Fashion, Culture, and Identity.* Chicago: University of Chicago Press.
Dear, P. (1992) "From truth to disinterestedness in the seventeenth century." *Social Studies of Science* 22: 619–631.
DeNora, T. (1995) *Beethoven and the Construction of Genius: Musical Politics in Vienna 1792–1803.* Berkeley: University of California Press.
Dickie G. (1996) *The Century of Taste: The Philosophical Odyssey of Taste in the Eighteenth Century.* New York: Oxford University Press.
Dimaggio, P. (1987) "Classification in art." *American Sociological Review* 52: 440–455.
Donner, W. (1991) "The sensory evaluation of wines." In: W. Donner, *The Liberal Self: John Stuart Mill's Moral and Political Philosophy.* Ithaca: Cornell University Press, pp. 83–91.
Ellis, C. and Flaherty, M.G. (eds.) (1992) *Investigating Subjectivity: Research on Lived Experience.* Newbury Park, CA: Sage.
Foucault, M. (1988 [1984]) *The History of Sexuality.* Vol. 3: *The Care of the Self*, tr. R. Hurley. New York: Vintage.
Gerard, A. (1780 [1759]) *An Essay on Taste*, 3rd ed. Edinburgh: J. Bell and W. Creech.
Gieryn, T.F. (1994) "Objectivity for these times." *Perspectives on Science* 2: 324–349.
Guilbaut, S. (1983) *How New York Stole the Idea of Modern Art*, tr. A. Goldhammer. Chicago: University of Chicago Press.
Hall, D.E. (2004) "Subjectivity." London: Routledge.
Haraway, D.J. (1991 [1985]) "A cyborg manifesto: Science, technology, and socialist-feminism in the late 20th century." In: D.J. Haraway, *Simians, Cyborgs, and Women: The Reinvention of Nature.* New York: Routledge, pp. 149–191.
Hennion, A. (2001) "Music lovers: Taste as performance." *Theory, Culture, and Society* 18: 1–22.
Hennion, A. (2005) "Pragmatics of taste." In: M.D. Jacobs and N.W. Hanrahan (eds.), *The Blackwell Companion to the Sociology of Culture.* Oxford: Blackwell, pp. 131–144.
Hennion, A. (2007) "Those things that hold us together: Taste and sociology." *Cultural Sociology* 1: 97–114.
Hennion, A. and Teil, G. (2004) "Le goût du vin: pour une sociologie de l'attention." In: V. Nahoum-Grappe and O. Vincent (eds.), *Le Goût des Belles Choses.* Paris: Éditions de la Maison des Sciences de l'Homme, pp. 111–126.
Hume, D. (1758 [1757]) "Of the standard of taste." In: D. Hume, *Essays and Treatises on Several Subjects*, new ed. London: A. Millar, pp. 134–146.

Jasanoff, S. (2011) "The practices of objectivity in regulatory science." In: C. Camic, N. Gross and M. Lamont (eds.), *Social Knowledge in the Making*. Chicago: University of Chicago Press, pp. 307–338.

Johnston, J. and Baumann, S. (2007) "Democracy versus distinction: A study of omnivorousness in gourmet food writing." *American Journal of Sociology* 113: 165–204.

Jones, P. (1993) "Hume's literary and aesthetic theory." In: D.F. Norton (ed.), *The Cambridge Companion to Hume*. New York: Cambridge University Press, pp. 255–280.

Kant, I. (1914 [1790]) *Kant's Critique of Judgment*, tr. J.H. Bernard. London: Macmillan.

Kant, I. (2006 [1798]) *Anthropology from a Pragmatic Point of View*, ed. Robert B. Louden. Cambridge: Cambridge University Press.

Korsmeyer, C. (1999) *Making Sense of Taste: Taste, Food, and Philosophy*. Ithaca, NY: Cornell University Press.

Kuhn, T.S. (1962) *The Structure of Scientific Revolutions*. Chicago: University of Chicago Press.

Kuhn, T.S. (1977 [1973]) "Objectivity, value judgment, and theory choice." In: T.S. Kuhn, *The Essential Tension: Selected Studies in Scientific Tradition and Change*. Chicago: University of Chicago Press, pp. 320–339 [Machette Lecture, delivered at Furman University, 30 November 1973].

Lamont, M. (1992) *Money, Morals, and Manners: The Culture of the French and American Upper-Middle Class*. Chicago: University of Chicago Press.

Lamont, M. (2009) *How Professors Think: Inside the Curious World of Academic Judgment*. Cambridge, MA: Harvard University Press.

Lieberson, S. (2000) *A Matter of Taste: How Names, Fashions, and Culture Change*. New Haven: Yale University Press.

McCormick, L. (2009) "Higher, faster, louder: Representations of the international music competition." *Cultural Sociology* 3: 5–30.

Markley, R. (1983) "Objectivity as ideology: Boyle, Newton and the languages of science." *Genre* 16: 355–372.

Meiselman, H.L. and Schutz, H.G. (2003) "History of food acceptance research in the US Army." *Appetite* 40: 199–216.

Miller, P. (1992) "Accounting and objectivity: The invention of calculating selves and calculable spaces." *Annals of Scholarship* 9: 61–86.

Mitroff, I. (1974) *The Subjective Side of Science: A Philosophical Inquiry into the Psychology of the Apollo Moon Scientists*. New York: American Elsevier.

Noxon, J. (1961) "Hume's opinion of critics." *Journal of Aesthetics and Art Criticism* 20: 157–162.

Peterson, R.A. and Kern, R.M. (1996) "Changing highbrow taste: From snob to omnivore." *American Sociological Review* 61: 900–907.

Peyram, D.R., Polemis, B.W., Kamen, J.M., Eindhoven, J. and Pligrim, J. (1960) *Food Preferences of Men in the U.S. Armed Forces*. Chicago: Quartermaster Food and Container Institute for the Armed Forces.

Peyram, D.R. and Pilgrim, F.J. (1957) "Hedonic scale method of measuring food preferences." *Food Technology* 11: 9–14.

Peyram, D.R., Pilgrim, F.J. and Peterson, M.S. (eds.) (1954) *Food Acceptance Testing Methodology, A Symposium Sponsored by the Quartermaster Food and Container Institute for the Armed Forces 8–9 October 1953*. Washington, DC: National Academy of Sciences-National Research Council.

Peyram, D.R. and Swartz, V.W. (1950) "Measurement of sensory differences." *Food Technology* 4: 390 – 395.
Pickering, A. (1991) "Objectivity and the mangle of practice." *Annals of Scholarship* 8: 409 – 425.
Polanyi, M. (1950) "Freedom in science." *Bulletin of the Atomic Scientists* 6(7): 195 – 198, 224.
Polanyi, M. (1958) *Personal Knowledge: Towards a Post-Critical Philosophy.* Chicago: University of Chicago Press.
Poovey, M. (1998) *A History of the Modern Fact: Problems of Knowledge in the Sciences of Wealth and Society.* Chicago: University of Chicago Press.
Porter, T.M. (1995) *Trust in Numbers: The Pursuit of Objectivity in Science and Public Life.* Princeton: Princeton University Press.
Reid, T. (1788) *Essays on the Active Powers of Man.* Edinburgh: John Bell.
Rorty, R. (1987) "Science as solidarity." In: J.S. Nelson, A. Megill and D.N. McCloskey (eds.) *The Rhetoric of the Human Sciences.* Madison: University of Wisconsin Press, pp. 38 – 52.
Scheffler, I. (1967) *Science and Subjectivity.* Indianapolis: Bobbs-Merrill.
Schutz, A. (1964 [1951]) "Making music together: A study in social relationship." In: A. Schutz, *Collected Papers.* Vol. 2: *Studies in Social Theory*, ed. Arvid Brodersen. The Hague: Nijhoff, pp. 159 – 178.
Shapin, S. (1994) *A Social History of Truth: Civility and Science in Seventeenth-Century England.* Chicago: University of Chicago Press.
Shapin, S. (1999) "Rarely pure and never simple: Talking about truth." *Configurations* 7: 1 – 14.
Shapin, S. (2012) "The tastes of wine: Notes towards a cultural history." *Rivista di Estetica*, n.s. 51: 49 – 94.
Shapin, S. (2016) "A taste of science: Making the subjective objective in the California wine world." *Social Studies of Science* 46(3): 436 – 460.
Shapin, S. and Schaffer, S. (1985) *Leviathan and the Air-Pump: Hobbes, Boyle, and the Experimental Life.* Princeton: Princeton University Press.
Shrum, W.C. (1996) *Fringe and Fortune: The Role of Critics in High and Popular Art.* Princeton: Princeton University Press.
Simmel, G. (1957 [1904]) "Fashion." *American Journal of Sociology* 62: 541 – 558.
Sjöström, L.B., Cairncross, S.E. and Caul, J.F. (1957) "Methodology of the flavor profile." *Food Technology* 11(9): 2 – 25 (suppl.).
Smith, B.H. (1988) *Contingencies of Value: Alternative Perspectives for Critical Theory.* Cambridge, MA: Harvard University Press.
Solomon, R.J. (1998) *Objectivity in the Making: Francis Bacon and the Politics of Inquiry.* Baltimore: Johns Hopkins University Press.
Stengers, I. (2000 [1993]) *The Invention of Modern Science: Theory Out of Bounds*, tr. D.W. Smith. Minneapolis: University of Minnesota Press.
Stern, D. (1991) "Are disagreements about taste possible? A discussion of Kant's antinomy of taste." *Iowa Review* 21(2): 66 – 71.
Stone, H.S. and Sidel, J.L. (2004) *Sensory Evaluation Practices*, 3rd ed. San Diego, CA: Elsevier Academic.
Taylor, C. (1989) *Sources of the Self: The Making of the Modern Identity.* Cambridge: Cambridge University Press.

Teil, G.T. and Hennion, A. (2004) "Discovering quality or performing taste? A sociology of the amateur." In: M. Harvey, A. McKeekin and A. Warde (eds.), *Qualities of Food.* Manchester: Manchester University Press, pp. 19 – 37.

Veblen, T. (1899) *The Theory of the Leisure Class: An Economic Study in the Evolution of Institutions.* New York: Macmillan.

Dimitri Ginev

Studies of Empirical Ontology and Ontological Difference

Abstract: While supporting the anti-foundational ontological turn in science and technology studies, the author criticizes in the present article the tendency to radical empiricization of empirical ontology. The article discusses two crucial arguments against this tendency. On the cognitivist argument, the empirical immediacy is inevitably shaped and mediated by non-empirical assumptions. According to the hermeneutic argument which is of much greater importance, any empirically immediate state of affairs is the upshot of actualizing possibilities projected by interrelated practices upon horizons of practical existence. Thus, the actually given as empirical immediacy is ineluctably "produced" within the potentiality for practical being. Following this argument, a non-empirical extension of empirical ontology is suggested. Starting-point of this extension is the integration of radical reflexivity in ethnographic descriptions of multiple realities. A further step consists in the introduction of double hermeneutics in the studies of empirical ontology. Finally, the significance of ontological difference for these studies comes under scrutiny.

In this chapter, I argue against the radical empiricization of ontology. The claim will begin to emerge that a kind of hermeneutic (non-empirical) ontological reflection has to complement the studies of empirical ontology. Roughly, I will seek to unfold the thesis that the unavoidability of "ontological difference" (or, the difference between empirical description of multiple entities in interrelated practices and hermeneutic analysis of situated constitution of meaning) provides a crucial argument against the full-fledged empiricization of ontology. The claim will be advocated that Melvin Pollner's way of integrating radical reflexivity in ethnomethodology is also a way of introducing a methodology of double hermeneutics that deals with multiple entities and realities by taking into consideration ontological difference. The conjugation of endogenous reflexivity (generated by a network of humans and nonhumans) and researcher's radical reflexivity requires more than ontic description. This conjugation, recast in terms of double hermeneutics, allows one to make sense of multiple realities in their potentiality for being.

https://doi.org/10.1515/9783110551563-008

I The Non-Empirical Assumptions in the Radical Empiricization of Ontology

On a central claim of the so-called "empirical ontology" (as a program within Science and Technology Studies), realities are enacted in practices (Law and Lien 2012). Empirical ontology is an initiative that promotes a way out of relativist-epistemological perspectivism. By putting all participants in a system of orchestrated practices on a par, the methodology of perspectivism dissects each particular entity enacted in practices, thereby representing it as a manifold of separate objects whose existences depend on the practitioners/participants' standpoints. By contrast, empirical ontology offers a holist approach. The network of practices is put first in this ontological program. An entity enacted in this network does not get dissected and scattered in perspective-dependent objects. It rather gets multiplied and stratified in its own being. Put differently, it becomes a multiple entity without losing its ontic unity/identity. The task of empirical ontology is to grasp this unity within the network of practices. Accordingly, the focus on a particular practice is limited to the question of how the practice weaves its relations with other practices whereby the interrelatedness enacts entities. By implication, the enacted entities have their modes of existence in overlapping practices. Thus, the program of empirical ontology is about interrelated practices in flux that only allows the existence(s) of entities-enacted-in-practices. The champions of the ontological turn in Science and Technology Studies [STS] argue that their approach provides resources for investigating how techno-scientific practices change the world(s) materially, socially, morally, and politically. Following this approach, one scrutinizes the ways in which science and technology intervene the world(s) (Marres 2013, p. 422).

No doubt, empirical ontology goes hand in hand with an immense variety of versions of constructivism. But it is much more than a mere supplement to social constructivism. In his review of Mol (2002), Ashmore (2005) argues that exploring the ways of cognitive construction is still an epistemological enterprise whereas the practical intervention in the world is something that belongs to the investigatory purview of ontology.[1] Yet empirical ontology is an investigation

1 Ashmore stresses also that Mol's ontological approach to practices should not be read as endorsing the search for "Ontics, designed and destined to replace the tired old routines Epistemics" (Ashmore 2005, p. 829). On my reading, the champions of empirical ontology are not looking for a confrontation with epistemological programs. Yet, in contrast to older supporters of science-as-practice, they are guided by the view that there is no hypostatized body of knowledge separable from the epistemic practices. The latter, however, are inextricably implicated in the multiple realities that have to be studied ontologically. Thus, there is no knowledge that cannot

not only of interventions in worlds already made but also of the "degrees of alterity" of the worlds which science and technology bring into being (Woolgar and Lezaun 2013, p. 323). In this regard, the ontological approach in STS suggests ways of studying "multiple entities" that are constantly *in statu nascendi*. These entities engender in their turn "multiple realities" that are also emerging political realities. More specifically, the ways in which the different types of practices do the entities differently create emergent micro-political regimes of interaction within the networks of concerted practices (Brives 2013). The shift from (representational and/or normative) epistemology to ontology parallels the transition from science-as-knowledge to science-as-practice. Yet the ontological turn is by no means to be restricted to a moment of the praxeological turn. The ontological approach to practices and enacted entities has a lot of distinctive features that make it unique within the family of science-as-practice approaches. Let me briefly sketch out the main of these features.

The students of empirical ontology prefer to use the plural not only for realities and worlds. They speak of "ontologies" because they hold that each relatively autonomous body of orchestrated and concerted practices that enacts entities *sui generis* deserves its own "ontological model."[2] Thus, there is a growing diversification of ontologies in science and technology studies. The rationale behind the impetus of this diversification might be also formulated as follows: Different enactments of an object in different configurations of practices entail different "ontological models" of it. Thus considered, a particular empirical ontology seems essentially akin to a description of (what Heidegger calls) a "nexus of equipment" [*Zeugzusammenhang*].

Since orchestrated practices generate orders, the ontological approach in STS avoids assuming a grounding order lying behind the particular orchestrations of practices and enactments of entities. The avowal of the insurmountable diversity of orders expresses the commitment of STS (and part of the feminist critique of science) to post-metaphysical initiatives and agendas. Law and Lien (2012) demonstrate cogently the way in which the ontological approach undoes

---

be treated in terms of empirical ontology (in particular, the units of knowledge are no more than specific "multiple entities"), and, at the same time, there is no knowledge that can only be approached/analyzed from epistemological point of view. The champions of empirical ontology manage to overcome the traditional opposition between theory and practice. When Ashmore appeals in his review for a peace between Epistemics (which is dealing with the hot side of science, with novelty and controversy) and Ontics, he still commits to the traditional opposition, thereby adhering to a sort of Cartesian presuppositions.

2 'Model' here is to be understood not as a theoretical representation but as the outcome of a thick description that includes intervention in what gets described.

the very idea of grounding order. These authors insist on the clear distinction between the question of what exists through enactment (the question of empirical ontology) and the question of the general ordering of the cosmos. Focusing on practices rather than on stable social structures implies a full-fledged concentration on the former question. On a further claim, there are no "orders in themselves" but only orders generated by practices. Accordingly, ontological questions of ordering (creation of contingent orders) are detached from any kind of global ontology of the world-as-presence. The idea of "cosmos" (if any) turns into Whiteheadian totality of ordering processes.

Law and Lien provide a nice non-foundationalist picture of the levels of practices' interrelatedness. This picture is obtained by unfolding the aforementioned claim that there is no ordered ground separate from practices and their relations. All kinds of ordering in a domain of interrelated practices are provisional, expressing specific effects of the interrelatedness. Entities are meaningfully reshaped as a consequence of changing choreographies as "nexuses of equipment." No entity can do its own identity behind the interrelated practices. The creation of a "choreography" in which a synergy between humans and nonhumans takes place is the first level addressed by the empirical studies of ontology. A well-functioning choreography is one in which the involvements of entities in practices maintain the domain's persistent unity. The enacted entities are pieces of equipment indispensable for domain's functionality. Within a well-functioning choreography entities are characterized by their serviceability, conduciveness, usability, and manipulability. A second move consists in exploring "precarious choreographies" in which the interrelatedness of practices gets disturbed. A precarious choreography might, for instance, arise from the maladjustment of an entity (as a piece of equipment) to the operative configuration of practices. Entities become dysfunctional in such choreographies. But the most important move is the thick description of the "textures of ordering practices." A texture draws, as it were, a demarcation between artefacts (entities enacted in practices) and "natural objects." The ontological study of a texture should unveil the hinterland of invisible practices (and invisible relations) that make alleged natural objects artifacts by assigning to them a status of "actants" playing normative roles (Law and Lien 2012, pp. 369–371). In this regard, empirical ontology takes the shape of "ontology of artification" (transformation of supposedly natural states into artificial entities). In the texture, there are always "practices of Othering" that bring artification into being. What is more important, however, is that it stops to be a purely empirical ontology of a domain in its actual presence. It describes practices and enacted entities with regard to the possibilities of transforming natural objects into artifacts.

In anticipating my further discussion in the next section, I would say that the difference between "choreographies" and "textures" indicates in a tentative manner the ontological difference. More specifically, I tend to think that the distinction between a domain-as-a-diversity-of-choreographies (the actual and empirically given "nexuses of equipment") and a domain-as-a-texture (the potentiality for artification) corresponds to Heidegger's distinction between the (ontic) "work-world" and the (ontological) "worldhood" (Heidegger 1962, pp. 95–102). Choreographies are present states that can be studied empirically (in ontic manner), while the study of a texture should involve an (ontological) reflection upon the possibilities of "Othering" that arise out of the interrelatedness of practices. The "worldhood" is distinguished by continuity (continuous constitution of meaning and meaningful articulation of a domain) whereas the "work-world" is a discrete concatenation and multiplication of practices and entities.[3]

One is not able to unfold empirical ontology without a method. The ethnographic method of thick description proves to be the preferable one of unfolding empirical ontologies. On this method, the way of developing empirical ontology consists in scrutinizing the practices involved in the making of a relatively autonomous domain. The best case in point is Annemarie Mol's ethnography of (the domain of) hospital Z as this descriptive work is entangled with another one, namely "ethnography of atherosclerosis." The ontological vision of the multiple reality is achieved by ethnographic description of how the enacted entities (a disease in the first place) become a part of what is done within the interrelatedness of practices. This description ought to be carried out in a manner that would prevent one from admitting the existence of passive objects "in the middle" of the interrelated practices, "waiting to be seen from the point of view of seemingly endless series of perspectives" (Mol 2002, p. 5). The body, the patient, the doctor, the technician, the technology among many other entities are constantly reshaped and meaningfully re-constituted. The changing configurations of practices (and not the particular standpoints of the participants) are only responsible for objects' coming into being and disappearance. (This is also Mol's argu-

3 Latour's recent concept of the "modes of existence" is intended, on my reading, to suggest a unified description of the "work-world" and the "worldhood." Approaching the plurality of modes of being Latour has in sight is to be relied on a concept of experience that takes into consideration the wordly horizons in which one constructs the realities of existence, i.e. the realities as work-worlds. Only the complementary unity of horizon and constructed reality within this experience would allow one a description of the modes of existence beyond the "prison of epistemological divisions." Latour 2013, pp. 184–185.

ment for the irreducibility/irreplaceability of the ontological approach to/by traditional SSK constructivist-relativist-epistemological approaches.)

The objects do not become fragmented but multiplied, hanging together in various ways. By implication, the changing configurations of practices constitute ontic multiplications. The ethnographic thick description opens the avenue to unfolding ontologies of objects' manipulation-in-practices. This description is not only a method but an act of intervention as well. In this regard, Mol spells out the specificity of the ethnographic description's normativity. At issue is the question of how the ethnographer should intervene in the texture of practices in order to disclose the being (of multiple realities) which becomes continuously constituted. Important here is what Mol categorizes as a "third step" in the ethnographic description—the step of transforming this description into ontology of practical constitution of meaningful entities. In performing this step, one realizes that making ontology of a particular multiple reality is a part of the ontic-ethnographic description of practices one is engaged with. Phrased differently, distancing from disembodied contemplation requires that the researcher's descriptive practices ought to become a particular focus point of ontic description. Unfolding empirical ontology is first and foremost a reflexive participation in the described reality.[4] (Mol 2002, p. 153) The ontic study of the multiple entity of atherosclerosis as it is placed in the practices taking place in hospital Z has much to do with the distinction between knowing in medicine (about disease) and knowing about medicine. This is not epistemic but ontic distinction (i.e. a distinction between two kinds of practices taking place in the whole orchestration of hospital's practices). If I am correct in my reading of Mol's study, the researcher might manage to move successfully between "knowing in" and "knowing about" only by means of her reflexive participation in the multiple reality. This conclusion is closely related to issues of radical reflexivity I will discuss later.

No doubt, ethnographic thick description dominates the landscape of empirical ontology. Yet there is also another methodological tendency in the ontic studies typically advocated by Latour. This tendency is inspired by the ontological relevance of ethnomethodological description. The nexus between ethnomethods and life-world's orders implies an ontic dimension of the descriptive

4 The moment of empathy in this reflexive participation is not to be underestimated. Against the background of Mol's way of distinguishing between disease and illness, one is to state that the more the researcher involves her own epistemic practices in the scenario of ontic-ethnographic description, the more effectively she able to understand the ways of "living with disease," i.e. the particular illness as a psychosocial phenomenon (as opposed to disease as an object of biomedicine).

work. However, this dimension is by no means amenable to scrutinizing in the very process of ethnomethodological description. It rather remains hidden in this process.[5] For Garfinkel's followers, nothing in a social world can be taken for granted as a de-contextualized presence-at-hand. All entities get described as contextually accomplished entities. In other words, the description prevents one from hypostatizing objects. *Prima facie* there is no room for ontology (in the traditional, more or less metaphysical, sense) when one is entirely dealing with lived, immediate, unmediated, and congregational practices. There is no "ontological residue" that escapes the immediacy of ethnomethodological description. However, studying the ways in which actors produce orders and manage settings of their everyday activities amounts to investigating the modes of being in everyday life. This is why the description of actors' endogenous methods of creating life-worlds might lead to ontologies of everydayness.

Two modifications/extensions of this description are of crucial importance for the passage to empirical ontology (and as I will show later, to non-empirical ontology as well). First, one has to undertake a step beyond the level of "irremediable indexicality" on whose primacy the ethnomethodologists insist. Second, the capability of producing (normative) orders is to be ascribed not only to reflexive actors but to all "actants" (humans and nonhumans). Melvin Pollner's (1991) integration of "radical reflexivity" in ethnomethodology allows one to carry out both extensions. Following Garfinkel's tenet that social norms are not imposed factors that guide, determine, regulate or cause the social conduct in pre-defined scenes of action, Pollner suggests a detailed analysis of the reflexive accountability of action. He makes the case that the study of this accountability (brought into being by actors' endogenous reflexivity) depends on the researcher's radical reflexivity. It is this radical reflexivity that engenders critical self-questioning and appreciating the inventory (presuppositions, attitudes, concepts, devices, techniques, theoretical resources, and methods) of inquiry. Referentially reflexive appreciation of the ethnomethodological work is "radicalized when the appreciator is included within the scope of reflexivity, i.e., when the formulation of reflexivity—as well as every other feature of analysis—is appreciated as an endogenous achievement" (Pollner 1991, p. 372).

---

5 To be sure, in the tradition of ethnomethodology there are several interesting attempts at making the ontological dimension explicit. Let me only mention Eric Livingston's ontological approach to the mathematical work's life-world. However, such attempts have been always met with skepticism by those adherents to the tradition who admit that the engagement with ontology would transform enthomethodological description into interpretative theorizing, thereby restoring a sort of theoretical essentialism (Ginev 2013a).

As a corollary to Pollner's considerations, note that the more intensive the preoccupation with radical reflexivity, the more elaborate the ethnomethodological description would become. By problematizing her own inventory, the researcher more and more ceases to look at actors' normative orders and life-worlds as something empirically given, and begins to scrutinize them as particular actualizations of possibilities that remain in horizons of still not appropriated possibilities. This is why she reads the empirically actualized orders as open to further changes that might come into being by the appropriation of new possibilities. Instead of being apprehended as empirically given actualities, orders become regarded as "inscribed" on horizons of possibilities.

On another motif, radical reflexivity calls into question the immediate actuality given in ethnomethodological description since it casts doubts on the validity of the "intuitions and criteria" about empirical immediacy. In exercising this kind of reflexivity, one brings to naught any uncritically accepted entity or state as "actually given," and the attention is drawn to the ongoing constitution of all what allegedly exists as empirically given. The (hermeneutic) analysis of this constitution begins to complement the empirical description. As a consequence, one starts out to approach the actors' endogenous reflexivity with regard to its potentiality to constitute a meaningful reality. The potentiality for constitution is not externally (explanatory) added to what is actually present, but revealed as inherently operating in the interrelatedness of practices which is ontologically studied. Accordingly, the first step I indicated above is put into effect: Ethnomethodological description is extended in a manner that allows one to go beyond "irremediable indexicality" and to look for ontology of everydayness (constituted meaningfully through endogenous reflexivity). Intensifying the preoccupation with radical reflexivity is also a prerequisite for making the second step. The researcher begins to realize that the physicality of nonhumans involved in humans' action and interaction participates in the constitution of orders and life-words as well. The capability to effectuating norms is to be assigned not only to the actors but to all "actants" (in Latour's Greimasian sense).

The question I discussed in the foregoing considerations can be also formulated as follows: Are the contingent orders of multiple entities (and realities of enacting practices) characterized by an actual being in itself, or they are rather distinguished by a potentiality for being? To be sure, there are many good testimonies to the claim that the new studies of ontology dispense with the concept of "being's actual presence." Thus, the champions of empirical ontology are interested in unveiling worlds and realities in the making. Empirical studies of ontology are looking for how entities come to be in relational, fluid, and more or less indeterminate practical modes of being-in-the-world (or, "modes of existence"). Despite these testimonies, however, there are two (an epistemological and a hermeneutic) crucial arguments that (purely) empirical ontology cannot avoid a hypostatization of the actual being of what it deals with. On the epistemological argument, the empirical immediacy is inevitably shaped by non-empirical assumptions (or, "prejudices"). Thus, the empirical immediacy is always mediated by such assumptions. According to the hermeneutic argument, any empirically immediate state of affairs is the upshot of actualizing possibilities projected by interrelated practices upon horizons of practical existence. Thus, the "actually given" as empirical immediacy is ineluctably "produced" within the potentiality of existence.

It is my contention that the studies of empirical ontology do not have resources to deal properly with these two arguments. I am not going to elaborate on the critical consequences following from the arguments. Let me only tentatively underscore the following point: Regardless of how strong is the stress on processual ordering, the search for a radical "empiricization" of ontology rehabilitates the priority of actuality over potentiality as this priority is launched by "metaphysics of presence." It is impossible—so the epistemological argument goes—to have an empirical description without presupposing an epistemic-representational attitude, and accordingly, to restrict the research work to dealing with an actual presence. (Thus, though representational epistemology has been solemnly banished, the epistemic representation of what is actual comes through a backdoor in each program that struggles for an "empiricization without remainder." This is true even when epistemic representation gets achieved by means of "practical intervention."[6]) The abovementioned attitude inevitably places emphasis upon what gets actually represented regardless of whether the latter is a given (stable and static) state or processes of ordering. All kinds of empirical investigations are epistemologically doomed to be committed to thematizing actualities. This is why in a (purely) empirical-ontological study, there is no room for radical reflexivity that radically might call into question all empirical immediacy of what gets described.

This criticism puts the question as to whether it is possible at all to address the task of empirical ontology without committing to a version of (non-empirical) constitutional analysis of meaning (in the sense of the phenomenological tradition). No doubt, the empirical stance in doing ontology ought to be reflexively enlightened about its own non-empirical assumptions that "make possible the empirical immediacy of each particular ontological study. In a reflexive manner

6 Notoriously, Hacking's epistemology puts much emphasis upon the contradistinction between representing and intervening. In fact, however, being still committed to the primacy of the subject-object cut, this epistemology only makes intervening a privileged method of epistemic representation.

again, these assumptions have to be taken into consideration in constructing empirical ontology. Pollner's radical reflexivity is to be implemented to the non-empirical (epistemological) assumptions of empirical ontology as well. Yet in what follows, I will pay attention exclusively to the hermeneutic argument, leaving aside the meta-epistemological critique of the anti-epistemological position held by the students of empirical ontology.[7] In the perspective of this argument, radical reflexivity provides the access to scrutinizing those aspects of the constitution of meaning (as an ontological issue) which are not amenable to immediate empirical study. In enabling one to integrate interpretative approach to the situated constitution of meaning in the empirical description of a multiple reality—so my argument goes—radical reflexivity paves the way for having recourse to ontological difference in the studies of empirical ontology.

II Specifying the Idea of Ontological Difference with Regard to an Extended Version of Empirical Ontology

A tendency to an internal critique of radical empiricization is already operative in the tradition of the studies of empirical ontology. In an illuminating study, Noortje Marres (2013) introduces the interesting distinction between empirical and experimental ontology. On her account, empirical ontology deals with transformations of entities taking place in a domain where practical, technological, and scientific kinds of experience merge whereby the transformations might produce political effects. The circulation of power accompanying these transformations is at issue in empirical ontology. Nonetheless, this kind of ontology is still committed to the classical (humans-centered) concept of politics. By contrast, experimental ontology follows the tenets of actor-network theory, and ascribes moral and political capacities to nonhumans. This program goes beyond the empirical studies of ontology in equipping (in a more radical fashion) nonhumans and environments with normative features (Marres and Lezaun 2011). On experimental ontology, politics exists as a leeway of possible normative engagements. On another formulation, politics is projected upon a horizon of possible accomplishments that can come into being through the deployment of devices, objects and settings. Marres's program has an experimental character because it ex-

7 I am using the expression "meta-epistemological critique" in order to underline that this critique is inspired not by the search for an epistemological alternative to empirical ontology. The aim is rather to uncover (by implementing reflexive-epistemological tactics) the "bad epistemology" tacitly involved in those versions of empirical ontology which insist on "empiricization without remainder."

plores the possible interventions in the world (and their political consequences) in terms of "experiments with the world." The outcome of such experiments consists in getting the political profiles of various (actual and potential) configurations of practices. In this regard, experimental ontology means the ontology of a domain as a leeway of its possible states.[8]

Furthermore, the "ontologization of politics" in terms of experimental ontology characterizes politics itself in its potentiality, i. e. not in its empirical stability but in terms of ongoing actualization of possibilities. There is always an empirically untranslatable (or, a trans-empirical) moment inherent in this characterization. With regard to this moment, Marres insists on overcoming the distinction between constituted and constituting ontologies. The activation of possible accomplishments affects the ways in which nonhumans exert influence over existing orders and regimes of power, thereby playing (new) political roles. Accordingly, experimental ontology offers a distinctive way of how to make sense of nonhumans enacted in practices in terms of "political entities." The political contributions of nonhumans are to be located on the constituting side. The politics of nonhumans depends entirely on how projected possibilities will be appropriated (not by humans but by trans-human interrelatedness of practices) in the course of articulating a particular domain.[9] In this regard, Woolgar and Lezaun spell out the view that the ontic studies of the constitution of multiple realities necessitate (or enable) a "new form of political normativity." The way in which they suggest to "rethink politics through ontology" leads to a concept of political normativity predicated on the potentiality for being of the political.

---

8 In (post-metaphysical) political philosophy one introduces the distinction between politics (*la politique*) and the political (*le politique*). The latter refers to the post-ideological (beyond the traditional Left and the traditional Right) constitution of political topics within the multiplicity of social practices, while the former is reserved for the practices of conventional politics (Marchart 2007, p. 156). The political implications of Marres's experimental ontology are much closer to the political than to politics. More generally, the ontological tradition in STS tends to treat (with good arguments) the institutionalized political power as not ontologically primordial force. On several authors, this power gets constituted within the trans-subjectivity of being-involved-in-practices. Accordingly, politics is about relations between statuses and power, whereas the political refers to "ontological politics" (Woolgar and Lezaun 2013) as it is put into play by humans and nonhumans' accomplishments within orchestrated practices.

9 As I pointed out, Marres's position is by no means an exception. As a rule, empirical studies of ontology tacitly admit a difference between ontic description and ontological reflection. Mol is after the difference between the ethnographic description of the "multiple body" (and other multiple entities) and the constitution of multiplicity. She makes the case that if one begins to study the interferences between the enactments of multiple entities (such as atherosclerosis and sex difference), then the complexities start to grow exponentially (Mol 2002, p. 151). The growth of complexity is precisely the theme of the ontological reflection.

More specifically, they stress the diversity of possible trajectories of "ontological politics" engendered by enactments of multiple entities. By implication, the possible ways of "political constitution of humans and non-humans is in the very constitution of these entities in those terms (human and non-human)" (Woolgar and Lezaun 2013, p. 334).

The program of experimental ontology as exposed by Marres, however, seems to be underdeveloped in one respect. It does not take into account the endogenous reflexivity generated by orchestrated practices in which the nonhumans get enacted. In saying this, I take up the motifs of reflexivity as they were discussed in the preceding section. A possible reason for the deficiency being indicated lies in the assumption that by addressing endogenous reflexivity one would rehabilitate the human actors' privilege position. Yet this assumption ceases to be valid if one goes on not to restrict endogenous reflexivity to the human actors' reflexivity. Granted that it is engendered by a whole domain of interrelated practices, endogenous reflexivity hinges not only on the humans' self-interpretation. It proves to be essentially caused by the nonhumans' involvements and enactments as well. In other words, endogenous reflexivity refers to two different but intertwined things: the actors' cognitive capability of reflexive accountability (in the sense in which ethnomethodologists oppose the view of social actors as "judgmental dopes") and the reflexive properties brought into play by the interrelatedness of practices. An illustration of how these two dimensions of endogenous reflexivity complement each other is the change of the normative design of practices' interrelatedness accomplished at once "behind practitioners' backs" and through practitioners' self-interpretative control. Only by having recourse to endogenous reflexivity,—so the argument for supplementing Marres's experimental ontology goes—one is able to ascribe normative (moral and political) capacities to nonhumans. In attributing reflexivity to the whole being-involved-in-practices that constantly create adjustable and regulable order, one makes an important step in introducing ontological difference in the interpretative study of entities' enactments in practices.[10]

At this point, one should appeal again to Pollner's radical reflexivity. To reiterate, the more one intensifies this reflexivity, the more one reflects upon the domain of practices in its potentiality for being. As a consequence, one is no longer inclined to admit that the present situatedness of the entities undergoing multiplication is the only empirically possible state of affairs. In the perspective of radical reflexivity, the particular practices and entities are not only situated in

10 For the distinction between two kinds of endogenous reflexivity ascribed accordingly to actors and the accountability embedded in action, see Czyzewski 1994.

the actual (empirically given) configurations of practices but in horizons of possibilities as well. These horizons are not to be disentangled from the mode of being-involved-in-practices. Radical reflexivity shows that what gets situated (enacted and multiplied) in practices is constantly transcended by a horizon of possibilities. Only by ignoring this transcendence brought into being by the interplay of practices and possibilities, one can (uncritically) accept the empirical immediacy of what gets enacted as a multiple entity/reality. The horizon remains finite in each particular configuration of practices (there is a finite number of possibilities that can be appropriated in/by such a configuration), but with regard to the infinity of possible configurations of practices the horizon is inexhaustible. By implication, the multiple entities and realities addressed by the studies of empirical ontology are constantly in a state of situated transcendence. Approaching this state requires a (non-empirical) ontological reflection.[11]

I will call "double hermeneutics" the way in which one relates radical reflexivity to the search for unveiling endogenous reflexivity as embodied in the interrelatedness of practices one is exploring. In elaborating on this relation, one is guided by the intention to reveal the potentiality for being (and accordingly, the ongoing situated transcendence) of the multiple reality constituted by (and within) this interrelatedness. Thus considered, double hermeneutics is a methodological strategy for doing justice of ontological difference in the ontic study of multiple entities enacted in practices. Double hermeneutics consists of ontological reflection and ontic-interpretative description. The reflection upon situated transcendence which is entitled to reveal the constitution of multiple entities in their potentiality (i.e. as embedded in horizons of possibilities) is ontological reflection that ineluctably makes use of transcendental arguments. By contrast, ontic-interpretative (ethnographic or ethnomethodological) description of how these entities circulate in changing configurations of practices is an empirical inquiry. Methodologically, double hermeneutics refers to the ways in which ontological reflection (upon the situated constitution of meaning) fore-structures the delineation of the empirical interpretation's objects of inquiry by disclosing the

11 In the Heideggerian tradition of hermeneutic phenomenology, empirical ontology (i.e. studies of domains' ontic structures) is dichotomously opposed to 'transcendental ontology" (existential hermeneutics of the meaning of being). It is the methodology of double hermeneutics that manages to overcome this dichotomous opposition. Regardless of how significant the difference is, there is no cleavage between both types of ontology. Both types work rather in concert. The unfoldment of an interpretative description (and narrative) of multiple entities enacted in a multiple reality of concerted practices requires a cooperation between empirical studies of ontic orders in the making and ontological reflections about the integrity of a specific mode of being-in-the-world (Ginev 2011, pp. 37–51).

tendency to actualizing possibilities within the interrelatedness of practices under study (Ginev 2013b, Ginev 2014). At issue in the fore-structuring is the question of how these objects exist in a horizon of possibilities that might be appropriated. It goes without saying, however, that double hermeneutics is something more than a relation of fore-structuring between empirical and non-empirical methods.[12]

In making use of hermeneutic phenomenology's terms, one is to state that ontic-interpretative description refers to domain's "factuality" of concerted practices and multiple entities, while ontological reflection (as launched and guided by radical reflexivity) deals with domain's "facticity." (The distinction between "work-world" and "worldhood" as discussed earlier is in fact a special case of the distinction between factuality and facticity.) On this account, factuality consists in the totality of thematically given entities and "choreographies" (in the sense discussed previously). Factuality embraces, as it were, the whole of entities and practices composing domain's actual reality. Furthermore, factuality refers to both domain's normative orders and networks of causal relations. Domain's empirical ontology should make sense of these orders and networks by describing procedurally the enactments of entities in practices. By contrast, facticity is the ongoing constitution of meaning through appropriating possibilities projected by the interrelatedness of practices. Given the situated transcendence of what gets constituted meaningfully, the appropriation and actualization of possibilities takes place within the same interrelatedness. Coming to grips with facticity requires hermeneutic-ontological reflection upon the interpretative interplay of practices and possibilities.[13]

12 The methodology of double hermeneutics takes into account the dual status of interpretation that is at once a cognitive procedure and an "existential phenomenon." Interpretation as existential phenomenon is to be addressed by ontology of "practices and possibilities." Situated transcendence has a character of hermeneutic circularity. Stressing this character is the argument that there is a dimension of the interpretative that is irreducible to interpretation as a particular cognitive procedure. This is why in the tradition of hermeneutic phenomenology the interpretation which appropriates possibilities and "articulates the world" is treated as an "existentiale" (a principal characteristic of the meaning of being/existence).

13 The distinction between "factuality" and "facticity" is the most straightforward way of explicating the idea of the ontological difference. It allows one to come to grips with the difference between empirical ontology and (non-empirical) ontology of the constitution of meaning and the meaningful articulation of a domain of orchestrated practices. The latter is ontology of the potentiality for being (qua ongoing constitution) of such a domain. At issue in this ontology is the question of how the interrelatedness of practices projects possibilities that get appropriated and actualized within the same interrelatedness. There is here a hermeneutic circle (between projected horizon and particular meanings contextually constituted), and for that reason

To stress again, situated transcendence (of multiple entities and realities) is what in (purely) empirical ontology remains inaccessible. The relation of factuality to facticity brings to the fore the relativity of situated transcendence: Factuality is always situated in facticity, whereas facticity constantly transcends domain's actual reality. Yet both the way of situatedness (as actual state within a leeway of possible states) and the way of transcendence (as inexhaustible horizon of projected possibilities) are continuously changing as a result of continuous actualizations of possibilities that constitute meaning. By placing emphasis upon the hermeneutic fore-structuring of empirical ontology by reflection upon domain's potentiality for being, double hermeneutics makes the relativity of situated transcendence its principal theme. Thus considered, the hermeneutic fore-structuring relativizes ontological difference within the diverse scenarios of studying multiple entities and realities.

Integrating ontological difference in the studies of empirical ontology changes the thematic focus of investigation. More appropriate to the hermeneutically extended version of empirical ontology are not local realities like "hospital Z," but, for instance, a global redescription of a disease. A purely empirical (ethnographic) study maintains its character by describing clearly localizable (in space and time) practices. Yet if the interrelatedness in which entities get enacted and multiplied is dispersed in many (physically disconnected) places, and at each of these places the "choreographies" are distinguished by its own regime of temporality (of production and reproduction of entities and states), then obviously the temporal-spatial unity of the interrelatedness is not immediately (empirically) given. Nonetheless, the coordinated kinds of practices (taking place—to stick with the example—in a global redescription of a disease) presuppose a non-empirical temporal-spatial unity, i.e. (social) being that requires for its analysis a non-empirical ontological reflection.

A classical case in point is the redescription of diabetes mellitus by transforming it from metabolic into endocrinal disease. The metabolic character of the disease was determined (before the 1920s) by the observation that the excess of sugar in the blood could not be metabolized normally in cells. Led by this observation, clinicians and laboratory scientists devised technics of studying sugar's intermediary metabolism.[14] The disease was placed in practices of measurement and quantification of metabolic intermediary and end products. The apex of the disease's "metabolic period" was the invention (in 1922) of effective ther-

---

one might insist the "being of interpretation" (as "existentiale") reveals the "being of meaning constitution."

14 The ketonic bodies (as end-products in urine of diabetic subjects) were distinguished to be the main entity which contains the secret of diabetes's metabolic status.

apeutic insulin. At that time, due to the success of the specific treatment with insulin, one began to consider the deficiency of the endocrinal pancreas to be the cause of the disease, and accordingly, to redescribe diabetes mellitus in terms of endocrinal disease (Sinding 2004). Interestingly enough, the redescription of the disease coincided historically with the emancipation of endocrinology both as scientific domain and medical specialty. It was the reconstruction of the entire endocrine network that brought this emancipation into being. The redescription of diabetes mellitus took place in a new configuration of practices that included practices of combining laboratory science and clinical medicine (like practices of specifying the pancreatogenic causes of diabetes), practices of composing new diets and regimens that are germane to the disease's endocrinal character, practices of implementing large-scale health policies, trial practices in a local health-care system, etc. These kinds of practices were strongly disconnected in terms of space and time. Accordingly, diabetes as endocrinal pathology (violation of clinical norms established by endocrinology and biochemistry) was empirically engendered at various places and within various temporal regimes of producing and reproducing multiple entities. Behind the diversity of (social) origins of diabetes-as-endocrinal-disease, however, all practices of the disease's redescription were uniquely configured. It was not that the new configuration occupied a "site" already (somehow) indicated and delineated. Rather, the very configuring of practices of different kinds constituted its own temporal-spatial site. This constitution precisely is a specific topic of (non-empirical) ontological reflection.

After the redescription of the disease, the multiple entity of diabetes mellitus began to exist in the new site of its multiplication in the interrelatedness of various kinds of practices. Again, this is a site that cannot be physically localized. It unifies efforts in establishing diabetes's etiology, laboratory science's identifications of the disease, explanatory approaches in the theoretical terms of endocrinology and molecular biology, strategies of clinical treatment (like performing pancreas transplants, and rodent islet transplants, and beta cells replacement therapy), policies of patients' social treatment, and policies of prevention of diabetes. Several other entities (e.g. pancreatic beta cells, biosynthesis of insulin, and the glucose fatty acid cycle) got multiplied at this site as well. Being non-localizable in time and space, the site at which the redescription of diabetes mellitus took place is only characterized by horizons of temporality and spatiality, i.e. horizons of possibilities whose actualizations bring into being particular (empirical) localizations in time and space.

I call "chronotope" the unity of temporal and spatial horizons circumscribing a "site." The interrelatedness of practices creates its own chronotope that has to be approached by ontological reflection supposedly complementing empirical description. In other words, site and interrelatedness are "equi-primordial" in the constitution of the social. To reiterate, there are no pre-given sites that wait to be occupied by social practices. Though not exclusively restricted to, the ontological reflection should be predominantly oriented towards the non-localizability (in time and space) of the interrelated practices in which the disease becomes redescribed as a new multiple entity. It is a reflection that should in a hermeneutic-ontological manner describe the co-constitution of the site of a particular social reality and the orchestration of particular social practices.

To be sure, the ontological concept of "site of the social" has its origin in various versions of social theory. On Schatzki's practice theory as such a particular version, one admits that the interrelatedness constitutes a specific site of the social. The aim of "site ontology" of the social's "embedded situatedness" consists in preventing one from any kind of reifying the social (Schatzki 2002, pp. 149–155). The social is always identified with the ongoing constitution of a site where empirical localizability of social entities in practices becomes possible. Seen in the perspective of "site ontology," the studies of empirical ontology are highly inventive in describing sites of the formation of multiple realities. Yet they tend to overlook the (non-empirical) unity of spatiality and temporality characterizing such sites. Accordingly, they assume the sites' "immediate presence," thereby treating time and space also as present (empirically given) characteristics of the social that becomes manifested in a particular site. Yet if one admits that a site is the situated transcendence of orchestrated practices which brings into being the continuity of practices' production and reproduction of meaningful multiple entities, then one ought to dispense with the admission of site's actual presence-in-time-and-space. The empirical immediacy of temporal dynamics and the actual presence of spatial relations of practices are always in horizons of temporality and spatiality.

The unity of temporality and spatiality (which I called "chronotope") belongs to the ongoing constitution of a site. In contrast to measurable time and space (with a certain metrics) which are always empirically given, this unity exists in its potentiality. Chronotope is a horizon of constituting temporal-spatial meaning of the particular entities and practices within the interrelatedness of practices. (Yet the reversal of this claim is also valid: the orchestration of practices takes place within the chronotope the orchestrated practices engender. In the perspective of ontological difference, site is the way in which interrelated practices create spatiality in the sense that the interrelatedness "makes room" for multiple entities that it enacts. By the same token, the interrelatedness creates a regime of temporalizing this spatiality. The unity of "making room" and temporalizing spatiality is a horizon of possibilities that constantly get actualized in the multiple reality. By implication, the reflection upon site-as-chronotope fore-structures the empirical description of how the domain's particular entities and practices exist in time and space.

III Conclusion

Following a tendency in STS tradition of empirical ontology, I tried to adumbrate a move from radical reflexivity to double hermeneutics that integrates ontological difference in the empirical studies of multiple entities and realities. This move is in line, in my view, with the observation that the turn to ontology should not be seen as a way of grounding the empirical study of practices in a theory of what is ready-made (Woolgar and Lezaun 2013, p. 336). Doubtless, there is "idiosyncratic critical sensibility" involved in the reluctance to take the world at face value. It is this sensibility that has to be assisted by a methodology of double hermeneutics. Thus, while the turn to ontology ought to continue to be an essentially empirical enterprise, critical sensitivity should be extended to cover the non-empirical dimensions of ontological interpretation.

As indicated earlier, the studies of empirical ontology demonstrate a clear commitment to post-metaphysical initiatives and agendas. The further engagement of these studies with radical reflexivity, double hermeneutics, and ontological difference will enhance their dialogue with hermeneutic phenomenology and other traditions of interpretative theorizing in which this commitment is of prime importance.

References

Ashmore, M. (2005) Book review: "The life inside/the left-hand side." *Social Studies of Science* 35(5): 827–830.

Brives, C. (2013) "Identifying ontologies in a clinical trial." *Social Studies of Science* 43(3): 397–416.

Czyzewski, M. (1994) "Reflexivity of actors versus reflexivity of accounts." *Theory, Culture & Society* 11: 161–168.

Ginev, D. (2011) *The Tenets of Cognitive Existentialism*. Athens, OH: Ohio University Press.

Ginev, D. (2013a) "Ethnomethodololgical and hermeneutic-phenomenological perspectives on scientific practices." *Human Studies* 36: 277–305.

Ginev, D. (2013b) "Hermeneutic pre-normativity." *Philosophical Forum* 44(3): 275–294.

Ginev, D. (2014) "Social practices from the viewpoint of trans-subjective existentialism." *European Journal of Social Theory* 17: 77–94.

Heidegger, M. (1962) *Being and Time*, tr. J. Macquarrie and E. Robinson. San Francisco: Harper Collins.

Latour, B. (2013) *An Investigation into the Modes of Existence: An Anthropology of the Moderns*. Cambridge, MA: Harvard University Press.

Law, J. and Lien, M.E. (2012) "Slippery: Field notes in empirical ontology." *Social Studies of Science* 43(3): 363–378.

Marchart, O. (2007) *Post-Foundational Political Thought*. Edinburgh: Edinburgh University Press.

Marres, N. (2013) "Why political ontology must be experimentalized: On eco-show homes as devices of participation." *Social Studies of Science* 43(3): 417–443.

Marres, N. and Lezaun, J. (2011) "Materials and devices of the public: An introduction." *Economy and Society* 40(4): 489–509.

Mol, A. (2002) *The Body Multiple: Ontology in Medical Practice*. Durham, NC: Duke University Press.

Pollner, M. (1991) "Left of ethnomethodology: The rise and decline of radical reflexivity." *American Sociological Review* 56: 370–380.

Schatzki, T. (2002) *The Site of the Social: A Philosophical Account of the Constitution of Social Life and Change*. University Park: Pennsylvania State University Press.

Sinding, C. (2004) "The specificity of medical facts: The case of diabetology." *Studies in History and Philosophy of Biological and Biomedical Sciences* 35: 545–559.

Woolgar, S. and Lezaun, J. (2013) "The wrong bin bag: A turn to ontology in science and technology studies?" *Social Studies of Science* 43(3): 321–340.

Babette Babich

Hermeneutics and Its Discontents in Philosophy of Science: On Bruno Latour, the "Science Wars", Mockery, and Immortal Models

Abstract: Themes discussed include a hermeneutic of hermeneutic philosophy of science, along with the hegemony of analytic style in university philosophy in the US and Europe as well as the rhetoric of power, highlighting the politics of mockery using the example of Alan Sokal's hoax as this sought to exclude other voices in the academy, especially philosophy of science. In addition to reviewing Sokal's attack on Bruno Latour, Latour's own "biography" of an investigation is read as articulating a doubled hermeneutic reflection on modernity including both field ethnography and lab-ethnography. The further question of the viability of a hermeneutics of science in general, both natural and social is raised, thematising Patrick Heelan's "readable technologies" as metaphor for scientific research practice. Including a discussion of peer review and the editorial vicissitudes of journal publication, this chapter also addresses the politics of scientific models using the metaphor of immortality, zombie-style.

I Science Wars

The so-called science wars would seem to have been thoroughly fought and utterly decided on the side of the angels.[1] It seems, in today's era of post truth, we need science and reason more than ever. We might even be said to need a present-day Galileo to stand up to some of the attacks on science from so many sides. But hermeneutically considered, historically considered, as Paul Feyerabend reminds us in his essays on *Science for a Free Society*, things were not cut and dried when it came to the original Galileo, the "pushy patron saint of science." More than pushy, as Feyerabend liked to repeat in conversation with the author, Galileo was "a crook." Feyerabend's colorful and hyperbolic description is not far from the truth and, by any standard, Galileo was an opportunist: capable of giving his word (to Cardinal Bellarmine) and capable of breaking it. Speaking of the

1 Stengers 1977.

https://doi.org/10.1515/9783110551563-009

contest between rational discourse schemata or models,[2] or more methodologically, in *Against Method*, Feyerabend points out that Galileo offers "arguments in appearance only," making the case he makes for science via rhetoric or more bluntly still, via "propaganda." Thus Galileo did what all science does,[3] using "*psychological tricks* in addition to whatever reasons he has to offer."[4] Feyerabend's judgment contravenes a received prejudice concerning the objective manner in which we suppose that modern science came to be modern science.

To his credit as a historian of science, Feyerabend's account follows the historical record more closely than the image of Galileo as martyr[5] persecuted by the church. Bertolt Brecht's *Galileo* is, by contrast, a modern morality tale like Jean Anouilh's *Antigone* and in many other philosophical accounts, it can seem that Galileo is revered as a saint of truth in the face of the Harry Potteresque "dark" arts of the church.[6] Science is the hero, as we know but, just to the extent that today's church no longer has the power to play the role allotted to it, science (or its public voice) is compelled to cast about for a suitably dark alternative enemy and it has found it in the various names of relativism and constructivism and not less as in the case of Sokal's original 'fake news,' structuralism, deconstruction, and postmodernism, alt- and post-truth.

As arbiters and defenders of science, what is important is that we modern intellectuals declare ourselves opposed to the side being mocked or 'parodied' and thereby ally ourselves with the winning side, the side of the enlightenment. But as, at least one mainstream scholar, P.M.S. Hacker has observed, there

> are far too many philosophers who take their task to be to sing the *Hallelujah Chorus* to the sciences. It seems to me we should be serious, and one hopes helpful, conceptual critics of the sciences. (Hacker 2010)

---

2 Feyerabend 1985, here on models, p. 158. On the claim that Bellarmine was more respectful of alternate viewpoints, i.e., less dogmatic, than Galileo, see p. 166.

3 See among his other studies, Latour 1976 as well as Latour and Woolgar 1986 [1979], among, recently, not nearly as many others as there might be.

4 Feyerabend 1993 [1975]). Of course, it is not for nothing that John Horgan was moved to title, only somewhat tongue in cheek his "Profile: Paul Karl Feyerabend—The Worst Enemy of Science" (Horgan 1993). See further, Preston, Munévar and Lamb 2000.

5 On Galileo, Alan Chalmers is most comprehensive but there are others, such as more sustainedly, Finocchiaro 2010. And in the history of science, see Nicholas Jolley or indeed the general shift in the field over the last twenty years. And see too Heelan 1994.

6 I am making the points as Feyerabend has highlighted them both in his published work and in conversation with me, but the point is highly complex and involves rhetoric all the way down. See for a slightly different reading, drawing on Stengers, Pelchat 2003.

Hacker's recommendation, modest as it is, to be "serious, and ... helpful, conceptual critics of the sciences," is a minority voice among philosophers and public intellectuals of all disciplinary stripes. For, in the wake of the science wars, the science side counts as the winning side and it is in accord with this that Alan Sokal had originally articulated his so-called "hoax." Significantly, Sokal's hoax elicited no debate apart from uniformly scandalized response: for no one came out opposed to Sokal's position.[7] Indeed, the entire hoax took place on just one side, with Sokal himself playing both sides in a dispute he authorized (and this, among other things, is the reason it was not, despite his insistence that it was, a "parody"). No one took the side of postmodern science in the so-called science wars, and to this day, few scholars have undertaken to defend hermeneutics,[8] not even Bruno Latour.

Thus when Sokal, a physicist, in an interview in *Le Nouvel Observateur*, raises the question in the light of media attention that was the aftermath of his hoax, "Are our philosophers imposters?",[9] it is important to emphasize that Sokal takes the term "philosopher" very broadly, including as he does whole other disciplinary fields, including Donna Haraway's biology (and her feminist history of consciousness) and Stanley Aronowitz's sociology together with Luce Irigaray's linguistics and psychology (count in Lacan as well), all along with the same Derrida

---

7 Typically, discussions of Sokal's hoax attack the humanities and the supposed failure of peer review. And the discipline of science studies, especially in history and sociology, which had had some critical elements quickly jettisoned those components in the wake of the media success of the hoax. Without exception, discussion of Sokal's work lionized his achievements. See most recently Corneliussen 2017 and Ruark 2017.

8 My own essay on Sokal was an exception and it remains one of the only critical responses to Sokal. Indeed, it is rarely, if ever, cited and from the start it was astoundingly difficult get into print: I sent it everywhere, even writing to Tracy Strong, who had originally emailed me about Sokal's hoax (at the time he was editor of *Political Theory*), to ask that he consider it. No luck. Finally, a bowdlerized version (courtesy of Paul Piccone's *Telos*) was published under a title that was not mine: "Physics vs. *Social Text:* The Anatomy of a Hoax" (Babich 1996). A year later it was published in *Common Knowledge*, thanks to the graciousness of an editor, Jeffrey Perl (who organized a special section around my essay, including an essay by Feyerabend and another by Barry Allen), with its original title: "The Hermeneutics of a Hoax" (Babich 1997). If articles are turned down all the time, for all kinds of reasons, this article happened to have been presented at a conference on *Hermeneutics and the History of Science*, at Stony Brook in June of 1996, which yielded not one but *two* sets of conference *proceedings*, the point of which "proceedings" being to ensure the dissemination of the papers presented: firstly in an issue of *Man and World*, edited by Robert Scharff, who excluded my contribution, which was also then excluded from the volume edited by Robert Crease. The political aspect of editorial gatekeeping is taken up in the context of coastal engineering in the fifth section below.

9 [*Nos philosophes sont-ils des imposteurs* ?] Sokal 1997b.

analytic philosophers were then anxious to denounce (not a lot has changed). Thus even after his fake news text and its decoder-ring bookend (*didn't mean it, how could you not know?*), Sokal mocked "The Philosophical Mystifications of Professor Latour."[10] But would *Social Text* (or *Le Monde*) have published the latter without the 'hoax' orchestrated between two publications, with the blessing of two sets of editors, one set supposed to have been hoodwinked, *Social Text*, the other, unveiled as the editorial locus of truth, *Lingua Franca*, (at the time, the academic equivalent of *Fox News*)? The achievement was a staged or "post-truth" event.

It is the mockery that matters now, because it is this that Sokal was permitted to publish about Latour, a fair amount of it elliptical, including this damning paragraph:

> I will not detail for the readers of *Le Monde*, explicating the "scientific formation" manifested by Latour in his essay on the Einsteinian theory of relativity, that which was presented as a "contribution to the sociology of the delegation" (*Social Studies of Science* 18, pages 3–44, 1988). These details appear in the book Jean Bricmont and myself are currently in the process of writing on *The scientific impostures of (post) modern philosophers*. Suffice it to say that certain colleagues suspect that Latour's article was, just as mine was, a parody. (Sokal 1997a)

Sokal continues to play the science card, natural scientist contra social scientist, distinguishing *inexact* from *exact* sciences, a rank-ordering move, i.e., my science is more scientific than yours:

> Latour accordingly pretends to address the sociology of science but his expose is confused: he mixes up ontology and epistemology and attacks claims that no one holds. "In place of recognizing a science holding absolute exactitude in its knowledge, one recognizes in its place the quality of the collective experience it demonstrates"—yet who today claims that science furnishes 'absolute exactitudes.' (Sokal 1997a)

---

10 Sokal 1997a. This did not go away quietly, to be sure. See Joerg Lau (2002), The argument here in 2002 against "political ecology" and against indeed the ecology of things, of non-human objects, has in the interim gone over in the field of political theory and philosophy not to mention media ecology to Latour's side, at least and arguably more rather than not. Lau's essay was written as a review of the German translation of Latour's *Politiques de la nature. Comment faire entrer les sciences en démocratie* (Latour 1999) (already cited in English and cf., too, Latour, *Das Parlament der Dinge* (Latour 2001) but see Latour 1991a, where he speaks of the idea of a 'democracy extended to things', a project since executed with some panache. See also for one approach to this question, Schmidgen 2014, pp. 108 ff.

At issue is expert power and public voice: at issue, who should be permitted to speak and who should be silenced.

Thus Sokal's ambition, which was largely if obviously in the case of Latour not completely successful (which does not mean that it was without effect for Latour himself), was to silence these and related voices, using the tactic of discrediting, after which the idea was to have these names and all their writings fall from mention: as if they had never been on the horizon of scientiifc exchange. To this day, *non-mention* is the way scientific authority continues to work: it determines who gets funding and is the engine of nothing less than the vetting and thus the literal "genesis and development" of today's scientific facts.[11]

Where philosophy traditionally serves as handmaiden or servant—the old word is "ancilla"—to theology, *sine qua non* as it is for theological reflection, the new modus of philosophy has ambitions to serve science, telling science what it can and cannot do. There are troubles with this ambition and the physicists have been reluctant to welcome the philosophers as either methodological instructors or logic coaches. Thus Stephen Hawking declared, some years ago attracting media attention—and never himself bothering to retract the claim—"Philosophy is dead." (Warman 2011)

II Les "Pseudos": Science vs. Pseudoscience

Given the economic constraints of the current day in the academy, the growing trend in almost all disciplines is that of suppression by threat: say what everyone else says or (and this is a real threat) you won't be hired, you won't be tenured, you won't be published, or if you are, you won't be read. To this extent, the ongoing non-citation of outlier views is deliberate and yields nothing less than what Thomas Kuhn called "normal science." Thus Latour offered his own recent reflections on the "disciplining" of anthropology,[12] departing from just that very hermeneutic philosophic sociology of ethnographic science of both field ethnography and lab ethnography as Latour practiced both of these kinds, relating the history, the bio-graphy of this practice. It is important to underline that this aca-

11 I have elsewhere written about what is done when academic authors dismiss the work of a university scientist by belittling him as a "pseudoscientist." See Babich 2015. The tactic is rhetorical one: a matter of disciplining, and it makes and breaks careers and, indeed (*both* during a lifetime *and* posthumously), reputations.

12 Latour 2013.

demic story of a lifetime,[13] that is, just as Latour underscores, not a matter of *autobiography*, was offered as it was across several books, and several platforms, including workshop collectives and the internet as well as online publications and books, thus entailing that Latour's own reflections are to be ranged under what Anthony Giddens and, in this current volume, both Dimitri Ginev and Simon Glynn call a *double hermeneutics.*[14] Latour thematizes just this double hermeneutic: the ethnographer is barred from observing the practice of the "whites," reflexively redoubling the ethnographer's own doubled hermeneutics. Here, broadly speaking, we might say that the "whites" refer to the natural sciences entailing that anthropology and other social sciences are excluded from the greater philosophic conversation on science. Indeed, it is only recently, after severe criticisms in part related to anxiety about constructivism and in part related to the Sokal hoax, and consequent retrenchments that for decades limited the purview of Science Technology Studies, seemingly gutting the so-called Strong Program in the process, that some ginger efforts have been made to return to Latour's lab ethnography.[15]

Taking his own point of departure from a reflection on Etienne Souriau's "different" scientific "*modes d'existence*,"[16] Latour invited 'open'[17] exchange on the movement in philosophy known as the "speculative turn."[18] The Souriau

---

13 Reflectively different in kind, for example, from either Martin Gardner's (2013) confidently pseudo-bashing autobiography or Paul Rabinow's (2011) Foucault-themed reflections or Geertz's (1996) own auto-reflections.

14 See Ginev 1998 as well as for contextualization with reference to Luhmann, Leydesdorff (2006) and Lynch 1993. Note that Mike Gane offers an illustration of Comte's double hermeneutics, which Gane analyses as a "two-fold hermeneutic" in the context of a discussion of Latour and Comte. Gane 2006, pp. 95–97. And see too, on Latour, with respect to Alfred Schutz, Bischur (2013). And see too more generally, the contributions to Maranhão and Streck (2003).

15 See Sormani (2016).

16 Souriau 2009.

17 Of course it was not really 'open.' See note below.

18 The speculative turn also goes by the name of OOO (and there are other names). It is true to say that Latour engaged this movement quite in his own fashion (this has ever been his wont) going beyond what some analytic (and some self-describedly so) "continental" scholars might call "experimental philosophy" towards what mattered for Latour and his studies of laboratory science including his turn to political ontology and thus to things environmentally, empirically encountered as we find them as they act. As Latour explained (and although he meant this literally it would turn out to have disputed significance for those scholars who took his internet-disseminated call seriously): "I invite my co-investigators to help me find the guiding thread of the experience by becoming attentive to several regimes of truth, which I call modes of existence, after the strange book by Etienne Souriau, recently republished, that features this phrase in its title" Latour 2012, here p. 1.

text to which Latour, along with his co-editor Isabelle Stengers, referred was initially published in 1943,[19] permitting in this context Latour to explain his approach to anthropology of science not as ethnography and not as social studies of science and technology but as philosophy of science as such. I note that some saw this invitation as a venture to bring disparate voices to dialogue in the philosophical academy.[20] But what was at stake was more than a matter of diversification but all about the exclusion that was already and from the start an exclusion of Latour's own voice.

Thus one might read Latour's *We Have Never Been Modern*[21] as a contribution to what might be counted as a national or "territorial" geography of science, not just European and non-European, not just French and southern Californian (San Diegan), but into the interstices of the academy of analyses tolerated and analyses barred. Inevitably this is a matter of translation and cultural formation. Thus what Latour offers is one of the first of its kind since Pierre Duhem's almost unread *German Science*[22] or Paul Forman's (1971) argument that a conceptual culture of philosophy would be indispensable (and for all kinds of reasons ultimately to be lacking) for understanding, in the title of one his articles on his thesis, "Weimar Culture, Causality, and Quantum Theory." Forman's thesis was both completely received (or successful) *and* misunderstood, a matter of inevitable dispute to this day inasmuch as the 'culture' of philosophy Forman was pointing to was nothing less than continental philosophy, the kind of philosophy foregrounding hermeneutics and phenomenology etc., the very philosophy advanced by the philosopher and physicist, Patrick Aidan Heelan (1965, 1994, 2016, etc.) It matters to observe that the contributors to Carson et al. (2011) although celebrating Forman as they were, did not, rather of necessity, have a formation in this particular culture of philosophy (and which might have aided them in unpacking Forman's arguments) owing to the dominion of analytic approaches in professional Anglophone philosophy over the last several decades—a rise to power that began, according to Reiner Schürmann (1985, 1994) already

19 Souriau 2009.

20 This it was not to do and when the project had run its course the players were the same names in the Latour camp (and in the camp of speculative philosophy) that had been involved at the start. No others. To be sure, here and there there were little virtual fisticuffs on Twitter, but little to write home about and nothing Latour would have noticed in any case. I discuss this more socio-political dimension in a longer version of this essay (Babich 2017), and see in particular (in French), Babich 2018.

21 Latour 1991b. It matters that Latour writes an afterword to the French translation of Fleck 2008.

22 Duhem 1991 [1916].

in the US as early as the 1960s, and which was certainly well established as an almost hegemony as the current author can attest by the 1970s. Several things obscure this claim, not the least of which is the habit of analytically formed scholars to regard themselves (and insist on being named by others) as continental if the themes (or names) they study are continental.[23] But there are additional difficulties to reading the Forman thesis because historical discussions of the rise of analytic hegemony in university philosophy are politically clouded (Weimar culture is perhaps all the cloud one needs but McCumber and others add McCarthyism in the US).[24] Here what is essential is the conceptual criticism Hacker had emphasized as quoted above and Forman's thesis remains salient just where what is at stake is both high philosophy and high physics. Nevertheless,[25] students of history and philosophy of science do not as a rule learn the actual history of contemporary academic philosophy but only what analytic philosophers call the history of philosophy, not even when what is at stake concerns, as Forman's thesis concerned the time span 1918–1927, an interval including the publication of Heidegger's *Being and Time*.

For his own part, Latour's concern is not Forman's and neither hermeneutics nor phenomenology are thematic for Latour, although he draws on the resources of both approaches. Significant, with respect to ethnography and double hermeneutics, is Latour's reflection on reflection: we investigators, philosophers, thinkers, researchers, ethnographers, we "whites," perpetually manage to fail to put ourselves *as investigators* in question.

To "the classical question of philosophy 'what is the being of technology, science, religion?'" is added the question favored by so-called object-oriented ontology, which Latour rearticulates, thereby "pluralizing" the question: "what are the beings appropriate to technology, science, religion, and how have the Moderns tried to approach them?"[26] And of course favoring the focus on things, this could be similarly varied. In his own reflection, Latour invokes his teacher at Dijon, André Malet, to reflect that the "science" of reading, including classical and theological philology presupposes a specific anthropology of reception. As is by now familiar, we note the absence of the word hermeneutics when speaking of hermeneutics:

---

23 Thus Gary Gutting gets to count as continental having written on Foucault which would make Ian Hacking continental too, and why not, as I understand: he lives in France? It also makes the late analytic Heideggerian Bert Dreyfus 'continental' and of course Brian Leiter is continental as well.

24 See McCumber 1996 and see further Glendinning 2006 and Cutrofello 2004.

25 See Shapin 1992 and Kusch 2005.

26 Latour 2012, here p. 2.

> the Biblical text finally became comprehensible, revealed as a lengthy process of transformations, inventions, glosses, and diverse rationalizations which, taken together, sketched out a layer of interpretations that played out—this is the essential point—each in its own way the question of fidelity or treason: faithful or falsified invention, impious reworking or astounding rediscovery?[27]

If Clifford Geertz almost patented the practice of talking hermeneutics without saying the word—lock, stock, and cockfight barrel[28]—Latour is also telling his readers and himself, his own biography (*bien entendu*, under negation: "Not to tell my life story—if a system is solid, one need not be overly concerned with its author—but rather to sketch the biography").[29] The apology here is my own but in his own voice Latour tells us that he knows of "no other author who has so stubbornly pursued the same research project for twenty-five years, day after day, while filling up the same files in response to the same sets of questions," also informing us of the challenges he faced, together with "a wife and child," in order to make the discovery in "the Abidjan of 1973–75 ... all at once the most predatory forms of capitalism, the methods of ethnography, and the puzzles of anthropology."[30] The effects of this insight are articulated further in his more recent book[31] to the height of persuasion, revealing the obstacles encountered along the way as sources of both affirmation and desolation.

For Latour,

> one puzzling question in particular that has never left me: why do we use the ideas of modernity, the modernizing frontier, the contrast between modern and premodern, before we even apply to those who call themselves civilizers the same methods of investigation that we apply to the "others"—those whom we claim, if not to civilize entirely, then at least to modernize a little?[32]

I am not able to develop this point as I seek to address it elsewhere but it applies to the distinction to be drawn between science and pseudoscience as well as to the status to be claimed in order to be named a philosopher of science like Ludwik Fleck (not to mention Heidegger or Nietzsche). Thus Latour can continue to reflect on what he names a "flagrant asymmetry," which we may also regard as

---

27 Latour 2012, p. 3.

28 But see for a discussion, largely via Ricoeur, of Geertz on space and place, Aucoin 2017. And for further discussion of anthropology and hermeneutics, see Kämpf 2013 and see too in the same collection, Dallmayr 2013.

29 Latour 2012, p. 4.

30 Latour 2012, p. 4..

31 Latour 2013.

32 Latour 2012, p. 4.

the default of hermeneutics, simple and above all doubled or reflexive, observing as the key question perhaps of social science as a science that

> ... the Whites anthropologized the Blacks, yes, quite well, but they avoided anthropologizing themselves. Or else they did so in a falsely distant, "exotic" fashion, by focusing on the most archaic aspects of their own society—communal festivals, belief in astrology, first communion meals—and not on what I was seeing with my own eyes (eyes educated, it is true, by a collective reading of *L'Anti-Oedipe*): industrial technologies, economization, "development," scientific reasoning, and so on: in other words, everything that makes up the structural heart of the expanding empires.[33]

Latour's path in search of symmetry (and asymmetry) may be illuminated by the cover of Latour and Woolgar's *Laboratory Life* (1986 [1979]), not the words themselves of that fatal subtitle *The Construction of Scientific Facts* (I write about this elsewhere)[34] but a legend on a book cover: "Introduction by Jonas Salk." To this extent, Latour's transgression—it was not a "violation," of scientific objectivity as much as it was a documention of the process—took him to his on-going success (or influence) in the guise of his own study of neuropeptides qua actors qua actants, and that "violation" was his attention to the scientists themselves in the laboratory itself.

Latour's own success (if this is what matters) crystalized when his attention shifted to the things themselves, the objects as such, the "nonhuman characters." Thereby, and just this is an achievement for objectivity, one excluded the human from the human sciences, excluding the agency of human agents along with human social practice. For Latour:

> I suddenly understood that the non-human characters had their own adventures that we could track, so long as we abandoned the illusion that they were ontologically different from the human characters. The only thing that counted was their agency, their power to act and the diverse figurations they were given.[35]

This question of investigation and influence returns, as every reader of Latour's reflections will go on to discover for themselves and to rediscover, if they care to do this, for the rest of their lives. Here it is enough to presage the point in terms

---

33 Latour 2012, p. 5.

34 Note the scare word "construction" as this would perturb both Ian Hacking and not less Bruno Latour himself as critics (not only the likes of Alan Sokal) turned the term against them by using it to characterize their own work—this sensitivity engendered no fewer than two books one by Hacking and another, earlier at the same press by Latour.

35 Latour 2012, pp. 6–7.

of Latour's own rueful musing on what response he might have had had one ever indeed thought to ask him about his own "philosophy" (Latour brackets this reflection, writing parenthetically):

> (Not to worry: no one has ever asked me that question, since the tumultuous quarrels over relativism and the science wars have in the meantime turned me into a mere sociologist, adherent of a "social construction" according to which "everything is equal," objective science and magic, superstition and flying saucers ...).[36]

Rules and the roles of demarcation remain and in Latour's little list of relativized damnations, Feyerabend's famous damnation, astrology, no longer rates a mention. And to this day in the academy one cannot or, better: may not—not if one wishes to have one's projects find funding, not if one wishes a university appointment—say anything but what the received view allows.

At stake are issues that should concern us whatever our formation in our deepest prejudices as academics, members of the university profession and that is *the life of the mind*, to use Hannah Arendt's formulation for what Arendt conveyed as politically as she did. Thus, to note a sociolinguistic hermeneutic assumption, we remain convinced that if only our discourse were clear enough, if only our style were rightly framed, with just the right words, the right punctuation, we might, have success in our grasp. This conviction preserves the power of those in power. We thereby pretend style has no play (we suppose anything can be said 'clearly') and influential scholars declare there is no distinction between analytic and continental philosophy (this is what has been learned by most younger scholars *and* it has truth inasmuch as the only philosophical kind left standing is analytic), and that the only thing that decides a grant application, publication success, a university post is *quality*, a conviction enthusiastically repeated by those with grants, regular publications, job security, etc.

In a 'post-truth' era, in these days of so-called 'fake news,' it is sobering to note one consequential reflection on the fallout from Sokal's hoax, quite apart from the violence and fading relevance of his attacks on Bruno Latour and others. Because, as we may be learning, the method of using mockery or what Sokal calls parody to attack a scholarly colleague whose claims one does not like, like witch-hunting in the past, can cover any number of sins without needing to make a logical case at all. As the historian Ellen Schrecker observes: "Today is the culmination of 40 years of attacks on academic expertise. It's fine if you

---

36 Latour 2012, p. 13. In a recent reading from the side of the humanities of Serres and Latour, the word hermeneutics appears once as a reference to Ricoeur. See Connor 2016.

want to make fun of deconstruction, but it's not fine if you make fun of climate change."[37]

Faults one may wish to lay to the account of so-called 'deconstructionists' and 'postmodernists' can come to haunt more respectable scientists in an era of generic denial of expertise, extending as Schrecker emphasizes, to the science authority we wish to claim on climate change and so on. Thus science itself polices its more speculative voices, especially on controversial topics including vaccines and homeopathy (we already have the truth)[38] or the industry assertion that cell phone radiation is just fine (does everyone not have a cell phone? Is not WiFI or WLAN omnipresent?), or the political assurances that fracking is perfectly good for the environment, dams grand for the Amazon, and GMOs likewise fine and so on and so on.

Indeed, it can be hard not to wonder if the language of 'post-truth' itself is not a bullying tactic, just as Sokal's hoax was a bullying tactic, deployed in his case from the side of hard science, against the softer, social kind, and in our era of political concern, deployed by a regime nostalgic for a single media voice and anxious to silence different voices.

III Beyond the 'Good' and the 'Bad'

Recall Nietzsche's (in context stridently misogynist, as Nietzsche's theme here is feminine fashion allure) reflection in *Beyond Good and Evil:*

> It is "the slave" in the vain man's blood, a remnant of the craftiness of the slave ... which seeks to *seduce* him to good opinions about himself; it is likewise the slave who immediately afterwards falls down before these opinions as if he himself had not called them forth. (BGE 261)

If such seductive persuasions correspond to slavish atavism as Nietzsche says, what else drives our responses to books, to looks, to Facebook and Twitter but also to our colleagues and our university research interests? Where in the face of all these "prejudices" as Nietzsche speaks of them, as he argues that such prejudices characterize not only philosophy but also science and even logic and mathematics, where shall we find the old enlightenment ideals of objectivity, science, truth? Or is this just part of the problem?

37 Cited in Ruark 2017 and Corneliusson 2017, among others.
38 See further Babich 2015.

Overall, the philosophical question of good and bad includes the challenge of knowing which is which. Familiar to us since Plato, how can we tell friends from enemies? Thus we may recall the popular cultural case of Alan Rickman's Severus Snape as he played the character of this originally reviled, qua overly severe, teacher[39] ultimately shown however to have been a hero (by which is meant that he was on Harry Potter's side in the Harry Potter series): supposed enemies can turn out to be *really* good despite appearing to have been *really* bad. Yet what if those we think bad are not villains but "interesting people" (as Rickman himself once put it)? Why is goodness assumed to be recognizable and why is it assumed that what is good would be something that would favor us (or Harry Potter)? Are we sure we would know the good if we encountered it, or that our taste would suffice as a test? For Nietzsche, there is a circle here and he elsewhere writes, in some seriousness I believe, that it is a great pity that nature does not single out excellent human beings with a kind of glow or beam of light such that one might know them with certainty rather than guess and deduce and be misled and disappointed as Nietzsche himself was and to his pain.

What are we to do about bad science or about scholars we regard as lacking? The academy is an institution formed to make such judgments: we do not want poor or bad scholars and we assume that a person who holds an appointment has a certain level of achieved excellence although this did not halt Sokal in his efforts to attack Latour, Derrida, et al and it does not stop us when we reject proposals for inadequacy. I am speaking of the assessments made by peers, who have—as this is the point of being a peer—a very personal stake in the same game.

In part, but only in part, this complex inter-involvement is one of the reasons, writing in the *Journal of the Royal Society of Medicines*, Richard Smith offers when he assesses peer review as a "flawed process."[40] Smith is not the only one to make this kind of observation, minimally as he makes it. But, as one congressman observes in a congressional review of the NSF in testimony given forty years earlier than Smith's essay, peer review is patently

> an incestuous buddy system that frequently stifles new ideas and scientific breakthroughs, while carving up the multi-million dollar federal research and education pie in a monopoly game of grantsmanship.[41]

---

39 See for a discussion of Snape as teacher, Babich 2016b.

40 Smith 2006.

41 Arizona Congressman John Conlan to a July 1975 hearing on the NSF peer review system. Cited in Cole, Rubin, and Cole, (1978), p. 11.

In the case of science (this was the heart of the Sokal hoax), peer review can cover over fraud, bogus results, plagiarism, or, in the case of Sokal himself who passed peer review, after all, fakery. And in the case of both scientific and humanities scholarship what is at stake are assessments of quality.

IV Philosophical Canons, Reading Texts, Reading Technologies

In the case of both the natural and the social sciences, there can be no greater pitfall than the conviction that hermeneutics is limited to texts and text practices. Much rather the "text" in each case when it comes to hermeneutics concerns the matter, i. e., the 'things,' as Heidegger transformed Husserl's phenomenology, themselves. In science, such 'things' correspond in each case to a disciplinary transform. But when György Márkus wrote a *petitio principii* into his title, which he doubtless did for rhetorical effect: "Why Is There No Hermeneutics of Natural Sciences,"[42] Markus himself never read the positions his title wrote out of existence from the start quite in spite of his thematic focus on *reading*.

Begging the question, Markus automatically, this is the way presumption works, overlooked Patrick Heelan's arguments (in book and article form) for a hermeneutic philosophy of physics, specifically advanced with reference to quantum mechanics. Nor did Markus read Joseph J. Kockelmans nor Ted Kisiel, just to name some Anglophone names (of course there are German and other names, and, of course, there are Hungarian and Bulgarian and Italian other names) of the leading proponents of the very same possibility of the hermeneutics of natural science Markus sought to rule out of court, a tactic not dissimilar to Sokal's practice. Heelan, however read Markus with characteristic generosity and responded to his points in scholarly if gently didactic fashion: "There is a Hermeneutic Philosophy of Natural Science."[43] And that might have been the beginning of a discussion but it was not and Markus knew no more of Heelan's argument after Heelan replied to him than he had known to begin with.

---

42 Markus 1987.

43 Heelan 1989. See also, addressing Markus, Ginev 2006, pp. 63–65. Regrettably although Paul Rabinow 2011 foregrounds Markus and his "haunting' challenge, Rabinow claims, writing a decade and a half after Markus' original publication that no one had responded to Markus' challenge: Rabinow 2011, p. 178. To make this claim Rabinow had to overlook Heelan's reply in the very journal where Marcus's essay had first appeared. To aid Markus himself, Heelan's essay was also translated into Hungarian in 2001.

Circularity—circular arguments included—has closure as a virtue and it seems that one can one win academic one upmanship by the expedient of ignoring a critic or a respondent rather than by taking the time to reply to them and to engage in a conversation that may show you not only the limits of their case but and always potentially your own.

To mistakenly limit hermeneutics to a textual practice (as Markus does), i. e., to the "interpretive encounter of a reader with a text"[44] misses the metaphor of the text as experimental setup or instrumental context articulated in and through Heelan's language of 'readable technologies.' As Heelan argues, the scientific experimentalist[45] is not "reading" his instruments as one reads a text but rather as one might "read"—metaphorically speaking—a painting, a landscape, a face, a gesture, or, or selecting points of significance in a data set, or, in the case of the social sciences, a community practice. To be sure, Heelan's insight may be connected, as he himself connects it, not only with Heidegger but also with Michael Polanyi and Norwood Russell Hanson as much as with Ludwik Fleck, who engaged both sociology *and* ethnography in his own classic discussion of the genesis of a scientific fact.

V. Models: Data-Vicissitudes and Textbook Timelessness

The above hermeneutic points may be illuminated with a final example on real politics in the science of climate change in connection with environmental science and the 'politics' of scientific modelling. In his book, *Useless Arithmetic: Why Environmental Scientists Can't Predict the Future*, co-authored with his daughter, Linda Pilkey-Jarvis, the coastal scientist, Orrin H. Pilkey discusses the politics of journal practices, including peer review practices, as these directly shape a science as such, defining knowledge regimes in the process. Thus the Pilkeys relate some of the challenges involved in the unresolved (and unresolvable), problem of shoreline erosion, locus of today's highly politicized debate regarding climate change, reflecting "the negative global impact of the greenhouse effect."[46] The pattern the Pilkeys trace has less to do with shoreline erosion (although their theme is shoreline erosion) than the difficulty of addressing *not* a science-illiterate public but research publication with respect to journal (and

---

44 Nordmann 2008.

45 Of special value here is Rheinberger 1997.

46 Pilkey/Pilkey-Jarvis 2007, p. 92.

by extension: textbook) editors concerning nothing so crucial as a model and the very theoretical idea of modeling as such.

Pilkey explains that

> Criticism of quantitative beach modeling is either avoided or suppressed by applied beach modelers. Instead of debating the issue in order to recognize the limitation of models, consultants and the Corps of Engineers erect a stone wall between the modelers and their critics.[47]

To be sure, Pilkey assumes that debate on models flourishes in the (ideal) research sciences even as he knows it to be suppressed in (in fact) his own field:

> Research scientists thrive in an environment of criticism and analysis, but in the technical coastal modeling literature, criticisms are nearly non-existent and the models remain unchallenged. To criticize is an almost ungentlemanly thing to do.[48]

For Pilkey, the modelers (and in this case, the engineers) knowingly apply a bad model, justifying the practice by saying that "it is all that they have at this time."[49] The problem for Pilkey concerns the limitations of the model which is presented as if it might someday be improved. Instead, Pilkey emphasizes that when it comes to coastal models: "nothing better is coming along. They can never be quantitatively modeled with sufficient accuracy for engineering purposes."[50] The result is a proliferation of zombie, i.e., 'immortal' models.

At issue is not merely complexity (beaches cannot be quantitatively modeled) but empirical practice, the standard account of comparing predictions with results, Pilkey writes:

> Long term monitoring is almost non-existent, and meaningful objective comparisons of model predictions and the results is virtually non-existent.[51]

The problem of zombie models in science is complex and the Pilkey's epigraph from *The Sea of Cortez* by John Steinbeck and Ed Rickets is on point:

---

47 Pilkey/Pilkey-Jarvis 2007, p. 136.
48 Ibid.
49 Ibid.
50 Pilkey /Pilkey-Jarvis 2007, p. 137.
51 Pilkey/Pilkey-Jarvis 2007, p. 137. The "refrain" in question, as Orrin refers to it, was uttered by Robert Dean and James Houston, then Head of the U.S. Army Corps of Engineering Coastal Engineering Research Center in a review responding to Pilkey/Dixon 1996.

> There is one great difficulty with a good hypothesis. When it is completed and rounded, the corners smoothed, the content cohesive and coherent; it is likely to become a thing in itself, a work of art ... One hates to disturb it. Even if subsequent information should shoot a hole in it, one hates to tear it down because it was once beautiful and whole.[52]

Such a "perfect" hypothesis is the Brunn Rule, "the single most widely used mathematical model to predict the outcome of a natural process on the surface of the earth. Its heuristic appeal and simplicity are apparently irresistible."[53] Arguing that the having of the model means that the coastal engineer goes on proposing engineering solutions—year after year—in the face of failure and despite negative feedback—the authors call for an alternative to this routine dependence on "bad models" emphasizing that only such bad models are available. That is why they are immortal.

This can be hard to understand for both the public and the bureaucrats who use such engineer's models oblivious to the "limitations of modelled predictions."[54] And yet, on Pilkey's account, to raise questions contra a standard model is sufficient reason for editors to bar an author from publication.[55]

There are two issues at stake: one is the patently socio-political issue of challenging a received view (this is not done) and the other has to do with the seeming deathlessness, or zombie 'immortality' of models in science:

> Clearly, the mathematical modelling community believed so strongly in models that it insisted on using them even when there was no scientific basis for their application. The discredited Brunn Rule predicts how much shoreline erosion will be created by sea-level rise and since no other model claims to do this, the Brunn Rule remains in widespread use. [Similarly] The maximum sustainable yield is a concept that fishery models are still using as a means to preserve fish population despite the fact that the concept was discredited thirty years ago.[56]

Given quantitative pressures in today's social science, rational choice (even including a direct parallel with hermeneutics in economics),[57] the standard culture

---

52 Pilkey/Pilkey-Jarvis 2007, p. 92.

53 Pilkey/Pilkey-Jarvis 2007, p. 109. See for a technical discussion of the model in question, Pilkey and Cooper 2004.

54 Pilkey/Pilkey-Jarvis 2007, p. xii.

55 "The editor of the principle coastal engineering journal of the American Society of Civic Engineers informed a mutual friend that he would never allow a paper by me to be published. And he kept his word." Pilkey/Pilkey-Jarvis, 2007, p. 136.

56 Pilkey/Pilkey-Jarvis 2007, p. xiii.

57 Koppla/Whitman 2004. The conjunction is not entirely unprecedented and goes back some time (even Nietzsche and certainly Bataille drew inspiration from economic notions). See the

of science, not to mention the potential scope of computer-generated data on the basis of a given model, the irrelevance of the predictive power of the model for its deployment can seem minor.

Practical questions of a hermeneutic kind are essential to the standard invocation of the working powers of science and technology. And yet if, as in this case, the applied and the pure, the natural and the social sciences go hand in glove with what the idealization of science in our culture. Hence although the authors themselves are scientists—having written their book for the sake of applying that same science to applied engineering to better, more efficient end-results—the critical dissonance that is part of the Pilkeys' arguments tends to alienate some readers. By contrast more readers will find it easier to read an author like Naomi Oreskes, who is more "readable" owing to her politically judicious criticism of the political uses of science (big tobacco being a perfect fall guy, the Army Corps of Engineers, even *after* Hurricane Katrina, even *after* a federal judge held the Corps "accountable for the destruction of most of New Orleans,"[58] much less so). Hence readers have tended to challenged by *Useless Arithmetic* and its insistent call for *more science* when it comes to the deployment of models.

The example of shoreline modelling, beaches and storms and sand, concern engineering, an *applied science*, yet these considerations bear on sociology and technology and science studies. The Pilkeys do not use the word "hermeneutics," but their description of the dominant paradigm in their field as a "fig leaf" for other interests, masking the subjective concerns haunting practices assumed objective, has limited the reception of their work.[59] This is regrettable as the mathematician, Ralph Abraham, argues, invoking "the hermeneutical circle that

---

contributions, particularly that of Philip Mirowski, to Lavoie 1990. For a discussion of Lavoie himself see the introduction to High 2006 which delineates layers of interpretation (more turtles) in addition to the hermeneutic. Cf. here Wayne Froman's chapter in the same volume: Froman 2006, pp. 164 ff. and see especially Gary Madison's contribution. In addition to Madison's first two books, see his (1989) and his (1994). See too Mirowski's monograph, now its second edition, Mirowski 2000.

58 Grunwald 2009.

59 Carpenter in his review (2013) points to the general appreciation of computer models and focuses, despite a positive review, on just those instances where models work. A more insightful review pointing to the authors' push for "more adaptive management practices" is on offer in Cockerill 2007. And in a review published in *Nature*, Roger Pielke, Jr. explicates the cognitive dissonance for scientists committed to precisely the opposite conviction contra the author's central claim regarding "'the virtual impossibility of accurate quantitative modelling to predict the outcome of natural processes on the Earth's surface'." Pielke 2007, p. 35–36.

drives the advance of science"[60] in the context of the "modeling of complex dynamical systems" and the "misuse of mathematical modeling" in the Pilkeys' instantiations of these cases as (to repeat Abraham's own summary of the modeling strategies already listed above) as

> including the collapse of Atlantic cod stocks, prediction of stock prices, body counts during the Vietnam war, the safety of nuclear waste storage at Yucca Mountain in Nevada, the rise of sea levels due to global climate warming, shoreline erosion, toxicity of abandoned open-pit mines, and the spread of non-indigenous plants.[61]

The Pilkeys' critical project requires hermeneutics. But if Abraham draws conclusions which may upset some journalistic science writers and delight others (on Global Warming and climate change—we are after all, with a century or two of measurement data not exactly replete with rich sample material one way or the other), Abraham's point is unambiguous, going further than the authors of *Useless Arithmetic:*

> policy makers with their own agendas may fool people (and themselves) into accepting risky policies by misrepresenting simulated data as prediction. This is what the Pilkeys mean by useless arithmetic. But it is worse than useless, it is dangerous.[62]

Pilkey himself invokes an iconic example to illustrate the "measurement of sand transport" (useful, as one might assume, for those involved with shore-erosion management simply in order to know how much sand to order at any given time, just to know what was displaced so to perhaps compensate). But not only are the models not particularly helpful, the tests of the same are inconclusive. Thus:

> Sam Smith, an Australian coastal engineer, thought he had a solution in measuring the storm problem. He spread a dump truck load of blue-dyed fluorescent sand along a Gold Coast beach in Australia as a typhoon approached the shore. Smith figured he would be able to find at least a few grains and thus learn the direction in which sand was moved. After the storm, however, not a single blue sand grain was found.[63]

I cite this as it exemplifies a hermeneutic insight into science otherwise advanced by Nietzsche, along with the revelation of the contrary results of the experiment—one part Canute, one part Lewis Carrol and nursery rhymes about

60 Abraham 2009, p. 1.
61 Abraham 2009, p. 2.
62 Abraham 2009, p. 2.
63 Pilkey and Pilkey-Jarvis 2007, p. 123.

maids sweeping the sea shore. At issue is the ocean itself and the wave, chaos and disorder and regularity. This is the reference to complexity as one finds it in Nietzsche's own high Kantian reference to causality and its noumenal complexity:

> *Die wahre Welt der Ursachen ist uns verborgen*; sie ist unsaglich komplizierter. Der Intellekt und die Sinne sind ein vor allem vereinfachter Apparat. [*The true world of causes is concealed from us*. The intellect and the senses are above all a simplifying apparatus.][64]

Nietzsche's point is not directed to the externality of the world and focuses on nothing less than consciousness, the self, the ego as a collimated kind of "end-phenomenon" as he names it, of what we perceive of ourselves in terms of what we call our "feeling willing thinking," the "causes of which are unknown to us" apart from the "succession" of the same "end-phenomena."[65] For Nietzsche there is no kind of fundamental spiritual or intellectual reality at the base of these appearances. Once again "*the true world of causes is concealed from us*."[66] It is in that sense that Nietzsche emphasizes "the unspeakable complexity" of that world and it is concomitant with that same complexity that he writes that "the intellect and the senses are above all a simplifying apparatus."[67] The simplifying note he adds is intended as an explication: all one needs for a sense of this is to study the body: physiology as such. Add political and cultural history to that, sociology, politics, what have you, complexities only increase.

The difficulty here (this what Abraham named "dangerous") concerns more than the differences between engineering- and science-based approaches but policy making: nothing other than the politics of environmental science not on the level of legislation and enforcement but politics on the level of science itself as indeed of technology as such.[68]

---

64 Nietzsche, KSA 11, 34 [46], p. 434. My translation. See too Simon 1989. And on Kant and Nietzsche, including other references to the literature, see Babich 2016a. Günter Abel in his closing chapter to the essays included in his co-edited volume, *Nietzsches Wissenschaftsphilosophie* refers to Goodman and his "ways of worldmaking" and art to address some of this also invokes Feyerabend. Abel 2011. For me this is at the heart of Alwin Mittasch's approach to Nietzsche, especially the language of a chemistry of sensations and sensibility, including broad parallels with Paneth or Schrödinger.

65 Nietzsche, KSA 11, 34 [46], p. 434. My translation.

66 Nietzsche, KSA 11, 34 [46], p. 434. My translation.

67 Nietzsche, KSA 11, 34 [46], p. 434. My translation.

68 Some scholars do explore this conjunction. See, for example, Sarewitz 1996 as well as Winner 1988. What can pass unread in today's age that endorses a recovery of Simondon and Souriau can be the very classic and otherwise increasingly excluded Ellul 1967.

VI. Conclusion: Politics and Hermeneutic Philosophy of Science

Philosophy of science has a political side even if political theorists themselves, subtribe as they are of the discipline of political science, tend to be charry of pointing this out. If Max Weber is an exception as is Bruno Latour, Latour himself is also a model example of the disastrous consequences of hinting that there might be a social element in science—political, sociological, anthropological.[69] Tarred with consructivism and saddled with the rubric of postmodernism, Latour turned away from his original efforts, decisively as far as I can see, not only for his own work but in social science and technology studies overall, in order to sidestep the negative press associated with what was (then) decried as social construction and its various discontents.[70]

If Alasdair MacIntyre has had[71] the rare confidence required to point to the influence of the political in what counts and what can be counted as a fact,[72] the very pointing to the social, let alone the political, not to speak of hermeneutics, has made many philosophers of science uncomfortable, even disquieting thinkers in science studies as in the sociology of science and technology.

Yet in recent years there has been both an efflorescence of hermeneutics *and* a step away from hermeneutics in the social sciences themselves and in philosophical expressions bearing on the social sciences.[73] Perhaps this has to do, as the above discussion would suggest, with an aspiration towards objective status on the model of the natural sciences (which as both Kockelmans and Heelan argue in this volume likewise include hermeneutical elements) or perhaps this simply reflects disciplinary shifts at the level of the university, or, in philosophy this may have to do with changes in formation and the near exclusive dominance of analytic conventions.[74] In any case, hermeneutics remains an indispensable

---

69 See Latour 1999. See for one, largely conventional reading, Brown 2009.

70 See again, already cited above, the concluding sections of Babich 2017.

71 For a discussion, see Dolling 2002.

72 I refer to Macintyre's discussion of "The Idea of Social Science" in *After Virtue*. To me it is regrettable that MacIntyre who discusses Winch and Durkheim in addition to Goffman, does not himself draw a connection to hermeneutics. See however Laitinen 2015. And see too, specifically on Gadamer, MacIntyre 2002.

73 For Kockelmans on the social sciences, in addition to his chapter in the current volume, see Kockelmans 1976, 1978 and 1979.

74 See Babich 2012. There is another set of complex questions among the many remaining beyond the scope of this essay which would allow one to determine the consequences of choosing for phenomenology over hermeneutics in a certain tradition at least in sociology, to wit Ferguson ingredient in any account, contemporary or historical, of scientific practice and to that same extent indispensable for any philosophy of science that means to proceed along the path of science.

References

Abel, Günter (2011). "Die Aktualität der Wissenschaftsphilosophie Nietzsches." In: Helmut Heit, Günter Abel, and Marco Brusotti, (eds.) *Nietzsches Wissenschaftsphilosophie. Hintergründe, Wirkungen und Aktualität.* Berlin: de Gruyter, pp. 481–530.

Arvan, Marcus (2014) "A Campaign for Better Philosophy Citation Practices?" April 24, 2014. Online: http://philosopherscocoon.typepad.com/blog/2014/04/a-campaign-for-better-philosophy-citation-practices.html. Last accessed 05.24.2017

Aucoin, Pauline McKenzie (2017) "Toward an Anthropological Understanding of Space and Place." In: Bruce B. Janz (ed.), *Place, Space and Hermeneutics*, Frankfurt a.M.: Springer, pp. 395–412.

Babich, Babette (2003) "Paradigms and Thoughtstyles: Incommensurability and its Cold War Discontents from Kuhn's Harvard to Fleck's Unsung Lvov." *Social Epistemology* 17: 97–107.

Babich, Babette (2010) "Towards a Critical Philosophy of Science: Continental Beginnings and Bugbears, Whigs and Waterbears." *International Journal of the Philosophy of Science* 24 (4): 343–391.

Babich, Babette (2011) *Nietzsches Wissenschaftsphilosophie.* Oxford: Peter Lang.

Babich, Babette (2012) *La fin de la pensée.* Paris: L'Harmattan.

Babich, Babette (2014) "Nietzsche's *Antichrist:* The Birth of Modern Science out of the Spirit of Religion." In: Markus Enders and Holger Zaborowski (eds.), *Jahrbuch für Religionsphilosophie.* Freiburg i. Br.: Alber, pp. 134–154.

Babich, Babette (2015) "Calling Science Pseudoscience: Fleck's Archaeologies, Latour's Biography, and Demarcation or AIDS Denialism, Homeopathy, and Syphilis." *International Studies in the Philosophy of Science.* Vol. 29, Nr. 1 (2015): 1–39.

Babich, Babette (2016a) "Nietzsche's Critique: Reading Kant's Critical Philosophy." In: Mark Conard (ed.), *Nietzsche and the Philosophers.* Lanham, MD: Rowman Littlefield, pp. 171–192.

Babich, Babette (2016b) "Getting to Hogwarts: Michael Oakeshott, Ivan Illich, and J.K. Rowling on 'School'." In: David Bakhurst and Paul Fairfield (eds.), *Education and Conversation: Exploring Oakeshott's Legacy.* London: Bloomsbury, pp. 199–218.

Babich, Babette (2017) "Are They Good? Are They Bad? Double Hermeneutics and Citation in Philosophy, Asphodel and Alan Rickman, Bruno Latour and the 'Science Wars'." In: Paula Angelova, Jaassen Andreev, Emil Lessky (eds.) *Das Interpretative Universum.* Würzburg: Königshausen & Neumann, pp. 259–290.

Babich, Babette (2018) " Les " pseudosciences " à l'aune de l'échelle des valeurs de l'université. " *Diversité linguistique et culturelle, appropriations, réceptions*

2006, and some of the contributions in the present volume bear witness to this influence, as it also grows out of Schütz 1967.

Francophonies, formations à distance, migrances. Réflexions épistémologiques et interventions. Actes du colloque de Tours (9–10.06.16). Forthcoming.
Bardini, Thierry (2011) *Junkware*. Minneapolis: University of Minnesota Press.
Bischur, Daniel (2013), "Scientific Practice and the World of Working" in: Michael Staudigl and George Berguno (eds.) *Schutzian Phenomenology and Hermeneutic Traditions*, Springer: Frankfurt a.M., pp. 126–198.
Carson, Cathryn, Alexei Kojevnikov, and Helmuth Trischler (eds.) (2011) *Weimar Culture and Quantum Mechanics: Selected Papers by Paul Forman and Contemporary Perspectives on the Forman Thesis*. Hackensack, N.J.: World Scientific Publishing.
Cole, Stephen, Leonard Rubin, Jonathan R. Cole, (1978) *Peer Review in the National Science Foundation: Phase One of a Study : Prepared for the Committee on Science and Public Policy of the National Academy of Sciences*. Washington, DC: National Academies.
Connor, Steven (2016) "Decomposing the Humanities." *New Literary History* 47(2 & 3, Spring & Summer), pp. 275–288.
Corneliussen, Steven T. (2017) "Commentators Reexamine Physicist Alan Sokal's Purposeful 1996 Parody Paper: 'Transgressing the Boundaries: Towards a Transformative Hermeneutics of Quantum Gravity' Still Packs a Sly Punch," *Physics Today* 26 Jan.
Cutrofello, Andrew (2004) *Continental Philosophy: A Contemporary Introduction*. London: Routledge.
Dallmayr, Fred. (2013) "The Return of Philosophical Anthropology." In: Ananta Kumar Giri and John Clammer (eds.) *Philosophy and Anthropology: Border Crossing and Transformations*. London: Anthem Press, pp. 367–378.
Duhem, Pierre (1991 [1916]) *German Science. Some Reflections on German Science. German Science and German Virtues*, tr. John Lyon. La Salle: Open Court.
Feyerabend, Paul (1985) "Galileo and the Tyranny of Truth." In: G.V. Coyne (ed.) *The Galileo Affair: A Meeting of Faith and Science, Proceedings of the Cracow Conference, May 24–27, 1984*. Citta del Vaticano: Specola Vaticana, pp. 155–166.
Feyerabend, Paul (1993 [1975]) *Against Method*. London: Verso.
Finocchiaro, Maurice (2010) *Defending Copernicus and Galileo: Critical Reasoning in the Two Affairs*. Frankfurt a.M.: Springer.
Fleck, Ludwik (1979) *On the Genesis and Development of a Scientific Fact*. Chicago: University of Chicago Press.
Fleck, Ludwik (2008) *Genèse et développement d'un fait scientifique*, tr. Nathalie Jas. Paris: Champs scientifique.
Forman, Paul (1971) "Weimar Culture, Causality, and Quantum Theory, 1918–1927: Adaptation by German Physicists and Mathematicians to a Hostile Intellectual Environment." *Historical Studies in the Physical Sciences*, 3(1), pp 1–115.
Gardener, Martin (2013) *Undiluted Hocus-Pocus: The Autobiography of Martin Gardner*. Princeton: Princeton University Press.
Gane, Mike (2006) *Auguste Comte*. London: Routledge.
Geertz, Clifford (1996) After the Fact: Two Countries, Four Decades, One Anthropologist. Cambridge: Harvard University Press.
Ginev, Dimitri (1998) "Rhetoric and Double Hermeneutics in the Human Sciences." *Human Studies* 21: 259–271.
Ginev, Dimitri (2006) The Context of Constitution: Beyond the Edge of Epistemological Justification. Frankfurt a.M.: Springer.

Glendinning, Simon (2006) *The Idea of Continental Philosophy.* Edinburgh: Edinburgh University Press.
Heelan, Patrick A. (1965) *Quantum Mechanics and Objectivity.* Nijhoff: The Hague.
Heelan, Patrick A. (1989) "Yes! There is a Hermeneutic Philosophy of Natural Science: Rejoinder to Markus." *Science in Context* 3: 469–480.
Heelan, Patrick A. (1994) "Galileo, Luther, and the Hermeneutics of Natural Science" in: T. J. Stapleton (ed.) *The Question of Hermeneutics*, Dordrecht: Kluwer, pp. 363–375.
Heelan, Patrick A. (2016) *The Observable.* Oxford/Bern: Peter Lang.
Heidegger, Martin (1996) *Hölderlin's Hymn "The Ister"*, tr. William McNeill and Julia Davis. Bloomington: Indiana University Press.
Horgan, John (1993) "Profile: Paul Karl Feyerabend—The Worst Enemy of Science." *Scientific American* 268(5): 36–37.
Kämpf, Heike (2013) "The Engagement of Philosophy and Anthropology in the Interpretive Turn and Beyond: Towards an Anthropology of the Contemporary." In: Ananta Kumar Giri and John Clammer (eds.) *Philosophy and Anthropology: Border Crossing and Transformations.* London: Anthem Press, pp. 89–104.
Kusch, Martin (2005) *Psychologism: The Sociology of Philosophical Knowledge.* London: Routledge.
Latour, Bruno (1976) *The Force of Knowledge: The Scientific Dimension of Society.* Cambridge: Cambridge University Press.
Latour, Bruno (1991a) *Nous n'avons jamais été modernes. Essai d'anthropologie symétrique.* Paris: La Découverte.
Latour, Bruno (1991b) *We Have Never Been Modern.* New York: Harvester Wheatsheaf.
Latour, Bruno (1999) *Politiques de la nature. Comment faire entrer les sciences en démocratie.* Paris: La Découverte.
Latour, Bruno (2001) *Das Parlament der Dinge.* Frankfurt a.M.: Suhrkamp.
Latour, Bruno (2012) "Biography of an Investigation: On a Book about Modes of Existence. Draft of an Article for a Dossier on AIME," tr. Cathy Porter. *Archives de philosophie* 75 (4): 1–20.
Latour, Bruno (2013) *An Inquiry Into Modes of Existence: Anthropology of the Moderns.* Harvard: Harvard University Press.
Latour, Bruno and Woolgar, Steve (1986 [1979]) *Laboratory Life: The Construction of Scientific Facts.* London: Sage.
Lau, Joerg (2002) "Bescheidwisser in die Politik." *Die Zeit*, March 7, 2002.
Leydesdorff, Loet (2006) *The Knowledge-Based Economy: Modeled, Measured, Simulated.* Boca Raton: Universal-Publishers.
Lynch, William (1993) "What Does the Double Hermeneutic Explain/Justify?" *Social Epistemology* 7(2): 193–204.
Márkus, György (1987) "Why is there no Hemeneutics of Natural Sciences. Some Preliminary Theses." *Science in Context* 1 (1): 5–51.
Maranhão, Tullio and Bernhard Streck (eds.) (2003) *Translation and Ethnography: The Anthropological Challenge of Intercultural Understanding* (Tucson: University of Arizona Press, 2003
McCumber, John (1996) *Time in the Ditch: American Philosophy and the McCarthy Era.* Evanston: Northwestern University Press.

Nietzsche, Friedrich (1980) *Kritische Studienausgabe*, (eds.) Giorgio Colli and Mazzino Montinari. Berlin: de Gruyter.

Pelchat, Yolande (2003) *L'obsession de la différence: récit d'une biotechnologie*. Laval: Presses Université Laval.

Preston, John, Munévar, Gonzalo and Lamb, David (eds.) (2000) *The Worst Enemy of Science? Essays in Memory of Paul Feyerabend*. Oxford: Oxford University Press.

Rabinow, Paul (2011) *The Accompaniment: Assembling the Contemporary*. Chicago: University of Chicago Press.

Ringer, Fritz (1969) *The Decline of the German Mandarins: The German Academic Community, 1890–1933*. Cambridge: Harvard University Press.

Ruark, Jennifer 2017, "Anatomy of a Hoax: Bait and Switch. How the physicist Alan Sokal hoodwinked a group of humanists and why, 20 years later, it still matters. An oral history" *Chronical of Higher Education*, January 01.

Schmidgen, Henning (2014) *Bruno Latour in Pieces: An Intellectual Biography*. New York: Fordham University Press.

Schürmann, Reiner (1985) "De la philosophie aux États-Unis" *Le temps de la réflexion* 6: 303–321.

Schürmann, Reiner (1994) "Concerning Philosophy in the United States" *Social Research*, 61 (I, Spring): 89–113.

Shapin, Steven (1992) "Discipline and Bounding: The History and Sociology of Science as Seen through the Externalism-Internalism Debate" *History of Science* 30: 333–369.

Simon, Joseph (1989) *Philosophie des Zeichens*. Berlin/New York: De Gruyter.

Smith, Richard (2006) "Peer Review: A Flawed Process at the Heart of Science and Journals," *J R Soc Med.*, 99(4) Apr.: 178–182.

Sokal, Alan (1997a) "Pourquoi j'ai écrit ma parodie." *Le Monde*, January 31.

Sokal, Alan (1997b) "Nos philosophes sont-ils des imposteurs?" *Le Nouvel Observateur* 1716, pp. 116–118.

Sormani, Philippe (2016) *Respecifying Lab Ethnography: An Ethnomethodological Study of Experimental Physics*. London: Routledge.

Souriau, Étienne (2009) *Les différents modes d'existence. Suivi de Du mode d'existence de l'oeuvre à faire avec une présentation par Isabelle Stengers et Bruno Latour*. Paris: Presses Universitaires de France.

Stengers, Isabelle (1977) *Cosmopolitiques*. Vol. 1: *La guerre des sciences*. Paris/Le Plessis-Robinson: La Découverte.

Warman, Matt (2011) "Stephen Hawking Tells Google 'Philosophy is Dead'." *Telegraph*, 17 May.

Gary Madison

On the Importance of Getting Things Straight

Abstract: It is surely rather curious that phenomenological (or philosophical) hermeneutics, which is a systematic theory of human understanding in all its various forms, has been, and continues to be, so widely misunderstood. Perhaps, though, this is not such a surprising phenomenon after all, since, as phenomenology has shown, human understanding is of such a nature that it invariably tends to misunderstand itself. It is nevertheless somewhat odd—but perhaps also revealing—that the two chief ways in which hermeneutics is commonly misunderstood are diametrically opposed to one another.

The main charge that philosophers of a traditionalist ("modernist") sort generally level against hermeneutics is that, by rejecting modern epistemologism and its notion of truth as the correspondence of subjective states of mind to an "objective," in-itself reality (the mind as a "mirror of nature"—what elsewhere I have referred to as referentialist-representationalism), hermeneutics leads directly (or by means of a "slippery slope") to an all-out, truth-denying *relativism*. In calling into question the traditional notion of truth (and thus also the traditional notion of reality as something "univocal" in itself), hermeneutics, it is claimed, embraces a form of irrationalism that undermines any and all claims to universally valid knowledge. It is in this regard yet another instance of the post-Nietzschean nihilism so prevalent in postmodern thought.[1]

On the other side of the ledger, critics of a "postmodern" sort, who are often themselves avowed relativists fully prepared to sacrifice philosophy's traditional claim to knowledge (the "end of philosophy"), tend to be equally dismissive of hermeneutics—but for an altogether different reason. For them, hermeneutics, far from having broken with traditional metaphysics, is nothing more than the old "essentialism" (the "metaphysics of presence") dressed up in new (and perhaps more seductive) garb. Jacques Derrida once sought to portray Gadamer as (as Gadamer summed it up) "a lost sheep in the dried up pastures of metaphy-

1 See in this regard Madison 1994a.

https://doi.org/10.1515/9783110551563-010

sics." And one of Derrida's leading spokespersons, John D. Caputo, flatly accused Gadamer of being "a closet essentialist."[2]

Simple logic dictates that these two mutually exclusive charges leveled against hermeneutics cannot both be right. Either one is true and the other is false—or perhaps neither is true. Logic alone cannot of course decide the issue; before one can properly assess any particular ideational position, it is first necessary to determine (as Plato would say) the "kind" of position it is, i.e., the conceptual category into which it falls. Now, as hermeneuticists themselves view the matter, hermeneutics is fully a form of postmodern thought—but one that differs in highly significant ways from other forms of postmodernism. Although many people still fail to appreciate the fact, phenomenological hermeneutics incorporates a genuinely deconstructive strategy inasmuch as it conscientiously rejects the modernistic objectivism of pre-phenomenological, Romantic hermeneutics. According to Richard E. Palmer, it is important to see "the unfolding of the hermeneutical problematic in terms of the philosophical critique of the metaphysics of modernity," and he has pointed out how such a critique generates the need for a deconstructive strategy very much akin in a number of ways to Derridian deconstruction.[3] Hermeneutics is decidedly postmodern in that, like classical phenomenology of which it is a logical extension, it seeks deliberately to set aside the guiding prejudices of modern philosophy.[4]

To be sure, hermeneutics is not "postmodern" in the negative sense in which most critics of postmodernism understand the term. Unlike other forms of postmodern thought (which could perhaps be grouped together under the heading "post-structuralist," for want of a better term), hermeneutics does not seek to undermine the traditional notions of "truth," "reality," and "knowledge" in such a way as to leave nothing in their place (this is indeed nihilism). Hermeneutical deconstruction is in fact eminently reconstructive in that it seeks to work out a genuinely nonfoundationalist and nonessentialist understanding of these traditional, core concepts of philosophy. This is, as one might say, "the difference that makes a difference." Unlike other forms of postmodernism, hermeneutics is not merely *anti*-metaphysical; it is genuinely *post*-metaphysical.[5]

---

2 See Michelfelder and Palmer 1989, pp. 50, 258–264. Time has a way, fortunately, of correcting many misunderstandings, and both Derrida and Caputo have over the years come to appreciate better the genuinely postmetaphysical significance of hermeneutics; see in this regard: Caputo 2004.

3 See Palmer 1984, p. 233.

4 For a detailed treatment of this issue, see Madison 2004b.

5 For a fuller discussion of this matter, see my (2001a).

All of this is something that Saulius Geniusas fully appreciates. In his chapter to follow, "Hans-Georg Gadamer's Concept of the Horizon," S.G. (as I shall henceforth refer to him) seeks to set the record straight by showing how hermeneutics escapes the age-old metaphysical opposition between *essentialism* and *relativism*, which is to say, between *universalism* and *particularism*. Hermeneutics is, quite simply, *neither* essentialist *nor* relativist; unlike other forms of postmodernism which tend merely to substitute the latter term of the opposition (relativism, particularism) for the former (essentialism, universalism), hermeneutics is a thoroughgoing attempt to move beyond, as Richard Bernstein would say, both objectivism and relativism.[6] As S.G. points out, the relation between the universal and the particular is in fact "the heart of the hermeneutical problem," and the pivotal issue in this connection is Gadamer's notion of "application," since for Gadamer all understanding comes down to a matter of "applying something universal to a particular situation." There could be no philosophical understanding of anything without an appeal to universals [*individuum ineffabile est*], but universals, as Gadamer has shown, do not exist fully defined in their own right or in any metaphysical sense of the term; they exist only in their application to particular situations. The relation between the "universal" (e.g., the meaning of a text or an ethical norm) and the "particular" (e.g., various interpretations of the text's meaning or applications of the norm to particular situations) is not a vertical or hierarchical relation of logical subsumption but a lateral or circular one of co-determination. Understanding (grasping the universal) is always of a particularizing or "applicational" and context-sensitive nature; it is not a matter of logical deduction but, as in jurisprudence, a matter of practical reasoning or *phronesis*. In other words, understanding is inseparable from interpretation. As S.G. says speaking of the notion of "appropriation" (i.e., "application"): "The task of interpretation is, while being guided by the text, to reveal its continuing significance, to bring it out of the past into the living present."

While Gadamer's notion of "application" and his understanding of the relation between the universal and the particular is anything but simplistic, it is really not all that difficult to comprehend by anyone who takes the time to do so. However, as S.G. rightly observes, Gadamer's views on this matter have been subject to a number of misunderstandings and misplaced criticisms. In addressing some of these misguided criticisms S.G. wants to show how Gadamer's hermeneutics not only makes perfectly good sense but how it is also supremely positioned for dealing with the challenge confronting humanity in today's rapidly globalizing world. This is an issue to which I shall return in my final remarks;

6 See Bernstein 1983.

S.G. himself approaches it via the detour of a critique of Richard Kearney's misportrayal of Gadamer's hermeneutics.

As illustrative of the way Gadamer's work can be grossly misread, this is a particularly well chosen example, although I must confess that I was shocked to see that Kearney, who in his various presentations of contemporary Continental philosophy has shown himself to be an excellent hermeneut, should nevertheless have so profoundly misconstrued Gadamer's position. Kearney maintains that the relation between self and other is the central hermeneutical problem—and he is absolutely right to do so. In opposition to, as S.G. points out, both "the mainstream metaphysical tradition which largely ignores the question of the Other" as well as "some postmodern thinkers who externalize alterity to the point that there can be no communication between self and other," Kearney advocates a "diacritical hermeneutics" which "discovers the other in the self and the self in the other." For Kearney (a former student of Paul Ricoeur), Ricoeur's hermeneutics is a prime instance of such a "diacritical" approach. This is all well and good, but where Kearney goes seriously wrong is in claiming that this does not describe Gadamer's own treatment of the relation between self and other. I, for my part as a former student of both Ricoeur and Gadamer, have no hesitation whatsoever in asserting that on this score there is no significant difference between the two, however much Kearney may go out of his way to find one. Indeed, S.G. shows very nicely how, in attempting to elaborate a "nonhegemonic" notion of appropriation, Ricoeur actually appeals to Gadamer's writings on the subject in the course of working out his own position.

Ricoeur does, of course, have his differences with Gadamer, but these are of a secondary nature. While Ricoeur was always sympathetic to Gadamer's attempt to work out a fundamental ontology of human understanding, he also felt that, because of Gadamer's focus on the ontological question, he did not pay sufficient attention to properly methodological issues and to the relationship between hermeneutics and the other human sciences. Ricoeur thus viewed the specificity of his own endeavors as consisting in the elaboration of a "methodological" hermeneutics that would serve as a complement to Gadamer's "ontological" hermeneutics. This was not, however, a difference over fundamentals (Ricoeur always viewed ontology as the "promised land" of hermeneutics). As students of classical phenomenology, both Gadamer and Ricoeur were in fact, as hermeneuticists, engaged in a common endeavor, and the basic strategies they pursued in this regard were strikingly similar. For both of them, it was always necessary to do battle simultaneously on two fronts: against, on the one hand, the objectivism of Romantic hermeneutics (and traditional metaphysics more generally) and, on the other hand, the relativism extolled by a number of postmodernists (who assert that since no single interpretation of a text or anything else can—as hermeneutics itself maintains—legitimately claim to be the one and only correct or valid interpretation, a state of glorious, free-wheeling interpretational anarchy must necessarily prevail).

It is thus rather astounding that Kearney should categorize Gadamer's hermeneutics as a form of Romantic hermeneutics and, accordingly, of being a "hermeneutics of appropriation" in the "bad" sense of the term, i.e., one which abolishes otherness by absorbing it into the horizon of the self.[7] However strange such a reading of Gadamer may be to, as S.G. says, "anyone who has listened to what Gadamer actually had to say," there is nevertheless, he allows, an ambiguity in Gadamer's notion of a "fusion of horizons" that can give rise to such a charge on the part of the unwary. Thus the question S.G. seeks to confront in his paper is: "Why does Gadamer simultaneously speak of the oneness and the multiplicity of horizons? Why is he reluctant to tell us whether there are many horizons or just one?" In the last analysis there is, of course, only one horizon, just as there is only one all-encompassing lifeworld which is the common home of us all (this world being, as Husserl said, the "horizon of all horizons"). But, as S.G. rightly argues, this oneness of the hermeneutical horizon is no way diminishes the genuinely *dialogical* character of Gadamer's hermeneutics, and in no way does it subsume, à la Hegel, multiplicity into a homogeneous oneness.

To be more specific, there is one horizon not in any absolutist sense (in the sense in which objectivists assert that there is one single, self-identical, "real" world) but only in the sense that, while everyone has his or her own individual horizon (of a personal or socio-cultural sort), there is nothing that in principle prevents any individual from entering into genuine contact with any other individual and penetrating to some degree or another into his or her own world. This is what the notion of a "fusion of horizons" is meant to express: the presence of the other in the self and the self in the other. As Gadamer says in a text quoted by S.G.: "Understanding is always the fusion of horizons supposedly existing by themselves." Perhaps it would be better in this connection to speak not of a "fusion of horizons" but rather of a "merging of horizons," since the term "fusion" can be easily be misunderstood to imply a kind of oneness of an "essentialist" sort that for Gadamer does not, and could never, exist. However that may be, the phenomenological fact of the matter is that it is meaningless to speak of a fixed or "closed" horizon. Horizons are, *per definitionem*, "open": Horizons

---

7 For a detailed overview of the main tenets of philosophical hermeneutics (as well as the crucial differences between it and Romantic hermeneutics), see my (1994b). For an analysis of how Gadamer's phenomenological hermeneutics differs in decisive ways from the neo-Romantic hermeneutics of D. Hirsch, see my (1988).

move with us when we move, and it is precisely by broadening our own horizons that we are able to enter into contact with what is distant and alien.

One of the great merits of S.G.'s paper is the way in which he manages to show how Gadamer's notion of a fusion of horizons provides for a genuinely non-oppositional way of conceiving the relation between oneness and multiplicity, between universality and particularity. One thing that Kearney rightly insists upon is that what he refers to as "today's challenge" is, as S.G. puts it, "that of respecting the specificity of the other while not schismatically dividing the other from the self." This is precisely where a great deal of present-day thought falls lamentably short, dominated as it is by the currently very fashionable paradigm of cultural incommensurability. As S.G. pertinently observes in this regard, "Our age ... is obsessed with schismatically separating the other from the self." Any would-be ethics which sets "alterity" in opposition to "ipseity" and which asserts that the relation between self and other is of a non-reciprocal, "asymmetrical" nature (the other, according to this "ethics of the Other," being a non-negotiable demand imposed upon the self and having absolute priority over the self's own concerns) is one which, ignoring as it does the role that self-interest necessarily plays in all human relationships and the need for mutuality in all just dealings with the other, is thoroughly utopian in its impracticality and its irrelevance to the everyday world of social reality.[8]

The obsession with "alterity" on the part of the "politically correct" testifies to what are undoubtedly praiseworthy motives (a concern to respect the "otherness" of the other), but it is nevertheless both wrong in theory and pernicious in practice. From a theoretical point of view, cultural incommensurabilism rests on an altogether erroneous concept of "culture." The basic assumption of that form of relativism that could be labeled "culturalism" is that cultures are somehow self-contained, internally consistent, self-subsistent "wholes." But this is not really the case at all. Every culture is in actuality a *mélange* of a multitude of beliefs and practices that are often only haphazardly related and are sometimes even inconsistent, and many of which, moreover, are borrowings from other cultures (borrowings which in the normal course of events are rapidly "indigenized"). Cultures are like languages in that they are immensely porous, and the inter-cultural exchange of ideas (as to what is true or what is of value) is as primordial a human phenomenon as is the exchange of material goods. In the real world, there is, as there always has been, an on-going and never-ending "merging of horizons." This is a basic fact of human life. The norm in human affairs is not cultural "self-identity" but cultural "hybridity."

8 For an extended discussion of this issue, see Madison 2000.

The incommensurabilist paradigm is also pernicious in practice in that, as S.G. points out, "by not acknowledging any bond between different cultures, languages, or subjectivities," this stance actually legitimates a sublime *indifference* to otherness. This is a classic instance of what economic theory refers to as the phenomenon of "unintended consequences." Not only that. Since in the real world we often cannot avoid having dealings with others, then—if it is indeed the case as cultural relativists maintain that dialogue in the hermeneutical sense of the term (the presence of the other in the self and the self in the other; the "fusion of horizons supposedly existing by themselves") is not a real possibility that we should strive to put into practice wherever possible—it follows that the only kind of relation that can obtain between the self and the other must be one of domination, or attempted domination, of one over the other.[9] This is something that no tolerant relativist would intentionally endorse, but it is nevertheless the logical consequence of the incommensurabilist stance. It is therefore for both theoretical and practical—which is to say, moral—reasons that hermeneutics rejects those forms of postmodern thought which elevate particularity over universality in such a way as to make it impossible to conceive of a kind of "oneness" of horizons that is in no way hegemonic.

The key insight in this regard that dominates all of Gadamer's work is that there is, or need be, no contradiction between "openness" to the other and "belongingness" to one's own cultural horizon. This is something that S.G. recognizes when he asserts that the oneness of the horizon in Gadamer's thought "reveals the *correlative* nature of ipseity and alterity" (emphasis added). And thus, as S.G. very nicely says, "the open-ended oneness of the horizon liberates both the other and the self from their anonymity by returning them to the infinity of dialogue." It is precisely by means of this infinite dialogue between the self and the other, this "boundless communication" as Karl Jaspers referred to it, that self and other are enabled to achieve self-identity by becoming, each thanks to the other, the unique individuals that they themselves are.

As S.G. importantly recognizes, Gadamer's nonessentialist and nonhegemonic (i.e., postmetaphysical) way of reconceptualizing universality is of "a nor-

9 Of course, one does not seek to engage in dialogue with, for instance, terrorists who *a priori* refuse all dialogue and possible accommodation (who, in other words, want not to negotiate differences but only to blow up the negotiating table). When the other becomes an implacable threat to one's own very existence, the only option is to seek to "contain" or remove the other by whatever means possible. The prerequisite for genuine dialogue is what Gadamer called "good will," i.e., the will and desire to reach a mutually satisfying agreement with the other. Where such a will is lacking on the part of the other, the only rules that apply are those of *Realpolitik*, which is to say, the rules of unflinching self-interest.

mative kind." Gadamer's defense of the oneness of horizons against all forms of cultural relativism has far-ranging ethical implications. The distinctive feature of hermeneutical theory in general is that it is never theory for theory's sake but is essentially and always theory geared to practice and is, in the last analysis, theory that exists only for the sake of practice.[10] As Gadamer ever insisted, hermeneutics is *scientia practica*. It is therefore altogether appropriate that S.G. should raise the issue of hermeneutics' relevance to "today's social and political challenges." This is where the importance of getting things straight becomes most clearly manifest. As I asserted in a tribute to Gadamer shortly after his death: In these globalizing times when a "clash of civilizations"—between, above all, Islam and the Western world—looms on the horizon, Gadamer's "philosophy of dialogue" is of the utmost relevance. It, or something very much like it, is really the only basis on which could ever be conducted what President Khatami of Iran has called a "dialogue of civilizations."[11] And in a text that S.G. cites in his paper, I went on to maintain that the crucial issue of our times is that of working out, by means of dialogue or communicative rationality, a *universal* ethic (based on the notion of universal human rights) that would be capable of reconciling universally binding ethical/political norms with the undeniable fact of cultural diversity.[12] It is my belief that the hermeneutical notion of "application" is such as to provide us with the theoretical framework necessary for a constructing a "new world order" of such a sort.

As the 20th century was drawing to a close, Gadamer said of the phenomenon of globalization ("the worldwide interwovenness of economies"): "Isolation from the rest of the world is no longer possible. Humanity today is sitting in a rowboat, as it were, and we must steer this boat in such a way that we do not all crash into the rocks."[13] The supreme effect of globalization is to abolish the distances that have largely prevailed hitherto between the various cultures of the world, between the self and the other. If this seemingly irreversible process is not to result in a world-wide confrontation between different cultures, it is imperative that economic integration and the technological unification of the world be accompanied by the working out of a genuinely global ethics, and this is a task that Gadamer's hermeneutics is eminently well-placed to address.

10 For a fuller discussion of this matter, see Madison 2001b.

11 Madison, "In Memoriam Hans-Georg Gadamer," *Symposium* 6, Nr. 1 (Spring/Printemps 2002): 6–9. For a discussion of Samuel P. Huntington's notion of a coming "clash of civilizations," see my (2004a).

12 See Madison 2002.

13 Hans-Georg Gadamer in Palmer 2001, p. 81.

With someone like Richard Kearney in mind, it may be noted that Ricoeur has also devoted a good deal of his attention to this issue—which should be enough to dispel the notion that there is any great divide separating these two outstanding thinkers of our times as regards the relation between self and other.[14] For both Ricoeur and Gadamer, the supreme task of philosophy in today's world must be that of discovering in each great cultural tradition the prospects for a dialogue in which the cultural identity of each is respected while at the same time each is called upon to reach out to the others in an attempt to discover universal values common to all. The fact that both Gadamer and Ricoeur should view the challenge confronting philosophy in a global age in much the same way is in itself a clear indication that there is a distinctive logic or, as Ricoeur would say, "inner dynamic" to the hermeneutical position that both he and Gadamer have sought to lay out in ways that are not only fully compatible but that together go to make up a well-defined alternative to, on the one hand, an unacceptable, hegemonic sort of "oneness" and, on the other, a ruinous, cultural relativism. S.G. is to be commended for setting the record straight on this crucial issue.

References

Bernstein, Richard J. (1983) *Beyond Objectivism and Relativism: Science, Hermeneutics, and Praxis*. Philadelphia: University of Pennsylvania.

Caputo, Jack (2004) "Good Will and the Hermeneutics of Friendship: Gadamer, Derrida, and Madison." *Symposium* (Special Issue: "Working Through Postmodernity: Essays in Honor of Gary B. Madison"), 8 (2): 213–225.

Madison, Gary (1988) "A Critique of Hirsch's *Validity*." In: Gary Madison, *The Hermeneutics of Postmodernity: Figures and Themes*. Bloomington: Indiana University Press, pp. 5–7.

Madison, Gary (1978) "Eine Kritik an Hirschs Begriff der 'Richtigkeit.'" In: Hans-Georg Gadamer and Gottfried Boehm (eds.), *Seminar: Die Hermeneutik und die Wissenschaften*. Frankfurt a.M.: Suhrkamp, pp. 393–425.

Madison, Gary (1994a) "Hermeneutical Integrity: A Guide for the Perplexed." In J. Peter Boettke and L. David Prychitko (eds.), *The Market Process: Essays in Contemporary Austrian Economics*. Aldershot: Ashgate, pp. 201–211.

Madison, Gary (1994b) "Hermeneutics: Gadamer and Ricoeur." In: Richard Kearney (ed.), *Continental Philosophy in the 20th Century*. Routledge History of Philosophy, Vol. 8. London: Routledge, pp. 290–349.

Madison, Gary (2000) "The Moral Self and the Anonymous Other." *Arobase* 4(1–2): 238–255.

14 For a discussion of Ricoeur's position in this matter, see Madison 2003.

Madison, Gary (2001a) "Coping with Nietzsche's Legacy: Rorty, Derrida, Gadamer." In: Gary Madison, *The Politics of Postmodernity: Essays in Applied Hermeneutics.* Dordrecht: Kluwer, 13–30.

Madison, Gary (2001b) "The Theory of Practice/The Practice of Theory." In: Gary Madison, *The Politics of Postmodernity.* Dordrecht: Kluwer, pp. 137–160.

Madison, Gary (2002a) "In Memoriam Hans-Georg Gadamer," *Symposium* 6(1) (Spring/Printemps): 6–9.

Madison, Gary (2002b) "Gadamer's Legacy." In: *Symposium* 6(2): 135–147.

Madison, Gary (2003) "Paul Ricoeur: Philosopher of Being-Human (*Zuoren*)." In: Andrzej Wiercinski (ed.), *Between Suspicion and Sympathy: Paul Ricoeur's Unstable Equilibrium.* Toronto: The Hermeneutic Press, pp. 481–501.

Madison, Gary (2004a) "Globalization: Past, Present, Future." In: Bart De Schutter and Johan Pas (eds.), *About Globalisation: Views on the Trajectory of Mondialisation.* Brussels: VUB Press, pp. 308–318:

Madison, Gary (2004b) "The Interpretive Turn in Phenomenology: A Philosophical History." *Symposium* (Special Issue: "Working Through Postmodernity: Essays in Honor of Gary B. Madison"); 8(2): 397–467.

Michelfelder Diane P. and Palmer, Richard E. (eds.) (1989) *Dialogue and Deconstruction: The Gadamer-Derrida Encounter.* Albany: State University of New York Press.

Palmer, Richard E. (1984) "The Scope of Hermeneutics and the Problem of Critique and the Crisis of Modernity." *Texte: Revue de critique et de théorie littéraire*, 3: 229–239.

Palmer, Richard E. (ed.) (2001) *Gadamer in Conversation: Reflections and Commentary.* New Haven: Yale University Press.

Saulius Geniusas

Hans-Georg Gadamer's Concept of the Horizon and Its Ethico-Political Critique

Abstract. Here I focus on the relevance of Gadamer's hermeneutics in the context of today's socio-political concerns. I engage in the ethically and politically motivated critique of Gadamer's hermeneutics, which suggests that Gadamer fails to offer a satisfactory account of the relation between ipseity and alterity. I argue against the view that Gadamer's hermeneutics overlooks the otherness of the Other. Thus I further criticize the perspective that it abandons the selfhood of the self. While focusing on the dialectic of oneness and multiplicity, I contend that for Gadamer, just as the one is irreducibly multiple, so multiplicity is ultimately one. While addressing the relation between universality and particularity, I suggest that for Gadamer, this relation is not vertical, but circular. Taking as my focus Gadamer's concept of *Horizontverschmelzung*, I argue that the fusion of the horizons abolishes neither the self, nor the Other, but raises both to a higher universality. The oneness of the horizon(s) thereby proves to be the dialogue that we ourselves are.

From the very first page of *Truth and Method* onwards, Gadamer speaks of the *phenomenon of understanding* as *the hermeneutical problem*, while in one of its best-known definitions, understanding is said to be "the fusion of the horizons supposedly existing by themselves."[1] It is therefore hard to overestimate the significance of the fusion of the horizons for Gadamer's hermeneutics, since it provides an answer to "the heart of the hermeneutical problem"[2]—the question concerning the relationship between the particular and the universal. While the *application* of the universal to the particular is said to be *the central hermeneutical problem*, understanding is characterized as "a special case of applying something universal to a particular situation."[3] Although Gadamer repeatedly tells us that application is never to be taken in a technical and hegemonic sense, that it is fundamentally dialogical and open-ended, his hermeneutical analysis of universality and particularity has led to a number of misunderstandings and misplaced criticisms.

1 Gadamer 2003, p. 306.
2 Gadamer 2003, p. 312.
3 Gadamer 2003, p. 312.

https://doi.org/10.1515/9783110551563-011

Gadamer's hermeneutics is often characterized as hegemonic and often criticized for being unable to account for genuine alterity. Supposedly, the sublation of the Other, brought about in the fusion of the horizons, does not preserve but rather eradicates otherness; supposedly, in the context of contemporary social concerns the hermeneutic model is incapable of hearing what the Other has to say. Thus Robert Bernasconi criticizes Gadamer for not being able to offer an account of a common experience, which can be summarized in the following phrase: "You cannot be yourself and understand me."[4] This is what women say to men, the poor to the rich, the victim to the oppressor, the target of racism to the racist. According to Bernasconi, this is the sociopolitical framework that Gadamer prefers to ignore and these are the obstacles that cannot be overcome by Gadamer's hermeneutical strategy.

Yet on what basis is one to claim that the often-encountered indifference to the Other (and to the self) signifies a *conceptual impossibility* of genuine contact between ipseity and alterity? Who is this "I myself," devoid of any *possible* change and any genuine contact with Others? Who is this "you yourself," who *by definition* can never understand me? Are the implied conceptions of selfhood and otherness in this critique not, as Gadamer would argue, a kind of Robinson Crusoe dream?[5] To distance the other from the self by abolishing any contact between them—does this path lead us to an accurate understanding of "genuine otherness?"

These questions are meant to suggest that Gadamer's hermeneutics provides us with the resources needed to answer Bernasconi's critique. Nonetheless, I would argue that this critique is indicative of the general context within which one should test the ethical and political relevance of Gadamer's hermeneutics. In what follows, I will do so by focusing on Gadamer's concept of *Horizontverschmelzung*. "You cannot be yourself and understand me"—where else is one to experience the full significance of Gadamer's hermeneutics if not in such a framework? One cannot rest content with the common sociopolitical experiences of not being heard, of ignoring the other's claim, or of overpowering the Other under the pretext of openness. Gadamer's unveiling of the presuppositions that underlie the incommensurabilist stance and the normative force of his emphasis on openness in our contact with the Other gain their full force in these and similar experiences. Hence the necessity to discover the self in the Other and the Other in the self, which the fusion of the horizons aims to achieve.

4 Bernasconi 1995.

5 See Gadamer 2003, p. 304.

Gadamer's fusion of the horizons is expressive of a distinct stance one can take on the relation between ipseity and alterity. Yet admittedly, the fact that this fusion is described in such an ambiguous way—as the fusion of horizons *supposedly existing by themselves*—has made it easy to miss the crucial features of his hermeneutical standpoint. Why does Gadamer simultaneously speak of the oneness and the multiplicity of horizons? Why is he reluctant to tell us whether there are many horizons or just one? And if the latter is the case, are we still justified in calling his hermeneutics dialogical?

With these questions in mind, I want to turn to Richard Kearney's critique of Gadamer, which he articulates while defending the specificity of Paul Ricoeur's hermeneutics. Making *Truth and Method* vulnerable to those dangers that Kearney sees present in Gadamer's discussion of the fusion of the horizons will constitute the detour and the confrontation through which I will then aim to unfold the relevance and the limits of the oneness of the hermeneutical horizon(s).

I

In "Between Oneself and Another: Paul Ricoeur's Diacritical Hermeneutics," Richard Kearney presents the relation between self and Other as the central hermeneutical problem. According to Kearney, there are three paradigmatic ways for the relation between ipseity and alterity to be dealt with and therefore hermeneutics itself can be divided into three types: *romantic*, *radical*, and *diacritical*. Schleiermacher, Dilthey, and, surprisingly, Gadamer are said to be the main representatives of romantic hermeneutics, characteristic of which is the attempt to unite the self and the Other in the event of appropriation. At the other extreme, Caputo's radical hermeneutics rejects the model of appropriation and addresses the unmediated and "sublime" nature of alterity, invoking an irreducible dissymmetry between self and Other. In between these positions lies diacritical hermeneutics, inspired by Ricoeur, which "obviates both the congenial communion of fused horizons and the apocalyptic rupture of non-communion,"[6] while exploring the inter-communion of distinct but not incomparable selves.

Within this typology, one encounters the specificity of Ricoeur's hermeneutics in how it deals with what Kearney terms "today's challenge"—that of acknowledging a difference between self and Other while avoiding a schismatic

6 Kearney 2003, p. 155.

split. In contrast to the mainstream metaphysical tradition which largely ignores the question of the Other, and in contrast to some postmodern thinkers who externalize alterity to the point that there can be no communication between self and Other, the central task of Ricoeur's hermeneutics is that of "building paths between the worlds of *autos* and *heteros*," of "charting a course between the extremes of tautology and heterology."[7] Diacritical hermeneutics discovers the Other in the self and the self in the Other; it supplements the critique of the self with the critique of the Other; its task is that of making the foreign more familiar and the familiar more foreign. It distinguishes between different kinds of selves and Others ("Not all 'selves' are evil and not all 'others' are angelic,"[8]) while refusing to accept the excesses of mainstream metaphysics and postmodernism. Thus, Ricoeur's works are not representative of "modern" philosophical reflection, which has been centered on the subject; nor does it share the "postmodern" fixation on otherness. Ricoeur's hermeneutics offers new ways of interpreting oneself in terms of otherness.

Let us attend to Kearney's critique of Gadamer in more detail. Gadamer is grouped together with Schleiermacher and Dilthey because the purpose of all three is "to unite the consciousness of one subject with that of the other,"[9] Kearney labels this approach "hermeneutics of appropriation" while emphasizing the meaning of the German *Aneignung*—"becoming one with." Since becoming one presupposes a more original difference, Kearney is critical of this style of hermeneutics because, supposedly, it eliminates what it presupposes—the otherness of the Other—as it recovers "some lost original consciousness by way of rendering what is past contemporaneous with the present."[10] This is how Kearney interprets Gadamer's reconciliation of our own understanding and that of strangers in the fusion of the horizons.

My analysis of this critique will follow three steps. First, I will show how distant Kearney's dissatisfaction with Gadamer is from Gadamer's hermeneutics. Although I believe this distance is apparent to anyone who has listened to what Gadamer actually had to say, the true challenge of Kearney's critique lies in the fact that it finds textual support. Thus, secondly, I will bring to light the textual support that underlies Kearney's position and in this way point to certain ambiguities present in *Truth and Method*. Finally, I will confront these ambiguities directly, demonstrating how one is to overcome them.

---

7 Kearney 2003, p. 150.
8 Kearney 2003, p. 150.
9 Kearney 2003, pp. 154–155.
10 Kearney 2003, p. 155.

II

Neither Kearney's claim that Gadamer is a proponent of romantic hermeneutics, nor the way he presents Gadamer's position as a "hermeneutics of appropriation" fits Gadamer's texts. The claim that Gadamer's hermeneutics is a romantic project ignores two central features which distance Gadamer from both Schleiermacher and Dilthey. Gadamer's hermeneutics springs from the rejection of two distinctive elements of romantic hermeneutics—of *psychologism* and *objectivism*, which Gadamer finds present in both Schleiermacher and Dilthey. *Psychologism* can be characterized by two interrelated claims: 1) the goal of interpretation is to trace the path from the textual expression to that originary experience which can characterize the inner life of the author; 2) the meaning of the text is fixed by the intention of the author. *Objectivism* can be characterized by two interrelated claims as well: 1) the intention of the author provides the text with a *fixed* object which serves as a condition of possibility of interpretation's *objectivity*; 2) interpretation must follow certain rules so that it can be rigorously methodological, and therefore objective. Gadamer embraces two themes which were of central significance to both Schleiermacher and Dilthey—the universality of the hermeneutic problem and the hermeneutic circle. However, he does not accept these themes blindly, but rather offers their reinterpretation.[11] Thus even though Gadamer's rejection of psychologism and objectivism is not a single-handed denunciation of the principles and concerns of romantic hermeneutics, it nonetheless indicates a crucial distance between Gadamer and the romantics, which both challenges and contradicts Kearney's critical claims.

Kearney's description of Gadamer's hermeneutics as a "hermeneutics of appropriation" is surprising, since this accusation directly echoes Gadamer's critique of Hegel. Being fully aware that Hegel's concerns overlap with those of hermeneutics—both are concerned with the fusion of the present and history—Gadamer distances himself from Hegel when he claims that the basis of hermeneutics is not an absolute mediation of history and truth; that the fusion of the horizons is not a fusion of the whole past in the present; that understanding is not an abolition of finiteness in the infinity of knowledge. Contra Kearney, Gadamer's hermeneutics does not signify the abolition of otherness in the fusion of the horizons, for even though Gadamer acknowledges Hegel's logical superi-

11 For an elegant overview of those themes that link the 20th-century hermeneutics to the romantic hermeneutics and those elements which distance them from each other, see Westphal 2002.

ority over his critics, "the arguments of reflective philosophy cannot ultimately obscure the fact that there is some truth in the critique of speculative thought based on the standpoint of finite human consciousness."[12]

The ultimate truth of the critics of speculative thought lies in the realization that otherness is never abolished in the hermeneutic fusion of the horizons: as Gadamer provocatively tells us, we understand *only* if we understand differently. We can take this to mean that the worry about the abolition of otherness is just as significant for Gadamer as it is for Kearney. Consider in this regard Gadamer's following claims: "[there] constantly arises the danger of 'appropriating' the other person in one's own understanding and thereby failing to recognize his or her otherness."[13] "It is constantly necessary to guard against overhastily assimilating the past to our own expectations of meaning."[14] In light of these claims, Kearney's labeling of Gadamer's hermeneutics as "hermeneutics of appropriation" proves to be no less unjustified than his claim that Gadamer's hermeneutics is a romantic project.

Moreover, Kearney's typology of hermeneutic styles, by introducing a lacuna between Gadamer and Ricoeur, is hardly justified not only in light of Gadamer's, but also in light of Ricoeur's works. For instance, in his conclusion to *Interpretation Theory*, Ricoeur addresses some misconceptions of what he terms "hermeneutic appropriation," chief among which are the assertions that 1) appropriation is a return to the romanticist claim to a "congenial" coincidence with the "genius" of the author, and 2) the hermeneutic task is the understanding of the original addressee of the text. Ricoeur turns for support to Gadamer while addressing these misconceptions. He claims that Gadamer has already shown why the second misconception is flawed: "the letters of Paul are no less addressed to me than to the Romans, the Galatians, the Corinthians, and the Ephesians."[15] Ricoeur's repudiation of the first misconception is more significant in the present context:

> [A]ppropriation has nothing to do with any kind of person to person appeal. It is instead close to what Gadamer calls a fusion of horizons: the world horizon of the reader is fused with the world horizon of the writer. And the ideality of the text is the mediating link in this process of horizon fusing.[16]

12 Gadamer 2003, p. 344.
13 Gadamer 2003, p. 299n.
14 Gadamer 2003, p. 305.
15 Ricoeur 1976, p. 93.
16 Ricoeur 1976, p. 93.

Kearney's critique of Gadamer fails to account for the close relation between Ricoeur's and Gadamer's hermeneutics. Even more importantly, this critique violates *Truth and Method* so strongly that it is hard to see the reasons that motivate Kearney's accusations. Yet only if these reasons are reconstructed can Kearney's text constitute a true challenge and provoke one to revisit some tensions in *Truth and Method.*

III

Kearney's position seems less surprising in the face of the following passage from *Truth and Method:*

> Historical consciousness is aware of its own otherness and hence foregrounds the horizon of the past from its own. On the other hand, it is itself ... only something superimposed upon continuing tradition, and hence it immediately recombines with what it has foregrounded itself from in order to become one with itself again in the unity of the historical horizon that it thus acquires.[17]

This account, or, as will soon become apparent, this *feature* of the fusions of the horizons strengthens Kearney's accusations. If the otherness of the Other is projected only so that it could be immediately reconquered in the unity of the horizon, are we dealing with genuine alterity? As Gadamer goes on to tell us, "in the process of understanding, a real fusing of horizons occurs—which means that as the historical horizon is projected, it is simulaneously superseded."[18] If otherness appears only so that it could be superseded, i.e., *abolished*, and if *Truth and Method* invites us to acknowledge that this abolition should be *immediate*, is one justified in calling Gadamer's hermeneutics the "hermeneutics of openess?" It seems that the very moment one acquires the conditions for the appearance of otherness, Gadamer eradicates them in "the true fusion of the horizons." But if such is the case, then what at the outset seemed to be a philosophy of openness, now proves to be a hermeneutics of violence; or so Kearney's critique of Gadamer seems to suggest.

These are the implications of Kearney's critique: What at the outset appears to be a fusion of sameness and otherness, in truth is a projection of sameness; what at the outset appears to be openness to the Other, in truth is a suppression of otherness. Kearney's accusations directed at Gadamer echo in the context

17 Gadamer 2003, p. 306.
18 Gadamer 2003, p. 307.

of today's widespread and rapidly growing concern that social and political interactions only hide behind the rhetoric of openness the suppression and even abolition of otherness. Kearney's accusations, if correct, would render Gadamer's hermeneutics impotent in the context of today's social and political dangers. But do the problems that accompany the unprecedented interaction on a global scale point to the powerlessness of Gadamer's hermeneutics, or do they, on the contrary, reveal the strength of his stance?

Let us ask: What enables Gadamer to speak of overtaking the past consciousness in the present horizon of understanding,[19] of immediately recombining with otherness,[20] and of superseding the projected historical horizon?[21] The reconciliation that the fusion of the horizons brings forth presupposes the *oneness and unity of the horizon* as the possibility of the hermeneutic interaction. Although it might seem that the fusion of the horizons presupposes an original difference between them, Gadamer repeatedly insists that a non-dialectical understanding of difference does not do justice to the hermeneutic phenomenon. Gadamer writes: "When our historical consciousness transposes itself into historical horizons, this does not entail passing into alien worlds unconnected in any way with our own; instead, they together constitute the one great horizon that moves from within."[22] As he further observes, "understanding is always the fusion of the horizons supposedly existing by themselves."[23]

This is the ultimate provocation that Kearney offers: we should not take the façade of openness to the Other at its face value but find a way to account for the *oneness* of the horizon. Kearney's challenge boils down to two interrelated questions: 1) Why does Gadamer speak of the oneness of the horizon? 2) How is this oneness to be understood in the context of *Truth and Method?*

IV

Two interrelated qualifications render Kearney's critique questionable: 1) Gadamer's conception of the oneness of the horizons lacks positive determinations; 2) Gadamer's account of oneness is *dialectical*. If nothing linked the horizons of ipseity and alterity, understanding would involve an empathetic transposition

19 Gadamer 2003, p. 307.
20 Gadamer 2003, p. 306.
21 Gadamer 2003, p. 307.
22 Gadamer 2003, p. 304.
23 Gadamer 2003, p. 306.

from the self to the Other. Moreover, a suspension of all presuppositions and an abandonment of all truths and beliefs would be a necessary requirement for understanding otherness. This, however, is exactly the position which Gadamer relentlessly criticizes. As he repeatedly tells us, "transposing ourselves consists neither in the empathy of one individual for another nor in subordinating another person to our own standards; rather, it always involves rising to a higher universality that overcomes not only our own particularity but also that of the other."[24] *There are no closed horizons*—such is the minimal requirement of Gadamer's account of understanding. The oneness of the horizon is the expression Gadamer chooses to make this requirement explicit. Therefore, Gadamer's account of the oneness of the horizon essentially lacks positive determinations, since all it says about the relation between self and Other is that they are never so distant that they cannot enter into dialogue with each other. In short, for Gadamer, no self and no Other is in principle beyond dialogue, beyond understanding.

This negative qualification is closely linked to Gadamer's *dialectical* account of the oneness of the horizon. Gadamer describes understanding as the fusion of horizons which *supposedly exist by themselves.* He is reluctant to tell us whether there is one or many horizons, arguably, because one of the leading ambitions of his hermeneutics to overcome what he sees as a false dichotomy between oneness and multiplicity. Gadamer's interpretation of the fusion of the horizons is dialectical through and through, for it aims to show that the one is ultimately multiple, and that multiplicity is ultimately one. This is the Hegelian background of Gadamer's fusions of the horizons.

Hegel's dialectical account of identity and difference mocks the proponents of pure identity: if someone promises to teach me what God is, he wrote, but only informs me that God is God, my expectations are cheated. For Hegel, the overcoming of abstract identity was, arguably, more significant than the abandonment of pure difference, or so the critics of modernity's obsession with the subject persistently suggest. We seem to suffer from the other extreme: our age is obsessed with schismatically separating the Other from the self, with, as Kearney has it, externalizing "the category of alterity to the point that any contact with the self smacks of betrayal or contamination."[25]

Following in the footsteps of Hegel, Gadamer's hermeneutics reveals the fictionality of the incommensurable difference:

24 Gadamer 2003, p. 305.
25 Kearney 2003, p. 149.

> Are there such things as closed horizons? ... Or is this a romantic refraction, a kind of Robinson Crusoe dream of historical enlightenment, the fiction of an unattainable island, as artificial as Crusoe himself? Just as the individual is never simply an individual because he is always in understanding with others, so too the closed horizon that is supposed to enclose a culture is an abstraction.[26]

A dialectic of oneness and difference is one of the central hermeneutic preconditions, since it reveals the meaning of the hermeneutic "belonging," of the commonality of the enabling prejudices. Hermeneutics starts from the presupposition that a bond links the interpreter to the interpreted. However, this presupposition does not signify the abolition of the Other, but quite on the contrary, it is the condition of possibility that underlies the appearance of otherness. Thus hermeneutics "is based on a polarity of familiarity and strangeness ... [The tension] is in the play between the traditionary text's strangeness and familiarity to us ... *The true locus of hermeneutics is this in-between.*"[27]

Such, then, is the meaning of Gadamer's negative and dialectical account of the oneness of the horizon: No horizons are incommensurable, since dialogue, in principle, has no limitations. Although each and every dialogue runs the risk of not reaching out to the Other and beyond the rhetoric of openness merely subordinating otherness to the interpreter's claim, it is always possible to recognize these limitations. Gadamer's open-ended dialectic is concerned with making these limitations explicit, as his critique of Hegel shows. Moreover, the very fact that, while being critical of Hegel, Gadamer does not share the anti-Hegelian sentiment and does not distance otherness from the self to the point that there is no communication between them, indicates not the weakness, but the strength of his hermeneutics in the context of the present social concerns. For if Kearney is right in characterizing today's challenge as that of respecting the specificity of the Other while not schismatically dividing the Other from the self, Gadamer's hermeneutics, as the next section will show, offers the necessary resources to address this challenge.

V

Gadamer's hermeneutics overcomes the shortcomings of the incommensurabilist stance, seen often as the only tolerant and respectful attitude to the Other. By not acknowledging any bond between different cultures, languages, or subjectiv-

---

26 Gadamer 2003, p. 304.
27 Gadamer 2003, p. 295.

ities, no matter how nameless this bond might be, this stance, Gadamer's hermeneutics suggests, hides behind the surface an *indifference* to otherness. Only if there is a bond between the Other and the self, only if the fusion of the horizons presupposes a certain unity, can the Other make a claim upon me. The oneness of the horizon does not mean a suppression of otherness, but rather points to the fact that, as James Risser has it, "Gadamer's hermeneutics is concerned with the opening of shared life in which one is able to hear the voice of the other."[28] The very fact that Gadamer is most cautious in not providing this bond with much content is revealing: It indicates his concern that this link should remain only a condition for hearing the Other and does not overpower and ignore her uniqueness. Thus in "The Limitation of the Expert" Gadamer writes: "What we truly have in common and what unites us remains ... without a voice. Probably we are harvesting the fruits of a long training in the perception of differences and in the sensibility demanded by it" (Gadamer 1982, p. 192). In the face of today's social and political challenges, it is simply not enough to claim that the only way to retain otherness is to grant it such a distant status that any contact with the self would smack of betrayal. As Gary B. Madison insightfully remarks, here one encounters one of the greatest merits of Gadamer's hermeneutics:

The overriding question today is, as Bassam Tibi formulates it:

> [H]ow can we combine the need for common rules and norms in international society with the reality of enormous cultural diversity?" One thing that is clear is that any viable global ethic capable of providing an alternative to a global clash of civilizations must provide for "common rules and norms," i.e., values that are themselves global. Nothing like this is to be expected from the cultural incommensurabilists.[29]

Tibi's concern is so closely linked to what Kearney calls "today's challenge" that they both can be seen as two formulations of the same problem. Gadamer's hermeneutics answers them both by showing that the relation between the universal and the particular is not that of logical subsumption, but rather of co-determination. For Gadamer, the relation between universality and particularity is not vertical or hierarchical, but rather lateral and circular. For this very reason, his universalism is nonessentialist and nonhegemonic, yet of a normative kind, allowing for the possibility of a philosophical critique of existing practices.[30] The oneness of the horizon renders this circularity non-technical

---

28 Risser 2002, p. 167.

29 Madison 2002, p. 139.

30 In this regard, see Madison 2002, p. 140.

and therefore non-violent, for it reveals that the universal is not to be imposed on the particular, but rather that the particular finds its way to the universal on its own. But even this language is misleading, for it carries the connotation of a universal which is, supposedly, "set in stone," of the universal "in-itself," as if all that remained for us to do was to apply it mechanically to different cultures and individuals. Gadamer's appropriation and reinterpretation of *phronesis* shows that principles can be adopted only in a context-sensitive way, that, as Madison has it, there is "no universal formula for the implementation of universal values."[31] Adoption of universal principles and laws always involves a creative adaptation of them. The hermeneutical co-determination of the universal and the particular means that, as the particular approaches the universal, it is both changed by and itself changes the universal. Precisely therefore it does not make sense to ask whether the self overpowers the Other or whether the Other overpowers the self in the fusion of the horizons, for a crucial aim of Gadamer's hermeneutics is to unfold a certain oneness, a certain medium, or "the shared life," within which both the self and the Other constantly gain new meanings and determinations. Here we find an implied respect for the particularity of the Other which is for Gadamer of a potentially decisive nature:

> We may perhaps survive as a humanity if we would be able to learn that we may not simply exploit our means of power and effective possibilities, but must learn to ... respect the other as an other, whether it is nature or the grown cultures of peoples and nations, and if we would be able to learn to experience the other and the others, as the other of our self, in order to participate with one another.[32]

All of this means that, for Gadamer, the oneness is both a *presupposition* and an *achievement*, that Gadamer uses the term both *descriptively*, to reveal the conditions of understanding, and that the term carries a *normative force*, since it is a task and a goal to be achieved in the face of social and political challenges. In both cases, oneness is accompanied by otherness. In case of oneness as a presupposition of understanding, otherness manifests itself as the condition of interpretation's objectivity: without otherness, there can be no interpretation. Yet oneness is also an achievement: the task of interpretation is, while being guided by the text, to reveal its continuing significance, to bring it out of the past into the living present. This is achieved not by overcoming the temporal distance that separates us from the original text, but by revealing distance as a positive and a

---

31 Madison 2002, p. 141.
32 Gadamer 1977, p. 41.

productive condition which enables understanding.[33] We thereby stumble across one of the central reasons why to understand is always to understand differently: temporal distance does not separate us from the meaning of the text, but rather links us to it in a genuine way, thereby revealing the significance of the hermeneutical belonging.

Here one encounters an answer to Kearney's claim that Gadamer's fusion of horizons abolishes otherness in the event of appropriation. Gadamer retains a difference between understanding and otherness, be it that of a text, a culture, or an individual. As is most clearly manifested in Gadamer's account of play, each and every work transcends itself as an original creation in the event of interpretation: a piece of music becomes actual when being performed, just as a novel becomes actual in the activity of reading. The meaning of a text or a text-analog cannot be reduced either to the intentions of the author, or to any particular interpretation of it. But if no single interpretation has the means of exhausting the interpreted object, Kearney's critique loses its basis. Since the hermeneutical reconquering, or as Gadamer sometimes says, of reconstruction, is not to be understood in a psychological sense, one cannot claim that the task of Gadamer's hermeneutics is to abolish otherness in the event of understanding. Such a claim would suppress what a critique has no right to ignore, namely, a clear separation not only between the individuality of the text's author and the text's meaning, but also between the interpretation's particularity and the overflow of the text's capabilities. Hence, the normative character of the oneness of the horizon shows why Kearney's critique of Gadamer is an instance of misplaced criticism. Just as otherness is not exhausted in appropriation, so the act of appropriation should not be understood as the subjection of the Other to the self, but as the rising of the Other and the self to a higher universality.

VI

The significance of the oneness of the horizon manifests itself in the context of Gadamer's reinterpretation of understanding as a *hermeneutic circle* and in the context of his reinterpretation of the *history of the effect*. According to Gadamer, the advantage of Heideggerian hermeneutics over that of Schleiermacher's lies in the abandonment of formalism and psychologism, which are the characteristic features of the romantic interpretation of the hermeneutic circle.

---

33 Gadamer 2003, p. 297.

The circle is neither subjective nor objective, because the anticipation of meaning which governs the understanding of a text "is not an act of subjectivity, but proceeds from the commonality that binds us to the tradition."[34] Since Gadamer identifies the tradition itself (rather than closed subjectivities) as the ultimate origin of the anticipation of meaning, he conceives of the hermeneutical circle not psychologically, but ontologically. Precisely because our anticipatory prejudices have an ontological status, understanding possesses an ontological structure. Thus in this context, the oneness of the horizon—that is, commonality, anticipation and tradition—plays the role of the necessary condition which justifies the ontological account of the hermeneutic circle. But how is this ontology of understanding to be understood? How is one to account for the anticipation as the bond with the tradition? Can one speak of the "ideology" of fundamental questioning into which we inevitably fall? I shall return to these questions in the following section.

In a similar way, the oneness of the horizon is implied in Gadamer's description of the history of effect. "In all understanding, whether we are expressly aware of it or not, the efficacy of history is at work."[35] The effect of history does not depend on being recognized, nor is it a supplement to historical inquiry; it is, rather, an intrinsic element in all understanding. While it is incumbent upon us to become aware of it, since on this awareness our knowledge of the subject matter and of ourselves largely rests, the explicit awareness of the history of effect is "as hybrid a statement as when Hegel speaks of absolute knowledge."[36] The very fact that we can never explicitly know the full effect of history demonstrates the hermeneutical significance of the oneness of the horizon. Being an element of understanding, it is effectual already "in finding the right questions to ask."[37] The hermeneutic circle and the history of effect, as far as they are explications of the oneness of the horizon, are so closely tied together, that it would be no exaggeration to suggest that they are two formulations of the same phenomenon. While the account of the hermeneutic circle unfolds the subjective side of the oneness of the horizon (that of our enabling prejudices), the history of effect reveals the objective side of the same phenomenon (that of history and tradition). Moreover, while unfolding the significance of the oneness of the horizon, both themes lead directly to Gadamer's analysis of the question/answer dialectic.[38] Their true significance, Gadamer

34 Gadamer 2003, p. 293.
35 Gadamer 2003, p. 301.
36 Gadamer 2003, p. 301.
37 Gadamer 2003, p. 301.
38 See Gadamer 2003, pp. 369–381.

tells us, is to be witnessed in *finding the right questions to ask.* But if this is the ultimate meaning of the oneness of the horizon, is one justified in speaking of a merely negative role that this oneness plays? What if the problematic character of Gadamer's hermeneutics lies not only in overlooking the Other, as Kearney suggests, but also in overlooking the self? After all, does the equation of the interpreter's question and the question of the tradition not lead one to the hermeneutics of the Fundamental Questions thereby implying the disappearance of the subject?

VII

One might argue that Gadamer's hermeneutics downplays the significance of the self in the process of understanding. One could ground such a view in the insight that Gadamer's hermeneutics reduces the individuality of the interpreter to the generality of the tradition, thereby abolishing the originality of the self. On this basis, one might further object that Gadamer ignores the uniqueness and the freedom of the self, that it transforms the self into a tool in the hands of some anonymous force, which determines from the outset the questions asked by the interpreter. Following such a line of reasoning, one might wonder if, contra Kearney, one shouldn't say that the weakness of Gadamer's hermeneutics lies not in the subjection of the Other to the self, but in the subjection of both the Other and the self to the impulses of Fundamental Questioning. Indeed, why not say that Gadamer's "hermeneutics of belonging" marks the abandonment of the self and the Other to the presumed oneness of the horizon?

In light of this set of concerns, one should stress that Gadamer's hermeneutics is just as opposed to "permanent problems" in philosophy as it is to the "history of problems."[39] If one is to speak meaningfully of fundamental questions in the context of Gadamer's hermeneutics, one must acknowledge that these "fundamental questions" must be each time asked differently. Gadamer's question/answer logic does not terminate in a list of supposedly "fundamental questions," which underlie a multiplicity of texts; quite on the contrary, this logic culminates in the realization that one and the same text can provoke in the interpreter an irreducible multiplicity of questions. The question/answer logic thereby provides an account of the hermeneutical fact that one and the

39 "History of problems would truly be history only if it acknowledged that the identity of the problem is an empty abstraction and permitted itself to be transformed into questioning," Gadamer 2003, p. 375.

same text cannot be reduced to a collection of specific statements, that a text has the potential to reveal a different face in different times and places. The question/answer logic develops the oneness of the horizon not in the direction of the abolishment of the difference between the past and the present, but rather in the direction of the acknowledgment that the past still speaks to us and that it speaks differently from how it spoke before.

One can therefore say that the oneness of horizon(s) is not a recovery of some lost original consciousness by rendering the past contemporaneous with the present. Having taken the detour of question and answer, the fusion of horizons proves to be a notion that explodes the subject/object dichotomy by rendering the question "who thinks whom" meaningless. The interpreter alters the text while the text alters the interpreter, and it does not take one far to ask who thinks whom, for each is simultaneously in play. The fusion of horizons thereby implicates an irreducible confusion of voices in which the interpreter and the text are inextricably tied to each other in a way that forbids one from defining either in separation from the other.

One should not take this to mean that the fusion of horizons abolishes the individuality of the self, although it does mean that the self in Gadamer is neither a primary principle, nor an unalterable presence. The indissoluble bond between the interpreter and the text is rooted neither in the self nor in the Other. Rather, we always already find ourselves within the bond that ties our own selves to Others and our identities are continuously enriched by this bond. As Gadamer has it, the text addresses questions to the interpreter and only in response to these questions can the interpreter begin to question the text. One can take this to mean that the subject is not the ultimate origin of meaning, but that s/he responds to the proposals of meaning, which are rooted in the oneness of the hermeneutical horizon(s). This oneness both liberates the text from its alienation by bringing it into the living present and constitutes the identity of the interpreter, for it is by approaching the text, by letting oneself be questioned by it, that the interpreter's prejudices are tested.[40]

Such, then, is the first essential determination of the oneness of the horizons: this oneness is a necessary presupposition of interpretation. In this sense, it does not merely secure the grounds of interpretation's objectivity; it is not merely a word which, by overcoming the shortcomings of psychologism, accounts for the referential character of interpretation. Being always already

40 "All understanding is ultimately self understanding," Gadamer 2003, p. 260; "It is true in every case that a person who understands, understands himself, projecting himself upon his possibilities," p. 260.

there, the oneness of the horizon is that which renders the text plurivocal: What the text says is revealed in the interplay of questions and answers that unfold in the dialogue between the interpreter and the text. While the bond that links the interpreter to the interpreted is to be acknowledged, at the same time it is to remain nameless, for by linking the text to anyone who "complies with the text's injunction," the oneness of the horizon extends in a plurality of directions, thereby remaining indeterminate and open-ended. The oneness of the horizon thereby proves to be essentially dialectical: the meaning of the *oneness* lies in the elucidation and encouragement of a *plurality* of fusions of horizons.

Within such a framework, interpretation cannot be approached as something added to the original text, as if the latter were a set of fixed statements, but rather manifests itself in uncovering the implicit meaning of the text. This, however, does not exhaust the presuppositional character of the oneness of the horizon. Just as the oneness of the horizon reveals the shortcomings of the incommensurabilist stance by showing the abstractness of non-dialogical difference, so likewise the question/answer logic reveals the abstractness of the non-dialogical self. The self-understanding of the interpreter is constituted within the oneness of the horizon; the self is a partner in dialogue and is invited to respond to the proposals of meaning, which derive from the text. This means that the self in Gadamer's hermeneutics does not play merely a passive role; rather, the self manifests itself as the one who actively responds to the Other, as the one who constitutes sense in virtue of an active response.

We thereby stumble against the second essential determination of the oneness of the horizon: this oneness is not merely a presupposition but also an achievement. The meaning of the text and the self-understanding of the interpreter are constituted in the interplay of questions and answers provided both by the reader and the text. What we face here is a genuinely dialogical encounter between the interpreter and the text. This means that it is not enough merely to hear the questions of the text. It is necessary to respond in a way that constitutes the text's meaning, thereby achieving a more thorough understanding of oneself.

The question/answer logic marks the culmination of Gadamer's account of the oneness of the horizon. This oneness, no matter how indeterminate it might be, proves to be the "conversation that we ourselves are."[41] The oneness of the horizon reveals the correlative nature of ipseity and alterity: Gadamer's account of the self and the Other goes hand-in-hand with his account of the Other in the self and the self in the Other. Just as there is no text without inter-

---

41 Gadamer 2003, p. 378.

pretation, so also there is no interpretation without the text. By extension, just as there is no self without the Other, so also there is no Other without the self. Moreover, the very fact that Gadamer's dialectic is open-ended—that human understanding is essentially finite—means that there are new Others to be discovered and new forms of self-understanding to be reached. One could thus say that the open-ended oneness of the horizon liberates both the Other and the self from their anonymity by re-turning them to the infinity of dialogue.

Acknowledgements

This essay is a revised version of my "On the Oneness of the Hermeneutical Horizon(s)," which was published, along with Gary B. Madison's critical response to it, in the inaugural issue of *PhaenEx: Journal of Existential and Phenomenological Theory and Cult*ure 1(1) (2006): 231–256.

References

Bernasconi, Robert (1995) "'You Do Not Know What I Am Talking About': Alterity and the Hermeneutical Ideal." In: Lawrence Schmidt (ed.), *The Specter of Relativism: Truth, Dialogue, and Phronesis in Philosophical Hermeneutics*. Evanston, IL: Northwestern University Press, pp. 178–195.

Gadamer, Hans-Georg (1977) "Reflections on My Philosophical Journey." In: Lewis Hahn (ed.), *The Philosophy of Hans-Georg Gadamer. The Library of Living Philosophers*. Chicago: Open Court, pp. 3–64.

Gadamer, Hans-Georg (2003) *Truth and Method*, tr. Joel Weinsheimer and Donald G. Marshall. New York: Continuum.

Kearney, Richard (2003) "Between Oneself and Another: Paul Ricoeur's Diacritical Hermeneutics." In: Andrzej Wiercinski (ed.), *Between Suspicion and Sympathy: Paul Ricoeur's Unstable Equilibrium*. Toronto: The Hermeneutic Press, pp. 149–161.

Madison, Gary B. (2002) "Gadamer's Legacy." *Symposium* 6(2): 135–147.

Ricoeur, Paul (1976) *Interpretation Theory: Discourse and the Surplus of Meaning*. Fort Worth: Texas Christian University Press.

Risser, James (2002) "Shared Life." *Symposium* 6(2): 167–180.

Westphal, Merold (2002) "Hermeneutical Finitude from Schleiermacher to Derrida." In: *Between the Human and the Divine: Philosophical and Theological Hermeneutics*. Toronto: The Hermeneutic Press, pp. 50–66.

III Practice and Application: Hermeneutics, Social Theory

Duška Franeta

Gadamer's Hermeneutics as Practical Philosophy

Abstract: The aim of the first part of this chapter is to show the network of the most relevant concepts of philosophic hermeneutics and to present their vital connection to Aristotle's idea of practical philosophy. The author elaborates the fundamental notions of prejudice, hermeneutical circle, tradition, situation, effective-historical consciousness, fusion of horizons and application. The explanation of the mentioned concepts intends to legitimize Gadamer's central thesis that our understanding is never mere subject-oriented behavior. On the contrary, it is always historically limited. In this context, the notion of prejudice loses its negative connotation and represents not only the link with our tradition, but also the original source of all our judgments. The second part of the paper deals with the universal requirement of the method of natural sciences by contrast with experiences of art and the humanities (*Geisteswissenschaften*). One cannot recognize the meaning of humanities once they are excluded from the horizon of praxis. Moreover, humanities are moral sciences and the concept of progress, so common in the terminology of natural sciences, cannot be applied to them. Their very purpose is human self-understanding.

I Hermeneutics and Praxis

One of the first lessons in philosophy is certainly Aristotle's division of philosophy into theoretical [*theoria*], practical [*praxis*] and poetical [*poiesis*]. We will examine differences between the first and the second one: theoretical philosophy that includes mathematics, physics and the first philosophy (metaphysics) is occupied with eternal issues, while practical philosophy (ethics, politics, economy) is occupied with changeable, temporal issues that 'could be and could not be.' The difference is clear: what depends on man gets his temporal nature. In the field of practical philosophy, there are no universals given in advance that could be cognized and afterwards in an unchanged form utilized: the field of *praxis* depends on concrete situation. That is a logical consequence of Aristotle's comprehension of the mistake that Socrates made in his intellectual ethics—Socrates completely omits concepts of *pathos* and *ethos*, which leads him into identification of virtue and knowledge. Only in an ideal, eternal, divine world could knowledge and virtue be identified so that there would not exist a mere sign of

https://doi.org/10.1515/9783110551563-012

possibility for the foundation of human action and the field of praxis. Practical philosophy would have been lost there and fully subjected to theoretical philosophy. The purpose of practical philosophy is not comprehension of the thing-in-itself, but learning how to relate to things, as it is in Aristotle's ethics—ethics does not investigate virtue in order to know what it is, but to know how one could acquire it. Cognition is here subjected to praxis, since it is impossible without it.

Aristotle divides virtues into virtues of character and intellectual virtues, and the latter into the ones related to cognition and others related to judgment. While the first are concerned with principles that are eternal and theoretical, the second relate to the possible aspects of this changeable world. There are two of the latter virtues: *techne* and *phronesis* (practical reason). *Techne* corresponds to the poetical field (rhetoric, poetics, dialectics), since it refers to things that do not have an inner purpose, but their purpose is in produced works of art. On the other hand, *phronesis* is a medium that helps us to get our bearing in the world of *praxis:* it is concerned with action that has an immanent purpose, that is to say, whose purpose is in the proper action. There are no universal principles at disposal in this field, rather one should behave in a particular situation according to the general rules. So, the illogical and temporary character of human soul (is there any other?, Gadamer would probably remark) is not omitted, as in Socrates' theory. The aim of *phronesis* is to find the appropriate measure for things. Practical knowledge cannot be developed as methodical science. It should not have the eternal ideas as a model, it should rather be presented in an outline (*typos*), due to the specific character of its 'subject.'

In the field of *praxis* the purpose is immanent and the aim cannot be separated from the means. Each part gives sense to the whole and the other way round. In other words: if a purpose is proper, i.e., good action, the means by which we acquire it cannot be bad.

According to Gadamer, hermeneutic philosophy is the heir of an older tradition of practical philosophy. Its main question, how is understanding possible, is completely situated within the horizon of *praxis*. Starting from Heidegger's definition of being as time, and understanding as the mode of being or *Dasein*, Gadamer comes to an insight that the historical character of every understanding is a principle of hermeneutics. He seeks something that is common to every understanding, and it is its definitive and historical character. Understanding is always temporary and, therefore, belongs to the field of praxis. This claim is outlined by a detailed explanation of a whole network of notions, which Gadamer uses to define hermeneutical experience.

I.1 Hermeneutics as Practical Philosophy: Basic Concepts—Hermeneutical Circle and Prejudices

'The whole should be understood from the part, and the part should be understood out of the whole,' this is an old hermeneutical principle originating from the practice of interpretation of ancient texts. People noticed long ago that certain concepts or elements of a text cannot be examined independently from the meaning of the whole text, for their meaning changes according to its unfolding. Dependence is mutual: individual text elements change their meaning following the whole, just like the whole changes with its parts. Thus, interpretation is characterized by a certain inner unfolding of meaning. In Heidegger's writings, hermeneutical circle has an ontological status. He emphasizes that this circle must not be interpreted as logical fallacy *circulus vitiosus*, and that it represents the basic structure of cognition in general. Hermeneutical circle, unlike the scientific method, does not require absolutely and once forever defined and limited concepts—quite the contrary, the scientific definition alone that seeks strict, fixed notions, leads, generally, to *circulus vitiosus* or axioms that cannot be defined. On the other hand, regarding the hermeneutical principle of the meaning mediation between the whole and its part, hermeneutical circle is ontologically positive. The hermeneutical circle, contrary to formal logic, allows a flow of time and a flux of meaning. It does not fix concepts eternally, but like practical philosophy, it develops them only in outline. They always remain elastic enough, so that their contents can support a certain change. Every understanding moves in outlines, since every understanding is finite and already in time. The claim concerning limits and temporal character of understanding implies that there is no 'zero understanding,' which does not mean that there is no understanding at all, or that every understanding is incorrect. Therefore, the possibility of changes in understanding does not mean value neutrality, but the awareness of the limits of our preconceptions. The concept of preconceptions does not imply personal limitations, character or biased approach or what Francis Bacon named *idolae* of the cave. Preconceptions are called prejudices [*das Vorurteil*] by Gadamer and by using them he tries to explain the structure and the process of understanding.

An illustrative example of hermeneutical circle is the study of the history of philosophy. Every time we try to identify a certain standpoint as philosophic, we have already approached it with a more or less formed opinion what philosophy actually is. By adopting the meaning of the concept of philosophy characteristic of that standpoint, our original general concept moves and changes. Yet, our original concept determines what can be considered a concept of philosophy at all. So, the whole and the part mutually and productively determine each other. Contrary to the meaninglessness of *circulus vitiousus*, the openness and productivity of hermeneutical circle are transparent. Hermeneutical circle is paradigmatic for any understanding and we can enter it only by virtue of our prejudices. Prejudices represent the original structure of all our understandings that is always mediated by tradition. Considering the fact that understanding is constantly dependent on tradition by means of always present prejudices, Gadamer adds that understanding is never a mere subjective act.

The unfolding of understanding is situated within a circle—there is no Archimedean point outside of it. Thomas Kuhn, a scientist and the author of the famous book *Structure of Scientific Revolution*,[1] concerned with the history of science comes across the concept of hermeneutical circle, and once, trying to explain it to his students, says:

> When reading the works of an important thinker, look first for the apparent absurdities in the text and ask yourself how a sensible person could have written them. When you find an answer, I continue, when those passages make sense, then you may find that more central passages, the once you previously thought you had understood, have changed their meaning. (Kuhn 1977, p. xii)

I.2 Definition of Prejudices

In his analysis of prejudices, Gadamer starts from the structure of German word: *das Vorurteil* (pre-judice). Prejudice is a soil where our judgment is grown, i.e., judgment made before the final examination of all moments that determine a thing.[2] However, Gadamer tends to dismiss the negative connotation that haunts this notion since the Enlightenment movement. By investigating the relation to prejudices in this age, he tries to release them from the footprints of ideology.

Discrediting of prejudices is a necessary consequence of the thought that tries to make a complete break-up with tradition. That attempt is present in the Enlightenment assault on three concepts: tradition, prejudice and authority.

The story of breaking up with the Middle Ages style of thought is a commonplace today: the attempt of changing hundreds of years of long dogmatism of the church with a brand new start is symbolized by, at least in the field of philosophy, Bacon and Descartes. The absolute doubt of René Descartes is exemplary for this break-up. Descartes considers our thoughts revolutionary enough for they alone can free us from all our limits. The pure method of mathematics should

1 Kuhn, (1970).

2 Gadamer, 2004, p. 273.

be the basis of this assignment. Francis Bacon introduces his famous critique of *idolae*. *Idolae* are deceitful pictures—concepts, solidly grounded in human reason, which disenable us from approaching truth. Bacon classifies them so that the people can recognize and eradicate them.

There are four types of *idolae:*

1. *Idolae* of the tribe—that originate from human nature and relate to the fact that people consider their senses and reason to be the general yardstick, and that the universe is such as we apprehend and perceive it. Our conception of the world is always human-like, and therefore, the value of science is not theoretical, but practically utilitarian: it serves to enlarge our power.
2. *Idolae* of the cave are concerned with individuals, their character, and education ... so that everyone judges by himself and not according to the real nature of things.
3. *Idolae* of the square refer to language mistakes made in communication and to the limits of our reason due to a definite number of possibilities of expression.
4. *Idolae* of the theater originate from the socio-historical nature of human life that is always grounded in a philosophy, religion, way of thought ...

'*Magna restauratio*' is necessary for all these prejudices present in human thought. A more extensive examination of this classification would offer a more complete picture of the ground of the scientific thought in general. However, regarding our intention, it is enough just to emphasize the general reform-praising attitude.

The attitude to prejudice is even more explicitly expressed in the revolutionary era of France, the Enlightenment movement. This movement points at two sorts of prejudice: the prejudice of human observation and the prejudice of hurry. The source of the latter is negligence, the source of the former is blind subordination to authority. The Enlightenment movement seeks the final break-up with tradition by means of denial of its authority and by making one and only legitimate tribunal out of the human reason [*der Verstand*]. Blinded by the faith in idealized omnipotent human reason, they examine tradition that they allegedly understand and assess more competently. They believe it is possible to free yourself from your prejudices and to become a valid judge by just one stroke of Cartesian doubt. The Cartesian method should smartly eliminate our burden of obsolete, preconceived ideas. Gadamer calls this attitude "prejudice of prejudices," and says that it closes the possibility of understanding our historical and finite nature. Prejudice of Enlightenment is the prejudice of absolute reason that does not accept the historical limits of human beings. It is connected with a belief in the infinite might of reason that represents the looked-for Archimedes point. By radical refusal of Middle Ages-characteristic dogmatism, the Enlightenment movement enters a new form of dogmatism, glorifying itself alone.

Romanticism and historicism make the same mistake. Romanticism is overturned historicism (and therefore, another misconception): there is idealized *mythos* (romanticism) on one side, and absolute *logos* (Enlightenment) on the other. The mythical world has an advantage over the 'reasonable' one, and the tendency to restore the old is inadequately exaggerated. Historical science of the 19th century is a parasite of this confrontation of *mythos* and *logos*, which by imitating Romanticism's praise of ancient times observes all epochs as relative. What all these cases have in common is a radical break-up with tradition and glorification of the omnipotent subject representing the one and only judge, either explicitly or implicitly. Gadamer asserts "... history does not belong to us; we belong to it ... The focus of subjectivity is a distorting mirror." (Gadamer 2004, p. 278) Before we gain understanding of ourselves through reflection, we understand ourselves intuitively within our family, society, state ... "The self-awareness of the individual is only a flickering in the closed circuits of historical life. That is why the prejudices of the individual, far more than his judgments, constitute the historical reality of his being." (Ibid.) Here we encounter the central thesis of Gadamer's work again: the result of historical hermeneutical circle is that understanding is never a mere subjective act.

Contrary to the attitude characteristic of the Enlightenment era, hermeneutics assesses prejudices both positively and negatively. There is no genuine negative connotation in the concept of prejudice. Gadamer wants to rehabilitate authority and tradition by showing that prejudices are universal conditions of understanding. He states that authority is by and far connected to cognition, and only then to obedience. That is the basis for the authority of teachers and experts and owing to their better acquaintance with certain fields we trust them. Yet, that belief is not blind, it is grounded on certain reasons that showed their competence in the field. Tradition is one of the forms of authority that was also established due to certain valid reasons. (Gadamer says that the privilege of ancient ethics over the ethics of the Age of Reason lies in the very recognition of tradition that enables transition from ethics to politics. The moral of the Enlightenment epoch is abstract and revolutionary. Symbolized by the opposition of Being and Ought, it disables moral consciousness to exit into reality without revolution.) Gadamer claims that preservation of tradition is a free act as well as an act of change. As revolution requires legitimacy, tradition demands a constant rational re-affirmation. Recognition of tradition does not mean an uncritical acceptance, but a refusal of abstract opposition of tradition and history, history and knowledge. "In other words, we have to recognize the element of tradition in historical research [*das Verhalten* – D. F.] and inquire into its hermeneutic productivity." (Gadamer 2004, p. 284)

The practical world, Husserl's *Lebenswelt* always places us, owing to tradition, in a network of certain prejudices that are our starting point. Our finite understanding is always situated in a historical process. That flow of history is characterized by a permanent mediation of past and present. By means of prejudices that are at our disposal, we enter hermeneutical circle of understanding. One should be aware that they represent an outline that we always start our understanding with. They are a positive starting point, parts that move together with the sense of the whole. We should keep them at a constant critical distance. Similar to reading a text: we try to strengthen the author's arguments as much as possible, so that we could understand them. What is at issue is the unfolding of common, inter-subjective, historical meaning that we cannot encounter if we hold our own horizons closed. Our prejudices tie us to tradition and by means of them we open ourselves to it. Their positive sense lies in the fact that they enable us to understand history as well as ourselves. In opening our horizons we never come to a definitive situation; although the anticipation of meaning becomes clearer, hermeneutical circle cannot be closed. That is the effect of the temporality of human being and understanding. We cannot in advance separate positive and negative prejudices—we must not forget that we are always situated in the world of praxis. Practical knowledge does not consist of rigid principles, but of moveable outlines. Hermeneutics is an heir of practical philosophy.

Hermeneutics critically asks how positive and negative prejudices could be separated, yet only on the basis of the historical consciousness and examination of tradition. The understanding that unites what is present and different takes place only in a dialogue with tradition.

I.3 The Concept of Effective-Historical Consciousness

Every historical horizon is situated within the frame of already existing effective-historical consciousness. It opens the past horizons to us in a particular, always limited manner. We should widen these horizons yet always warn ourselves against the deceitful pretension to absolute knowledge of the effective history.

The concept of effective-historical consciousness implies a certain ambiguity. Primarily, it represents the influence of effective history on us, but on the other hand, it is equal with our consciousness of hermeneutical situation. The consciousness of situation can never be full, since we are always its integral part. Situation cannot become the object of our cognition; we can only more or less illuminate it. That is the effect of our limits and limits of our understanding.

Every situation is characterized by a certain horizon. Husserl used to play with this notion in the final phase of his work, but always meant it as something that restricts our view on the environment. Gadamer explicitly denotes the concept of horizon positively—as a possibility to adequately comprehend and compare close and distant things. To have a horizon means to be able to clearly measure and understand the importance of things within their frame. Yet, concerning this issue, philosophic hermeneutics asks an important question: how do we approach different horizons, so that we could understand them?

It is crucial to note that Gadamer asserts that there is neither a present horizon-in-itself, nor distinguished historical horizons. Neither horizon nor situation can become part of 'objective' knowledge that would be analyzed, precisely defined and then used. A complete change of horizons that would make us forget our prejudices is impossible. What really takes place during the process of understanding is the formation of a common situation of communication. It is the only way to let the other side express itself. The horizon of the present is neither closed nor it can be separated from the past, but it grows inside of it—that is the real meaning of the above-mentioned assertion that there is no particular horizon-in-itself. Genuine interweavement of all horizons is at issue—by understanding the past ones, we build a huge, common horizon that is permanently on move. Likewise the above-mentioned hermeneutical circle is determined by the constant mutual influence of its parts and its whole, a huge horizon is influenced by a smaller and vice versa. When we try to understand someone, we never lose ourselves, but approach a more general ground that represents our common space. Similarly, as we interpret texts, we must not fix the meanings, so that the meaning of the whole could be outlined. Particular meanings give a new sense to the whole, but, on the other hand, the unfolding of the whole presents us with a new self-understanding. Only by understanding others, we approach ourselves. We cannot place ourselves in parenthesis if we want to meet the Other. We cannot remove all prejudices—even if we could, all paths of understanding would be inevitably closed. Gadamer's analysis of aesthetic and historical consciousness shows what difficulties these attempts imply. In *Truth and Method*, the process of approaching different horizons is entitled "fusion of horizons." By the fusion of horizons we encounter the Different, enabling it to speak freely.

I.4 The Problem of Application

Traditional hermeneutics divides the hermeneutical problem into understanding [*subtilitas intelligendi*], interpretation [*subtilitas explicanda*] and application [*subtilitas applicandi*]. The concept of subtleness [*subtilitas*] implies a sophisticated skill and distance from purely intellectual method. It adequately corresponds to the complexity of practical *Lebenswelt* that includes, as Aristotle puts it, the illogical and temporary part of the soul.

The three mentioned elements—understanding, interpretation and application—are always in an unbreakable unity. The way of approaching the Other, described as the fusion of horizons, shows that understanding is always interpretation. Understanding presupposes a particular horizon and prejudices and therefore corresponding restrictions as well. Thus, we always interpret the Other, never meeting the thing-in-itself. The unity of understanding and interpretation is the most apparent in the case of translation from foreign languages—every translator is forced to interpret the sense of a text given in another language, due to the limits imposed by his own language and his own understanding of the text, and to either highlight or neglect some elements of the text. There is no identical, neutral translation—it is clear to everyone who ever tried to translate anything. Gadamer adds that a good translation is always simpler than the original.

Application, as an integral part of understanding, implies the above-mentioned concept of situation. We can never have an 'objective' knowledge of situation, since it is always open. The inclusion of application into understanding means that the hermeneutical situation is essentially practical: we cannot gain a general knowledge from which we would deduce singular cases. 'The whole must be understood from its parts and the other way round.' Hermeneutical knowledge is always given in an outline, as a direction, since it is the only way not to lose a singular case in the universality of principles. By means of application, understanding is transformed into historical events. Encountering singular cases, it becomes history. Therefore, it can never turn into science.

I.5 Understanding Is a Form of Experience

Juristic hermeneutics is an excellent example of the unity of application and understanding. Justness of the court that allows one not to hold strictly to norms shows that law, as a practical field, cannot be applied like mathematics without losing its meaning. Human relations correspond to human issues. The unity of being and reason should be respected, otherwise the field of *praxis* turns into an empty universal concept—that is also the essence of Aristotle's critique of Plato's concept of Good. Once again, we encounter Aristotle's speech on practical and moral knowledge.[3] Moral knowledge cannot become science since it cannot be applied dogmatically. The very manner of approach is central to moral knowledge. It does not have a particular purpose and cannot be subjected to it. The means cannot be subjected to the purpose in an inadequate way, for means and purpose in this field cannot really be separated. The fact that final purpose is unattainable and constantly 'open' makes purpose and means inseparable. Furthermore, moral knowledge cannot be acquired in a classical way, it is intrinsic. We realize and improve it by application and in "dialogue with the Other and ourselves." Full participation of personality is essential to moral knowledge and self-reflection is inevitable. Heteronomous morality is not to be defined as moral consciousness.

The integration of application into understanding indicates that knowledge and action are essentially interrelated and that subsequent application of principles to life is inadequate. What makes understanding possible is application, its interrelatedness with the *Lebenswelt.*

II Natural Sciences and Humanities [*die Geisteswissenschaften*]

One of the 'results' of Gadamer's hermeneutics is the explanation of the position and meaning of humanities. Objectivistic-relativistic attitude present within aesthetic and historical consciousness, formed on the basis of the Cartesian idealization of method and 'getting rid of all prejudices' characteristic to the Enlightenment movement, has led to the considerable misunderstanding of the essence of humanities. Owing to the abovementioned loss of meaning, humanities conform to the methodical demand of natural sciences in order to find a solid ground to stand on. However, the effect of this conformity is that their own purpose becomes dubious. Out of the narrow horizon of the scientific method, it is simply impossible to recognize *raison d'être* of humanities.

Already in the preface to *Truth and Method*, Gadamer emphasizes the fact that his intention is not to found humanities. It would be contrary to his whole project. What he actually wants is to answer the question "How is understanding possible?" and that leads him inevitably into the field of humanities. He does not want to say that the methodological work in humanities is needless,

3 Aristotle, 1925, Book VI.

or to doubt in modern science and its rapid progress, but to find what is common to every form of understanding. Concerning that issue, he says:

> The phenomenon of understanding not only pervades all human relations to the world. It also has an independent validity within science, and it resists any attempt to reinterpret it in terms of scientific method. The following investigations start with the resistance in modern science itself to the universal claim of scientific method. They are concerned to seek experience of truth that transcends the domain of scientific method wherever the experience is to be found, and to inquire into its legitimacy. Hence, the human sciences are connected to modes of experience that lie outside science: with the experiences of philosophy, of art, and of history itself. These are all modes of experience in which a truth is communicated that cannot be verified by the methodological means proper to science. (Gadamer 2004, p. xxi)

Humanities are, essentially, moral sciences, asserts Gadamer. In other words, he deems that they completely belong to the field of *praxis*. Their aim is not to cognize a particular and defined object and its purpose. Quite the contrary, their meaning is in human self-understanding. They are concerned with temporal issues, that is, human issues.

Thus, they cannot be subjected to the idealized scientific method. By undergoing the control of method, they become meaningless, since they cannot be 'technified' as natural sciences—their immanent purpose cannot be made technically useful at all. Their meaning is in a characteristic experience of truth, which presents a universal genuine experience. They fully demonstrate to us the historical aspect of understanding. Hermeneutics describes what humanities really are, and in what way they are a part of our experience of the world. By placing humanities in the frame of their real meaning, hermeneutics shows that the difference between natural sciences and humanities is not the question of method, but the much greater issue of the aim of cognition. It is opposed to the monopoly of the scientific method that tends to deprive of truth all other sorts of experience. Moreover, its comprehension of the historical aspect of understanding as being of *Dasein* represents its pretension to universality. It does not mean questioning the results of contemporary science, but the uncovering of the horizons from which every science stems as primarily human. On the other hand, this research has practical important effects as well: restoring the credibility of the field of *praxis* and regaining its autonomy. It appears to be the only way of overcoming the above-mentioned crisis of meaning and preserving the human community.

Consequently, the interpretation of the title *Truth and Method* as opposed alternatives is invalid. Gadamer did not intend to oppose truth to method, but only to denounce the universal methodical pretension over truth. It seems that the given analysis suggests that truth is an essentially practical concept. According to the 'tradition' of modern philosophy, it means that there is no truth-in-itself [*an sich*]: furthermore, truth is always human and temporal, and it cannot be considered outside its context. Yet, this does not imply its relativity.

The universal pretension of hermeneutics is based on the universally historical character of our understanding. Therefore, philosophy preserves a part of its traditional aims, but, on the other hand, it is essentially restricted by the imperative of development of the hermeneutical consciousness. It loses a great deal of its former pretentious tasks: it has neither the obligation to constitute the world any more, nor to have the last word over our experience. It does not have the role of the highest tribunal for science—in the contemporary world it would sound, to say the least, comical: by enlightening our interweavement with horizons, it presents a corrective for our more or less blind comprehension and intentions. By virtue of understanding things, it tries to find an appropriate measure for them.

A major theme running through entire Gadamer's work is the claim that it is impossible to build a modern science out of the field of *praxis* in a sensible manner. Definition of humanities as moral sciences, whose subject is man and his knowledge of himself, implies their essential integrity. Owing to their common, immanent purpose, they cannot be truly studied as completely autonomous fields. That is one of the consequences deduced from the hermeneutical comprehension of humanities. Due to the fact that all of them are concerned with man's knowledge of himself and due to their identical orientation, their full and permanent cooperation is necessary. The renewal of this ancient union of the field of *praxis* seems to be the only way of regaining their lost credibility.

In other words: by separating them both from the pretension of proving the 'progress' in the sense of contemporary science and from subjecting 'idealized objects' to the inappropriate method, humanities will come back to their original sense and will inevitably be oriented towards each other. How is it at all possible to engage in politics, and not in the same time to deal with ethics, or to deal with ethics notwithstanding law? Observed from the hermeneutical position, that demand appears to be a mere universalism of methodical consciousness of humanities. The politics that does not care for ethics and the field of *praxis* always has an instrumental purpose.

Given to the perplexity of the field of humanities, the contemporary science that surprises us with new achievements day by day, is even urged to give answers and make decisions that completely surpass its competence. The result is a characteristic reduction of the world to a scientific-technical gallop that must not be stopped, while natural science cannot really answer the issues of the field of *praxis*. In an old terminology, that fact strikes us as alienation. In this respect, a question should be raised: how should the rehabilitation of the field of *praxis* be realized?

II.1 On the Request for the Rehabilitation of the Field of *Praxis*

A more extensive study of contemporary society could probably very vividly outline the influence that the "universal-methodical" scientific consciousness has on human self-understanding. Similar pieces of research have already been made: it would not reveal anything new. Let me mention just one of Gadamer's examples: the analysis of the distortion of the meaning and diminishing of the significance of art caused by the prevailing acceptance of the aesthetic consciousness. Researches into the so-called technocratic societies, notwithstanding their justification, are exemplary as well.

Two other questions are particularly emphasized: Gadamer has already been occupied with both of them. The first one is the problem of contemporary education and the dilemmas connected with it, while the other is the question of the universal competence of experts. Later on in the text, an attempt will be made to show how these two questions could be considered from the horizon opened by philosophic hermeneutics.

Before focusing on the mentioned problems, it is necessary to draw one's attention to a dilemma and critique of Gadamer's hermeneutics. In short: in a rough formulation, the critique is related to the attitude that philosophic hermeneutics, regarding the central place of the application in the concept of understanding, inevitably goes beyond philosophy. Gadamer opposes that attitude completely. The questions, which will be elaborated here in short, and which Gadamer explicitly deals with (at least with the second one),elicit the mentioned dilemma. The problem is the following: Does philosophic hermeneutics has the right to be acquitted of its concrete consequences? In spite of Gadamer's denial, it seems that there is no real answer given, since in his text one may find *pros* as well as *contras*.

II.2 The Problem of the Universal Competence of Experts

The above-mentioned loss of meaning and therefore self-confidence of the humanities resulted in their surrender to the myth of progressive natural sciences. There is another effect that is similarly severe—decisions of social-political life are ever more being conceded to scientific experts. Their role is, certainly, of an undeniable importance: the field of knowledge has become so wide today that it is impossible for an individual to access and remember all information. Therefore, it is inevitable to rely on the authority of experts. However, there is a question whether competence in a certain field allows one to play a role of the leader of civilization. There are many examples which appropriately illustrate this problem: the best one is perhaps in the area of human genetics. It seems that decisions which modern science tends to take have such relevance that they can change the entire social life on the planet. It is undeniable that the work of scientists cannot be separated from the social-political life and that a firm division of facts and values is just another human misconception. Yet, can they really make such important social-political decisions by themselves alone? Can they alone answer these so crucially relevant questions, such as the question of the Good of the human race? Gadamer maintains that the question of the Good cannot be answered by any expert or any science. That answer would presuppose that the Good could be treated theoretically, which is the actual basis of every dogmatic doctrine. The knowledge of the Good is always connected with an individual case, from which the whole draws its sense as well. Ethics cannot be practiced as a set of rules, without losing its meaning: what is necessary is responsible individual reasoning. Global decisions of experts threaten to endanger this responsibility: "Science and its responsibility should replace man's own responsibility." (Gadamer 1999, p. 101) Modern science not only tends to answer the question of the whole society; it is also compelled to do it, since people expect it. The intention of this critique is not to question the responsible thought of scientists. Quite the contrary, the aim is to show that science alone cannot solve the subtlety of problems of the world of praxis on the basis of the universal horizon of progress. It does not have the right to take the responsibility of the whole society on itself: for the purpose of science (its progress) cannot make universal social decisions legitimate.

Which solution does Gadamer suggest? The rehabilitation of the autonomy of the field of praxis as a universal horizon of our lives is what according to Gadamer is to be done. Only in a dialogue with history and tradition, which humanities practice, is that possible. From this standpoint, it is clear that the request for the universality of the scientific method is invalid and that science appertains to the immanent purpose of the practical philosophy. As Husserl puts it, science itself grows on the ground of a *Lebenswelt*. Hermeneutics adds that every question of science limits a certain horizon and consequently influences the *Lebenswelt*. This reciprocal influence between science and *Lebenswelt* prohibits their separation and fosters their unity. Science separated from the *Lebenswelt* is meaningless, yet it alone changes the *Lebenswelt*.

Serious problems related to this point begin with a question: "How?" How can we make the whole society feel so responsible that they appropriately respond to scientific dilemmas? How can the scientific language be translated into everyday language? Finally, how can we waken people from their individual slumber to questions concerning common social responsibility? In order that the field of *praxis* could follow the bloom of natural sciences, it must be independent. The question is whether we should produce experts in this field as well, so that we might rely on their answers? The reflections above imply that the answer is a negative one. It does not mean that there is no commitment or serious work in humanities, but it means something important for the very meaning of their work: they tend to contribute to human self-understanding and that refers to the whole society. Therefore, the humanities offer their insights to the whole of humankind that should, in turn, responsibly accept them. In this respect, they do not want to convert a scientist into an expert, but into a human being.

II.3 Remarks Concerning the Problem of Contemporary Education

The above-mentioned problems directly raise the question of organization of contemporary education. Just a few elements that connect this issue to the results of philosophic hermeneutics will be outlined here.

Apparently, Western *Fach* [or discipline]-oriented education is becoming more questionable day by day. The demand in modern society for experts is undeniable, yet it is becoming clear that such education is subjected to the imperative of universality of scientific methodology and progress. The effects of this orientation have already been mentioned: the amnesty of individuals from taking responsibility for their society.

On the other hand, the issue of education at universities and corresponding studies of humanities is another crucial problem. If we access humanities in the manner hermeneutics observes them, that is to say, as moral sciences in the broad sense of that word, a strict differentiation of individual departments does not reflect their purpose. It seems that this illegitimate separation of "subjects" (how complicated it is to define a "subject" in humanities has already been shown) is inappropriate to their purpose. Some European universities have been aware of this for a longer period and they practice interdisciplinary studies of humanities. The return to this original sense of the humanities should not mean a radical change, but only the recognition of their common purpose that always directs them one to another.

Acknowledgments

This paper was published in Croatian, (Duška Dobrosavljev, "Gadamerova hermeneutika kao praktička filozofija," *Filozofska istraživanja*, Vol. 23, No. 88 (2003): 127–152 and, including some changes, in English as Dobrosavljev, "Gadamer's Hermeneutics as Practical Philosophy," *Facta Universitatis. Series: Philosophy, Sociology and Psychology*, Vol. 2, No. 9 (2002): 605–618. This chapter has been stylistically modified from its earlier version.

References

Aristotle (1925) *Ethica Nicomachea*. Transl. by W. D. Ross, Oxford: Clarendon Press.

Bernstein, Richard J. (1983) *Beyond Objectivism and Relativism: Science, Hermeneutics and Praxis*. Oxford: Blackwell.

Bernstein Richard J. (2000) *Odgovornost filozofa*. Belgrade: Beogradski krug.

Braun, Hermann (1971) *Zum Verhältnis von Hermeneutik und Ontologie, Hermeneutik und Dialektik*. Vol. 2. Tübingen: Mohr.

Bubner, Rüdiger, Cramer, Konrad and Wiehl Reiner (eds.) (1970) *Hermeneutik und Dialektik*. Vol. 1. Tübingen: Mohr.

Delo. Belgrade: Nolit, 4–5, godina XIX.

Dilthey, Wilhelm(1968) *Gesammelte Schriften*. Band V: *Die geistige Welt. Einleitung in die Philosophie des Lebens I Abhandlungen zur Grundlegung der Geisteswissenschaften*. Stuttgart: B. G. Teubner.

Dilthey, Wilhelm (1968) *Gesammelte Schriften*. Band VII: *Der Aufbau der geschichtlichen Welt in den Geisteswissenschaften*. Stuttgart: B. G. Teubner.

Gadamer, Hans-Georg (1999) *Evropsko nasleđe*. Trans. by Božidar Zec. Beograd: Plato. [Translation from: Gadamer, Hans-Georg (1995) *Das Erbe Europas*, Frankfurt am Main: Suhrkamp Verlag]

Gadamer, Hans-Georg (1987) *Gesammelte Werke*. Vol. 3: *Neuere Philosophie 1. Hegel, Husserl, Heidegger*. Tübingen: Mohr.

Gadamer, Hans-Georg (2004) *Truth and Method*. London and New York: Continuum.

Gadamer, Hans-Georg (1997) *Zukunft ist Herkunft*. Jena: Friedrich Schiller Universität.

Gledišta (*Topic of the issue: Hermeneutics and Science*). Belgrade: Univerzitet u Beogradu, 3–4, 1990.

Habermas, Jürgen (1969). *Erkenntnis und Interesse*. Frankfurt am Main: Suhrkamp.

Heidegger, Martin (2001) *Sein und Zeit*. Tübingen: Max Niemeyer.

Heidegger, Martin (1967) *Vom Wesen der Wahrheit*. Frankfurt am Main: Vittorio Klostermann.

Husserl, Edmund (1954). *Die Krisis der europäischen Wissenschaften und die transzendentale Phänomenologie*. Haag: Martinus Nijhoff.

Karnezis, G. K. (1987) "Gadamer, Art and Play." Online: https://www.svcc.edu/academics/classes/murray/gadamer/gadartpl.htm

Kuhn, Thomas, S. (1970) *The Structure of Scientific Revolutions*. Chicago: University of Chicago Press.

Kuhn, Thomas S. (1977) *The Essential Tension*. Chicago and London: The University of Chicago Press.

Lammi, Walter, "The Conflict of *Paideias* in Gadamer's Thought". Online: https://www.bu.edu/wcp/Papers/Educ/EducLamm.htm

Landgrebe, Ludwig (1952) *Philosophie der Gegenwart*. Bonn: Athenäum-Verlag.

Merleau-Ponty, Maurice (1976) *Phénoménologie de la perception*. Paris: Gallimard.

Pavić, Željko (1997) *Metafizika i hermeneutika*. Zagreb: Hrvatsko filozofsko društvo.

Rorty, Richard (1979) *Philosophy and the Mirror of Nature*. New Jersey: Princeton University Press.

Rorty, Richard (1994). *Consequences of Pragmatism*. Minneapolis: University of Minnesota Press.

Šarčević, Abdulah (1981) *Iskustvo i vrijeme*. Sarajevo: Svijetlost.

Urbančić, Ivan (1976) *Temelji metode moći*. Belgrade: Mladost.

Vukadinović, Đorđe (1998) *Habermasova odbrana moderne*. Master's thesis. Belgrade.

Bernt Schnettler, Hubert Knoblauch & Jürgen Raab

The 'New' Sociology of Knowledge

Abstract: The methodological and conceptual advances referred to below are based on a particular research tradition. In order to understand its implications, it is necessary to recall its main aspects. The sociology of knowledge was developed in a characteristic context, first as philosophical reflection on the conditions of human thinking and reasoning, and later evolving into a specific sociological perspective on the social conditions of knowledge production and dissemination. The social character of thinking has been observed: from Bacon to Marx, many theorists have been concerned to emphasize problems of ideology and to criticize the distorting effects that social influences have upon individual thinking. Conversely, thinking and knowledge production depend fundamentally on their social genesis.

I Sociology of Knowledge

Today, the field of the sociology of knowledge has become so wide-ranging that it is impossible to summarize it here.[1] But one of its major twists is decisive for understanding the basis of the present work: the so-called new sociology of knowledge. This sociology is associated with the work of two classic, third generation sociologists, namely Peter L. Berger and Thomas Luckmann. They are regarded as among the most notable leading social theorists, whose works reinforce interpretive sociology. Together with the works of Max Weber and Emile Durkheim, their seminal book on the *Social Construction of Reality* is classified as one of the ten most important books in sociology. The impact of their wide-ranging opus goes far beyond the discipline of sociology and includes works on methodology, the phenomenology of the life-world, religion, identity and morality. Of central relevance for the new approach on sociology of knowledge is especially Luckmann's theory of action, knowledge and communication.

It is important to underscore Luckmann's influence in connecting the classical European intellectual legacy with modern American traditions of thought. In theoretical terms, the 'new' sociology of knowledge draws on the work of the sociologist and philosopher Alfred Schutz, whose scientific program aimed to create a phenomenological proto-sociology to provide a comprehensive and univer-

1 See Knoblauch 2005 for a comprehensive overview.

https://doi.org/10.1515/9783110551563-013

sal foundation for the social sciences. However, Berger's and Luckmann's work does not refer to this foundational level. Instead, it is erected upon an insight that is formulated in the later published *Structures of the Life-World* (Schutz and Luckmann 1973, 1989) but orientated to the successive problems of historical social structure and the production of reality. Luckmann's own contribution to this was his development of a theory of action, together with a genuine sociological theory of language and communication. This is connected with constitutional analyses of the structures of interactive and communicative processes, such as those exemplified in empirical studies on oral genres or moral exchange processes.

In the late 1960s, Luckmann and Berger formulated their thesis about the "social construction of reality," which provided a coherent frame for, and gave inner unity to, this broad research field (Berger and Luckmann 1991 [1966]). In their book of the same name, their argument, anchored in an understanding of sociology both as empirical *and* as real science, drew on Max Weber's notion of *Wirklichkeitswissenschaft*. In so doing, it continues the path opened by a sociological currently called "*Verstehende Soziologie*," which is one of the early origins of current interpretive social science. It places special emphasis on the hermeneutical tradition of German and Central European Sociology. Berger and Luckmann adopted the goal of placing the sociology of knowledge, which until then had played only a minor role at the margins of social theory, at the center of a re-oriented, general theory of action and society. Its main characteristic consists in abandoning narrower conceptions in the sociology of knowledge, i.e., those primarily preoccupied with specialized forms of knowledge, such as intellectual reasoning or the more sophisticated and refined forms associated with specific domains in society (cultural production, science, arts, politics etc.).

Instead, the structure of *knowledge in everyday life* is taken as the all-encompassing ground from which other forms of knowledge are but specific derivations. It is due to this common property that everyday life comes into focus. The main methodological resources used by the authors are phenomenological descriptions and analytic reconstructions of the constitutional processes of social action and knowledge. The purpose of this 'new' sociology of knowledge is to answer complex questions such as: how is reality socially generated? How are individuals' everyday perceptions and actions shaped by socially preestablished patterns and forms? How do societies create, transmit and reproduce what they believe they 'know' and define as 'reality'? How does the social and historical order arise in and through human action and interaction? Moreover, how does it, once it has emerged, present individuals with an objectively experience-able 'reality,' working to invest their actions and identities with meaning? And finally: how do these social constructs in turn influence their constructors?

The perspective that finds expression in these questions is one of fundamental existential and situational boundedness, as well as of the relativity and contingency, not only of all human knowledge, but also of what is understood as reality. This might be said to be the basic axiom of the most prominent line of development in the sociology of knowledge. This line is generally referred to as 'social constructivism' (Knoblauch 1999; Knorr Cetina 1989) although neither Luckmann nor Berger use this term to describe their theory. In sociology in general, and the sociology of knowledge in particular, there is now an almost overwhelming diversity of overlapping theoretical approaches. Social constructivism is not currently among the most-discussed theoretical alternatives, although its potential is far from being acknowledged. There have been serious efforts to demonstrate its continuing theoretical potential and the contributions it has made to general theoretical advancement in sociology (Endreß 2002). Albeit using different conceptual means, the aim of this book is to push in the same direction. The following work endeavors to contribute to this by showing in an exemplary manner the continuities and further developments of social constructivism, the aim is at once to engender discussion on points of convergence with other constructivist and knowledge-oriented sociological approaches.

The following chapters are arranged according to a specific structure, system and program. The chief interest involves revealing the theoretical foundations, and above all the key developments, of this line of conceptual thinking, as well as the inseparable methodological and theoretical considerations that arise from the empirical analyses upon which it rests. The argument is therefore constructed according to a principle of 'layering.' It entails several analytical levels, the results of which are progressively superimposed and aggregated, in an order of ascent that goes from the nuclear level of interaction to the institutional spheres of social reality and ultimately the level of society itself. The argument begins by analyzing the small-scale structures in the interior of interaction orders, building up to more complex socially, culturally and historically specific institutions of human action. This corresponds to the constitutive logic of the underlying thinking. Constitution starts with the 'egological perspective.' This means that subjectivity is conceived as the constitutive and indispensable condition of any social process. But unlike other sociological theories that start out from models of individual action, a phenomenologically orientated sociology does not operate with a reductionist idea of single actors. Its 'methodological individualism' does not derive from some prerequisite of austerity for the formulation of postulates. Models of action that universalize the drive to maximize expected subjective utility do so in order to reduce the confusing multiplicity of motifs that might engender human activity. They thereby strive to meet the scientific obligation of brevity and parsimony. But they are thereby also seriously incompatible with the general human condition, which, intricate and irremediably multiple, is diverse and even contradictory. It is important to emphasize two things about the concept of 'individualism' being argued for here. First, it is not a concept tied to scientific necessities of theoretical brevity, but a fact that reflects fundamental and universal human conditions. In this sense, it is the result of a certain epistemological 'realism.' Second, it is based on the only evidence to which we have 'undistorted,' or at least 'unmediated,' access, i. e. our own experience. Third, it is crucial to stress that social construction *starts* out with subjectivity and strongly argues against any theory that tries to exclude subjectivity from its conceptual outline. But it does not end with the egological perspective nor is it accurate to label it a 'subjectivist' approach. On the contrary, it is a core element of social constructionism that individual action is complemented with, and inseparably tied to, interaction. In other words, subjectivity and sociality are not only coexistent but co-emergent.

The aforementioned 'layering' takes the meaning-constituting performance of consciousness and the subject-relatedness of the human life-world as its point of departure. It then goes on to look at that aspect of the life-world that is relevant for sociology: the 'minor' social institutions that are negotiated in processes of social exchange, in which subjective meaning patterns are solidified into intersubjectively shared structures of 'knowledge.' Knowledge here is construed as socially objectified meaning, broadly defined to include a wide array of human forms of socially established, shared and apprehended meaning patterns. These patterns originate in human action and interaction, which in turn are transferable and proceed to 'determine' individual action, interpretation and knowledge. Finally, these patterns may lead to reformulations of the argument of social construction. This new orientation and concretization of the knowledge-sociological approach has been labeled a 'paradigm change' in the construction of reality in *communication* (Knoblauch 1995; Luckmann 1997). Before sketching this line of development, however, it is necessary to clarify some key aspects of the social constructivist tradition and the extent to which it differs from other theories that are likewise called "constructivist."

II Variants of Constructivism

Over the past decades, 'constructivism' has been used to describe a wide range of theories, which have emerged as a broad movement crossing the boundaries of the most varied scientific disciplines. Variants of constructivism have proliferated since the 1960s. Apart from sociology, major constructivist theories have been developed in biology, philosophy and psychology. The number and range of publications with the term 'social construction' in their title has become simply unwieldy, stretching from topics as diverse as the 'social construction of emotions,' of the 'mind' and of 'gender,' the 'social construction of illness,' of the 'postmodern' or of 'technology,' etc. A detailed list with references can be found in Ian Hacking (1999). The catalogue of studies that draw on social constructivism, at least rhetorically, is constantly expanding. However, the theoretical positions to which the works refer continue to be countable, even if seldom sharply demarcated:

(1) One of the most influential theories sociological theories of constructivism is tied to a concept of 'radical construction,' which stems from the philosophical works of Ernst von Glasersfeld and the physicist Heinz von Foerster. Together with ideas developed by the neurobiologists Humberto Maturana and Francisco Varela, this epistemology laid the ground for an influential reorientation of social theory in the German-speaking social sciences, namely Niklas Luhmann's autopoietic systems theory. According to Luhmann, 'radical constructivism' is the fundamental epistemological principle of this complex theory (Luhmann 1997). This version of constructivism is 'radical' insofar as it posits that social systems emerge from a single principle, requiring no further material than the process from which they arise. On this view, social reality is not created by action or interaction. It needs no antecedent and is created solely through 'communication,' which is the 'ultimate unit' of social systems. As Luhmann puts it, sometimes rather paradoxically, neither man, nor even consciousness, but only communication communicates—and thereby *creates*—social systems.

(2) A second major strand is referred to as 'social constructionism' (Burr 1995). Despite the lack of cross-fertilization, and regardless of its explicit opposition to 'conservative' social theories like Luhmann's, its tenets partly overlap with those of autopoietic systems theory. Social constructionism is particularly strong in Anglo-Saxon countries and often connected with 'discourse theories': notwithstanding the clear theoretical differences, 'discourse' plays a similar role to the one that Luhmann ascribes to 'communication'. The difference between them lies in the role played by processes of power in theories of discourse, but both social constructionism and systems theory focus on communicative processes: both stress that social reality is—mainly or even exclusively—created in and by communication. And finally, the central interface of both approaches can be reduced, roughly, to the formula that the subject (the actor) arises essentially from discourse or communication.

(3) The third and last viewpoint, however, places systems theory and 'social constructionism' in opposition to the earlier version of social constructivism. As early as the 1960s, Peter L. Berger and Thomas Luckmann reduced the sociology of knowledge to a formula that was to guide all of sociological constructivism: the "*social construction of reality*" (Berger and Luckmann 1991 [1966])[2] The book of the same title became a modern classic of (knowledge) sociology and still counts as one of the most important since it is one of the most read and cited works in sociology, but also in prominent 'neighboring' disciplines such as philosophy, theology and cultural anthropology, as well as literature studies and history.[3]

Berger and Luckmann's theory starts out from the assumption that the reality in which we all live is fabricated in and through our actions. Reality is argued to consist in the small or large institutions of action; and what reality means is determined by what these institutions recognize as knowledge and transmit by means of language. It therefore does not exist without people. Instead, people first create reality in and through their actions. And what is sociologically important in this is the fact that they do not do this alone, since reality becomes objective in its being shared by several persons and thus its intersubjectivity. There are two unique aspects to the theory of social construction. First, Berger and Luckmann manage to avoid the sociologism of systems theory and 'social constructionism.' They argue that reality is constructed in social action, but, as Hacking (1999) properly states: "They did not claim that everything is a social construct, including, say, the taste of honey and the planet Mars. [...] They did not claim that nothing can exist unless it is socially constructed." Second, Berger and Luckmann assume that social reality is constructed in action. Actions for their part are impossible without an individualized consciousness. This idea is the central postulate of the sociological theoretical tradition that starts with Max Weber's analysis of the subjective meaning of action. It has been substantially elaborated further by Alfred Schutz's phenomenological constitution analysis of consciousness and the everyday life-world.

---

2 It should be noted that the authors laid the groundwork for this approach in an earlier article: Berger and Luckmann 1963.

3 The English edition of the book alone sold hundreds of thousands of copies—a remarkable success for a sociological work. Apart from German, the book has been translated into French, Spanish, Italian, Portuguese, Catalonian, Polish, Swedish, Russian, Slovenian, Japanese and Chinese.

III Action and Interaction in Everyday Life

This theory and research tradition draws its inspiration from Max Weber's *methodological individualism.* As is well known, for Weber the goal of sociological analysis is the reconstruction of the subjectively intended meanings upon which actors base their actions. In this connection, not only ought we recall Weber's action-theoretical foundation of sociology, but also his clear rejection of any sort of concept of 'collective actors':

> For still other cognitive purposes as, for instance, juristic, or for practical ends, it may [...] be convenient or even indispensable to treat social collectivities, such as states, associations, business corporations, foundations, as if they were individual persons [...] But for the subjective interpretation of action in sociological work these collectivities must be treated as solely the resultants and modes of organization of the particular acts of individual persons, since these alone can be treated as agents in a course of subjectively understandable action. [...] for sociological purposes there is no such thing as a collective personality which "acts." When reference is made in a sociological context to a "state," a "nation," a "corporation," a "family," or an "army corps," or to similar collectivities, what is meant is, on the contrary, only a certain kind of development of actual or possible social actions of individual persons.[4]

The principle of methodological individualism is a safeguard against abstractions of the meaning of action from acting subjects—which is philosophically imaginable but sociologically detrimental—thereby avoiding any reification of the latter: social action can never be understood as detached from acting subjects.

Another essential feature is the Weberian specification that meaningfulness is not limited to a special case of rationality. Weber showed that modern economic activity is guided by meaningful orientations whose contents are by no means solely 'rationally' calculated, but in large measure arise from religious convictions. Weber clearly demonstrated this connection in the case of Protestantism (cf. Weber 1988). However, his conception of the meaningfulness that guides action remains unclear. Alfred Schütz's objection, for example, is that Weber completely failed to define the basic concept of 'understanding sociology' (cf. Schütz 1991, pp. 24 ff.; for further detail: Eberle 1999). Schütz's intensive work in phenomenology led him, amongst other things, to concentrate on the key question of what meaningful action is. From the assumption that phenomenology makes possible, justifiable, and even definitively provable, statements, he attempted to grasp the concept of meaning, which he approached through a phenomenolog-

4 Weber 1997 [1897].

ical analysis of the processes that occur in the consciousness of actors. Schütz understands the specific meaning of actions as a form of intentionality characterized by a special time structure, namely a plan "*modi futuri exacti*" (Schütz 1932): something is to be achieved with previously planned actions.[5]

In one respect, meaningful action becomes social by being 'socialized': we acquire relevant aspects of our action-knowledge and our action-competencies from social others. Action in Weber's sense—and likewise Schütz's—is, however, also social when oriented to others. These 'others' do not have to be human subjects by any means, for we can also act socially toward sweet potatoes, insofar as we assume that they are themselves meaningfully acting subjects. In some cultures 'universal projection' can also go beyond the domain to which it is limited in our culture. Magical forces and gods are also often viewed as actors (cf. Luckmann 1980b); and more latterly also some technological, 'artificially intelligent' constructions have been described as semi-social hybrids (Latour 1995). The most common forms of social action are directed at other people, however. This is not because we experience them as similar to ourselves and therefore assume a corresponding reciprocity, but instead because of the fact that others can respond to social actions in a somewhat predictable manner, due to the pre-design. The predictability of the response to social action thus presupposes the reciprocity of perspectives and relevancies (Schütz 1932). Only for this reason can the other person respond, as expected, to our outstretched right hand, by extending his own right hand and shaking it, and only for this reason does he view our question—e. g. as to his well-being—as a sufficiently relevant grounds for replying.

Social action has, however, very many far-reaching consequences, since in a certain sense it generates its own experiential space. While sweet potatoes, gods and hybrids are very unreliable action partners and appear to us only occasionally in dreams, trances, and fictional or theoretical (con)texts, with social actions we create what Schütz refers to as the *world of everyday life* (cf. Eberle 1993a; Knoblauch, Kurt and Soeffner 2005). Not infrequently is the everyday life-world equated with the 'life-world' [*Lebenswelt*], the 'everyday world' [*Alltagswelt*] or simply 'everyday' [*Alltag*]—here, however, it is necessary to avoid a popular misunderstanding. Schütz regards the everyday life-world as merely one, albeit the dominant, 'order' of the life-world: the life-world constitutes the overarching horizon of meaning for "multiple realities" (Schütz 1971), for

5 Naturally not all actions are always pre-planned, because they can, so to speak, be 'automatized' through consciousness' ability to sediment and routinize. The plan-like character [*Entwurfscharakter*] is thereby only clearly specifiable for actions that must of necessity be newly—or continually—planned (cf. for more details: Luckmann 1992; Knoblauch 1999a).

which reason it can also be referred to as the "totality of the worlds of meaning" (Honer 1999, p. 64). The everyday life-world stands out from the various other life-worlds or meaning-domains of dream and fantasy as well as theorizing. It circumscribes its own unmistakable domain of reality, which is, of course, circumscribed in its turn. This region is not real 'in itself,' but created with a special state of consciousness: that "relatively natural world view" (Scheler 1928) which "includes all modifications of attitude and alertness—viz., the tension of consciousness present with the normal adult" (Schütz and Luckmann 1984, p. 47; English: 1974, p. 21). Moreover, it is constituted in practical action. The natural attitude is one in which we are pragmatically oriented. By contrast, what we experience subjectively as the everyday life-world is first constituted through our meaningful action, our understanding of action and mutual acts of achieving understanding. The everyday life-world is just that unique domain of reality in which we perceive others in their physical co-presence, and act, interact and communicate with them (cf. also Grathoff 1978; Soeffner 1989).

But how do the 'objects,' events and experiences of the everyday life-world concretely confront the individual? What share does consciousness have in experience? Is it a matter of a shared style of experience? And what role do society and history play? In two essays, Luckmann deals with the foundations of these questions. The first, *Lebenswelt: Modebegriff oder Forschungsprogramm (Life-world: Fashionable Concept or Research Program)*, describes the design of a research program oriented to a proto-sociology for the phenomenological description and analysis of the everyday life-world, its invariant structures, its layering and knowledge constitution—they form the foundation of a social-scientific basic theory. The second is called *Lebensweltliche Zeitkategorien, Zeitstrukturen des Alltags und der Ort des "historischen Bewußtseins"* [*Life-world Temporal Categories, Temporal Structures of the Everyday and the Location of "Historical Consciousness"*] and deals with the temporal structuring of the life-world and thereby with a central problem of the general matrix of human action and human experience of reality around which the project of proto-sociology is oriented: what is universally human about the temporality of human experience, and what is social-historical and how much?

The ideas that Luckmann presents here doubtless owe much to Schützian analyses of the life-world, to typifications and relevance systems and thereby also to Edmund Husserl's transcendental phenomenology. Yet this theory also diverges remarkably from the latter—and at least for Schütz[6]—from the founding

---

6 Srubar points to the late Schutz's 'turn' to anthropology. To the insight, namely, "that a theory of the life-world must be built up not on the transcendental, but rather on a philosophico-an-figures of transcendental philosophical, instigating a major shift that emphasizes sociology's anthropological as opposed to phenomenological foundations. From the perspective of the philosophical anthropology that underpins Luckmann's theoretical structure, the *conditio humana* is characterized by its "dual nature" and "eccentric positionality" [*exzentrische Positionalität*] (Plessner 1975): on the one hand, man with his body is part of nature; on the other, he possesses mind, a self and so also a principle that differs from nature, and is independent of, or even opposed to, it (Scheler 1928). On the basis of this naturally given form of existence, its instinct reduction and the "world openness" based upon it, the biologically "imperfect being" [Mängelwesen] (Gehlen 1964) is forced to form a "second nature"—a cultural one. So, man is forced, by nature, to be an artefact and at the same time a product of his own self-making, because it is up to him to create this reality, this "second fatherland in which he finds his homeland (Heimat) and absolute rootedness" (Plessner 1975, p. 316).

These simplified references suffice to show the role of anthropology. Anthropology does not reveal the epistemological foundations of the constitution of meaning. Instead, what it makes clear is the necessity, indeed even the obligation, to construct reality socially. This is a reality that people create collectively and thereafter continue to share, that they defend against competing plans and regularly—at least in part—work to change or even alter completely.

IV Institutions

Where phenomenological, *proto*-sociological analysis investigates the constitution of the invariant structures of the life-world through acts of consciousness, the *sociological* analysis that 'builds upon' it aims to understand the construction of individual and societal stocks of knowledge and social institutions through social action.[7] Anthropological conditions and the work of consciousness, then, form 'only' the constitutional logical frame within which social construction can occur; since whatever people do together, they do it within the limits of their body and the structures of human consciousness. However, as Srubar maintains, in discussing Schütz, it is equally crucial to see that "meaning-giving acts [are] not exclusively to be sought in the subject's conscious domain" (Srubar 1991, p. 172). Action in society is not merely oriented around solitary plans. In-

thropological foundation whose statements clarify the mundane *conditio humana*, but do not concern their ultimate ground and meaning" (Srubar 1988, p. 275 f.).

7 On the distinction between 'constitution' and 'construction' cf. Luckmann 1999b, on proto-sociology cf. Luckmann 1990.

stead, it occurs primarily in interaction processes from which intersubjectively shared patterns of interpretation and action arise. These patterns are socially negotiated or carried out, maintained or changed; however, they are always first and foremost individual, weakly contoured and 'fleeting' forms that increasingly sediment and harden after repeated attempts. In this way, overcoming their original particularity and subjectivity, they congeal into predictable, objectified components of reality: into "structures with their own weight" (Gehlen 1964, p, 71), namely social institutions.

Social institutions arise wherever groups of actors are confronted with a recurrent social problem and are compelled routinely to resolve it. This requires them to develop typical solutions for equally typical social-action problems. This is the case for all the ways in which people live, work and communicate together, as well as for questions concerning the spread, stabilization and limitation of political power, and obviously also for experiences of extraordinary situations. The regular repetition of interpretive patterns and the equally regular coordination of actions that are derived from, and referring to, them is the thing that drives the institutionalization process forward, relieves actors of the task of always having to develop new solutions or 'answers,' and makes each actor comprehensible, and thereby calculable, to others in terms of their perception, feeling, thinking and acting.

Widespread typifications and habitualizations in the end become social institutions through transmission and legitimation.[8] Transmission is an essential moment in the sedimentation and making permanent of interpretive and action patterns. For it is first their transmission to third parties—their social 'inheritance'—that detaches them from specific actors, and/or from historically unique circumstances, and turns them into *typical situations*—the ultimate basis of their objectivity. But social institutions must also be given a higher meaning via processes of legitimation, which explains their 'rational,' pragmatic relevance or emphasizes their comprehensive symbolic meaning. These processes thus mediate an intersubjectively shared 'knowledge-in-order-to.'

As mentioned earlier, whereas *meaning* is created on an initial level in individual consciousness, *knowledge* refers to a society's socially objectified, and therefore legitimate, interpretations of meaning. This social knowledge extends from 'simple' physical capabilities, such as the 'art' of eating or walking, to highly complex forms of special theoretical knowledge, such as techniques of fly fishing. However, there is a universal condition of such knowledge: it must be subjectively acquired, either through one's own experiences or through the 'detour'

8 On 'legitimation' cf. Berger and Luckmann 1969, Ch. II.2, as well as Luckmann 1987.

of concrete exemplifications of actual producers of legitimation, i.e. knowledge experts of every stripe.[9] What the individual represents as his life-world and what he thinks he knows about it are the result of subjective experiences, social actions and, above all, socialized experiences. In the standard empirical case, the latter is derived from a social stock of knowledge: from the meaning reservoir that the subject encounters as something historically pre-given and socially imposed—as a "socio-historical a priori" (Luckmann 1980a, p. 127).

Such ideas do not simply link Thomas Luckmann with Max Weber and Alfred Schutz, but express the empirical-scientific consensus that Luckmann shares with diverse theorists from Emile Durkheim and Marcel Mauss to Maurice Halbwachs, from Max Scheler, Karl Mannheim and Alfred Weber to Robert Merton. This consensus concerns the social character of knowledge and its action-orienting function. Subjective and societal knowledge stocks are socially produced and determined, they are socially mediated and distributed, not to mention the essential precondition of all human action.

In his essay "*Individuelles Handeln und gesellschaftliches Wissen*" [Individual Action and Social Knowledge], Luckmann asks about just this structural connection of subjective and societal knowledge stocks and directs his argument at an analytic differentiation of various levels of 'determination' of individual action. Biologically conditioned differences in gender and age produce different knowledge stocks: women tend to know more about menstruation, old people about age-related illnesses, and so on. But further differentiations also arise to produce separate stocks of special knowledge that are assigned to experts such as priests and shamans, blacksmiths and physicians. The more complex and differentiated the social world, the more the overall societal knowledge stock increases in volume and the more the quality and extent of intersubjectively shared knowledge decreases. The sociologically most important level of societal knowledge distribution is therefore the social structure: general knowledge about it is separate from special knowledge, access to processes of knowledge acquisition are regulated and systematically limited to typical societal members. The social-structural differentiation of class, level and milieu-specific knowledge variants—what Pierre Bourdieu called the social distribution of 'symbolic capital'—is a generative and simultaneously stabilizing moment in the system of social inequalities.

While *Individuelles Handeln* deals with the knowledge-dependent preconditions of human action, in *Wirklichkeit als Arbeit* [Reality as Work] Luckmann shows that, although other human actions also construct reality, work is the

---

9 On the structure of expert knowledge cf. Schütz 1972, Sprondel 1979, as well as Hitzler, Honer and Maeder 1994.

most important way of doing so. The concept of work here contains more than its common, everyday sense to include, together with all the economic and financial implications, all forms of social action through which an intended change is effected in nature or the social world. As a result, work forms the basic category of the social attribution of responsibility and the social construction of reality. Only based on these considerations, as Luckmann clearly shows, can the development of the societal organization of work and the work-mediating experience of reality be reconstructed; and only in this way is it then possible to show that work has quite distinct connotations in various cultures and societies, as well as in different historical epochs. Consequently, there is a core of meaning inherent in all ways of understanding work, which is tightly wrapped and thus usually concealed, around which all other layers of meaning are grouped. It is Luckmann's achievement to have uncovered this core of meaning.

V Limits of the Life-World

Luckmann's empirical work began with research on the sociology of religion (cf. Luckmann 1957, 1959, 1960). His contribution to the sociology of religion is, however, by no means limited to sociological studies on the church. In fact, he became one of the keenest ever critics of a one-sided cultural pessimism as regards the seemingly inevitable secularization of religion in modern society. Luckmann can thus be attributed with providing a major impulse toward a renaissance of the sociology of religion is thus attributable to Thomas Luckmann (Luckmann 1963, 1967). He developed a sociology of religion that, free of uni-dimensional critiques of religion and research limited to the sociology of the church, understood, according to a view of sociology as science of reality, human experiences and social-historical developments as defined by the interior world and human nature. In this purview, *religiosity* becomes an inescapable basic aspect of human existence and *religion* a central characteristic of all social reality.

Luckmann's functionalist definition of religion has attracted great attention. Due to its intention to include the greatest possible spectrum of contents and social forms, it is regarded as one of the broadest: it is "the fundamental function of 'religion' ... to transform the members of a natural group into actors within an historically developed societal order" (Luckmann 1991, p. 165). By contrast to other societal forms of knowledge and interpretive authority—such as science, economics, politics, law or art, which also perform this fundamental social function—religion is a structural element in the construction of social realities. The reason for this is because, by assigning them to levels of 'sanctified' meaning that is set against and also transcends everyday life, it is even possible to legitimize the sense of everyday customs and the activities of profane life. Consequently, as an intersubjectively shared reservoir of meaning that shores up and legitimates interpretations and behaviors as no other, religion does more than merely free the individual, in the same sense as any other social institution, from "the virtually impossible task of creating a system of meaning—however rudimentary—on his own" (Luckmann 1991, p. 89). Instead, derives its objectively binding character from its function of justifying interpretations on the basis of an ultimate, unquestionable authority. For Durkheim, religion is no more than a different, albeit more idealized expression of society, defined in terms of its integrative and symbolizing contributions. Luckmann, by contrast, does not seek to provide a functional determination of religion, but instead looks at it from the stance of the sociology of knowledge. This led him to develop a theory of transcendence as the foundation of a sociology of religion.

The theme of transcendence deals with the limits of the human life-world. In addition, Luckmann's explicative and interpretive argument is, in the first instance, both anthropological and phenomenological. The "insurmountable dual aspect" located in the "eccentric positionality" of human existence (Plessner 1975) not only creates the contradictory unity of mind and body (cf. II.), but also manifests itself in the individual's experience of being simultaneously an individual and a social creature. This paradoxical dual existence enables a person to be simultaneously aware of himself, his experiential and action knowledge, and of his life-world. For this reason, it runs the permanent danger of confusing and isolating him. In order to avoid this naturally given "insecurity and uncertainty, whose experience is our common fate" (Simmel 1995, p. 72), the individual needs—likewise imposed by nature—to transcend his own experience and permanently exceed himself: Because "the process of transcendence ... is immanent in life itself,' man turns out to be 'the born boundary crosser" (Simmel 2000, p. 297).

For Luckmann the experience of transcendence has its original source in man's corporeality. In addition, his theory requires that he uncover the structure of intersubjectivity itself as boundary crossing. Born incomplete, and thereby dependent on the social other, man only becomes human—and an individual—among his own kind because "the individuation of consciousness is a possibility of the human organism which is realized only in social processes" (Luckmann 1991, p. 83; English: 1967, p. 46; cf. also Knoblauch 1991). A precondition for this development is the human ability to set oneself apart from ongoing events, as well as the stimuli and reactions of the biological organism. This going beyond biological nature is only possible in a social context, i.e. through interaction with others in which the individual finds himself more or less 'mirrored' in their behavior, he begins to see himself through the eyes of others, thus acquiring the ability to assume roles and thereby also the chance to develop a personal identity.[10]

The origins of *religiosity* lie in the experience of transcendence, in the naturally posed task of gaining access to what one is not oneself. This disposition to religiosity is an innate attribute of human existence, and is where *religion* as a socially institutionalized form of dealing with specific experiences of transcendence derives (cf. on this also Soeffner 2000).

More specifically, specifying the aspects of religious experience, Luckmann, drawing on Alfred Schütz, describes three levels of transcendence. He uses the term *minor* transcendencies to describe everything that goes beyond direct, contemporary and pragmatic everyday experience in a temporal or spatial regard. *Middle* transcendencies differ in that what is experienced is only indirectly accessible: by contrast to everyday temporal and spatial dimensions, which are still within reach, the border against which one comes up is uncrossable, not even be potentially crossed. Instead, they involve interactive and communicative processes in which actors 'step outside themselves,' acting and interpreting—through signs, symbols or rituals—which they both embody and in which they decode an inaccessible 'within.' While the demarcations of the minor and middle transcendencies are drawn into the reality domain of the everyday, the *major* transcendencies are characterized by the fact that in them a reality other than 'profane' everyday life is experienceable. This is the case, for example, in ecstasies and dreams, in questions concerning the meaning of our existence or in the intimate knowledge about death (i.e. the 'mysterious' and 'strange,' the peculiarly pleasing or frightening extraordinary experiences it elicits). If grasped as direct knowledge of a different, 'sacred' sphere of reality, such major transcendences must, in principle of the sign-dependency—the mediatedness—of human perception and action, be articulated and mediated with the expressive possibilities of ordinary experience: through amulets, icons or sacrificial rites—generally: through signs, symbols and symbolic forms as the indicators and media of the transcendental (see cf. on this Knoblauch 2001).

So Luckmann does not locate the original 'site' of experiences of transcendence in numinous, or other-worldly, existence, but instead—upstream of any metaphysics—with individuals in their life-worlds. On the primary and fundamental level, religiosity assumes an intersubjectively shared social form, which Luckmann refers to as a *Weltansicht* (world view). Usually, it includes linguisti-

10 Luckmann refers hereby to the social-psychological analyses of Mead, who understands 'taking the role of the other' to mean taking account of, or anticipating in one's own action plans and actions, the social other's perspectives and modes of reaction (Mead 1973). On the specific ties between social psychology and the sociology of knowledge see also Eberle 1993b.

cally transmitted typifications, interpretive and behavioral schemas that guide routine knowledge and action: elementary typifications of things ('meadows,' 'horses,' 'blue'), rudimentary know-how concerning dealing with persons, things and events ('a full moon precedes a change in the weather') as well as moral regulations concerning what can and what ought to be done ('on Friday you are not allowed to eat meat'). Such a world view is interpreted as entirely religious, because it gives meaning to all aspects of worldly experience, which makes it possible for people to deal with it in interpretation and action. And only by building upon this world view can a separate meaning domain crystallize which then appears as 'sacred,' precisely what Luckmann calls the *sacred cosmos*. The latter defines those special experiences and the domain of reality of major transcendencies. As such, it extends beyond the everyday and finds its expression in forms which, as mentioned earlier, are based on the behavioral patterns, images and everyday language of a specific world-view. These then sediment to form a specific, historically and socially objectified form of social knowledge and action: *religion*.

In archaic societies the differentiation of social functions is still limited, such that personal identity, social structure and religion tightly overlap. Religion, which is more or less demarcated sacrally, affects behavior-steering institutions to a great extent, and religious interpretive patterns and themes give an unambiguous answer to the major typical crises that regularly intrude on the lives of individuals and the group, as for example the death of a mother or a sudden epidemic in a village. Only in traditional major cultures is the sacred cosmos definitely excluded from the everyday in an institutional sense. It is only with the expansion of written culture and the production of economic surpluses that it becomes possible to train experts to structure and codify 'higher forms of knowledge.' As written, religion not only receives a socially perceptible 'basis' as a regular and systematized interpretive system, but is also biographically experienceable as a profiled dimension or as numinous. Beyond this, institutional roles such as 'father,' 'mother,' 'bachelor,' etc. are loaded with a special significance and thereby either idealized or marginalized. This affects the conditions for their fulfillment and their perception in everyday social life.

In modern industrial societies the sphere of authority of the sacred cosmos, which once stood as the 'official model of religion' and legitimated society in its totality, loses its influence over other institutional domains. The domains of economy and science, law and politics—exemplary theoreticians of which are Machiavelli and Galileo, Smith and Kant—are given their own independent legitimations, giving rise to specific forms of political action, distinct economic and juridical rationalities, as well as specific forms of scientific logic none of which any longer need the support of religion. Because it is required that these forms of legitimation be given preference in their own specific domains, institutionalized religion increasingly loses plausibility for the lives of individuals: while it is still taught, its significance is often only rhetorical, and at most mere lip service is paid to its supposed status as the "official model."

Luckmann developed the connection between religiosity and religion, as well as the theory of transcendencies, in his work *The Invisible Religion*, first published in 1967. In the postscript to the German edition these basic insights are further expanded and clarified. In two other essays presented, *Die religiöse Situation in Europa* and *Schrumpfende Transzendenzen, expandierende Religion* [Shrinking Transcendencies, Expanding Religion], Thomas Luckmann argues with different emphases against the dominant interpretation, according to which the differentiation of the social structure and concomitant institutional specialization of religion leads to these transcendencies losing all meaning, or even disappearing from the modern world to leave behind a religious vacuum.

As he puts it, if experiences of transcendence are universal components of human life, and religiosity describes an anthropological disposition, then religion will always assume new forms in processes of social change. During such periods, it is no longer required for experiences of transcendence to be expressed in the form of traditionally recognizable institutions and conceptions. In one respect, worldly ideologies such as communism, fascism or anarchism try to co-opt the function of religious meaning systems; in part, because they explicitly draw on institutionalized religions in their self-staging, from which they even demonstratively distance themselves in other contexts. In another respect, there is a clear tendency toward a 'privatization' of religion, which is apparent in two directions. First, religion separates itself from church institutions and spreads into the sphere of short-term and group-like organizational forms, such as self-help groups, cliques and other meaning-giving communities. Second, religiously relevant topics increasingly shift to the subjective domain, equivalent to a shrinking of transcendencies: contents increasingly move into the center of the sacred cosmos of modern societies which belong less to the major, other-worldly than to the middle and minor trancendencies of everyday life. Aspects such as corporeal self-experience and sexual behavior, self-realization and consciousness expansion, personal happiness and family well-being come to occupy a central position in religious strivings. This "subjectivization of religion" (Knoblauch 1997a) has the effect that individuals even understand themselves as the origin and source of religion.[11] However, this tendency—as stated above—by no means

11 That the subjectivization of belief already had roots in the modern type of individuality 'created' by Luther was convincingly argued by Soeffner 1992.

leads to an isolated and individualized exercise of religion by the individuals who are 'sanctified' in this way. Instead, new social forms of the religious are added to existing conventional religions, socially expressed in institutions like psychoanalysis, therapeutic cults and the 'New Age' movement (Knoblauch 1989). One thing is quite decisive, however: the forms of the religious change, the fundamental conditions for the socialization of religious groups and the modes of their social visibility are primarily due to new media and market-conforming communication structures. Insofar as believers find themselves in and on television (Keppler 1995; Reichertz 2000), and the Internet brings laymen together, and communities with permanent members also become 'event communities' coming together only episodically to celebrate important occasions, we can see the necessarily communicative construction of religion (cf. Knoblauch 1997b, 1999b).

VI The Turn to Communicative Construction

Berger and Luckmann (1969) describe the social construction of reality as a dialectical process in which analytical distinctions must be made between externalization, objectification and internalization. This division adheres to the basic problem of sociology, which is that of understanding and explaining the relationship between the individual and society. Externalization refers accordingly to a process in which subjective meaning is constituted in consciousness and then externalized, which explains individual sociality anthropologically and phenomenologically. Objectification describes the course in which the thus externalized becomes a reality through social processes of institutionalization and legitimation. Finally, it is the internalization of the socially objectified—of action patterns and the meanings tied to them—which enables the individual to develop and permanently establish a personal identity, a process through which individuals are ultimately integrated into the world.

Impressive as this dialectic may ultimately appear, through its managing to link consciousness and society together in such a way that they cannot be isolated into different 'systems' by any theoretical sleight of hand—neither Luckmann nor Berger made much use of it. The reason for this may be because the complex 'interactions' between these three levels proved to be too abstract to be able to grasp the process of social construction in its concrete development. As such, they thought is practical to clarify the social function of language, insofar as it overarches and permeates all levels.

As can be seen in processes of externalization, in which individuals outwardly transmit their inner, directly experienced life impulses and thereby give expression to their subjective meaning conceptions, linguistic forms of expression clearly take precedence with regard to other systems of signs and symbols. Language is just as dominant in the objectification of solitary typifications, interpretive and action schemes for intersubjectively shared and collectively binding societal world views. Because language, "as objectively available sign system," is what first "bestows a status of incipient anonymity on sedimented experiences by detaching them from their original context of concrete individual biographies and making them generally available to all who share, or may in future share, in the sign system in question" (Berger and Luckmann 1969, p. 72; English: 1967, p. 68).

Linguistic ability and linguistic activities thus are the actual prerequisites for the construction of social order as an endless process in which reality is socially defined, redefined, sedimented and changed (cf. Luckmann 1979a). This is why language ultimately proves to be the most important bearer and mediator of social knowledge stocks which, while through being internalized by individuals is not determining, constitutes the largely prefiguring pre-established reference points for their orientations and action in everyday life.

On the basis of this prominent status, communicative action—first of all, the use of language, then increasingly, also of non-verbal forms of expression—takes a central position in Luckmann's theoretical and empirical work on the key processes in social situations where action-orienting knowledge becomes socially distributed (Luckmann 1971, 1975, 1979a).[12] The opening of the sociology of knowledge for communication does justice to the change in the meaning of communication in society itself, as well as in social theory. Second, and above all, it brings about a theoretical expansion and new empirical-methodological orientation of the sociology of knowledge, with which it reacted to the new tasks being posed: social scientific constitution analysis of acts of understanding in their elementary details.

Alfred Schutz emphasized the importance of communication very early. The everyday life-world not only has priority over other domains of reality, because in it 'pragmatic motivation' dominates and humans can effectively change things, but also because in it communication takes place with others (Schütz 1971, p. 265). Since the early 1980s, however, a notable turn toward communication can be shown for all German-language theoretical sociology. It was on the basis of Schütz and Luckmann's *Strukturen der Lebenswelt* [Structures of the Life-World] (1979) that Jürgen Habermas developed his *Theorie des kommunikativen Handelns* [Theory of Communicative Action] (1981). And in *Soziale Systeme*

12 Cf. Auer 1999, who treats Luckmann as a 'classic' in this context.

(1984), Niklas Luhmann made an 'autopoietic' turn in which communication is treated as the basic process of society as a whole (see above).[13]

Moreover, in the domain of empirical research, a range of new research approaches were developed, including ethnomethodology, conversation analysis, the ethnography of communication and certain hermeneutic procedures, all of which display a methodological and theoretical proximity to the social-constructivist sociology of knowledge and whose 'interpretive' access became possible in new ways through more widely-available auditory and audio-visual recording techniques.

Although communication assumes a central value in the quasi-'timeless' scheme of the sociology of knowledge, its significance is not based solely on its theoretical-analytical weight, but is above all derived from concrete developments in contemporary society. Thus, the turn to communication displays traces of an unmistakably social-diagnostic nature insofar as it takes account of the increasing significance of communicative action in modern societies. The rapid specialization of knowledge makes it necessary to link together various special knowledge areas: these processes, not to mention theoretical reflection on them, would not even be possible without the existence of increasingly market-like forms of communication. This effect is strengthened by the parallel spread and refinement of communication technologies, leading to a multiplication and qualitative 'enrichment' of communication activities, a fact which thus drives the growing presence of the media in everyday life and perception (cf. Soeffner and Raab 1998). Ultimately, the growing pluralization of life-worlds is causing a decline in intersubjectively shared knowledge stocks. As Habermas has rightly noted, this development, which can also be understood as 'detraditionalization' (cf. Beck 1986; Schulze 1992), is forcing people to communicate: since it can no longer be assumed that there will be a fairly uniform distribution of elements of social knowledge, it is urgently necessary for acts of understanding to articulate, renegotiate and retransmit already objectified knowledge contents in social sub-domains; i.e. to communicate. However, the social-constructivist sociology of knowledge by no means shares Habermas's hope that this communication would tend to take a rational course. Instead, it presupposes that we have to assume a 'secondary traditionalization' of communication: in communicative action stable forms and patterns increasingly develop—analogous to institutions—that provide people with a frame of orientation in the rapidly changing flow of communication.

13 This thesis is explained in detail in Knoblauch 1995.

When they orient, social actors use such patterns and forms, ones that are usually embedded in institutions, then, when they interpret and act, reaffirm and reach agreement among themselves. They mark communicative action and form, as Thomas Luckmann emphasizes in his discussion in *Der kommunikative Aufbau der sozialen Welt und die Sozialwissenschaften* [The Communicative Construction of the Social World and the Social Sciences], "the more or less self-evident and binding foundation for the introduction of 'natural' human organisms into an 'artificial' socio-historical world." In order to study these routinized processes, constitutive for the social construction of reality in which knowledge is represented, processed, stored and handed on and which structure action, Thomas Luckmann, drawing on Vološinov (1975) and Bachtin (1986), developed a sociology of communicative interpretive and representational forms—a theory and methodology of 'communicative genres.'

Its founding premises are decisive: every symbolic or communicative action is subject to rules that pattern behavior and thus provide a certain structuring of communicative events. Of course, not all communicative processes in human societies are sediment in genre-like communicative forms of action, similar to the way in which those who participate in communication always orient their actions to the pre-given forms of a genre. Thus there are communicative acts in which actors continually plan their actions spontaneously and perform them 'under their own direction.' These 'spontaneous' communicative processes stand in contrast to ones in which the participants' courses of action are determined over a certain period of time by an overall pattern such that the combination of individual communicative elements is more or less obligatorily socially pre-given. Thus 'sedimented' forms can then be recognized as communicative genres. These forms are components of the social knowledge stock available to actors, "a society's communicative household" (Luckmann 1988), and are typically observable in concrete communicative action.

The need to find orientation in communicative genres derives, first, from the fact that in every society there are recurring elementary communicative problems: how can events or experiences, conceptions or opinions, states of affairs or knowledge contents be dealt with, summarized and transmitted according to various criteria for meaning? Moreover: how is this stylistically and 'technically' possible? Communicative genres offer answers to these questions. They are the more or less effective, and more or less binding, solutions for the specific communication problems that typically arise in society: repeating everyday proverbs, telling jokes or fables, presenting an eulogy or writing a lonely-hearts ad, criticizing, professing love or recalling the legend of a saint—with which the broad spectrum of typical communication problem situations and their 'solutions' is only hinted at—are things that facilitate the management of communication problems. Finally, communicative genres are means and 'programs' for the construction of intersubjective meaning: as communicative guidelines they objectify style units of meaning and in this way make possible traditions of meaning setting (cf. Schütz and Luckmann 1984, p. 13).

Luckmann's considerations in *Zur Methodologie (mündlicher) kommunikativer Gattungen* [On the Methodology of (Oral) Communicative Genres] start from this theoretical conception. In this work, Luckmann shows, in an exemplary manner, that sociological theory construction must always be testable against social reality, or, conversely, that, if based on and guided by theory, empirical work must of necessity lead to meaningful results. Methodically, genre analysis must solve a translation problem. The typical forms of understanding of a culture and a society—the first-order constructions (Schütz 1971)—have to be transformed into a 'universal,' culture- and epoch-dependent data corpus that permits of comparisons: i. e. into second-order constructions (ibid.). As such, empirical genre analysis is focused not on giving a taxonomy of patterns or the illustration of 'pure' types in Weber's sense—since communicative genres are not static dimensions, but instead 'develop' in interaction and so display a temporal structure. These temporal courses of events must be systematically and methodically studied in order to reconstruct them. Genre analysis thus displays a certain proximity to sequence analysis as a hermeneutic procedure (cf. Oevermann et al. 1979; Soeffner 1989), as it also does to ethnomethodological conversation analysis. At the same time, however, it claims to go beyond these two methodical instruments. With its special emphasis on historical and cultural comparison, it aims to grasp the different degrees of sedimentation of genres, their subtypes, which it differentiates substantively, as well as their situative action contexts and frame conditions, e. g., through the description of their respective "internal" and "external structures."

Building on the foundation of the sociology of knowledge and drawing on the theoretical and empirical conception of communicative genres, a wave of studies on 'sedimented' communication forms developed. Besides works in linguistics, particularly text linguistics (Knoblauch and Günthner 1994, 2000), there are, above all, analyses on the sociology of language, i. e. phenomena from gossip (Bergmann 1987) to conversions (Ulmer 1988) and argumentation (Keppler 1994; Knoblauch 1991). If informal communicative acts were the initial focus of attention in genre analyses, with the study of linguistic interactions in institutional contexts (cf. Bergmann 1999; Christmann 1999) and the study of media communication forms (exemplary: Keppler 1996, 2001; Knoblauch and Raab 2001), two new focuses became particularly interesting for genre research.[14]

Indeed, the empirical works show with great clarity the particular new orientation of social constructivism. Knoblauch (1995), for example, gives communication a central role as a constitutive element for the social order. For their part, Bergmann and Luckmann (1999/2000) no longer regarded their research results on morals as contributions to the social, but as bearing on the 'communicative construction' of reality: morals are carried less by institutions than by communication between people, where it naturally must assume a certain indirection.

Luckmann gives strong expression to the constitutive meaning of linguistic activity for societal life and for the forming of social orders as well as for the related turn of social theory to communication. He points out that the shift in emphasis to the communicative aspects of social action means neither a turning away from an action-theoretical orientation—as is demanded by the system-theoretical 'shift' from action to communication—nor a paradigm change in Kuhn's sense (1973). Much more, the paradigmatic opening for the particularities of communicative acts means an empirical expansion of the sociology of knowledge: the reconstruction of everyday practices that are constitutive of meaning—of social behavior and the social structures that condition and arise from it—should make it possible to uncover the fundamental structures of human social life.

References

Auer, Peter (1999), *Sprachliche Interaktion. Eine Einführung anhand von 22 Klassikern*, Berlin: de Gruyter.

Bachtin, Michail M. (1986), *Speech Genres and Other Late Essays*, Vern N. McGee, trans. Austin; University of Texas Press.

Beck, Ulrich (1986), *Risikogesellschaft. Auf dem Weg in eine andere Moderne.* Frankfurt a. M: Suhrkamp.

Berger, Peter L. und Thomas Luckmann (1963) "Sociology of Religion and Sociology of Knowledge," *Sociology and Social Research* 47, 61–73.

Berger, Peter L. und Thomas Luckmann (1969), *Die gesellschaftliche Konstruktion der Wirklichkeit. Eine Theorie der Wissenssoziologie*, Frankfurt a. M.: Fischer (engl. *The Social Construction of Reality. A Treatise in the Sociology of Knowledge*, New York: Anchor, 1966)

Bergmann, Jörg R. (1987), *Klatsch. Zur Sozialform der diskreten Indiskretion,* Berlin: de Gruyter.

14 An overview of the breadth of the research fields is found in the contributions in Knoblauch (1996).

Bergmann, Jörg R. (1999), "Diskrete Exploration. Über die moralische Sinnstruktur eines psychoanalytischen Frageformats" in: J. Bergmann und Th. Luckmann (eds.), *Kommunikative Konstruktion von Moral, Bd. 2: Von der Moral zu den Moralen*, Wiesbaden: Westdeutscher, pp.169–190.

Bergmann, Jörg R. und Thomas Luckmann (1999) (eds.), *Kommunikative Konstruktion von Moral, Band I: Struktur und Dynamik der Formen moralischer Kommunikation, Band II: Von der Moral zu den Moralen*, Wiesbaden: Westdeutscher.

Burr, Vivien (1995), *An Introduction to Social Constructionism*, London: Routledge.

Christmann, Gabriele (1999), Moralisierungsaskese in der Kommunikation von Ökologiegruppen, in: J. Bergmann und Th. Luckmann (eds.), *Kommunikative Konstruktion von Moral, Bd. 2: Von der Moral zu den Moralen*, Wiesbaden: Westdeutscher, pp. 191–214.

Eberle, Thomas S. (1993a), "Schütz' Lebensweltanalyse: Soziologie oder Protosoziologie." In: A. Bäumer und M. Benedikt (eds.), *Gelehrtenrepublik – Lebenswelt*, Wien: Passagenverlag, pp. 293–320.

Eberle, Thomas S. (1993b), "Social Psychology and the Sociology of Knowledge," *Aprendizja, Revista de Psicologia Social* 8, pp. 5–13.

Eberle, Thomas S. (1999), "Sinnadäquanz und Kausaladäquanz bei Max Weber und Alfred Schütz." In: R. Hitzler, J. Reichertz und N. Schröer (eds.), *Hermeneutische Wissenssoziologie. Standpunkte zur Theorie der Interpretation*, Konstanz: UVK, Universitätsverlag, pp. 97–119

Gehlen, Arnold (1978), *Der Mensch. Seine Natur und seine Stellung in der Welt*, Wiesbaden: Athenaion.

Grathoff, Richard (1978), Alltag und Lebenswelt als Gegenstand der phänomenologischen Sozialtheorie, in: K. Hammerich und M. Klein (eds.), *Materialien zur Soziologie des Alltags, Sonderheft der Kölner Zeitschrift für Soziologie und Sozialpsychologie* 20, pp. 67–85.

Günthner, Susanne und Hubert Knoblauch (1994), Forms are the food of faith‹. Gattungen als Muster kommunikativen Handelns, in: *Kölner Zeitschrift für Soziologie und Sozialpsychologie* 46, pp. 693–723

Habermas, Jürgen (1981), *Theorie des kommunikativen Handelns*, Frankfurt a. M.: Suhrkamp.

Hacking, Ian (1999), *Was heißt ›soziale Konstruktion‹? Zur Konjunktur einer Kampfvokabel in den Wissenschaften*, Frankfurt a. M.: Fischer Taschenbuch.

Hitzler, Ronald, Anne Honer und Christoph Maeder (eds.)(1994), *Expertenwissen. Die institutionalisierte Kompetenz zur Konstruktion von Wirklichkeit*, Wiesbaden: Westdeutscher.

Honer, Anne (1999), Bausteine zu einer lebensweltorientierten Wissenssoziologie, in: R. Hitzler, J. Reichertz und N. Schröer (eds.), *Hermeneutische Wissenssoziologie. Standpunkte zur Theorie der Interpretation*, Konstanz: UVK, Universitätsverlag Konstanz, pp. 51–67.

Keppler, Angela (1994), *Tischgespräche. Über Formen kommunikativer Vergemeinschaftung am Beispiel der Konversation in Familien*, Frankfurt a. M.: Suhrkamp.

Keppler, Angela (1995), Die Kommunion des Dabeiseins. Formen des Sakralen in der Fernsehunterhaltung, in: *Rundfunk und Fernsehen* 43, 4, 301–311.

Keppler, Angela (1996), Interaktion ohne reales Gegenüber. Zur Wahrnehmung medialer Akteure im Fernsehen, in: P. Vorderer (ed.), *Fernsehen als ›Beziehungskiste‹. Personale Beziehungen und Interaktionen mit TV-Personen*, Wiesbaden: Westdeutscher, pp. 11–24.

Keppler, Angela (2001), "Media Communications and Social Interaction: Perspectives on Action-Theory Based Reception Research." *Communications* 26, 169 – 179.

Knoblauch, Hubert (1989), Das unsichtbare neue Zeitalter. ›New Age‹, privatisierte Religion und kultisches Milieu." *Kölner Zeitschrift für Soziologie und Sozialpsychologie* 3, 504 – 525.

Knoblauch, Hubert (1991), "Die Verflüchtigung der Religion ins Religiöse." In: Thomas Luckmann, *Die unsichtbare Religion*, Frankfurt a. M., 7 – 41.

Knoblauch, Hubert (1995), *Kommunikationskultur. Zur kommunikativen Konstruktion kultureller Kontexte*, Berlin/New York: de Gruyter.

Knoblauch, Hubert (1996), *Kommunikative Lebenswelten. Zur Ethnographie einer geschwätzigen Gesellschaft*, Konstanz: UVK, Universitätsverlag Konstanz.

Knoblauch, Hubert (1997a), "Die Sichtbarkeit der unsichtbaren Religion. Subjektivierung, Märkte und die religiöse Kommunikation." *Zeitschrift für Religionswissenschaft* 5, 179 – 202.

Knoblauch, Hubert (1997b), "Transzendenzerfahrung und symbolische Kommunikation. Die phänomenologisch orientierte Soziologie und die kommunikative Konstruktion der Religion." In: H. Tyrell, V. Krech und H. Knoblauch (eds.), *Religion als Kommunikation*, Würzburg: Ergon, pp. 147 – 186.

Knoblauch, Hubert (1999a), "Zwischen System und Sozialkonstruktivismus? Unterschiede und Überschneidungen zwischen Systemtheorie und Sozialkonstruktivismus." In: R. Hitzler, J. Reichertz und N. Schröer (eds.), *Hermeneutische Wissenssoziologie. Standpunkte zur Theorie der Interpretation*, Konstanz: UVK, Universitätsverlag Konstanz, pp. 213 – 235.

Knoblauch, Hubert (1999b), "Populäre Religion. Markt, Medien und die Popularisierung der Religion." In: A. Honer, R. Kurt und J. Reichertz (eds.), *Diesseitsreligion. Zur Deutung der Bedeutung moderner Kultur*, Konstanz: UVK, Universitätsverlag Konstanz, pp. 201 – 222.

Knoblauch, Hubert (2001), "Gelebte Allegorien. Symbole, Metaphern und die Nahtoderfahrung." In: G. von Graevenitz, S. Rieger und F. Thürlemann (eds.), *Die Unvermeidlichkeit der Bilder*, Tübingen: Gunter Narr Verlag, pp. 255 – 270.

Knoblauch, Hubert und Susanne Günthner (2000), "Textlinguistik und Sozialwissenschaften." In: K. Brinker, G. Antos, W. Heinemann und S. F. Sager (eds.), *Text und Gesprächslinguistik. Linguistics of Text and Conversation*, Berlin/New York, 1. Halbb., 811 – 819.

Knoblauch, Hubert, Ronald Kurt und Hans-Georg Soeffner, "Zur kommunikativen Ordnung der Lebenswelt. Alfred Schütz' Theorie der Zeichen, Sprache und Kommunikation." In: *Alfred Schütz. Die kommunikative Ordnung der Lebenswelt* (Alfred Schütz Gesamtausgabe), Konstanz : UVK, Universitätsverlag Konstanz. Forthcoming.

Knoblauch, Hubert und Jürgen Raab (2001), "Genres and the Aesthetics of Advertisement Spots." In: H. Knoblauch und H. Kotthoff (Hg.), *Verbal Art across Cultures. The Aesthetics and Proto-Aestehtics of Communication*, Tübingen: Gunter Narr Verlag, pp. 195 – 219.

Knorr-Cetina, Karin (1989), "Spielarten des Konstruktivismus. Einige Notizen und Anmerkungen." *Soziale Welt* 40, pp. 86 – 96.

Kuhn, Thomas S. (1973), *Die Struktur wissenschaftlicher Revolutionen*, Frankfurt a. M.: Suhrkamp.

Latour, Bruno (1995), *Wir sind nie modern gewesen. Versuch einer symmetrischen Anthropologie*, Berlin

Luckmann, Thomas (1957), "The Evangelical Academies: An Experiment in German Protestantism." *Christianity and Crisis* 17, 4, pp. 68 – 70.

Luckmann, Thomas (1959), "Four Protestant Parishes in Germany: A Study in the Sociology of Religion." *Social Research* 26, pp. 423–448.
Luckmann, Thomas (1960), "Vier protestantische Kirchengemeinden. Bericht über eine vergleichende Untersuchung." In: D. Goldschmidt, H. Greiner und H. Schelsly (eds.), *Soziologie der Kirchengemeinde*, Stuttgart: Enke, pp. 132–144.
Luckmann, Thomas (1963), *Zum Problem der Religion in der modernen Gesellschaft. Institution, Person und Weltanschauung*, Freiburg/Br.: Rombach.
Luckmann, Thomas (1967), *The Invisible Religion*, New York: Macmillan.
Luckmann, Thomas (1971), "Vorschläge zur Richtung der soziologischen Erforschung der Sprache." In: R. Kjolseth und F. Sack (eds.), *Zur Soziologie der Sprache* (Sonderheft der Kölner Zeitschrift für Soziologie und Sozialpsychologie 15), pp. 36–47.
Luckmann, Thomas (1975), *Sociology of Language*, Indianapolis: Bobbs-Merrill.
Luckmann, Thomas (1979a), "Soziologie der Sprache." In: R. König (ed.), *Handbuch der empirischen Sozialforschung*, Bd. 13, Stuttgart: Enke, 1–116
Luckmann, Thomas (1979b), "Persönliche Identität und Lebenslauf—Gesellschaftliche Voraussetzungen." In: G. Klingenstein, H. Lutz und O. Stourzh (eds.), *Biographie und Geschichtswissenschaft*, (Wiener Beiträge zur Geschichte der Neuzeit, Bd. 6), Vienna: Verlag für Geschichte und Politik, 1979, pp. 29–46, also in: H. G. Brose und B. Hildenbrand (eds.) (1988), *Vom Ende des Individuums zur Individualität ohne Ende*, Opladen: Springer, pp. 73–88.
Luckmann, Thomas (1979c), "Persönliche Identität, soziale Rolle und Rollendistanz." In: O. Marquard und K. Stierle (eds.), *Identität* (Poetik und Hermeneutik, Bd. VIII), München: Fink, pp. 293–313.
Luckmann, Thomas (1980a), *Lebenswelt und Gesellschaft. Grundstrukturen und geschichtliche Wandlung*, Paderborn: Schöningh.
Luckmann, Thomas (1980b), "Über die Grenzen der Sozialwelt." In: Luckmann, *Lebenswelt und Gesellschaft. Grundstrukturen und geschichtliche Wandlung*, Paderborn: Schöningh, pp. 56–92.
Luckmann, Thomas (1981), "Vorüberlegungen zum Verhältnis von Alltagswissen und Wissenschaft." In: P. Janich (ed.), *Wissenschaftstheorie und Wissenschaftsforschung*, München: Beck, pp. 39–51.
Luckmann, Thomas (1985), "Über die Funktion der Religion." In: P. Koslowski (ed.), *Die religiöse Dimension der Gesellschaft*, Tübingen: Mohr Siebeck, pp. 26–41.
Luckmann, Thomas (1986), "Zeit und Identität: Innere, soziale und historische Zeit." In: F. Fürstenberg und I. Mörth (eds.), *Zeit als Strukturelement von Lebenswelt und Gesellschaft*, Linz: Trauner, pp. 135–174.
Luckmann, Thomas (1987), "Comments on Legitimation." *Current Sociology* 35, 2, 109–117.
Luckmann, Thomas (1988), "Kommunikative Gattungen im kommunikativen Haushalt einer Gesellschaft." In: G. Smolka-Koerdt, P. M. Spangenberg und D. Tilmann-Bartylla (eds.), *Der Ursprung der Literatur*, München: Fink, pp. 279–288.
Luckmann, Thomas (1989), "Zum Verhältnis von Alltagswissen und Wissenschaft." In: K. Rebel (ed.), *Wissenschaftstransfer in der Weiterbildung: der Beitrag der Wissenssoziologie*, Weinheim/Basel: Beltz, pp. 28–35.
Luckmann, Thomas (1990), "Towards a Science of the Subjective Paradigm: Protosociology." In: *Critique and Humanism* (Special Issue), pp. 9–15.

Luckmann, Thomas (1991), *Die unsichtbare Religion*, Frankfurt a. M.: Suhrkamp (engl. *Invisible Religion*, New York/London: Macmillan, 1967)
Luckmann, Thomas (1992), *Theorie sozialen Handelns*, Berlin/New York: de Gruyter.
Luckmann, Thomas (1996a), "Die intersubjektive Konstitution der Moral." In: *Arbeitspapiere Moralprojekt*, Nr. 1, Konstanz/Gießen, Februar (abbreviated version in: J. Bergmann und Th. Luckmann (eds.) (1999), *Kommunikative Konstruktion von Moral. Bd. 1: Struktur und Dynamik der Formen moralischer Kommunikation*, Wiesbaden: Westdeutscher, pp. 13–38).
Luckmann, Thomas (1996b), "Über Moral und moralische Kommunikation in der modernen Gesellschaft." *Sociologia Internationalis* 34, I, pp. 1–11.
Luckmann, Thomas (1997), "The moral order of modern societies, moral communication and indirect moralising." In: *Public Lectures*, 17, Collegium Budapest/Institute for Advanced Study (abgedruckt in: M. Wicke (ed.), *Konfigurationen lebensweltlicher Strukturphänomene. Soziologische Varianten phänomenologisch-hermeneutischer Welterschließung*, (Festschrift für Hansfried Kellner zum 60. Geburtstag), Opladen: Westdeutscher, pp. 11–24.
Luckmann, Thomas (1998a), "Moralpredigten in der modernen Gesellschaft?" In: H. Tyrell, V. Krech und H. Knoblauch (eds.), *Religion als Kommunikation*, Würzburg: Ergon, 391–416.
Luckmann, Thomas (ed.) (1998b), *Moral im Alltag. Sinnvermittlung und moralische Kommunikation in intermediären Institutionen*, Gütersloh: Verl. Bertelsmann-Stiftung.
Luckmann, Thomas (1999a), "Moralpredigten." In: J. Bergmann und T. Luckmann (eds.), *Kommunikative Konstruktion von Moral. Bd. 2: Von der Moral zu den Moralen*, Wiesbaden, 80–112
Luckmann, Thomas (1999b), "Wirklichkeiten: individuelle Konstitution und gesellschaftliche Konstruktion." In: R. Hitzler, J. Reichertz und N. Schröer (eds.), *Hermeneutische Wissenssoziologie. Standpunkte zur Theorie der Interpretation*, Konstanz; UVK, Universitätsverlag Konstanz, pp. 17–28.
Luckmann, Thomas (2002), *Wissen und Gesellschaft*, Konstanz: UVK, Universitätsverlag Konstanz.
Luckmann, Thomas und Peter L. Berger (1995), *Modernität, Pluralismus und Sinnkrise. Die Orientierung des modernen Menschen*, Gütersloh: Verlag Bertelsmann-Stiftung.
Luhmann, Niklas (1984), *Soziale Systeme. Grundriß einer allgemeinen Theorie*, Frankfurt a. M.: Suhrkamp.
Luhmann, Niklas (1997), *Die Gesellschaft der Gesellschaft*, Frankfurt a. M.: Suhrkamp.
Mead, George H. (1973), *Geist, Identität und Gesellschaft aus der Sicht des Sozialbehaviorismus*, Frankfurt a. M.: Suhrkamp, [1934].
Oevermann, Ulrich, Tillmann Allert, Elisabeth Konau und Jürgen Krambeck (1979), "Die Methodologie einer ›objektiven Hermeneutik‹ und ihre allgemeine forschungslogische Bedeutung in den Sozialwissenschaften." In: H.-G. Soeffner (ed.), *Interpretative Verfahren in den Sozial- und Textwissenschaften*, Stuttgart: Metzler, pp. 352–434.
Plessner, Helmuth (1975), *Die Stufen des Organischen und der Mensch. Einleitung in die philosophische Anthropologie*, Berlin/New York: de Gruyter [1928].
Reichertz, Jo (2000), *Die Frohe Botschaft des Fernsehens. Kulturwissenschaftliche Untersuchungen medialer Diesseitsreligion*, Konstanz: UVK, Universitätsverlag Konstanz.
Scheler, Max (1983), *Die Stellung des Menschen im Kosmos*, Bern/München: Francke [1928].

Schnettler, Bernt (2003), "Sociability. Reconstructing the ethnotheory of cooperation." In: A. Müller und A. Kieser (eds.), *Communication in Organizations*, Frankfurt a. M.: Suhrkamp, p. 201–218.

Schulze, Gerhard (1992), *Die Erlebnisgesellschaft. Kultursoziologie der Gegenwart*, Frankfurt a. M.: Suhrkamp.

Schütz, Alfred (1971), "Symbol, Wirklichkeit und Gesellschaft." In: ders., *Gesammelte Aufsätze I*, Den Haag: Nijhoff, pp. 237–411.

Schütz, Alfred (1972), "Der gut informierte Bürger." In: ders., *Gesammelte Aufsätze II*, Den Haag: Nijhoff, pp. 85–101.

Schütz, Alfred (1991), *Der sinnhafte Aufbau der sozialen Welt*, Frankfurt a. M.: Suhrkamp [1932]

Schütz, Alfred und Thomas Luckmann (1979), *Strukturen der Lebenswelt, Bd. 1*, Frankfurt a. M.: Suhrkamp.

Schütz, Alfred und Thomas Luckmann (1984), *Strukturen der Lebenswelt, Bd. 2*, Frankfurt a. M.: Suhrkamp.

Simmel, Georg (1995), "Die Religion." In: Simmel, *Philosophie der Mode. Die Religion. Kant und Goethe. Schopenhauer und Nietzsche*, Frankfurt a. M.: Suhrkamp, pp. 39–118.

Simmel, Georg (2000), "Vorformen der Idee. Aus den Studien zu einer Metaphysik." In: Simmel, *Aufsätze und Abhandlungen 1908–1918, Band II*, Frankfurt a. M.: Suhrkamp, pp. 252–298.

Soeffner, Hans-Georg (1989), *Alltag der Auslegung – Die Auslegung des Alltag. Zur wissenssoziologischen Konzeption einer sozialwissenschaftlichen Hermeneutik*, Frankfurt a. M.: Suhrkamp.

Soeffner, Hans-Georg (1992), "Luther—Der Weg von der Kollektivität des Glaubens zu einem lutherisch-protestantischen Individualitätstypus." In: ders., *Die Ordnung der Rituale. Die Auslegung des Alltags 2*, Frankfurt a. M.: Suhrkamp, pp. 20–75.

Soeffner, Hans-Georg und Jürgen Raab (1998), "Sehtechniken – Die Medialisierung des Sehens." In: W. Rammert (ed.), *Technik und Sozialtheorie*, Frankfurt a. M.: Suhrkamp, pp. 121–148.

Soeffner, Hans-Georg (2000), "Das Ebenbild in der Bilderwelt. Religiosität und die Religionen." In: ders., *Gesellschaft ohne Baldachin*, Weilerswist: Velbrück Wissenschaft, pp. 97–123.

Sprondel, Walter M. (1979), "›Experte‹ und ›Laie‹, Zur Entwicklung von Typenbegriffen in der Wissenssoziologie." In: Sprondel and R. Grathoff (eds.), *Alfred Schütz und die Idee ders Alltags in den Sozialwissenschaften*, Stuttgart: Enke, pp. 140–154.

Srubar, Ilja (1988), *Kosmion. Die Genese der pragmatischen Lebensweltheorie von Alfred Schütz und ihr anthropologischer Hintergrund*, Frankfurt a. M.: Suhrkamp.

Srubar, Ilja (1991), "›Phänomenologische Soziologie‹ als Theorie und Forschung." In: M. Herzog and C. F. Graumann (eds.), *Sinn und Erfahrung*, Heidelberg: Asanger, pp. 169–182.

Ulmer, Bernd (1988), "Konversionserzählungen als rekonstruktive Gattung. Erzählerische Strategien bei der Rekonstruktion eines Bekehrungserlebnisses." *Zeitschrift für Soziologie* 17, 19–33.

Vološinov, Valentin N. (1975), *Marxismus und Sprachphilosophie. Grundlegende Probleme der soziologischen Methode in der Sprachwissenschaft*, Frankfurt a. M. : Suhrkamp [1929].

Weber, Max (1984), *Soziologische Grundbegriffe*, Tübingen: J.C.B. Mohr, [1921].

Weber, Max (1988), "Die protestantische Ethik und der Geist des Kapitalismus." In: Weber, *Gesammelte Aufsätze zur Religionssoziologie I*, Tübingen: J.C.B. Mohr, 1–206 [1921].

Didier de Robillard

Taking Plurality Seriously with Michel De Certeau: From History to 'Reception Sociolinguistics'

Abstract: It is not sufficient to try to keep the human sciences in statu quo, under the intellectual spell of Cartesian and positive epistemology with an over-sprinkling of added-on ethics. Human sciences should rather tap other resources. Michel de Certeau's work is one of such, concerned as he is with alterity, plurality and diversity. His reflexions about history can then easily be translated to sociolinguistics, and move towards providing it with a hermeneutic reception perspective. This does not reduce to "sociology of reception," but embraces deriving all the consequences from the fact that a sociolinguist, just like anybody else, phenomenologically and hermeneutically receives all the data and experience his or her research is based upon.

I Michel de Certeau: *Isn't He a Historian?*

With the majority of scholars in the human sciences, one might without a doubt think that work that is pluralist can take place in non-pluralistic epistemological frameworks, inspired, perhaps by pragmatism. This type of undertaking has been generalized in theories and methodologies, derived, for example, from symbolic interactionism.

One might—to the contrary—also think that most of these undertakings are, paradoxically, incapable of studying pluralism *without* objectifying it,[1] which obviously gives rise to a contradiction. In that case, one would need to undertake research in forms of thought that approach the question differently. To simplify: if one allows that the epistemology of the human sciences is presently composed of two major approaches—the hermeneutic ones and the others—and if one also admits that most of the perspectives of the human sciences are structured non-hermeneutically (pragmatism, cognitivism, socio-constructivism), it is worthwhile to engage the hermeneutic approaches.[2] These approaches place plurality at the heart of their undertaking and not only in appendices dealing with polit-

1 Robillard 2012. See, for a recent synthesis, Robillard 2016.
2 Robillard 2008a and Robillard 2010.

https://doi.org/10.1515/9783110551563-014

ical objectives or ethical imperatives: in that case such concerns are attached, *a posteriori*, and as a form of compensation, to non-pluralist approaches. In addition to those approaches that I have been able to explore,[3] we find certain scholars, like Michel de Certeau, who perhaps make theoretical freedom the foundation for work on pluralism: they merit the close attention of scholars concerned with the question of plurality. To be sure, de Certeau is not himself a socio-linguist but, as we shall see, his work can, in more ways than one, be easily appropriated for a sociolinguistics that would center on plurality: this is likewise not to say that his work is foreign to sociolinguistics. Moreover, de Certeau's constant preoccupation with questions of alterity makes him a relevant reference for whoever wishes to integrate this latter problematic into sociolinguistics (and, as any other human science, how could sociolinguistics escape that it is chiefly concerned with diversity).

II Diffuse Portraits of Michel de Certeau: The Man and the Historian

It is unfortunate that Michel de Certeau is largely familiar to sociolinguists only by way of his collaborative sociolinguistic book, *Une Politique de la langue: La Révolution française et les patois: l'enquête de Grégoire* [*A Politics of Language: the French Revolution and Patois: the Investigations of Henri Grégoire*], first published in 1975.[4] For scholars of sociolinguistics, this work is often the tree that hides the forest. It tends to obscure his other work, work that would be of the utmost general interest to sociolinguistics, were it inclined to take the question of plurality seriously.

Sketching an account of Michel de Certeau, François Dosse calls attention to the fact that, as he partakes of too many categories, de Certeau "suffers from being unclassifiable"[5]: a Jesuit, a historian, an anthropologist, a sociologist, a theologian, a co-founder in 1964 of the Freudian school of Paris. For Dosse,

> moved by the desire for an elsewhere, a desire for an other ... he did not cease to be moved towards an alterity in as much as this provokes an alteration of identity and thus gives rise to a renewal of a constant journey towards creation and innovation.[6]

3 Robillard, ed., 2010, Robillard, 2016.

4 Certeau, Julia and Revel 1975.

5 Dosse 2003, p. 1.

6 Dosse 2003, p. 1.

Dosse thus relates de Certeau to Edward Said, the intellectual of exile, the man who does not let himself be halted either by the accumulation of his works, nor by the fact that he occupies legitimate institutional positions.

In what way? By showing himself, as he did in a most intense fashion, like an over-exposed photograph. He will always have been, as Michel Foucault said, "at the edge of a cliff". Constantly taking risks, for the path that leads to the other puts one's own identify and certainties into risk ... There is thus an intense unity between de Certeau's life and work, to the point that his life, in a certain fashion, was his work.[7]

As Dosse continues,

> As the final point of his work [de Certeau] proposes a definition of mysticism that corresponds precisely to his own journey. 'The mystic is the person who cannot stop walking and who, with the certain knowledge of that which he lacks, knows of each locale and of each object that this is *not that*, that one may not dwell *here* nor remain content with *that*.

Consequently, one understands that one can only make fluid or out-of-focus portraits of Michel de Certeau, portraits where there is always "too much" as well as something bygone as there is also always something "missing" to the extent that it is still coming to birth. In what follows, I rely both on texts from de Certeau as well as on Dosse's account, from which, however, I shall distance myself—yet another reason this portrait will be "out of focus," as it will not attempt to reconcile two or three contradictory portraits, a quality for which I draw inspiration from the Certeaulian thought on plurality.

III Michel de Certeau and his Double—According to François Dosse

For Dosse, de Certeau organizes his understanding of work in history, and consequently in the human sciences, around three ideas: history articulates itself on a social plane; it is a practice that sets certain techniques to work; and it is a practice in which writing has a particular saliency. The following extracts from Dosse are clear enough that I need add nothing to them.

A social plane:

> First of all, it is the product of a social plane from which it emerges in the manner that consumer commodities are produced in business enterprises. Along this line, it insists on the

7 Dosse 2003, p. 1.

> very concept of making in that which is its strongest instrumental acceptation. "In history, any doctrine that foregoes its relation to society is abstract ... Scientific discourses that do not speak of their relation to the social body will not be able to articulate a practice. They would cease to be scientific".[8]

A practice:

> Secondly, history is a practice. It is never the simple noble speech of a disinterested and disincarnated interpretation. To the contrary, it is always mediated by technique and the borders between document and the construction thereof are constantly displaced ... In this understanding, the historian is he who masters a certain number of techniques dealing with the establishing of sources, with their classification and redistribution in relation to another space by using a certain number of operators.[9]

A writing:

> The attention that Michel de Certeau brings to the particular manner of writing history in no ways means that he would limit this discipline only to its discursive dimension: "In fact, historian-writing—or historiography—remains controlled by the practices that give rise to it; even more, it is itself a social practice." As the very place of historical realization, by its double nature as a mirror-writing that returns one to the present as the fictional fabricator of secrets and lies as well as to truth as a performative writing, historian-writing is caught in a fundamentally ambivalent relationship. The performative role of history comes down to permitting "a practice to situate itself in relation to its other, to the past".[10]

In this sketch by Dosse, one may see why historians are interested in studying de Certeau: as during the 1970's he raised questions about several ways of writing history that still remain today in high regard—those of the *Annales* school, for instance. An early 21st century sociolinguist who would wish to question the growing hegemonic faith in the "corpus," or in field data, even the recent fascination with "big data," might thus find in de Certeau some critical illumination. Nonetheless, while Dosse claims to perceive a "brilliant unity in de Certeau between his life and his work, to the point that in a certain manner his life was his work,"[11] it seems to me that his portrait of this incandescent personality remains a portrait of a historian who, quite surprisingly from this point of view, is far more classical than what one might have expected from that portrait. The aim of my essay is to work on this opening by mining material from the texts of

8 Dosse 2003, p. 6.
9 Dosse 2003, pp. 6–7.
10 Dosse 2003, p. 7, here citing Certeau 1975.
11 Dosse 2003, p. 1.

de Certeau (which, for a hermeneutic, is no guarantee of truth, but at least provides fuel for the debate).

IV A More Hermeneutical Michel de Certeau

It seems to me useful to direct our attention to certain reflections by de Certeau that yield a different picture. This "direction" (orientation [*sens*]) of reading is in fact suggested by Dosse himself in his long discussion detailing the intimate relation between de Certeau and Said, as well as in the portrait he draws of de Certeau, details of which were noted above, as they are in the actual coherence of his portrait of de Certeau.

One might thus pose the question like this: when de Certeau invokes history and partly thereby the human sciences, even if one cannot assimilate the human sciences as such to history, is he speaking of "his" conception of history, or else of history in general to which he would attach quite new ideas and critiques? One must be struck by analogies between de Certeau's reflections[12] and Hans-Georg Gadamer's hermeneutic conceptualizations, whereas Dosse, while speaking of a "hermeneutic of the other,"[13] cites only Paul Ricoeur.

V Knowledge, Exclusion, Domination, and Plurality

De Certeau holds that

> A structure characteristic of modern western culture probably shows itself in this historiography: intelligibility establishes itself in a relation to the other; it 'shifts' (or progresses) by modifying that which it makes its 'other' ... [and] this displays itself as knowing what to say about that which the other silences and guarantees the interpretative work of a ('human') science by the border that differentiates it from a region which waits for it to be known.[14]

Probably alluding to Michel Foucault (1926–1984), de Certeau raises the stakes, writing that medicine, like historiography, is born "from a separation between

---

12 Michel de Certeau, in the texts referred to here, does not clearly acknowledge hermeneutics as a source of inspiration. He is more probably inspired by psychoanalysis. However, his writing has hermeneutic undertones as he must have been acquainted with hermeneutics, as a Jesuit, theologian, etc.

13 Dosse 2003, p. 4.

14 Certeau 1975, p. 9.

the knowing that gives rise to discourse and the silent body that sustains it";[15] the authority of science "finds its confirmation in the avowal drawn from that which is dominated" (thus knowledge of/over the other, human knowledge, is formed).[16] Thus, de Certeau himself questions the reductions that the human sciences must bring about in order to exist as such, precisely when they undertake the project of exploring human plurality.

VI Knowledge and (Ir)rationality

This deliberate and forceful[17] foundational exclusion makes for a certain rigor ("Exclusion is always necessary for the establishing of rigor";[18] "*In the West, the group (or the individual) authorizes himself by that which it excludes ...*")[19] and this has a price: the amputation of the human phenomenon from one part of the complexity that is, for it, defining. Thus simplified, the human phenomenon becomes thinkable rationally, precisely because amputated, but it henceforth becomes unthinkable in a global sense, such that that which has been removed "*returns despite everything on the margins and faults of discourse: 'resistances,' 'survivals' or delays discretely trouble the nice ordering of a 'progress' or an 'interpretative system'*."[20] To say the least, the result is ambivalent: "In its progress, historical science sees the growth of the silent regions of that which it lacks."[21]

The more the discipline of the human sciences wishes to "methodologize" itself (in the strict sense of a method held to be independent of the objects of its concern), the more it is logically constrained to restrict the field of that which is meaningful for it. All the more, it thus proliferates objects that it makes *strange*, objects that it categorizes as incoherent or non-existent—because it has put on blinders. As an illustration, one might call upon certain kinds of (socio)linguistics, which can be centered on language provided it is reduced to its stable and homogeneous features; these are logically constrained to ask what to say about patois, dialects, "creoles," "interlanguages," "interlects"[22]

---

15 Certeau 1975, p. 10.
16 Certeau 1975, p. 10.
17 Certeau 1975, p. 10.
18 Certeau 1975, p. 48.
19 Certeau 1975, p. 10. Italics in original.
20 Certeau 1975, p. 10. Italics in original.
21 Certeau 1975, p. 52.
22 Prudent 1981; Robillard 2013.

which do not appear autonomous because they cannot find any relevance in its rigid rigor. In this last case, one can only note the coincidence between the appearance of these purist conceptions of language and the construction of nation-states that wish to be monolingual, with watertight borders,[23] as if it were the task of linguistics to legitimate by a narrow conception of language a narrow conception of nation, certain nations of which were then in a fierce rivalry, in particular Germany and France.[24] In the same manner, if one follows de Certeau, one may ask if one cannot reproach the human sciences with having advanced a restrictive picture of the others, which immediately minimizes the interest of what might be said about plurality, and shrinks plurality to nonsense.

VII Knowledge, Social and Institutional Anchoring, and (Ir) rational

The intellectual activity of the human sciences and thus of sociolinguistics, hollowed out as it were from the inside by an imperative to simplification, can nevertheless be efficient, as it is both made necessary and sustained by institutions. For de Certeau, a prominent fiction of the writing of history at least since Machiavelli is to illustrate how much the world owes to the activities of political powers as historians assimilate themselves to "the position of the subject of action—that of the Prince."[25] One cannot avoid thinking that since the development of large European states – a development corresponding to the birth of linguistics as a scientific discipline – the role of linguistics has been to defend a kind of "system" language, something that for the moment sociolinguists, despite their protestations of a pluralistic faith, have taken over without either criticizing or adapting it, thus remaining trapped inside the epistemology of structural linguistics.

In such work, the historian sees himself or herself instrumentalized into a technician[26] by the political and by institutions: it is from these that he receives

---

23 Baggioni 1997.

24 See Bergounioux 1992 on the difficulties that French linguistics has in opening itself to variation.

25 Certeau 1975, p. 14.

26 This term here and elsewhere in this text refers to Heidegger's problematization. According to Heidegger, our modern times are only more visibly technical than has always been in the West in the past because what defines a technical epoch is neither technology nor machinery, which are only symptoms of a far earlier foundational choice putting thinking rationally or technically on top of everything else (technology is an effect of that, not a cause). That choice was made, for orders that make history through the historian, just as this happened to sociolinguists justifying narrow conceptions of the state as we just saw above. This introduces a certain number of dissonances to the rather conformist portrait Dosse sketches. Thus Michel de Certeau brings out a set of foundational contradictions in the work of the historian for which Dosse seems to have no account. When the historian speaks of others, no matter what he may try, he will appear to take responsibility for them, while, on the contrary, when he reflects on his practices, "the historian discovers constraints that take their origin from well before his activity and that go back to previous organizations of which this work is a symptom and not the source."[27] Consequently the historian is required to recognize that the exclusion that grounds his legitimacy cannot be sustained, because

> thus grounded on a rift between a past that is its object and a present that is the scene of its practice, history continually rediscovers the present in its object and the past in its practices. It is inhabited by the strangeness that it seeks and it imposes its law on distant regions that it conquers believing that it gives them life.[28]

The historian is a prestidigitator: his work is viciously circular. In fact, concerning other disciplines in addition to history that he criticizes, and in particular in criticism of Bourdieu and Foucault, de Certeau shows how they have in common a fairly perverse way of proceeding: "one part (observable because circumscribed) is held to represent the (in-definite) totality of practices,"[29] "although initially obscure, tacit and distant, it is nevertheless inverted in the element that clarifies the theory and sustains the discourse."[30] Thus for example, in sociolinguistics, one might set a hypothetical general problematic that would consist in asking oneself whether globalization does not transform cultural practices or languages into merchandise, or whether the discourse of men does not produce masculine domination, etc. ... This perspective shrinks reality by means of a whole series of implicit simplifiers that are not subjected to critique (in particular: what is a man, what is a woman, what is merchandise, what is a language). *It is only thanks to this simplification that the experience one may have of others or any "corpus" or "field data" becomes immediately readable,* because by this hy-

---

Heidegger, by the early thinkers interpreting Plato and Aristotle, which results in the tendency in the human sciences to overvalue "objective" anonymous data and reasoning over more "inhabited" and humane ones. This grounds the term "technolinguistics" in this article (as opposed to ontolinguistics).

27 Certeau 1975, p. 47.

28 Certeau 1975, p. 48.

29 Certeau 1990, p. 99.

30 Certeau 1990, p. 99.

pothesis one has eliminated all that might trouble the picture that one might have of it. Then, with the help of certain transcribed "interactions" "field data" or "corpus," one can "show," for example, that in fact languages are truly merchandised, that men are dominant, for one has eliminated all complexity. There only remains to reverse the logic: "You see very well that my hypothesis is verified!": the corpus (a simplified metonymy of the world) concludes the magic trick set up by the reductive hypothesis,[31] but manages only to convince those who already thought that the corpus or "field data" is the royal road of the human sciences (a faith that has many followers in our times), thus, in effect that there is only one manner to build knowledge, the manner that is attributed, sometimes stereotypically, to the hard sciences.

For this reason de Certeau finds that one must turn one's attention towards the inaugural simplifying hypothesis: the researcher can in many different ways combine the hypotheses held by the institutions, political parties, ideologies, together with his own *arché:*

> This lacuna, the marking of a place [= the historical process] in a text and put into question by the text, finally sends us back to that which archeology[32] designates without being able to express it: the relation of the logos *to an* archè, *a 'principle' or 'beginning' that is its other. This other on which it rests and that makes it possible, can always be placed "before" by historiography, or designate it as that which, from the 'real' authorizes representation, but is not identical to it. The* archè *is not of that which can be said. It insinuates itself only into the text through the work of division or with the evocation of death.*[33]

In several passages, de Certeau invokes the idea of an anterior foundational event that authorizes a certain way of looking at things, of a certain perspective following from it, that renders it acceptable because it also exists in the expectation horizon of others. He thus takes the example of Freud, or Marx, who, after and in their writings, authorize certain understandings of the world, that would have been rejected prior to that writing—or, more prosaically, prior to a film like Jacques Tati's *Playtime* (1967), which modifies the manner of seeing a city.[34]

> One must probably recognize here, on the one hand, the relation of reason to will—... and on the other the paradoxical relation that the universality of a scientific rigor maintains with the particularity of historical conjectures .... At the bottom of the human sciences,

31 Robillard 2014.

32 This critique clearly challenges Michel Foucault's *Archaeology of Knowledge*.

33 Certeau 1975, p. 23.

34 Certeau 1987, p. 210.

> there is an articulation with that which they silence. *That which* they presuppose, how should one designate it?[35]

This *archè* is thus neither totally irrational nor totally explainable: this ties de Certeau to phenomenologico-hermeneutic scholars and considerably weakens sciences when these pretend to be wholly rational and to give themselves the objective of an explication of everything by discourse. Understanding is rather here a partly enigmatic activity that is neither totally rational, nor totally irrational—in fact it escapes these categories because phenomenological understanding is other than in these explicit categories. It is not always the case of an 'in-between': if the non-rational element deals with a key element of reasoning, the whole proof is weakened from the point of view of rationality. In the final analysis, for much sociolinguistic work, the basic hypothesis only resists because it is constituted as a stereotype shared by a community of sociolinguists, who therefore take for granted and validate this particular hypothesis simply because it is foundational to or emblematic of their homogeneous community. For things to go another way, an alterity of thought such as that brought by de Certeau is necessary.

VIII Understanding What "Understanding" Others Means

> What might one do as an historian, if not to defy luck, is to pose questions, that is to say understand? But to understand is not to escape into ideology, nor to give an obscure word to that which remains hidden. It is to have to find in historical information itself that which would make it thinkable.[36]

In this perspective,

> 'to understand' ... is to each time ask something other than that which was wanting to be said; [in religious history] it is to interrogate those about that which they teach us on a social status found in the collective or personal forms of a spiritual life; it is to understand, under the aspect of a representation of society that which *founded* society, from *their* point of view ... That which was theirs to explain by a truth (God, providence, etc ...) has become that which renders their explications intelligible to us. We postulate an encoding which is the inverse of the encoding relevant in the historical period we are studying.[37]

35 Certeau 1987, p. 201.
36 Certeau 1975, p. 123.
37 Certeau 1975, p. 148.

De Certeau thus criticizes historians as incapable of following their own logic to its end, a logic that would consist in explicitly making history from that which they are, from the place they occupy socio-historically (in his own perspective, this would be to make religious history explicitly as a Christian). One would not be arrested by caricatured categories, but would go as far as possible to the specific, the biographical, indeed, the instantaneous. The exigencies of this history, in which others acquire meaning from that which constitutes meaning for the historian himself, is rather replaced by an ersatz in which historians choose objects 'objectively' tied to a thematic, then insert them into an anachronistic problematic implicitly borrowed from contemporary concerns. For example, history as done by a member of a minority group that lays claim to that which differentiates it from others (a requirement for de Certeau), would find itself replaced by the history of minority objects, inserted into the problematic of the history of the construction of minorities by the homogenizing logic of majorities. It seems to me that with this requirement for a critical approach to 'history,' an approach that is at the same time a critique of history, de Certeau partly escapes the synthesis of Certeaulian thought made by Dosse.

One can easily extrapolate these claims to other human sciences, all of which should try to understand the answers that others bring to their (the researchers') own questions; but one should start from questions that the researcher asks himself, in, from and to his own coherence, influenced by that which he is, has been, wishes to become, by the stereotypes that he shares with those he addresses—those who validate his work, assure his promotions, publish his articles.

From this point of view, the "reading" that allows meaning to come forward cannot be reduced to an activity organized by a framework, nor assimilated to a simple "decoding." In fact, for de Certeau,[38] the supposed "literal" meaning has no other foundation or legitimacy than that furnished by institutions that decide what will be "in the signs" and what is "added on." "From this point of view, the 'literal' meaning is the index and the effect of a social power, that of an elite."[39] In contrast, since elites have declared themselves to be "true" interpreters, this immediately produces readings and does so because of the meanings excluded by institutions, meanings that are strange, orthodoxies and heresies.[40] One must go back to the origins of this conception of meaning in the context of the Catholic Church, which has defended it against the more liberal understanding of the

38 Certeau 1975, p. 47.
39 Certeau 1990, p. 248.
40 Certeau 1990, p. 248.

Reformers, inasmuch as and in order to remain "catholic" (universal), it found it had to understand itself as the sole authority of meaning, a conception often still present in contemporary human sciences.

De Certeau thus invites us to freer, heterodox, readings, for he finds that individuals forced in the impoverishing and simplifying categories that legitimate the rigor of the sciences never make the readings predictable from these categories.

> But where the scientific apparatus (ours) is led to share the illusion of the powers to which it owes itself, that is to suppose the many transformed by the conquests and the victories of an expansionist productivity, it is always good to remember that one should not take people to be idiots.[41]

In a more contemporary formulation: One may choose to oppose globalization by establishing homogenous categories of individuals (whom one then takes to be desperately conformist idiots completely enthralled by that actuality) in order to show that they are the great victims of phenomena that surpass them. The scholar then sets himself up as a hero able to escape such determinisms and thus able to work for the emancipation of these docile masses. Such is not the choice of de Certeau who would rather select a conception of the human that, without being able to struggle head-on against phenomena such as globalization and capitalism, nevertheless, much like the sailor who uses the power of the wind to tack against it, remains capable of cunning, or of poaching a different meaning, *which explains at the same time how the researcher himself would be able to avoid being taken prisoner by and in these phenomena from which he would otherwise not be able to emancipate himself* (this is harder to explain in the other hypothesis, unless one postulate a group of the "elect" and/or the emancipating power of the scientific methodological formation).

IX From History to Sociolinguistics

As the proposals of de Certeau that I have chosen to rehearse cut to a great extent across the human sciences, the transition from history to sociolinguistics is, so to say, superfluous. One can nonetheless attempt to make it explicit by taking up certain Certeaulian themes in relation to sociolinguistics.

On which Exclusions is Sociolinguistics Based?

---

41 Certeau 1990, p. 255.

For de Certeau, the most important unspoken [*non-dit*] in and of history is death: history claims to take symbolic control of the dead, in order to present them in discourse as if they still lived. This is the paradox of the writing of history: to bring the dead to life in the imagined consequences of the present. Likewise, sociolinguistics tries, first, to make others (through their discourses) live; secondly, to make them live in their consequences for others; and thirdly, to translate them into coherence with these others. For this to be conceivable, the language-speech-discourse dimension must be reducible to communication and the ontological function itself must appear as communication, such that it can be mastered, made knowable by others—this is the case in approaches inspired by pragmatism. In fact, if the languages-speech-discourse have first of all an ontological value (the hermeneutic hypothesis), then the researcher, who is human, and only partially appears in language, cannot master or rigorously control the discourse of others in order reliably to extract meaning from it. If he tries, he will most probably instill precisely that which he thinks to extract. To hold, as do Heidegger and Gadamer, the ontological function (and the historical dimension, which more or less has to do with death and thus brings de Certeau closer to the Heideggerian hermeneutic) in a priority position, is to uncover the profound contradictions of the human sciences, in particular when to know others who pretend to use only that which they get from signs.

At the bottom, the human sciences "know" their place in the world by experiencing others;[42] they know it from the point of view of the researcher, something that must each time carefully be made as clear as possible. In fact, however, the researcher is himself a being with multiple identities, from which he can constitute meaning for other such multiples in a widely varying fashion.

X Towards Sociolinguistics of Reception

If the humanities share de Certeau's problematization, they are also close to the field that I have been exploring for some years—the field of the hermeneutic human sciences, although they are not completely coincident.[43] In this undertaking—as de Certeau argues—the human sciences are not completely rational. Thus, to give themselves the appearance of rigor and credibility, they simplify and amputate, albeit invisibly. Likewise, if "to understand" is a basic problem

42 Robillard 2008a and b.

43 I cannot summarize this here but in any case it would not be useful as the main stages of that which occupies us can be found in texts indicated in the footnotes here.

in the human sciences, then the problem set for us is to problematize that which contemporary sociolinguistics silences, a sociolinguistics that is mostly positivist or pragmatist (symbolic interactionism, ethnomethodology, "complex thought," and so forth). What is raised is whatdrives it—the question of its *archè*.

What Might Be the Archè of the Sociolinguist?

A good candidate is meaning, understood as an indissociable process of understanding and self-production (for the researcher; for the others in question) and of research. Naturally, (socio)linguistics is most concerned with the meaning of others, but with a meaning with clipped wings, technologized, and conditioned to be compatible with the limits of that which "makes for" science: a technological epoch. All this makes the sociolinguistics of today a somewhat byzantine applied discipline: a discipline established implicitly by an anticipated epistemological censure. Many sociolinguists whose work focus on near-to-hand "action" thus limit themselves to epistemologies compatible with this aim, something that implicitly and without argument eliminates the others. That which guides the epistemology of an important sector of sociolinguistics is thus the focus on action and immediate intervention. This leads to a diminishing of the quality and richness of the epistemological argument (and therefore of the formation of young researchers): there are fewer diversified strains, fewer contradictory ones, fewer strains with a more mediated relation with action (which does not make them less effective).

Sociolinguistics has inherited from technolinguistics an 'unthought' [*impensé*] that has never been subjectged to critique. It is the unthought of a science founded on the rational and thus on the apparent rationality of *traces* that would give meaning. This is what de Certeau rejects, as he also does a focusing on the production of meaning that renders the process of understanding invisible, taking them matter-of-factly. To renew itself—superficially—sociolinguistics has then completely coherently borrowed pragmatics, "complex thought"[44] and pragmatisms, without however ever questioning this heritage. Sociolinguists know very well the place of experiential meaning and of understanding, but their work cannot take these into explicit account, unless it were to admit the "non-scientificity" of their undertaking, which, as they are subject to institutions, would necessarily be according to dominant criteria analogous to those of the police and judges. Rather than qualitatively changing (and choosing to

44 Thus one would have to make elsewhere a critique (crypto-cybernetic, with reference to genetics, etc. ...) that cannot be accomplished here. See Lafontaine 2004.

put stress on comprehension by the researcher, thus freeing themselves in part from signs), they have chosen two modes of escape.

Ever More Signs

The first is a flight forwards, to the quantitative, by a constant increasing in the *quantity* of the signs of which one takes account, while all the while restricting oneself to signs: the sentence, the discourse, gestures, intonations, the managing of space, context (reduced to signs), history (frozen in the 'facts').

Such extensions of signifiers take over the empty space formed by the obscuring of the *archè* because they remain reduced to frozen signs, signs transformed into objects, including the historical and contextual elements. This is dead meaning, understood as crystalized into a frozen configuration of interdependent and differential signs (one will recognize meaning as found in de Saussure, or in the Foucault of *Les mots et les choses*). But it is the living meaning (unstable, fluid, chaotic) that would be pertinent and effective in another manner, a meaning chosen to be meaningful.

Many sociolinguists try to succeed on both contradictory fronts and this is what makes their work at once practically pertinent and epistemologically subject to criticism. Despite a strict methodological conformism (setting out of the corpus, of interactions, of field data), they try to arrive at conclusions that are much more ambitious than this methodology can coherently allow.[45] A frequent example of this consists in engaging in a discourse about the intentions of the subjects, apparently drawn from some scraps of interactions, or from some piece of corpus or field data. One can have confidence in the honesty of the researcher's interpretation, as one may of the pertinence of the conclusions at which he arrives. This does not erase the damage done by all that remains: that is left implicit. It is thus legitimate to discuss the move full of the implicit, the move that, by the means of a rhetoric of diversion and omission that cannot be discussed fully here, remains unthought.[46] In doing so, one remains prudent enough never to make explicit that the corpus, the interactions or field data, would be the most important elements of the approach; one does so by giving prominence to the corpus, all the while leaving in the shadows the interaction processes evoked by de Certeau. This reduces the importance of the researcher to very little, an importance to which Certeau has called attention. Indeed, according to him, it is the crucial element.

---

45 Robillard 2014

46 Robillard 2015.

Ever More Benevolent

The second compensatory strategy consists in excusing oneself from an always implicit reproach. It is achieved by declarations that seek to redeem the researcher from this dissimulation and can be called "empowerment," sometimes "militancy," even "compassion."[47] These stances are certainly quite respectable and have their usefulness and pertinence in relation to quite actual problems, but nevertheless cannot compensate for a lack of epistemological reflection. This has the aspect of the "second work" of French ethnologists,[48] something that cannot compensate for the symbolic violence done to humans that one has pretended to make transparent, humans given over to the pretended omniscience of the researcher with their alterity and thus their existence dissolved.

The circle is exemplarily vicious: to justify their existence, sociolinguists are led to affirm that tongues, languages, discourse are instruments of power, the study of which is therefore pertinent. They thus try to make sense of tongues, languages and discourses for their studies, all the while attempting to exonerate themselves from personally assuming any position of power in the interpretation of others, or vindicate to always side with the weak and dominated (which is almost an avowal that they have exerted some sort of interpretive power in their research). By this very problematizing of their discipline, they therefore condemn themselves to an epistemological incoherence in the quizzical form of a redemption for an enigmatic fault, all the more so as this discussion is never made explicit.[49] They try to convince that they can understand others fully, while this is just not the most important issue, as we know from de Certeau.[50]

Even so, certain sociolinguists assume in their work the stance of the "interpretivist." In this case, however, in order to be coherent, they should be more explicit as to how their singularity permits their interpretations: this is a basic ethical and political requirement, especially when one plays the role of an expert in relation to institutions that are responsible for populations whose future this expertise may affect.[51] A similar reproach applies to democratic institutions, which should not admit expertise resting on such weakly problematized grounds. The fact that everyone seems to accommodate themselves easily to these practices suggests that each finds something in them. The institutions thus easily discharge some of their responsibilities onto the researchers, with

47 See the contributions to Férréol and Jucquois 2004 on this issue.

48 Debaene 2010.

49 See Robillard 2012 for a different argument.

50 See Robillard 2012 for a different argument.

51 As we know, any research, whether geared towards expertise or not can be mobilized expertise-wise.

the sense that they have brought about a workable "description" of "reality"—and the researchers build careers, find funding, are encouraged by their universities, for in particular such institutional relations allow one better to place oneself in the competition of selling research operations and the training of new scholars. I have elsewhere[52] given an example of a research program in which one cannot easily determine if the researcher is independent from his sources of financing—something quite troubling as a researcher who is aligned with the orientation of his funder can then only marginally play the role of a researcher and rather merges substantially with his backer. Not to be explicit on the process of interpretation and/or to cut it off comes down to the exercise of a kind of opaque and somewhat irrational power, all the while pretending the opposite.

One understands thus how "empowerment," militancy and compassion can find themselves mobilized as a form of tactic diversion and made explicit, while the process of interpretation on which research rests remains implicit. In consequence, this turns attention away from the basic problem: it demobilizes all critique (who would want to critique nice "humanists"?) and provides a foregone answer to any eventual critique, for this postulated power is supposed to manifest only perspectives that are just, ethical, politically correct, made as they are by righteous, compassionate, militant humanists, always with the guarantee that any slippage be excluded—something that is hard to sustain. The eradication of French plurilingualism, as with that of colonization, was also partially made with the self-proclaimed best intentions. The recurrence and the power of these denials in anticipation of a problem that is never made explicit, accompanied as they are by self-proclaimed good will, translates to an *archè*, that, according to de Certeau, always returns.

I need now only to conclude by insisting on the central idea of Certeaulian perspectives: it is indispensable to place the central epistemological questions of sociolinguistics into question so as at last to confront them, knowing all the while in advance that, in face of the *archè*, one has always lost, for it is constitutive of he who problematizes it. One can never make it disappear, one can never hide it; one can only attempt to problematize it in a provisional manner in order to extract more that is positive than negative.

One may do this by taking as example "speech acts." This means that one would be centrally concerned with the problem of the reception, itself only partly rational, of "speech acts." This would lead to giving another, albeit concurrent, interpretation to those given by Bourdieu and Austin in their debate on "speech acts." Bourdieu insists on the idea that it is the relation of social power that ren-

52 Robillard, 2010.

ders "speech acts" efficacious, whereas for Austin it is the linguistic properties and formal conformity of these "acts."

The hermeneutic point of view, as broached above by de Certeau, does not deny these conclusions but insists on the idea that *what renders them efficacious is also the fact that the intended receiver* [le destinataire] *is invested in them, confers meaning on them.* Leaving aside instances of coercion, may one appoint to a post, marry, cast a spell, teach someone for whom these practices or certain of their modalities and significations are foreign? In certain cases, the essential quality of the efficaciousness of a "speech act" may be, at bottom, *an "activity of comprehending and believing in a 'speech act'"* without which a "speech act" would, from the pragmatic point of view, remain simply an incantation or would require coercion: it is interesting to note here that if the human sciences, without questioning, share with the police and the courts a strong passion for *traces* (signs, corpus, fields), it is because they hold themselves capable of giving meaning to others, without their participation, and eventually against their will, which is the symbolic violence the French ethnologists in Vincent Debaene's book want to redeem by a "second" book restoring both the "informants'" and the researchers' humanity.

One will have recognized here the kind of radical questioning that hermeneutic perspectives bring when one applies them to the human sciences.[53] This has multiple consequences that one must patiently examine by building the *sociolinguistics of reception* necessary to pluralist perspectives that take pluralism seriously, assuming therefore that plurality can lead all the way to incomprehension, including to that of the researcher. In doing so, one moves the ethical and political problems from the periphery (as a kind of escort) of sociolinguistics to its very heart. The discourse that haunts sociolinguistics and accompanies its protestations of humanism and political benevolence gives way to a reflection on the consequences of grounding a sociolinguistics that takes plurality seriously, not only as a matter for a non-coherent study, but as a pluralist undertaking that goes to its very core: an epistemologically pluralist sociolinguistics and thus a sociolinguistics of reception.

Translated by Tracy B. Strong

53 See, for example, Gadamer 1976 [1960]; Robillard 2008b, Robillard 2012.

Acknowledgments

This article was published in an earlier version as "Prendre la diversité au sérieux avec Michel de Certeau: de l'histoire à des sociolinguistiques de la réception," in: "Pluralité linguistique et culturelle: actualité de la recherche en sociolinguistique," *Cahiers Internationaux de Sociolinguistique* 5, (2013): 23–40. I thank Tracy Strong for his translation (including the quotations), which I find better than the original (no wonder for a hermeneutic, provided the translator is talented). The French version of this text benefited from comments from Marc Debono, Véronique Castelloti and Isabelle Pierozak, for which they must be thanked. I however take full responsibility for the content of this article.

References

Baggioni, Daniel (1997) *Langues et nations en Europe.* Paris: Payot.

Bergounioux, Gabriel (1992) "Linguistique et variation: repères historiques." *Langages* (Hétérogénéité et variation: Labov, un bilan) 108: 114–124.

Certeau, Michel de (1975) *L'Ecriture de l'histoire.* Paris: Gallimard.

Certeau, Michel de (1987) *La faiblesse de croire.* Paris: Seuil.

Certeau, Michel de (1990) *L'invention du quotidien.* Vol. 1: *Arts de faire.* Paris: Gallimard.

Certeau, Michel de, Julia, Dominique and Revel, Jacques (1975) *Une politique de la langue: La Révolution française et les patois.* Paris: Gallimard.

Debaene, Vincent (2010) *L'adieu au voyage. L'ethnologie française entre science et littérature.* Paris: Gallimard.

Dosse, François (2013) "Michel de Certeau, un historien de l'altérité." Conference paper presented in Mexico, September 2003. Online: http://www.culturahistorica.es/dosse/dosse_certeau_historien.pdf. Consulted March 26, 2013.

Férréol, Gilles and Jucquois, Guy (eds.) (2004) *Dictionnaire de l'altérité et des relations interculturelles.* Paris: Armand Colin.

Gadamer, Hans-Georg 1976 [1960] *Vérité et méthode. Les grandes lignes d'une herméneutique philosophique.* Paris: Seuil.

Lafontaine, Céline (2004) *L'empire cybernétique. Des machines à penser à la pensée machine.* Paris, Seuil.

Prudent, Lambert-Félix (1981) "Diglossie et interlecte." *Langages* 15, No. 61: 13–38

Robillard, Didier de (2008a) *Perspectives alterlinguistiques.* Vol. 1: *Démons.* Paris: L'Harmattan

Robillard, Didier de (2008b) *Perspectives alterlinguistiques.* Vol.2: *Ornithorynques.* Paris: L'Harmattan.

Robillard, Didier de (2012) "Diversité, sens: enjeux." In: Marc Debono and Cécile Goï (eds.), *Regards interdisciplinaires sur l'épistémologie du divers. Interculturel, herméneutique et interventions didactiques.* Fernelmont: Éditions Modulaires Européennes, pp. 195–216.

Robillard, Didier de (2013) "'Interlecte': Outil ou point de vue épistémologique sur 'la' linguistique et les langues? Sémiotique ou herméneutique?" In: Jacky Simonin and

Sylvie Wharton (eds.), *Sociolinguistique des langues en contact, modèles, théories. Dictionnaire encyclopédique des termes et concepts.* Lyon: ENS Editions Editions de l'Ecole Nationale Supérieure de Lyon, 2013, pp. 265–283.

Robillard, Didier de (2014) "La magie des signes: *Elémentaire mon cher Watson!* Réflexivité, 'pratiques réelles', 'corpus', 'interactions' et autres 'données-produites'." In: Gilles Forlot and Fanny Martin (eds.), *Regards sociolinguistiques contemporains. Terrains, espaces et complexités de la recherche.* Paris: L'Harmattan, pp. 39–55.

Robillard, Didier de (2015) "Quelles 'langues' sont les français régionaux? Un point de vue phénoménologique-herméneutique." In: Marie-Madeleine Bertucci (ed.), *Les français régionaux dans l'espace francophone.* Hamburg: Peter Lang, pp. 46–57.

Robillard, Didier de (2016) "Fenêtres sur une sociolinguistique de la réception ou phénoménologique-herméneutique, ou sur des SHS qualitatives à programme fort." Online in: *Glottopol* 28, http://glottopol.univ-rouen.fr/telecharger/numero_28/gpl28_07robillard.pdf.

Robillard, Didier de (ed.) (2010) *Réflexivité, herméneutique: vers un paradigme de recherche?* Cahiers de sociolinguistique 14. Rennes: Presses de l'Université de Rennes.

Robillard, Didier de, (2010), " DYLAN, un exemple parmi d'autres des coûts et difficultés du travail de la diversité : naît-on, ou devient-on divers ? ", Cahiers de l'ACEDLE, 2010, volume 7, n° 1, 35 – 61.

Barry Allen

Pragmatism and Hermeneutics

Abstract: Rorty occasionally invokes "hermeneutics" as a term for his philosophical point of view, either explaining pragmatism in terms of hermeneutics or vice versa. However, compared to hermeneutical thinkers like Gadamer or Vattimo, this pragmatic hermeneutics is far more pragmatic than it is hermeneutic, and eventually Rorty drops the effort to enlist hermeneutics among the allies and avatars of pragmatism. What is at stake in the confrontation between pragmatism and hermeneutics is nothing other than the point and value of philosophy. Hermeneutical ontology may be post-metaphysical but is it probably not post-philosophical in the sense that Rorty anticipates for his new pragmatism.

It can be surprising to realize that the word pragmatism scarcely appears in Richard Rorty's *Philosophy and the Mirror of Nature.* Certainly it is not used as an epitome for Rorty's point of view in that book. The preferred description of his philosophy there is epistemological behaviorism, a not very memorable term Rorty abandoned soon after that first, break-out book from 1979. Epistemological behaviorism quickly became anti-representationalism, and these thoughts on truth and knowledge blended with thoughts on literature and politics to form Rorty's version of pragmatism. *Philosophy and the Mirror of Nature* was written for professional consumption in a way none of the later books are. He did not have reach out to Analytic epistemologists, because he was already one of them, though writing as it were on his way out the door. There is a motto over that door; it is the title of chapter seven: *From Epistemology to Hermeneutics.*

Hermeneutics was not a word much heard around Analytic departments in 1979. It was a provocation to use it prominently in his book, or so I found it then, reading it over the holidays during my first year in a fastidiously Analytic graduate program. Rorty's reference to hermeneutics was, of course, inspired by the work of Hans-Georg Gadamer, one of several exotic authors Rorty insinuated into his argument. I for one was thrilled, and immediately wanted to know more about hermeneutics, deconstruction, post-structuralism, Heidegger, Foucault, Derrida, and of course Gadamer. Christmas the next year I was reading *Truth and Method.*

Analytic theorists of knowledge were Rorty's his first audience for *Mirror of Nature*, and to them hermeneutics was a very black box indeed. That left Rorty plenty of leeway in interpretation. He introduces hermeneutics as a new way for analytic philosophers to think about what Kuhn and Quine have accomplished, a

https://doi.org/10.1515/9783110551563-015

continental version of Quine's holism and anti-essentialism, and a historicism that accommodates Kuhn's most radical insights. Apart from this suggestive comparison Rorty has little to say about hermeneutics. What he does say is characteristically negative; hermeneutics is defined by what it is not. He says hermeneutics "is what we get when we are no longer epistemological" (Rorty 1979, p. 325). Its major accomplishment is to have overcome the idea of a human being as essentially a knower of essences (Rorty 1979, p. 364).

In other words hermeneutics accomplishes a negative—an escape, a liberation—*and nothing beyond that*, no new, alternative, wiser philosophical point of view. This is tendentious but in a well-meaning way. It was useful at the time and eventually made new things possible in Analytic departments. The point of Rorty's intervention against epistemology was not to advance hermeneutics as a better alternative. The point was to change the conversation, to stop talking and thinking in epistemological terms. The contribution of hermeneutics to this agenda is merely negative. It offers a thoughtful way of setting aside the idea of a neutral epistemological matrix for the evaluation of claims, without becoming "irrationalist." Hermeneutic rationality, on this reading, celebrates the dilettante. Rorty says, "For hermeneutics, to be rational is to be willing to refrain from epistemology ... and to be willing to pick up the jargon of the interlocutor rather than translating it into one's own" (Rorty 1979, p. 318). Hermeneutics is only one of those ladders that we kick away after scaling the wall of the prison called Epistemology (Rorty 1991, p. 103). I think that is why "hermeneutic" was quickly dropped from Rorty's philosophical self-description. In his interpretation it does not add anything to *pragmatic*. Gadamer is invoked mainly to make the same negative, anti-Platonic, anti-Cartesian objections to epistemology that Rorty reads into a long list of thinkers: Nietzsche, Heidegger, Derrida, Davidson, Sellers, Quine, and of course the classical American pragmatists. I think Rorty realized that, these negative points apart, the difference between pragmatism and Gadamer's hermeneutical ontology is more significant than the similarity. It took longer for him to reach the same conclusion about Heidegger.

The negative mode seems congenial to Rorty. A lot of energy is directed at what not to think, what to give up, get over, abandon, drop, overcome, set aside. Rorty tries, with uneven success, to stay at this melancholy level, destroying old temples without erecting a new one. Pragmatism, as an American philosophy, is constitutionally disinclined to establish a church.[1] Rorty is not remotely

1 Citing Harold Bloom's discussion (in *The American Religion*) of the American tradition of founding new churches, Rorty says, "Of course, shortly after one of those private American churches is founded, it develops its own little Vatican and becomes one more horrible authoritarian institution." Rorty 2005, p. 70.

as diligent as Gadamer in constructing a philosophical theory of conversation—or anything else. I sometimes think that any thoughts verging on the constructive-theoretical have been extracted from him under duress. His preference is for laconic suggestions in place of the laborious arguments epistemologists (and hermeneuts) spend careers on. I am not surprised that experts think Rorty's use of Gadamer glosses over important details. Important, of course, for people more committed to hermeneutics than Rorty was when he wrote *Philosophy and the Mirror of Nature.* Already in that first book he is following what becomes the usual pattern: agree with and appropriate interesting interlocutors like Gadamer, Derrida, or Heidegger on their anti-Platonic, anti-Cartesian, anti-epistemological points, and fudge the rest.

So the hermeneutics of *Philosophy and the Mirror of Nature* were not all that hermeneutical, and soon dropped out of Rorty's work. Some friends of hermeneutics think this blurring of the difference with pragmatism is a genuine insight from which *hermeneutics* might change in a desirable way. Santiago Zabala sees an antidogmatic stance as the common presupposition linking both pragmatism and hermeneutics to the politics of democracy. "Both pragmatism and hermeneutics," he says, "arose not merely in revolt against all authoritarian theories of truth but were also impelled by the intention to improve the way in which men understand each other." He believes that the postmetaphysical thought exemplified by Vattimo's hermeneutical ontology (as well as Rorty's pragmatism) "reduces the weight of objective structures and the violence of dogmatism." This should, he believes, strengthen "the capacity of culture to annul all the reasons for conflict and to assume the program of secularization as its task."[2]

Other friends of hermeneutics thinks that had Rorty been more rigorously hermeneutical he would have avoided conclusions that he himself considers troubling. The troubling conclusions come down to the irrationality with which Rorty is supposedly obliged (by his assumptions) to view conversations across communities. On this view, justification is a strictly internal matter among peers. Only in their eyes can one be reasonable. The gulf between communities is an abyss of unreason. It can be bridged only by a persuasion that is not rational and cannot defend itself against the charge of violence. This is a dreary relativism though I do not see Rorty trapped in it. Supposedly for Rorty being grounded in one's community establishes who is an "*appropriate interlocutor.*" But, *an interlocutor?* Another human being with whom you might have a conversation? No. No community, no solidarity, "grounds" the mere possibility of a conversation. With enough trouble any human being can have a con-

2 Zabala 2005, p. 9, 14.

versation with any other. But these potential interlocutors are vastly many and far apart compared to those nearer at hand, with whom one feels solidarity and acknowledges an obligation of justification. Justifying oneself in others' eyes is only one of the things we do with words. It is important, to be sure, especially because of the link justification makes between what we believe and what we are motivated to do. But not every conversation pursues justification.

An idea Rorty left undeveloped after *Mirror of Nature* distinguishes between normal and abnormal discourse. The difference is explained by analogy to Kuhn's idea of normal and revolutionary science. To some unimaginative readers Kuhn seemed to sacrifice revolutionary scientific change to irrational, sociological causes. Rorty invokes Gadamer's hermeneutics as a philosophically sophisticated defense of the "reasonableness" of abnormal discourse (Rorty 1979, p. 363). Abnormal conversations go on across interlocutory barriers as dramatic as you can imagine precisely because no one is trying to win an argument or prove something and make others change their beliefs. It is enough get your view across and get something of the other's, even if you're not sure you *fully* understand, or have to agree to differ. One may still learn something, even something important. But nobody has won an argument, no one is logically compelled to change beliefs on pain of irrationality. That is what is interesting and valuable about abnormal conversations.

Conversations within the solidarity community are not all the conversations there are. They are only the normal, practical ones. That leaves all the abnormal, impractical conversations of pure curiosity. Normal discourse among peers is symmetrical, with interlocutors really working to justify themselves and mobilize social action. Abnormal conversations are not symmetrical in this way. They are instead characterized by the dialogical openness of interlocutors who have opted to pursue hermeneutical understanding rather than achieve theoretical or practical closure. Perhaps the idea of conversation in *Mirror of Nature* owes more to Michael Oakeshott's "conversation of mankind" than to Gadamer and hermeneutics. The "conversation of mankind" is not a Socratic dialogue.[3] Oakeshott was not trying to explain the same phenomenon on the same level as Gadamer pitches his hermeneutics of dialogue. Oakeshott makes it clear in his beautifully conceived essay that what he calls the *conversation of mankind* is one possible sort of conversation and a peculiar one at that.

He was interested in the intersubjective and intergenerational communication of poetic images—the historical conversation of poetry. The relevant concept of poetry is a broad one, embracing any images. Possibly it could be made to ac-

3 See Oakeshott 1962.

commodate the images of revolutionary science, though Oakeshott considers science as what, since Kuhn, we have learned to call normal science and as such governed by principles distinct from poetic revery. The conversation of mankind is not scientific, moral, or practical but *contemplative*. Oakeshott calls it an inconsequent adventure. There is no premeditated achievement. What impels it is solely delight. It leads only to more complex images, not to well-justified conclusions. So what good is it? To be indifferent to this conversation, not to care about the images of another place, another time, another self, is for Oakeshott the definition of barbarism. The motivation for entering into the conversation of mankind is the imaginative cultivation of the self. Foreshadowing Rorty's argument in "The Contingency of Selfhood" (a chapter of *Contingency, Irony, and Solidarity*) Oakeshott explains selfhood as an activity, not a substance or thing; specifically, the activity of imagining, and making images of desire. This description of poetry in the conversation of mankind may well be the prototype of abnormal discourse in *Mirror of Nature*, and may retain a subterranean influence on Rorty's ideas about the imagination, romanticism, and the power of redescription.

To hermeneutic philosophers Rorty sometimes seems overly committed to a propositional picture of the mind as nothing but a set of beliefs and other propositional attitudes that we change more or less at will. Hermeneutic philosophers reply that a human being is not fundamentally an entity holding beliefs but an actor in the world. An interlocutor is irreducible to an alternative set of propositional attitudes. Changing your mind is not solely changing beliefs. It requires a willingness to see a point. A kind of openness to the world, including others, comes before belief and makes change of belief possible. That is all true, of course. But despite some definite propositional bias Rorty's picture of the mind is a long way from a Cartesian homunculus rearranging its beliefs like cards in a poker hand. This misreading of pragmatism is an example of how, in trying to evade a theory, pragmatists are spontaneously read by non-pragmatists as offering a new theory. I think Rorty might say that it may be convenient for certain purposes to regard people as calculating networks of belief and desire, but that is not the master perspective disclosing essential human nature. On the contrary, it is the abiding thought of pragmatism, from James and Dewey to Putnam and Rorty, that there is no substance to the world, no self-identical natures or essences.

Pragmatists are rhetorical opportunists—there is that much in common with the sophists of Socratic times. *Of course* there is more to people than their beliefs. *What* more depends on context. What are you trying to do? Persuade them, seduce them, praise, humiliate, psychoanalyze them, teach them how to march? However, I think Rorty would be cool to the idea that there is a *philosoph-*

ical or *hermeneutical* or *ontological* context in which we reflect on the essence of all things human. Gadamer rightly insisted that the closed horizon that is supposed to enclose a culture is an abstraction. That is certainly true. We are never bound to one standpoint. Language itself places us in a space of different viewpoints and makes us agile perspective-switchers. That could be an argument against some anthropologists of culture and some philosophers of community, but Rorty is not committed to this picture of impermeable communities incapable of reasonable communication.

It should be possible to conceive an encounter between human beings of however different background without summoning either universal rationality or brute force. That is the dilemma hermeneutical philosophers sometimes try to force upon Rorty. Having abandoned universal rationality he supposedly has no alternative to a force that only seems reasonable to the master class that wields it. Rorty does say that the difference between rational and irrational persuasion can only be applied within language games, not across them or in the shift from one to another (Rorty 1989, p. 47). I think the idea is that understanding the change from, say, Ptolemaic to Galilean astronomy, is not like understanding an argument whose validity can be assessed independently of the history that embeds it—and very much favors Galileo. Something similar might apply at a personal level when someone changes political or religious affiliation. I do not think such changes are matters that hermeneutics sheds much light on. The norms of dialogical reason described in hermeneutical philosophy are a model for conversations with others but not for this order of spiritual conversion.

The symmetrical, normal conversations with peers, where we pursue justification with others with whom we already have a lot in common, are never more than half the story. There is always more—the abnormal discourse, the liberal ethnography, the journalistic curiosity, the stroll through the bazaar before retiring to the club. Impermeable communities contradict a well-known thesis of Donald Davidson's—a thesis Rorty champions as a tenet of pragmatism. He regards Davidson as having refuted the idea that there are untranslatable languages, incommensurable conceptual schemes, or impermeable communities that cannot talk with each other.[4] So it is unlikely that Rorty would implicate himself in the picture of impermeable communities. Impermeable communities are also hard to reconcile with his description of moral progress. He says, "Think of moral progress as a matter of increasing *sensitivity*, increasing responsiveness to the needs of a larger and larger variety of people and things ... being able to respond to the needs of ever more inclusive groups of people" (Rorty 1999,

4 See Davidson 1984 and Richard Rorty, "Pragmatism, Davidson, and Truth," in Rorty 1991.

p. 81). This openness to others and change does not require the superfluous supplement of a philosophical theory. Its "ground" (if you want to call it that) is in feeling and politics, not ontology.

Hermeneutical thinkers emphasize that the reasonableness of even the most abnormal conversation is secure if only the participants agree on a common subject matter; are not hostile, but rather share a commitment to understanding; and are responsive rather than patronizing, approaching the other as an individual with a potentially worthwhile point of view. I do not see anything in this description that Rorty could not agree with were there a compelling need to have a serious theory of abnormal discourse. I suspect he did not feel that need, however, or see the point of sweating the details as Gadamer and others do to fine-tune their hermeneutics of dialogue. The important thing about abnormal discourse is to acknowledge its right to exist and let it happen, not to *theorize* it.

Twenty years after *Mirror of Nature*, Rorty sees hermeneutics as a bid to be the successor subject for philosophy after Nietzsche and Heidegger swept the decks of modern subjectivism. Of course Rorty has no enthusiasm for ensuring that something called Philosophy with a suitably pretentious mandate (Being) has a voice in any possible mutation of Western culture. He dismisses such efforts as typical of European rather than American philosophy, which (he says) appreciates that the overcoming of Platonic and Cartesian categories means the undoing of philosophy as such (Rorty 1999, pp. xx–xxi). He says, "The real question about the utility of the old Platonic dualisms is whether or not their deployment weakens our sense of human solidarity" (Rorty 1999, p. xv). So too presumably the utility of hermeneutics. An artist invited to participate in a symposium on aesthetics eloquently explained that aesthetics is for art what ornithology is for the birds. So too what hermeneutics is for dialogue and conversation. It is probably harmless, though it would be intellectual hubris, both absurd and dangerous, to think that a good theory of dialogue will make dialogue more consistently preferred over violence. A more reasonable theory of hermeneutical reason will not make us more reasonable in conversations we do not want to have.

I do not want to suggest that pragmatism is a better philosophy than hermeneutics. It is not a philosophy, whereas philosophical hermeneutics apparently is, though Vattimo denies it. "Hermeneutics is not a philosophy but the enunciation of historical existence itself in the age at the end of metaphysics."[5] When I say that pragmatism is not a philosophy I mean that it is not offered as worthwhile on its own or for its own sake (for *understanding*). It is a therapeutic inter-

5 Vattimo 2005, p. 45.

vention, a perlocutionary act, an effort to change the world and not just interpret it. It is not part of pragmatism to say how we should think if we do not think epistemologically. That is for the future to decide. It will not emerge from the principles of a new philosophy, because where Rorty wants to go is on the other side of the whole idea of philosophy.

That may be what is finally at stake in the confrontation between pragmatism and hermeneutical ontology—the point and value of philosophical discourse. Why ontology, hermeneutical or any other variety? Rorty was implacably skeptical of the point or value of anything that looks at all like everything from Parmenides to Heidegger. Too much of Gadamer (the bits that resemble Heidegger more than pragmatism) looks like more of that. Hermeneutical ontology may be post-metaphysical but is it post-philosophical? Probably not. What needs to be clarified, then, is what to expect from hermeneutics, what good it does, its educational value, its contribution to what Rorty eventually wanted to call cultural politics. What is the point of finding new and better ways than Hegel or Heidegger to carry on a conversation with the philosophical tradition? Explaining that would be the most practical way to impress the value of hermeneutics on a pragmatist who is skeptical of the contemplative bias in Western philosophy.

References

Davidson, Donald (1984) "On the Very Idea of a Conceptual Scheme." In: Donald Davidson, *Inquiries Concerning Truth and Interpretation*. Oxford: Oxford University Press, pp. 183–198.

Oakeshott, Michael (1962) "The Voice of Poetry in the Conversation of Mankind." In: Michael Oakeshott, *Rationalism in Politics*. London: Methuen, pp. 197–247.

Rorty, Richard (2005) "Atheism and Anticlericism." In: Richard Rorty and Gianni Vattimo, *The Future of Religion*, ed. Santiago Zabala. New York: Columbia University Press, pp. 29–42.

Rorty, Richard (1979) *Philosophy and the Mirror of Nature*. Princeton: Princeton University Press.

Rorty, Richard (1989) *Contingency, Irony, and Solidarity*. Cambridge: Cambridge University Press.

Rorty, Richard (1991) *Objectivity, Relativism, and Truth, Philosophical Papers*, vol. 1. Cambridge: Cambridge University Press

Rorty, Richard (1999) *Philosophy and Social Hope*. Harmondsworth: Penguin.

Vattimo, Gianni (2005) "The Age of Interpretation." In: Richard Rorty and Gianni Vattimo, *The Future of Religion*, ed. Santiago Zabala. New York: Columbia University Press, pp. 43–54.

Zabala, Santiago (2005) "A Religion Without Theists or Atheists." In: Richard Rorty and Gianni Vattimo, *The Future of Religion*, ed. Santiago Zabala. New York: Columbia University Press, pp. 1–28.

Paul Fairfield

Make It Scientific: Theories of Education from Dewey to Gadamer

Abstract: Faculties of education have long aligned their discipline with the social sciences. The faculty and the discipline of education assert a claim to scientificity in ways largely reminiscent of the early days of sociology, psychology, political science, and other established disciplines of the social sciences. Old debates in the philosophy of education often appear to have been superseded by developments in learning theory and developmental psychology in particular, leaving behind once and for all contested notions of *Bildung*, progressive versus conservative education, and various other ideas that resist translation into the scientific.

I Corporate Scientism

While showing signs of continuity with the progressive movement, recent educational trends have taken a decided turn toward the scientific, the technical, and the managerial. The matter of how students learn—different categories of students at different stages of development—has become the dominant issue in the contemporary discipline of education. While John Dewey had already posed the question a century ago of "how we think," his approach to this question was unapologetically philosophical and indeed phenomenological. The current thinking, by contrast, is framed strictly within a vocabulary of empirical and developmental psychology, a non-phenomenological and ostensibly apolitical methodology. Education, according to this new orthodoxy, is essentially a scientific matter and its central question is one of technique: how (not whether or why) to bring about certain predetermined educational outcomes. These outcomes are often described in vaguely progressive terms; the language of individual growth and autonomy, of creativity and critical thinking, now enjoys very broad appeal and is often coupled with a more political terminology of empowerment and democratic equality. To all appearances the scientific spirit of progressive education lives on, yet on closer inspection it could be more accurately said that certain Deweyan themes have been thoroughly transformed to lend legitimacy to a trend that Dewey himself would have certainly rejected.

The broad outlines of this trend are as follows. It includes a decided emphasis on technology, an exhortation toward managerial efficiency and cost-effectiveness, the concept of the student as consumer and the educator as resource,

https://doi.org/10.1515/9783110551563-016

service provider, or facilitator of a kind, student-centeredness, an emphasis on learning outcomes conceived as measurable results of one kind or another, general skills of problem solving and critical thinking, the acquisition of useful information, particularly in the areas of mathematics and science, cognitive and psycho-social development, the various and growing number of learning styles, individual autonomy, education as a commodity, and so on. Increasingly it is the language not only of science and technology but of the marketplace that dominates the discourse of education. A general mind set of technology and of empirical and economic rationality is now so entrenched, and its basic orientation so contrary to Dewey's stance, that its connection with progressive education is increasingly difficult to see.

Perhaps the most accurate description of the current thinking in education remains one put forward by Jean-François Lyotard in *The Postmodern Condition*, in which he pronounced a diagnosis of the state of education, research, and knowledge in general in the second half of the 20th century. To be educated, he wrote, now means to have mastered the various bits of information that are necessary for the maintenance of efficiency and for the optimizing of technological and economic use-value. According to the new standard of performativity, "The question (overt or implied) now asked by the professionalist student, the state, or institutions of higher education is no longer 'Is it true?' but 'What use is it?' In the context of the mercantilization of knowledge, more often than not this question is equivalent to: 'Is it saleable?' And in the context of power-growth: 'Is it efficient?'" Knowledge in postmodernity has been reduced to a commodity, and along with it the whole business of education, particularly at the postsecondary level which was the focus of Lyotard's analysis. Values of experimentation, inventiveness, and judgment become subordinated within a new ethos that is at once positivistic and corporate. It is the performativity and efficiency of the economic system that drives the entire process, while "[t]he old principle that the acquisition of knowledge is indissociable from the training (*Bildung*) of minds, or even of individuals, is becoming obsolete and will become ever more so." As education and research are absorbed within a logic of the marketplace, "[k]nowledge is and will be produced in order to be sold, it is and will be consumed in order to be valorized in a new production: in both cases, the goal is exchange."[1] The essential business of educational institutions, accordingly, is the production and consumption of information which must itself be useful in an economic sense. Its utility consists in the credentials with which it supplies students intent on entering the workforce and little, perhaps nothing, besides.

1 Lyotard 1984, p. 51, 4.

Lyotard pronounced this diagnosis in 1979 and the trend that he described continues to gain momentum in the present information age, as the economy becomes increasingly oriented toward technology and informational knowledge and as social and political institutions become ever more beholden to instrumental rationality. He, of course, is not alone in his diagnosis. It has been a frequent observation among continental philosophers for over a century that scientific and technological rationality has assumed an altogether dominant presence in the conduct of social life no less than in the science of nature. Hans-Georg Gadamer remarked upon this phenomenon in 1965 in the following terms:

> What appears to me to characterize our epoch is not the surprising control of nature we have achieved, but the development of scientific methods to guide the life of society. Only with this achievement has the victorious course of modern science, beginning in the nineteenth century, become a dominant social factor. The scientific tendencies of thought underlying our civilization have in our time pervaded all aspects of social praxis. Scientific market research, scientific warfare, scientific diplomacy, scientific rearing of the younger generation, scientific leadership of the people—the application of science to all these fields gives expertise a commanding position in the economy of society.[2]

Max Weber's description of the "iron cage of rationality," Martin Heidegger's analysis of "science-technology," and Michel Foucault's "regimes of truth" all have relevance here. What all depict in one fashion or another is the hegemony of scientific and technological ways of thinking within social reality and the consequent delegitimation of ways of thinking and knowing that do not fit this model. Unsurprising, education is no exception. Here as well, a kind of managerial positivism has largely displaced progressivism, even as the language of progressive education continues to have a place in the current thinking.

Let us use the expression corporate scientism to refer to the general phenomenon that Lyotard and many other educational theorists have called to our attention. The first principle of this view is that education should be scientific. Why this should be so is a question seldom answered and seldom asked. As a branch of social science, educational research must be strictly empirical and draw upon the latest findings of empirical psychology, learning theory, cognitive science, sociology, and any other field that will support its claim to constitute a legitimate form of scientific knowledge and an independent discipline within the university. Educational research must above all strive to be rigorously empirical and concerned with means far more than ends. If it cannot be entirely apolitical or value-free, as the older philosophical positivism urged, it must approach evaluative matters in as empirical and technical a manner as the subject will permit.

---

2 Gadamer 1992, p. 165.

Whenever possible, quantitative methods are employed, and if it cannot be denied that qualitative "methods" have a place, one suspects the concession is somewhat grudging, the positivist dichotomy of fact and value still having considerable purchase. As Derek Briton observes regarding adult education in particular:

> The commonsense assumption that the modern practice of adult education is a disinterested, *scientific* endeavor that need not, indeed, *should not* concern itself with moral and political questions has become all but impossible to question because the field's normative base can no longer be addressed within its narrowly defined, depoliticized, dehistoricized, technicist, professional discourse.[3]

The managerial or corporate dimension of the current thinking is sufficiently evident, I trust, to require little demonstration. The marketing material of educational faculties alone is unambiguous in its descriptions of the research conducted therein and the decided emphasis on professional credentials. As one group of observers notes,

> The new theoretical emphases are on statistics and the countable, on observation and testing, on the useful and on "what works." Its new watchwords are skills, competences and techniques, flexibility, independence, targets and performance indicators, qualifications and credentials, learning outcomes. Profound objections, from both theoretical and practical perspectives, to established shibboleths are angrily dismissed as idle or self-indulgent diversions from brute educational necessities .... The standard under which this movement marches is itself that of "raising standards."[4]

Two other theorists writing in the same volume similarly lament this new "rhetoric of the marketplace":

> Headteachers' conference bars rang to the sound of "marketing strategies," "mission statements" and "business plans," "performance measures" and "performance-related pay"; parents became "customers" or "clients"; heads of department were constituted into "senior management teams" and became "line managers." Schools "delivered" "products" in the most "cost-effective" ways they could invent.[5]

Surely, one frequently hears, no right-thinking person could oppose raising standards or evidence-based (which always means empirical evidence) learning outcomes, even while the gloss that is put on these terms is resolutely if not

3 Briton 1996, p. 9.
4 Blake, Smeyers, Smith and Standish 2003, p. 8.
5 Bridges and Jonathon 2003, p. 29.

crudely economic. The aim is to produce a certain kind of subject and a certain kind of worker: one that is efficient, informed, technically competent, and skilled in the execution of tasks spelled out in advance, perhaps not especially creative or reflective unless this can be disciplined by technique and turned to profitable use. In the end, one must have a product. It matters only as a secondary issue whether this be a good or a service, a trade or a profession, but one must have the necessary preparation and credentials to enter the workforce, and education is properly a means to this end. Students themselves are consumers of a service, but it is as future producers that they are trained.

This new corporatism is encouraged by governments that continually warn of impending economic crisis if education is permitted to go its own way or underemphasize science, technology, and mathematics. Anxiety regarding economic preparedness is instilled in students' consciousness, and in such a way that even the fashionable political language of empowerment becomes translated in many minds into issues of competitive advantage and the relative speed at which one is likely to ascend the corporate ladder. The values of autonomy and freedom shrink down to the freedom to consume and the secure knowledge that this will not be easily jeopardized in the event of economic downturn. Corporate scientism has little use for the intangibles of education or for anything that cannot be brought within an ethos of scientific and economic rationality. The arts and humanities in particular are regularly, and quite inevitably, deemed unnecessary luxuries in comparison with the natural sciences and mathematics, with all the utilitarian benefits that the latter disciplines provide. Defenders of the arts and humanities who are now obligated to plead their case within a vocabulary that is foreign, if not antithetical, to these disciplines themselves are engaged in a losing cause. No cost-benefit analysis redeems the study of music or philosophy. The problem here is not that we are unable to provide such an accounting, without resorting to clever but inauthentic marketing, but that we are required to do so.

Perhaps the most fundamental problem with this latest form of scientism is its tendency to regard education in general as a mere means to an end. When this view prevails, it is perfectly irrelevant what end education is thought a means of achieving, whether it be economic success or any other. Whatever the ultimate ends of the educative process are, they are nothing outside of that process itself. Education serves, and has always served, as a means of attaining practical and economic ends, yet at a more fundamental level of analysis it is also an end in itself. The practice of education is an art in which an inventive mind mediates between any findings of empirical research and the student's consciousness. While education undoubtedly benefits from empirical investigation into human psychology and cognition, the essence of education remains the search for understanding and self-understanding that occurs between educators, students, and the subject matter. The imperative to "make it scientific," whether it be for purposes of disciplinary legitimation or simply because in an age of science the imperative has become something of an axiom, will not succeed in transforming what is by its nature an art and a practice into a science or technique. Regarding this art on a behaviorist model, for instance, or as any kind of closed causal system in which learning is construed as a certain kind of effect and teaching a certain cause or technology, constitutes a profound misunderstanding of this practice and an absurd overestimation of what science can achieve.

An additional difficulty with the new corporate scientism is that it leaves little room for genuine agency on the part of students and educators alike. Cognitive development itself presupposes a level of personal and intellectual agency together with the conditions that make this possible. The educated mind is fundamentally one with a capacity for freethinking, an inventive and self-directing agent. It is the human being who is able and vitally concerned to participate in the conversation that is its culture, who is therefore knowledgeable of the ideas that make up that conversation and, no less important, capable of taking it further and relating it to one's own existence. Education at a more fundamental level of analysis is not an outcome but a life process that has no end beyond itself. Educational institutions no more approximate corporations than students are human capital in the making or laboratory rats in a behaviorist's maze. Their purpose far exceeds instilling virtues of adaptation and efficiency, but includes such economically useless qualities as inquisitiveness, wonder, originality, and self-understanding. There is still a place for such values in a scientific age, and if these and similar intellectual virtues are being de-emphasized and consequently unlearned in the rage to make it scientific then it is not only our educational institutions that are in trouble. What students must ultimately learn is the art of thinking, yet this is precisely what defies empirical metrics, measurable outcomes, and standardization.

There is no doubt that knowledge derived from psychology, cognitive science, sociology, and other branches of social science have profitably informed our understanding of education, particularly regarding issues of means: how students of different descriptions and at different maturational levels successfully integrate new knowledge into an established conceptual framework and how our pedagogical practices may be adjusted in this light. Enormous quantities of empirical study have devoted themselves to this purpose for some decades now, however what too much of this research overlooks is that the question of how learning takes place is not only an empirical matter but a properly philosophical one, and that as a philosophical question it calls upon the resources of phenomenology and hermeneutics. Empirical questions regarding the means of education remain subordinate to the matter of its ends. Here again we are faced with a philosophical question for which science will not help us. Empirical investigation will never disclose what the whole enterprise is for. It cannot account for which learning outcomes we ought to seek and why, which subject matters are of relative importance and why, or any other question pertaining to ends. Education is a matter about which we may certainly ask scientific questions, but a science itself it is not. Treating it as one narrows rather than deepens our understanding of it and causes us to overlook the often tenuous connection between empirical research and the actual practices of teaching and learning. Inferences drawn from the realm of empirical study to what actually takes place in classrooms are often less than obvious, and educators obliged to bridge these worlds are often and understandably at a loss as to how to do this. The confusion itself is instructive, I would suggest, and affects very little whether education succeeds or fails. Educational success depends to a great extent on the intangibles and unquantifiables of the classroom, which is to say precisely that which no method can teach. There is no technique for instilling a fascination with history, a sense of justice, or a capacity for inventive interpretation.

It is on this last point that Lyotard placed his emphasis. The heart and soul of education, on his account, is the student's capacity for novelty in fashioning ideas and in questioning received bodies of knowledge. Research and education are likewise centered around dissension rather than consensus. Success occurs when we are able to invent novel moves within settled language games or to invent new language games and thus "disturb the order of 'reason.'"[7] The truest indicator of educational success is that for which there is no science and no method: the power of the imagination to destabilize what presently passes for knowledge and to invent new ways of seeing the world. The conditions that would make this possible are not present when imperatives of scientificity and performativity gain a dominant position, effectively creating a world that is ever more an object of calculation and administration and of means over ends.

II What Is Education?

Scientifically conceived, the discipline of education is an applied science—one might say a technology—which brings empirical research findings from psychology and cognate fields to bear on what happens in classrooms in ways that pro-

7 Lyotard 1984, p. 61.

mote efficiency in learning and measurable outcomes. Hermeneutically conceived, education may be defined as (1) the art (2) by which students are brought into a given field of study (3) by fostering capacities and knowledge (4) that often defy objective quantification and (5) that form the soul. Let us briefly analyze each of these claims.

1. Education is neither a science nor any master- or meta-discipline of the university but an art. Informed by disciplines both empirical (psychology in particular) and humanistic (philosophy of education), it is not a science unto itself, and apart from its standing in the university as a vocational school its claim to being a separate faculty or discipline must be regarded as dubious. There is no prospect of education becoming a purely scientific, technical, or otherwise non-philosophical discipline, despite the efforts of many educationalists to transform the ultimate questions of this practice into purely technical issues. For as long as research in this field continues to be conceived on the model of applied science alone, it will continue to impose upon education a nomenclature and a way of thinking that miss a good deal of its point.

The point would perhaps be obvious were the imperative to make it scientific less ubiquitous than it is in an age of science. When science is a worldview rather than a contingent way of thinking and interpreting the world—as Friedrich Nietzsche put it, "an interpretation and exegesis of the world (to suit us, if I may say so!) and *not* a world-explanation"—intellectual respectability itself requires that we plead every case before this court, that no matter what we are speaking about or what we have to say about it we shall say it in this language.[8] In such conditions, disciplines of the arts and humanities are compelled to legitimate themselves in a language they do not speak and by standards that are foreign to the disciplines themselves, rather as a hockey player is judged by how well he can execute a triple axel. It is in this condition that education now finds itself—trying to legitimate its standing in the university as a scientific discipline and, accordingly, an appropriately separate faculty. It is neither.

2. The fundamental aim of this art is to initiate students into what Michael Oakeshott called "the conversation of mankind" or one of its specialized tributaries.[9] As a parent teaches a child to speak the language, walk, or throw a baseball, the professional educator initiates students into a given form of knowledge and trains them as participants. In every case the learner is being intentionally

8 Nietzsche, BGE 14, trans. Kaufmann (Nietzsche 1989, p. 21)..

9 Michael Oakeshott defined education as "an initiation into the skill and partnership of this conversation in which we learn to recognize the voices, to distinguish the proper occasions of utterance, and in which we acquire the intellectual and moral habits appropriate to conversation." Oakeshott 1991, pp. 490–491.

brought into something—a discipline, practice, or art—that belongs to the way of life into which they are initiated and so come into their own. This kind of learning is life-long and involves a fair amount of self-education. The entire process is driven by the student and is at most supported by the teacher.

The model of joining a conversation is central here. This, of course, is a central theme in Gadamer's hermeneutics and was described in *Truth and Method* as an art of informal and undogmatic communication on the model of Platonic dialogue, in which Socrates comports himself not as one in possession of the truth but as one who professes his ignorance in the encounter with an interlocutor. True wisdom, he famously insisted, is the possession of the gods; human beings may pursue and indeed love wisdom, but we are only ever on the way to acquiring it, and acquiring it in association with other rational beings. One does not pursue knowledge alone, but only ever on a common basis, and rather often without formal methods. Language is best regarded, phenomenologically speaking, as the practice of dialogue in which reciprocity, freedom, and equality between speakers is the only morality, and power, while never altogether eliminable from human affairs, requires constant vigilance from participants. The point of a dialogue is the search for what is true, what is good, and what things mean, and none in the conversation possesses special expertise in these matters.

There are two paradigmatic dialogical acts, which are speaking and listening. Participation involves a constant back-and-forth between what another has to say and the creative response of the individual. Fundamentally, the act of speaking is a responding to what another has said, and a response that crucially anticipates its possible truth value. The other has addressed me, and it behooves me to take their claim to truth or meaning seriously, which means to regard it in its strongest light rather than to be searching continually for evidence of incoherence or errors in reasoning. The accent on receptivity and the anticipation of truth does not entail an uncritical posture but that where this preliminary expectation is not present there is no genuine listening and learning. Gadamer described not only an expressive but an importantly receptive dimension of dialogue which has special importance for education. We do not control the direction a dialogue takes but allow ourselves to be taken up in a process that has a life of its own. Where it is genuine, rather than an empty catchphrase or a veneer for a certain kind of politicization, dialogue is governed by a spirit of egalitarian reciprocity in which all are responsible for what they say and no one, be it teacher or student, is above the fray. The dialogical ideal recognizes the educational value of uncertainty and of processes of fallibilist interpretation and judgment that largely define us as rational beings. Quite apart from the secure possession of information, a mark of educational success is the cultivation of habits of mind that may or may not translate into outcomes of some determinate and measurable kind. The dialogical view expresses a conception of knowledge, reason, and truth as praxial categories for which there are no foundations but the conversation itself. To know is to participate in social practices of inquiry and interpretation that culminate in understanding, not in objective certainties. It is defined by the pursuit and the love of wisdom in the Greek sense and not by its altogether secure possession.

An important mark of educational success, as Dewey well noted, is that one is a politically engaged citizen capable of forming judgments in an intelligent and pragmatic fashion. A more hermeneutical (and not at all un-Deweyan) way of saying this is that education properly initiates students into the dialogue that is our culture or tradition. It is concerned far less with the content of students' beliefs than with their ability to form their own and to participate as equals in the conversation of mankind. It is not uncommon for students or anyone else to be afflicted with blinding prejudices of one kind or another, and the work of education surely involves leading students to see how their apparent certainties are in fact interpretations and judgments that might have been otherwise. The best way this is accomplished is still to expose students to others' ideas since, as Gadamer knew, it is in dialogical exchanges that one's prejudices are called into play and can become an object of awareness. Conversation requires that we risk our point of view and often our parochialism in encountering unfamiliar texts and ideas. This is how our prejudices, be they true or false, are brought to light and potentially seen through rather than by any expertocratic bestowing of enlightenment on the part of the educator. If we regard culture itself on the model of a conversation that constitutes our historical facticity and affords a fundamental orientation to consciousness then education can be conceived as the process by which the younger generation learns to participate in dialogical processes that precede us rather than any mere acquisition of information or credentials. Becoming literate in any discipline means developing capacities of intellectual agency, and where agency signifies not only that one knows how the conversation has unfolded to this point but how to carry it further.

The salient facts about conversation as Gadamer spoke of it are fundamentally two: reciprocity and openness. All education, hermeneutically conceived, is an education in thinking, where this is conceived not in terms of the straightforward mastery of information but more fundamentally as an affair of language. Thought itself is "this infinite dialogue with ourselves," and an education in it may be spoken of as a gradual process of "growing up in the midst of this interior conversation with ourselves, which is always simultaneously the anticipation of conversation with others and the introduction of others into the conversation with ourselves." It is in this conversation that "the world begins to open up and achieve order in all the domains of experience," in which meanings are understood and truths are discerned. No technique governs this art; no empirical or evidence-based pedagogy tells us how it is done or how to measure success, however, as is the case with any art and any skill, practice and habit-formation are imperative. In education students become habituated not only to acquiring facts but to raising questions and pursuing them with patience and persistence, to listening and discerning, to judging, criticizing, imagining, and other cognitive skills that resist our efforts at quantification and formalization. Dialogue itself is an art that no method governs but the dialectic of question and answer. Gadamer emphasized the priority in this art of the questioning act since it is this that brings the object that is to be known into the open and that is also inseparable from the event of insight. "The real nature of the sudden idea," he noted, "is perhaps less that a solution occurs to us like an answer to a riddle than that a question occurs to us that breaks through into the open and thereby makes an answer possible. Every sudden idea has the structure of a question."[15] The art of thinking is nothing else than the art of questioning, of learning both to discern what is questionable and to formulate the question that brings the matter into the open.

What Gadamer spoke of as the play structure of language refers to the back-and-forth of question and answer which characterizes knowledge in general. "Knowledge is dialectical from the ground up," he noted, in the sense that it emerges from the movement of statement and reply which belongs to all genuine conversation.[16] Reciprocity and equality fundamentally characterize the relation between speakers in a process over which no one altogether presides, including in an educational context the professor. While their role includes the important matter of informing the students of certain matters, it is not to play the expert but to inquire, as Dewey often put it, with the students into a given problem or question. The professor, from this point of view, is less "professing" what they know than guiding the course of inquiry in a direction that is productive and educationally worthwhile. The equality between speakers is not an equality of knowledge but one in which professors and students are free to question and to assert anything they wish as well as obliged to defend their answers.

3. Education crucially bears upon the cultivation of intellectual agency and virtues of mind, including the various forms of knowing how and knowing that. To cultivate or foster is not to cause. A farmer cultivates the land in the sense not that they cause the growth of a crop but provide the conditions that make growth possible, and the outcome will be what it will be. Teachers, by the same token, do not grow the mind but create the environment that makes growth—a process

15 Gadamer 1989, pp. 542–543, 366.

16 Gadamer 1989, p. 365.

that in every case emerges from within—optimal. No pedagogical art, however evidence-based it is purported to be, brings about this result of itself any more than a farmer can guarantee that a crop will turn out well. A sizable element of fortune presides over the outcome of any art, no matter how dutifully we follow our "best practices."

So long as the learning process aims at the gradual attainment of intellectual maturity, indications of its success will be found not in tests scores or other quasi-objective indicators alone but in the cultivation of habits and capacities of mind of the kind that are called forth in dialogue. Becoming competent interlocutors requires practice at all stages of the learning process. One learns to judge, as Aristotle remarked, by judging, and one learns to participate in dialogue by participating, not only by being informed of whatever consensus or discoveries at which others have arrived. It is an important prerequisite of such participation that one knows the history of the conversation to which one will offer a contribution, but it is a prerequisite nonetheless and not an end in itself. The art of conversation requires much of its participants, from inventiveness to listening and a hospitality to others' views. It requires a renunciation of false self-certainty and an orientation toward process over outcomes. This last issue is a virtual impossibility for teachers at the primary and secondary levels who are required both to teach a standardized and information-driven curriculum and to prepare students to write standardized tests, and in a great variety of ways to ensure certain measurable outcomes. The highest achievements in education—a certain restlessness of mind, a passion for understanding for its own sake, curiosity, originality, critical capacity, and similar habits of mind—are not quantifiable outcomes and no standardized examination can test for their presence. The impatience for process and intangibles, or for any educational values that defy reduction to the utilitarian calculus, is profoundly antithetical to dialogue, the conditions and spirit of which are incommensurable with the scientistic and technological bent of many contemporary educationalists.

4. Education is a life process which, like anything that can be so described, resists the language of metrics, quantification, planning, managerialism, and outcomes. The language of art, process, cultivation, agency, and so on gets us to the heart of what education is, and what it speaks of are largely intangible and qualitative matters of precisely the kind that many educational policymakers regard as an accessory. It is these matters that make it possible for the young to join in the intellectual life of their culture and their importance, accordingly, is ultimate. Despite monumental efforts of the empirically minded to formalize all such matters, it cannot be done without the kind of distortion that happens whenever we flatten an art into a technique. There are matters that defy objective

measure, and they include most everything that we encounter in the deeper waters of our existence.

The reply will be that educators have long had methods of assessing their students' learning in the form of examinations, essays, and other assignments which can be graded with some claim to objectivity, including in disciplines of the arts and humanities. A professor of history or English is well able to distinguish an A essay from a B; this much is clear. The reply to the objection is that it can indeed be expected that grades provide a roughly accurate measure of a student's work, but not of their learning. What a student learns in a given course of inquiry—and not only in the present but perhaps years into the future—is incalculable and unknowable to the educator and often to the student. The consciousness of the student is forever inaccessible to the teacher, who will often presume to know how much a student has learned on the basis of their graded work, but it is not unusual for a sizable discrepancy to emerge between these two matters. Every educator knows that students with high grades do not necessarily learn more than their lower graded peers, which is one reason why grades are sometimes considered a necessary evil—necessary, that is, for institutional reasons and unfortunate for their inability to measure learning rather than task completion. When our primary educational goals are defined in terms of the acquisition of information there is little difficulty in measuring this, but when we are aiming higher, objective assessment is a difficult matter indeed.

5. Education forms the soul. There is a "rising up to humanity" that happens here, a process that is well captured in the notion of *Bildung* and that Dewey conceptualized as a form of growth. One is initiated into something that at first lies outside of the self, yet it is oneself into which one grows. Gadamer provided a hermeneutical analysis of this notion in Part One of *Truth and Method.*

Part of his project in that book was to rehabilitate for the human sciences several guiding concepts of the humanist tradition, including one whose implications for education are not far to seek. Originating in medieval mysticism, *Bildung* (culture) is an idea that found its way into modern German idealism in the writings of Johann Gottfried Herder, Wilhelm von Humboldt, and G.W.F. Hegel in particular before undergoing something of a deterioration toward the end of the 19th century. The disrepute into which this idea fell was owing to its association in many minds with cultural and intellectual snobbery. *Bildung*, many came to believe, belongs to the affluent and the elite, although this is not what the term meant in the humanist tradition and it is not at all what was intended by the philosophers just listed.[18] The word refers to a life task that belongs to

18 As Graeme Nicholson has pointed out, "*Bildung* took on a bourgeois coloring during the 19th every human being, and while it occurs both within and without educational institutions it has special importance for what happens within them. In *Bildung* we are not pursuing a particular end-state, a condition of "being cultured" or "sophisticated," but are, as Herder expressed it, "rising up to humanity through culture." The word connotes a process rather than an outcome, and while it aims at the transformation of the self it does not proceed in any single direction but toward a general cultivation not only of given talents but of capacities of mind that take one beyond the immediacy of the self and toward some conception of the universal. In Humboldt's words, "when in our language we say *Bildung*, we mean something both higher and more inward, namely the disposition of mind which, from the knowledge and the feeling of the total intellectual and moral endeavor, flows harmoniously into sensibility and character."[19]

Gadamer cited with approval Hegel's notion of *Bildung* as a break from human naturalness and immediacy in order to cultivate higher capacities of thought: "'In this sphere he is not, by nature, what he should be'—and hence he needs *Bildung*." "What he should be," for Hegel, is to be understood in terms of "rising to the universal," where this refers to a life process of transcending the self in its immediate circumstances and taking up an idea that partakes of a higher universality. This is accomplished, to take Hegel's example, in work; this form of activity finds one becoming disciplined in a fashion in view of the task at hand and is formed in so doing. "Whoever abandons himself to his particularity," as Gadamer put it,

> is ungebildet ("unformed")—e. g., if someone gives way to blind anger without measure or sense of proportion. Hegel shows that basically such a man is lacking in the power of abstraction. He cannot turn his gaze from himself towards something universal, from which his own particular being is determined in measure and proportion.[21]

century that would make it repugnant to authors like Nietzsche and Heidegger. As with the English word 'gentleman,' it was the tone of snobbery that came to prevail, for *ein gebildeter Herr* was a German term that in the 19th century accomplished the same effect—marking a social distinction." Nicholson 2010, p. 72. Clearly, this is not what the term meant in the humanist tradition or in the writings of early modern German thinkers like Hegel and Herder. For Gadamer, *Bildung* is a life task that belongs to everyone, and it occurs both inside and outside educational institutions. It has no socio-economic connotation but is more the nature of a process and project that aims at the transformation of the self, and not in any single direction. People can be well educated and otherwise have rather little in common.

19 Cited in Gadamer 1989, pp. 10 – 11.

21 Gadamer 1989, p. 12.

Work cultivates a capacity for abstraction in the sense that in laboring upon an object one is forming it in light of an idea at the same time that one is forming the self. Work requires a self-forgetfulness and a self-overcoming in order to accomplish a task, a cultivation of sensibilities that transform the individual and impart a sense of oneself. In being initiated into a profession, for instance, students are developing a range of skills and habits that take them out of the immediacy of interest and desire and transform them in light of what it means to be a professional in a given field. Becoming a historian is a rising to the universal in this sense; the student develops a general conception of what a historian is, what form of work is involved and what it takes to accomplish it, what capacities of thought, work habits, and so on, require cultivation, the effect of which is to become a different self. One becomes a servant of a kind and makes oneself answerable to the demands that every profession makes, yet not in a sense that intimates mere conformity. One makes one's profession one's own as we learn to find our way about a language or any dimension of a lifeworld; we become ourselves in the same gesture that has us learning to serve something beyond ourselves.

Bildung requires a distancing from the given, an orientation toward the universal, and that one make oneself at home in a world that is initially unfamiliar. In Gadamer's words, "to recognize one's own in the alien, to become at home in it, is the basic movement of spirit, whose being consists only in returning to itself from what is other." The same process of "getting beyond his naturalness" characterizes the acquisition of language and culture, this universal life task of becoming at home in a world in the same process in which one is formed by it. It is a process of ascending not only from ignorance to knowledge but from particularity to universality, nature to culture, and immaturity to maturity. It is a formation that happens through cultivating habits, broadening horizons, and becoming exposed and receptive to ideas whatever their source. In this process, it is not only our reason narrowly conceived that is cultivated but a range of capacities that Gadamer referred to as senses. Thus "someone who has an aesthetic sense knows how to distinguish between the beautiful and the ugly, high and low quality,"[22] much as the student of philosophy develops a facility with concepts, a sense of whether an idea is plausible and worth pursuing or whether it may be left aside. Common sense as well consists not in any mere possession of information but in a practical sensibility and a judgment that is broadly shared by members of a historical community and a sense of what that community holds in common. "Thus," as Gadamer put it, the educated or "cultivated con-

---

22 Gadamer 1989, p. 17.

sciousness has in fact more the character of a sense"—of how to do things, how to see what is required, form distinctions and judgments, and respond to whatever situations we encounter. It is a consciousness that is "active in all directions," and accordingly is a "universal and common sense."[23] One may say that the basic structure of *Bildung* is the dialectic of venture and return. Learning is a venturing toward the unknown and strange, an undertaking that involves risk and in which another can play at most a supporting role. It is followed by a return to the familiar, but no longer as the self whom one was. Education is transformative in this sense; it forms the self in a process that is dialectical and lifelong.

In becoming educated one takes up one's culture in such a way as to make it one's own, much as in joining a profession one is not merely conforming to established ways of doing things but adding one's originality to the received ways. For Gadamer, in learning about one's tradition or culture (and other cultures no less) one learns not only in the limited sense that it speaks and one listens but that one also answers or enters into a dialogue with the past. I must appropriate my culture, make it my own and see myself in it, indeed become myself in it, and in a process in which I also transform elements of the culture itself. For Gadamer, the true mark of *Bildung* is precisely an openness to what is alien: "the general characteristic of *Bildung* [is] keeping oneself open to what is other—to other, more universal points of view." The cultivated mind is not only well informed in a particular discipline but has more the character of a sense than mere information—a sense that is at once universal and common, including a sense of what is important and good, a sense of history, an aesthetic sense, and some others. Common sense, for instance, is far more than any mere matter of possessing information but consists in a sense of what is shared by the members of a historical community, a sense of how to do things including how to form various kinds of judgments.

The concept of *Bildung* as Gadamer spoke of it refers to both the process of becoming formed in a certain way and also the result of that process. The process itself is not a technical one but is a kind of inner development that is characterized by a break from what is given in our natures. In Gadamer's words, "Man is characterized by the break with the immediate and the natural that the intellectual, rational side of his nature demands of him."[24] Culture and humanity itself are values to which the human being aspires and must not be regarded as givens of our existence. It is, as Hegel stated, a life task of every human being to rise

23 Gadamer 1989, p. 14, 17.
24 Gadamer 1989, p. 12, 13, 14.

above the circumstances in which we find ourselves and to pursue an idea of one kind or another.

Corporate scientism knows nothing of this or may well regard all such talk as anachronism in an age of science. Education is in every case an education in thinking—and for as long as the latter remains an art then so too is the practice that endeavors to cultivate it.

References

Blake, Nigel, Smeyers, Paul, Smith, Richard D. and Standish, Paul (2003) "Introduction." In: Nigel Blake, Paul Smeyers, Richard D. Smith and Paul Standish (eds.), *The Blackwell Guide to the Philosophy of Education*. Malden: Blackwell, pp. 1–18.

Bridges David and Jonathon, Ruth (2003) "Education and the Market." In: Nigel Blake, Paul Smeyers, Richard D. Smith and Paul Standish (eds.), *The Blackwell Guide to the Philosophy of Education*. Malden: Blackwell, pp. 126–145.

Briton, Derek (1996) *The Modern Practice of Adult Education: A Postmodern Critique*. Albany: State University of New York Press.

Dewey, John (2008) *Democracy and Education*. Middle Works Vol. 9: *1916*. Carbondale: Southern Illinois University Press.

Gadamer, Hans-Georg (1989) *Truth and Method*, tr. J. Weinsheimer and D.G. Marshall. New York: Continuum.

Gadamer, Hans-Georg (1992) "The Idea of the University—Yesterday, Today, Tomorrow." In: *Hans-Georg Gadamer on Education, Poetry, and History: Applied Hermeneutics*, tr. Lawrence Schmidt and Monica Reuss, ed. Dieter Misgeld and Graeme Nicholson. Albany: State University of New York Press, pp. 47–60.

Lyotard, Jean-François (1984) *The Postmodern Condition: A Report on Knowledge*, tr. Geoff Bennington and Brian Massumi. Minneapolis: University of Minnesota Press.

Nicholson, Graeme (2010) "The Education of the Teacher." In: Paul Fairfield (ed.), *Education, Dialogue and Hermeneutics*. London: Continuum, pp. 61–76.

Nietzsche, Friedrich (1989) *Beyond Good and Evil*, tr. W. Kaufmann. New York: Vintage.

Oakeshott, Michael (1991) *Rationalism in Politics*. Indianapolis: Liberty Fund.

IV Truth and Life: Life-Philosophy and History, Psychology and Theology

Simon Glynn

The Hermeneutical Human and Social Sciences

Abstract: Hermeneutic *interpretation*, coming to prominence in the exegesis of scriptural texts and later in the understanding of legal texts, is no less useful, and indeed is arguably indispensible, to the understanding of human experience (both sensory and private) and dispositions, and the social, cultural political, economic and historical action, interactions, relations and institutions etc. which they give rise to or instantiate, while it is, somewhat surprisingly, no less indispensable to the natural sciences.

I Introduction: Hermeneutic Interpretation

While Heidegger maintains that hermeneutics, concerned with the interpretive derivation of meaning and correct understanding, can be traced back, via Plato, to Parmenides and Heraclitus,[1] it was with the Reformation's attempt to divine the supposedly true meanings of the scriptures that it rose to prominence. Thus contra the Fundamentalists, who, failing to recognize (or at least publically acknowledge) their interpretations of the scriptures as interpretations, insisted that the scriptures had a literal meaning, which they claimed to be evident to them at least, others, aware of apparent incoherencies and contradictions, within the scriptures, argued that it was only by interpreting each *text* in *context* that we could truly understand it.

And as with scriptural texts, so too with legal and literary texts, cultural artifacts, theatrical performances, and *human behavior* more generally, and concomitantly therefore with *social, cultural, historical, political and economic etc. action, interaction and relations, and the institutions they instantiate;* all of which may be *understood* by *interpreting* them in terms of the *contexts* in which they arise and operate. Furthermore hermeneutic interpretation is also usefully, even indispensible, to understanding the *experiences*, both sensory and non-sensory or private (e.g. emotions, thoughts, ideas, memories, fantasies, dreams etc.) not to mention the *dispositions* (e.g. values, attitudes, beliefs and aspirations etc.) underlying and informing such actions and interactions etc..

1 See for instance Heidegger 1971, 1975a, 1976 and Heidegger 1962, Section 44, pp. 256–273.

https://doi.org/10.1515/9783110551563-017

II From Objectivistic Observation and Causal Explanation to Hermeneutic Interpretation and Understanding

Thus against those who council applying the *objective epistemologies, quantitative methods and causal explanations* of the natural sciences to the human and social sciences also, it is argued that such an approach, useful as it might be in the study of physical objects, their properties, relations and interactions, is at best of limited relevance, and at worst simply misleading, when applied to the study of human subjects, their actions, social relations and interactions, and that it is only by hermeneutically interpreting, and thus *understanding the qualitative meaning and/or significance* of subjects' *experiences,* (both sensory and non-sensory) *and dispositions* which in furnishing the foundations and motives that give rise to the projects and goals which provide the *reasons* for individual's *choices*, that we may come to truly understand and, where appropriate, confidently predict human behavior and the social, cultural, historical, political and economic etc. actions, interactions and relations etc. associated therewith. A position with which Wilhelm Dilthey, who insisted that whereas "Nature we explain; Man we understand,"[2] concurred.

Beginning at the most fundamental level then, like the meaning of the term "volume," for instance, which is hermeneutically dependent upon context, varying as it does depending upon whether I ask you "What volume of gasoline does your car's gas tank hold," to "Turn up the volume of your radio," or to "Pass me the volume by Byron off the bookcase," the significance of even the most basic *sensation*, such as my aching limbs, depends upon whether it follows a "work out," in which context it might well be *understood* to be a healthy reaction, or whether it came about during a period of relative inactivity, in which context it might well be *interpreted* as an indicator of the onset of a bout of, say, influenza, or following much drink, when it might be *understood* as a hangover.

And as with *sensations*, so too with non-sensory or private *experiences and dispositions*, and the *behavior*, etc., resulting therefrom. For instance the *feeling* of *guilt* which some people, particularly adolescents, not uncommonly experience when first engaging in sexual relations, and which may therefore influence their *behavior or actions*, and *interactions*, can be interpreted in a number of different, context dependent, ways. For instance, given that parent(s) routinely attempt to control any *behavior* of their children they regarded as, and proclaimed to be, "bad," by the actual, or threatened, withdrawal of parental affection, support and protection, and/or corporal punishment, which is to say by provoking

2 Dilthey 1957, p. 144 as quoted by Schrag 1980, p. 101.

the child's *anxiety*, it is quite understandable that, upon entering adulthood, the individual might tend to associate certain *feelings* of anxiety with moral guilt. In which case s/he may well tend, even absent parental admonishment, to interpret, and thus understand, the anxiety, not unreasonably resulting from unfamiliar sexual activity, as indicative, symptomatic, or even a manifestation or experience, of guilt, and therefore perhaps desist from it.

Nor is this necessarily to imply that *feelings* of guilt and the concomitant *disposition* to regard adolescent sexual interactions as immoral are always the consequence, rather than the cause of, or reason for, an individual's anxiety regarding them. For, quite clearly, such *feelings* may, conversely, derive from religious, social or cultural taboos grounded upon an understanding that the enhanced level of commitment that marriage implies may help protect the heightened emotions arising from sexual relations from being crushed by a breakdown of the relationship, and/or help insure adequate social stability and economic support for any child that might result, concomitantly avoiding the prospect of facing the potentially unpleasant choice between abortion or an unwanted child which might otherwise result.

As such examples demonstrate then, *human experiences, both sensory and non-sensory, and dispositions, as well as the behavior, or actions and socio-interactions to which they give rise, may be understood, and, were appropriate, even predicted, by interpreting them within the contexts in which they appear or arise.*

III From Hermeneutics to Its Structuralist Implications

Furthermore, Dilthey also insists that, hermeneutic interpretation is indispensible to the understanding of *political, and cultural* etc., *relations*, as well as the *institutions* which they instantiate. As he tells us:

> A rigorous hermeneutic of social organizations is needed in addition to single textual works .... Hermeneutics is possible here because between a people and a state, between believers and a church, between scientific life and a university there stands a relation in which a general outlook and unitary form of life find a structural coherence in which they express themselves. There is here the relation of parts to the whole, in which the parts receive meaning from the whole, and the whole receives sense from the parts; these categories of interpretation have their correlate in the structural coherence of the organization, by which it realizes its goal teleologically.[3]

3 Wilhelm Dilthey, quoted in Polkinghorne 1983, p. 221, quoting Earmarth 1978, p. 303.

However note that here Dilthey is extending the understanding of hermeneutics beyond that hitherto explicated. For while, as shifts in the meaning or significance of the term "volume," and of the experience of aching limbs, for example, demonstrate, the words or "parts receive meaning from the whole" context which surrounds them, he is here further claiming that, on the other hand, "the whole receives sense from the parts." That is to say that not only do the *parts* (the people, the believers and the scientific life) *derive their meaning or significance* (as the people of a state, congregants of a church, and constituents of a university) *from the whole,* (the state, the church, and the university) *but this whole receives sense from, or is constituted as such by, the very structurally related parts* (the people, the believers and the scientific life) *to which it gives meaning.* An act of mutual co-constitution which, like the attempt to pull oneself up by one's own bootstraps, may initially appear somewhat counterintuitive, if not paradoxical.

And yet, returning to that paradigm of meaning and hermeneutic interpretation, language, isn't just such "bootstrapping" precisely what happens with the learning of a (first at least) language? Coming across a new word (or part), which we initially do not understand, we usually (as in the case of the term "volume") attempt to understanding it by paying attention to the *context* in which it appears. However if this proves insufficient, we may then look the word up in a dictionary, in which each word is defined by its relationship to other words, which are, in turn, defined by other words until eventually, coming full *hermeneutic circle,* we encounter the first, or/and some of the earlier, word(s) with which we began. Thus, each of the individual "*parts,*" or words is indeed *ultimately* defined by, or "receives meaning from," its *relations to all the other parts* or words constitutive of the whole, *to which the same applies.*

Thus, as in the sentence, "The mill-wright on my right thinks it right that some rite should accompany the right of everyone to write what they think is right" (modified from Arthur Koestler) *the meaning of each individual part or word* (cf. *parole*) *receives meaning from the structurally related totality* (cf. *le langue*) *which "receives sense from the parts"*(cf. *parole*) *which collectively constitute it.*[4] A *hermeneutic circle* that is an instantiation of the *Structuralist* linguistics of

4 There are seven *semantically* distinguishable meanings attaching to the seven *phonetically* indistinguishable terms in this sentence, and although it is true that they may be *graphically* distinguished into four groups, (wright, right, rite & write), given the *graphic and phonetic* indistinguishability of four *semantically* distinguishable uses of the term "right," as well as the fact that those whose acquaintance with the sentence is purely *phonetic* can nevertheless distinguish all seven *semantic* differences, it should be clear that it is the seven different *contexts* in which the term appears, that enables us to distinguish the seven different *semantic meanings* it takes on;

Ferdinand de Saussure.[5] A *Structural Holism*, in accordance with which, as just demonstrated, the relations between the parts [*parole*] and the whole [*le langue*] are crucial to the understanding of language, just as, or so Dilthey is claiming, they also are to the understanding of social, political and cultural etc. relations, interactions and institutions etc. and those individuals who engage in and constitute them.

IV Structural Hermeneutics: Identity, Dialectics and Consciousness

For instance, as with the meanings of words, an individual's social identity is also, as *per* holistic ontology in general, differentially, or relationally, defined. For example, if I am identifiable as a Caucasian, male, professor and father, I am so identified in relation to, non-Caucasians, females, my students and my children; just as, *vice versa*, they are identified as such in relation to Caucasians (more specific racial designations being defined by their relations to other races as well of course) males, their professor or professors, and their father, respectively; the identity of each being dependent upon, and thus co-constituted by, its relations to the others, to which, to come full hermeneutic circle, the same applies. Furthermore, moving beyond the relationship between individuals or parts, to "the relation of parts to the whole," for instance that between "a people and a state," it is apparent that so far from the state, or indeed society etc., being reified entities, existing if not wholly independently of, at least in exterior relation to, the totality of individuals who appear, dialectically, both to influence and to be influenced by it, rather, like language as a whole (cf. *le langue)* the state or society is, most fundamentally, the structured totality of the individual elements (cf. *parole*) or people who constitute it. While not unlike the way in which the linguistic system as a whole constitutes and delineates the meanings of the individual parts, or words, which collectively constituted it, society, or to be more specific the *structure of* social *relations* and *interactions* also constitutes and delineate—as exemplified by our previous discussion of the rational for, and transmission of, sexual mores—many of the, particularly non-sensory, experiences, dispositions and behaviors of those individuals who both constitute, and derive their identities from, it. An insight which in serving to deconstruct

contexts which the very terms whose meanings are in question are also instrumental in constituting.

5 See Saussure 1959 [1916].

the traditional notion of dialectical interaction in favor of holistic part/whole relations, (dis)solves many of the problems and paradoxes, associated with the former.

Furthermore, just as the particular structural relations between individual linguistic terms delineate *what* they mean, while it is by virtue of structure *per se that* they have any meaning or significance whatsoever, so too with the meaning and significance of human experiences, behavior, and dispositions etc., as well as social actions, interactions and relations etc. Beginning then with language, just as an unstructured aggregate of clicks, accompanied by silence, when structured, as Morse Code, have meaning, so too do bumps on a page, structured as Brail, lines on a page, structured as conventional writing, and certain sorts of sounds, structured as speech. While applying this same analysis more generally, the human *behavior* of chasing an inflated animal skin around a field can, when structured in a certain way, become football, while the difference between the *feeling* of lust and the *experience* of love, for instance, would also seem to rest upon structure; stimulus/response giving way to, or being superseded by, a meaningful or significant, loving, *relationship* on account of the relationship's structure. Although—returning from the fact *that* relationships may be meaningful or significant to *what* that meaning or significance may be, here too, as with the meanings of words—the *feelings* and *dispositions or attitudes* etc. one may have regarding such relations can, of course, change with changes in context (including, of course, the relationship's own history) and may therefore, similarly, be subject to interpretation and re-interpretation.

Moreover, the very phenomena of meaning or significance *per se* would seem to presuppose a conscious subject, and hence consciousness, which also arises from structure. Thus just as the properties of water (e. g. wetness, freezing and boiling points etc.) which are vastly different from those of the two gasses, hydrogen and oxygen, from which it is exclusively constituted, may be understood as arising or *emerging* from the molecular *structuring* of $2H_2$ and O_2, to form $2H_2O$, so too consciousness *per se*, beginning with the experiencing or awareness of sensations, may—like the emergence of life by virtue of the (cyclical) structuring of carbon atoms into molecules, and of cells by virtue of the biological structuring of organic matter thus derived—be understood as emerging from the structuring of cells into a nervous system, and sensory organs; more complex consciousness emerging by virtue of the structural infolding of the nervous system, which forms a brain.[6]

6 For a fuller, and more detailed, version of the discussion contained in this section see Glynn 2005a.

V Contexts and Concepts: The Contextual Delineation of Concepts, the Conceptual Mediation of Experience and the Structuralist Hermeneutics of "Perception"

Returning to our earlier concern with *particular* meanings or significance, clearly particular meanings are delineated by concepts, which are indispensible to thought. Thus language, being a system not only of *signifiers*, or words, but of the concepts *signified* thereby,[7] is, in addition to being a medium of communication, also, a medium or "vehicle" of thought. As Saussure, for instance, referring to phonic language, tells us:

> Language can ... be compared with a sheet of paper: thought is the front and sound the back; one cannot cut the front without cutting the back at the same time; likewise in language, one can neither divide sound from thought nor thought from sound; the division could be accomplished only by abstraction ...[8]

Indeed it would seem that not only can we think in language, but that we *can only* think in language, whether symbolic, iconic (in the case of those who think "visually") or indexical;[9] the "linguistic" signifiers, whether phonic (as here per Saussure), graphic, tactile (as in Brail), or of any other form, being correlated with the concepts signified by them. Thus like our concepts, whose significance or meanings are contextually defined or delineated by our language,[10] which also articulates them, so too are our *thoughts.*

Furthermore as Immanuel Kant famously claimed, and as the cognitive experiments of the *Gestalt* psychologists and of Ames and his school, empirically demonstrate, the *sensible* (or sensory experience) is inextricably intertwined with the *intelligible* (or understanding); even *our empirical perceptions being mediated, and thereby,* as Heidegger affirms,[11] *delineated, as are our "perceptions" in the broader sense of our understanding of their meaning or significance, by our*

---

7 For instance, the concept of a table being variously signified in English, Spanish and Latin, respectively, by the signifier, table, mesa or mensa.

8 Saussure 1959 [1916], p. 113.

9 Now insofar as we may extend our notion of language in this manner, the claim that we think in language appears to be something of a tautology, in that any medium of thought will be designated a "language."

10 See our "volume" and "mill-wright ..." examples.

11 On this issue, see for example, Martin Heidegger, "What is a Thing," reprinted in part as "Modern Science, Metaphysics and Mathematics" (Heidegger 1975b), and Heidegger 1962, Section 32, pp. 188–195.

"conceptions and/or preconceptions,"[12] (hereinafter (pre)conceptions), *which is* then *ultimately to say by our language.*

For example, in the well-known *Gestalt* duck/rabbit experiment, having been told that they are going to view a drawing of a rabbit, individuals observing an outline on a piece of paper *see it as* the drawing of a rabbit. However, being told that what they are observing is a drawing of a duck they will *see it as* the drawing of a duck. While moving from the simple perception of objects to understanding actions, interactions and relations, whereas a Newtonian will "perceive" the falling to Earth of an unsupported object as a manifestation of *gravity*, an Aristotelian will "perceive" the very same motion as a manifestation of an earthly body's *striving* to reach its earthly home.

And similarly with our *personal* or private experiences, both sensory and non-sensory (i.e. psychological states), as well as our "perception" or understanding of socio-political affairs etc. Thus, those unfamiliar with Inuit language, which has many different terms for differing shades of white, are reportedly unable to perceive the many shades of white which those familiar with the language are, while, as for non-sensory experiences it is noticeable that melancholia for example, which was previously a prevalent emotion, is, with the exception of those familiar with Jane Austin novels and the like, scarcely evident today. Nor is it merely that it is not much spoken about, but rather it seems that it is not much felt either.

Thus just as it is widely understood, by those who have reasonable competence in more than one language, that some ideas or concepts which are readily articulable in one language, are not necessarily translatable into, another, so too, it would seem, with our physical and mental, experiences; those accessible to one linguistic community being by no means *necessarily* accessible to another.[13]

Moving on to our "perceptions" in the more general sense of our *understanding*, the decline of the British automobile industry in the 1970s, for example, was *"perceived" or understood* by management as symptomatic of a recalcitrant workforce, and by workers as symptomatic of poor management. When Japanese auto companies, using the same British workforce, set up successfully production facilities in Britain, the workers took this as proof of their view. To which British management replied that having been obstructionist to them, the workforce

---

12 Indeed the very ambiguity of terms like "perception," "observation" and "view" etc., straddling as they do both the narrower (empirical or experiential) sense and wider "sense," (of comprehending or understanding) attested precisely to this point.

13 See Whorf 1964 and Harré 1989. And Paul Bowles, amongst others, has noted the difference in, supposedly archetypical, dreams between cultures.

was far more compliant with Japanese management, to which the British workers responded that that was because Japanese managers were better at managing them, and thus to work for. And so the argument proceeded, each side interpreting, and thus "understanding," the situation, *Gestalt* like, upon the basis of their own preconceptions.

VI The Double X 2, or Double Double Hermeneutic of the Human and Social Sciences

Furthermore there is no reason to suppose that (pre)conceptions and context play any less a role in the "perceptions" and understanding that human and social scientists may have of individual subjects' experiences etc. and social actors actions etc., than in the understanding which such subjects and actors may themselves have of them.. As Zygmunt Bauman affirms regarding social actors for example:

> There is no difference ... between the sense actors make of their actions, and the meaning assigned to this action by an ... external observer for that matter; all are equally in a basically similar process of meaning-construction-through interpretation.[14]

The understand that a scientist may attempt to gain of a subject's understanding, will then clearly rest upon the scientist's interpretation of what s/he takes to be the subject's interpretation, or Double Hermeneutic, which will thus be informed by, and consequently reflect, the scientist's, second order, (pre)conceptions regarding the subject's (pre)conceptions. As Alfred Schutz affirms:

> ... the concepts formed by the social scientist are constructs of the constructs formed in the commonsense thinking by actors on the social scene ... constructs formed at the second level.[15]

VII Difficulties of Interpretation

Let us assume for the moment that scientists have ready access to subjects willing to articulate their understanding of their *experiences, both sensory and non-sensory* (e.g. psychological feelings, thoughts, ideas, memories, fantasies,

---

14 Bauman 1978, p. 181.

15 Schutz 1962, Vol. I, p. 246; see also p. 243.

dreams etc.), *dispositions* (e.g. values, attitudes, beliefs, aspirations etc.) etc., *motives* and *intentions*, along with their understanding of the *social interactions relations and institutions* etc. in which they participate. Even in such ideal circumstances the scientist's understanding of the subject's understanding, remains problematic for a number of reasons. (i) The subject may not be fully, or perhaps even partly, conscious of his/her, therefore *unconscious*, psychological experiences, dispositions, motives and intentions etc., while (ii) even if s/he is, given that all meaning and significance is *context* dependent, then, unless s/he is also fully aware of, and completely understands, the context(s) (e.g. social, political, economic or cultural etc. interactions, relations and institutions etc.) in which they arise and/or operate, s/he may nevertheless fail to (fully) understand them, (iii) a limitation exacerbated by the fact that, being mediated by *(pre)conceptions*, the subject's understanding may still be far from definitive. Furthermore, even if the subject's understanding of all this were entirely unproblematic, turning to the scientist, (iv) so far from the subject's *account* offering the scientist immediate insight into the subject's understanding, this account is itself no less in need of interpretation than is the understanding which it is supposed to illuminate. Moreover (v) like the subjects' understanding, that of any scientist is, of course, mediated by his/her (the scientist's) *preconceptions*, and may therefore also be far from definitive. While (vi) even if the (pre)conceptions which mediate the scientist's understanding, of the subject's supposedly definitive understanding were entirely appropriate, given that all meaning and significance is *context* dependent, then, for this reason alone it may transcend the scientist's understanding. And (vii) these same limitations, of *mediating concept and contextual* relativism, also necessarily apply to any Third Party (e.g. Marxist, Freudian, etc.) interpretation and understanding of subjects' experiences, dispositions, motives, intentions etc. and the social actions, interactions, relations and institutions etc. associated therewith, which the scientist may deploy.

Furthermore (viii) we have seen that there cannot, even in principle, be any *absolute*, or context independent or/and conceptually unmediated, definitive understanding, nor therefore any "objectively" given set of facts, *correspondence*, or at least conformity, to which might stand as the criterion by which all, often competing and sometimes even conflicting, interpretations might be judged. Consequently, as Hans-Georg Gadamer has concluded, "... understanding is not merely a reproductive but always a productive attitude ..."[16] Bauman puts it even more baldly. "All meaning results from interpretation; it is something to be construct-

---

16 Gadamer 1975, p. 264.

ed, not discovered."[17] In which case, all claims to the understanding of the meaning or significance of any experience etc. relation or event etc. if not the very notion of truth itself, would appear to be problematic!

VIII The Human and Social, and the Natural Sciences, Compared but not Contrasted

Deprived of a contextually and conceptually independent, objective, referent to which they might otherwise have been required to conform, the interpretation and understanding of human and social scientists', and for that matter their subjects, as *contextually* and *conceptually relative*, may therefore seem somewhat *arbitrary.* The perceptions and understanding of the human and social sciences therefore appear to be epistemologically inferior to the natural sciences, whose understanding and theoretical explanations, supposedly grounded upon ostensibly presuppositionless and context independent, empirical perceptions of the therefore putatively objective" facts to which they are supposedly constrained to correspond or conform, therefore seem *non-relative* and *non-arbitrary.*

However things are not what they seem. Indeed, in light of the previously discussed demonstration by the *Gestaltists*, that even our most basic empirical perceptions are contextually and/or conceptually relative, then so too, of course, derived from such perceptions as they are, are the apparent "facts" of the natural sciences, if not also any theoretical understanding of them. As Heidegger affirms:

> The greatness and superiority of the natural sciences during the sixteenth and seventeenth centuries rests in the fact that all the scientists were philosophers. They understood that there are no mere facts but that a fact is only what it is in the light of the fundamental conception ...[18]

Indeed nowhere is this more evident than in the earlier example of differences in the Aristotelian and Newtonian "perceptions" or/and understanding of the falling to Earth of unsupported objects as supposedly manifestations of their "earthly nature" and gravity respectively; an understanding subsequently superseded by the notion of the graviton, and then by Einstein's *reconception* of such a putative force (gravity) or entity (graviton) as geometry; the alleged curvature of

17 Bauman 1978, p. 181.

18 Martin Heidegger, "What is a Thing," reprinted in part as Heidegger 1975b, pp. 247–248.

space apparently being the current "flavor of the month" by which we are to account for such behavior.

Yet, although contextually and/or conceptually *relative*, nevertheless such *perceptions and understanding* are clearly *not unconstrained*, and consequently are *far from arbitrary.* For as with the Gestalt picture, which can plausibly be perceivable as being of a duck, or/and of a rabbit, but which could not be *coherently* interpreted, nor therefore plausibly perceived as of, say, The 1812 Overture, or a university, so too with the observations, observation statements and explanations of the sciences in general (human and social, no less than the natural) which, other things being equal, are then normally *constrained by coherence, as opposed to the correspondence, criteria.*[19] That is to say that notwithstanding the hermeneutically interpretive, contextually and/or conceptually relative, nature of our perceptions or/and understanding it is usually only if and insofar as such "perceptions" are *coherent* that they are regarded as at all plausible. But why?

In answer let us begin by noting that in addition to requiring that the *explicit* theoretical conceptions of the sciences be *intrinsically coherent with our observations* of the supposed "facts"—which facts, being, as we have seen, already mediated by, often *implicit*, theoretical (pre)conceptions, is to say *coherent with these implicit (pre)conceptions*[20]—we also normally require them to be *extrinsically coherent* with other, widely accepted, explicit theoretical conceptions. Moreover we additionally judge them by their *simplicity relative to the extensiveness* of the field to which they apply, not to mention, where applicable, by their *predictive* capacity.[21] Now the most significant feature of all these requirements is, of

---

19 While wavicles, understood as both particles and not particles, but waves, positrons, understood as electrons moving backwards in time, and neutrinos, understood as massless particles, are all logically incoherent, and are consequently seen, as *per* epistemologically sophisticated physicists at least, as ontologically inexistent posits, they are nevertheless adopted primarily because of their pragmatic utility in facilitating predictions.

20 Given the conceptual or theoretical mediation of even our most basic perceptions, clashes between theories and empirical "facts" should therefore be understood not as "falsifications" of theories by facts, but, as Imre Lakatos affirms "inconsistencies" between the explicitly theoretical conceptions of the sciences, and the conceptions implicitly informing our supposedly immediate "perceptions" of the "facts." (Lakatos and Musgrave 1970, p. 99])

21 Note, while some theories are predictive, others simply aimed at providing an understanding. Nor should we make the common, mistake of *necessarily* equating predictive capacity, with "truth," as should be evident from the capacity of the geocentric cosmology to predict sunrises and sunsets for example. The "truth" of the geocentric view being challenged, of course, by the pragmatic utility, measured both by simplicity and extensiveness (See FN 24 for the latter and the *text* prior to it for the former) of the heliocentric.

course, their *pragmatic utility*, in which case it should now be clear that it is precisely in service of such *pragmatic utility*, that *coherence*, both *intrinsic* and *extrinsic*, and, of course *simplicity relative to extensiveness*, normally constrain what might otherwise be the arbitrary interpretations of the sciences. Indeed, in line with the notion of falsification,[22] articulated by Karl Popper in relation to the universal theories of the natural sciences, in so far as they make claims or adopt views which transcend, or extend beyond, the available "facts," the *theoretical* conceptions of the natural sciences, no less than those of the human and social sciences, are adopted tentatively; being abandoned only if and when they are refuted by any *supposedly* "factual" evidence that may become available; and often then only if a more, or at least equally, pragmatic alternative is available.

Nor, given the conceptual mediation, and hermeneutic or interpretive nature, of even our most basic perceptions, is it the case, as some have suggested, that the supposed "facts" and "factual" evidence of the natural sciences are less susceptible to conceptual reinterpretation in order to accommodate theoretical conceptions (or ideologies) than those of the human and social sciences; the theoretical conceptions of the natural sciences consequently having no greater verisimilitude than those of the human and social sciences. To give but one, of many, examples, having formed the hypothesis that heavenly bodies move in circular orbits, Galileo interpreted his telescopic observation of elliptical orbits as the illusory product of imperfections in his telescope's lenses. Clearly then, as Popper affirms, in the natural, no less than the human and social sciences "... observations, and even more so observation statements and statements of experimental results ... are always ... *interpretations in the light of theories.*"[23] Theories or theoretical conceptions which, far from arbitrary, are judged by their pragmatic utility.

However, against this view it will surely be objected that, as Galileo's conflict with the Church, regarding his rejection of the geocentric for the heliocentric cos-

---

22 This holds that while certain theories—including, but, as we shall see later, not necessarily limited to, the universal claims of the sciences—can never be definitively proven true, they nevertheless gain greater credibility the greater the number, diversity and stringency of observations which fail to refute them. It is, in other words, the demand that where *correspondence* of theories to the (entire range of) facts to which they supposedly apply cannot be ascertained, then—*coherence of theories with facts being a necessary, though not, of course, sufficient condition of their correspondence to the facts*,—they should at least be *coherent* with all known facts. A demand which, as we have seen (see FN 20) is a demand for the coherence of the *explicit* theories of science with the *implicit* theoretical conceptions mediating our "perceptions" of the supposed "facts."

23 Popper 1959, p. 107 n. 3.

mology of Aristarchus and Copernicus *appears* to demonstrate, even the apparently greater pragmatic utility of the latter theory—enabling as it does the replacement of the relative complexity of Ptolemaic epicycles by the simpler, and more extensive, elliptical orbits of Johannes Kepler[24]—did not prevent it from being rejected on account of its inconsistency with, and thus threatened disruption of, widely held traditional beliefs (articulated in the scriptures),[25] which placed Earth, and therefore by implication "Man," (sic) supposedly made by God in "his" (sic) image, at the center of the universe. However so far from refuting the claimed centrality of pragmatic utility, this incident is demonstrative of it; pragmatism in the narrower sense of enabling easier calculation, giving way to a wider notion of pragmatism understood as the avoidance of the disruption of the political, social and cultural etc. upheaval that might have resulted from an open refutation of the supposedly "authoritative," views of the Church. A dynamic indicative, as Thomas Kuhn has noted,[26] of *the significance of cultural, social and/or political consensus, in grounding the natural sciences, and thus of the fundamental role of the human and social sciences in the understanding of epistemological verification in general.*

IX Evolving Contexts and Interpretations

Now just as changing concepts and conceptual frameworks may change our *constitutive* "understanding" of the "facts," so too, of course, will changing *contexts.* Take, for example, the *feeling* of stress or anxiety provoked in a student by his/her failure to obtain a passing grade for a class. Although this may lead the student to abandon his/her studies, and may therefore initially be *interpreted* and thus *"perceived,"* as having a negative effect on his/her intellectual development, on the other hand it may result in his/her redoubling of effort, and eventually excelling as a consequence, and may therefore be *"perceived,"* in this context, as having had an altogether positive effect. Alternatively, if the student's initially failure was a consequence of an irremediable lack of aptitude it may act to alert the him/her to this, and to persuade her/him to switch to an area of study for which s/he may have much greater aptitude, which may result in her/his immense satisfaction. In either event then, what may, in the initial context, have been *interpreted or "perceived"* as a rather unfortunate state of affairs,

24 More extensive in that unlike Ptolemaic epicycles, Galilean view applies to all planets, including Earth, and does not depend on insisting upon the Sun's *contrasting* "circular" motion.
25 See Joshua 10:12 (King James Bible).
26 See Kuhn 1962.

inimical to the student's overall development, might well come in a broader, retrospective, context, conversely, to be "*perceived*," both by the student, and indeed by human or social scientists, as a fortunate eventuality.

And just as our *feelings* about, or "perceptions" of, our *experiences* may change with context, so too may our moral *dispositions*, for example. Thus to return to our earlier discussion of the rational for the moral taboo against extra-marital sexual relations, this, it will be remembered, could help insure that individuals were not faced with the unpleasant choice between abortion or an unwanted child. Given such a rational, clearly then one might, in the context of the widespread availability of reliable contraception (e.g. the "pill") predict the widespread change that occurred in the moral disposition of many regarding extra-marital sex.

Turning now then to focus upon the *relation between contexts and concepts*, and returning to the adolescent's feeling of guilt when engaging in sexual relations, this was rooted in the *context* of his/her early upbringing, which led him/her later to *conceive* of, and thus interpret and "perceive," the anxiety accompanying unfamiliar sexual activity as indicative, or even as a manifestation, of his/her "badness" or moral guilt. However, upon being made aware, perhaps by a psychoanalyst, of this s/he may subsequently come to *reconceptualize* his/her feeling of anxiety, and consequently adopt a different disposition regarding sexual relations. Thus *by contextualizing the subject's (in this case) feelings and dispositions in a way that s/he had not, the outside observer* (e.g. psychoanalyst) *may gain, and offer the subject, a different, and perhaps better*[27] *understanding of her/his (the subject's) feelings and dispositions than s/he (the subject) initially had her/himself.*

X The Masters of Suspicion

And just as subjects may not always have a clear and/or adequate "perception" or understanding of the meaning or significance of their feelings and dispositions, so too with their other experiences (e.g. dreams, fantasies, memories and thoughts etc.) actions, intentions, interactions and relations etc. A limitation

---

27 The interpretation and "understanding" of the outside observer is no less contextually and conceptually informed or delineated and mediated, than that of the subject. Consequently the term *better* here can, for reasons we have explicated at length, only be indicative of relative pragmatic utility, resulting (as in this case) from a broader, or more extensive, context, in terms of which such feelings and dispositions may be understood, but which may, in other cases, result from a simpler or more intrinsically and/or extrinsically coherent interpretation.

which—as the "Masters of Suspicion," as Paul Ricoeur has dubbed Freud, Marx, and Nietzsche, have all shown—is, as above, attributable to a failure to fully comprehend, the true extent or significance of different and/or broader *contexts* in which they are embedded, and/or the variety of *conceptual* frameworks which may facilitate understanding.

For instance, a poor and beleaguered rural working class US male, lacking much efficacy in his daily life, may come to blame this upon restrictions placed upon him by government and the associated legal system. Consequently he may support the Republican Party, which promises to reduce taxes, and to resist attempts to restrict his freedom to carry a high powered firearm, in the belief that he is thus "freeing" himself from oppression. And although this might be so, it might alternatively be interpreted as a case of what Marx would have referred to as "false consciousness," in that he fails to recognize that if he and those like him were to vote for a socialist government, which intervened more fully in their lives, they might, apparently paradoxically, well end up more free in many ways, and perhaps even overall. For not only would the vast majority of the greater tax burden that a socialist government might be expected to impose probably fall upon corporations and those in higher income brackets, but he and his family would likely benefit from a corresponding increase in the availability of health care, education and social services more generally, as well as higher minimum wages and better working conditions. While greater regulation of access to firearms may render him and his family free, or at least freer, of the threat of being shot. Overall then they might be very much freer of preventable illness, opportunity limiting ignorance, poverty, and work place and other dangers.

However even were the worker fully appraised and accepting, of this, he might remain reluctant to give up his gun for some reason that he may not be able to articulate convincingly even to himself. Upon further analysis it might seem to a Freudian that his lack of day to day efficacy in his (e.g. economic, political, social, cultural etc.) life might well be linked, in some less than fully conscious manner, to a general sense of emasculation, which, a gun, as a symbol of potency and a potential source of actual power, may be coherently interpreted as helping to ameliorate.

Furthermore, notwithstanding the New Testament message of proto-passivism (e.g. turning the other cheek) this gun toting individual may nevertheless consider himself a God fearing Christian, and may indeed in many ways be just that; having an abundance of compassion and concern for his family and his neighbors, all of whom he may be more than willing to help, even at the cost of considerable effort and sacrifice on his part. However, far from such behavior being *necessarily and always* understandable, *primarily* as an act of self-abnegating for purely altruistic reasons, following Nietzsche it may be alternatively interpreted as being motivated by "The Will to Power," in that the subject's temporary self-overcoming or sacrificing of his immediate self-interest, may, in the context of Christian beliefs, be understood by him as facilitating his ascent to an infinite heavenly reward. An "ethical egoism"[28] which, insofar as he may have absorbed the Christian teaching not only that "the last will be first" but also that "the first will be last," may be supplemented by more than a little *schadenfreude*, or pleasure in the contemplation of the ultimate misfortune of the presently more fortunate.

As previously then, in such cases it seems at least possible, as Ricoeur would have it, to "... understand an author/actor" and/or the true significance of her/his *actions and intentions* etc. "better than s/he understood (them) her/himself."[29] A possibility which, as our examples suggest, arises precisely by virtue of outside observers having a degree of critical or reflective distance, and consequent awareness of contexts and/or conceptual frameworks, that the subjects they are studying, do not.

XI The Intentional Fallacy

Not unlike the artist then, who may not be consciously aware of historical, political, economic, social, cultural, biographical etc. circumstances which may nevertheless have played a significant role in shaping his/her sensibility etc., and who consequently fails to fully appreciate the significance, of his/her work, similarly our subject may be unaware of the primary motivation for his reluctance to part with his gun, not to mention for his attachment to Christianity, and may concomitantly fail to fully appreciate the *intentions* motivating and guiding his or her actions.

Furthermore, shifting focus from the *context of* a work or act's *production or origin*, to the *context of* its *reception*, just as Leonardo could not possibly have envisioned, much less *intended*, the meaning or significance that the Mona Lisa was to have, so too the future significance of an action may be entirely unimaginable, much less intended, by social actors. Thus the First World War is generally regarded as an unintended consequence of the assassination of Arch-

28 Ethical egoism, in its descriptive form, is the doctrine that people ultimately promote their own self-interest in one way or another.

29 Quoted by Paul Ricoeur, in Ricoeur 1981, p. 151. My addition in parentheses. Note my caveat (see note 27) regarding the term "*better*" in accordance with which "*true*" as expressed here, is to be equated with pragmatic.

duke Ferdinand, which seems only have been intended to facilitate breaking away of the Austro-Hungarian empire's south-Slave provinces. Or again, the extraction of large war reparations from post First World War Germany, widely interpreted as having been intended to block the reconstruction of a powerful and militarized German state, nevertheless, in handicapping German economic recovery, and thus delegitimizing the ruling Junker elite, is widely understood to have paved the way for the rise of fascism, and thus to the very militarized German state it had been intended to prevent.

Not dissimilarly, the US financing, through the Pakistani Intelligence Service, of the *Mujahidin*, or holy warriors, as a countervailing force to the "godless Soviet communists," was surely not intended to give rise, as it did, to *al-Qaida*. While the significant consequences of the US lead invasion of Iraq—which included the demonstration of the relative impotency of the invader, the refutation of previously widely held beliefs regarding US moral rectitude and commitment to human rights, the massive number of civilian non-combatant casualties, and the resulting stoking of anti US sentiment and recruitment into the resistance, and the rise of the Islamic State in the Levant (ISIL) which collectively increased US vulnerability to attack—must surely have been vastly different from the consequences Dick Cheney, and "Sorcerer's Apprentice" Bush, had intended. Indeed as Election Supervisor Theresa LePour can most surely testify, when a butterfly ballot flaps its wings in Palm Beach County, the unintended consequence may well be the catastrophe of 600,000 non-combatant civilian deaths in Iraq, and, arguably, the ongoing legacy of terrorism in the Middle East![30]

In sum then, it should be clear that, even when a subject's intentions may be unambiguously clear to him/her self, not only may s/he fail to fully grasp the many factors which may have shaped, and thus give meaning, to his/her actions, but also their unforeseen (and in some cases at last unforeseeable) and thus unintended consequences. While, as previously, an outside observer may, by virtue of a critical reflective distance, have access to a wide variety of alternative *conceptual* frameworks (e.g. Marxist, Freudian, Nietzschean etc.) and/or different, and perhaps developing, *contexts*, which may enable him/her to understand the significance or meaning of subjects' experiences or *feelings* (of "guilt"),

30 Thus as in Chaos Theory, in which the flapping of a butterfly's wings influences the formation and path of a hurricane, and changes world history, the infamous Butterfly Ballot, which arguably cost Al Gore 25 Electoral College votes by virtue of Florida's "winner take all" system, resulted in Georg W. Bush's US Presidency, while had Al Gore become President it is extremely doubtful that the US would have gone to war with Iraq, which had nothing at all to do with 9/11!

(moral) *dispositions*, and, as we now see, *intentions* and *actions* or *behavior*, better[31] than such subjects do themselves.

Nevertheless actor's *intentions remain important*, for irrespective of whether or not they are realized by his/her actions, *an understanding of subjects' intentions may facilitate the prediction of future individual and/or social behavior or actions.* For instance, while an invasion may be interpreted as motivated by a desire for security, other interpretations may include, but are by no means limited to, the desire to topple a despot, to spread democracy, or as a prelude to a resource grab etc., while an understanding of which of these intentions, either individually or collectively, motivated the actors would clearly be useful in attempting to predict such actors' future behavior.

XII Belonging and Estrangement: Self Evidence versus Critical Distance; The Sociological and Anthropological Dilemma?

Now just as the understanding of subjects etc. and their actions etc. may be facilitated by a certain critical or reflective distance, so too with understanding societies and/or cultures; although sometimes such distance may result in an uncomprehending estrangement. For example, the story is told of a two space probes to Earth, one sent by Martians and the other by Venusians. The first, landing on a Los Angeles freeway, sends back imagery from which the Martians conclude that Earthlings are about 4 to 7 feet high, 12 to 20 feet long, travel around at 50 – 70 miles per hour, and have eyes which light up at night. The second, landing in a Hollywood cemetery and, probing Earth, discovers a number of biodegraded corpses with well-preserved breast implants, from which the Venusians conclude that these Earthlings were most surely members of a fertility cult. Now while we might be tempted to dismiss the Martians' interpretation as so obviously incoherent as to be false, we might, despite initial resistance to the Venusians', nevertheless subsequently conclude, upon reflection, that it may have something to it.

In the first case then, *belonging to or participating in* a society enables the rejection of what, for reasons known to the insider, are clearly incoherent, and thus spurious, interpretations offered by outsiders, whereas in the second case, it is precisely the outsiders' *estrangement, detachment, or critical reflective distance, from* the society and its culture which results in what the insider or par-

31 "Better," it should be remembered can, in light of what we have seen, only mean a more coherent and/or simpler and extensive etc., and thus potentially pragmatic, understanding.

ticipant may ultimately acknowledge to be a better understanding of it than they had. And far from this presenting us with a contradiction it is merely indicative of the fact that *for cultural anthropologists, and indeed for psychologists, sociologists, political analysts and other human and social scientists, the combination of proximity and reflective distance, which is to say of familiarity with the subject at hand, and the alternative, broadening if not broader, perspectives of the estranged, is likely* (as with returning from a period of estrangement occasioned by foreign travel for instance) *to assist in the comprehensive and insightful understanding of individuals, societies and cultures etc.*

Take, for instance, the insistence by many schools in Britain that pupils wear uniforms. Noting that those schools which require uniforms tend to be private, while those which do not are more likely to be government or state schools, an *outside* observer might, not unreasonably, conclude that this is yet another example of the infamously entrenched British class system. However those more *familiar* with the situation may note that even some government schools insist that students wear uniforms, while some private schools do not; a circumstance which may seem to undermine the initial, outside observer's, interpretation. However yet closer examination may reveal that those private schools not requiring uniforms often have a preponderance of children from the households of reasonably well off writers, journalists, artists, designers and other creative professionals, who, so far from necessarily being adverse to class privilege, tend to interpret uniforms as imposing what they regard as an unwelcome uniformity upon children who they may hope will succeed in preserving their relative privilege precisely by virtue of their creative originality, while, on the other hand, the uniform requirement of some government schools may be interpreted as aspirational.

Alternatively however, it is noteworthy that in replacing the individual forms of dress by which socio-economic status is often asserted, uniforms may very well be interpreted precisely as an attempt to undermine class distinctions, or, perhaps as an attempt to move students beyond a distracting, and often deleterious, obsession with their clothing, to an educationally more salient interest in ideas etc.

XIII The Conflicts of Interpretation: Complementary, Supplementary, Mutually Exclusive and Jointly Sufficient

Reflecting upon the profusion of interpretations above, and remembering that so far from being able to establish the definitive correspondence of any interpretation or interpretations to an objective, contextually un-situated and conceptually unmediated understanding, it is clear that we have consequently come to judge interpretations in terms of their coherence, simplicity and extensiveness, which is to say pragmatically in terms of their utility. In which case noting that by no means are all of the immediately preceding interpretations of school uniforms mutually exclusive, it seems that those that are not may *supplement* or *complement* one another. Thus while some state schools' and some private schools' adoption, and some private schools' rejection of, school uniforms, may be interpreted, as initially above, as *complementary* attempts to secure class privilege, this in no way necessarily invalidates the *supplementary* interpretation of their adoption as shielding students from the distracting consideration of fashion. While even the apparently *contradictory* claims that school uniforms were, on the one hand an attempt to secure, and on the other an attempt to undermine, class distinctions, are not, at least in this case, entirely irreconcilable, in that, within the *extrinsic* context of association with students of other schools, school uniforms may be interpreted as an attempt to affirm class distinction, within the *intrinsic* context of students in the same school, they may be interpreted as undermining class distinctions which might be more readily evident without a uniform dress code.

Applying such insights to the, altogether more consequential,Second Gulf War, interpretations of the reasons underlying it have included, but are by no means limited to, a) retribution for 9/11, b) fear of Iraq's supposed Weapons of Mass Destruction (WMD), c) a desire to rid Iraq of a vicious and nasty dictator, d) a desire to bring democracy to Iraq, e) the desire to support women's rights, and so on.

Let us then apply the aforementioned logic of falsification—in accordance with which we reject theories which are incoherent with the known "facts"[32] in so far as such "facts" are coherently "perceived" or conceived of—to these various theoretical explanations.

Given that none of the hijackers was an Iraqi, and that bin Laden, a devout Wahhabi (Salafist) had denounced Saddam Hussein—who had persecuted Muslim fundamentalists, and presided over the killing of many Iranian and Southern Iraqi Muslims, and who was much feared by bin Laden's major benefactors, the Saudi Wahhabi Princes—as apostate, it would not seem plausible the two would have made common cause. Consequently whatever the reason or reasons for the invasion or Iraq, retribution for 9/11 does not appear to be a credible one.

Turning next to the much touted fear of Iraq's alleged nuclear Weapons of Mass Destruction, while —notwithstanding its misrepresentation as the blatantly

32 See notes 19 – 22.

false claim that one cannot prove a negative[33]—Donald Rumsfeld's claim that "Absence of evidence is not *necessarily* evidence of absence," is most certainly a corollary of the logic of falsification, nevertheless the United Nations Security Council's supervision, in the aftermath of the First Gulf War, of the destruction of Iraq's chemical, biological and missile facilities, and, in cooperation with the International Atomic Energy Agency, of the elimination of nuclear facilities, together with extensive post 9/11 inspections, and interviews with Iraqi engineers known to have the *potential* capacity to contribute to such programs (whose accounts of the projects they claimed to have been working on, were checked against the actual existence and state of those projects) provided strong justification for the view that Iraq neither had any serviceable weapons of this sort, nor any potential for producing nuclear weapons, even in the medium term.[34]

As for the desire to get rid of a brutal dictator, and foster democracy, given the United States' foreign policy record,[35] and its systematic and widespread violation of human rights at Guantanamo and elsewhere, such an explanation would seem wholly implausible, not to say *insufficient*, as so too, in light of US support of the Saudi regime, would its support of women's rights.

On the other hand the Bush Administration's disbanding of the Iraqi military, and de-Ba'athification of the administration, seems not inconsistent with the hypothesis that its *principle* goal was to reconfigure the Iraqi state; an interpretation which almost immediately gained further credence from Paul Bremer's rewriting of the Iraqi constitution, and the US supported transition from the Coa-

33 Thus, for instance, the facts that it does *not* appear to be snowing in my room as I write this, and that an individual *cannot* be both more than 10 feet and less than 3 feet tall at the same time, are negatives which I can prove empirically and rationally, respectively.

34 And this irrespective of the fact that, having been frequently at war with Iran, which was thought to be developing nuclear weapons capabilities, the Iraqi regime had had every incentive to give the impression of having a developed nuclear weapons program.

35 This record includes, but is by no means limited to, active participation in and/or support for the overthrowing of the democratically elected governments of Muhammad Mosaddegh in Iran, Jacobo Arbenz in Guatemala, Salvador Allende in Chile, Papandreou in Greece, and latterly Mohamed Morsi in Egypt, and US support of the often brutal dictatorships of Mohammad Pahlavi the "Shah" of Iran, General Rios Mott in Guatemala, General Augusto Pinochet in Chile, Colonel George Papadopoulos & Co. in Greece, and General Abdel el-Sisi in Egypt, which replaced them. And this not to mention US support for the attempted coup against the democratically elected Chavez government in Venezuela, its support of General Suharto in Indonesia, Ferdinand Marcos in the Philippines, Somoza and the Contras in Nicaragua and El Salvador, General Paz and Battalion 316 in Honduras and of former Air Chief Marshall Hosni Mubarak in Egypt, as well as of the House of Saud, not, of course, forgetting the US government's supplying of helicopter gunships to Saddam Hussein in 1984, when he was already known as a major human rights violator etc. etc.

lition Provisional Authority, to the Iraq Interim Government, and its shepherding in of the Iraqi Transitional Government, and, subsequently the Al Maliki administration. But to what end? Clearly such an *interpretation*, and the *understanding* and *explanation* it attempts to provide, stands in need of substantial *supplementation.*

A wholly plausible, *supplementary*, understanding is that the desire to reconfigure the Iraqi state was motivated by an attempt by the US to gain strategic control over the Middle East, perhaps with the help and support of its Israeli allies, and the concomitant *complimentary* attemptly to insure Israel's security. But again, to what end? To which a wholly plausible, additional, *supplement*, would seem to be, in order to secure access to extensive oil reserves.[36] A view which gains greater credibility in light of the facts that: a) amongst the most significant aspects of the series of Bremer authored orders and laws, which the interim government was prohibited from changing, was one opening up the Iraqi economy and resources to foreign ownership, b) that the US and the UK, which were at the forefront of the war, both also lead the world in experience in oil exploration and extraction, and c) in underutilized or excess capacity in this regard, d) that immediately post invasion a much greater emphasis was placed upon securing oil facilities than upon preventing looting and revenge killings amongst the general Iraqi population, e) that the three countries, France, China and Russia, which objected most strongly to the invasion, were the very ones which already had existing contracts with Iraq to extract its oil, f) that the "Cheney Report" emanating from US Vice President, and ex-Chairman and CEO of oil logistics company Halliburton, Dick Cheney, projected US importation of oil raising from its then current level of 50 %, to 66 % by 2020, not to mention the fact that g) no fewer than eight of Bush's senior White House staff and advisors were then or previously, as was Bush and his father, either owners, chairmen or CEO's, lawyers, and/or corporate lobbyists, of or for oil and/or gas corporations.[37]

Here then we see that while, like any such theory, the "oil hypothesis," as we might call it, cannot be definitively proven, its extensive coherence, not only with the initially articulated "facts," but with this wide or extensive range of additional factors (a–g)—any of which, while even if, arguably insufficient of itself to support this hypothesis, certainly appear, in combination, to approach the

---

36 Thus Iraq's, at that time proven, 100 Billion Barrel reserves placed it second to Saudi Arabia, with 261 Billion Barrels, while, in light of the post First Gulf War sanctions and technological embargo placed on Iraq, and the resulting unavailability of advanced oil detection techniques, it was widely held that actual reserves were very much, perhaps as many as an additional 200 Billion Barrels, higher. See Klare 2002, pp. 6–7.

37 For a fuller discussion and analysis of the Iraq war see Glynn 2005.

level of joint sufficiency ("the perfect storm")—renders it increasingly credible; the more so in the absence of any equally extensive and coherent alternative.

XIV Conclusion

In conclusion, clearly hermeneutic considerations and criteria, as deployed by the human and social sciences, are no different from those by which the natural sciences may attempt to determine the plausibility or credibility, if not the ultimate veracity, of so many of their, equivalently ultimately unverifiable, theoretical claims. While no less obvious is the fact that this same hermeneutic approach, used here to determine the plausibility and/or credibility of *theoretical claims* regarding *the meaning and/or significance of* human intentions, and political acts, is no less applicable to attempts to establish the plausibility and/or credibility of *theoretical claims* regarding *the meaning and/or significance of* human experiences both sensory and non-sensory (e.g. thoughts, ideas, feelings, memories, fantasies and dreams etc.) dispositions (e,g, values, attitudes and beliefs etc.) and behavior, as well as of social, historical and cultural etc. interactions, relations and institutions etc. Moreover, we have seen that hermeneutic interpretation, is not only a useful, but indispensible, and at some level unavoidable, component of understanding, and as such is central not only to the human and social, but the natural sciences also.

References

Bauman, Zygmunt (1978) *Hermeneutics and the Social Sciences*. London: Hutchinson.

Dilthey, Wilhelm (1957) *Die Geistige Welt*. In: Wilhelm Dilthey, *Gesammelte Schriften*, Vol. 5. Stuttgart: Teubner.

Earmarth, Michael (1978) *Wilhelm Dilthey: The Critique of Historical Reason*. Chicago: University of Chicago Press.

Gadamer, Hans-Georg (1975) *Truth and Method*, 2nd ed. London: Sheed and Ward.

Glynn, Simon (2005) "Deconstructing Terrorism." *The Philosophical Forum* 36(1): pp. 113–128.

Harré, Rom (1989) *The Social Construction of Emotions*. Oxford: Blackwell.

Heidegger, Martin (1962) *Being and Time*, tr. J. Macquarrie and E. Robinson. New York: Harper and Row.

Heidegger, Martin (1971) "Plato's Doctrine of Truth," tr. J. Barlow. In: W. Barrett and H. Atkins (eds.), *Philosophy in the 20th Century*. New York: Random House, pp. 251–270.

Heidegger, Martin (1975a) "Aletheia (Heraclitus Fragment B. 16) and Moira (Parmenides VIII, 3, 4–41)." In: Martin Heidegger, *Early Greek Thinking*, tr. David Krell and F. Capuzzi. New York: Harper and Row, pp. 79–101.

Heidegger, Martin (1975b) "Modern Science, Metaphysics and Mathematics." In: Martin Heidegger, *Basic Writings*, tr. and ed. D. Krell. New York: Harper and Row, pp. 243–282.

Heidegger, Martin (1976) "On the Essence of Truth." In: Martin Heidegger, *Basic Writings*, tr. and ed. D. Krell. New York: Harper and Row, pp. 113–141.

Klare, Michael T. (2002) "Oiling the Wheels of War." *The Nation*, October, 7, 2002.

Kuhn, Thomas (1962) *The Structure of Scientific Revolutions*. Chicago: University of Chicago Press.

Lakatos, Imre and Musgrave, Alan (1970) *Criticism and the Growth of Knowledge*. Cambridge: Cambridge University Press.

Polkinghorne, Donald (1983) *Methodology for the Human Sciences*. Albany: State University of New York Press.

Popper, Karl (1959) *The Logic of Scientific Discovery*. London: Hutchinson.

Ricoeur, Paul (1981) *Hermeneutics and the Human Science*, ed. J.B. Thompson. Cambridge: Cambridge University Press.

Saussure, Ferdinand de (1959 [1916]) *Course in General Linguistics*. New York: New York Philosophical Library.

Schrag, Calvin (1980) *Radical Reflection*. Indiana: Perdue University Press.

Schutz, Alfred (1962) "Concept and Theory Formation in the Social Sciences." In: Alfred Schutz, *Collected Papers*. The Hague: Nijhoff.

Whorf, Benjamin Lee (1964) *Language, Thought and Reality*, ed. John B. Carroll. Boston: MIT Press.

Harald Seubert

Life, Metaphysics, History: Reflections on the Contemporary Relevance of Dilthey's Philosophy of Life

Abstract: In his speech given on his seventieth birthday, Dilthey came to a remarkable and alarming conclusion recollecting a dream in which Raphael's *School of Athens* came to life. The philosophers separated into three groups—positivism, freedom idealism and objective idealism— arguing amongst themselves and unable to agree on anything. Every school had its own coherent system of concepts of how to perceive the world. From this, Dilthey gains an insight into the irreversible downside of freedom that stems from historical awareness, as he conjures repeatedly in his later work: "the pure light of truth presents itself as a differently refracted beam" [*das reine Licht der Wahrheit ... in verschieden gebrochenem Strahl*].[1]

I

Beginning with his 1877 essay on Goethe and poetic imagining [*Goethe und die dichterische Phantasie*], Wilhelm Dilthey highlighted the central role of the concept of life which later became the foundation of his *The Formation of the Historical World in the Human Sciences.*[2] Dilthey would only make a few adjustments here which demonstrate the importance of this formulation over time:[3]

> In life, my self is given to me in its milieu, feeling of my existence, a behavior and an attitude toward people and things around me; They exert a pressure on me or give me strength and joy of being, they make demands on me and they occupy a space in my existence. Thus everything and every person receives their own power and color from my life-realities. The

1 Wilhelm Dilthey, DGS VIII, p. 224. Henceforth: cited in the text by volume and page number. *Aufbau der geschichtlichen Welt in den Geisteswissenschaften.* Translations of Dilthey's work follows the German. It is in every case my own translation in cooperation with Hanna Rebiai (Basle, Jerusalem).

2 See Dilthey, *Aufbau der geschichtlichen Welt in den Geisteswissenschaften* in Dilthey, Volume III of SW.

3 See for this topic also the stimulating anthology: Orth 1985. It mainly concerns certain aspects of Dilthey's philosophy of life—hence regarding its reception, clearer today after Heidegger—that illustrate the topicality of his work in that area.

https://doi.org/10.1515/9783110551563-018

> finite nature of that which is bounded by birth and death, constrained by the pressure of reality, awakens in me the longing for something permanent, invariable, taken away from the pressure of things, and the stars to which I look up, are the symbols of such eternal intangible world. In everything that surrounds me, I re-experience what I have experienced myself. At dusk, I look down upon a quiet city at my feet; The lights that appear in the houses one by one are the expression of a protected, peaceful existence. This content of life in my own self, in my different states, in man himself, and in things around me, forms their value of life, in contrast to other values which are attributed to them by their effects. [4]

This text shows the basic idea which in a comparative study with Husserl's phenomenology, would later lead Georg Misch to draw the concise conclusion: "the 'reference to life' moves into the role of intentionality." [*Der 'Lebensbezug' rückt in die Rolle der Intentionalität.*][5] It also foreshadows the ineluctability and pre-reflexivity of life contexts and experiencing consciousness. Dilthey points that out by saying: "Here, life encompasses life." [*Leben erfasst hier Leben*] He wanted people to understand that realizing life and having realized it is the same thing and they form an inseparable 'whole.' Insofar, in an ingenious anticipation of the main idea of the early Heidegger and varying a *topos* of classic practical philosophy,[6] the foundation of the human sciences is 'self-interpretation' of life. This also means that life *in itself*, without relying on a distance-taking perspective, is 'decentered' with regard to world relations and the complex unit of meaning [*komplexe Bedeutungseinheit*] of internal and external relations. In a programmatic sentence, Dilthey states that there is a consistent self-consciousness of the mind and its contents.[7] As demonstrated impressively by

---

4 "Im Leben ist mir mein Selbst in seinem Milieu gegeben, Gefühl meines Daseins, ein Verhalten und eine Stellungnahme zu Menschen und Dingen um mich her; sie üben einen Druck auf mich oder sie führen mir Kraft und Daseinsfreude zu, sie stellen Anforderungen an mich und sie nehmen einen Raum in meiner Existenz ein. So empfangen jedes Ding und jede Person aus meinen Lebensbezügen eine eigene Kraft und Färbung. Die Endlichkeit des von Geburt und Tod umgrenzten, vom Druck der Wirklichkeit eingeschränkten Daseins, erweckt in mir die Sehnsucht nach einem Dauernden, Wechsellosen, dem Druck der Dinge Entnommenen, und mir werden die Sterne, zu denen ich aufblicke, zum Sinnbild einer solchen ewigen unanrührbaren Welt. In allem, was mich umgibt, erlebe ich nach, was ich selbst erfahren habe. Ich sehe in der Abenddämmerung hinab auf eine stille Stadt zu meinen Füßen; die Lichter, die in den Häusern nacheinander aufgehen, sind mir der Ausdruck eines geschützten, friedlichen Daseins. Dieser Gehalt an Leben in meinem eigenen Selbst, meinen Zuständen, den Menschen und Dingen um mich her bildet den Lebenswert derselben, im Unterschied von den Werten, die ihnen durch ihre Wirkungen zukommen. Dilthey 1957, p. 113; see also DGS VII, p. 131 f.; p. 228 f.

5 G. Misch in Dilthey, DGS V, p. LVIII; cf. G. Misch (1967 [1931]).

6 It needs to be referred to Heidegger's early lectures on philosophy of life, especially GA 58, p. 59, 60 and 63.

7 "ein einheitliches Selbstbewusstsein des Geistes und seines gesamten Inhaltes." (VIII, p. 207)

Bollnow,[8] the philosophy of life is one of Dilthey's key issues. When Dilthey speaks about life he means human life. There is no possibility of pantheism:[9]

> There appears to be something strange to us in nature which we can never fully comprehend intuitively; There is a regularity in it which has nothing to do with the regularity of our own intuition. It is the gap between us and nature that rises up to our consciousness.[10]

Life foremost is 'motion'—an idea that Heidegger will pick up on in his early conception of categories. Even in a state of deepest contemplation the ego does not discover itself as "substance, entity, given fact."[11] Dilthey objects to Plato and Husserl, who fully agreed with Plato in this respect, that every ideative fixation determines "the term of developing, fluent things [*die werdenden fließenden Dinge im Begriff*] and then adds the term of flow as a supplement to it."[12] A contrary reading is obviously just as possible—and regarding the inner problem genealogy of Plato's dialogues perhaps more probable[13] according to which the ideas are supposed to stop the flux of life in order to deal with the threat of radical Heracliteanism.

It is striking that Dilthey uses term-theoretical and semantic categories for his considerations of the reality and significance of life.[14] However, life cannot be distinguished from itself: "it only refers to itself."[15] Therewith, the realization of life shifted unambiguously in the horizon of life. Realization only transpires in

---

8 Cf. Bollnow 1967 [1936]; even though newer research does not find Dilthey's center of philosophy of life that important any more, I consider it the central issue—even if that means referring to Dilthey's later work in particular. Due to maturation, this of course unveiled some of his concepts more clearly. For the critical point of view cf. Fellmann 1993, pp. 108 ff. See also some fundamental articles: Frithjof Rodi, "Der Strukturzusammenhang des Lebens" and "Diltheys Kritik der historischen Vernunft—Programm oder System?," in: Rodi 2003, pp. 17 ff. and pp. 36 ff.

9 Cf. Bollnow 1967 [1936], pp. 43 ff. See also the articles by F. Rodi mentioned in the footnote above.

10 "Es scheint uns in der Natur etwas Fremdes zu sein, was wir niemals ganz gefühlsmäßig realisieren können; eine Gesetzmäßigkeit ist in ihr, die mit der Gesetzmäßigkeit unseres Gefühlsverlaufs nichts zu tun hat. Es ist die Kluft, die zwischen uns und der Natur ist, die uns zum Bewusstsein kommt" (VII, p. 58).

11 "Substanz, Sein, Gegebenheit] but always "as life, action, energy" [als Leben, Tätigkeit, Energie] (V, p. 157).

12 [*dann den Begriff des Fließens zur Ergänzung*] (V, p. 112

13 I refer to the conception of ideology compared to Heraclitus' flow theory, and regarding mortality experience i.a. to *Phaidon* 100a ff. See also: Seubert 2004, pp. 200 ff.

14 "Jede Lebensäußerung hat eine Bedeutung, sofern sie als ein Zeichen etwas ausdrückt, als ein Ausdruck auf etwas hinweist, das dem Leben angehört" (VII, p. 234).

15 "Es ist in ihm keine Sonderung, auf der beruhen könnte, dass es etwas bedeutete, außer ihm selbst." Ibid.

anticipation, *hypothetically* and *proleptically.* Aiming to fully understand life would mean to step out of life and have a look at it from a distance. Only dead things can be fully understood. This consideration was already made by Aristotle in connection with his conception of human *eudaimonia.*[16]

Dilthey uncovers this, with respect to the metaphysical relation between part and whole which he understands as a category of life, even though life cannot be split into these components. As long as you are part of life as a whole you do not have the means to distinguish clearly between part and whole.

> One would have to await the end of the course of the life and could, only in the hour of death, have a look over the whole, from which the relationship between its parts could be ascertained. One would have to wait for the end of the story to have the complete material in order to determine its meaning.[17]

This is the reason for an interaction between meaning and life. On occasion, Dilthey defines meaning as "comprehensive category which makes life construable."[18] But he also suggests that meaning can only be grasped by looking at the relation between part and whole. As depicted, this unavailable relationship evokes its '*conditio sine qua non.*'[19]

II

If you locate this approach in the period of upheaval of philosophy in the 19th century after Hegel's death, it has certain affinities with the radical renunciation of reason and metaphysics represented by Nietzsche but also the philosophers in the lineage of Feuerbach, Kierkegaard and Marx. But it also exposes the problem of different metaphysical forms of thought (this understanding of metaphysics which is impressively constituted in his memory of his dream prevents him from speaking undifferentiatedly of 'the metaphysic') and the mediation of a unification of reason and reality as it was displayed in Hegel's system. Dilthey views this as an '*hiatus irrationalis*' of world and theoretical rationality, depicting this in allegories that, owing to the genesis of the 19th century have similarities to

16 Aristotle, *Nicomachean Ethics* I, 11, 1100a ff.

17 "Man müsste das Ende des Lebenslaufes abwarten und könnte in der Todesstunde erst das Ganze überschauen, von dem aus die Beziehung seiner Teile feststellbar wäre. Man müsste das Ende der Geschichte erst abwarten, um für die Bestimmung ihrer Bedeutung das vollständige Material zu besitzen" (VII, p. 233).

18 "umfassende Kategorie, unter welcher das Leben auffaßbar wird." (VII, p. 232).

19 "Es ist eine Beziehung, die niemals ganz vollzogen wird." Ibid.

some positions that do not recognize mediating mind and reality as an important philosophical issue. Consider his statement that a subject who is merely driven by thought must be bloodless. Hegel's idea of concepts, Dilthey suggests, acts as a logical grasp of reality of life and that is why it actually undermines its concrescence.

It is the subtle double view—the Janus-faced viewpoint in two directions—that makes Dilthey's way of thinking so appealing.

Dilthey's '*Phänomenologie der Metaphysik*' does not just deny metaphysical forms of thought their legitimacy. He actually offers a blueprint of a 'critical view'[20] when he points out the ground- and placelessness of metaphysical thoughts which is attributable to the fact that they ignore the foundation—the context of life. The 'critical view' is not displayed by Dilthey despite his extensive preliminary work. To this it is also required to mark the sector of inference that contributed to the categories by fixation of specific moments in life.[21] An approach to do that could be inspired by his conception of 'immanent theology' based on the ineluctability of context of life (VII, p. 154; ct. also V, p. 238, 272). Systematically it would resemble Kant's third critique but go beyond aesthetical judgments.[22] Dilthey conceives theology as a reciprocal, purposeful relation of different respects and activities of life—cognitive, emotive and volitional. He tried to combine some of Kant's conclusions regarding theoretical and practical reason, natural phenomena and the noumenal world of morality.

Due to the ambivalence of the '*Phänomenologie der Metaphysik*,' it also tends to rescue and preserve metaphysical conceptualization, at least as far as it remains indispensable for unveiling its own underlying layers of life. In a remarkable letter of December 1869, Dilthey admits this to himself *à contre-coeur:*

> As far as I recognize metaphysics at all, and in the sense in which I am doing it, I now believe I have laid the ground [...] against my will, since today I do not attribute value to sys-

---

20 With this I refer to Michael Theunissen's characterization of Hegel's *Logik:* Theunissen 1980, see also: Fulda, Horstmann and Theunissen 1980.

21 Therefore, you have to go beyond Manfred Riedel's approach in "Von der Phänomenologie der Metaphysik zur Lebensphilosophie. Diltheys Konzeption einer Kritik der historsichen Vernunft" in: Riedel 1978, pp. 44–64, here p. 63. A doxographical summary of several metaphysical topoi is not important. It is mainly about various thought-tectonics.

22 [Soweit ich überhaupt Metaphysik anerkenne, und in dem Sinne, in welchem ich es tue, glaube ich nunmehr den Grund gelegt zu haben [...]. Gegen meinen Willen, der ich Systemen nicht Wert zuschreibe heute, entsteht etwas, was einem System leider sehr ähnlich sieht. Es kann wenigstens den Hintergrund meiner Untersuchungen bilden.] Rudolph Makkreel highlights these judgments in consideration of the factual connection of Dilthey's peotics and aesthetics. Cf. Makkreel 1991. See also Rodi 1969.

> tems, something emerges which unfortunately looks very similar to a system. It can at least form the background of my investigations.[23]

Looking at current philosophical problems it can be quite appealing to mirror critique and preservation of metaphysical tradition one to an other. Because of the high—and as it appears to me not very satisfying—sophistication involved, the second aspect of that mirroring needs special attention. Here, the entanglement of life and world can serve as starting points. Dilthey criticized the Cartesian distinction between *res cogitans* and *res extensa* just as Heidegger did later.[24] Life stands always in relation to 'liveliness.' Therefore, the endeavor to recognize the existence of the outside world from the I or the ego ("*von dem Ich aus*") seems absurd.[25] That consciousness and world are equi-primordial does not result "from one train of thought" [*nicht aus einem Denkzusammenhang*] as Dilthey emphasizes. Prior to the act of thinking, life is experienced through "drive, volition and sentiment" [*In Trieb, Wille und Gefühl*] (V, p. 95).

According to his 'theorem of consciousness/phenomenality,' Dilthey understands consciousness as the place that contains the whole world and its objects[26]:

> As far as these objects that appear to me extend, so far does the connection of my ideas extend, too. What is found in them, the force that smashes, the glowing heat that melts, everything down to the innermost of the objects is fact of my consciousness, and this thing is so to speak a composition of such spiritual facts.[27]

This theorem is accompanied by a second one, detecting the relation between objects of consciousness in the 'totality of our spiritual life.' It shows, in accordance with an early idealistic fundamental impulse, that awareness cannot be

---

23 C. Misch 1933, p. 274 (letters from December 1869). Cf.: "Übersicht meines Systems," DGS VIII, pp. 176 ff.

24 "Die Besinnung über das Selbst ist [......] zugleich die [sc. Reflexion] über seinen Bezug zu einer äußeren Wirklichkeit" (VIII, p. 39).

25 "Seit Descartes ist man am Brückenschlagen" (Yorck-Correspondence, p. 55).

26 "Ort, welcher diese ganze, scheinbar so unermessliche Außenwelt einschließt, (den) Stoff, aus welchem alle Objekte [...] sind", (XIX, p. 59).

27 "So weit sich diese mir erscheinenden Objekte erstrecken, so weit erstreckt sich der Zusammenhang meiner Vorstellungen. Was in ihnen angetroffen wird, die Härte, welche zertrümmert, die glühende Hitze, welche schmilzt, alles bis ins Innerste der Objekte ist Tatsache meines Bewusstseins, und das Ding ist sozusagen eine Zusammensetzung von solchen geistigen Tatsachen" (XIX, p. 59).

thought of as some kind of self-objectification[28] and neither does it follow the analogy of substance and accident. In fact, consciousness is handed to us in a pre-reflexive way and we can only point it out but we cannot analyze it or understand it in a propositional way. In experiencing life, the equiprimordiality of world and self reveals itself—this idea here is not at all in accordance with the basic tenor of early idealism. World and self; one comes with the other in a primordial interaction. Therefore, to say 'I' cannot be regarded as the origin of self-consciousness and ego. Here, Dilthey agrees with Husserl's *Logical Investigations*.

To be sure, Dilthey holds on to the transcendental term of '*Setzen*' which was largely shaped by Fichte (for example: "*unser Selbst setzen wir nur, indem wir eine Welt setzen*"). But, like a cross-section through the different basic ideas of German idealism, Dilthey also wonders when "the contents of consciousness and the act of being conscious becomes one and the subject-object-relationship is dissolved."[29] He searches in essence for the union of the act of being conscious and its content as this union is the reason we experience life in its totality.[30] From this synthesis-point of experience—a unity of material and form, of receptivity and spontaneity[31]—we have to differentiate the numerous relations between world and self. In addition, a system context can only be gained through the analytic synthesis-point by taking a close look at every single moment that it contains in order to contrast them with each other. Dilthey articulates this contrasting analysis in a famous phrase: "Something that is there, comes to be noticable." [*Etwas, das da ist, wird merklich*] (VII, p. 122). In his unpublished elaboration of a second volume of *Einleitung in die Geisteswissenschaften* he discusses the union of self-consciousness more comprehensively based on his theorem of consciousness. The fact that our self-consciousness is aware of its act of being conscious as *uno actu*, which is why we experience our reality, means:

> What happens in this act of touch, so to speak, is life itself -not a theoretical process, but that, which is expressed by us with the term "experience" ; oppression and counter-pres-

---

28 Cf. here: Henrich 1999, especially pp. 49 ff. ("Subjektivität als Prinzip") and pp. 194 ff. ("Bewusstes Leben und Metaphysik"). Typically, Henrich never really refers to Dilthey.

29 "Inhalt des Bewusstseins und der Bewusstseinsakt selbst für das Bewusstsein nicht außer einander sind, d. h. sich nicht wie Subjekt und Objekt gegenüber steht." See here the whole extent of the debate between Kant, Fichte and Herbart in "Breslauer Ausarbeitung," DGS XIX, pp. 155 ff. Dilthey refers to them when he speaks of 'abstract philosophy.'

30 "Alles, was für uns da ist, ist im Erlebnis als ein in der Gegenwart Gegebenes da" (VII, p. 230).

31 Dilthey, DGS VII, p. 84 f.

> sure, position opposite to things which are position in and of themselves, the power of life within us and around us, which is experienced in joy and pain, in fear and hope, in grief over what is invariably burdening, in bliss over that, which is outside of the self, opposite and in regard to it, constantly experienced and which is there: the I, it is not a spectator who is sitting in front of the stage of the world, but action and counter-action, in which, no matter whether kings or fools and idiots operate in it, the same reality of facts is to be experienced overpoweringly. Thus, those who are in it, where never talk into believing, by any philosophers, that everything is imagination, is stage and not reality.[32]

Impetus and resistance are primary realities of our life and the self finds and realizes itself in them. It is striking that Dilthey uses the pre-idealistic term of ego [*Selbstgefühl*] that was, *inter alia*, shaped by Leibniz.[33] He considers it the essence of the phenomenon of self-consciousness.

III

In a letter to Althoff from 1882 Dilthey wants his "*Phänomenologie der Metaphysik*,"[34] namely the second book of the preface, to be understood as a venture with parallels to Hegel's *The Phenomenology of the Spirit*. By referring to Hegel, Dilthey opposes the "de-realization of the spirit" [*Entwirklichung des Geistes*][35] which was a common notion in his day.

Dilthey refers to Hegel's idea of an 'objective spirit' when he talks about the 'objectification of life' and wants to define the term and content of 'humanities' through it.[36] Of course, this cannot be seen as an externalization. It is much more a characteristic of life to aim for objectification. This is also indicated, as Boll-

32 "Was in diesem Akte der Berührung sozusagen sich vollzieht, ist das Leben – —nicht ein theoretischer Vorgang, sondern was in dem Ausdruck Erlebnis von uns bezeichnet wird, Druck und Gegendruck, Position den Dingen gegenüber, die selber Position ist, Lebensmacht in uns und um uns, welche in Lust und Schmerz, in Furcht und Hoffnung, in Gram über das, was unüberwindlich lastet, in Seligkeit über das, was draußen dem Selbst sich zu eigen gegen hat, beständig erfahren wird und da ist: nicht ein Zuschauer, das Ich, der vor der Bühne der Welt sitzt, sondern Handlung und Gegenhandlung selber, in dem, gleichviel, ob Könige darin fungieren oder Narren und Tölpel, dieselbe Tatsächlichkeit übermächtig erfahren wird. Daher es denen, die darin stehen, nie ein Philosoph eingeredet hat, das alles sei Vorstellung, Bühne nicht Wirklichkeit" (XIX, p. 153).

33 Cf. Frank 2002.

34 You can find the letter in: Dilthey, DGS V, p. 434.

35 See also Strube 2003, pp. 93 ff.

36 "Ihr Umfang reicht so weit wie das Verstehen, und das Verstehen hat nun seinen einheitlichen Gegenstand in der Objektivierung des Lebens" (VII, p. 148).

now already strikingly emphasized, by Dilthey's idea of life and history merging into each other. The line between these terms is blurred.[37] In his correspondence with Yorck, the entanglement of philosophy of life and history climaxes for Dilthey in the following statement: "Just as much as nature, I am history [*Gerade so wie Natur bin ich Geschichte*]" (p. 71). *Ipso facto*, "the human is a historic creature" [*der Mensch ein geschichtliches Wesen*] (VII, p. 291). "Ich bin so bis in nicht mehr erforschbare Tiefen meines Selbst ein historisches Wesen" (VII, p. 278).

Dilthey wants objectifications to be understood in the sense of manifestation and institutionalization: they range from expressing a fleeting sentiment "to a centenarian reign of a constitution or a breach of law."[38] In this respect, the objectification of life also provides sedimentation of forms of life in products of history, i.e. "the realization of spirit in the sensory world" [*Realisierung des Geistes in der Sinnenwelt*] (VII, p. 147). It should be noted that Dilthey's 'vocation of man' as a 'historical entity' (VII, p. 291) is connected to the objectification of life. This creates commonalities in terms of variation of the old practical-philosophical and hermeneutic intention of a "*sensus communis*," and of Aristotle's teaching of culture as our second nature.[39] The relation between the internal and external [*die Beziehung des Äußeren und Inneren*] is determining for objectifications. This idea is similar to Hegel's concept of institutions; they are products of and shaped by one mind only.[40] Dilthey sticks with Vico's '*verum et factum convertuntur*'-principle but adapts it to the objectifying, common mind's ability to reach a consensus. We can only understand and experience life through objectifications. They are articulations of past lives which they only perceive in a flawed, fragmentary way. Dilthey has to distance himself from Hegel's term 'objective spirit.' He calls it 'profound and fortunate' (VII, p. 148) because he recognizes Hegel's philosophy of the mind as a construct based on reason-*logos*, but he himself is concerned with the analysis of things given to us through experience.

---

37 "Leben [...] ist seinem Stoffe nach eins mit der Geschichte [...]. Geschichte ist nur das Leben, aufgefaßt unter dem Gesichtspunkt des Ganzen der Menschheit, das einen Zusammenhang bildet" (VII, p. 256).

38 "bis zur jahrhunderlangen Herrschaft einer Verfassung oder eines Rechtsbruchs." (VII, p. 147).

39 "Von der Verteilung der Bäume in einem Park, der Anordnung der Häuser in einer Straße, dem zweckmäßigen Werkzeug des Handwerkers bis zu dem Strafurteil ist um uns stündlich geschichtlich Gewordenes" (VII, p. 147).

40 "Sonach ist diese Objektivation überall bezogen im Verstehen auf das Erleben, in welchem der Lebenseinheit sich ihr eigener Gehalt erschließt und den aller anderen zu deuten gestattet." Ibid.

The ineluctability and inexhaustibility of life's and experience's totality point to their finite nature in particular, as well as on 'nowadays' "feeling of frailty, the power of dark drives, the suffering of darkness and illusions, and the finiteness of everything that is."[41] Even though the act of experiencing something is unfathomable because our mind can never fully grasp the experienced object, Dilthey understands humanistic research, based on life's starting point and objectifications, as an interlocking [*Ineinandergreifen*] of "critique, interpretation and procedure which produces an understanding of an historic event"[42]; an historian, according to Ranke, cannot be the eyepiece that only has to focus on 'what actually happened.' This demarcation plays a central role in Dilthey's letter to Yorck. The remains and ruins of the past cannot be translated back to a full life:

> Just like raw material in the industry is subjected to several kinds of processing, in the same way, the remnants of the past are raised to full historical understanding through various procedures.[43]

Ranke's ideal of pure description cannot be binding in Dilthey's sense because the 'historic world' only evolves in the rayon of humanities as understood life—a consideration that is closely linked to Dilthey's concept of humanities as transformed practical philosophy. The 'historical world' cannot be comprehended as a "copy of reality that exists separately from it" [*Abschrift einer außer [sc. ihr] befindlichen Wirklichkeit*]. Interdependency only emerges in itself. That is why Dilthey's 'philosophical history' never runs into danger of an 'intuitive divinatory.' It also does not commit to an aprioristic theory of history, as the history-philosophical approaches of Windelband's and Rickert's Neo-Kantianism do. In an allusion to Kant, Dilthey speaks of a 'critique of historical reason' which focuses on explaining how history presents itself 'to us.'[44] Nevertheless, Dilthey's theory was rightly accused in an independent further development of the issue of missing the ratio of difference of (former) depiction and discontinued visualization

41 "Gefühl der Gebrechlichkeit, der Macht des dunklen Triebes, des Leiden an den Dunkelheiten und den Illusionen, der Endlichkeit in allem, was Leben ist." Ibid,

42 "Kritik, Auslegung und [dem] Verfahren, welches die Einheit in dem Verständnis eines historischen Vorgangs herbeiführt." (VII, p. 161 f.)

43 "Wie Rohstoff in der Industrie mehreren Arten der Bearbeitung unterworfen wird, so werden auch die Reste der Vergangenheit durch verschiedene Prozeduren hindurch zum vollen geschichtlichen Verständnis erhoben" (VII, p. 161 f.).

44 Cf. Dilthey, VIII, pp. 304–310.

which is essential for historical insights.[45] Because his starting point is the totality of life, Dilthey is mired in an immediacy that is unable to grasp the multifaceted nature of past events:

The coincidence of "objectivation of life" and "unitary object of understanding" has its basis in missing the difference between representability and representation.[46]

This observation by Stephan Otto is basically justified yet it needs to be altered: Dilthey does ponder the idea of a modal-difference between reality and possibility, at least not in his correspondence with Yorck. Additionally, it is inevitable for Dilthey's philosophy of life to take the ineluctability of life as the basis of every synthesis or mediation. The problem that Otto addresses applies to every historic-philosophical context. The reason why it cannot be solved is found in in the roots of Dilthey's philosophy of life.

In a fashion akin to the basic structure of Plato's dialogues that start with a debate on supposedly peripheral questions and lead up to core of the *logos*,[47] Dilthey's construction of a historical world starts at a certain point of life because solitary individualities are "intersecting points of different systems"[48] of interactions. Despite every prudent effort to gain distance, the interdependence of mankind and history in Dilthey's approach cannot be detached from immediacy as it remains intertwined in the totality of the context of life: in the "interdependence of unity of life with the outside world."[49] Here, Dilthey finds his fundamental maxim come true; he wants "to understand life out of itself" [*das Leben aus ihm selber verstehen zu wollen*] and "dive deeper and deeper into the historical world in order to find its soul."[50]

At least Dilthey's late work is able to prove the stepped sequence of the construction of an historical world, of the logic of humanities and a meta-philosophy[51] as an explication of the context of life. Due to his specific and highly differ-

---

45 [Der Ineinsfall von "Objektivation des Lebens" und "einheitlichem Gegenstand des Verstehens" hat seinen Grund im Verfehlen der Differenz von Darstellbarkeit und Darstellung] Otto 1992, pp. 78 ff., especially p. 84. Cf. also Diwald 1963.

46 Otto 1992, p. 84.

47 This is a crucial point in Schleiermacher's interpretation of Plato. It also plays a vital role in the correspondence between Dilthey and Yorck because Dilthey wanted, in connection with his work on the "life of Schleiermacher," to develop a well-founded opinion on the inner, and relatively chronological connection in Plato's dialogues. Cf. Schleiermacher 1996, pp. 21 ff.

48 "Kreuzungspunkte der verschiedenen Systeme" (V, p. 63)

49 "Wechselwirkung der Lebenseinheit mit der Außenwelt" (XIX, p. 100).

50 "in die geschichtliche Welt immer tiefer einzudringen, um gleichsam ihre Seele zu vernehmen" (V, p. 4).

51 Qua 'philosophy of philosophy,' see volume VIII of Dilthey's *Gesammelte Schriften*.

entiated concept of metaphysics, Dilthey can continue the venture of a 'philosophy of philosophy' of classical German philosophy and poetry that started with Friedrich Schlegel and Hegel. Against the historian of materialism, Lange, he argued that metaphysics is not 'poetry,' "but the expression of the metaphysical consciousness in conceptual symbols."[52] Transcendental philosophy should converge to this 'metaphysical consciousness.'

IV

When one discusses the topicality of Dilthey's philosophy of life, one must understand that systematic and historical issues are inextricably interwoven. With respect to his own philosophical situation, Dilthey could serve as a bridge for today's discourses regarding the upheaval in philosophical history in the 19th century in order to keep, last but not least, Hegel's concern for the spirit's content of life awake. That the life of conception does not have to be understood as a mere intelligible and logos-like subjectivity, as Dilthey took it from Hegel's *Logik*, leads to the track of being able to expatiate reason in the life context of the interdependence of individuality and universality.[53] The tectonic quakes between Hegel and Nietzsche, Heidegger or Wittgenstein shaped modern philosophy significantly. Dilthey's concept could work here as *medius terminus* of contrast that might be able to maintain a dialogue between these sides. Of particular importance, as already demonstrated, is Dilthey's exposure of the consciousness out of the context of life. His theory of the connection of life and its investigative reorientation to itself can resolve the major problem of Heidegger's philosophy of '*Da-sein*' that is unable to explain how a self realizes its relation to the world. To this day, all discussions about the 'death of the subject' are incapable of preventing the question of its hermeneutics and, last but not least, the practical philosophical question of *phronesis* to arise again. Dilthey's discussions of life-consciousness would offer great benefit to this context, for which, paradigmatically, the late Foucault will stand firm.[54] Even Nietzsche's deconstruction of the 'fictions' of the 'I' requires a context of life which is of course not shown.[55]

---

52 "sondern der Ausdruck des metaphysischen Bewusstseins in den begrifflichen Symbolen." (II, p. 497).

53 Cf. the thoughts founded on Hegel by Robert B. Brandom (1994), especially pp. 689 ff. Also: Brandom 2000.

54 See Foucault 2001.

55 Cf. Ricoeur 1995—no mention of Dilthey. See also: Ricoeur 2004, and it is worth remarking the reflections here by Tengelyi (1998).

Dilthey's impressive, solid, yet constantly changing conception refers back to the classical period of German philosophy and theology between Hegel, Humboldt and Schleiermacher. However, he should not be absolutized. His notably illustrated depiction of his 'hermeneutic situation' in the beginning of *Einleitung in die Geisteswissenschaften* shows that he is a modern theorist of equal significance with Max Weber. Dilthey regards the time after 1848, the time of the industrial revolution and resulting political turmoil, as an epochal crisis without comparison in history. Modern technology, abandonment of a considerate lifestyle in individual professions and a partialization of production processes degrade society into a 'machine operation'[56] whose operations remain maintained but are obscure to its individuals. Even though Hegel had already anticipated some of these diagnostic assessments, Dilthey, based on his own reflections, also recognized a major turning point between the classical period around 1800 and his own day and era. He states there is no way back to that classical period that ended with Fontane's *Before the Storm* [*Vor dem Sturm*] and during which his research was mostly devoted to young Hegel and Schleiermacher.

> Now the dams are torn down and we sail on the high seas. We are a part of the thought movement of Europe, we are a link in its social movement [...]. Now still, we are making quite new demands on the guiding ideas and emotions which would be up to the storm that roars around us.[57]

It is only against this background that Manfred Riedel's observation becomes genuinely valid. Dilthey's position is characterized by the peculiar ambivalence "to participate in the matters it is distancing itself from."[58] This is of special importance regarding metaphysical traditions. Unlike more recent conceptions in the 20th century, Dilthey neither gets caught up in a twist or 'overcoming,'[59] nor yet in a negation of an alleged metaphysical compulsion that is dialectically followed by a "solidarity with metaphysics in the face of its fall";[60] nor in an *Epoché* of the big metaphysical questions that must not be confused with a com-

---

56 See Riedel 1981, pp. 9 ff., especially p. 13 f.
57 "Nun sind die Dämme niedergerissen und wir fahren auf hoher See. Wir sind ein Teil in der Gedankenbewegung Europas, wir sind ein Glied in seiner sozialen Bewegung [...]. Nun stellen wir doch ganz neue Forderungen an die leitenden Ideen und Gefühle, welche dem Sturm gewachsen wären, der uns umbraust." Dilthey 1922, p. 798.
58 "sie an dem, woran sie sich kehrt, noch in ihrer Distanzierung teilhat." Riedel 1981, p. 15.
59 Like Heidegger did who more and more used the term of a twist [*Verwindung*] of metaphysics than of 'overcoming' it. Cf., *pars pro toto*, Heidegger 1990, pp. 67 ff. Heidegger's approach has nothing to do with post-metaphysical thinking. That is only a cheap and groundless suspicion.
60 "Solidarität mit der Metaphysik im Angesicht ihres Sturzes." Adorno 1982, p. 400.

plete substitution.[61] Dilthey's phenomenology of metaphysics is rather based on finding metaphysical categories in the foundation of life. This assumes that the concept of life carries all differences, which were characterized as abstractions in the categories of the first philosophy, inside itself. Despite of the wide range of Dilthey's *Phänomenologie der Metaphysik*, starting with Aristotle, and extending to scholasticism and ending with classical German philosophy, it can still count as an unfinished draft.[62]

In this regard the tectonics of Dilthey's *Grundwissenschaft* is of special interest to us. Referring to it might be worthwhile inasmuch as it entails that you cannot take a *Grundwissenschaft* for granted. Yet, it is a 'first science' which, according to Manfred Riedel's correct conclusion of the tectonics of this approach,[63] mean that

> The theory of the mind and its methods [...] is not preceded by a logic and theory of knowledge, but on the contrary, it is attempted, on the basis of a self-reflection of its own history, principles and methods, to extend logic and theory of knowledge beyond traditional boundaries, and to develop this 'First' science- which is nonexistent – to take over as a basic science the function of the justification and regulation of the research of humanities.[64]

This refers to the demand of an aprioristic pre-science that can only be found by going back in history and looking at the eventful and ineluctable foundation of life: this attempt should not be underestimated because it brings late modern science explanation, lived life and phronesis together.

In this attempt, Dilthey combines his recalled dream with an endless approximation to the truth that is only gradually comprehensible. You are always on the

---

61 This approach of not a suspension but a bracketing is exposed by Hans Blumenberg. Cf. Blumenberg 1986, pp. 313 ff.

62 Cf. Dilthey, DGS II passim. See also an essential work for Dilthey, recommended by Yorck: Braniß 1834.

63 "den Geisteswissenschaften und ihren Methoden [...] nicht eine Logik und Erkenntnistheorie *voraus*geschickt (werde), sondern es wird umgekehrt versucht, auf der Grundlage einer Selbstreflexion ihrer Geschichte, Grundsätze und Methoden, die Logik und Erkenntnistheorie über traditionelle Grenzen hinaus zu erweitern und jene nicht vorhandene "erste" Wissenschaft auszuarbeiten, die dann als Grundwissenschaft die Funktion der Rechtfertigung und Regelgebung der geisteswissenschaftlichen Forschung übernehmen soll. Cf. Riedel 1978, p. 100- However, Riedel's attempt to distinguish between a "logic of history" [*Logik der Geschichte*] which is associated with traditional philosophy of history and Dilthey's co-founded "logic of historical research process" [*Logik des historischen Forschungsprozesses*] (ibid.) is not reasonable. On the contrary, regarding Dilthey's ideas both have to be understood as inseparable and engaging one another.

64 Riedel, ibid., p. 100 f.

way to find the truth but you never really attain it (E. Grassi)—this is certainly an indication of Dilthey's lasting topicality.

References

Adorno, Theodor ([3]1982) *Negative Dialektik.* Frankfurt a.M.: Suhrkamp.
Blumenberg, Hans (1986) *Lebenszeit und Weltzeit.* Frankfurt a.M.: Suhrkamp.
Bollnow, Otto Friedrich ([3]1967 [1936]) *Dilthey, Eine Einführung in seine Philosophie.* Stuttgart, Berlin/Cologne/Mainz: Novalis.
Brandom, Robert B. (1994) *Making it Explicit.* Cambridge: Harvard University Press.
Brandom, Robert B. (2000) *Articulating Reasons. An Introduction to Inferentialism.* Cambridge: Harvard University Press.
Braniß, Julius Christlieb (1834) *System der Metaphysik.* Breslau: Grass, Barth und Comp.
Dilthey, Wilhelm (1922) *Das Leben Schleiermachers.* Berlin/Leipzig: H. Mulert.
Dilthey, Wilhelm ([13]1957) *Das Erlebnis und die Dichtung. Lessing, Goethe, Novalis, Hölderlin,* Göttingen: Vandenhoeck & Ruprecht.
Diwald, H. (1963) *Wilhelm Dilthey. Erkenntnistheorie und Philosophie der Geschichte.* Göttingen/Berlin/Frankfurt a.M.: Musterschmidt.
Fellmann, F. (1993) *Lebensphilosophie. Elemente einer Theorie der Selbsterfahrung.* Reinbek: Rowohlt.
Foucault, Michel (2001) *L'herméneutique du sujet.* Paris: Cours au Collège de France.
Frank, Manfred (2002) *Selbstgefühl. Eine historisch-systematische Erkundung.* Frankfurt a.M.: Suhrkamp.
Fulda, Hans Friedrich, Horstmann, Rolf-Peter and Theunissen, Michael (eds.) (1980) *Kritische Darstellung der Metaphysik. Eine Diskussion über Hegels "Logik."* Frankfurt a.M.: Suhrkamp.
Heidegger, Martin ([7]1990) "Überwindung der Metaphysik." In: *Vorträge und Aufsätze.* Pfullingen: Neske, pp. 67–97.
Henrich, Dieter (1999) *Bewusstes Leben. Untersuchungen zum Verhältnis von Subjektivität und Metaphysik.* Stuttgart: Reclam.
Makkreel, Rudolph (1991) *Dilthey: Philosoph der Geisteswissenschaften.* Frankfurt a.M.: Suhrkamp.
Misch, C. (ed.) (1933) *Der junge Dilthey.* Leipzig/Berlin: Teubner.
Misch, Georg (1967 [1931]) *Lebensphilosophie und Phänomenologie. Eine Auseinandersetzung der Dilthey'schen Richtung mit Heidegger und Husserl.* Stuttgart: Teubner.
Orth, Ernst W. (ed.) (1985) *Dilthey und die Philosophie der Gegenwart.* Freiburg/Munich: Alber.
Otto, Stephan (1992) *Rekonstruktion der Geschichte. Zur Kritik der historischen Vernunft. Part 2: Systematische Ausarbeitung.* Munich: Fink.
Ricoeur, Paul (1995) *Oneself as Another*, tr. Kathleen Blamey. Chicago: University of Chicago Press.
Ricoeur, Paul (2004) *Gedächtnis, Geschichte, Vergessen.* Munich: Fink.
Riedel, Manfred (1978) "Von der Phänomenologie der Metaphysik zur Lebensphilosophie. Diltheys Konzeption einer Kritik der historischen Vernunft" in: Manfred Riedel, *Verstehen oder Erklären?* Stuttgart: Klett-Cotta 1978, pp. 44–64.

Riedel, Manfred (1978) *Verstehen oder Erklären?* Stuttgart: Klett-Cotta.
Riedel, Manfred (1981) "Einleitung." In: Wilhelm Dilthey, *Der Aufbau der geschichtlichen Welt in den Geisteswissenschaften*. Frankfurt a.M.: Suhrkamp, pp. 9–81.
Rodi, Frithjof (2003) *Das strukturierte Ganze. Studien zum Werk von Wilhelm Dilthey.* Weilerswist: Velbrück.
Rodi, Fritjhof (1969) *Morphologie und Hermeneutik. Diltheys Ästhetik.* Stuttgart/Berlin/Cologne/Mainz: Kohlhammer.
Schleiermacher, F.D.E. (1996) *Über die Philosophie Platons*, ed. P.M. Steiner. Hamburg: Meiner.
Seubert, Harald (2004) *Polis und Nomos. Untersuchungen zu Platons Rechtslehre*. Berlin: Duncker & Humblot.
Strube, Claudius (2003) "Die ontologische Wiederentdeckung des deutschen Idealismus." In: Harald Seubert (ed.), *Heideggers Zwiegespräch mit dem deutschen Idealismus.* Cologne/Weimar/Vienna: Böhlau.
Tengelyi, Laszlo (1998) *Der Zwitterbegriff der Lebensgeschichte*. Munich: Fink.
Theunissen, Michael (1980) *Sein und Schein. Die kritische Funktion der Hegelschen Logik.* Frankfurt a.M.: Suhrkamp.

Leonard Lawlor

Four Fundamental Aspects of the Reversal of Platonism

Abstract: This essay attempts to conceive precisely what is included in the idea of reversing Platonism. It shows that there are four fundamental aspects that derive from Plato's dialogues. First, the aspect of thought conceived as interior monologue, from the *Theatetus*. Second, multiplicity, which comes from the *Parmenides*. Third, the aspect of an involuntary stimulus to think, from the *Republic*, Book VII. Finally, the aspect of imagining political life on the basis of the conception of the soul, from the *Republic*, Book II. These four aspects revolve around two more fundamental ideas: the reversal of Platonism (as Deleuze has shown), conceiving the ideas (forms or essences) as events and (as Derrida has implied) reducing violence to the very least violence. I attempt to actualize this aim by a "hyperbolic *Gelassenheit*" (letting be), the only genuine reversal of Platonism.

In a simple reading of Nietzsche's definition of the reversal of Platonism, we value this world in itself, immanently, and no longer value it in relation to transcendent forms such as the Platonic idea of the good. In other words, the revaluation of existence means that existence is measured neither in terms of an origin from which existence might be said to have fallen nor in terms of an end toward which existence might be said to be advancing. More precisely, we must say that the reversal of Platonism means that the duration of existence has no beginning and it has no end. It has no primary origin and no ultimate destination. In the reversal, the time of duration becomes unlimited, and time itself looks to be composed of nothing but fragments and remainders. While we started out from a well-known definition of the reversal of Platonism, we have ended up in a complicated idea. The reversal of Platonism leads us to the idea of time imagined as a line that has no terminal points, a line that never bends itself back into a circle. It leads us to the imagination of an unlimited straight line. It seems to me that, despite all the reflections on time that have taken place across the last one hundred years, the implications of the idea of unlimited time remain, at the least, under-determined, and, more likely, I think, the implications remain largely unknown. In the 20th century, Deleuze of course is the great philosopher of the reversal of Platonism. In his 1968 *Difference and Repetition*, he assigns the reversal of Platonism as the task of contemporary phi-

https://doi.org/10.1515/9783110551563-019

losophy.[1] It is, however, in his 1969 *The Logic of Sense* that Deleuze gives us the most precise definition of the reversal of Platonism. There, he says, “To reverse Platonism is first and foremost to depose essences and to substitute *events* in their place.”[2] The question that therefore drives the investigation in which we shall engage is: what is an event? As we shall see, we arrive at an answer to the question of event only if we conceive the event in terms of the straight, unlimited line of time. We know we have experienced an event when the two questions of its primary origin and its ultimate destination are and remain necessarily unanswerable. In other words, an event is happening when we cannot say with certainty of an event what happened and what is going to happen. In fact, if one *can* answer these questions, then one knows that one has not *really* experienced an event. And if one thinks one can answer these questions, then one has not really broken free of Platonism.

There is however a second part to our question of the event. Not only are we seeking the definition of an event, but also we are seeking the means to make ourselves acutely aware of the event. By calling the awareness acute, sharp, even painful, we see that the experience of the event is in fact an experience of violence. Indeed, the experience of the event is the experience of fundamental violence. And, as you might expect from this characterization, the experience is deeply connected to death. It is not the case, as we shall see, that one must die to experience the event. Yet, one must undergo a negation of one’s will, one must suffer an accident in which things get mixed up, one must be infected with a plague, or one must be wounded in a battle. It is only by means of the wound that one becomes acutely aware of the event, so acutely aware that one can finally see. The vision however does not complete the event. The vision only allows one to have the chance to produce a work, a work of art, or a work of philosophy. The event happens only when the work is produced, only when the work attains a kind of “eternity” that transforms it into a “remainder.” With the work, we know we have experienced an event—even though the unlimited becoming of the work implies that the event never really happens. The event is always still to come. We have of course returned, through the work, to the unlimited straight line of time. By stressing the unlimited straight line of time—by stressing that no matter how far we go out into the future, there is always still another “to come”—we shall finally be able to refine our understanding of the reversal of Platonism. Insofar as Platonism wills the end of time, insofar as it wills that all existence constantly approximate a *telos*, it wills, we shall argue, the very worst violence.

---

1 Deleuze 1968, p. 82; English translation: Deleuze 1995, p. 59.
2 Deleuze 1969, p. 69; English translation: Deleuze 1990, p. 53, my emphasis.

Thus the reversal of Platonism amounts not to willing, but to letting the event ceaselessly continue to happen. Letting the event happen without end, letting all the ends of the event happen implies that the reversal of Platonism is a hyperbolic response to the hyperbolic will of Platonism. Of course, such a hyperbolic *Gelassenheit* makes us think not only of Heidegger but also of Derrida.[3]

Here and in what follows there are echoes and allusions to the works and ideas of Derrida, Deleuze and Heidegger. Yet, the purpose of the current project does not lie in producing another commentary on their works. Instead, we shall attempt to appropriate their thinking in a way that will open up new possibilities of thinking and acting. The idea that we must first appropriate is immanence since, of course, both Derrida and Deleuze, and especially Deleuze, begin their thinking in immanence. While this point is not often recognized, and despite their well-known criticisms of phenomenology, both Derrida and Deleuze belong within the phenomenological tradition. Thus, in order to understand what immanence means, we are going to start with internal, subjective experience. After all, it is impossible to reverse Platonism without passing through a phase of Cartesianism. The phase of Cartesianism means that we must examine the "*cogito*," or, in Greek, it means that we must examine "*dianoia*." The Greek term here brings us to the first of our four reference points in Plato himself. Perhaps it is surprising to see us turn so quickly to Plato when all we have spoken of is the reversal of Platonism. Yet, as Deleuze has pointed out, Plato himself was the first philosopher to begin the movement of the reversal of Platonism.[4] Our first reference point is the *Theatetus* (189c–190a). Here Plato says that thinking is interior monologue. To define thinking as interior monologue means that thinking is equivalent to hearing-oneself-speak. Therefore what we shall engage in first is a phenomenology of hearing-oneself-speak. By means of this phenomenology, we shall be able to approach the definition of the reversal of Platonism in terms of the event.

I The Phenomenology of Hearing-Oneself-Speak and Some of Its Implications

If this investigation is to be a genuine phenomenological investigation, we must enact the *epoché*. In agreement with the epoché, we turn back from the objects of

3 Derrida 1992. English translation: Derrida 1995.

4 Deleuze, "Platon et les simulacres" in: Deleuze 1969, pp. 292–307; English translation: Deleuze 1990, pp. 253–266.

our experience to the experience itself. Following the basic trajectory of the phenomenological movement, we must not stop with the epoché. We must radicalize it with the universalization of the transcendental reduction.[5] Through its strict universalization, the reduction relates all beings, that is, all constituted things, including me as a psychological subject, back to an experience that is itself extra-psychological and even pre-ontic. The universalization of the reduction takes us therefore to a level of experience that is non-existent and (to speak like Derrida) "ultra-transcendental."[6] Through the universalization of the reduction, what we experience resembles nothing that we grasped in the natural experience of objects or subjects. What has come into view, where have we landed due to the universal reduction? Below the functioning of the natural experience of objects, we find *pure* auto-affection. As we anticipated, at first glance pure auto-affection looks to be interior monologue, hearing-oneself-speak.

Now, let us pursue the investigation of the pure auto-affection of hearing-oneself-speak. Auto-affection *seems* to include two aspects. *First*, I seem to hear myself speak at the very moment that I speak; and, *second*, I seem to hear my own self speak. The question we must ask is clear: is it really the case that in hearing-oneself-speak, one hears oneself speak *at this very moment* and that one really hears *one's own* self? In other words, is auto-affection really that pure? What we are going to pay particular attention to in the investigation is these "seems." This is how auto-affection seems to take place. When I engage in interior monologue, when, in short, thinking takes place—it *seems* as though I hear myself speak at the very moment I speak. It *seems* as though my interior voice is not required to pass outside of myself, as though it is not required to traverse any space. So, my interior monologue seems to be immediate, immediately present, and not to involve anyone else. Interior monologue seems therefore to be different from the experience of me speaking to another. However, are we really, truly able to distinguish and separate interior monologue from external dialogue? When I speak in general, that is, with or without the intention of communication, some moment always comes prior to the speaking. The prior moment could be silence or noise, but something like a context precedes all speaking. The prior context implies that the present speaking, whether it is internal or

---

5 The discussion of *epoché* and the reduction is based on Edmund Husserl, "A. Abhandlungen. Der Encyclopaedia Britannica Artikel," in Husserl 1968, pp. 277–301; English translation in Husserl 1997, pp. 159–179. It is also based on the presentation of the phenomenological method in *Ideas I.* Husserl 1950; English translation: Husserl 1983. For a lucid and exhaustive treatment of the "Encyclopedia Britannica" essay, see Kockelmans 1994.

6 I have appropriated the term "ultra-transcendental" from Derrida. See Derrida 1967b, p. 14; English translation: Derrida 2011, p. 23.

external, whether it has the purpose of communication or not, is in a secondary position. The present speaking is necessarily a "second." In a few moments, below, by means of an eidetic variation, I shall attempt to demonstrate this claim about the necessity of the secondary position of present speaking. For now, however, we must recognize that the necessity is this: whenever I start to speak—to myself, to others, for the sake of phonation whatsoever—I find that some other speaking has already taken place and elapsed. There is always some elapsed moment that has expired, that has been lost and reduced to silence, even as something of that elapsed moment has been retained, even as something of it remains. Necessarily, my speaking is not a pure first time, even though it takes place right now. The secondary character of all speaking means that there is a delay between one speaking and another. This delay then functions as well in between speaking and hearing. Just as the apparent initiating speaking is in truth a "second," the hearing of the speaking is not immediate. In other words, the delay in interior monologue means that interior monologue is always involved in a process of mediation. We must therefore conclude from this description that my interior monologue in fact resembles my experience of external speech, in which a distance separates me from my hearer. I cannot, it is impossible for me to hear myself *immediately.* Regardless of whether the action is hearing or speaking, the action is a response to the past. Similar to the first necessity of the delay in time, we encounter another necessity. This second necessity appears despite the radicalization of the reduction, despite the universal bracketing of all natural beings. Here it is. In order to hear myself speak at this very moment, I must make use of the same phonemes as I use in communication (even if this monologue is not vocalized externally through my mouth, even if it does not have the purpose of communication). It is an irreducible or essential necessity that the silent words I form contain repeatable traits. This irreducible necessity means that, when I speak to myself, I speak with the sounds of others. In other words, it means that I find in myself other voices, which come from the past: the many voices are in me. I cannot, it is impossible for me to hear myself speak *all alone*. Others' voices contaminate the hearing of myself speaking.[7] Just as my present moment is never immediate, my interior monologue is never simply my own.

As noted earlier, I think that the implications of this description are unclear. Here are some of the implications of the description as far as I understand them. First, I think that the description shows, fundamentally, that auto-affection is

---

7 Fred Evans has developed an important conception of the voice in Evans 2008, see especially pp. 144–168 and 280–282.

based on a structure which consists of two contradictory forces.[8] On the one hand, there is always a present moment, a point or a singularization. Each thought I have, as I speak it, has a kind of novelty to it, giving it a singular location. It is important to realize that what makes the singular point novel is that its appearance is haphazard and determined by chance. Undoubtedly, this first force of singularization is the root of what we naturally call an event-like experience. Yet, this experience is not the experience of the event. It is only the experience of an accident, an accident due to the mixed up way in which the singular points succeed one another. As we shall see, more is required for an event than an accident. Now, let us turn to the other force in the structure we have been examining. Beside the singularizing force of chance, there is the universalizing force of repetition. As the description showed, the singularity of a thought, my present interior speech, is always connected back to some other thoughts in the past or its location is connected back to some other places elsewhere. Because of this necessary inseparability of the present thought to past thoughts, the present thought is necessarily composed of traits already used in the past, traits standing nearby. These traits are necessarily repeatable to infinity. The structure we have discovered therefore consists of the force of singularization and the force of universalization. These two forces of universalization and singularization are irreducibly connected to one another but without unification. In other words, these two forces are necessarily bound to one another and necessarily dis-unified. The paradoxical relation of the two forces implies that auto-affection is really, necessarily, at the same time, hetero-affection. The paradox is that the relation is heterogeneous and yet the alterity does not make a separation. The inseparability is a distribution of the unity into a duality. Or, more precisely, insofar as a new now is always, necessarily linked to repetition, the unity is distributed into a multiplicity.

The wording of this last formula for the structure implied in the description of hearing-oneself-speak (that is, "the one distributed into a multiplicity") brings us to the *second* fundamental aspect of the reversal of Platonism: the ancient problem of the one and the many in the labyrinthine discourse of the *Parmenides*. Here, Parmenides presents astonishing arguments that support the description of the structure we have just laid out: the one is the same as the many insofar as it is different from them, and unlike the many insofar as the

---

8 The description of hearing-oneself-speak and its implications have evolved out of years of reflection upon Jacques Derrida's *Voice and Phenomenon* (Derrida 2011), especially on its introduction and chapter 6.

one is the same as the many (147c–148c).[9] However, also in the *Parmenides*, we find this argument. It concerns the one touching itself, and therefore it concerns auto-affection. Parmenides argues that, if the one were to touch itself, it would have to be situated next to itself (148e). Yet, Parmenides counters by saying that the one does not have this "next to itself" distance since it is not two. He concludes that since it is not two, it cannot touch itself. In the structure we have been outlining, however, the one of the "auto" is necessarily distanced from itself and distributed into two. So, according to Parmenides' argumentation, we must be able to say that, since the structure is a "two," the structure in some way touches itself or makes contact with itself. How are we to understand this self-contact of the two forces?

We said that the two forces are contradictory. The terms with which we designated the two forces clearly indicate their contradictory character: the one is the force of singularization, while the second is the force of universalization. The contradictory character of the two forces means that the two are in competition with one another, the one overstepping the other. We might imagine the competition as a race, with the two forces going beyond one another on a straight line. But, the image of the competition does not really emphasis the back and forth of the two forces; it does not really capture the idea of them as forces. Therefore we could also imagine the contradictory character as a border-crossing. If we understand the "contra" of "contradiction" in its logical sense, then we must say that the two forces are the negation of one another. Or, taking up Heidegger's discourse on the "*Ereignis*," we could say that, even though the two forces are appropriate (*geeignet*) to one another, the one dis-appropriates (*enteignet*) itself into the other. Through the language of appropriation and disappropriation, we have retained the negative relation. But also we see now that the relation between the two forces—the one dis-appropriates itself into the other like an infection—is one of "pain." The two forces are trying to annihilate one another. The self-contact of the two forces is a struggle, and the distance between them is not a threshold (as Heidegger would say), but a battlefield. Therefore by pursuing the implications of the description of auto-affection, we have entered into what we could call, following Deleuze, "chaos," or, following Derrida, we could call it "fundamental violence."[10]The

---

9 I have used the Fowler English translation and the Cornford English translation of the *Parmenides*. Plato 1939 and Plato 1961.

10 For chaos, see Deleuze 1969, pp. 129–131; English translation: Deleuze 1990, pp. 106–107. See also Deleuze and Guattari 1991, pp. 44–45; English translation: Deleuze and Guattari 1994, p. 42. Derrida does not use the precise phrase "fundamental violence." Yet, such a concept is implied in Violence and Metaphysics" since he engages Levinas' thought at the level of the

paradoxical relation of the two forces has taken us very far from the apparently peaceful experience of my own interior monologue. What defines, therefore, the structure of auto-affection is the necessary inseparability of the two forces. A moment ago, I said that I think that an eidetic variation would be able to demonstrate the necessity of the present speaking coming second, as if it is always a response to the past. You can see in this wording—"always a response to the past"—that the eidetic variation really concerns the experience of time.

So let us imagine any experience in any domain. We could imagine an experience in the domain of the everyday, in the practical, the arts, the theoretical sciences, or in mathematics. No matter what the experience and no matter what the domain, we see that, each and every time, the experience involves a before and an after. As we imagine a variety of experiences, we never find an experience in which there is a before with no other before prior to it; likewise, we never find an after that does not have another after coming later than it. In other words, it is not possible to imagine a present moment or a now-point that does not come after a previous point and that does not remember a past moment. No matter what now-point I think of, there is always a prior retention. Likewise, it is not possible to imagine a retention that does not come before and that does not anticipate another now-point. In other words, there is no repetition without the supervenience of a singularity and there is no singularity without the supervenience of universality. If this imaginative exercise has disclosed a truth about the structure, then we must say that, within the structure, it is impossible to speak of an origin in the traditional sense, a principle (or *arché*), a unitary starting point, complete in itself, an unprecedented beginning. Instead, the origin is always *origin-heterogeneous*, that is, the origin is heterogeneous from the start or what starts is itself heterogeneous to the very idea of origin.[11] Likewise, if there is always another singularity beyond every repetition, then we cannot speak of an end in the traditional sense, a purpose (or *telos*), a unitary stopping point, complete in itself, with nothing left over. Instead, the end is always *end-heterogeneous*, that is, the end is in the end, finally, heterogeneous or what finishes is heterogeneous to the very idea of an end. In short, there is no original principle and there is no final purpose. We see now that the experience we have been describing is not just the experience of hetero-affection, it is also the experience of origin-heterogeneous and end-heterogeneous.

---

transcendental. See Derrida 1967a, especially, pp. 171–172 and 191–192; English translation: Derrida 1978, especially, pp. 116–117 and 130–131.

11 I have appropriated "origin-heterogeneous" from Derrida. Derrida 1987, pp. 176–178; English translation: Derrida 1989, pp. 107–108.

The lack of an original principle and of a final purpose also tells us something about the forces in this inseparable but heterogeneous way. A strong force would be one that is based on a principle from which it would derive all of its functions or it would be based on a purpose toward which it would orient all of its functions. Because the two forces function *without* an *arché* and *without* a *telos*, we *cannot* describe these forces at the bottom of auto-affection as strong. They are *weak* precisely because they are neither archeological nor teleological. Yet, despite their weakness, the forces continue to work, to function, and to struggle. And, while we cannot say that the two forces of universalization and singularization are "the forces of things," we can say that they are the forces included in *all* experiences of things. Although we have shown how auto-affection is structured like a war with itself—it is as if the interior monologue is saying, "I am at war with myself"—we have never left the level that conditions and generates all experience of all things. We have never left the depth of the ultra-transcendental.

II The Experience of the Event

We reached the ultra-transcendental level by following the phenomenological method of the universal epoché. It was as if we had merely "leaped" out of the natural attitude into the depth of the experience, a leap made possible by "our perfect freedom," as Husserl says in *Ideas I* (§31). Yet, later in *The Crisis of European Sciences*, Husserl says that this "shorter way" of the leap into the transcendental level—this is the Cartesian way, of course—has "a great shortcoming."[12] The shortcoming, for Husserl, lies in the fact that the shorter way places us in an experience that seems to lack any content. Then, because it lacks content, it is "all too easy right at the beginning to fall back into the naïve-natural attitude."[13] Thus in the Cartesian way, it is not clear that one is not copying the transcendental level off the naïve level of natural experience. It is not clear that one has escaped a vicious circle. As we know from *The Crisis*, Husserl thinks that a "preparatory explication" of the *epoché* is necessary to avoid this shortcoming. In other words, we must engage in a criticism of the history of philosophy in order to show how the transcendental level differs from all other philosophical positions. In short, something like a genealogy is required to show us how to

---

12 Husserl 1976, §43; English translation: Husserl 1970, §43. Ludwig Landgrebe's "Husserl's Departure from Cartesianism" helped me a great deal in the writing of this paragraph. See Landgrebe 1981, especially, pp. 98–99.
13 Husserl 1976, §43; Husserl 1970, §43.

reach the ultra-transcendental experience. Yet, in order to escape the vicious circle, something else is required. If the epoché or even the genealogy is taken up on the basis of "our perfect freedom," it amounts to an act of will. In an act of will, one is directed toward something one already has a sense of. One projects a series of means in order to reach a goal that one has outlined in advance. The will always seems to be about recognition.

Therefore, once again, we have not escaped the vicious circle: we reach only that which we had projected ahead of time, something we are able to re-cognize. Through an act of will, no change occurs in me: at the other end of the action, I find myself again. In other words, I have not become other, I am not thinking otherwise. Unlike an act of will, what is required is an experience that is *undergone*, a *negative* experience that throws all accepted opinions into question. The question of the experience brings us to the *third* fundamental aspect of the reversal of Platonism. It comes from Book VII in the *Republic* (522c–524b).[14] Appearing after the allegory of the cave, there is a well-known illustration. The illustration is supposed to answer the question of what sensation would motivate one to ascend from the depths of the cave. In other words, Socrates is trying to tell Glaucon how certain kinds of sensations provoke "thought" (here again the word is "*dianoia*"). The sensation is *not*, Socrates stresses, that of things "far away"; the sensation is *not* "shadow paintings." It is simply the sensation of Socrates' hand being held up to Glaucon's vision. In particular, it is Socrates' hand composed of only three fingers, the index, the middle, and the little finger. The question is not whether the fingers held up are fingers; the question is not whether Glaucon is able to recognize these fingers as fingers.[15] Instead, the question is whether the middle finger is big or small. It seems to be at once both big (in relation to the pinky finger) and small (in relation to the index finger). The sensation of the middle finger is a *mixture* of big and small. According to Plato, it is this simultaneously contradictory sensation that provokes thought. The type of sensation Plato is pointing toward is the paradox of mixtures. This whole experience of contradictory sensations, however, does not bring us to the experience of the event. Socrates holding his hand in front of his student Glaucon is too friendly. My clasping your hand in a handshake is not disturbing. These experiences have no danger to them. However, we know the dangers involved in the experience of alcohol and of hallucinogenic drugs. Indeed, Deleuze has more than suggested that these experiences might have a philosophical function. He suggests a

14 I have used the Shorey English translation, and the Bloom English translation of the *Republic*. Plato 1987 and Plato 1968.

15 Deleuze 1964, pp. 122–123; Deleuze 2003, 100–101.

philosophical function for drunkenness because, for Deleuze, the event is like a plague, a wound, or a battle.[16] In fact, Deleuze says, "the battle is not one example of an event among others ..., [it is] the [event] in its essence."[17] The battle is the event in its essence because, *first*, it involves mixtures, deep mixtures down in the battlefield, mixtures in this case of bodies, the soldiers clashing. The mixtures consist in accidents and chance encounters. The accidents and chances taken make the battle singular, unlike any other battle. Here we have the force of singularization that we described earlier. However, a series of chance accidents does not make an event. If the event were nothing more than a series of accidents, it would indeed be the simple equivalent to drunkenness. There is a *second* reason why the battle is the event in its essence. Due to the chance mixtures of bodies on the battlefield, a soldier comes to be mortally wounded. Being caused by the mixture, the wound is an effect. It is the effect of the soldier risking his life in the abyss of the battle; he has risked and lost. Due to the mortal wound, the soldier has become aware, painfully aware that he is going to die. The awareness of his wound blinds him to the means and the purposes of the battle. The blindness to the battle's causes, however, releases the soldier enough to able to see the battle in its unlimitedness hovering above the battlefield. What does the soldier see? It is the vision of *impersonal* death. This soldier, who has a proper name, is dying, his person is dying from the wound. Yet, what he sees is other soldiers dying, whose names he does not know; he sees them dying and that they never stop dying.[18] It is the vision of incessant dying and being lost —and not just incessant dying of unknown soldiers, but also animals perishing, and country sides and cities being destroyed. It is the vision of life in its endless struggle with death. This vision is why the event is horrifying. In this intuition, chaos has risen from the depths to the surface. Because the surface that the vision sees never comes to an end, the vision itself cannot be grasped. It is this vision of death never ceasing, never ending, never accomplishing itself, never making itself be over once and for all, this vision cannot be thought. The inability to stop the struggle is the impotence of the event. It is, however, a powerlessness that includes a kind of power.

So far, we have seen that the experience of the event involves two features. On the one hand, it involves the depth of mixtures, chance relations of cause and effect, accidents, which make this battle a battle unlike any other. This is the force of singularization. On the other hand, however, there is the force of univer-

16 Deleuze 1969, p. 177; Deleuze 1990, p. 151.

17 Deleuze 1969, p. 122; Deleuze 1990, p. 100. Deleuze capitalizes the word "event" in the phrase "Event in its essence."

18 Deleuze 1969, p. 178; Deleuze 1990, p. 152.

salization. Through the effect of being wounded, one is forced to see, intuit, have a vision of the battle; the battle rises to the surface and is no longer limited to the accidents. Without end, incessantly singularities pass away, as if a plague is taking place. There is, however, a third feature of the experience of the event. *It is the most important feature.* The mortally wounded soldier has no choice in relation to the two forces we have just described. The effect of the battle is that he is dying and others are incessantly dying. Although the vision of the battle's incessant deaths cannot be grasped, cannot be thought, the unthinkable must be thought, the ingraspable must be grasped. Due to the force of universalization, something remains of the singularities as they pass away. In this moment of grace between life and death, the mortally wounded soldier is able to effectuate the battle differently, *against* the incessant deaths being caused in the battle. *Counter* to the accidental, *de facto* characteristics of the battle, he is able to select traits from the battle that are ideal and *de jure*. In other words, he is able to create an ideal sense of the battle. In still other words, he is able to create a philosophical concept or an artwork. Responding to the vision, the mortally wounded soldier, through the selection of traits, a selection that is like a single act of violence, includes all violence and all mortal events in one single event—a book, a speech, a picture, a song, or a concept—that denounces and deposes all violence and all death.[19] The mortally wounded soldier must write the story of the battle—in order to liberate it, as Deleuze says, "always for other times" and "to make us go farther than we would have ever believed possible."[20]

This third feature of the experience of the event amounts to what Deleuze in *The Logic of Sense* calls "counter-effectuation." Effectuation, which is the deep, accidental mixture of bodies, takes place in the present. The counter-effectuation in the artwork, in a novel, in a concept, makes the battle "eternal." The counter-effectuation is "eternal" not in the sense of an eternal present that never changes or of a circle of time that constantly returns to the present. The experience of the event is "eternal" in the sense of being non-present, that is, it is the experience of the openness of an unlimited past and future.[21] The experience of the event is no longer simply the present of effectuation; instead, the battle is always to come and always already passed. That is, as an ideal sense, the battle appears to lack an origin; but also, as an ideal sense, it exceeds all actual fulfillments. In this

19 Deleuze 1969, p. 179; Deleuze 1990, p. 152–153.

20 Deleuze 1969, p. 188; Deleuze 1990, p. 161.The importance of writing in Deleuze (and Guattari) is seen in 1st Plateau of *A Thousand Plateaus*. I have argued for the importance of writing (either a story or a philosophical concept) in Deleuze's thought, and in particular to his concept of becoming in my (2008).

21 Deleuze 1969, p. 78; Deleuze 1990, p. 61.

sense, the event has never taken place and never will take place. What is the experience of the event? It is the grasping in a work of the ungraspable vision of incessant struggle: endless fundamental violence. The terrible nature of the event means that we really do not know, in the strong sense, what happened and what is going to happen.

III Conclusion: What Happened? What Is Going to Happen?

Like the vision of the mortally wounded soldier, Nietzsche's Zarathustra has a vision of unlimited time.[22] Zarathustra's vision of the moment standing at a gateway over a road that stretches far out of sight, this is the image for eternity: a straight line without a termination point, a straight line that never bends itself back into a circle. Earlier, we had tried to provide this image of the unlimited straight line with conceptual determination by referring to the features of origin-heterogeneous and end-heterogeneous. Let us return again to these conceptual determinations. In relation to these conceptual determinations, I think that it is harder for us to understand the idea of end-heterogeneous than the idea of origin-heterogeneous. In other words, it seems to me that it is more difficult for us to imagine the world continuing without end than to imagine the past extending indefinitely. Yet, if I have understood the idea of end-heterogeneous correctly, it contests the very idea of a complete apocalypse; end-heterogeneous asserts that the world—or something—will continue indefinitely. End-heterogeneous implies that there is always a remainder. The concept of remainder is defined by two features. On the one hand, a remainder indicates that something has been lost and gone away. And, insofar as the remainder indicates loss, it is truly the end of a singular world. However, on the other hand, insofar as the remainder remains, it indicates that something more is coming. And, insofar as the remainder indicates more, it is truly the promise of other worlds. Yet, I cannot know what is coming. I cannot know whether what is coming is the best or the worst.

The claim of non-knowledge returns us to the question of Platonism. Platonism thinks that it knows what is coming. By positing absolute and transcendent values, it thinks there is an absolute or ultimate end and an absolute or primary origin. Through this knowledge, metaphysics in fact knows nothing of the "eternity" of the event. Metaphysics, however, not only posits absolute and transcen-

22 Friedrich Nietzsche, Z III, "Vom Gesicht und Rätsel," KSA 4, pp 197–202; English translation: Nietzsche 1968, pp. 267–272.

dent values, it also wills the means to achieve the fulfillment of these values. As we saw at the beginning, such a will reduces the value of this world, of existence to being nothing more than a function of this end and purpose. But the reduction of value is not the only result of the metaphysical will. When the metaphysical will wills the means to achieve the end, it thinks it is willing the good. Such a teleology implies the willing that all of existence, all of life, all remainders be brought to the end. In truth, however, this willing can have no other outcome than the absolute and hyperbolic elimination of all remainders. In short, the metaphysical will does not will the best; it wills the worst. Thus we see the stakes in the reversal of Platonism are more extensive than a problem within the history of philosophy. The stakes, simply, are more violent.

If our ultra-transcendental investigation of auto-affection is correct, there can be no denying that the apocalypse willed by metaphysics is impossible. Yet, despite its impossibility, what the metaphysical will wills is a constantly increasing approximation to this apocalypse. Perhaps we can understand globalization only in reference to this constantly increasing approximation. As it encloses the earth in a globe, it aims at the complete obliteration of remainders. How are we able to reverse the incessant obliteration of remainders? If metaphysics thinks that it knows the one value or purpose for existence, then the reversal must base itself in the *non-knowledge* of the heterogeneity of origin and end. We do not know the answer to the questions of what happened and what is going to happen. In short, the reversal amounts to a vision, an acute awareness of not knowing what is coming. Then, just as the metaphysical will is hyperbolic—it wills that all remainders march toward the end—the reversal must be hyperbolic. It must let every single remainder be, without exception. Through this *Gelassenheit*, as Heidegger would say, the reversal "values" (but "value" does not seem to be the right word here) every possible remainder, every imaginable remainder and, especially, all of what they indicate is coming, every single end that they might indicate. The reversal of Platonism therefore does not aim for the worst violence, but for the *least violence*.

There is one more question. Is this hyperbolic *Gelassenheit* equivalent to what we were calling "counter-effectuation"? Is it equivalent to the experience of the event? We know already that the answer to this question is "no." The unlimited *Gelassenheit* becomes a counter-effectuation *only if* it results in a work. It remains nothing but an accident unless it produces a work of art or a work of philosophy. But what is the purpose of the work? The question of the work's purpose brings us to the *fourth* and last fundamental aspect of the reversal of Platonism. It comes from the *Republic*, Book II (368c–369b). There Socrates suggests to Glaucon that they investigate the constitution of the soul by looking at the bigger image of the constitution of the *polis*. A couple of books later, of course, we land with Plato in the ideal city. As we have seen however, the reversal of Platonism in fact starts, not from the larger political image, but from the smaller psychological image. It starts with the soul, with internal subjective experience; it starts with interior monologue. An implication of our investigation of pure auto-affection, an implication we left in the dark above, is this: the heterogeneity of auto-affection—that auto-affection is always in fact hetero-affection—means that, instead of an identical or unified self, I find, inside myself, an other. The other in me turns the "I," the self, into a "we." But this "we," it also, is heterogeneous, and therefore not strictly a "we" at all. The self is a "we" and yet the "we" is absent. In other words, we can say that *the people is lacking*. Then the question becomes: how are we to call the people forth? How are we to make them come? This calling forth, we see now, is the purpose of the work. The purpose of a work of art or a work of philosophy lies in calling forth a new people. But the unlimited straight line of time implies the work can only and must necessarily call forth a new people, a "*demos*," that always remains *to come*. In this way, we see, finally, that the reversal of Platonism does not land us in an ideal city. It places us in a land that has no borders, where the people are so aware of being at war with themselves that they never stop letting themselves become other than what they are.

References

Deleuze, Gilles (1964) *Proust et les signes*, Paris: Presses Universitaires de France.
Deleuze, Gilles (1968) *Différence et répétition*. Paris: Presses Universitaires de France.
Deleuze, Gilles (1969) *Logique du sens*. Paris: Minuit.
Deleuze, Gilles (1990) *Logic of Sense*, tr. Mark Lester and Charles Stivale, ed. Constantin Boundas. New York: Columbia University Press.
Deleuze, Gilles (1995) *Difference and Repetition*, tr. Paul Patton. New York: Columbia University Press.
Deleuze, Gilles (2003) *Proust and Signs. The Complete Text*, tr. Richard Howard Minneapolis: University of Minnesota.
Deleuze, Gilles and Guattari, Félix (1991) *Qu'est-ce que la philosophie?* Paris: Minuit.
Deleuze, Gilles and Guattari, Félix (1994) *What Is Philosophy?*, tr. Hugh Tomlinson and Graham Burchell. New York: Columbia University Press.
Derrida, Jacques (1967a) "Violence et métaphysique." in Jacques Derrida, *L'écriture et la différence*. Paris: Points Seuil, pp. 117–227.
Derrida, Jacques (1967b) *La voix et le phénomène*. Paris: Presses Universitaires de France.
Derrida, Jacques (1978) "Violence and Metaphysics," tr. Alan Bass. In: Jacques Derrida, *Writing and Difference*. Chicago: University of Chicago Press, pp. 79–153.
Derrida, Jacques (1987) *De l'esprit*. Paris: Galilée.
Derrida, Jacques (1989) *Of Spirit*, tr. Geoff Bennington and Rachel Bowlby. Chicago: University of Chicago Press.

Derrida, Jacques (1992) "'Il faut bien manger,' ou calcu du sujet." In: Jacques Derrida, *Points de suspension, Entretiens*. Paris: Galilée, pp. 269–302.
Derrida, Jacques (1995) "'Eating Well,' or the Caculation of the Subject," tr. Peter Connor and Avital Ronell. In: Jacques Derrida, *Points ... Interviews, 1974–1994*, ed. Elizabeth Weber. Stanford: Stanford University Press, pp. 255–287.
Derrida, Jacques (2011) *Voice and Phenomenon*, tr. Leonard Lawlor. Evanston, IL: Northwestern University Press.
Evans, Fred (2008) *The Multivoiced Body: Society and Communication in the Age of Diversity.* New York: Columbia University Press.
Husserl, Edmund (1950) *Ideen zu einer reinen Phänomenologie und Phänomenologischen Philosophie. Erstes Buch.* In: Edmund Husserl, *Husserliana*, vol. 3. The Hague: Nijhoff.
Husserl, Edmund (1968) *Phänomenologische Psychologie.* The Hague: Nijhoff.
Husserl, Edmund (1970) *The Crisis of European Sciences and Transcendental Phenomenology*, tr. David Carr. Evanston: Northwestern University Press.
Husserl, Edmund (1976) *Die Krisis der Europäischen Wissenschaft und die Transzendentale Phänomenologie.* In: Edmund Husserl, *Husserliana*, vol. 6. The Hague: Nijhoff.
Husserl, Edmund (1983) *Ideas Pertaining to a Pure Phenomenology and to a Phenomenological Philosophy*, First Book, tr. Fred Kersten. The Hague: Nijhoff.
Husserl, Edmund (1997) *Psychological and Transcendental Phenomenology and the Confrontation with Heidegger* (1927–1931), tr. and ed. Thomas Sheehan and Richard E. Palmer. Dordrecht: Kluwer.
Kockelmans, Joseph J. (1994) *Edmund Husserl's Phenomenology.* West Lafayette, IN: Purdue University Press.
Landgrebe, Ludwig (1981) "Husserl's Departure from Cartesianism." In: Ludwig Landgrebe, *The Phenomenology of Edmund Husserl*, ed. with an introduction by Donn Welton. Ithaca, NY: Cornell University Press, pp. 66–121.
Lawlor, Leonard (2008) "Following the Rats: An Essay on the Concept of Becoming-Animal in Deleuze and Guattari." *Sub-Stance* (The Political Animal, Issue 117) 37(3): 169–187.
Nietzsche, Friedrich (1968) *The Portable Nietzsche*, tr. Walter Kaufmann. New York: Viking.
Plato (1939) *Cratylus, Parmenides, Greater Hippias, Lesser Hippias*, tr. Harold North Fowler. Cambridge, MA: Harvard University Press.
Plato (1961) "Parmenides," tr. F.M. Cornford. In: *The Collected Dialogues of Plato*, ed. Edith Hamilton and Huntington Cairns. Princeton, NJ: Princeton University Press.
Plato (1968) *The Republic of Plato*, tr. Allan Bloom. New York: Basic Books.
Plato (1987) *Republic* II, tr. Paul Shorey. Cambridge, MA: Harvard University Press.
Sallis, John (1986) *Being and Logos: The Way of Platonic Dialogue.* Atlantic Highlands, NJ: Humanities Press.

Robert C. Scharff

Heidegger: Hermeneutics as "Preparation" for Thinking

Abstract: Heidegger's unsympathetic reaction to Husserl's "theoretical-scientific attitude" in his *Logos* article is well-known. What is not so well-known is Dilthey's role in Heidegger's forming this reaction. In fact, it is Dilthey's idea of understanding historical life "in its own terms" that inspired Heidegger's early, and quite un-Husserlian, conception of phenomenology as a philosophy requiring "hermeneutical" preparation; and in this context, it is also through Dilthey that Heidegger came to think that in Nietzsche's second *Untimely Mediation*, he "understood more about [being historical] than he made known."

During a 1917 exchange about the role of logic in philosophy, Heidegger wrote to Rickert that as far he was concerned,

> Pure logic is something extreme, a disguised criminal assault on the living mind—[and this is so] even if [its idea of] "absolute validity" makes it appealing to all those who are terrified of relativism, and if it attracts and comforts [so-called] "critical" realists obsessed about their precious "external world." (Heidegger/Rickert 2002, p. 38)[1]

Obviously, Heidegger is not launching an assault on good reasoning. Rather, he knows that "Pure Logic" and "Absolute Validity" have become powerful cultural metaphors that promote an undeservedly dominant philosophical outlook—an outlook achieved by expanding the model of cognition in the natural sciences, driving an epistemic wedge between "purely logical" thought and the allegedly sloppy ruminations of everyday life, and then calling the former the only genuine model for objective knowledge and the latter, its forgettable and merely sub-

---

1 [*Die reine Logik ist ein Extrem, eine verkappte Vergewaltigung des lebendigen Geistes—sosehr auch die 'absolute Geltung' als Empfehlung alle vom Relativismus Verängstigten und um die Existenz der lieben 'Außenwelt' so bekümmerten 'kritischen' Realisten anlockt und sanft beruhigt*]. Heidegger/Rickert 2002, p. 38. "Rape" is perhaps the more obvious translation of *Vergewaltigung*, but "violent assault" seems to come closer here since in German it is used as a legal term to cover more than just rape (which is often rendered "*sexuelle Verwaltigung*," precisely for this reason). "*Lieben*" is clearly sarcastic. I ignore here some surprising features of this exchange, e.g., its early date, and the fact that Heidegger, the student, had the sort of relationship with Rickert, the teacher, that allows for such frankness.

https://doi.org/10.1515/9783110551563-020

jective origin. As the passage suggests, the young Heidegger is already intensely concerned with becoming a philosopher who does not think from this outlook.[2] And if he regards this generally Cartesian and specifically neo-Kantian stance toward lived experience as bordering on the philosophically criminal, it is certainly no surprise that he is also critical of the "theoretical-scientific attitude" he finds in Husserl's famous *Logos* article.[3]

At the very same time, however, Heidegger is also giving high praise to Dilthey, who wants to understand life "in its own terms" by using special categories drawn from life itself instead of concepts theoretically imposed upon it. And still more important is Dilthey's ontologically pluralistic way of depicting nature and history, not just as different research topics, but as different "expressions of life" that require natural and human scientists to think differently. To understand instead of explain, he says, human scientists must become "interpreters of historical life" instead of being observant theorizers of nature. They must "be" the kind of thinkers who derive their sense of what they are studying, not from a pre-established method or regional ontology, but directly through a conscious enhancement of their own lived sense of the "whole sphere of experience," where we are just as much related to understandable others as we are to externally encountered objects.[4]

It is in this context—where Heidegger is eagerly learning from Dilthey about understanding life in its own terms—that we may recall *Sein und Zeit*'s famous remark about Nietzsche's second *Untimely Meditation*—namely that in it, Nietzsche seems to "understand more than he makes known to us" about being-historical. (Heidegger 1962, p. 448)). I will return to this remark, but first a bit more about Heidegger's retrieval of Dilthey.

---

2 Indeed, a lead question in a number of the early lecture courses is how to respond to his culture's scientistic assault on the minds of aspiring philosophers—a question, he says, that is made all the more urgent because the tendency to privilege "theorizing" and "objectification" seems to come so naturally to us Heidegger 2000, pp. 94–96 [GA 56/57: 112–14].

3 Husserl's phenomenology, Heidegger frequently says, isn't very phenomenological. See, e.g., Heidegger 2000, pp. 92–93 [GA 56/57: 109–10], where Husserl is said to betray his own "principle of principles" (Heidegger refers to *Ideas I*, §24), by assuming that there must be some sort of reflective separation between life and the study of it, even for phenomenology. Cf., Heidegger 1985, pp. 75–80 [GA 20: 103–11].

4 In GA 59, Heidegger contrasts Dilthey's "immanent illumination of life experience that remains in this experience itself and does not step out and turn it into objectivity" (Heidegger 2010, p. 131 [GA 59: 171] and generally §§16–19) with Natorp's devitalization or "de-vivification" of life through his theoretical reconstruction of it (§§17, 20). I will return to the glaringly implicated but unasked question here, viz., "who" is philosophically qualified to *distinguish* various ways of expressing the concerns of life?

1 Dilthey and the "Sphere of Lived Experience"

At first, Dilthey treated the idea of understanding life in its own terms primarily in relation to his plan for an epistemology of the human sciences. He described himself as making room for such sciences, more or less side-by-side with the natural sciences, with each type possessing its own method, purpose, and subject matter. Eventually, however, he began to realize that an epistemologist of either sort of science is faced with a wider problem. If natural science "explains" and human science "understands," then the ultimate epistemic task must be to show how explaining and understanding are *both* existential possibilities. Hence, by the end of his life, Dilthey had developed an ambiguous stance toward both kinds of science, continuing to portray their differences epistemologically, but also as "manifesting life" in fundamentally different ways.

Heidegger saw clearly the radical implication of the later Dilthey's expanded epistemological vision: The effort to understand life in its own terms ultimately requires a kind of philosophy that does not start with epistemology—that is, a philosophy that does not begin by taking the usual "reflective" distance from life, and then conceptually reconstructing one or two scientific methods and leaving them side by side. Rather, one needs a philosophy that begins more deeply embedded in experience and cultivates a *Selbstbesinnung*—that is, a mindfully enhanced, but undistanced awareness of the living-through of life—so that one sees how life itself can be the origin of multiple expressive possibilities, some scientific, some not. Only such a philosophy—a "phenomenological" philosophy, says Heidegger—would "sink back down into life as such," "experientially go along with the experiencing of life," and thus be in a position to describe life's "intensifications" pluralistically. For the traditional epistemological mind, of course, a philosophy that takes no distance from life is impossible. As everyone knows, lived experience is a kind of "puzzling presence of determinacy prior to all theoretical description...for which one invents the convenient title of 'the irrational.'"[5] Within two years, Heidegger is calling this "puzzling presence"

5 Heidegger 2000, pp. 188, 99 [GA 56/57: 220, 187]. I prefer "determinacy" to Sadler's "something determinate," because I think that Heidegger may well be using Hegel's "*Bestimmtheit*" in a provocative fashion here. This quote is from the War Emergency Semester 1919, and it is clear evidence of what Theodore Kisiel calls Heidegger's "phenomenological breakthrough." As I argue elsewhere, without his extensive study of Dilthey, at least somewhat earlier than his study of Husserl, there would have been no such breakthrough. See Scharff 2013. "*Steigerung*" (intensification) is a wonderfully phenomenological choice; in German, it also means increase, heighten, escalate, boost, improve, enhance...perhaps here all of them.

our facticity, urging us to discover in it "what goes on in philosophy before it becomes what it is," and assigning this task to "hermeneutics."[6]

Even in 1919, however, Heidegger is already preoccupied with the task if not the name of a hermeneutics of philosophy's own facticity, and with the question of how to move away from the traditional epistemological stance of modern philosophy and back into life.[7] So much noise has always been made about Heidegger's Ontological Turn that the question of "who" is capable of making such a turn is often neglected. As he puts it in WS 1923/24, Dilthey's writings show us that when the issue is how best to become philosophically responsive to the things themselves, it is wrong to privilege the natural scientific imagery of "known knowledge"—not because it makes some things ontologically invisible, but because it only makes *objects encountered by a theorizing consciousness* visible in a phenomenological way. However generously defined and universalized, "knowing" remains only one manifestation of *Sorge*. In Heidegger's phrasing, "everything that crosses the path of this [predominant mode of] care is cared for in such a way that what is not cared for is not just 'merely not there' but is instead cared for as something that does not have to be there" (Heidegger 2006, p. 62 [GA 17: 85]). From the viewpoint of known knowledge, the non-objective is present, sort of, but not in a way that matters philosophically. A second kind of science, or any extra-scientific practice, or any account of how things are "experienced"—none of these phenomena have to be there, when the issue is the understanding of What Really Is. Hence, a phenomenological philosophy's first question must be a preliminary one: How does thinking avoid being trapped in this "self-ensnaring" circularity? How is it that we are already engaged with our surroundings, such that even when it becomes obvious that life is articulated in *various* ways, only one way continues to be sanctioned? And now that this unwarranted hegemony is revealed, what is to be done?

It is in relation to this line of questioning that Heidegger sees Dilthey's real promise. What Dilthey's work discloses is that his initial problem regarding the human sciences "is not a separate [epistemic or regionally ontological] problem

---

6 Heidegger 1999, pp. 15–16, 46, 40 [GA 63: 20, 58, 51]. In *Being and Time* (Heidegger 1962), the analysis of Dasein is, of course, the ultimate expression of this interest. That this is ultimately going to require something like a full-dress *Daseinsanalytik* seems clear in retrospect between the lines in every chapter of GA 63.

7 There is of course a longer story here involving much more than just our inheritance of a Cartesian legacy, or indeed of the question of inheriting itself, as a human characteristic. But this is a short paper, and as far as I can see, Heidegger's concern for "who" philosophizes—as opposed to what tools a rational mind uses to think in certain well-recognized ways—informs his thought from beginning to end, but is most accessible *as a topic* in the early lectures.

but the expression [*Ausdruck*] of an ultimate philosophical motive: to interpret life from out of itself, [that is,] primordially."[8] It is this motive that animates Dilthey's life-long, "restive" [*unruhig*] path "toward the question of life" (Heidegger 1962, pp. 72–73). To follow out this path is to realize that in the end, we must come to an understanding that historical-human life is not just an object of scientific research but is also "the root of the sciences." And "hermeneutics is the way this understanding enlightens itself" (Ibid., pp. 450). Only a "hermeneutically enlightened" thinker—that is, an aspiring phenomenologist who is actually *being* phenomenological—can understand life in its own terms, no matter what its manifestations.

With this insight, says Heidegger, we come as far as Dilthey can take us. Regarding who and how we are, and regarding the fact that in spite of our apparent inclination to theorize from a distance, we can learn to "sink back down into" life itself and "experientially go along with experience" in various ways, without "assaulting" this experience with a pre-established method—on these issues, Dilthey has nothing explicit to say. For all its promise, the direction of his inquiries remains anchored by his original epistemological mission. He deserves credit for having disclosed a proto-phenomenological "standpoint of life." But he never makes this standpoint itself an actual topic, let alone consider what it is like to take such a standpoint, and so he never interprets it as a possible *philosophical* orientation that is only sometimes concerned with the life's *scientific* articulations.

Yet if Dilthey never considers these issues, he leaves some clues concerning how *we* might do so. Given life's historical character, he says, its "first categorical determination" must be "temporality."[9] This late remark gives us two things to consider. First, the temporality Dilthey has in mind is *Zeitlichkeit*, "lived time," not *Zeit*, the traditional notion of cosmic or world time. The very description of historical life as a process, says Dilthey, already intimates how different this experiential sense of time is. Life is lived "through" time, not "in" it. Our experience is structured by a sense of presently-going-into-the-future-as-having-already-been that is lived through as a unified process before it is conceptually seg-

---

8 Heidegger 2010, p. 119 [GA 59: 154]. "Expression" is *Ausdruck*, which is Dilthey's favored term for manifestations of life, whether they are purely theoretical, involve moral and practical actions, or reveal the depths of experience in an especially palpable way, as in poetry and art. I discuss this appropriation of Dilthey in detail in Scharff 2015, pp. 167–174; 246–256.

9 In full: "Temporality is contained in life as its first categorical determination, the one that is fundamental for all the others. The expression 'passage of life' already points to this temporality. Time [*Zeit*] is there for us, by means of [*vermöge*] the gathering unity of our conscious awareness" (Dilthey 2002, pp. 214–15).

mented. But second, Dilthey's characterization of this temporality is always somewhat defensive. He says it is "another" kind of time that needs "special" categories that are "not" theoretical.

Taking these two considerations together, we may conclude as follows. On the one hand, what is actually *displayed* in Dilthey's work is not just an expanded epistemology, but the possibility of a philosophy that would begin with a heightened awareness of what really goes on in life, such that it can be temporally articulated in various ways in response to various sorts of lived-through engagements with our surroundings. Yet on the other hand, the defensive cast of Dilthey's language shows how his work is as much hindered as furthered by the intellectual context in which he pursues it. The inherited philosophical and cultural atmosphere in which Dilthey tries to understand life in its own terms did not just evoke criticism from others. It often mars his own accounts of what he is doing—as, for example, when he settles for characterizing human science as a "second" kind of science and assures us that it is really "objective," too, in its own way. In short, we can say that Dilthey arrives at his present task, intellectually "burdened" by an inheritance that prevents him from taking up this task in a way that is fully responsive to his currently experienced need. Here, of course, I use Nietzsche's language. His second *Untimely Meditation* addresses just this sort of "burdensomeness," and so can shed further light on the temporality Dilthey identifies as lying at the heart of our historical life experience.

2 What Nietzsche "Understands" About Historical Life

My aim, says Nietzsche in the second *Untimely Meditation*, is to consider a "need for historical science...quite different from that of the spoiled idler in the garden of knowledge."[10] Note that Nietzsche turns first, not to his topic but rather to his sense of *who he is* when he asks, How might we require *Historie* "for life"? In

10 Nietzsche 1997, pp. 60 – 61. Hereafter UM2. It is useful to remember that the title of this essay is "*Die Nutzen und Nachteil der Historie* [not *Geschichte*] *für das Lebens.*" As Heidegger remarks, apropos this line, "It is not a matter of expanding our stock of knowledge, but rather *seeing with different eyes*, so that we can discover what ordinary views and opinions are *not* able to see and do not need to see for their immediate purposes" (Heidegger 2016, pp. 18 – 19 [GA 46: 21 – 22], my emphasis. GA 46 critically traces Nietzsche's own path, but always with the idea of its retrieval in mind. There is something right but also opaque, e.g., about contrasting the seemingly "unhistorical" character of animal's existence with the "historical" character of human existence. See n.11.

what sense must we be "needy," such that monumental, antiquarian, and critical history—which are "poisons" when they merely "instruct" us, but are somehow "life-giving" in the right doses—might be "advantageous" to us? For Nietzsche as for Heidegger, to address *these* questions is to show a concern for what it means to *be historical*, rather than just an intellectual interest in the past.

Our existence, he says, is an "always imperfect tense that never becomes a perfect one" (UM2, 61). Like Dilthey, Nietzsche sees life as involving a special sort of experienced temporality. In a famous metaphor that has sometimes been hilariously misunderstood as expressing Nietzsche's "biological" outlook, he contrasts human existence with animal life. Beasts in the field, he says, seem to

> know nothing of yesterday or today but merely leap about, eat, rest, digest, leap about again, and so continue from morning to night, day after day, tethered to the moment and enthralled by its pleasures or displeasures, and thus neither melancholy nor bored.[11]

Nietzsche is not making an empirical claim about herd animals here. His point is about how the appearance of such a life, real or not, might sometimes strike *us*. Think of it: An existence that is never boring or distressing, where pleasures and displeasures are neither anticipated nor missed, and where the contentment of the moment occurs and passes, again and again, automatically and effortlessly. In a word, animals can seem to us to live "unhistorically," entirely for the moment, and we know, alas, that we do not. For us, a beast's apparently easy and accidental happiness is never possible, because our "present" is never just a "now."

Of course we can chose to conceive our lives as a series of moments. But what our lives *are* to us, directly and experientially, is not a string of separate units. Every lived moment is thick with a sense of the past and the future. Every present, says Nietzsche, comes to us already infused with our "having been," that is, with a historically determinate sense of who and how we under-

11 UM2, p. 59. In my reading, I stick closely to the direction of Nietzsche's own analysis of *Historie* and its relation to human life. In Heidegger's later reading of UM 2, this analysis is followed "thoughtfully" from the beginning, i. e., in relation to the ontological questions left unasked and determinations left vague. So, e. g., Heidegger makes much of a double sense in which humans and animals can be "compared," in order to show that Nietzsche rightly pushes us toward the philosophical question of the "specialness" of human beings, not just their biological difference; for the issue is not whether human beings are "superior" to animals (an idea that is basically a kind of confused and muddled mixture of biological and philosophical ideas) but instead the fact that it is from out of human life that the questions of animality, forgetting/remembering, being historical/unhistorical, etc., arise in the first place (Heidegger 2016, pp. 18–42 [GA 46: 21–52]).

stand ourselves to be. We are always already "da," Heidegger will say, simultaneously blessed and cursed with lingering thoughts and habits that prefigure how it seems things will be, have been, and thus already "live" in all our thoughts and deeds. Unlike Nietzsche's beasts, this temporal prefiguration is unavoidable for us—not because our wills are too weak to stop it but because we are living out an inheritance that is inevitably there as something *to* forget, remember, and struggle with.

It is in terms of this sense of the lived time of historical beings that Nietzsche explains our threefold need for historical knowledge.[12] The echo of this discussion in *Being and Time*'s chapter on historicity and temporality is unmistakable. In both accounts, the central ontological fact about us is our uneasy historicity. Past events and old theories may be gone; but their *having been enacted* still shapes our inherited sense of what there is and what it means. Yet who we have become is never quite suited to deal with how we currently find ourselves, and we know this because we are already "burdened" with the prospect of an unsatisfactory future. Historical knowledge promises to illuminate how we unsatisfactorily "are" to ourselves. It is our entrée to the Delphic invitation to "Know thyself."[13] Monumental, antiquarian, and critical histories are thus not professional specializations; they are ways in which *Historie* can "belong to the living person" (UM2, p. 67). It is only in this possible "belonging" that historical knowledge might be *nützlich*—that is, useful, of service, advantageous as a source of existential awakening in light of present need.

Historians and philosophical pragmatists do not understand this need. They have pledged to come *to* life with their methods, their theories, their problem-solving mentality, and their "outcomes-based" assessments, instead of starting *from* life and responding to its experienced rather than conceptually pre-shaped

---

12 In general, Nietzsche's account of the three histories is well-known. *Monumental history* identifies exemplary individuals who can inspire us to see great possibilities. *Antiquarian history*'s comprehensive reconstructions of the past can awaken an appreciation for the way our inheritance makes possible genuine growth, not merely arbitrary change. *Critical history* can move us to assess and finally condemn this same inheritance by reminding us that we still suffer from the injustices that remain part of it. Together, the three histories illuminate in their advantages the three phases of the lived time—or better, historicity—that Dilthey identifies but never analyzes. For detailed discussion, see Scharff 2015, pp. 199–215.

13 UM2, p. 122. Thus in my view, Nietzsche also shares the sense that inherited burdensomeness already comes back at us *from* the future. Burdensomness is not a mere projection from an unsatisfactory present, and this makes all the difference in determining the "philosophical motivation" for Socratic self-understanding. If one sees that motivation as arising from the present, it can only be a matter of anger about one's inheritance or something like a "theoretical" picture of what we can do "now" to twist free of it. No wonder liberation *theories* never satisfy....

dissatisfactions. For those in "need," the test comes "from within" the life they are aspiring to live, and it is specific to this need. This is the point Nietzsche stresses. He intends to work out a *lived relation* with historical science—that is, to analyze three ways in which knowledge of the human past can strengthen our capacity to feel and respond to the "burden" of our inheritance, to quicken our sense of a lack of fit between what we have already become and what we currently experience, and to educate our sense of how we might yet be.

3 Retrieving Dilthey and Nietzsche for Our Sake

I have explained briefly how Heidegger hermeneutically *retrieves* Dilthey and Nietzsche's understanding of temporality. But let me emphasize that he also asks, in a *destructive* vein: How is it possible for them to show us so much of life's genuinely historical-temporal condition but fail to tell us about it? Put quickly, it is because they do not entirely know "who" they are. Neither of them fully recognizes how the very temporality they disclose to us, functions in their own thinking in a way that reinforces their tendency to give tradition-bound accounts of this very functioning. Dilthey's wider epistemological "problem" and Nietzsche's "burdensome" inheritance are not, as they assume, phenomena that originate in what they are just *presently* attending to. Rather, they manifest *inherited issues*, expressive of a natural-scientistic tradition and experienced by Dilthey and Nietzsche as present problems only because these issues already come back toward them as demands from a projected *future*. Phenomenologically speaking, Dilthey is right to privilege temporality over cosmic time, and Nietzsche, this temporality's futurity; but they mistakenly assume they can defuse the burdensomeness of the traditional counter-treatments of such phenomena through acts of *present* resolve.

What is missing in Dilthey and Nietzsche is an analysis of how traditional dogma prevents their explicitly telling us what they understand—an analysis, as Heidegger's *Sein und Zeit* puts it, of how in everyday life we are

> not only inclined to be caught up in the world of ordinary affairs so that we fall into interpreting ourselves in its reflected light [but also]...to fall in with a tradition we have more or less explicitly taken hold of—a tradition that deprives us of providing our own guidance in asking questions and making choices.[14]

---

14 Heidegger 1962, p. 42–43. My choice of "dogmas" is deliberate and is intended to draw a comparison to Heidegger's reference to the three dogmas, or roadblocks, that seem to prevent a productive way of raising the Being-question again (Ibid., pp. 2–4). I also think it's important

What Heidegger calls "falling in with a tradition" is always the leading feature of being-historical. It dominates our initial condition—as Dilthey and Nietzsche demonstrate in their struggle to describe their projects, while being *both* caught up in the ordinary and traditional *and also* motivated by convictions that something less familiar, obvious, and oppressive is possible. The source of the traditional impediments to their saying appropriately what is most important to them is *existence itself in its movement away from an awareness of its own movement.* Thus Dilthey, who already "has" an orthodox conception of science, assumes that even studying life in its own terms must somehow be accomplished "scientifically." And Nietzsche often tries to further creative life by repeatedly overstating in combative and anti-traditional terms how to take the right dose of something that is already poisonously overvalued.

Hence, to retrieve what Dilthey and Nietzsche understand about historicity, we must focus *right there, at the place where they are living through* a tradition-burdened effort to further non-standard possibilities—and we must do so while taking with us what we have learned from their writings, namely, that in any struggle to become who we are, our past "*does not follow along after us but rather always already goes ahead of us.*"[15] Our default condition is to "fall into" interpreting *ourselves* in the reflected light of everyday involvements and traditional tendencies. Doing better, says Heidegger, means learning *how* to be "futural" (Heidegger 1992, p. 20 [GA 64: 123]).

Yet all of this can be *said* too easily. *Achieving* such an interpretive focus requires refusing to depict being-historical as a topic or object and instead attempting to mindfully experience being-historical as the very condition *we already live through in the process of trying to ask about it.* Fallenness is not a hazard to be avoided or "authentically" conquered. It is something we always take with us,

---

not to lose the "always-alreadiness" intended in "*ausdrücklich ergriffenen Tradition*" by translating "*ergriffenen*" as something like "*seize*," or "*take up.*" The point is that "*ergriffenen*" characterizes an aspect of our condition that involves more than just a passive and mindless "absorbing," but also something less than an active and deliberate "embracing."

15 Heidegger 1962, p. 41, emphasis altered. I draw on 1927 language, but the idea is already present in the 1920 Jaspers review: "The proper [*eigentlich*] experience of having-myself extends historically into the past of the 'I.' This past is not like an appendage that the 'I' drags along with itself, but rather is experienced historically as the past of an 'I' *within a horizon of expectations already placed ahead of itself by itself* ....The phenomenological explication of how of this enactment of experience accords with its fundamental historical sense is the most important task in the entire complex of problems relating to the phenomena of existence...[and] little is to be gained in this regard from an external account of the psychical that stresses the interaction of past and future states working together in 'consciousness'" (Heidegger 1998, pp. 27–28 [GA 9: 31–31], my emphasis]). See also, Kisiel and Sheehan (2007), pp. 114–115, pp. 139–140.

something that informs our corporeal, linguistic, cultural, social, and intellectual embodiment—and no more obviously so than when we announce proudly that we have already become post-positivist or post-modern. A really phenomenological philosophy acknowledges and acts from this double sense of being-historical. But there is more. Even the best phenomenology, warns Heidegger, never finally *becomes* phenomenological. It can only provide an adequate counterthrust to the weight of tradition in its *practice*; it can "prove itself only through itself," he says, with no advance embrace of a well-prepared standpoint or method.[16] To picture a philosophizing that throws off its traditional impediments and communes with the things themselves is to imagine *not* being-historical. Hence, any philosophy that wishes to be stimulated more by life's burdens than by social convention and tradition, must be mindful that a concern for "being-historical *fallingly*" must remain co-extensive with its actual practice.

4 Coda: Being-historical in Technoscientific Times

After *Sein und Zeit*, as we know, Heidegger's further consideration of our "insurmountably historical" condition eventually led him to see that *Verfallen* is ultimately not a human weakness, nor even entirely understandable in terms of Dasein. Yet as we retrace this thought-path, it is worth remembering why Heidegger retrieved Dilthey and Nietzsche in the first place. I think it is probably true that only something like Heidegger's Being-question, taken up and followed through to the possibility of thinking at the end of a dismantled onto-theological tradition, can actually open us up to considering how "the world civilization just now beginning might someday overcome its technoscientific-industrial character

---

16 Heidegger 2000, p. 93 [GA 56/57:110]; cf. Heidegger 2001, p. 31 [GA 61: 39–40]; Heidegger 1999, p. 37 [GA 63:46]. Here is the "phenomenological" meaning of the idea of a presuppositionless philosophy. It does not mean starting with Nothing from Nowhere, which is in any case just a distorted conception of "being" a conscious knower. Rather, it means continuously struggling and practicing to "be" phenomenologically comported, without availing oneself of any preconceptions about what sort of "standpoint" one must have to do so (Heidegger 2013, p. 92 [GA 58: 109]). So Husserl is partially right. Life as lived as well as its manifestations are not just given to us; they must be won (Ibid., p. 29 [24]). For Husserl himself, life *as lived* ultimately proved elusive. The *Umwelt* that the young Heidegger would have phenomenology "sink back into" remains for Husserl a "merely cultural" site of worldviews spun by "noble spirits" and of naïve beliefs about nature—making it, as Heidegger puts it in *Being and Time*'s introduction, a "mere aspect" of what transcendental phenomenologists cognize in essentialist terms rather than the characteristic way in which existence is "had" as is described by hermeneutic phenomenologists (Heidegger 1962, p. 44).

as the sole criterion for our journey through the world."[17] But I see a prior question: Hermeneutically speaking, is our 2017 any more encouraging of a phenomenological philosophy of thoughtful openness than Heidegger's 1919? I think the answer is clearly, No.

What has been and is still going on, is that Dasein is "being-interpreted" such that we "are" either socially determined entities or rational animals—and thus related to everything as either practical agents expressing cultural preferences or objective minds calculating natural events.[18] Of course, practical agents and calculating minds do not ask about technology's essence, let alone imagine working out of a free relation with it. Rather, "one" simply assumes that whatever seems experientially burdensome about science and technology will find its solution in making them still more useful, efficient, and rational.[19] No immanent analysis of the "world" in which one "puts scientific theory into technological practice," whether eagerly or reluctantly, will ever lead to a "thoughtful questioning" *of* technoscience. To make such questioning possible, one must first learn to "become" a thoughtful questioner instead of just "falling into" being and remaining a practical agent or calculating mind.

In the meantime, our current conception of a "developed" world still resonates with 19th century positivism, as does our continuing to privilege mathematical reasoning, visual perception, the primary realness of the logical and the material, the idea that there is a technique (and a machine) for everything, and that true intelligibility is a function of explicit, criteria-tested, comprehensive theoriz-

17 Heidegger 1972, p. 60 [GA 14: 75]. "[E]very attempt to gain insight into the supposed task of thinking finds itself moved to review the whole of the history of philosophy. Not only this, but it is even forced to think the historicity of that which grants a possible history to philosophy" (Ibid.).

18 Heidegger 1999, 28–52 [GA 63: 35–66. To get behind this, Heidegger suggests, for the time being we should just "assume that everything asserted in philosophy is pure, incontrovertible truth," set it aside, and move on to the hermeneutical task of considering how the reigning "philosophies" interpret (mostly without acknowledgement) "who" philosophers "are." Of course for this task, "no methodology or philosophical logic could give a proper explanation...because it would itself have to be a theory in the same sense as this philosophy itself" (Heidegger 1999, 46 [GA 63: 58). It is misleading, I think, for van Buren to call being-interpreted [*Ausgelegtheit*] a forerunner of *das Man* in *Sein und Zeit* (Heidegger 1999, pp. 116–117n.36), because this ignores what Heidegger also clearly intends to include here, viz., the way we "fall in with a tradition..." such that "what one says" becomes codified in philosophical "dogma."

19 Heidegger 1977, p. 3 [GA 7: 7]. A solution, in other words, that typically involves utilitarian and positivist accounts of "what everyone knows" about technology and science (Ibid., pp. 4–6 [GA 7: 8–9].

ing.[20] Modern philosophy thus remains *our* “burdensome” inheritance. Our default position remains that Reality is only properly encountered at an “informed” distance from experience. “Techniques” insure that everyone does the distance-taking the same way. “Education” means learning these techniques. And of course, critically assessing this state-of-affairs might be of interest to historians, social theorists, psychoanalysts, and biographers, but it is “not philosophy.”

All of this makes Heidegger’s early struggle to appropriate Dilthey and Nietzsche at Husserl’s expense especially attractive to me. Preparing to “be” a philosopher who avoids technique-happiness, cultivates a *Besinnung* that takes no distance from lived experience, has no interest in founding a philosophical school, and seeks a language that is “not yet” representational—all of these “preliminaries” seem to me something well worth “retrieving” from Heidegger’s early lectures, all the more so because there we find them so often expressed in problematic, disorganized, tradition-bound—in short, “destructible”—language. For this forces us to make their retrieval *our* retrieval, where hermeneutic adjustments for differences of time and place are obviously necessary, not optional.[21]

Acknowledgements

A version of this essay, with extended analysis of Nietzsche’s discussion of the three histories is available in the Conference Proceedings of the 2017 Heidegger Circle meeting at <http://www.heideggercircle.org/history.html>. My thanks to Daniel Dahlstrom, Robert Crease, Eugene Gendlin, and Natalie Nenadic for discussions of early drafts.

References

Dilthey, Wilhelm (2002) *Selected Works, Vol. 3: The Formation of the Historical World in the Human Sciences*, tr. Rudolf A. Makkreel, et al. Princeton: Princeton University Press.

Heidegger, Martin /Heinrich Rickert (2002) *Briefe 1912 bis 1933 u. Andere Dokumente*, Alfred Denker (ed.) Frankfurt a. M.: Klostermann.

Heidegger, Martin (1975–) *Gesamtausgabe* [GA], Frankfurt: Klostermann, 102 vols ff.

---

20 On the relation between Comte’s conception of the third, scientific stage of human progress and the latent positivism of our third-stage-like conception of the “developed” world, see Scharff (2017) and (2010). See also, Scharff 2015, pp. 147–54.

21 “We shall never experience our relationship to the essence of technology so long as we merely conceive and push forward the technological, put up with it, or evade it” (Heidegger 1977, p. 3 [GA 7: 7]).

Heidegger, Martin (1962). *Being and Time*, tr. John Macquarrie and Edward Robinson. New York: Harper and Row. [GA 2]

Heidegger, Martin (1972) *On Time and Being*, tr. Joan Stambaugh. New York: Harper and Row. [GA 14]

Heidegger, Martin (1977) *The Question Concerning Technology and Other Essays*, tr. William Lovitt. New York: Harper and Row. [GA 7, translations of the first, second, and fourth essay]

Heidegger, Martin (1985) *History and the Concept of Time: Prolegomena*, tr. Theodore Kisiel. Bloomington: Indiana University Press. [GA 20]

Heidegger, Martin (1992) *The Concept of Time*, tr. William McNeill. Oxford: Blackwell [Bilingual edition, incorporates GA 64: 105–25]

Heidegger, Martin (1998) *Pathmarks*, tr. John van Buren. Cambridge, Cambridge University Press. [GA 9]

Heidegger, Martin (1999) *Ontology—Hermeneutics of Facticity*, tr. John van Buren. Bloomington: Indiana University Press. [GA 63]

Heidegger, Martin (2000) *Towards the Definition of Philosophy*, tr. Ted Sadler. New York: Continuum. [GA 56/57]

Heidegger, Martin (2001) *Phenomenological Interpretations of Aristotle: Initiations into Phenomenological Research*, tr. Richard Rojcewicz. Bloomington: Indiana University Press [GA 61]

Heidegger, Martin (2006) *Introduction to Phenomenological Research*, tr. Daniel O. Dahlstrom. Bloomington: Indiana University Press [GA 17]

Heidegger, Martin (2010) *Phenomenology of Intuition and Expression*, tr. Tracy Colony. New York: Continuum. [GA 59]

Heidegger, Martin (2013) *Basic Problems of Phenomenology: Winter Semester 1919/1920*, tr. Scott M. Campbell. New York: Bloomsbury [GA 58]

Heidegger, Martin (2016) *Interpretation of Nietzsche's Second Untimely Meditation*, tr. Ullrich Haase and Mark Sinclair. Bloomington: Indiana University Press. [GA 46]

Kisiel, Theodore and Thomas Sheehan (eds.) (2007) *Becoming Heidegger: On the Trail of His Early Occasional Writings, 1910–1927*. Evanston: Northwestern University Press.

Nietzsche, Friedrich (1997) *Untimely Meditations*, tr. R.J. Hollingdale. Cambridge: Cambridge University Press.

Scharff, Robert C. (2010) "Comte's Positivist Dream, Our Post-Positivist Problem." In: Dean Moyar (ed.) *The Routledge Companion to Nineteenth Century Philosophy*, New York: Routledge, pp. 435–66.

Scharff, Robert C. (2013) "Becoming a Philosopher: What Heidegger Learned from Dilthey, 1919–25," *British Journal for the History of Philosophy* 21(1), pp. 122–142.

Scharff, Robert C. (2015) *How History Matters to Philosophy: Reconsidering Philosophy's Past After Positivism*, New York: Routledge.

Scharff, Robert C. (2017) "Living After Positivism, But Not Without It." In: Andrew Wernick (ed.) *The Anthem Companion to Auguste Comte*, London: Anthem, pp. 227–246.

Scharff, Robert C. (2018) "Phenomenology without 'Guidelines': The Young Heidegger's Retrieval of Husserl." Under review.

David B. Allison

Hermeneutic Reflections on Descartes' Introduction to His *Meditations on First Philosophy*

Abstract: In these extracts reflecting on Descartes' Introduction to *Meditations on First Philosophy* we undertake to read between the Descartes project, reviewing Descartes' own account of his own project. By way of a close and critical reading, the key method of any hermeneutic approach to a philosophical text, the essay seeks to explore, in a parallel to Ranke's ideal of history as it itself actually was [*eigentlich gewesen*], what Descartes 'actually' says. In the end, this articulates Descartes' epistemological project beyond its usual interpretative scheme.

I General Introductory Remarks

In a text written in 1647—"Comments on a Certain Broadsheet"—Descartes makes a reference back to his *Meditations:*

> I wrote that we cannot doubt that our mind exists, because from the very fact that we are doubting, it follows that our mind exists, but for all that, we *can* doubt whether any *bodies exist in the world.* From this I concluded and demonstrated that we clearly perceive the *mind as an existing thing or substance*, even though we have no conception of any *body* whatever and even deny that any bodies exist, and *hence* that the concept of the *mind* does not in itself involve any concept of *body.* (CSM I, p. 301)[1]

Two important things to note here, among others: (1) that *substance* seems to be equated with *existence*, and (2) that *the concept of mind* does not involve any *concept of body.*

We know that Descartes will retrieve the *cogito* from doubt, that *he will be a thinking thing*—a thing which, as he says in Meditation II (Paragraph 8, CSM II, p. 19), "doubts, affirms, denies, wills, refuses, which also imagines and feels"—what he will term a mind *or* soul *or* understanding *or* reason. Now, each of these terms has an extension as wide as the history of philosophy itself.

1 Citations here follow Descartes in *The Philosophical Writings of Descartes*, ed. J. Cottingham, R. Stoothoff and D. Murdoch, 2 vols. Cambridge: Cambridge University Press, 1985 [henceforth CSM].

https://doi.org/10.1515/9783110551563-021

Yet what does Descartes return to, time and again? To the term "a *thinking* thing," "a thing which *thinks*." (emphasis added) Later, in *The Principles of Philosophy* (Principle IX, Pt. I, CSM I, p. 195), he defines thought in the following way:

> By the term 'thought,' I understand everything which we are aware of as happening within us, in so far as we have awareness of it. Hence, thinking is to be identified here not merely with understanding, willing, and imagining, but also with sensory awareness [i. e., "feeling": *sentir*—DBA]. For if I say 'I am seeing, or I am walking, therefore I exist', and take this as applying to vision or walking as bodily activities, then the conclusion is not absolutely certain. This is because, as often happens during sleep, it is possible for me to thin*k* I am seeing or walking, though my eyes are closed and I am not moving about; such thoughts might even be possible if I had no body at all. But *if* I take 'seeing' or 'walking' to apply to the action of my thought or feeling i. e., to the awareness which is in me, which makes me seem to be seeing or walking, then the conclusion is quite certain, since it relates to the mind, which alone has the sensation [the feeling: *sentir*—DBA] or thought that it is seeing or walking.

Here, thought seems to be all that which is present to me, all that I am conscious of: "Everything which we are *aware of as happening within us*," he says (emphasis added). The list of terms which defines a thinking thing in Meditation II (CSM II, p. 19) thus seems to require an addition: if each member on that list was a kind of consciousness, then this reading of *The Principles* seems to add another important dimension to the thinking, namely, the addition of self-consciousness. And the difference between the two is precisely the self, the "I," the ego of the *ego cogito.*

Now, what is so striking about this? About the self which thinks? Simply that it will be the origin of modern thought per se. This is Descartes' introduction of the coherent problematic of consciousness—to be taken up by Leibniz and Locke (who will use the exact same terms as Descartes: e. g., this "thinking thing" or "ego" that he speaks of repeatedly in his *Essay*), right through the empiricists, Kant, Hegel, etc., into contemporary thought.

Ego, self, or I, together with *consciousness* and *self-consciousness*. We have already seen in the *Discourse on Method* that Descartes had denied the ancient view of the soul. Here, in the *Meditations*, he will develop his critique, or rather, his proper account of it. The traditional view attributed an organic function to the soul, together with the functions of awareness and thinking. Descartes *separates* these two functions and conceives of the soul as a *function of consciousness*. The thinking self is then made opposed to the extended self; the result is the celebrated Cartesian dualism, mind and machine.

But where, precisely, is the opposition? In some sense, we know that the thought or mind depends on body: for example, in the *Discourse on Method*,

Part 6, Paragraph 2, (CSM I, p. 143), he said, "The mind depends so much on the temperament and disposition of the bodily organs" ... that it is medicine which will make men wiser. Also, there are the frequent affirmations in the *Regulae* that the imagination depends on the body; and, we recall in Meditation II, Paragraph 6, he observed that "one cannot feel without body," etc., etc. In this sense, according to the order of being, mind depends on body (this *ordo essendi*, of course, was the point of Henry More's objection of nullibism). Yet, from the standpoint of consciousness, mind is a truth prior to the truth of the body. In this sense, it is distinct from the body—that is, according to the order of reason or knowledge—the *ordo cognoscendi.* At the same time, and from the standpoint of consciousness, the thinking thing is: he will call it a *substance*, that is: an *existence.* It *ex-ists*, it stands forth to itself in self-consciousness: it is aware of its thoughts immediately.

Why has it been that the consciousness doctrine, perhaps, if anything, remains as the historical legacy from Descartes? Why have the attacks on it been so weak? Perhaps the strongest attack is the kind ventured by Nietzsche, Freud, Marx, and Heidegger—each of whom will claim that consciousness and self-consciousness are *not* all so evident, so clear and distinct, and that consciousness belies its hidden and obscure origins. Yet, in a very special sense, these are precisely Cartesian objections: for *Descartes* of the *Meditations*, the "I," "ego," or "self," that is, the source of consciousness is never exposed as a datum for inspection. What is examined is the *cogito*, or rather, the thinking as such, the thoughts themselves, the *cogitationes.*

But the self who doubts is not examined. It arises, or is constituted *by*, as he will say, "a continual succession of antecedents." On the one hand, as we have seen, the self has its origin in the body-machine, in the mechanical account of its activities, actions, passions, habits, etc.—and more of this is given us in detail in the final work, *The Passions of the Soul.* On the other hand, the self is historical: it is constituted by the acts of consciousness themselves—and in this sense, the Cartesian self somehow achieves itself, creates itself, as a work of resolution. It dictates, for example, a method by means of which it can increase its own wisdom. It resolves to pursue the course of mastery and self-mastery. By art, it frees itself from nature in order to overcome its own limitations, and thus, to conquer nature. And with this stroke, the unity of man with nature becomes broken.

In a traditional way, then, the project of mastery corresponds to psychophysical dualism—it involves two distinct orders: the organic and the cognitive. For the human being, the thinking self exercises mastery over the organic—the individual sets an end for himself and constitutes his own self according to the order he legislates (that is, according to felicity, wisdom, health, sweetness in this life, etc.). Likewise for nature as a whole: the order by which we understand and master nature is—as he says in the *Discourse*—arbitrary. A fictionalized nature results from the model of mathematics. Thus, e. g., Cartesian nature is no longer beneficent, no longer directive, purposive, teleological, no longer eschatological.

To follow out this reading of Cartesian dualism—as a separation of function and as a domination of one function by the other—is also to see the perplexity that ensues for the tradition stemming from Descartes. What does thought do? What is the order of the self? Is the world of body now its object? Its source? Its constituted product?

With the traditional understanding of Cartesian dualism, one half of the dualism is invariably denied or dropped: idealism or materialism ensue. In any case, this is what we shall have to pursue in our reading of the *Meditations*—namely, to examine the agency and the effects of the Cartesian doctrine of consciousness. Already, we anticipate that it shall relate to, or at least in some important ways, it shall connect up with, the broader Cartesian themes of selfhood, mastery, mathematics, physics, Cartesian metaphysics and epistemology.

Our approach to this complex set of issues shall be through a close analysis of the famous Cartesian *doubt* of the First Meditation, and we shall center particularly on the questions of (1) the nature of deception, (2) the possibility of certainty, and (3) the status of God and demon.

II Introduction to the First Meditation: *Dedication* and *Preface*

What are the hermeneutico-phenomenological intentions of the *Meditations?* At the very start, the book's intentions seem to be *apologetic*, that is: they seem to attempt a defense of Christian doctrine. That is what *apologetics* means: a theological discourse, which pleads, or argues, in defense of the Christian faith. The term comes from the Greek: *apo* and *logos*. A speech or discourse *for*, or *about*, or *in favor of.*

So, the intention of the *Meditations* seems to be apologetic: he seems to be defending the faith and he seeks protection from the Sorbonne for this book—which he calls "this just or excellent treatise." Now what are the contents of this just treatise? The contents are his considerations upon what he calls "the two questions" respecting God and the soul. What is the stated purpose of such an apologetic treatise? To persuade infidels of religion and moral virtue. Or, as Mr. Cottingham would have it, to persuade "unbelievers" of religion and moral virtue.

The intended audience of the *Meditations*, then, will be infidels and atheists. Why is this? Because Descartes holds philosophy and theology to be quite distinct. As he will say in the *Dedication* [—to those most learned and distinguished men, the Dean and Doctors of the sacred Faculty of Theology at Paris], in Paragraph 2 (CSM II, p. 3).

> It is quite enough for us faithful ones to accept by means of faith the fact that the human soul does not perish with the body and that God exists.

Sure, it is quite enough for us—we, of the faith—but *not for them.* As he would say, "we must believe in the existence of God because it is a doctrine of Holy Scripture, and conversely, that we must believe Holy Scripture because it comes from God."

They, however, would accuse us of *circular reasoning:* they would admonish us by saying that we *believe* in God *because* we have *faith* in Holy *Scripture*—we have faith in faith. What we believe in is the cause of our belief.

Thus the adversaries, the infidels and atheists, will determine the mode of discourse, and this will be natural reason, logical argumentation. Now, note that this is curious in that it seems as if the adversary would have to suspend reason, precisely in order to assert belief in God. Also, the very terms infidel and atheist are themselves designations of faith and not reason. It is also interesting in that Descartes makes no mention that his natural reasoning would tend to bolster or corroborate the faith of the already faithful.

All of this points out Descartes' extreme separation of faith and reason. For St. Thomas, it was not unreasonable to give our assent to truths of faith, precisely because these truths of faith are said to be beyond reason, i.e., they are held to be higher than reason. Thus, he—St. Thomas—claims the utility of reason in the service of faith. Or, in short, that *philosophy* is ultimately *dependent on*—ancillary to—*theology.* But there is absolutely none of this for Descartes. Indeed, from his "Comments on a Certain Broadsheet," he would say as much (CSM I, p. 301).

> For, since we were born men before we became Christians, we cannot believe that anyone would seriously embrace opinions which he thinks contrary to that right reason which constitutes being a man, simply in order to cling to the faith which makes him a Christian.[2]

As to the explicit separation of faith and reason in the *Meditations*, we already note the following remark in Paragraph 6, CSM II, p. 8, of the *Preface to the Reader*—and this is just below the middle of Paragraph 6—"Those who do not bother to grasp the proper order of my reasons and the connection between them, but merely try to carp at individual sentences, as is the fashion, will not get much

2 From CSM I, p. 301.

benefit from reading this book." Such readers must, he says, "deliver themselves from every source of prejudice." Moreover, in Paragraph 6 of the *Dedication*, CSM II, p. 6, he says "The reasons by which he proves that God exists, and that the human soul differs from the body"—should "be treated as very exact demonstrations." Or, in Paragraph 4 of the *Dedication* (CSM II, p. 4): all the proofs of God and the soul, of which he will select certain ones are put forward "precisely and clearly" as "demonstrative proofs." Or, again, in Paragraph 5 of the *Dedication* (CSM II, p. 4), they "are as certain and evident as the proofs of geometry" ... "and no proposition is put forward in a book without there being a conclusive demonstration available."

It seems clear, then, that the *mode of discourse* will be *right reason*, and that the *criteria for evaluating his arguments* will be the deductive certainty required by *logic* or geometrical *proof.*

The means for evaluating what are, after all, articles of faith in this case, thus seems to be reason. This is a claim, we remember, from the Fourth *Discourse on Method*, Paragraph 8, CSM I, p. 131: "For after all, whether we are awake or asleep, we ought never to let ourselves be convinced except by the evidence of our reason." He will *repeat* this kind of claim in the last words of his very next book, *The Principles of Philosophy,* where he says, "I would not wish anyone to believe anything except what he is convinced of by evident and irrefutable reasoning."[3]

So much then, for the apologetic intention. Within the *Dedication* to those most learned and distinguished men of the Sorbonne, and within the *Preface to the Reader,* the apologetic intention seems to be well-stated. The same criteria seem to be affirmed elsewhere.

Yet, there are some troubling problems with the apologetic intention: Indeed, I think we can specify seven points of difficulty concerning this apologetic intention:

1) We see little indication of reason's confirming the faith of the faithful.
2) Thus, reason appears to be in conflict with faith, and this is opposed to the traditional teaching of, e.g., St. Thomas.
3) Descartes shall be writing according to *the most ancient method,* i.e., according to the task of seeking "truth"—as he says in Paragraph 4, CSM II, p. 4, of the *Dedication.* But, in this case, what is oldest or most ancient is of course *pagan,* quite *unchristian.*
4) Another troubling issue is that the subject matter of the apologetic intention is remarkably vague:

3 Descartes, *The Principles of Philosophy,* CSM II, p. 291 (Part IV, princ.207

a) Paragraph 2 of the *Dedication*, e.g., speaks of "The two questions respecting God and the soul."
b) Again, in Paragraph 2: "That the human soul *does not die* with the body and that God exists."
c) Paragraph 4: "That God exists and that the human soul is *distinct* from the body."
d) Paragraph 6: "That God exists and that the human soul *differs* from the body."
e) Again, Paragraph 6: "The existence of God and the *real and true distinction* between the human soul and the body."

Note that the first formulation is referred to as "the two questions"—Cottingham has "topics"—and that the last is referred to as "these beliefs" (and this is in the footnote 1, CSM II, p. 6). Thus, what we find here is really several quite distinct formulations of the subject matter, all lumped together as "the two questions."

5) These "two questions," rather sloppily articulated in the *Dedication*, are held up to us in the first paragraph of the *Preface to the Reader*—yet there, he claims to have already discussed them in an earlier book, one he wrote four years before the *Meditations*, namely, in his *Discourse on Method*. Interestingly, he mentions that he wrote the earlier *Discourse on Method*—not in Latin, but in French. Why? He says he wrote it for the benefit of weak minds, who couldn't read Latin. Now in a situation like this, when an author who very rarely quotes himself does so in such a striking manner, it is usually worthwhile to track down that reference. If we track it down, we find that it occurs in the fifth part of the *Discourse on Method*, Paragraph 12, CSM I, p. 141, and it says the following:

> Next to the error of those who deny God, which I think I have already sufficiently refuted, there is none which is more effectual in leading weak minds from the straight path of virtue, than to imagine that the soul of the brute (i.e., of animals) is of the same nature as our own, and that in consequence, after this life we have nothing to fear or to hope for, any more than the flies and ants.

So, there, in the *Discourse on Method*, it seems that weak minds fear to think of themselves just as perishable in their being as flies and ants. Here, in Paragraph 6 of the *Dedication*, he appeals to the Dean and Doctors of the Sacred Faculty of Theology at the Sorbonne to defend precisely these so-called proofs—of God and soul. Why should they defend them? Because, Descartes reminds them, "It is for you to judge the advantage that would come from establishing these beliefs firmly, since you see the disorders which come from their being doubted." Or, in

Paragraph 2 of the *Dedication*, he says, "Few people would prefer the right to what is useful, if they did not fear God or have the expectation of an afterlife."

What is a bit odd about this, of course, is that we have seen just how importantly Descartes himself sees utility, usefulness—from the *Regulae* right through the *Passions of the Soul.* In fact reason itself is important precisely because it is useful in the service of the passions, the emotions, the human sensibility. Indeed the doctrine of mastery over nature was framed to enable us to live well and to enjoy the fruits of this life. That the tree of philosophy, with its branches of medicine, mechanics, and morals, was grown for its fruits. That the art of scientific method gives the knowledge of all that can be known by man. In fact, in Paragraph 4 of the *Dedication* Descartes even says "I have cultivated a method for the resolution of difficulties of every kind in the sciences."—no small claim. Few people, indeed, would prefer the right to the useful, were they not restrained by the fear of God or the expectation of an after-life.

6) Not only is the apologetic subject matter somewhat vague, and that it seems to contradict Descartes' own major teaching of utility, of mastery, in the *Discourse on Method*, but there are still further reasons for lessening its stated importance. After his repeated insistence that the mode of discourse would be right reason, he sums up his account in Paragraph 5 of the *Dedication*, on the bottom of CSM II, p. 4:

> The present treatise contains everything that I have been able to accomplish in this area. Not that I have attempted to collect here all the different arguments that could be put forward to serve as proofs of the subject, for this does not seem worthwhile except in cases where no single argument is regarded as certain. What I have done is to take merely the principal and most important arguments [note the plural] and develop them in such a way that I would now venture to put them forward as very certain and evident demonstrations. I will add that these proofs are of such a kind that I reckon they leave no room for the possibility that the human mind will ever discover any better ones.

Thus it doesn't seem necessary to give more than one proof of God unless no single proof was certain. And what does Descartes himself do in the *Meditations?* He gives three proofs. What does he say about the proofs? None could be better. Also, all that he could accomplish in these matters is contained in this treatise.

On to point 7:

7) What does Descartes demand, what does he require, of his audience? Not only that they follow right reason and really treat these proofs as veritable demonstrations, but also—and he says this in Paragraph 5 of the *Dedication*—also that the reader (1) be free of prejudice, (2) that the reader detach himself from the senses.

Yet this first requirement ironically describes the learned and distinguished Dean and Doctors of the Sacred Faculty of Theology. That is, ironically, it points out precisely those people who are the most prejudiced—those people who, in fact, tolerate circular reasoning out of faith, out of their own pre-existing belief, their pre-judgments or prejudices.

But, furthermore, the second requirement follows from the first. Belief in the teaching of the senses, that is, the ordinary belief in what we learn through our own sense experience, is also a prejudice. And why is that? Because, ultimately, it gives us a false understanding of nature. Sense experience does not teach us about a mathematically conceived nature; sense experience does not give us scientific nature—rather, sense experience gives us a lot of hard, soft, sweet, sour, pleasant, light and bright, drippy, yucky, loud and smelly nature. As Descartes himself would say in a later work, *The Principles of Philosophy*, "The first and principal cause of error stem from the prejudices of childhood"[4]—and the error consists simply in believing the testimony of the five senses, and by grasping the world, or nature, in terms of these sense qualities, instead of understanding it according to magnitude, figure, quantity, and movement—i. e., according to what he takes to be the "simple natures," or the "analytical" simples, or, what will later be called the doctrine of primary qualities.

The sense qualities are subjectively experienced, on the one hand, while, on the other, mathematical magnitude, is objectively conceived and quantifiable. The former concerns the *qualitative* aspect of our *experience* of things, the latter the *quantitative* aspect, the *objective nature of things themselves*. The former is *secondary* to the latter, at least in terms of *scientific* understanding. Sight, sound, smell, taste, and touch may vary from person to person, and the experiences *we* have will thus vary among us, as will the judgments based upon these varying tastes, and experiences. But three-dimensional space-time, which envelops every object, and in terms of which every object can be mathematically defined, doesn't. The geometrically conceived figure is the same for everyone: it can be precisely defined, measured, duplicated by anyone, anywhere, verified and judged valid in terms of mathematical rules—even if you don't have a taste for mathematics. And every object, no matter how tasty, smelly, or pleasing it may be to you—or may not be to someone else—every object, any object, can be expressed mathematically, by the sciences of physics, mechanics, and dynamics. And that is useful.

All the same, for the apologetic intention, these two requirements demanded of the reader (namely, to be free from prejudice, to be detached from the senses),

4 *The Principles of Philosophy*, Part I, princ. 71, CSM I, pp. 218–219.

these could be understood in another way. They could concern the prejudices of infidels and atheists. Atheists, for example, have the prejudice that there is no immaterial, and hence, immortal soul, which will go to heaven—and in this respect they are materialists. They, like flies and ants, will doubtless suffer corruption upon death—at least this is what they believe, as materialists. Hence they treat certain other tenets of Christian doctrine with some suspicion as well (miracles, grace, beatitude, heaven, angels, etc.). As for the infidels, certainly Averroes —following Aristotle—they also denied any compelling reasons for personal immortality, since the soul is held to be the form of the body. And this, among other things, accounts for the violence of the attacks against the Averroist heresy—for example, Petrarch's *Contra Averroistes*, or even his *De Ignorantia*—where he claimed that the Averroists were impious and pestiferous fools, worthy only of censorious rebuke. Also, and to push this a bit, the political wars of the Ottoman Turks were ravaging the Europe of the Holy Roman Empire. For them, of course, the Christians were the infidels.

Now all this leads us to the second intention of the *Meditations*, which is perhaps best expressed in the very first paragraph of the First Meditation:

> Some years ago I was struck by the large number of falsehoods that I had accepted as true in my childhood, and but the highly doubtful nature of the whole edifice that I had subsequently based on them. I realized that it was necessary, once in the course of my life, to demolish all the opinions I had formerly received and start again right from the foundations if I wanted to establish anything at all in the sciences that was stable and likely to last.

Hardly a *suspicion* of this concern with the sciences in the *Dedication.*

Curieux.

In the *Preface to the Reader*, this second intention—the theoretical or scientific intention—is barely discernible. In Paragraph 6 of his *Preface to the Reader*, Descartes had remarked that he will tackle the questions concerning "God and the human soul, and this time I am also going to deal with the foundations of first philosophy in its entirety."

What should be noted here, however, is that these "two questions" of God and the soul are traditionally supposed to be among the very contents of metaphysics, i.e., of first philosophy—so, how do we explain this? This seeming redundancy? Perhaps the previous sentence directs us to the more obvious theoretical intention Descartes might have in mind. There, at the end of the previous paragraph, Paragraph 5 of the *Preface*, CSM II, on p. 8, he says "our minds must be regarded as finite and limited things, while God is infinite and beyond our comprehension." With this statement, the mind seems curiously identified with what could be defined as figure—that is, it might be seen to anticipate a doctrine of mathematics, which would exclude comprehension of anything without finitude and limit. In this sense, God would be incomprehensible indeed. Again, there is ample cause for suspicion when God is said to be incomprehensible. How, for example, would one have an idea of God or about God? How could one reasonably or rationally prove the existence of anything, which is literally incomprehensible?

I think what Descartes is attempting to do here is to make the *attentive reader* more aware of his theoretical intentions—thus suggesting to the attentive reader that the apologetic concerns are not really what the book is principally about. In other words, it seems that Descartes is really trying to separate physics from metaphysics, precisely in order to make the strong distinction between our scientific knowledge of bodies and the incomprehensibility of traditional metaphysical accounts of God and the immortal soul. Then, as now, the very term "metaphysical" had a secondary meaning: vague, abstract, speculative, and useless, with not too much sense of reality. Let the attentive reader stick with the claims for ascertaining certainty in the sciences, and let the Jesuits and the weak-minded hot-foot it after immortality. This suspicion seems to be confirmed in his Synopsis of the Second Meditation, on the top of CSM II, p. 10, where he says,

> But I have not pursued this topic any further in this book, first because these arguments are enough to show clearly enough that the decay of the body does not imply the destruction of the soul, and are hence enough to give mortals the hope of an after-life, and secondly because the premises which lead to the conclusion that the soul is immortal depend on an account of the whole of physics.

Now, I think that it is a reasonable suspicion that one *is not likely to deduce the immortality of the immaterial soul from physics.* What one might assert, however, is that the soul or mind is not extended, as are the bodies of physics. In this sense, physics may be said to exclude any scientific knowledge of the soul. Or of God, for that matter. If Descartes can say that all he needs for a complete elaboration of the sciences—of physics, mechanics, and dynamics—is mathematics, then God could simply be postulated as "infinite." Indeed, as a mathematician, infinity could easily be asserted in a formula: X+1, or X to the power of n. What to keep in mind, however, and this is extremely important for our reading, is that Descartes will often speak of the nature of mind, the nature of God, the nature of bodies, as well as about the existence of mind, the existence of God, and the existence of bodies. He will often speak both of the nature and the existence of something as well as about the nature or the existence of something. The nature of a centaur is a flying horse, fancifully depicted in Greek mythology. The existence of a centaur is not likely to be verified, however. The nature of a perfectly regular, equiangular triangle is well known to any high school freshman. Unfortunately, they do not exist in reality.

III Meditation One

With the stated theoretical intention of establishing a firm foundation of the sciences in mind, how does the First Meditation begin? Well, in a by now familiar way: it begins by resolution—he must act to overcome his own irresolution. In the beginning, then, is will, practice, resolution—and the theoretical intention will be effected by this will, just as in the *Discourse on Method*, where he resolved to form a method.

The first instance of will or resolution immediately follows: he wills to *doubt*. Yet, what controls this doubt? What directs it? Why, in fact, doubt at all? There must be some reason for doubting—some *ratio dubitandi*. And this means that doubt is determined, orchestrated, by some principle.

But in the same breath he says that if there is the slightest doubt concerning his former opinions, this justifies his doubting them all, the whole sum of his former opinions. Again, curious. What is the reason for this? None. The celebrated hyperbolic doubt thus does not follow from any reason or principle. Doubt is therefore not argued, and the hyperbolic doubt is not an argument. What is it, then? Quite simply, hyperbole—that is, exaggeration. He presents it as if it were a conclusion, but this hyperbolic doubt—which equates the teensie-weensiest bit of doubt with falsity—is a preposterous, that is, hyperbolic, conclusion. Thus, the rejection of the merely or possibly dubious facts or opinions is not an argued position at all. Rather, it has been willed, it has been resolved. The question we have to ask of Descartes, then, is why? Why start here? Why this seemingly arbitrary starting point, which, unlike ordinary doubt, or unlike argued doubt, simply excludes the dubitable, much less the likely, and even more curiously, the probable. "99 and 44/100 % pure" is fine for Ivory soap, but seemingly not for Descartes.

In a way, we see how far Descartes also excludes the entire tradition of philosophy by this move. Even the ancient pagans, such as Plato and Aristotle, vested trust (i. e., *pistis*) in the objects of the senses—even to the point of using them as the basis for attaining higher knowledge.

Now, at this point, some half-way through Paragraph 2 of the First Meditation, CSM II, on p. 12, Descartes *narrows* this hyperbolic doubt, and he renders it finite:

> For the purpose of rejecting all my opinions, it will be enough if I find in each of them at least some reason for doubt. And to do this I will not need to run through them all individually, which would be an endless task. Once the foundations of a building are undermined, anything built on them collapses of its own accord; so I will go straight for the basic principles upon which all my former opinions rested.

By doubting the old foundations hyperbolically, he can ascertain the certainty of new foundations. On the basis of a destructive work, he is enabled to find new, veridical foundations.

Thus, he doubts the senses. The reason now, for doubting the senses, is that they are sometimes deceptive. But—and this is a very big but—in what appears to be quite contrary to hyperbolic doubt, Descartes doesn't doubt all the senses. He only doubts the external senses, that is, he only doubts external sense perception. The problem is, however, that the external senses depend on the internal senses. That is, our images of the external world depend on our internal mental states, our own imagination, our particular temperaments, our passions. Thus, the first example he gives in Paragraph 4 is that of madness: those people who think they are made of glass, or who think they have heads made of earthenware or pumpkins—these people are mad! Me too, perhaps!

The second example of external dependency on the internal mental state, which is given in Paragraph 5, is that of dreaming. How do I discern external reality in my dreams? Thus, the real problem here is the status of images. In other words, to what extent do images distort external reality? The continued use of the dream, of dreaming, is a metaphor for the imagination. The first *hyperbolical conclusion* then, is that—of all things—*I am dreaming!* The whole analysis of Cartesian doubt will find its core in this problem: namely, the way we take the external upon the internal. Again, a memorable passage from *The Principles of Philosophy*, Part I, Principle 71, (CSM I, p. 218):

> It is here that the first and main cause of all our errors may be recognized. In our early childhood the mind was so closely tied to the body that it had no leisure for any thoughts except those by means of which it had sensory awareness of what was happening to the body [i.e., it had sensations]. It did not refer these thoughts to anything outside itself, but merely felt pain when something harmful was happening to the body and felt pleasure when something beneficial occurred. And when nothing very beneficial or harmful was happening to the body, the mind had various sensations [or, feelings] corresponding to the different areas where, and ways in which, the body was being stimulated, namely, what we call the sensations of tastes, smells, sounds, heat, cold, light, colors and so on —sensations which do not represent anything located outside our thought, but which vary according to the different movements which pass from all parts of our body to the part of the brain to which our mind is closely joined and united.

The error we make as children. This is to say that, traditionally, to be real is to be a particular thing—precisely Aristotle's mistake in beginning his philosophy with the sensible particulars, the *tode ti.* All our mistakes of sensation stem from this. Consequently, we do not know the nature of things: of body, extension, figure, proportion, number, etc.

Thus, we see the problem of dreams. Initially, our images depend on our temperaments. In this way, the external images become transformed by our internal sensibility, i.e., by our own various feelings and sensations. Therefore, we must somehow get outside the passions, outside the temperaments or personal sensibility, etc., in order to understand this error. The problem is effectively what has since become termed *the error of the natural attitude.* Or, to put this in still somewhat different terms, we must somehow overcome the *anthropomorphic* attitude.

The critique of traditional belief, or the critique of the traditional sciences, cannot, therefore, be based on the senses alone. Thus, the senses themselves must be criticized by something else—namely, by Cartesian science. But the problematic status of the *image*, of the *dream*, out of which one extracts *the mathematicals*, the analytical simples of Cartesian mathematics and physics, this is itself never really resolved. Cartesian dualism, therefore, is more rightly understood to be a form of *epistemological dualism*, i.e., the subject-object split, rather than the much more conventionally heralded psycho-physical dualism, i.e., the mind-body split.

IV Meditation Three: God

For purposes of method, the theses about mind and body remain metaphysically neutral in Meditation II. Both of these are argued for on the order of knowledge. Thus, I know that mind or soul, etc., is a thinking thing. Its nature—at least, so far as it is known by me—is to think. Likewise with body: so far as I know its nature, body is extension. Both claims, as we showed above, regarding the nature of mind and about the nature of body, are basically *epistemological* claims. That is, they are claims about what I can know of their respective natures. How is the conception of body as magnitude connected with the reality of really existent extended bodies? How is this connection made? It is simply asserted. Thus, 13 lines down on CSM II, p. 21, in Paragraph 12 of Meditation II, he had claimed:

> But what is this wax which can only be conceived by the understanding or the mind? it is of course the same wax which I see, which I touch, which I imagine, in short, the same wax that I knew from the start.

The assertion, then, amounts to the claim that what I know is similar to what I see, and that it exists. This is an assertion and it remains to be proven. In Meditation III, however, he will claim God as the guarantor for this knowledge. Hence, the *necessity for proving the existence of God.*

Let us look first at the organization of the Third Meditation. It can be divided into six parts:

1) CSM II, p. 24, Paragraph 1.
2) CSM II, p. 24, Paragraph 2.
3) CSM II, p. 24–25, Paragraphs 3 & 4.
4) *First* method of investigating ideas: CSM II, pp. 25–27, Paragraphs 5–12.
5) *Second* method of investigating ideas: *first proof* of God; CSM II, pp. 27–32, Paragraphs 13–26.
6) Divisibility of time; *second* proof of God; CSM II, pp. 32–36, Paragraphs 27–39.

Briefly stated:

Part I. *What* do I know? That I am a thinking thing.

Part II. *How* do I know this is *true?* Because it is clear and distinct. Truth is defined as clarity and distinctness.

Part III. The *referential character* of *images* is *not* clear and distinct. What *is* clear and distinct is only the fact *that* something is *present to consciousness.* Also, the truths of the cogito, mathematics, and the principle of noncontradiction are clear and distinct. *But, an omnipotent God* could *deceive* us even about *these* truths. Thus, truth gets reformulated, and is said to be clarity and distinctness, together with the knowledge that if there is a God, he is not a deceiver.

Part IV. Method one. Returning to what I know. No ideas give me the knowledge that what appears to be is, much less, that my ideas are similar to real things. The first method thus results in a *failure* to get *beyond* the image.

Part V. Hence, method two—what he calls "another way." There are ideas in my mind for which I can't be the adequate cause. Thus, God must be the adequate cause.

Once I prove God exists, I can prove that the *body* exists and the *world* exists. All the same, one might admit that this is somewhat of an odd progression, in that without the knowledge of God's existence, I couldn't know that the body exists. By this same train of reasoning, it would seem that an atheist would not know that he or she even had a body—and atheist or infidel would not know that he or she was a living, breathing, walking thing.

Part VI. We are presented with the *second proof* of God, by way of the *divisibility of time and recurrent creation.*

Now, we had good reason, in reading the Sorbonne Dedication letter and the *Preface to the Reader*, to be somewhat skeptical about Descartes' apologetic claims. Yet, here, God reappears in force as a guarantor of truth. It seems possible, then, that there might be a convergence of the theoretical and the apologetical claims. But, we must ask, is this a real convergence or is it only apparent?

Let us initially pose the "G" question. Does Descartes really *need* God? His preliminary considerations in Meditations I and II showed that the nature of body was extension, and, in Meditation II, that the mind is only a thinking thing. Also, there, we saw that there was no need for sensible or intelligible forms. After the mathematicals are asserted, Descartes finds this very sphere of truth to be the basis of the cogito. And, on this basis, he can doubt the world. Thus, Cartesian science proceeds to doubt the images, knowing full well that it can correct them. It remains problematic, then, in what respect Descartes really requires God. It *seems* that the whole of Meditation III labors, through God, to establish the existence of the objects *of* Cartesian science. *If* God exists, then the *world* exists.

Notice that the Third Meditation begins with the same characterization of the thinking thing that we found in Meditation II, i. e., the characterization of the *cogito* in terms of its activity. Thus, in Paragraph 1, of the Third Meditation, 6 lines down, on CSM II, p. 24 of the Cottingham edition, he says,

> I am a thing that thinks: that is, a thing that doubts, affirms, denies, understands a few things, is ignorant of many things, that loves, hates, is willing, is unwilling, and also, which imagines and feels.

These are activities, then, or modes of thought—modes, modifications, or, quite simply, ways, of thinking—as he says, that "certainly reside and are met with in me." But, by Paragraph 5, a significant shift occurs, and the activity of the mind is dropped: now, he only speaks of its contents. This will be the basis of discussing the mind for the rest of Meditation III. Of course, in speaking of the mind's activity, we would have to ask about its ontological or metaphysical status—other than merely in terms of its contents. Thus, *the whole question of the I, the me, the ego or self, of the ego cogito, is once again passed over.* Now, why should this be? Because it may be the bodily source of our knowledge about bodies. Through our bodies, we could know both about the existence and about the nature of body in general. In any case, the omission of the self or what is not known about the mind, leaves us back on the plane of *images*—and, Paragraph 1 tells us that he will explicitly exclude their referential status. Yet, what is an image, if not of something?

> I will now shut my eyes, stop my ears, and withdraw all my senses. I will eliminate from my thoughts all images of bodily things, or rather, since this is hardly possible, I will regard all such images as vacuous, false, and worthless.

Therefore, when Descartes defines *truth* in Paragraph 2, as *clarity and distinctness*, we are presented with a concept of truth that is bizarre indeed. Conventionally, the Aristotelian-Thomistic tradition holds truth to be an *adequation*, i.e., a correspondence, or a conformity between the mind and the thing: *veritas est adequatio intellectus ad rem.* But, now, for Descartes, if I have any content present to my mind, it is held to be true. Thus, the image *per se* is true, even though it gives us no evidence of anything at all beyond itself.

Whether or not it refers to things, I don't know. Hence, there cannot be a correspondence with things. This view will ultimately be developed through the empiricists' account of "impressions"—they will drop the use of the term 'image,' and will speak about *impressions* as the contents of consciousness. Thus, both Descartes and the empiricists seem to deny the intentionality of images, of thought contents. This intentional aspect had formerly been a characteristic understanding of images, at least since Plato, where the image or icon—*eikon*—derived from the capacity to make an image of something, or to recognize images as being images of something else in turn: *eikasia.*

Now, if this negative characterization of the image enables Descartes to provisionally sidestep the correspondence notion of truth, it also has an ostensibly positive side. It entails the thinking thing as the basis of the particular image. The thinking thing is prior to and more general than what I am thinking. Any candidate for truth, then, will be held up and judged by the cogito. Truth, then, is psychological: the image will have to be present to the cogito with clarity and distinctness. Now, this psychological presence to the cogito entails another psychological dimension, namely, that there be degrees of clarity and distinctness—and this bears on the degrees of priority in our own knowledge.

We already saw this with the wax example: what is most prior to our order of knowledge is most clear and distinct—this is *extension*, and it is more clear and more distinct than figure, for example, or flexibility, mutability. This priority of knowledge is also a logical priority. It is contradictory to say that figure does not presuppose extension, but the reverse doesn't hold. Psychologically, one could say that figure was less clear and distinct than extension, for extension is an absolutely simple concept, and it doesn't have the duality that figure has —it does not presuppose anything else.

So, clarity and distinctness thus have three functions:

1) psychological
2) logical [functions]

3) methodological

1) Psychologically, something, let us call it “X,” is indubitably present.
   a) forcibly present equals clear
   b) different from something else equals distinct
2) Logically, “X” is indubitable—and here, “indubitably” present means not self-contradictory.
3) Methodologically, “X” is prior to “Y” in our order of knowledge.

Again, the kind of truth we are given by these criteria, is interideational, i.e., it is a truth that takes place among or between ideas themselves. It is not one of correspondence or reference. Thus, figure might be indubitably present, and if I conceive of a triangle without self-contradiction, I satisfy a logical demand. But, if I understand this triangle as extension, then I grasp something more clearly and distinctly than figure. But, I still don't address any reference of the image to existence, however.

So, positively, then, the traditional notion of truth as correspondence is challenged on the basis of a *prior* truth, the truth about ourselves as thinking things, which claims an absolute priority for the order of knowledge. So, generally speaking, our images are clear and distinct so long as we don't try to interpret them, i.e., to assign them a reference. And this, of course, raises the principal issue of the Third Meditation: the status of the world as the cause of images, and the existence of God to guarantee the referential truth of these images. Thus, continuing in Paragraph 3, the top line CSM II, on p. 25 of Cottingham,

But there was something else which I used to assert, and which through habitual belief I thought I perceived clearly, although I did not in truth do so. This was that there were things outside me.

And to this, he adds at the beginning of Paragraph 4,

> But what about when I was considering something very simple and straightforward in arithmetic or geometry, for example, that two and three added together make five, and so on? Did I not see at least these things clearly enough to affirm their truth?

(It should be noted that this second case could well be an instance of clarity and distinctness, because the example of mathematics is drawn from the cogito, the very basis for clarity and distinctness.)

Nonetheless, an omnipotent God could suspend both kinds of claim: he can suspend existential and analytical truths. Why? 1) Because, since God is omnipotent, he is free to will anything at any time. Thus, he could will that 2 + 3 = 17, or, he could make justice mean anything. In fact, this characterization of God by

Descartes will be strongly objected to by Leibniz. Let me quote from a letter, likely written to Malebranche, in June of 1679:

> I am told that Descartes established so well the existence of God and the immortality of the soul. I fear that we are deceived by such beautiful words. For the God or perfect being of Descartes is not a God such as one imagines, and as one would wish, that is to say, just and wise, doing all things for the good of the creatures so far as is possible, but rather, he is something approaching the God of Spinoza, that is to say, the principle of things, and a certain sovereign *power* called primitive Nature, which puts all in action, and does all that can be done; which has no will nor understanding, since, according to Descartes, he does not have the good for the object of his will, nor the true for the object of his understanding. *For he did not wish that his God act according to some end*, and it is for that reason that he excluded from philosophy the quest for *final causes*, under this clever pretext that we are not capable of knowing the purposes of God. Leibniz, (1923–), p. 775.

Thus, a more theologically proper account would be the following: an omnipotent being can do this, he could will that 2 + 3 = 17, i.e., he could do anything, provided you only consider his power. But this power is held to be qualified by his goodness—they are traditionally held to be coextensive in God. We see Leibniz' objection, then, in that the Cartesian God appears as a simple power. He doesn't seem to be qualified in any way—but, in the *Meditations*, Descartes at least says God could deceive, but he won't, because "he is said to be good." Whether or not this kind of God will be proven—Leibniz thinks not—will remain to be seen.

In any case, here we see the motivation for Descartes to prove God's existence. God could make clarity and distinctness false! All the same, Descartes has to employ the principle of noncontradiction—the very foundation of logic —if he is to demonstrate anything logically. Is this a circularity? I have to use logic to prove that God would guarantee the validity of logic? That which I prove guarantees the means by which I prove it. Or, that I have to use the principle of noncontradiction to prove God syllogistically: only then, only by virtue of the logical conclusion, do I have the right to affirm the validity of my logical principles of proof.

Perhaps this can be stated in a somewhat different way. I need a guarantee that God wouldn't suspend the truths of reason—i.e., at the limit, the law of noncontradiction"? How do I do this? I assume that he will guarantee it. So, we could say:

a) The whole question of proof is logically circular. That is, I have to presuppose that which I attempt to prove.
b) It is not circular. Many commentators have claimed this, theologians in particular.

c) We could say, with Leibniz, that the whole question of proof, here, is simply one grand charade. At best, Descartes' God would be like Spinoza's God of nature.

The explicit proof of God begins with the second method—namely, to look at the "objective reality," that is, the content of my ideas. By representation, some ideas are said to have more reality than other ideas! But, is this a plausible way of approaching ideas? Do ideas themselves admit of degrees of reality? Is the idea of an angel any more or less real than the idea of the devil, or the idea of a recreational vehicle, or the very idea of Marshall Spector's new Fall wardrobe?

As for ideas of substances, we have a very smelly red herring introduced here. Because, Descartes knows nothing about substances—he only knows that the nature of body is extension and that he's a thinking thing. Suddenly, substance intrudes into the equation. If this seems to be an unlikely way of approaching God, let us see how he begins, with the first way or the first method of investigating ideas.

There are two ways, then, one that apparently fails and one that allegedly succeeds. In Paragraph 5, CSM II, on p. 25 of Cottingham, 4 lines from the bottom of the page, Descartes gives us a classification of thoughts that are immediately present to us:

> Some of my thoughts are as it were the images of things, and it is only in these cases that the term 'idea' is strictly appropriate—for example, when I think of [or: when I represent to myself] a man, of a chimera, of heaven or of an angel, or of God. Other thoughts have various additional forms: thus, when I will, or am afraid, or affirm, or deny, there is always a particular thing which I take as the object of my thought, but my thought includes something more than the likeness of that thing. Some thoughts in this category are called volitions or affections, while others are called judgments.

So, in Paragraph 5, then, Descartes offers us three types of thoughts, and these differ according to their *content*.

a) Images (ideas, properly speaking)
b) Thoughts accompanied by volitions or affections (image + concept)
c) Thoughts accompanied by judgments (images + concept)

Now, Descartes should be able to substitute the term "image" for "thought" in categories "b" and "c," but he doesn't. Why not? Because it would be hard to classify the *cogito* as an image, even as he seems to strain here by calling the idea of God an image.

But he goes on to a further classification of ideas in Paragraph 7, CSM II, on p. 26 of Cottingham:

> Among my ideas, some appear to be innate, some to be adventitious, i.e., foreign to me and coming from outside, and others have been made and invented by me. My understanding of what a thing is, what truth is, and what thought is, seems to derive simply from my own nature.

Thus, three kinds of ideas:
1) innate ideas
2) adventitious ideas
3) ideas made by me—that is, presumably, images made out of other, prior images, or ideas formed by abstraction

Now, while this definition is indeed wide, he gives an even more extensive one in his reply to Hobbes's *Objections*, the third set (CSM II, p. 127):

> Here my critic [Hobbes] wants the term 'idea' to be taken to refer simply to the images of material things which are depicted in the corporeal imagination. And if this is granted, it is easy for him to prove that there can be no proper idea of an angel or of God. But I make it quite clear in several places throughout the book, and in this passage in particular, that I am taking the word 'idea' to refer to whatever is immediately perceived by the mind. For example, when I want something, or am afraid of something, I simultaneously perceive that I want or am afraid; and this is why I count volition and fear among my ideas.

Descartes' definition of idea here, is so enormously broad as to be coextensive with thought. Indeed, he will say as much on p. 113 of CSM II, where he gives a set of definitions, following his replies to the Second Set of Objections. He says, "Idea. I understand this term to mean the form of any given thought." And, "Thought. I use this term to include everything that is within us in such a way that we are immediately aware of it."

The list in Paragraph **7**, CSM II, on p. 26, then, is a reclassification of ideas or thoughts with regard to their *origin*. First of all, then, according to this second classification by origin, what is an innate idea? It is nothing inscribed in us like a truth of conscience. Rather, it is a mode of thought, a way we think, and by which we can have the ability to recognize the truth of such things as the law of noncontradiction, figure, number, time, and the mathematicals. Let me give some references and citations on the sense he gives for *innate ideas*—that is, ideas which are born within me. He will often refer to these as "eternal truths."

1) Paragraph 3, Rule Four, of the *Regulae* (CSM I, p. 17):
   The human mind has within it a sort of spark of the divine, in which the first seeds of useful ways of thinking are sown, seeds which, however neglected and stifled by studies which impede them, often bear fruit of their own ac-

cord. This is our experience in the simplest of sciences, arithmetic, and geometry.

2) Paragraph 5 Rule Four, of the *Regulae* (CSM I, p. 18):
I am convinced that certain primary seeds of truth naturally implanted in human minds thrived vigorously in that unsophisticated and innocent age [of the Greek mathematicians] ... [which] enabled them to grasp true ideas in philosophy and mathematics.

3) Third Meditation, Paragraph 19, CSM II, p. 29:
As to my ideas of corporeal things, I can see nothing in them which is so great or excellent as to make it seem impossible that it originated in myself. For if I scrutinize them thoroughly and examine them one by one ... I notice that the things which I perceive clearly and distinctly in them are very few in number. This list comprises magnitude, or extension in length, breadth and depth; figure, which is formed by the boundaries of this extension; situation, which is a relation between various items possessing figure; and motion, or change in situation; to these may be added substance, duration and number.

4) *The Principles of Philosophy*, Part One, Principle 13 (CSM I, p. 197):
The mind, then, knowing itself, but still in doubt about all other things, looks around in all directions in order to extend its knowledge further. First of all, it finds within itself ideas of many things: and so long as it merely contemplates these ideas and does not affirm or deny the existence outside itself of anything resembling them, it cannot be mistaken. Next, it finds certain common notions from which it constructs various proofs; and, for as long as it attends to them, it is completely convinced of their truth. For example, the mind has within itself ideas of numbers and shapes, and it also has such common notions as: If you add equals to equals the results will be equal; from these it is easy to demonstrate that the three angles of a triangle equal two right angles, and so on.

5) *Principles*, Part One, Principle 49 (CSM I, p. 209):
when we recognize that it is impossible for anything to come from nothing, the proposition Nothing comes from nothing is regarded not as a really existing thing, or even as a mode of a thing, but as an eternal truth which resides within our mind. Such truths are termed common notions or axioms. The following are examples of this class: It is impossible for the same thing to be and to not be at the same time; What is done cannot be undone: He who thinks cannot but exist while he thinks: and countless others. It would not be easy to draw up a list of all of them; but nonetheless, we cannot fail to know them when the occasion for thinking about them arises.

6) *Principles* One, 55 (CSM I, p. 211):
We shall also have a very distinct understanding of duration, order, and

number, provided we do not mistakenly tack on to them any concept of substance. Instead we should regard the duration of a thing simply as a mode under which we conceive the thing in so far as it continues to exist. And similarly we should not regard order or number as anything separate from the things which are ordered and numbered, but should think of them simply as modes under which *we consider* the things in question.

7) *Principles* One, 57, 58 (CSM I, p. 212):
When time is distinguished from duration taken in the general sense and called the measure of movement, it is simply a mode of thought .... In the same way, number, when it is considered simply in the abstract or in general, and not in any created things, is merely a mode of thinking; and the same applies to all the general ideas, which in the Schools are understood by the name of universals.

8) *Principles* One, 75 (CSM I, p. 221):
We have within us knowledge of many propositions which are eternally true, such as "nothing comes from nothing." We shall also find that we have knowledge both of a corporeal or extended nature which is divisible, moveable, and so on ... When we contrast all this knowledge with the confused thoughts we had before, we will acquire the habit of forming clear and distinct concepts of all the things that can be known.

The *adventitious* idea. This is the image pure and simple. He gives several examples of adventitious ideas in Paragraph 7, "my hearing a noise, as I do now, or seeing the sun, or feeling the fire, comes from things which are located outside me, or so I have hitherto judged."

Those ideas made by me, again, seem to be presented as a mixing or associating, or abstracting of ideas. He gives as examples, the ideas of "sirens, hippogryphs, and the like."

Now, where do we get the idea of body as extension? Seemingly by the third way, for we saw in Meditation II that Descartes stripped sensible qualities off the wax by abstraction—a procedure he had earlier explained in *The Regulae*, Rules XII and XIV, which then permits an intuition by the mind. In any case, he's silent about it here—perhaps because he had to suppose the existence of the wax in Meditation II.

Thus the question arises, at first negatively: How do I get *from* the contents of consciousness, from ideas or images in my mind, *to* the world? If I simply remain on the level of a self-present idea, I don't risk falsity. Thus, in Paragraph 6, CSM II, p. 26, he will remark:

> And the chief and most common mistake which is to be found here consists in my judging that the ideas which are in me resemble, or conform to, things located outside me. Of course, if I considered just the ideas themselves simply as modes of my thought [or: ways of thinking] without referring them to anything else from the outside, they could scarcely give me any material for error.

Thus the move begins: if my judgments concern the references of images, then what can I learn from images about the world, i.e., what can I know about real bodies? Does the image accurately represent the nature of the thing? And here it doesn't seem to be so much a question of existence, at least not from the start. Nonetheless, methods 1 & 2 will raise this as a problem: which is more important for our judgments about ideas?—essence or existence? In any case, both essence and existence are in question. His first formulation about the referential status of images will concern the nature of things, in Paragraph 8, CSM II, on p. 26:

> But the chief question at this point concerns the ideas which I take to be derived from things existing outside me: what are my reasons for thinking that they resemble these things?

Why do I judge that my ideas resemble or, are similar to, objects outside me? Why? Well, he says, *Nature teaches me!* That's just the way I'm made. Here the argument is limited to the simple image, to *adventitious* ideas alone. Yet he objects to this "teaching of nature" because it is not based on indubitable principles. It is only a natural impulse or inclination that makes him think the image is similar to external things, and not the natural *light*, i.e., not the *principles of reason.* Natural inclination or impulse makes errors: it can't distinguish, oftentimes, between virtue and vice, and it oftentimes inclines me to evil, rather than to the good, as he remarks at some length in Paragraph 9.

What Descartes wants to say is that simple images can't give us the real nature of bodies, or of the existing world. Nonetheless, my natural inclination leads me to believe that they do—and thus it has to fail. But why doesn't Descartes explain how it fails? Because then he'd have to expose the presupposition that there are bodies, that bodies exist! Otherwise, we couldn't very well make mistakes about them. So, in any case, I'm not taught the similarity thesis by natural reason. The principles of natural reason are indubitable. Inclination is not indubitable, so it has to be the cause of error. Thus, reason or understanding is preserved at the expense of natural inclination. Incidentally, this is the faculty, which, for St. Thomas Aquinas, leads us to the Good! In his *Treatise on Law*, Art. 2, sec. 93, he remarks, "We have a natural inclination to the Good." "Natural inclination is, for man, to preserve his own being." Hobbes and Spinoza could likewise furnish analogous references. And, for Aquinas, reason would be the guide to the Good.

Cartesian physics, however, doesn't recognize the good, or incarnations of goodness, in the mathematical manifold. Also, for Cartesian physics and cosmology, the universe is in a sense homogeneous—it consists of extended bodies in an homogeneously extended space. There is no "great chain of being" here that would ascend from brute, formless matter, through informed matter, to pure forms, intelligible species, hosts of angels, and then on to the God who is pure act, *actus essendi*. Thus, for *Thomistic* physics, the created world points to God by degrees of goodness and by degrees of being or reality. Thus, the God of St. Thomas is at once *ens perfectissimum* and *ens realissimum*, as well as *ens omnipotens*.

In any case, the "teaching of nature," the "natural inclination," is dropped in Paragraph 9. On the one hand, Descartes wants to get outside of consciousness. The image must have its referent in the real world. If it doesn't, then the whole of Cartesian science is a rude sham for the groundlings. The problem is that I believe my image *corresponds to* reality. But do I have a scientifically justifiable basis for this assertion? No! This is why Descartes, bless his heart, will go through an apoplectic hocus-pocus in Meditation III to try and get a justifiable basis for it. Step one will exhaust images. Step two, what he calls "another way," i.e., a "second way," in Paragraph 13, will, ostensibly, get Descartes beyond his mind—but, all the same, this step occurs in an extraordinary fashion. Using illegitimate scholastic language, in the second way, he'll account for his knowledge of substance by claiming that, as a thinking thing, he may be the super-eminent cause of the objective content of his idea of extended substance. Got it? But still, realize that he hasn't gotten beyond the mind. Thus, he'll say that there is only one idea of which he can't account for his being the super-eminent cause, namely, God. So the ostensible move out of his mind doesn't occur until Paragraph 22, the top of CSM II, p. 31 in Cottingham. Thus, there is a God. God wouldn't deceive us. God, then, who is not a deceiver, guarantees our belief in the real existence of things, and that the nature of really existing things is to be extended. At a stroke, a *proof for the existence of the world*—and this satisfies the *scientific* intention—and a proof of the *existence of God*, which satisfies the *apologetic* intention. The great five cent synthesis! So, now, let us deal with this purported move. We return to the start of Paragraph 10, CSM II, on p. 27:

> And as for the other reason, since these ideas do not depend on my will, it does not follow that they must come from things located outside me. Just as the impulses which I was speaking of a moment ago seem opposed to my will, even though they are within me, so there may be some other faculty not yet fully known to me, which produces these ideas

> without any assistance from external things; this is, after all, just how I have always thought ideas are produced in me when I am dreaming.

Now, this mysterious faculty, which might produce these ideas, let us call it the "X" faculty, this might be the imagination, since it is said to produce images in me when I'm asleep. Much as we saw in the First Meditation. So here, again, we can find an answer to the question, "when does the thinking thing exist?" Only when I think—but if I think when I'm asleep, i. e., dreaming, then there is more to the thinking thing than awake, conscious thinking. But, all the same, this "X" faculty can't simply produce images in their entirety. As we saw, from Meditation One, Paragraph 6, it can make medleys and constructs out of a previously given content. Thus, *imagination* itself still presupposes a source of content—namely, the *adventitious* idea. Thus, we can't even explain the content of dreams without ultimately referring to extended bodies.

At this point in the Meditations, Descartes still doesn't know the thinking thing is incorporeal. Also, the status of this "X" faculty is something other than a function of the thinking thing as thinking. He says he doesn't know what it is. So, there must be the assumption that the "X" faculty is corporeal—what originates by it, then, doesn't originate from me, insofar as I know myself to be a thinking thing. I don't even know if I'm incorporeal. Suppose, then, that the thinking thing *is* corporeal. Then, either there are two sources of what is present to thought, or they are indistinguishable. So, there is reason to think they are separate—the operative assumption here, being that the thinking thing isn't corporeal!

So, finally, we get to the crucial Paragraph 11, CSM II, on p. 27: "And finally, even if these ideas did come from things other than myself, it would not follow that they must resemble those things.

There is a two-sided inquiry here: that which resembles and that which is resembled. Continuing, "Indeed, I think I have often discovered a great difference between an object and its idea in many cases."

Thus, two theses are asserted here. Descartes wants to prove:

A) Either my ideas do not come from objects outside me, or, that I do not know that objects exist outside me.
B) My ideas do not resemble objects outside me.

If A and B are true, then there is no knowledge of bodies outside of us. The first method or way tries to establish A and B. Therefore, no objects can justifiably be said to exist. Method two then tries to prove that God does exist.

What is the *relation* between these two theses? If thesis A is true—if my ideas do not come from objects outside me—then the question of *resemblance* doesn't arise. That is, if A is true, then B is true. Which is to say, I can make no claim about resemblance. But, if thesis A is false, thesis B may still be true. So, the stronger case would be to try to prove A first, and then let it entail B: if there is no existence, then there can't very well be any resemblance. Why not? Quite simply, because there is nothing to compare!

But if we look at these two theses the other way around, then the case must fail! If B is true, i.e., if my ideas do not resemble objects outside me—then A must be false. Why? Because in order to compare my idea with its referent, I must presuppose its referent! Whether or not they resemble objects, the very claim of resemblance entails the existence of that which is to be compared. I'm comparing two things: how can I compare them if they don't exist?

Thesis A goes to the root of the matter, and thesis B does not. So, what does ol' Renatus Cartesius do? He attempts to prove thesis B—a very odd procedure indeed, if he expects us to think that thesis B entails thesis A. If he proved A, then B would indeed follow. To be even more audacious, Descartes uses as his example to prove thesis B, the case of the sun!

In arguing thesis B, Descartes presents two candidates for a resembling idea, that is, in Paragraph 11, CSM II, on p. 27 of Cottingham:

> For example, there are two different ideas of the sun which I find within me. One of them, which is acquired, as it were, from the senses and which is a prime example of an idea which I reckon to come from an external source, makes the sun appear very small. The other idea is based on astronomical reasoning, that is, it is derived from certain notions which are innate in me (or else, it is constructed by me in some other way), and this idea shows the sun to be several times larger than the earth. Obviously, both these ideas cannot resemble the sun which exists outside me; and reason persuades me [*me fait croire*] that the idea which seems to have emanated most directly from the sun itself has in fact no resemblance to it at all.

There are two ideas given, then:

1) The *scientific idea* of the sun. This is elicited from certain innate ideas or it is formed by me in some manner.
2) An idea of the sun which results from the *image*, that is, an idea of the sun which is an *adventitious* idea.

Now, the two ideas can't resemble the same sun, and all reasoning tells me that the adventitious image is most dissimilar—which admission, of course, presupposes the existing sun, just in order to bear comparison! Or, on the other hand, the scientific idea is also dissimilar to the sun—which also presupposes the existence of the sun. The same would hold even if the adventitious idea proved to be more similar—but then, by definition, the world—i.e., the really existing sun—would be necessary.

What is curious about the two sun argument, as it is formulated, is that it is extremely weak. In fact, it must presuppose the existence of bodies. This is the conclusion that must be drawn from Paragraph 11. But Descartes doesn't draw this conclusion. In fact, he remains entirely silent about this. Rather, Descartes will say, in Paragraph 12, that it's blind impulse which makes him believe. And this raises the whole question of existence once more. Hence, the necessity for a second way.

To repeat this once again, the problem Descartes is faced with is the status of images. Of course, he argues from a representative theory of ideas. Berkeley and Hume will argue from a non-representative theory, where image will be replaced by the term 'impression.'

The image is a problem, for Descartes claims to know the sun by scientific reasoning—and in this sense, he can rectify the image. But without knowing that the sun exists, the elaborate scientific account seems to be a rather dubious construct. Much the same problem occurs here as it did with the *wax example* in the Second Meditation. Granted that I know the *nature* of bodies, i.e., that they are *extended*, how can I start from extension and arrive at wax and not a pumpkin? So here, too, if I start with extension, how do I get the sun and not wax? What we see here is that the scientific account must *presuppose* something that *it cannot prove*. Thus, the science is itself dubious! And if it is dubious, can it give us an adequate account of the world?

Let us briefly restate the *real problem* of the Third Meditation. How can we get *outside* the sphere of consciousness? The *first method* for investigating ideas takes us up to Paragraph 12. There, Descartes analyzed the *representational status of images* from the standpoint of interiority: How do I know that my ideas are (1) *caused by* external objects, and (2) that they resemble external objects? Well, natural inclination or blind impulse tells me. But, natural inclination is dubitable. It often inclines me towards evil and vice. Natural *reason*, which is indubitable, doesn't tell *me* that my ideas are caused by, or that they resemble, external objects. The belief that they do come from without and that they *resemble* external things does not seem to depend on my will, or on myself, as a thinking thing. Well, what, then? *Perhaps* there is an "X" faculty that belongs to me, yet which is unknown—which, we saw, left open the possibility that he is more than a thinking thing. It is possible that the "X faculty" is the imagination. In this case, he would also have to be bodily, and receive sensory impressions from figurate bodies at the outset.

Now, this line of reasoning seems the most plausible way of explaining Paragraph 10, CSM II, on p. 27. Nonetheless, Descartes quickly drops all talk of the "X faculty" and of the *existential* causal source of these images, these adventitious ideas, and he suggests, in Paragraph 11, that even if the images do come from without, there is no reason that the interior image should faithfully represent the nature of the exterior object. Thus, he centers on the weaker, yet more complex resemblance thesis, when he raises the question of the two suns. That is, I have two ideas of the sun, one derived from the senses, the other from astronomical reasonings—and these ideas are either innate, or formed by me. The former idea, derived from our senses, represents the sun to be extremely small; the latter idea, derived from astronomical reasonings, represents the sun as extremely large. Reason tells me both can't be similar to the sun and that the scientific idea is more similar.

The weakness of the argument is transparent: neither the scientific idea nor the adventitious idea could even be compared with the sun, unless one supposed the sun to exist. The *resemblance* thesis thus *presupposes* the *existence* thesis.

But what complicates this whole first method of investigating ideas is the fact that Descartes cannot claim the existence thesis! He has no *warrant* for it. Thus, the existence thesis is characterized in *negative* terms: i.e., external objects can't be assumed; they must be proven. From the standpoint of interiority, I do not know that objects exist outside me. In other words, according to what I do know, so far as I do know, my ideas do not come from objects without: I cannot assert that they do. Thus, to assert that one kind of *idea* or image more *closely resembles* a real *object* than another, is to make an *illicit inference*. It's *because* the inference is illicit that Descartes has to go on to the second way, the second method of investigating ideas, beginning in Paragraph 13, CSM II, on p. 27 of Cottingham.

Before we pursue this other way, what motivates the collapse of the first way, the first method of investigating ideas?

1) The *inference* from similarity to existence is *illicit*. Illicit, that is to say, presuppositional. It moves from the order of thought to the order of being, without being able to justify this move. The move is, therefore, an assertion.
2) Now, what this means, then, for Cartesian *science*, is that *there is no guarantee of its object*. Cartesian science has to *posit* its object.
3) Thus, while the internal mathematicals, the principle of noncontradiction, etc., are *true*, according to the criteria of clarity and distinctness, raised in Paragraph 2, CSM II, on p. 24 of Cottingham, they are *non-existential*. Truth, in this case, is only *interideational*. It does *not correspond* to anything *outside* the realm of ideas. This is why, in Paragraph 4, CSM II, p. 25, Descartes supplements the definition of truth as clarity and distinctness with the additional statement, that if there is an omnipotent God, he must not

> be a deceiver. That is, a good God wouldn't deceive me by suspending existential and analytical claims. To bring in the world and his own body, Descartes needs God as a guarantor.

All of which leads to the apparent convergence of the theoretical and apologetic intentions. Thus, the failure of the first method is necessitated by the required proof of God.

At which point, the question of Descartes' theological or apologetical sincerity arises. By eliminating sensible forms, intelligible forms, pure forms, intelligible species, etc., in Meditation Two—we don't seem to need a God as most real, as *ens realissimum*. By eliminating natural inclination, we eliminate the conventional faculty of recognizing *goodness* in the world and in ourselves. Thus, God as the source of goodness and as the highest good—the *ens perfectissimum*—also seems unlikely.

If a God remains, he is simply power, unqualified by goodness. Also, we have seen the charge of circularity arise. To prove God deductively, I must suppose the principle of non-contradiction. The conclusion must follow from the premises. Thus, I have to prove that there exists in fact a God—beyond my own ideas of one—a God who would intervene to guarantee *the means by which* I prove his own existence. Then, and only then, can I claim there is a world, or that I have a body. Now, either this is circular, or it is not circular, or, as Leibniz claimed, the whole affair is simply one grand charade.

Finally, what is gotten by God? A satisfactory resolution of the apologetic intention. Also a justifiable claim—*if* the argument does prove that God exists and that he would not deceive us—that the world exists: that, in short, Cartesian science would have a justifiably certain field of application.

Yet, we already saw, in the First Meditation, that Descartes had to presuppose the world in order to account for the contents of ideas: the imagination only makes arrangements and medleys of colors. We have to have a source of color from without. Also, in Meditation Two, with the wax example, we had to suppose the wax really existed in order to claim that its nature was extension: because, (a) we had to abstract away its sensible qualities, and (b), because it was claimed to be the same wax that we formerly saw, felt, smelled, and always believed in.

In conclusion, then, *existence is* a problem for Descartes. Either he has to simply presuppose that there is in fact a world, and that people indeed possess bodies—or, he has to deduce the external existence of God: and then, from God, the existence of the world. He has to do all this from the internal cogito, and without supposing that there is a world.

So, the "second way," or the "other way," in Paragraph 13, CSM II, on p. 27: "But *it* now occurs to me that there is another way of investigating whether some of the things of which I possess ideas within me exist outside of me." Now, this second way, or method, begins by discussing degrees of being within the idea. The representative idea of one thing may itself have a greater reality or being than the representative ide*a* of something else. This is what Descartes alleges. Paragraph 13, CSM II, p. 28 of Cottingham, line 3:

> Undoubtedly, the **ideas** which represent substances to me amount to something more and, so to speak [*pour ainsi dire*], contain within themselves more objective reality, i. e., participate by representation in a higher degree of being or perfection, than the ideas which merely represent modes or accidents.

Of course, a representative idea can't represent something other than itself, unless there is something other than itself to represent. That is, there is something representing, namely, the idea, and something represented. Thus, the content of idea "A" participates in a higher degree of being than the content of idea "B," only on the condition that what idea "A" represents, itself has a higher degree of reality than what is represented by idea "B." There must be a really existing "A" outside the mind. Yet, for Descartes, the whole argument concerning degrees of objective reality is attempted without any reference outside the mind. In short, does it make any sense to talk about degrees of representing reality without referring to that which is represented? Descartes wants to get outside the mind, but he starts out by contradicting himself—to prove his getting outside the mind, he has already presupposed that external referent!

Moreover, and what is curious, Descartes doesn't tell us what substance is, either. He proceeds to borrow the scholastic notion of objective reality, which is based on really existing external being, i. e., which presupposes the world, and he then combines it with his own notion that nothing exists outside the mind—i. e., that we have no knowledge of extra-mental reality—and he then moves in grand contradictory sweeps up to the deity.

In Paragraph 14, he will claim the following:

1) *That* there must be as much *reality* in the cause as in the effect.
2) *That* the effect *derives its reality* from its cause.
3) *That* what is *more perfect* cannot be derived from the *less perfect.*

BUT, all these are scholastic notions, and Descartes lets us know this by the ad hominem reference, further down, CSM II, on p. 28: "And this is transparently true, not only in the case of effects which possess what the philosophers call actual or formal reality, but also in the case of ideas, where one is considering only what they call objective reality."

So, the assumptions of the second argument concerning ideas are the following:

1) An idea has objective reality. That is, it has a represented content, and it is claimed to have degrees thereof (Paragraph 13, CSM II, p. 28).
2) The efficient and total cause must have as much reality as the effect. This is specified in Paragraph 14, CSM II, p. 28, to include
   a) formal cause (a cause is of the same kind or the same form as the effect),
   b) eminent cause (a cause that is of a higher kind or form than the effect)—he says he knows about efficient and total cause by the natural light—also, he claims that ideas and their content (the objective reality) must have adequate causes; the eminent cause, then, is not only an idea.
3) Thus, the cause of objective reality in the idea, i.e., the specific content, must be a thing (and not merely an idea) with at least as much reality in it, as the content of the idea represents!

These are the premises on which the argument is built. Yet, Descartes has offered no premise, no argument, for speaking about degrees of reality. Much less, he explicitly attributes the crucial notions of objective and formal reality to the tradition.

The extraordinary feature of the argument results precisely from his failure to discuss degrees of reality and different forms of reality. For what is being compared in the argument is my mind and its ideas: i.e., the ideas I find in my mind. What strikes us as being extraordinary in the comparison is the possibility that an idea can be more real than a thing. Let's look at this jocular Platonism CSM II, on p. 29, the second line from the beginning of Paragraph 16:

> But what is my conclusion to be? If the objective reality of any one of my ideas turns out to be so great that I clearly recognize the same reality does not reside in me, either formally or eminently, and hence that I myself cannot be its cause, it will necessarily follow that I am not alone in the world, but that some other thing which is the cause of this idea exists.

The argument is a simple modus ponens: P) Q. P therefore Q. *If* I cannot be the formal or eminent cause of the objective reality of an idea (i.e., P), *then* some being other than me is the case (Q). Implicitly, this being exists. Yet, this argument holds for *any one of my ideas.* Here he doesn't speak of his idea of a stone or of heat. He gives no examples. Why not? Because he really wants to take the argument further. He wants to show, on the one hand, that *if nothing else,* if there is nothing *other than* himself, then *he* is the cause of his *ideas.*

Therefore, *he, as thinking substance, can be*. Thus, he wants to show that *he can* be the cause of his *ideas* of the world, because he, too, is *substance*. This enables him to take the final step, namely, that there's only one idea that he can't be the cause of, namely, God. Thereby, he tries to pass over the world until after he can prove the existence of God.

The next stage, then, is to consider whether or not we *can* be the adequate cause of our thoughts about the world, about corporeal reality. After all, we don't know anything about what exists outside the mind.

What ideas, then, are the *candidates* for my knowledge about corporeal bodies, in Paragraph 19, toward the bottom CSM II, of p. 29?

> As to my ideas of corporeal things, I can see nothing in them which is so great or excellent as to make it seem impossible that it originated in myself. For if I scrutinize them thoroughly and examine them one by one, in the way in which I examined the idea of the wax yesterday, I notice that the things which I perceive clearly and distinctly in the are very few in number. The list comprises magnitude [*grandeur, magnitudinem*], or extension in length, breadth, and depth; figure, which is formed by the boundaries of this extension; situation, which is a relation between various items possessing figure; and motion, or change in situation; to these may be added substance, duration, and number. But as for all the rest, including light and colours, sounds, smells, tastes, heat and cold and the other tactile qualities, I think of these only in a very confused and obscure way, to the extent that I do not even know whether they are true or false, that is, whether the ideas I have of them are ideas of real things or of non-things.

Magnitude or extension in length, breadth, or depth; figure; situation; motion; substance; duration; number; light; colors; sounds; scents; tastes; heat; cold; tactile qualities. In short, Descartes seemingly has originated a whole panoply of *ideas* about body!

Then, Descartes turns against the image. Images are confused, he says, they contain a certain "material falsity," they may be chimeras, they may thus represent things which may not even exist!

At which point, in Paragraph 21, CSM II, on pp. 30–31, he restates the list, now diminished, of what can be held as clear and distinct. But now, he has replaced ideas as images with ideas as concepts. This will permit knowledge of extension, the extension thesis, to arise, without making it seem to depend on images. He once again gives the list of ideas, and he now inquires as to their source. First, the new list, in Paragraph 21:

> With regard to the clear and distinct ideas I have of corporeal things, it appears that I could have borrowed some of these from my idea of myself, namely, substance, duration, number, and anything else of this kind ... As for all the other qualities which make up the ideas of corporeal things, namely extension, figure, situation, and movement, these are not formally

> contained in me, since I am only a thinking thing; but since they are merely modes of a substance, and as it were, the garments under which corporeal substance appears to us, and I am a substance, it seems that they might.

What clear and distinct ideas we have then, about body, are the following:

Substance; extension duration; figure; number; situation; motion. Now, the addition of quantity or magnitude would make it equivalent to the list in Meditation One, Paragraph 7, CSM II, on p. 14. Number, here, however, would give us quantity, and number or figure could give us magnitude—whether numerical or geometrical.

Yet what warrant does Descartes have for including substance in this list? In the list of Paragraph 7, of the First Meditation, he had specified "corporeal nature and its extension." Nonetheless, the explicit term 'substance' seems to intrude here: in fact, he doesn't tell us at all *what it is*. On CSM II, p. 10, in the Synopsis, he had briefly mentioned it, saying, "Body, taken in the general sense, is a substance." But this mention appears to be little more than the Aristotelian statement that our knowledge of substance begins with particular things. What little he mentions of substance here, CSM II, on p. 30, Paragraph 21, doesn't amount to very much, either. If we say that substance is self-subsistence, as with the stone, Descartes fails to tell us what that is!

> For example, I think that a stone is a substance, or is a thing capable of existing independently, and I also think that I am a substance. Admittedly, I conceive of myself as a thing that thinks and is not extended.

So, let us tentatively drop substance from the list. It is not explained, and therefore, it doesn't add anything to our understanding.

In any case, both I and the stone have duration and number. They seem to apply both to me and to the stone. In this sense, I can be the formal cause of these concepts. Thus, he says, "I remember that ... I have various thoughts which I can count; it is in these ways that I acquire the ideas of duration and number, which I can transfer to other things." so what remains of my clear and distinct concepts of bodies? Can I be the cause of them? Again, referring to the list he gives in Paragraph 21, on CSM II, pp. 30–31, he states that he "could have borrowed some of these ideas from my idea of my self," and he concludes that these ideas "might be contained in me eminently." So, these concepts could be caused by me. They might be. Might be, or could be, is a rather weak way to conclude an argument, however. After all, they might not be caused by me. But why might? I might be the eminent cause of them. If I am a substance and rock, too, is a substance, it might be that the thinking thing is more excellent, more real, more perfect than a rock, a stone. But, has he even suggested what excellence is? Or reality, for that matter, much less perfection? No, quite simply.

The whole argument stands on eminent causation and degrees of reality, precisely those terms he slipped into the previous account in Paragraphs 14–16: precisely those terms he attributes to the scholastics and for which he offers no justification whatsoever. Apologetically, this is fine, for no self-respecting Thomist would object. But is Descartes a Thomist? Do these terms belong to the vocabulary of Cartesian mathematical physics? Hardly.

Is the thinking thing (or, let's say, mental substance) *more real* than a stone (i.e., a particular extended substance)? is it more *real* than the side of a mountain? Or more *real* than the combined realms of Brittany and Aquitaine? Or of France? The earth? Is it more real, more excellent, more perfect than the universe? *Ad absurdam*, buddy!

At which point, Descartes turns the argument to God, precisely by departing from the imperfection of his own mind. Out of the whole world, which might point to God, by virtue of its order, reason, coherency, excellence, goodness, etc., Descartes chooses one tiny chunk, his mind; and of that, one idea—which arises precisely from the imperfection of his mind.

All of this should make us somewhat suspicious, at the very least. The way to understand the argument, it seems, is otherwise than its rather weak, apparent character.

This last step of the argument, which relies on the scholastic doctrine of eminent causes, is the serious one. Since the thinking thing is not known to be body, and since we don't know what substance is, and since he offers no justification for degrees of reality, then the thinking cannot be known to be the cause of the remaining list of clear and distinct ideas about real bodies. That is, we don't know the mind to be the cause, the source of the ideas of extension; figure; situation; motion insofar as their content belongs peculiarly to real, existing bodies.

If we drop the unjustified premises of the argument, then, we are forced to conclude that bodies exist, and that bodies are the cause of my ideas about bodies. Therefore the world exists! Therefore the proof for the existence of God is superfluous. At least he doesn't need to prove God's existence to account for the world. What Descartes would have to do here, and what, of course, he fails to do, is to prove that he is the formal and efficient cause of the extension of the stone.

We remember the structure of the argument in Meditation One, Paragraph 6, CSM II, p. 13, before the onset of God and the demon. I examine the contents of consciousness, or, of the idea. I can't account for it unless objects outside me exist. While it is true that I'm a thinking thing, when I examine what is found within my thought, I'm forced to admit that its content is ultimately caused by bodies outside my thought.

The same regression takes place in the case of the wax example in the Second Meditation. I can't conceive or mentally intuit, grasp, the extension of the wax unless I presuppose that the wax really exists. Thus, the existence of the wax wasn't doubted. On the contrary, it was required, in order to know that its nature was to be extended. In fact, he even goes so far as to refer the reader back to the wax example on the bottom line of CSM II, p. 29. When we follow that reference—"I examined the idea of wax yesterday (Paragraph 19, CSM II, p. 29)"—when we follow that reference out, and read, back on CSM II, p. 21, Paragraph 12, of Meditation Two, his remark is the following:

> But what is this *wax which can only be conceived by the understanding or the mind? It is of course the same wax which I see, which I touch, which I imagine, in short the same wax that I knew it to be from the start.*

When we track back the reference, then, we realize that the wax has to exist for the analysis to be carried out in the first place. No existing wax, no *sameness* to the cases made in the example.

The presuppositionality of the world was also seen in the case of the two suns. In order to compare an image (whether scientific or adventitious) with the sun, I must perforce suppose that the sun exists and that it is extended.

Well, back to the big "G" question. What is the case with the first argument for God? Paragraph 22, on CSM II, p. 31, tells us.

> So, there remains only the idea of God; and I must consider whether there is anything in the idea which could not have originated in myself. By the name 'God' I understand a substance that is infinite, eternal, immutable, independent, all-knowing, all-powerful, and which created both myself and everything else (if anything else there be) that exists. All these attributes are such that, the more carefully I concentrate on them, the less possible it seems that the idea I have of them could have originated from me alone. So from what has been said it must be concluded that God necessarily exists.

What seems different about the idea of God, here, is that it's defined as a multiplicity—a multiplicity of divine attributes. Now, is this idea of a multiplicity itself clear and distinct? That is, can I hold infinity, eternality, immutability, independence, omniscience, omnipotence, and the notion by which I and everything else has been created. ... can I hold all this together as a unified idea and claim that it is clear and distinct? Most unlikely, good people! But what about the compatibility of these attributes? Moreover, what about God's goodness—without goodness, it seems as if Descartes can simply sidestep the whole question of theodicy. If

God isn't good, it doesn't seem too much of a problem to reconcile the traditional attributes of omnipotence and benevolence, for there is nothing to reconcile.

Recall, again, that a similar list of attributes was given CSM II, on p. 28, Paragraph 13: eternality, infinity, immutability, omniscience, creator of all things. But, once again, no goodness. As we have already seen, this failure to discuss the compatibility of these attributes, much less to reconcile these several concepts with God's goodness, results in a very peculiar God. One that at best seems co-extensive with power alone. If these attributes here, in Paragraph 22, or in Paragraph 13, or even in the *Fourth Discourse on Method*, Paragraph 4, is just a list, just a heap of attributes, then Descartes is extraordinarily careless—in which case, is this meant to be a serious proof? Indeed, in Paragraph 22, CSM II, on p. 31, he is careful to say, not by the idea of God, but by the name of God, I understand a substance that possesses these attributes.

The proof itself duplicates the previous step in the argument, and it depends on the unfounded concepts of substance, degrees of reality, and eminent causation.

Yet, in Paragraph 24, CSM II, on p. 31—*toujours* Cottingham—Descartes does claim to have a single notion, or idea, of God—one which—is *clear and distinct*. To be precise, he says in Paragraph 24, that he has a notion of the infinite—"That is, God." This is simply asserted as an identity. Then he refers to the notion of God in the next paragraph, Paragraph 25, as "This idea of God," which is then stated as being clear and distinct. But how can a finite being have an idea of the infinite? Seems remarkable, no? If we look ahead a bit, however, to the Fourth Meditation, Paragraph 8, towards the bottom of CSM II, p. 39, we discover how we can find the infinite within us! More precisely, Descartes finds within himself the infinite faculty of will: (this is 7 lines up from the bottom of CSM II, p. 31)

> I cannot complain that the will or freedom of choice which I received from God is not sufficiently extensive or perfect, since I know by experience that it is not restricted by any limits. Indeed, I think it is very noteworthy that there is nothing else in me which is so perfect and so great that the possibility of a further increase in its perfection or greatness is beyond my understanding. If, for example, I consider the faculty of comprehension, I immediately recognize that in my case it is extremely slight and extremely limited, and I at once form the idea of an other faculty which is much greater—indeed, supremely great and infinite; and from the very fact that I can form an idea of it, I perceive that **it** belongs to the nature of God .... It is only the will or freedom of choice, which I experience within me to be so great that the idea of any greater faculty is beyond my grasp; so much so that it is above all in virtue of the will that I understand myself to bear in some way the image and likeness of God.

Now, a few lines further on, an interesting definition of the will emerges: "The will simply consists in our ability to do or not to do something; that is, to affirm or deny, to pursue or avoid."

In any case, Descartes begins his *second proof of God* in Paragraph 29, on the top of CSM II, p. 33: "From whom would I derive my existence?" From myself? My parents? From a source less powerful than God? If not any of these, then I must suppose God. Of course, if I were the author of my own being, I should doubt nothing, and I should desire nothing. I'd give myself every perfection. That is, I would have done a much better job of it! The same problem would hold with regard to his parents. Also, this would lead to an infinite regress—way back past Lucy and the Olduvai Gorge! As for a source less than Divine, how, then, could Descartes obtain the ideas of the divine perfections, not to speak of their unity?

Thus, Descartes states his second argument for God, based on the divisibility of time, in Paragraph 31, just below the middle of page 33 in Cottingham:

> I do not escape the force of these arguments by supposing that I have always existed as I do now, as if it followed from this that there was no need to look for any author of my existence. For a lifespan can be divided into countless parts, each completely independent of the others, so that it does not follow from the fact that I existed a little while ago that I must exist now, unless there is some cause which, as it were, creates me afresh at this moment—that is, which *preserves* me.

In short:

- All *duration* of my life is infinitely divisible into parts (apparently, into moments of time).
- All the parts of *time* are independent of one another.

- Therefore: there must be a conserving cause for my existence.

The problem with the proof, of course, consists in the transition from the parts of time to the assertion that the being of things, in time, is likewise fragmented. (Remember in Paragraph 21, CSM II, on p. 31, where he said "I acquired the ideas of duration and number which I can then transfer to other things." Also, in *The Principles of Philosophy*, Part I, Principle 57 (CSM I, p. 212), where, he said, "When time is distinguished from duration, taken in the general sense, and called the measure of movement, it is simply a mode of thought.") These references should awaken our caution.

Now, here, Descartes seems to claim that beings are contingent upon moments of time. Does a thing depend, in the present, on its previous moment?

—which no longer is? Is this at all plausible? In any case, there is no reason to suspect that the possible independence of moments of time—which is a function of thought—in any way involves the being which is to be found within that time.

Of course, what is in question here, is the continued being of one thing, the thinking thing—but we don't even know whether it is bodily or immaterial! What its being even is remains a complete mystery to us at this point! For example, in Meditation Four, Paragraph 10, CSM II, on p. 41, he says:

> But now, besides the knowledge that I exist, in so far as I am a thinking thing, an idea of corporeal nature comes into my mind; and I happen to be in doubt as to whether the thinking nature which is in me, or rather by which I am what I am, is different from this corporeal nature or identical with it. I am making the further supposition that my intellect has not yet come upon any persuasive reason in favor or one alternative rather than the other.

Moreover, the very nature of the thinking thing itself is still up in the air. In Paragraph 32, on the bottom line of CSM II, p. 33, for instance, he says, "For since I am nothing but a thinking thing—or at least since I am now concerned only and precisely with that part of me which is a thinking thing ...."

Well, we are once again forced to ask if Descartes' proof is to be taken seriously. Is this a serious method of inquiry? When he questions the source of his own being, he neither knows what he is, or even, what kind of being he has! How, then, could he even tell that he *is* or *is not?*

C'mon, René, "Is you is, or is you ain't?" You putting' me on!

References

Descartes, René (1953) *Méditations*. In: *Œuvres et Lettres*, Paris: Gallimard. pp. 257f.

Leibniz, Gottfried Wilhelm (1923–) *Sämtliche Schriften und Briefe*, Series II, Volume 1, 2nd ed., Berlin: Akademie Verlag. pp. 775.

List of Contributors

Barry Allen is Professor of Philosophy at McMaster University, in Hamilton, Ontario, Canada. He is author of numerous articles as well as *Truth in Philosophy* (1993), *Knowledge and Civilization* (2004), and *Artifice and Design: Art and Technology in Human Experience* (2008).

David B. Allison (1944–2016) was Emeritus Professor of Philosophy at the State University of New York at Stony Brook. He is the author of *Reading the New Nietzsche* (2001) and editor of *The New Nietzsche* (1985) as well as, with Mark Roberts, *Disordered Mother or Disordered Diagnosis: Munchausen by Proxy Syndrome* (1998). He translated Jacques Derrida, *Speech and Phenomena and Other Essays* (1973) and Derrida's *Edmund Husserl's Origin of Geometry* (1977) in addition to several book collections. He was co-editor of *New Nietzsche Studies*, the journal founded in 1996 to honor his contributions to international Nietzsche scholarship.

Babette Babich is Professor of Philosophy at Fordham University in New York City. Author of over 250 articles/book chapters, a four time Fulbright fellow, Babich is editor of twelve collective volumes in addition to the journal, *New Nietzsche Studies*. Her eight books include *Un politique brisé. Le souci d'autrui, l'humanisme, et les juifs chez Heidegger* (2016), *The Hallelujah Effect: Music, Performance Practice, and Technology* (2016 [2013]), *La fin de la pensée?* (2012), *Words in Blood, Like Flowers* (2006), and *Nietzsches Wissenschaftsphilosophie* (2010 [Engl. [1994]).

Paul Fairfield is Associate Professor in the Department of Philosophy at Queen's and Adjunct Professor at the University of Ottawa. He is the author of more than eight books on topics ranging from education to hermeneutics, politics, and death in addition to editing many collections. Among his planned new books is a study of the philosophy of history entitled *Transitions: An Essay on Historical Change*.

Duška Franeta Associate Professor at the Faculty of Legal and Business Studies dr Lazar Vrkatić, in Novi Sad, Serbia. She has mostly written on hermeneutics and legal and ethical values and she authored *Human Dignity as Legal Value* (in Serbian, 2015), co-edited (with Evangelos Protopapadakis) *Applied Ethics* (in Serbian, 2014) and has translated several books from German into Serbian.

https://doi.org/10.1515/9783110551563-022

Saulius Geniusas is an Associate Professor of Philosophy at the Chinese University of Hong Kong. His work primarily engages Continental philosophy, especially phenomenology and hermeneutics. He is the author of *The Origins of the Horizon in Husserl's Phenomenology* (Springer 2012) and forty plus articles in various philosophy journals and anthologies.

Dimitri Ginev is Professor of Philosophy at Sofia University. He is founder and editor-in-chief of the journal *Studia Culturologica*. Among his books are: *Entre Anthroplogie et Hermeneutique* (2003), *Das hermeneutische Projekt Georg Mischs* (2011), and *Practices and Possibilities* (2013). His main interest of research is the history of modern hermeneutics.

Simon Glynn is Professor of Philosophy at Florida Atlantic University in Boca Raton, Florida. In addition to numerous articles and chapters in journals and books, he has been contributing editor of a number of books including *Sartre: An Investigation of Some Major Themes* (1987), *European Philosophy and the Human and Social Sciences* (1987), and contributing co-editor (with Babette Babich and Debra Bergoffen) of *Continental and Postmodern Perspectives in the Philosophy of Science* (1995).

Patrick Aidan Heelan (1926–2015) was a Belgian-Irish physicist and philosopher of science. He taught philosophy at Georgetown University and the State University of New York at Stony Brook as well as Fordham University, New York City, and, early on, at University College, Dublin. He is author of *Quantum Mechanics and Objectivity: The Physical Philosophy of Werner Heisenberg* (1964), *Space-Perception and the Philosophy of Science* (1983) and, posthumously, *The Observable: Heisenberg's Philosophy of Quantum Mechanics*, with prefaces by Michel Bitbol and Babette Babich (2015).

Hubert Knoblauch is Professor of Sociology, especially the theory of modern societies, at the Institute for Sociology of the Technical University of Berlin. He is the author of *Powerpoint, Communication, and the Knowledge* Society (2013) and co-editor (with R. Tuma and M. Jacobs) of *Culture, Communication, and Creativity: Reframing the Relations of Media, Knowledge, and Innovation in Society* (2014) and (with B. Schnettler, J. Raab, and H.-G. Soeffner) of *Video Analysis: Methodology and Methods: Qualitative Audiovisual Data Analysis in Sociology* (2009).

Joseph J. Kockelmans (1923–2008) was Director of the Interdisciplinary Graduate Program in the Humanities and Professor of Philosophy at The Pennsylvania State University. He was the author of numerous books including *Phenom-*

enological Psychology: The Dutch School (1987), *Philosophy of Science: The Historical Background* (1968), *Hermeneutic Phenomenology: Lectures and Essays* (1988), and *Edmund Husserls Phenomenology* (1994).

Hans-Herbert Koegler is Professor of Philosophy at the University of North Florida. He is author of *Michel Foucault* (2004) and *The Power of Dialogue: Critical Hermeneutics after Gadamer and Foucault* (1999).

Leonard Lawlor is the Edwin Erle Sparks Professor of Philosophy at Pennsylvania State University. He is the author of *The Implications of Immanence: Toward a New Concept of Life* (2006).

Gary Madison (1940–2016) was emeritus professor of philosophy at McMaster University, in Hamilton, Ontario. He was the author of, among other monographs, *Understanding: A Phenomenological-Pragmatic Analysis* (1982), *The Logic of Liberty* (1986) and the author of *The Politics of Postmodernity: Essays in Applied Hermeneutics* (2001) and *Hermeneutics of Postmodernity: Figures and Themes* (1990) and *On Suffering* (2013). Madison was editor, among other collections, of *Working Through Derrida* (1993).

Eric S. Nelson is Associate Professor at the Hong Kong University of Science and Technology. He has published over seventy articles and book chapters on Continental and Comparative philosophy. He is the author of *Chinese and Buddhist Philosophy in Early Twentieth-Century German Thought* (2017) and is currently working on the early modern German reception of Chinese philosophy. He is co-editor of the *Bloomsbury Companion to Heidegger* (2016), *Between Levinas and Heidegger* (2014), *Anthropologie und Geschichte: Studien zu Wilhelm Dilthey aus Anlass seines 100. Todestages* (2013), *Rethinking Facticity* (2008), and *Addressing Levinas* (2005) and guest editor of topic issues of *Frontiers of Philosophy in China* and the *Journal of Chinese Philosophy.*

Jürgen Raab is Professor of Sociology in the Division of Sociology of the Institute for Social Sciences at the University of Koblenz-Landau, Campus Landau. He is author of *Erving Goffman. Klassiker der Wissenssoziologie* (2014) and co-editor of *Grenzen der Bildinterpretation* (2014) *Materiale Visuelle Soziologie* (2016) as well as *Wissensforschung – Forschungswissen. Beiträge und Debatten zum 1. Sektionskongress der Wissenssoziologie* (2016).

Didier de Robillard is a sociolinguist initially specialized in Creole and Francophone societies. These research fields show the diversity of the corresponding societies as incompatible with the sole predominance of rationality in social sciences. He is author of *Perspectives alterlinguistiques* (vol. 1: *Demons*, vol. 2: *Ornithorynques* [2008]), and has edited an issue of *Glottopol* (No. 28, July 2016), *Epistémologie et histoire de la sociolinguistique* (http://glottopol.univ-rouen.fr/), featuring phenomenological and hermeneutic conceptions of sociolinguistics.

Robert C. Scharff is Professor of Philosophy Emeritus at the University of New Hampshire. He is author of *How History Matters to Philosophy* (2015), *Comte After Positivism* (2002), and numerous papers on 19th and 20th century positivism, postpositivism, and continental philosophy, and former editor of *Continental Philosophy Review* (1994–2005). He is currently finishing two manuscripts, *Becoming Phenomenological: The Young Heidegger on Dilthey* and *Husserl and Inheriting Technoscience: Ontological Inquiries and Empirical Turns.*

Bernt Schnettler is the Chair for Sociology of Culture and Religion, University of Bayreuth, Germany. He is author of *Thomas Luckmann* (2006) and *Zukunftsvisionen. Transzendenz-erfahrung und Alltagswelt* (2004). His most recent publications, co-edited with Hubert Knoblauch, Jürgen Raab and Hans-Georg Soeffner, include *Video-Analysis. Methodology and Methods. Qualitative Audiovisual Data Analysis in Sociology* (2009).

Harald Seubert is Professor of Philosophy and Religious Studies at STH Basel. He is author of many books, including, to name only two, *Max Weber interkulturell gelesen* (2006) and *Zwischen erstem und anderem Anfang. Heideggers Auseinandersetzung mit Nietzsche und die Sache seines Denkens* (2000).

Steven Shapin is Franklin L. Ford Research Professor of the History of Science at Harvard University, joining Harvard in 2004. He is author, with Simon Schaffer, of *Leviathan and the Air-Pump: Hobbes, Boyle, and the Experimental Life* (1985; 1989) and most recently of *The Scientific Life: A Moral History of a Late Modern Vocation* (2008).

Tracy Burr Strong is Professor of Political Theory and Philosophy at the University of Southampton (UK) and UCSD Distinguished Professor, *emeritus*. He is the author of numerous essays and several books, most recently: *Politics without Vision: Thinking without a Banister in the Twentieth Century* (2012). Present projects include a book on "Citizenship and Contestation in America," in addition to a book-length commentary on Nietzsche, *The Birth of Tragedy*, essays on music and language and politics since the 18th century, and on 19th-century American literature as political theory.

Index

https://doi.org/10.1515/9783110551563-023